P9-AQU-478

THE *unofficial* GUIDE®
TO London

4TH EDITION

ALSO AVAILABLE FROM JOHN WILEY & SONS, INC.:

Beyond Disney: The Unofficial Guide to Universal, Sea World,
 and the Best of Central Florida

Mini-Mickey: The Pocket-Sized Unofficial Guide to Walt Disney World

The Unofficial Guide to California with Kids

The Unofficial Guide to Central Italy: Florence, Rome, Tuscany, and Umbria

The Unofficial Guide to Chicago

The Unofficial Guide to Cruises

The Unofficial Guide to Disneyland

The Unofficial Guide to England

The Unofficial Guide to Florida

The Unofficial Guide to Hawaii

The Unofficial Guide to Las Vegas

The Unofficial Guide to Maui

The Unofficial Guide to Mexico's Best Beach Resorts

The Unofficial Guide to New Orleans

The Unofficial Guide to New York City

The Unofficial Guide to Paris

The Unofficial Guide to San Francisco

The Unofficial Guide to South Florida including Miami and the Keys

The Unofficial Guide to Walt Disney World

The Unofficial Guide to Walt Disney World for Grown-Ups

The Unofficial Guide to Walt Disney World with Kids

The Unofficial Guide to Washington, D.C.

THE *unofficial* GUIDE®
TO London

4TH EDITION

LESLEY LOGAN

WILEY

This is for Sylvana Grodin with thanks for the memories.

Lesley Logan is a freelance writer who has worked in publishing for over two decades as author of guidebooks, ghostwriter, copywriter, and editor. Originally from New York, she has lived in London for many years, and now enjoys dual citizenship of these two great countries.

Please note that prices fluctuate in the course of time, and travel information changes under the impact of many factors that influence the travel industry. We therefore suggest that you write or call ahead for confirmation when making your travel plans. Every effort has been made to ensure the accuracy of information throughout this book, and the contents of this publication are believed correct at the time of printing. Nevertheless, the publishers cannot accept responsibility for errors or omissions or for changes in details given in this guide or for the consequences of any reliance on the information provided by the same. Assessments of attractions and so forth are based upon the author's own experience, and therefore, descriptions given in this guide necessarily contain an element of subjective opinion, which may not reflect the publisher's opinion or dictate a reader's own experience on another occasion. Readers are invited to write the publisher with ideas, comments, and suggestions for future editions.

Published by:
John Wiley & Sons, Inc.
111 River Street
Hoboken, NJ 07030

Copyright © 2006 by Robert W. Sehlinger. All rights reserved. No part of this publication may be reproduced, stored in a retrieval system or transmitted in any form or by any means, electronic, mechanical, photocopying, recording, scanning or otherwise, except as permitted under Sections 107 or 108 of the 1976 United States Copyright Act, without either the prior written permission of the Publisher, or authorization through payment of the appropriate per-copy fee to the Copyright Clearance Center, 222 Rosewood Drive, Danvers, MA 01923, (978) 750-8400, fax (978) 750-4744, or on the web at www.copyright.com. You can contact the Publisher directly for permission by email at permreq@wiley.com or on the web at www.wiley.com/about/permission.

Wiley, the Wiley logo, and Unofficial Guide are registered trademarks of John Wiley & Sons, Inc. in the United States and other countries and may not be used without written permission. Used under license. All other trademarks are the property of their respective owners. John Wiley & Sons, Inc. is not associated with any product or vendor mentioned in this book.

Produced by Menasha Ridge Press

Cover design by Michael J. Freeland

Interior design by Vertigo Design

For information on our other products and services or to obtain technical support please contact our Customer Care Department within the U.S. at (800) 762-2974, outside the U.S. at (317) 572-3993 or fax (317) 572-4002.

John Wiley & Sons, Inc. also publishes its books in a variety of electronic formats. Some content that appears in print may not be available in electronic formats.

ISBN 0-7645-9537-7

Manufactured in the United States of America

5 4 3 2 1

CONTENTS

List of Maps VII
Acknowledgments VIII

Introduction 1
London Calling 1
About This Guide 3
How Information Is Organized 7

PART ONE **An Overview of London** 16
The Long Life of an Ancient City 16
British Culture: Queues, the Weather, and a Stiff Upper Lip 36
DIVIDED BY A COMMON LANGUAGE: A BRITISH/ENGLISH GLOSSARY 40–43

PART TWO **Planning Your Visit** 44
Airline Deals 44
Quick Check 46
The Weather 47
What to Bring 48
When to Go 50
Gathering Information 52
Special Considerations 53
A Calendar of Festivals and Events 59

PART THREE **Accommodations** 66
Selecting Accommodations 66
What to Expect 68
Hotel Ratings 80
HOW THE HOTELS COMPARE 82–84
Hotel Profiles 85

PART FOUR **Arriving and Getting Oriented** 148
Entering the Country 148

Getting into London 150
Getting Oriented in London 155
Things the Locals Already Know 157

PART FIVE **Getting Around 167**
Public Transportation 167
Getting around on Your Own 175

PART SIX **Sightseeing, Tours, and Attractions 178**
An Embarrassment of Riches 178
Tourist Information Centers 179
Touring 180
Outside London 184
NOT TO BE MISSED: A HIGHLY SUBJECTIVE LIST 185
Romantic London 185
Oh, Such a Perfect Day 186
Walking in and around London 189
For Museum Lovers 195
LONDON ATTRACTIONS BY NEIGHBORHOOD 196–199
Museums and Attractions 199
Green and Pleasant Lands: Parks of London 266
Greenwich 274

PART SEVEN **Children's London 276**
London with Children 276
Planning and Touring Tips 277
Recommended Attractions and Itineraries 277
Services for Families 284
Activities 285
Theaters 287
Where to Eat 288
Shopping for Children 289

PART EIGHT **Dining and Restaurants 293**
The Restaurants 296
LONDON RESTAURANTS BY CUISINE 298–300
LONDON RESTAURANTS BY NEIGHBORHOOD 300–301
Restaurant Profiles 305

PART NINE **Entertainment and Nightlife 356**
The London Scene 356
Theater 357
Laughs in London 362
Classical Music 363
Dance and Ballet 365
Opera 366

Live Jazz, Pop, and Rock 367
Dance Clubs 368
Bars and Pubs 369
Sex in the City 371
Gaming in the United Kingdom 372
Freeloader's Forum 373
LONDON NIGHTCLUBS 375
Nightclub Profiles 375

PART TEN Shopping 388
Wise Buys in London 389
Time to Shop 391
Paying Up 392
Salespeople's Attitudes and Behavior 396
The Chain Reaction 396
The Big Shopping Neighborhoods 397
Markets 403
Department Stores 406
Where to Find . . . 408

PART ELEVEN Exercise and Recreation 421
Spectator Sports 421
Participation Sports 426

Hotel Index 000
Restaurant Index 000
Subject Index 000

List of Maps

Central London 8–9
West End Accommodations 86–87
Westminster and Victoria Accommodations and Dining 88
The City Accommodations 89
Knightsbridge to South Kensington Accommodations 90–91
Marylebone to Notting Hill Gate Accommodations 92–93
West End Attractions 200–201
Westminster and Victoria Attractions 202
The City Attractions 203
Knightsbridge to South Kensington Attractions 204–205
Marylebone to Notting Hill Gate Attractions 206–207
The City Dining and Nightlife 306
West End Dining 308–309
Knightsbridge to South Kensington Dining and Nightlife 310–311
Marylebone to Notting Hill Gate Dining and Nightlife 312–313
West End Nightlife 376–377

ACKNOWLEDGMENTS

FIRST AND FOREMOST I WANT TO THANK Tom and Nora Logan without whom nothing, least of all this book, would be possible.

And to Bob Sehlinger and Molly Merkle of Menasha Ridge Press, thanks for a wonderful assignment

Many heartfelt thanks to the legions of anonymous curators, cab drivers, London Transport people, London Tourist Board employees, shopkeepers, waiters, concierges, hotel managers, bellhops, B&B owners, and people on the street, who generously gave me tips, information, guided tours, and unfailingly pointed me in the right direction.

Big thanks to all those who helped with the book, especially Emma Littlewood and the great food writer Richard Erlich, who wrote the previous editions' restaurant chapters which form the basis for the fourth edition's update, and into whose enormous shoes I humbly have stepped.

I also appreciated the letters and evaluations I received from so many readers, the kind and the critical. Your suggestions and your generosity in taking the time to write made me grateful to be able to continue updating the book, making right some wrongs, and learning from your own London experiences.

—*Lesley Logan*

INTRODUCTION

▌LONDON CALLING

LET'S JUST GET IT OUT OF THE WAY, SHALL WE? Dr. Samuel Johnson's quote about his beloved city is as famous as Big Ben: "When a man is tired of London, he is tired of Life, for there is in London all that Life can afford." Only in London could the words of an 18th-century writer be put to such persistent, modern public-relations use; it is exactly this easy—some might say surreal—conversation between past and present that makes London so appealing to its visitors and residents alike.

London is a historical free-for-all where, against the gorgeous Georgian facade of the Royal Academy, you'll find a series of seriously modern sculptures; where horse-drawn carriages and soldiers on horseback in full regalia barely merit a passing glance from Londoners in their cars; where the Liberty department store on the 18th-century Nash-designed Regent Street is housed in a Tudor building straight out of a fairy tale, and filled with the most cutting-edge products imaginable. This wonderful palimpsest of centuries—the layering of post–World War II London over Edwardian elegance, on top of Victorian glory, over 18th-century exuberance, under which the medieval and even the Roman city can be appreciated—is, especially to the North American eye, a miracle of conservation and civic pride. But if London was only the sum of its past, it would be an inert monument, and not the contemporary scene of a constantly evolving culture of theater, arts, music, and fashion for which it's justifiably celebrated.

In 1978, Bette Midler said of the time difference between the two cities, "When it's three o'clock in New York, it's still 1938 in London." Thirty years ago, this was a spot-on quip, referring to the gloom of post war austerity that still clung to London's coal-dirty buildings and lack of good food or central heating. Although to many of us, raised to believe that all stores should be open on Sunday and remain open past six on weekdays, and who would like to be able to take the tube (London's underground trains) home after midnight, London still has a way to go to rival the 24/7 charms of, say, New York. Yet despite the minor irritations and the major expenses of this vast city, over 25 million visitors a year come to experience this maddening place, swelling its population of almost 8 million. And that's not even counting the transient young people who, like Dick Whittington and his cat, come to London to seek fame and fortune, people from all over Great Britain, the European Union, the commonwealths and ex-colonies of England, looking for a stroke of luck, urban excitement, or their own history. They work in the service industries or on the streets, busking for pounds, or serving your soup, essential ingredients in the madcap stew that is London. Of course, all visitors to this capital quickly discover that London is no quaint theme park. It takes a bit of work, and visitors may struggle to reconcile the picture of London carried in their minds against the sometimes dirty, indifferent, and confusing modern reality of the place. But the payoff for a little footwork is huge.

London can be many cities to many people. Contrast Dr. Johnson's hymns of worship ("The happiness of London is not to be conceived but by those who have been in it . . .") with Percy Bysshe Shelley's assessment of early-19th-century London: "Hell is a city much like London—a populous and smoky city." People may have a wide range of feelings about London, but indifference is usually not one of them. It's rare for an English speaker to come here without a mental trunk full of preconceptions. Those of us of a certain age had an intimate acquaintance with the bells of St. Clements, London Bridge, and the Drury Lane home of the muffin man even before we knew the alphabet. When we could read, we inhaled deeply the pungent London of Charles Dickens, who captured the 19th-century city in all its degradation and beauty, who spent hours each night exploring his city on foot, and who left his unforgettable impressions on the pages of his novels and in the psyches of his readers. London has appeared as a character in so much literature, art, and films that it is a place we carry in our collective consciousness like a time-traveling dream.

Waking up to London is another story. To arrive here for the first time is to suddenly confront the fantasy with the fact. The most outstanding fact about London is its sprawling geography—there is nothing so neat as a "downtown" of London. It isn't so much one big city as a series of interconnected villages on a human-size scale, liberally dotted with breathing spaces of greenery. London can take a lifetime to explore fully, and a tourist with only a week to cover the major sights will be hard-pressed to take it all in. The best approach to London is to decide where your interests lie; you will soon discover that there are few interests known to humanity that London cannot entertain.

We want you to make the best of this best-of-all-possible cities. We want you to waste no time getting lost on the tube, or taking a taxi if walking is quicker. We don't want you to get such a bad case of museum legs that you can't make it to the theater that night, and we definitely don't want you to spend your hard-earned money buying anything that's cheaper back home. London is a great place for visitors—tourism is its second largest industry—and we love the fact that we anglophones can, for the most part, communicate with the locals without needing a course from Berlitz. We hope to identify and address any difficulties you might have in visiting London, so that you can pursue whatever course of entertainment you desire, efficiently and happily. And there's so much to be done. . .

London has the best museums in the world, the world-famous as well as some lesser-known ones. There are miles of parks, offering some of the loveliest natural scenery to be found in any metropolis. Part of London's charm lies in the sudden deluges from leaden skies that will just as quickly be sliced open with swords of sunlight. There are also the people of London, who speak in a rich concoction of accents, in over 200 languages, and represent multiple classes, nationalities, and political views. No matter what moves you—theater, architecture, sports, antiques, markets, designer clothing, contemporary art and old masters, heart-stopping cathedrals, smoky cafés, palaces, poetry readings, elegant casinos, lunatic nightclubs, pubs, horticulture, witchcraft, fencing, boating—there truly is, as the good doctor pointed out almost three centuries ago, "in London all that Life can afford."

ABOUT *this* GUIDE

WHY *UNOFFICIAL?*

MOST LONDON TRAVEL GUIDES FOLLOW the usual tracks of the typical tourist, automatically sending everyone to the well-known sights without offering any information about how to do this painlessly; recommending restaurants and hotels indiscriminately; and failing to recognize the limits of human endurance in sight-seeing. This guide is different: We understand that in a huge city like London it is essential for one to discriminate, make plans, whittle the town down to size, and be flexible when hours-long lines appear out of nowhere or when the clouds burst and you've forgotten your umbrella.

We'll tell you what we think of certain tourist traps, what the real story is on the famous restaurants and hotels, what the options are if you want to go off the beaten track, or how to spend a little less money on one thing so you can spend more on another. We'll complain about rip-offs, and we'll advise you on bargains. We also hope to give you the kind of information that will make you love London all the more—some of the endearing eccentricities that make you realize you're definitely not in Kansas anymore.

London is such a complex and sprawling city, so full of fantastic anecdote and incident, that it's hard to edit out the trivia—it's all great stuff, and the more tales you hear, the more you want to know. Every building and monument, every alley and lane has a story—fictional or historical, it hardly matters to the legions of authors, tour guides, and local characters who continue to document and embroider on the fascinating yarns of London. The longer you stay here, the larger London becomes in some ways. Each door that opens reveals ten windows through which to gaze. In the old days a visit to London was a rite of passage for the upper classes of North America, and they used to spend six months at it. You probably haven't got that luxury (unless you're here as an exchange student), so you have to be very efficient and organized if you want to make the most of your time. The majority of overseas visitors stay only for about five to ten days. How much can you squeeze into that time? How much do you want to see? What are your priorities, and how can they best be served? Like any worthy undertaking, preparation and strategy are key to unlocking London's charms. We have done the footwork: We've checked out the hotels to find the best deals and the most interesting buildings; we've eaten at all the best, semigood, and worst restaurants in town, keeping up with the latest trends and revisiting the old reliables. We've got the lowdown on the high life from those younger, heartier types who have crawled out of their fair share of clubs and casinos at daybreak. If a museum is dull, or there's a two-hour wait for an attraction that just isn't worth it, we'll tell you why—and we hope in the process to make your visit more fun, efficient, and economical.

We've tried in this book to anticipate the special needs of older people, families with young children, families with teenagers, solo travelers, and people with physical challenges.

London has hundreds of attractions, and we've tried to sort them based upon which are first rate, which are intended for those with special interests, and which are hype jobs. Obviously, even if you visit London dozens of times, you won't be able to see all that we describe to you, and by the time you have become an old London hand you'll have identified your own favorite haunts. But we want you to always have the option of exploring more and more of this endlessly interesting city, and we want to give you the best tips for doing so. We take things easy, the way we think you'll want to (remember, you're on *vacation*), but we don't take exploitation or stupidity lying down—we vote with our feet. If it isn't fun, if it isn't informative, if it isn't a reasonable deal, if there's a better alternative, we want you to know. We hope to keep the quality of your visit high and the holiday hell quotient low.

We cover attractions in these various ways because we want to make sure you can make informed decisions about which ones you'll enjoy most. For those of you who don't want to have to figure it all out yourself, we've listed a number of good commercial and customized tours on pages 180–183 in Part Six, Sightseeing, Tours, and Attractions.

Although we believe you'll get a pretty good workout just walking around, we've included a selection of exercise opportunities. Travel can be pretty hard on the body—airplane stiffness, up and down the underground stairs, strolling through galleries and streets—and it doesn't hurt to get some endorphins going at some point in your visit. Also, London has so many great restaurants and patisseries that you may well need a little calorie-corrective run or swim, unless you want to take home more than photos and souvenirs (try a few days of cream teas and you'll see what we mean).

Please do remember that prices and admission hours (and, worst of all, exchange rates) fluctuate. We have listed the most up-to-date information we can get, but it never hurts to double-check times in particular (if prices of attractions change, it is generally not by much). Remember, this is one of the busiest tourist towns in the world, so make your reservations early and reconfirm.

About Unofficial Guides

Readers care about authors' opinions. The authors, after all, are supposed to know what they are talking about. This, coupled with the fact that the traveler wants quick answers, dictates that travel authors should be explicit, prescriptive, and, above all, direct. The authors of the *Unofficial Guide* try to do just that. We spell out alternatives and recommend specific courses of action. We simplify complicated destinations and attractions to allow the traveler to feel in control in the most unfamiliar environments. Our objective is not to give the most information or all the information, but the most accessible, useful information. Of course, in a city like London, there are many hotels, restaurants, and attractions that are so closely woven into the fabric of the city that to omit them from our guide because we can't recommend them would be a disservice to our readers. We have included all the famous haunts, giving our opinion and experience of them, in the hopes that you will approach (or avoid) these institutions armed with the necessary intelligence.

An *Unofficial Guide* is a critical reference work; we focus on a travel destination that appears to be especially complex. Our authors and researchers are completely independent from the attractions, restaurants, and hotels we describe. The *Unofficial Guide to London* is designed for individuals and families traveling for fun as well as for business, and it will be especially helpful to those hopping "across the pond" for the first time. The guide is directed at value-conscious, consumer-oriented adults who seek a cost-effective but not overly-Spartan travel style.

SPECIAL FEATURES

- Vital information about traveling abroad
- Friendly introductions to London's "villages"
- Listings that are keyed to your interests, so you can pick and choose
- Advice to sightseers on how to avoid the worst crowds; advice to business travelers on how to avoid traffic and excessive costs
- Recommendations for lesser-known sights that are off the well-beaten tourist path but no less worthwhile
- Maps to make it easy to find places you want to go and to avoid other places
- A hotel section that helps you narrow down your choices quickly, according to your needs and preferences
- A table of contents and detailed index to help you find things fast

WHAT YOU WON'T GET

- Long, useless lists where everything looks the same
- Information that gets you to your destination at the worst possible time
- Information without advice on how to use it

HOW THIS GUIDE WAS RESEARCHED AND WRITTEN

IN PREPARING THIS WORK, WE TOOK NOTHING for granted. Each hotel, restaurant, shop, and attraction was visited by trained observers who conducted detailed evaluations and rated each according to formal criteria. Team members conducted interviews with tourists of all ages to determine what they enjoyed most and least during their London visit.

Though our observers are independent and impartial, they are otherwise "ordinary" travelers. Like you, they visited London as tourists or business travelers, noting their satisfaction or dissatisfaction.

The primary difference between the average tourist and the trained evaluator is the evaluator's skills in organization, preparation, and observation. A trained evaluator is responsible for more than just observing and cataloging. Observer teams use detailed checklists to analyze hotel rooms, restaurants, nightclubs, and attractions. Finally, evaluator ratings and observations are integrated with tourist reactions and the opinions of patrons for a comprehensive quality profile of each feature and service.

In compiling this guide, we recognize that a tourist's age, background, and interests will strongly influence his or her taste in London's wide array of attractions and will account for a preference for one sight or museum over another. Our sole objective is to provide the reader with sufficient description, critical evaluation, and pertinent data to make knowledgeable decisions according to individual tastes.

LETTERS, COMMENTS, AND QUESTIONS FROM READERS

WE EXPECT TO LEARN FROM OUR MISTAKES, as well as from the input of our readers, and to improve with each new book and edition. Many of those who use the *Unofficial Guides* write to us asking questions, making comments, or sharing their own discoveries and lessons learned in London. We appreciate all such input, both positive and critical, and encourage our readers to continue writing. Readers' comments and observations will frequently be incorporated into revised editions of the *Unofficial Guide* and will contribute immeasurably to its improvement.

How to Write the Author

Lesley Logan
The Unofficial Guide to London
P.O. Box 43673
Birmingham, AL 35243
UnofficialGuides@menasharidge.com

When you write, be sure to put your return address on your letter as well as on the envelope—sometimes envelopes and letters get separated. Remember, our work takes us out of the office for long periods of time, so forgive us if our response is delayed.

HOW INFORMATION *is* ORGANIZED

TO GIVE YOU FAST ACCESS TO INFORMATION about the best of London, we've organized material in several formats.

HOTELS

THERE ARE MANY HOTELS IN LONDON THAT are small, quirky, and unique. Even the world-class, well-known, and very expensive hotels can vary dramatically in room size and amenities, and a hotel priced somewhere in the middle of the price range can have under one charming roof and at a similar price both closet-size attic rooms and magnificent salons with French windows. The converted town houses, the updated terminus grand hotels, the homey B&Bs have only so much to work with— grade-listed historical buildings cannot make changes to the footprint and occasionally the interior space of a property, so making the rooms homogeneous is impossible. We have tried to stick to the hotels that are more reliable and consistent in their accommodations, and we have attempted to summarize this somewhat unwieldy and problematic subject in ratings and rankings that allow you to quickly crystallize your choice. We concentrate on the specific variables that differentiate one hotel from another: location, size, room quality, services, amenities, and cost.

central london

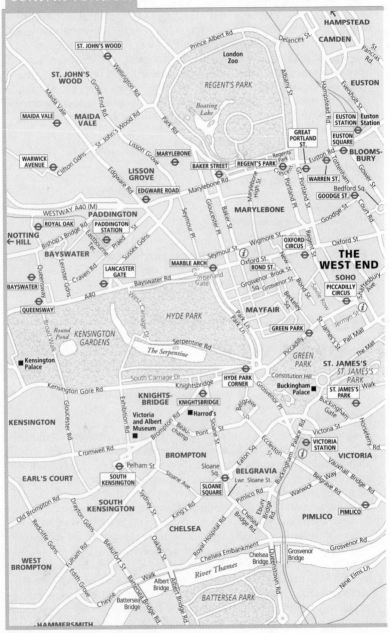

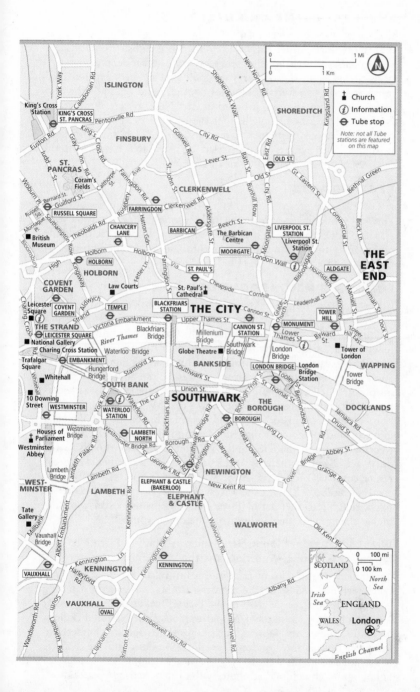

ENTERTAINMENT AND NIGHTLIFE

VISITORS FREQUENTLY TRY SEVERAL DIFFERENT clubs or nightspots during their stay in London. Since clubs so often have a very specific clientele and ambience, we believe that detailed descriptions are warranted, so that you don't end up in a lager-soaked moshpit when you were looking for cool jazz and Bellinis. The best nightspots in London are profiled in Part Nine, Entertainment and Nightlife. Be warned, though, that the popularity and character of clubs can change overnight; they can also go out of business without warning. We've made a point of selecting places that have withstood the tests of time and fluctuations of fashion.

RESTAURANTS

WE PROVIDE PLENTY OF DETAIL WHEN IT comes to restaurants. You will probably eat a dozen or more restaurant meals during your stay, and not even you can predict what you might be in the mood for on Saturday night. You can browse through our detailed profiles of the best restaurants in London before dining out.

LONDON'S NEIGHBORHOODS

ONCE YOU'VE DECIDED WHERE YOU'RE GOING, getting there becomes the issue. To help you do that, we refer consistently to a group of London's neighborhoods. Those are described briefly below to give you an idea of what they're about. All profiles of hotels, restaurants, attractions, and nightspots include neighborhood references. The post codes that appear at the end of an address are for the purpose of delivering mail and are known to the citizens as shorthand for a certain area. Everyone knows that SW1 is part of the royal borough of Westminster and includes the neighborhoods of Victoria, Pimlico, and parts of Knightsbridge and Belgravia. Chelsea and Kensington are in the SW3 and SW7 codes. Neighborhoods to the north are known by their "N" prefix followed by a number. They represent compass directions (N, S, W, E) that radiate generally from central London (C), with the lowest numbers being in the center of town, roughly to the east of Hyde Park. With some exceptions, the higher the number, the farther from the center you will be.

West End (includes Bloomsbury, Holborn, Mayfair, Piccadilly, Regent's Park, Soho, Waterloo, and the West End)

You'll likely spend a lot of time in this fun-filled, extended group of neighborhoods. Most of the theaters are here, as are the Charing Cross bookshops, St. Martin-in-the-Fields, Trafalgar Square, rowdy Leicester Square, Chinatown, Somerset House, the National Gallery, and pubs, pubs, pubs. Covent Garden has shops and street entertainment, as well as the London Transport Museum and the Theatre Museum. You might want to stay in a hotel around the West End or Soho, but it can get loud at night, with drunks roaring up and down side streets and tourists as far as the eye can see. Of course, that may be part of the appeal. Other attractions include the Royal Academy, the National Portrait Gallery, the Horse Guards Parade, the British Museum, and portions of Regent's, Green, and St. James's parks. The West End embraces the shopping of New and Old Bond Street, Oxford Street, Baker Street, Leicester Square, Carnaby Street, Neal's Yard, Covent Garden, and more. This area was the heart of London life in the centuries following the Great Fire of 1666, and remains the pulsating center of the entertainment industry in Soho, the legal profession in Lincoln's Inn, and the higher-education ivory towers of Bloomsbury's University of London Colleges, London School of Economics, and King's College. Blue plaques recording the London addresses of various historical giants abound in this area, from Handel and Karl Marx in Soho, to Virginia Woolf and her pals around the British Museum, to the various lords and ladies off Piccadilly, in grand old Mayfair. Mayfair is a very high-class area, in which you can find the most expensive shops in the world, including the bespoke clothing establishments of St. James and Jermyn streets and the international designers of Bond Street. There is every imaginable hotel here, except for inexpensive ones—here's where sheiks, celebs, and business high-flyers stay at the Atheneum, the Ritz, Brown's, Claridges, or the Savoy. Hatchard's, the oldest bookstore in London, is on Piccadilly, as are Fortnum and Mason's, and the Burlington and Piccadilly Arcade, dignified ancestors of the shopping mall. Nearby is Shepherds' Market, which in the 1600s was the site of the riotous saturnalia known as the May Fair and a place for the entertainers of the day—jugglers, fire eaters, boxers, prostitutes—to parade their talents. Today, Shepherds' Market is a mere shadow of its former self, but interesting nonetheless.

In fact, it is quite possible to have a rollicking great time in London without once stepping out of this area. Wandering all the side streets and mews of this area can take years; visiting the major sights in the area can eat up even a full-week's holiday; dodging all the traffic around here can start to wear on your nervous system; so be sure, even if you are staying in one of the many hotels in this area, to hop a bus and get into the other areas that are equally interesting.

The City (includes Barbican, Brixton, Clerkenwell, the East End, South Bank, Tower Hill, and Whitechapel)

This is the oldest part of London, where you'll find the magnificent and unsinkable St. Paul's Cathedral, the occasional whispers of a medieval past, and some remnants of the town that the occupying ancient Romans called Londinium—all of which managed to survive the devastating Blitz of World War II. This is also where most of the financial business of London is conducted. The area pretty much dies at night and on weekends, but during the day you'll find many good restaurants here, and lots of very antique pubs. The Bank of England

Museum and the Lloyd's of London building by Richard Rogers are here, along with some amusing architectural visions, such as the grasshopper on the top of the Stock Exchange and the glass high-rise known as "the gherkin" for its shape. The old markets—Smithfield's, Spitalfields, and Leadenhall—are fun to check out. This area also offers Victorian architecture, art galleries, churches, and the echoes of cockney English. The East End is, like so much of this crushingly expensive city, experiencing a bit of gentrification, as the prices of real estate in central London push people ever further afield. New luxury apartments, artsy nightspots, and even the Prince of Wales's School of Architecture now share the streets where Jack the Ripper stalked his prey and Sweeney Todd made mincemeat of his customers. Here, too, you can get boats to Greenwich, see some of the old Roman wall around London, or visit the ancient Tower of London and the Victorian marvel of Tower Bridge. You can walk across the Millenium Bridge, which spans both the Thames and the centuries between the old power station that houses the art of the Tate Modern and Christopher Wren's 17th-century Cathedral of St. Paul. It's a wonderful mélange of old and new (and, in the case of the re-creation of Shakespeare's Globe Theatre, the newly old), where modern needs push up against, but never overcome, the proud footprints of the past.

Westminster and Victoria (includes Belgravia and Pimlico)

This area runs from the seedy to the sublime. It encompasses the august halls of government and power in London in Whitehall, where there are statues everywhere memorializing the great and powerful of England: Cromwell, Lord Nelson, the two King Charleses, Winston Churchill, and others; all left out in the rain with pigeons desecrating them. There are plenty of hotels to go along with the preponderance of tourist attractions, such as the Houses of Parliament, the Queen's Gallery, Westminster Abbey, and the Tate Britain, which was built on the site of the infamous Milbank Penitentiary, where prisoners went mad from the strictly enforced silence. Due to the heavy concentration of World War II bombing in this area, there are patches of real ugliness here and there where rebuilding went on without any attention to architectural coherence. Much of Westminster simply closes down on the weekend—not the attractions but the eateries, which cater mainly to the business crowd. Pimlico, to the south of Westminster, has lots of cheap hotels and bedsits, but may not be the greatest place to be late at night. Buckingham Palace, which the Queen calls home; Number 10 Downing Street, official residence of the Prime Minister; and the Banqueting Hall where Charles II was beheaded neatly take the measure of power throughout England's history. There are magnificent vistas here—the fairy-tale view from Buckingham Palace across St. James's Park toward Westminster

Abbey will have you reaching for your camera, and who can ever have enough photos of Big Ben and the wildly neo-Gothic Houses of Parliament, now looked over by the graceful spectacle of the London Eye Ferris wheel? Belgravia is an enclave of ambassadors and billionaires, with enormous attached mansions, some of which are five houses strung together to make one gargantua, as in the humble home of the sultan of Brunei. On the Westminster Embankment you can watch the Thames flow past, or else jump on a sight-seeing boat that will take you to the Tower of London or Greenwich. The area also encompasses the great renaissance of the South Bank—the London Aquarium, the Marriott Hotel, the Royal Festival Hall and the National Theatre, the Hayward Gallery, the London Eye—as well as the ancient palace of Lambeth, where the archbishop of Canterbury lives. From the South Bank you get the very best views of the halls of Westminster and Big Ben, and year-round you can stroll along the promenade and enjoy the parade of life that is always marching by.

Knightsbridge, South Kensington, and Chelsea (includes Earl's Court)

This group of neighborhoods is the stronghold of the very wealthy— British aristocrats, movie stars, rock-and-roll gods, expatriate entrepreneurs, and sultans coexist peacefully in the splendor of Georgian town houses built around gorgeous private garden squares, or in deceptively simple mews houses that once stabled horses. Knightsbridge is mainly about shopping: besides Harrods, Harvey Nichols, and H&M, there are world-class designer shops on Sloane Street, Fulham Road, and Beauchamp Place. The auction house Bonhams is in Knightsbridge Village as is an assortment of secondhand designer-clothes shops (there are two on Chelsea's Elystan Street as well that are great for nabbing last year's fashions). Besides its expense and proximity to Hyde Park, Knightsbridge is also famous for having the most consonants in a row in any English word! The area is a very convenient place to stay, with buses and tube lines going from here to everywhere in London. The Victoria and Albert, Natural History, and Science museums are but a stone's throw from Hyde Park, through which you can horseback ride, skate, or bicycle. South Kensington was once known as Albertopolis and Museumland because of the Great Exhibition of 1851 that Prince Albert organized, whose collections of treasures and curiosities grew into these great museums that are as beautiful on the exterior as they are fascinating inside. There's also the Royal Albert Hall, the Royal Art College, Imperial College, and numerous learned societies, institutes, and foreign embassies in the area. South Kensington is known as Little France, thanks to the Lycee Français and the Institute Français in the middle of town. There are lots of great patisseries, a few good restaurants, and plenty of excellent hotels. Chelsea is to the south and boasts the famous King's Road, the once-swinging high street for 1960s hipsters, 1970s punks, 1980s yuppies, and 21st-century just-plain-rich folk. The now-ubiquitous, expensive, and unsuitable SUVs are referred to as "Chelsea tractors," obese vehicles with underweight, overwrought women on their mobile phones at the driving wheel. In the neighborhoods off King's Road are a multitude of blue plaques identifying the many writers and artists who once called Chelsea home: Oscar Wilde, George Eliot, Thomas Carlyle, Dante Gabriel Rossetti, Whistler . . . the list goes on and on. Chelsea is a very smart area in which to live—and the property prices reflect this, as do the pricetags in the swanky shops. A new pedestrianized area at the Sloane Square end of the King's Road is the Duke of York shopping enclave, which is a fine place to sit with a gelato and watch Chelsea residents and visitors as they go around maxing out their platinum plastic.

Marylebone to Notting Hill Gate (includes Kensington, Bayswater, Holland Park, and Regent's Park)

At the northern border of Hyde Park, Bayswater and Marylebone have a big Arab population (which made the Edgeware Road tube bombing of July 2005 so puzzling until it turned out the terrorists were home-grown British citizens who didn't give a toss who they hit). This is your best bet for fabulous Middle Eastern restaurants and some funky daily street markets. Here you'll find the Wallace Collection, Whiteley's Shopping Mall, skating rink and bowling alley, Regent's Canal Waterbus, the Sherlock Holmes Museum, Madame Tussaud's, and two horseback-riding stables that offer trots around Hyde Park. There are tons of cheap hotels here, some downright dismal, some of good value. Paddington Station is the terminus for the Heathrow Express, as well as for trains that serve the West Country and South Wales. There's a bit of a sleaze factor in Bayswater, with hooker hotels in the vicinity, but Marylebone is a charming little village north of bustling Oxford Street, with a number of unusual and excellent shops. Regent's Park houses the London Zoo, the London Central Mosque, Regent's Open Air Theatre, and it affords some of the most beautiful 18th-century vistas in London. Designed in concert with King George IV, who was regent at the time, this area is the crowning achievement of architect John Nash, even though it was a financial failure that was never completed.

When King William and Queen Mary moved their royal residence to the then far-flung country village of Kensington in 1689 for the king's health, their court followed suit, and lots of grand manors were built in this area. As rich attracts rich, in the following centuries the neighborhoods to the west and north, such as Notting Hill and the adjacent Holland Park, developed into exclusive places to live, as they remain. Kensington High Street is a big bustling shopping street, with a huge range of stores selling clothing, accessories, housewares, and electronics, as well as boasting a number of popular restaurants.

Kensington Church Street is lined with interesting, although expensive, antiques shops. Notting Hill, after its genteel heyday in Victorian times, became run-down enough to attract the new immigrants, and in the early 1960s, it was a Jamaican enclave. Before long, it started attracting idle trust-fund kids who were dubbed "trustafarians." It is a very hip, happening place, as its ever-increasing rents and roster of celebrity residents can attest. This is where the famous Portobello Market is, which is worth a look on Saturday as long as you're not prone to agoraphobia.

PART ONE

AN OVERVIEW
of LONDON

LONDON OFFERS SOMETHING FOR EVERY MOOD, desire, and interest, and there are so many ways to appreciate it. Music, sports, architecture, theater, fashion, antiques, gardens, nightlife . . . London is an amazing place today, but it takes on even more interesting dimensions when you know what it was yesterday. A bit of the history of this town on the Thames is just as useful for the discerning visitor as a street map. So, here we go.

THE LONG LIFE
of an ANCIENT CITY

LONDON'S HISTORY, PERHAPS BECAUSE THE city is situated on the banks of a wide river cutting through a large island, is initially one of invasion and conquest. Because of England's system of monarchy, her later history is one of bloody factionalism and revolving persecutions. As the empire began to take shape, British blood was shed on foreign soil, as England's sovereignty was propped up by the exploitation of foreign continents and by the labor of the impoverished workers in London. But throughout all of it, the history of the city of London has been the history of commerce: This port city has beckoned to artisans and sailors, farmers, prostitutes, and wheelers and dealers of all shades of corruption for two millennia. London shows no signs of flagging in its appeal in the third millennium.

Some of the highlights from London's past can be found in the Museum of London, where you can wander from the prehistoric banks of the Thames all the way through to the Millennium Bridge, seeing the everyday sights of London's long life that you won't find anywhere else, such as the underground heating system of Roman Londinium, or an Anderson shelter from the days of the Blitz. The museum's overall style is nostalgic and cheerful, although you do get to look into a dismal cell of the notorious Newgate Gaol. It's a great experience for the young and the old, the well-informed and the merely curious.

WHEN ROME RULED LONDINIUM

JULIUS CAESAR'S FAMOUS REMARK ABOUT how Britons were simply not good slave material was sour grapes: in 55 B.C. and 56 B.C., he tried to subdue England twice and failed. In A.D. 43, the Romans again sent an army to conquer the island. This time they built a bridge over the Thames at the narrowest crossing, near the present London Bridge. Soon, this Roman fort called Londinium grew into a thriving port of commerce, as luxury goods from all over the Roman Empire arrived and were exchanged for corn, iron, and—Julius Caesar notwithstanding—slaves. Roman historian Tacitus wrote that Londinium was "famed for commerce and crowded with merchants," a description that would remain accurate for the next 2,000 years (and will doubtless continue to do so). Roadways, the most ubiquitous and long-lasting feature of Roman rule, soon headed in every direction from this trading post and were well traveled by Romans and Britons in search of adventure and wealth. After a period of Pax Romana (peace imposed by ancient Rome on its dominions), the Roman rule became increasingly unbearable to the local tribes. Queen Boudicca (Also spelled Boudicea) of the Iceni tribe led a violent revolt, invading Londinium, massacring everyone in sight, and burning the camp to the ground. The revolution was short lived, however; Londinium was rebuilt with a huge wall around it, encompassing what is presently the City and Barbican area. A piece of the wall is preserved near the Museum of London, and there's a heart-stirring statue of the ferocious Boudicca by Westminster Bridge.

In 410, the sun was setting on the Roman Empire. The troops were withdrawn, leaving the sprouts of the newly-adopted Christian faith behind. London then went into a decline; when new invaders arrived, they superstitiously stayed away from the Roman ruins, which were soon buried in the silt of the river, not to be rediscovered until after the Blitz of World War II.

THE SAXON'S LUNDENWIC

AFTER THE SAXONS CAME OVER THE NORTH SEA in about 450 to settle in southeast England, London slowly began its rise from Roman ashes to again become a trading post, called Lundenwic. After presiding over a pagan society, King Ethelbert became a Christian convert, and the first cathedral of St. Paul was built. The Saxon kings spent most of the next five centuries fighting Viking invaders and fortifying their kingdom and its capital at Winchester, in the west country. London has King Alfred to thank for rebuilding it after Danish invaders left it in ruins, as well as for lighting a few other candles in those dark ages. The tenth century saw a new prosperity as neighborhoods and parishes were formed on the banks of the Thames River. In the 11th century, the Danes finally won the day, and England was forced to accept the Danish King Canute as its leader. He put London on the map as the capital of the kingdom, and by 1042, when Edward the Confessor took the scepter, London was poised on the brink of a great architectural leap forward. Westminster Abbey and the Palace at Westminster gave the raucous commercial port a dignity that was soon complemented by the construction of the White Tower, the tallest building at the Tower of London.

WILLIAM THE CONQUEROR

IN 1066, AT THE BATTLE OF HASTINGS, a Norman army led by William conquered the Saxon armies, and with that victory spelled a new dawn for London. William decided to have his coronation in Westminster Abbey, which has remained a tradition since that time. He saw that London was perfectly placed to be a rich capital and located the impressive stronghold of the White Tower on the Thames to show the inhabitants of this headstrong city just who was in charge. However, he was also a smart politician and granted freedoms to the Saxon-dominated church and the local governors that ensured a pleasant and profitable back-scratching for all concerned. London grew rich under the watchful eye of the monarchs, who knew the key to their power lay in the wealth and acquiescence of London's merchants and churchmen. In 1180, William Fitzstephen, in the preface to his *Life of Thomas à Becket*, sang high praises of London: "It is blessed by a wholesome climate . . . in the strength of its fortifications, in the nature of its site, the repute of its citizens, the honour of its matrons; happy in its sports, prolific in noble men. . . I can think of no other city with customs more admirable. . . The only plagues of London are the immoderate drinking of fools and the frequency of fires." He forgot that other plague of London: the plague.

A VIBRANT MEDIEVAL PORT

MEDIEVAL LONDON WAS A CRAZY SALAD OF streets, alleys, markets, outdoor brothels, bear-baiting pits, pubs, and theaters. The vibrancy of the streets was matched in energy by the jostling for power among the court, the burgesses, and the church. In 1215, the Magna Carta, which attempted to limit the excesses and power of the king and establish personal rights and political freedom for the nobility, was signed by King John, who was forced to do so by rebellious barons and the newly created lord mayor of London. Soon Parliament and the House of Commons were created, and England became a place of liberty and justice for at least a few more than before. Though the Magna Carta was designed to free the aristocracy from the despotism of a monarch, it contained the fateful word *freemen* and so signaled at least theoretical rights for the common people.

The port was thriving with houses and warehouses lining the river-banks, and the power of the guilds and merchants grew apace. The position of London as one of the world's great ports, crowded with thousands of people living in appalling sanitary conditions, led to the first outbreak of plague. The Black Death of 1348 traveled across the English Channel from the European continent, which was reeling from the disease. Nearly half of London's population succumbed to the plague, which was carried by rats that multiplied in the filthy streets and fetid sewers. The general unrest and loss of labor led to the ill-advised poll tax imposed in 1381 by a financially strapped court—a shilling a person, regardless of income or situation. The Peasant's Revolt, led by Jack Straw and Wat Tyler, put every future monarch on notice that Londoners had a breaking point that should be avoided. After a riotous spree of looting, burning, and murder, the rebels were overcome, and a young King Richard II restored order, but the point was well-taken: the poll tax was quietly dropped.

A new intellectual age dawned around this time. In the 1390s, Geoffrey Chaucer wrote *The Canterbury Tales,* and in 1476 William Caxton set up his printing press at Westminster. The numerous and wealthy monasteries became centers for teaching and learning, and literacy began creeping into the merchant and upper classes, setting the scene for the Renaissance culture of the Tudor era.

TUDOR LONDON

THE WAR OF THE ROSES BETWEEN THE FRACTIOUS factions of the House of Plantagenet—York and Lancaster—provided William Shakespeare with a superabundance of material for his tragedies. As he wrote in *Richard III: "England hath long been mad, and scarred herself; The brother blindly shed the brother's blood, The father rashly slaughtered his own son, The son, compelled been butcher to the sire: All this divided York and Lancaster."*

The bloody dynastic feud for the throne had relatively little effect on the daily lives of Londoners scrambling for a living, but when Richard III allegedly smothered the two young princes, the rightful heirs to the throne, in the Tower of London, the citizenry grew restless; few regretted the end of Richard's reign. Next came the Tudor dynasty, whose heirs were at least as ruthless when it came to insulting and disposing of relatives as any of the previous Plantagenets had been.

Henry VIII married his brother's widow, Catherine of Aragon, to keep the peace with Spain. After 20 years of marriage and one daughter, Mary, Henry fell in love with Anne Boleyn and decided he had to marry again in order to have a male heir. He cast off his wife, alienating the Catholic Church in Rome, which refused to grant him an annulment. Not one to take no for an answer, and a man who willingly threw out baby and bathtub with the bathwater, Henry reformed the church in England, styling himself as its supreme ruler. Then he went on a serial marital spree that left in its wake a total of six wives; as the nursery rhyme goes, "two beheaded, two divorced, one died, and one survived." Anne Boleyn, whose daughter was to become one of the most powerful monarchs of England, was executed at the tower, and her ghost apparently makes the rounds there nightly. (The Tower of London is as haunted a place as you can find in ghost-ridden London. Heads rolled like billiard balls there, innocent souls were racked and tortured regularly, and their tormented specters are well known to the people who remain there past nightfall.)

The most radical expression of this religious overhaul was in the dissolution of the monasteries, in which Henry took for the crown all the property of the Catholic cathedrals, churches, priories, convents, and monasteries in England. He destroyed huge numbers of beautiful gothic and medieval buildings, redistributing the land among the new, loyal-to-Henry aristocracy, creating new streets, houses, and courtyards where there had once been wealthy Catholic establishments. Resistant nuns and clergy were hung, drawn, and quartered; the army of crippled, diseased, and homeless who had been supported by the charity of the churches were thrown upon their own resources, and the streets of London resounded with the cries of their misery.

After Henry VIII died, syphilitic and obese, the six-year reign of the sickly child-king Edward didn't amount to much more than a vicious power struggle among his courtiers. When Bloody Mary, Henry's first daughter, became queen after Edward's early death, she put her half-sister, Elizabeth, in the Tower of London, and it was the Protestants' turn to have their property seized and be hung or burned alive. The daily spectacle of burning heretics at the marketplace of Smithfields finally disgusted even the Londoners accustomed to gruesome public punishments. In another turn of the dynasty, Elizabeth returned England to its still unsteady Protestant base, forestalling any Catholic overthrow by having her cousin, Mary Queen of Scots, executed at Fotheringay Castle in Northamptonshire in 1587. (Mary's son, King James I, ordered her body exhumed in 1612 and re-interred at Westminster Abbey, producing the grim irony of the two rival queens resting for eternity within a few feet of one another.)

THE ELIZABETHAN FLOWERING OF LONDON

WHAT WERE THE GOOD CITIZENS OF LONDON doing while all the royal kin-killing kerfuffle and musical thrones were being played out? Well, while the aristocrats built over-the-top estates from the remains of the monasteries, and Hyde Park became a happy hunting ground for King Henry VIII, the ordinary Londoner went about the usual daily rounds of earning and eating, fornicating and frolicking, marrying and burying. In 1586, William Shakespeare arrived in London, joining Ben Jonson, Christopher Marlowe, John Donne, and others of the day's glitterati in the boom years of English letters, helping record the uproar that was London. The city now had a population of 200,000 people, up from 50,000 in the 1300s, and more arrived every day. The great era of exploration was under way as the English plied the oceans in search of riches, returning with sugar, spice, coffee, and tobacco. Sir Thomas Gresham started the Royal Exchange from its humble beginnings as a coffeehouse and made London the world's most important financial center, a position it maintained into the early 20th century.

Although Queen Elizabeth could be as dangerous a friend (and relative) as she was a foe, she was devoted to the welfare of her kingdom and understood that her greatest power lay in the love her subjects had for her—she had an instinctive gift for public relations. Perhaps the greatest gift she gave the nation was her much vaunted virginity: By not marrying a foreign prince, she kept England solidly English for 45 prosperous years. By the end of her long reign, the memories of those ugly battles of succession had faded, but more cataclysms lay ahead for the monarchy and for London.

ROUNDHEADS AND RESTORATION

THE GUNPOWDER PLOT OF 1605, IN WHICH a group of Catholic conspirators, including Guy Fawkes, was thwarted in a plan to blow up King James I, his ministers, and Parliament at the Palace of Westminster, rather appropriately opened London's apocalyptic 17th century. King James died in 1625, leaving on the throne a somewhat backward son, Charles I.

Although at this time London was the wealthiest city in the world, Charles I simply could not leave well enough alone. Insisting on the divine right of kings, a philosophy that was anathema to the Parliament and businessmen of London, he started a civil war. The monarchist Cavaliers were defeated by the Puritan Roundheads, and Charles I was beheaded outside his beloved Banqueting Hall, which had been designed by Inigo Jones. It's the only part of the massive Palace of Westminster that remains intact, and the ceiling painting by Rubens will give you a hint of the megalomania that led to Charles I's downfall: the Stuart dynasty is depicted as sitting at the righthand of God, and glorified beyond all recognition is the short, awkward king who managed to lose his throne and his head. Although the majority of London had been on the side of the antiroyalist Commonwealth, 18 years of dour Puritan reign under Oliver Cromwell's rule, during which all fun was canceled, left the city gasping for a breath of fresh air. The diarist John Evelyn wrote at Cromwell's death that "it was the joyfullest funeral I ever saw, for there were none that cried but dogs." In 1661, London warmly welcomed the exiled Charles II back from France, "shouting with inexpressible joy" and watching undismayed when Charles ordered the exhumation of the three-year-old corpses of Cromwell and two cronies for the dubious purpose of hanging and beheading them publicly for the murder of his father. Perhaps the citizens thought it fitting punishment for the closing of theaters, brothels, and gambling houses.

1660S: PLAGUE AND FIRE

CHARLES II BARELY HAD TIME TO ADJUST HIS crown when disaster struck. In early 1665, the first cases of a second round of the bubonic plague were seen in London. Samuel Pepys, the great diarist, first heard of the outbreak in April, writing, "Great fear of the sickness here in the city, it being said that two or three houses are already shut up. God preserve us." The hot summer saw the outbreak burst into an epidemic, with affected houses painted with red crosses and shut up with a guard outside—people trapped inside died either of the plague or starvation. By September, red crosses bloomed everywhere, and the rattle of the death cart was heard in the streets with its mournful accompaniment, "Bring out your dead!" a wretched parody of the cries of the apple or mussel sellers that had been silenced by the calamity. On September 7, John Evelyn wrote, "I went all along the city and suburbs from Kent Street to St. James's, a dismal passage and dangerous, to see so many coffins exposed in the streets thin of people, the shops shut up and all mournful silence, as not knowing whose turn might be next."

It was not humanity's finest hour: The stricken were prevented from leaving their homes, or if they had escaped London, from traveling on roads. They were often pelted with rocks and dung at the outskirts of villages. Con artists and quacks sold phony cures, and the rich and powerful jumped ship like the rats who were carrying the plague. The problem was that no one had figured out that it was the rats'—or, more accurately, the fleas' on the rats—fault. Mistaking the disease as airborne, someone decided that the very cats and dogs who could have helped control the rats had to be destroyed, and the killing of 60,000 animals certainly added to the disaster. The horror and pain of the disease was unspeakable, dispatching an estimated 100,000 by the time this epidemic began to abate, around Christmas 1665, when the cold started to kill off the fleas. In February, the king returned to London to survey—in safety, he thought—the melancholy scene of a decimated London still smelling of rotted flesh. But the rough hand of fate hadn't finished with London yet.

On September 2, 1666, a baker's oven in Pudding Lane was left unbanked. Its sparks, teased out of the chimney by a stiff wind, fired like tinder the dry wood of summer-baked houses and ignited the city in a matter of hours. Pepys was called at three in the morning by a servant to look at the fire, and being used to little local fires in the cramped wooden alleys and byways of London, he "thought it to be on the back side of Mark Lane at the furthest . . . I thought it far enough off, and so went back to bed."

The lord mayor also brushed the fire off, saying "a woman might piss it out," and no measures were taken to control the conflagration until it was too late. Amazingly, only a handful of people lost their lives, one of them a servant in the house of the baker where the fire had started. John Evelyn describes a ghastly picture of the event two days after it started: "The burning still rages, and it was now gotten as far as the Inner Temple; all Fleet Street, the Old Bailey, Ludgate Hill, Warwick Lane, Newgate, Paul's Chain, Watling Street, now flaming, and most of it reduced to ashes; the stones of St. Paul's flew like grenados, the melting lead running down the streets in a stream, and the very pavements glowing with fiery redness, so as no horse nor man was able to tread on them, and the demolition had stopped all the passages, so that no help could be applied."

King Charles finally stepped in and did what the lord mayor should have done sooner: His navy blew up the houses in the way of the fire, creating a break in its path. After four grim days, the driving wind died down and the fire finally ended. In its wake lay an unrecognizable London, suffering untold losses in its architecture, treasures, books, and art. In all, 436 acres of London had been consumed by the fire: 13,200 houses, 87 parish houses and many of their churches, 44 merchants' halls, the Royal Exchange, the magnificent medieval Guildhall, and St. Paul's Cathedral. It was, if nothing else, an opportunity to rebuild the city along straight and reasonable lines, obliterating the medieval maze of streets that had contributed to the tragedy.

But this was not to be. Although both John Evelyn and the young Christopher Wren submitted designs for a new London with wide thoroughfares and sensible squares and circuses, the urgent need for housing and the legal problems of ownership of land assured that the rebuilding followed the original "plan" of medieval London somewhat faithfully. The main differences were that the lanes were widened to a mandatory 14 feet, and the buildings were made of stone. This was Wren's great opportunity, as he rebuilt 51 of the ruined churches, including St. Paul's Cathedral. Despite the loss of many of those edifices during World War II, Wren's name will forever be associated with the glory of that age, as London rose like a phoenix from the ashes of the fire into the magnificence of the 18th century.

GEORGIAN LONDON

TO MOST LONDON CONNOISSEURS, THE 1700S remain the very apex of the city's greatness: in architecture, literature, theater, painting, sculpture, in the building of stately homes and parks, in philosophy and sciences, there can be no other century to rival the verve and creativity of the 18th. The names of the artists, thinkers, and artisans of the day have come to define their disciplines: William Hogarth, Sir

Joshua Reynolds, Thomas Gainsborough (painting); Jonathan Swift, Henry Fielding, Oliver Goldsmith (literature); David Garrick (theater); Alexander Pope (poetry); John Nash, Robert Adams (architecture); Edward Gibbon (history); John Gay (opera); David Hume (philosophy); Capt. James Cook (exploration); Adam Smith (economics); James Watt (technology); and the naturalized British subject, composer George Frederic Handel. Of course, you can hardly mention London and the 18th century in the same breath without a bow to the looming figure of the formidable writer and lexicographer Dr. Samuel Johnson and his biographer and friend, James Boswell. There are countless other figures who made major breakthroughs in technology, medicine, and science in this robust century. There was something in the air, it would seem, and not just the stench of the tanneries, slaughterhouses, and privies. In the 100-year span of this period, London grew from 650,000 souls to close to a million. The small villages north and west of the city were embraced by London's expansion. Near the bucolic hamlet of Knightsbridge, a country house was bought and grandly rebuilt by the duke of Buckingham, later to go to King George III as a private royal residence.

The relatively dull 12-year reign of Queen Anne left her name to a wildflower and a style of furniture. She was the last of the Stuart line; the last monarch to veto an act of Parliament; and she was on the throne when England and Scotland were unified as Great Britain. In 1714 came the Hanoverian succession from Germany. Georges I through IV presided over the acquisition of imperial lands from Canada to Australia and the ignominious loss of the wealthy American colonies to the war of independence. They saw the rise of a new technology that revolutionized the cotton and wool trades of England. They watched as the Bastille was stormed, igniting the French Revolution, and managed to keep their crowns on while across the channel others were losing their heads. They continued to prefer the German language while ruling an English-speaking kingdom. Due to this oddity, the position of prime minister came to be necessary; thanks to the madness of King George and the dissolute lifestyle of the prince regent, the policy-making powers of the monarch were carefully whittled away by an increasingly powerful Parliament.

The expansion and progress of London were attended by an increase in crime, corruption, drinking, and poverty. Dr. Johnson, whose remark that "when a man is tired of London, he's tired of life" was not without its irony, wrote a poem about London that exposed this dark underbelly:

Here malice, rapine, accident, conspire,
And now a rabble rages, now a fire;
Their ambush here relentless ruffians lay,
And here the fell attorney prowls for prey;
Here falling houses thunder on your head,

And here a female atheist talks you dead. . .
Prepare for death if here at night you roam,
And sign your will before you sup from home. . .

There was an increasing polarization—due to the incipient Industrial Revolution—of London's society into owners and workers, rich and poor. The coarseness and insensitivity to the less fortunate on the part of the wealthy was truly shocking. Their entertainment included outings to the insane asylums for a laugh and attendance at public executions, where they were fleeced by locals who charged outrageous prices for a window seat overlooking Newgate Gaol's scaffold. There was one law for the rich and one for the poor; the criminals who weren't executed for the slightest offense were made to endure a grueling and often fatal passage to the new penal colony in Australia. It was only by the most repressive of measures that the revolution in France did not spread to London's gates, especially after the Gordon Riots of 1780, in which the Newgate Gaol was stormed and 300 were left dead. There were a few reformers and progressive thinkers, most memorably Jonathan Swift, who, with his "Modest Proposal" of solving the problem of the Irish poor by feeding their babies to the rich, refined a tradition of savage English satire and social commentary that found many talented exponents in the Victorian century.

VICTORIAN LONDON

QUEEN VICTORIA'S REIGN STARTED IN 1837, after the unlamented last gasp of Georgian rule by the grotesque George IV. He may have been the patron of John Nash, who developed Regent's Park and filled the city with white stucco-covered houses, but other than that, George IV didn't do much for London, although the extravagances and vices of his court certainly helped fill the coffers of moneylenders, gambling dens, and whorehouses. Princess Victoria was a woman of only 18 years when she became queen and gave her name to an age of change and reaction, reform and wretchedness, empire and exploitation.

There is another name so completely identified with 19th-century London that it has become an adjective describing it: Charles Dickens. He is never far from the hearts and minds of the London dweller; his face appears—appropriately for one who wrote so much about money's awful power—on the £10 note. It is the London of Dickens we tend to think of when we envision the 19th century: poor Bob Cratchit freezing in Scrooge's office; the convict Magwitch and Pip fleeing on the Thames under the cover of pea-soup fog; Oliver Twist asking for more food in the orphanage; the endless court case of Jarndyce versus Jarndyce. Dickens was an insomniac who walked the streets of London for hours every night, and in his travels he picked up the sounds and secrets of the city. He is as much the voice of 19th-century London as Pepys and John Evelyn were of the 17th. Through his deeply compassionate reporting and fiction, Dickens opened up the eyes of the middle class to the misery of the poor. He helped steer England toward a more humane course as reformers worked to abolish the slave trade, put limits on child labor, allow women to keep their own property, extend voting rights, and open the first state schools.

The Industrial Revolution didn't so much flower as detonate in the 19th century; its effects were not entirely salutary. The gulf widened between rich and poor, the landscape and atmosphere were degraded, and as people in the country lost their self-sustainability, they trickled into a city already bursting at the seams with immigrants from the far reaches of the empire. But with all that cheap labor available, London grew at an amazing rate. New houses were built in every direction, with formerly quiet outlying villages becoming part of London's urban scene. The first underground trains began operation, sewers were built, transatlantic cable laid, the first police force was established, over-ground train tracks originating in London crisscrossed the country, omnibuses were pulled through the streets by huge workhorses, streets were gaslit, and roads were laid all over the city. Museums, monuments, learned societies, and public libraries flourished. The Great Exhibition of 1851, organized by Victoria's husband, Prince Albert, showed the world that London was a city of cosmopolitan suavity and culture, firmly looking to the future.

That Karl Marx wrote *Das Kapital* while living in this two-faced city has a certain poetic logic. The terrible contrast between the shiny new city, with its shops and theaters, hotels and town houses, and the unmitigated squalor of the East End slums in many ways defined the Victorian Age. It's interesting to see how rosy with nostalgia that era has come to be: look at the industry that has sprung up around all things Victorian in the last 25 years. It couldn't have been all that much fun to be alive then: the sexual hypocrisy, claustrophobic class system, sexism, racism, xenophobia, and social Darwinism must have been about as much fun as a night out with Jack the Ripper. Yet it was a time in which enormous changes took place, a time in which terrible injustices were at last redressed, and a time of unforgettable literature and indelible heroes. After all, any age that could produce Florence Nightingale, Oscar Wilde, and Lewis Carroll can't be all bad.

WORLD WAR I

QUEEN VICTORIA MADE A PERFECT EXIT IN January 1901, keeping her era neatly defined by century. And now the 20th century dawned with poor old Bertie, prince of Wales, at last out from under his mother's long shadow to lend his own name of King Edward to a new age. It was a short reign—only a decade, a mere fraction of his mother's 64 years on the throne—but it was distinctive enough to earn the title of the Edwardian Age, which was England's last era to be named for a monarch. It was a clear cusp between the centuries, a time of accelerated progress during which motorcars became common, corsets came off, women demonstrated for the vote and smoked in public, and people started to challenge a number of tired Victorian verities. As a well-known sensualist of the time, King Edward helped usher in a more permissive era in which free love, divorce, and bohemian living arrangements were practiced without the terror of ostracism from an uptight moral majority. The famously free-thinking Bloomsbury Group formed around this time, during which artists and writers who lived in the then shabby-genteel neighborhood of the British Museum redefined not only their artistic disciplines but also their relationships. Virginia Woolf's famous quote, "In or about December 1910, human character changed," underscores the leap made in thought and behavior by this new generation.

In 1914, London and the British Empire enjoyed the zenith of their world power. The British pound sterling was as safe as gold and was the currency of international commerce all over the globe. There was peace and prosperity. Social activists were kept busy working to get the vote for women, get children out of the factory and into a classroom, and force legislation that would make the government responsible for its neediest citizens. But the shadow of the German zeppelins loomed above London. Despite the efforts of pacifists like George Bernard Shaw, England was plunged into the ghastly war fought across the English Channel that came close to wiping out an entire generation of young Englishmen. When it was over in 1918, the whole social order changed again. It was a completely different London, filled with emancipated working women and powered by electricity.

THE LONG WEEKEND: 1918–1939

THERE IS A SENSE THAT THIS PERIOD BETWEEN the two World Wars was a last glimmer of glamour for London. There is something to that, despite the ugly rumblings from the black-shirted British fascists led by Nazi-sympathizer Sir Oswald Mosley; despite the economic depression that left millions unemployed; and despite the terrible losses of life, limb, and hope during World War I. It may be that we view this interlude with an acute awareness of how much was soon to be buried under the Blitz, which makes any frivolity of that time seem more poignant than silly.

People embraced the work of humorist P. G. Wodehouse, which helped them shake off the blues of the war and depression. To this day, the country still loves Wodehouse's version of London between the wars: gin-soaked parties with bright young things, dim Right Honorables, creaking lords and terrifying aunts, the Drones Club, and of course the unflappable Jeeves and his young master Bertie Wooster. They inhabit a hilarious fictional world that reveals what made London laugh between cataclysms. Noël Coward, Cecil Beaton, Virginia Woolf, George Orwell, Nancy Mitford, W. H. Auden, and

T. S. Eliot are a few of the artists whose work also captures the various feelings of that time.

London gave Hollywood a run for its money, making movies with such luminaries as Sir Laurence Olivier, Peggy Ashcroft, Charles Laughton, and Alfred Hitchcock. Agatha Christie and Dorothy Sayers fed the increasing demand for murder mysteries. The West End was alive with plays, from melodramas to social realism. But nothing cooked up in the imagination could even come close to the real-life drama of 1936: the abdication of King Edward VIII for the woman he loved, the American divorcée Mrs. Wallis Simpson. Although the event was billed as a grave constitutional crisis, it was clear that the monarch of England was becoming increasingly irrelevant to the citizenry, except as gossip and newsreel fodder. The citizens were mainly concerned with their own lives as they joined trade unions, built suburban communities, and tried to figure out the map of the underground. In 1931, this tangled web was simplified into the sleek art deco design we know and love, and the population of eight million began using the tube to escape the brown-fogged city to ever-more distant reaches of residential London.

Meanwhile, across the English Channel, Europe was increasingly threatened by Adolf Hitler, dismissed in the early days by most intelligent Londoners as a twisted clown and admired by a shameful number of hate-filled fascists and dim-witted minor (and some major) nobility. They would all come to despise his name, as his Luftwaffe rained destruction on London, and Europe's fleeing Jews came to town with stories of concentration camps and genocide too horrible to believe.

THE BLITZ: "OUR FINEST HOUR"

WORLD WAR I, THE "WAR TO END ALL WARS," couldn't live up to that promise for long; only two decades after the armistice was signed, London was once again anxiously watching the skies over Whitehall. Though this time it wasn't the lumbering zeppelins, but the significantly more deadly Messerschmitts, Stukas, and the unpiloted "doodlebugs" that spelled disaster. The attack started in earnest on the sunny day of September 7, 1940, when hundreds of fighter planes and bombers buzzed up the Thames and destroyed docks, gasworks, and power stations. The Luftwaffe went on to bomb London nightly for 76 consecutive nights, dropping over 27,000 high explosives and thousands more incendiaries. The Blitz was on. The night of December 29, 1940 was the worst, with the city almost burned to the ground and St. Paul's Cathedral under serious threat. Children were hurriedly sent to the countryside or to America, but the royal family made a point of staying in town, even after nine bombs dropped on Buckingham Palace. People sheltered in the tube stations in staggeringly large numbers, sleeping on the ground or in bunk beds placed on the tracks and platforms. Above ground, civilians coped with bombed-out streets, nightly fires, disrupted railways, power and water failures, the destruction of their homes, and, most terribly, the deaths of their friends, neighbors, and families. Novelist Nancy Mitford described the scene vividly in a letter to a friend:

> I find my nerves are standing up to the thing better now—I don't tremble quite all the time as I did. . . NOBODY can have the slightest idea of what it is like until they've experienced it. As for the screaming bombs, they simply make your flesh creep but the whole thing is so fearful that they are actually only a slight added horror. The great fires everywhere, the awful din which never stops, and wave after wave after wave of aeroplanes, ambulances tearing up the street and the horrible unnatural blaze of lights from searchlights, etc.—all has to be experienced to be understood. Then in the morning the damage—people ring one another up to tell one how their houses are completely non-existent. . . People are beyond praise, everyone is red eyed and exhausted but you never hear a word of complaint or down-heartedness. It is most reassuring.

> —(Selina Hastings, Nancy Mitford [London: Hamish Hamilton, 1985], p. 134.)

The bombardment put to the test the famous English stiff upper lip, and London's amazing rise to the challenge earned the admiration of the rest of the country and the world. Prime Minister Winston Churchill was the voice of the people during those dark days, author of such unforgettable war cries as "we shall defend our island, whatever the cost may be, we shall fight on the beaches, we shall fight on the landing grounds, we shall fight in the fields and in the streets, we shall fight in the hills; we shall never surrender," and "Let us therefore brace ourselves to our duties, and so bear ourselves that, if the British Empire and its Commonwealth last for a thousand years, men will still say, 'This was their finest hour.'"

And so it was. Despite the thousands killed, the millions wounded and made homeless, the destruction of hundreds of thousands of dwelling places and buildings, and the nearly total destruction of the city and the East End, London carried on. The people lived in corrugated steel caves called Anderson shelters (to be replaced later by the heavier Morrison shelters) buried three feet underground. The homeless were sheltered by hotels—when the East End was first bombed, a huge crowd marched to the Savoy and demanded to be admitted, which they were—as well as by the not completely invulnerable tube stations. Brigades of men and women pulled all-night duties to put fires out in likely targets such as Westminster Abbey and St. Paul's Cathedral, saving some of the precious treasures of London's past. When the war finally ended, it could be well said of the blitzed Londoners that, again in the words of Churchill, "their will was resolute and remorseless, and as it proved, unconquerable."

SUNSET OF THE EMPIRE

IN 1948, ENGLAND LOST THE JEWEL OF HER colonial crown when India became independent, and over the next decade it continued to lose colonies around the world, as well as much of the shipping and manufacturing business that made her rich. The 1950s were spent cleaning up the wreckage of the Blitz and continuing to live under strict food rationing. There was a greyness in the city; gaps of bomb sites yawned among the old Victorian buildings that were still black with coal grime and sagging under the weight of the years. People abandoned the city for the suburbs, whose spread was contained by the public lands of the Green Belt on the outer perimeters of London. Yet London was buoyant; the welfare improvements of the Labour government helped people rebuild their lives and gave them a sense of security unknown up to that time. In 1946, Heathrow Airport was opened, followed by Gatwick Airport three years later; the city was quickly rebuilt with modern glass-and-steel towers (Samuel Johnson and Charles Dickens would weep with confusion if they time-traveled to their old haunts); and domestic laborsaving devices were new, plentiful, and affordable.

The most influential of these was certainly the television, on which people watched the colorful coronation of Queen Elizabeth II on June 2, 1953, from the comfort of their own armchairs. The prime minister, Harold Macmillan, said in 1959, "Most of our people never had it so good."

The Festival of Britain celebrated the centennial of Prince Albert's Great Exhibition, and it was on that site the South Bank Arts Centre came to be. The fog lifted, thanks to antipollution measures, and the future looked as bright as the sky on a clear day. A new age was indeed coming, and it was a doozy. After the war, a quarter of the map of the world had been colored with pink empire; by the mid-1960s, England had lost almost all of her colonial possessions.

THE SWINGING SIXTIES AND PUNK SEVENTIES

WHATEVER ENGLAND MAY HAVE LOST IN HER empire, London certainly compensated by becoming ground zero of the 1960s "youth quake." The iconic 1960s figures of the Beatles and James Bond joined the thinner ones of Twiggy and Julie Christie in making all things British very hip. England was swinging like a pendulum, and London, as always, was the epicenter of the groove. Movies such as *A Hard Day's Night, Blowup, To Sir with Love,* and *A Man for All Seasons* were worldwide hits. The comedy of Spike Milligan gave way to Monty Python. Michael Caine, Vanessa and Lynn Redgrave, Oliver Reed, and Terrence Stamp were among the many English stars who could pull off a Hollywood blockbuster as well as do Pinter or Shakespeare in the West End. Peter Sellers's Inspector Clouseau made him a superstar—a word and concept born in the bright light of the 1960s. Fashion designers of Carnaby Street and the King's Road started the miniskirt and bell-bottom trends, and fashion photographers like David Bailey became as famous as their subjects. The Rolling Stones, The Kinks, Cream, The Yardbirds, Led Zeppelin, The Who . . . London's bands in the 1960s were a veritable *Debrett's Peerage* of rock and roll. Twenty-something rock stars and their birds got their clothes at Granny Takes a Trip and Biba, drove around in Bentleys, and bought stately old piles in the country from hard-up toffs. *Hair* was performed in the West End, scandalizing audiences with its on-stage nudity. The Rolling Stones put on a free concert in Hyde Park, which was also the scene of political demonstrations and love-ins. Drugs, sex, and rock and roll became a way of life for many of the new generation.

No one did sex, drugs, and rock and roll better than the glam rockers and punks of the 1970s, who went to extremes. Green Mohawk hairdos, safety pins piercing cheeks, very high platform shoes, and in-your-face attitudes were the usual for the King's Road, where designer Vivienne Westwood and Malcolm McLaren (later manager of The Sex Pistols) had a punk-rock clothing shop—still there with the crazy backward-moving clock outside—under a series of interesting names ("Sex" was one, and "Too Fast to Live, Too Young to Die" another). If you told this peroxided punk goddess with the ripped shirts with zippers and chains that she would one day receive an Order of the British Empire from the Queen and have her own exhibition at the V&A, she would have told you to sod off, or words to that effect.

Feminism had many local, brilliant exponents, with Angela Carter writing in south London and Aussie expat Germaine Greer lecturing around the city. The literature of the day was pretty dark; Martin Amis's *Dead Babies* was a savage and chilling portrait of young people in 1970s London that opened the door to many imitators. *A Clockwork Orange,* filmed by Stanley Kubrick in 1972 from the novel by Anthony Burgess, was a surreal prediction of a London gone viciously mad in the not-too-distant future. Squatters took over entire buildings that were earmarked for renovation; value-added tax was introduced; and a Women's Year Rally coincided with the election of Margaret Thatcher as leader of the Conservative Party. By the time Sid Vicious of The Sex Pistols had stabbed his girlfriend and then overdosed in New York City, people were exhausted and disillusioned with the 1970s. It seemed time to get on to more upbeat pastimes—like making money, that old-time London passion.

THE THATCHER YEARS

WHEN MARGARET THATCHER WAS MADE prime minister in 1979, she announced the somewhat astonishing goal of returning to Victorian values. She axed 40,000 civil-service jobs, wrested control of London Transport away from the Greater London Council (GLC), and sold it to private investors. The gap between rich and poor became wider, as a very Victorian economic and social Darwinism—the survival of the fittest and fattest cats—took shape. After fighting constantly with the Labour-based Greater London Council over social services and privatization, she abolished the GLC altogether in 1986, and the building on the Thames that housed it stood empty until the Marriot Hotel and the Saachi Gallery moved in. People in the city were suddenly making piles of dough (as they were on Wall Street across the pond), property prices were sky-high, and the materialistic yuppie came to define the era in both England and the United States.

London in the 1980s also saw race riots in Brixton, the first cases of AIDS, strikes by tube- and steelworkers, and a ban on smoking on the London Underground after a fire at King's Cross killed 31 people. Homelessness rose most disturbingly, as Thatcherism ripped holes in the socialist safety net, and the real-estate boom took its toll on government housing. But all that money had a salubrious affect on the surface of London, as many of the old white stucco fronts of private homes and the marble of grand old buildings got a good old scrub, erasing years of coal smoke from their faces. Look at any photos of London in the mid-20th century and compare it to contemporary views: even allowing for sepia-toned discolorment, the change is startling. Throwing off the old habits of war cover, London became brightly lit, shining arc lights on its many monuments and museums. Even Harrods started lighting up, outlined in white bulbs that locals would say is tawdry but secretly admire. Another bright spot in the 1980s was of course the "fairy-tale" marriage of Princess Diana and Prince Charles at St. Paul's Cathedral in 1981, watched by millions on TV and providing a much-needed popularity punch to the boring old House of Windsor. In 1989, Thatcher closed out her decade by resigning (to put it nicely), and John Major took over as another Conservative prime minister.

COOL BRITANNIA: THE 1990S

THE 1990S STARTED WITH THE HISTORICAL joining of the French and English sides of the new tunnel beneath the English Channel, linking Paris and London with a three-hour train ride, whose duration gets shorter every decade (it's currently down to two and a half hours). The xenophobic fear that hordes of foreigners would breach London by rail never quite materialized, although the train surely had a part to play in the huge upsurge of tourism in the 1990s.

In 1992, the queen suffered her famous annus horribilis (you've got to love a queen who uses Latin the way we use slang). A fire at Windsor Castle caused extensive damage, Charles and Diana and Andrew and Fergie were having horrendously public marital troubles, and, worst of all, the richest woman in the world had to pay taxes for the first time in her life. Not one to leave books unbalanced—this is a woman who lived through the Blitz and food rationing—the queen decided to pay for the repair of Windsor Castle by opening Buckingham Palace to the public for two months a year. They're now raking in so much money that there was enough left over to upgrade the Queen's Gallery, where we can now see even more of the royal treasures.

The 1990s saw a number of cultural developments, such as the rise of the "Britpack" of young artists whose work made traditionalists wonder if they were losing touch: Damian Hirst's animal carcasses floating in formaldehyde, Chris Ofili's elephant dung Virgin Mary, and Tracy Emin's unmade bed won prizes and patrons. Brits started being funny again, with French and Saunders, Eddie Izzard, the Fast Show, and Blackadder hopping the pond to amuse Anglophones everywhere. By the time the Brit-pop explosion signaled the start of "Cool Britannia," everyone in the world knew that London was again the place to be. The Spice Girls, Oasis, All Saints, and Robbie Williams put British music back at the top of the charts. London Fashion Week became one of the hottest tickets in Europe, rivaling even Milan and Paris as the event in which to showcase new collections.

In May 1997, Tony Blair of the Labour Party was voted in as prime minister, signaling an end to the Conservative Party's 18-year run, and beginning a historic three-term reign. Blair ran on a platform of finding the "third way" between the policies of Tory and Labour, and he succeeded mainly in annoying both parties. The same year also saw the tragedy of Princess Diana's death in a car crash in Paris, and the resulting week of completely un-British mourning. It was a spasm of national grief that had Buckingham Palace doing backflips to appease the people who found fault with how the royal family responded to the tragedy. People stood in line for days to sign the condolence book at St. James's Palace, while a sea of flowers numbering in the millions was left at the gates of Kensington Palace. It was a London no one had ever seen before and will likely never see again.

Next up for London was the opening of the Millennium Dome, the much maligned and hyped exhibition to celebrate the turning of the century and the next millennium. To the bitter delight of its critics, the exhibition failed to draw the crowds anticipated, and plans on what to do with the hulking thing are still up in the air, but the latest plan is to develop it as an arena for sports and entertainment.

Another millennium damp squib was the Sir Charles Foster–designed footbridge over the Thames, connecting the Globe Theatre and St. Paul's Cathedral. While it beautifully fulfilled its design as a "blade of light" across the Thames, on the opening day it shook so dangerously that it had to be closed for a rethink, with everyone involved blaming each other for the humiliating foul-up. Now the bridge is fully operational and vies with the nearby Hungerford Bridge as the best walk across the Thames.

An unmitigated success, however, was the British Airways London Eye, the elegant Ferris wheel that now looms over the Thames with surprising grace, adding to the grandeur of views of Parliament Square and beyond. It was originally intended to be temporary with a five-year lease, but that's been extended to 20 years, and it is most likely that your great-grandchildren will be queuing up to take that stately ride.

A more mixed blessing to London was the election of its first mayor, one with actual power, unlike the honorary lord mayor. Former Greater London Council–head Ken Livingstone has been trying, with varying degrees of success, to make London a better place to live, with his first priority being to make the public transport system more efficient, apparently an impossible dream, despite the controversial congestion charge that was instituted in 2002 to reduce traffic in central London.

A NEW WORLD: AFTER SEPTEMBER 11

THE TERRORIST ATTACK ON THE PENTAGON in Washington, D.C., and the World Trade Center in New York City threw the world into a state of panic, and the hardest-hit business was the travel trade, from airlines to souvenir shops. London, an equally significant symbol of Western capitalism and culture as New York, went into the same high alert as the United States. Of course, London, having coped with the years of IRA terrorism, went quietly into action without much ado: permanently closing the street in front of the American Embassy, arresting suspected Al Qaeda members, and stepping up security in the Parliament and other high-profile institutions, such as the museums and cathedrals. The number of visitors to London dropped dramatically in the months following the attack, and the buoyant financial outlook of the 1990s gave way to a nervous slide in the stock market, real estate, and consumer goods. With the war in Iraq, tourism took an even greater hit as England and Prime Minister Tony Blair became partners with the United States in the coalition forces in the Middle East. Peace demonstrations in Hyde Park put the government on notice, and a rally in Trafalgar Square featured the toppling of a statue of George Bush. The period of tourists staying away in droves ironically corresponded to the completion of new hotels and restaurants responding to the trend of the 1990s, and by the time people began getting on planes again, the exchange rate of dollar-to-pound was topping out at $1.95, making even mid-range hotel prices of £150 a terrifying $292 a night.

The year 2002 was the Queen's Golden (50th) Jubilee, which turned out to be a total lovefest for Lizzie. The House of Windsor was royally entertained by a lineup of rock and roll's own royalty. Queen's Brian May kicked off a great concert in the garden at Buck House, playing "God Save the Queen" on his electric guitar on the palace roof, and Prince of Darkness Ozzy Osbourne managed to perform without swearing. The Queen certainly needed the cheering up, as she had recently lost her sister, Princess Margaret, and her mother, the Queen Mum Elizabeth, who was over 101 years of age when she died.

2005 was a momentous year: Prince Charles finally wed his mistress of 30 years, Camilla Parker-Bowles in April, making her the Duchess of Cornwall to mixed reactions. In May 2005, Tony Blair was reelected prime minister for a historically unprecedented third time for a Labour Party member. Two months later, on what has come to be called the 7/7 attacks, four British-born Muslim terrorists detonated four bombs on the underground and a bus, killing an estimated 55 innocent people, and producing the finest example of grace under fire seen since the Blitz. While American soldiers at a nearby military base were ordered to stay out of London for five days, Londoners were back on the tube the next day, and continued to be determined to display implacable calm in the face of the horror. The brave readiness of the fire, police, and medical personnel was equally impressive. Although when a second attack was attempted unsuccessfully one week later, many Londoners lost faith in the effectiveness of the anti-terror squads. The shooting of an innocent man at the Stockwell tube station further shook the citizens' confidence in the police.

On the same day as the 7/7 bombings, to less fanfare than was planned, London won the bid to host the 2012 Summer Olympic Games. It was an extraordinary day for the city.

Beleaguered mayor Ken Livingstone presided over the abolition of the traditional pigeonfeeding from Trafalgar Square, as well as the closing of its northern end to traffic, creating a pigeon-free, automobile-free pedestrian area. The controversial congestion charge reduced traffic in central London, according to those who should know, the taxi drivers, but it has been hard on shops and services. In July 2005 the charge was raised from five pounds to eight, in order to pay for an extension of the congestion area, which would make West London, to Earl's Court, subject to the eight pound congestion charge. (Despite the big names in retail protesting vociferously, and smaller businesses looking at increased running costs and reduced customer base, Ken Livingstone seems to consult only his own conscience in making decisions for London). The scheme relies on cameras and prepayments, and not surprisingly, in the first week almost 10,000 people were falsely accused of not paying. The tube saw an increase of 17,000 trips a day just a month after the congestion charge was introduced. The buses move a bit more freely in some areas, but actually have added time to their trip in other places. Retailers in the congestion areas have seen a distressing drop in business. The money raised by the congestion charge is supposed to be used to improve public transportation and quality of life in London, but at the time of publication, the city is still unwieldy and difficult for the citizen. Public transportation suffers from high fares and low expectations, and with the specter of terrorism hanging over it, it has been eschewed by visitors and locals alike. Tube strikes bring the city to a standstill often (though thankfully not with the regularity of Paris), automobile traffic is still bad, roadwork is constantly causing traffic jams, and the streets after midnight are rife with the shouts of drunken louts and the assault of the occasional mugger. Livingstone has plans to increase the police force to 35,000 by 2006, which should sort out the crime problems considerably, and pubs will be allowed to stay open past 11 p.m., a baffling "solution" to the public drunkenness associated with the drink-all-you-can-before-closing syndrome. To the delight of many, smoking is finally becoming an issue in London, and many restaurants are now smoke-free. By 2008, pubs that serve food will be required to be completely nonsmoking. Now if they could do something about the pollution from the diesel trucks and auto emissions, we might start breathing more easily.

The bottom line is that London is and always has been a big city with big problems, along with its myriad delights. But no matter what the century, London will *always* remain a fascinating, fast-paced, infuriating, and fun-filled destination of choice.

BRITISH CULTURE: QUEUES, *the* WEATHER, *and a* STIFF UPPER LIP

A FOREIGN TRIBE

THE MOST WONDERFUL THING ABOUT COMING to London is the opportunity for English-speaking transatlantics to learn more about a foreign culture than could be possible in any European city with a language barrier. That is not to say that there won't be communication problems, but at least you'll know the words, if not always the meaning behind them. The great misunderstandings are not in language but in nuance. This is a society based on the oblique and the tacit, with an intrinsic orderliness that springs from the old class system. You'll never understand it in the course of a visit, so just be polite and go along with the program. They're not going to change a hair for you.

George Bernard Shaw said that it is impossible for one Englishman to open his mouth without inviting the disdain of another. These days some people would very much like to believe that this is no longer true; whether it is still reality is open to argument. What is referred to as "BBC pronounciation" has wrought some changes in the various accents of England. Professor Henry Higgins, in Shaw's *Pygmalion*, had the entertaining ability to identify the very street on which a Londoner grew up by the accent. You don't have to be a linguist to be able to know who was raised in South London, East London, or in a boarding school, but these accents are no longer strictly defined by class. It is certain, however, that as a foreigner, you will never have to go through the process of having your class and social status sized up, judgments made, and conclusions drawn. You will likely be treated as an unknown, perhaps a novelty, and if you are American, with a curious combination of admiring amusement and the occasional flicker of contempt.

The primary exposure most Brits have to Americans is via Hollywood, and the Brits may check you out to see if the stereotype matches up with the real thing. You, of course, are free to do likewise. But trust me, you won't run into Mary Poppins, Bertie Wooster, Jeeves, James Bond, Miss Marple, or Austin Powers. You will find that they are not amused by any attempts to claim some kind of special kinship with them—this is essentially an island culture, insulated for centuries against all comers, and still in some ways quite impenetrable by outsiders. This gives Brits their strength, eccentricity, and quiet assumption of superiority. The wonderful thing about us transatlantics is how we buy into this assumption in an automatic, reflexive way. Americans, it has been observed, can go weak before an English accent—and it doesn't even have to be a "posh" accent, which we wouldn't necessarily recognize, because we've somehow trained ourselves to think of the English as indeed superior in intelligence and experience. It could be thought of as the *Masterpiece Theatre* complex, except that it existed long before television. Don't fall into that trap—we're just different, like apples and oranges, or, as the British say, chalk and cheese.

GET IN LINE: THE ENGLISH ART OF QUEUING

ALL THE RUMORS ARE TRUE: THE BRITISH QUEUE for everything. Even soccer hooligans queue for tickets and beer. To jump the queue is the height of bad manners, and to do so is to invite certain tut-tutting, muttered comments, and, in the case of soccer games, a punch in the face. In fact, it is such a breach of etiquette that it is about the only time the British will break another taboo, the one that prohibits raising one's voice in public (markets, pubs, and soccer stadiums notwithstanding). Nowadays, the order of the bus queue has been breached, and you no longer see neat single-file lines along the pavement, but, please, do not give a little old lady the elbow and jump ahead of her. You'll regret it.

Also, always stand to the right when riding on escalators—the locals, even if they have no intention of passing you, hate it when tourists stand two abreast and clog up the path.

WEATHER REPORTS

THE OLD SAW ABOUT HOW EVERYONE TALKS about the weather but no one does anything about it is not entirely true in London. The passion that the British have for talking about the weather amounts nearly to an interactive hobby. They will even go so far as to discuss it vigorously with complete strangers: As Dr. Johnson observed in the 18th century, "When two Englishmen meet, their first talk is of the weather." And frankly, it's rich material for discussion: London can easily go through four seasons in one day. The casting of aspersions on the abilities of the forecasters is a tried-and-true icebreaker and will pave the way for inquiries from the Brits about the extreme and interesting weather (tornadoes, blizzards, hurricanes, monsoons, sandstorms, and so on) of former colonial continents. As everyone must know by now, the famous London fogs of the past were a result of the coal burned in London, and a bona fide "pea-souper" hasn't been sighted since the early 1960s, after the Clean Air Act of 1956 put a stop to industrial pollution. The idea that it rains constantly in London is also a myth, although there isn't one Londoner who doesn't own at least one umbrella (called a brolly; over 7,000 are lost on London buses and trains a year), nor will you find too many visitors who haven't been forced to buy a rain poncho or umbrella on short notice. The once reliably cool summers have, like so much of the world, fallen prey to ferocious heat spells, which are made more hellish by the lack of air-conditioning on public transport, and in some restaurants and hotels. However, they are short-lived compared to the blistering heat of southern Europe.

AT YOUR SERVICE, SORT OF

A RECENT STUDY CONCLUDED THAT THE BRITISH complain more about poor service than the residents of any other country. However, it also concluded that this is because they have more to complain about. They have only recently realized that it's OK to enjoy good food; the deprivations and sacrifices of the postwar years cast a very long shadow. There's good food all over London now, and extra-virgin olive oil is no longer considered a foreign delicacy. However, they will not put iced water and a basket of bread on the table as a matter of course (worse, they may charge you a pound). They will not rush to take your order or bring you your bill. They will not take kindly to complaint—it's not so much that the customer is always wrong, but that the customer overestimates his or her importance. Don't take it personally: it's a British thing.

THE GREAT BRITISH RESERVE

THIS IS ALIVE AND WELL, STIFFENING THE upper lip and continuing to define "Englishness." You will see it manifested in the advertising, where wit and wordplay take precedence over volume, sloganeering, and repetition (although this may come to be a relic of the past, as vulgarity and briefly clad people in ads grow apace on the sides of buses and on billboards). It is apparent in the weather forecasts ("Today will be rather damp, with a possibility of patchy fog and maybe a spot of drizzle in between clear intervals") and on the tube at rush hour, where instead of mouthing off at an annoying commuter who refuses to move down in the carriage, passengers will mutter "excuse me's," issue irritated coughs, and initiate great flappings of newspapers. This quietude can be almost soothing and welcome to an American accustomed to the chattering hordes of compatriots asking personal questions and offering the usual too much information, but it can take a bit of getting used to at first and might leave the visitor feeling a little out in the cold. The traditional silence on buses and trains has been broken by people shouting into their mobile phones, but the prevailing mood on public transport can still be strangely meditative.

However, this reserve is not to be taken for granted. Road rage is a big problem in traffic-choked London, but luckily the gun laws are stringent enough that it results in shouting matches and fisticuffs rather than more serious consequences. And there is nothing quite so ominous to the uninitiated as the roar of 10,000 grown men at a soccer game singing with one voice, "You're shite and you know you are!" Not for them the cozy familiarity of the seventh-inning stretches and the lilting tones of "Take Me Out to the Ballgame."

A similar contradiction to the stereotype is found during the prime minister's question period in the House of Commons. Barely veiled or even naked insults are hurled by members of Parliament at one another, while howls of derision and guffaws of braying laughter render the institution more like a high-school classroom when the teacher has stepped out than a hallowed hall of government. There is something rather invigorating about this cacophony, and it gives you an idea of the healthy self-regard in which the English hold themselves. The great paradox is that they yield to no one, even if some of them get weak at the knees before the Queen.

TO DO OR NOT TO DO: THAT IS THE CULTURE

THERE WAS AN ARTICLE IN *THE SPECTATOR* magazine a few years ago in which the staff gave the worst possible advice to put in a tourist guide to London. They came up with, among others, "Introduce yourself and shake hands all around in your train compartment," and, "Try out the famous echo in the British Library Reading Room." As funny as we find this concept, we will resist temptation and will give you the following dos and don'ts guaranteed to be 100% valid.

- Don't call older people by their first names unless expressly asked to do so—it is considered normal not to use any names at all when addressing people.
- Don't expect people to introduce you to others. One can spend an entire evening with a group of people who introduce neither themselves nor their friends to you.

- Don't try to intervene in soccer arguments—it's a very serious subject, one no outsider can comprehend properly. Remember at games that the hooligans mean business.
- Don't take it personally when people act as if you're not there, correct your pronunciation, look at you as if you're daft when asking directions to "Lye-cester Square," act slightly exasperated by your inability to read a complex map of London, or try to run you down in the street. You'll get a lot of this—get used to it.
- Don't brag about how much sunlight you get at home; this will not endear you to anyone.
- Don't tell anyone that their accent is "cute." It is you who has the accent, and it is not considered remotely cute by the British.
- Don't gloat about the American Revolution or the sunset on the British Empire. Again, not cute.
- Do watch out for queues and take your place in them.
- Do be courteous; it's appreciated much more than friendliness.
- Do remember that this is a country of rules, rules, rules—and they aren't just making them up as they go along, though it sometimes seems that they are.
- Do be patient in restaurants and stores; use your vacation as an opportunity to slow down and practice your manners.
- Do learn to enjoy being called "love" and "darling" and "sweetheart" by certain strangers.
- Do prepare for your visit by reading as much as you can about London; when here, try to listen more than you speak. This is a very interesting place, and the people are fascinating. Make the most of your visit.

Divided by a Common Language: A British/English Glossary

Thanks to the broadcasting of television shows and films (in London, films are viewed at the cinema, as opposed to movies or flicks viewed at the theater), the British are more hip to our lingo than they may let on. But if your exposure to Brit-speak has been limited to watching some shows on PBS or A&E, you may need a bit of a leg up. We have provided a short glossary of some words you may not have caught watching *Pride and Prejudice* or *King Lear*. With the globalization of culture, it is almost quaint to assume that we English speakers might misunderstand each other, but just in case, here goes:

AMERICAN	ENGLISH
AT THE AIRPORT	
cart	trolley
bill	bank note

Divided by a Common Language:
A British/English Glossary *(continued)*

AMERICAN	ENGLISH
AT THE AIRPORT (CONTINUED)	
wallet	billfold/purse
telephone booth	telephone box/kiosk
ON THE ROAD	
baby carriage/stroller	pram/buggy
dead-end road	cul-de-sac
delivery truck	van
divided highway	dual carriageway
detour	diversion
gas	petrol
highway exit	motorway junction
hood (car)	bonnet
license plate	number plate/registration
minivans	people carriers
sedan car	saloon car
subway	underground or tube
overpass	flyover
one-way ticket	single journey
pull-off	lay-by
round-trip ticket	return ticket
station wagon	estate car
truck	lorry
trunk	boot
underpass	subway (pedestrian, under streets)
AT THE HOTEL	
antenna	aerial
apartment hotel	service flats
apartment building	block of flats, mansion block
baby crib	cot
baggage room	left-luggage office
bathe (verb)	bath (bathing—short "a" sound)
bathrobe	dressing gown
cot	extra bed or camp bed
call collect	reverse charges

Divided by a Common Language: A British/English Glossary (continued)

AMERICAN	ENGLISH
AT THE HOTEL (CONTINUED)	
closet	cupboard/wardrobe
comforter/quilt	eiderdown/duvet
elevator	lift
first floor	ground floor
second floor	first floor
long-distance call	trunk call
milk in coffee/tea or not	white or black
outlet/socket	power point
rent	let
vacuum	Hoover
washcloth	face flannel
IN A RESTAURANT OR FOOD STORE	
buffet	sideboard
can (of food)	tin
candy	sweets
check	bill
cookie	biscuit
cotton candy	candy floss
cracker	savoury biscuit
dessert	pudding
diaper	nappy
downtown	town center/high street
druggist/drugstore	chemist/chemist's shop
eggplant	aubergine
eraser	rubber
French fries	chips
hamburger meat	mince
hardware store	ironmonger
lima bean	broad bean
molasses	black treacle
potato chips	crisps
pit	stone

AMERICAN	ENGLISH
IN A RESTAURANT OR FOOD STORE (CONTINUED)	
Popsicle	ice lolly
raisin	sultana
smoked herring	kipper
zucchini	courgette
AT THE THEATER	
aisle	gangway
balcony	gallery/upper circle
intermission	interval
mezzanine/loge	dress circle
movie theater	cinema
IN THE MARKETS AND ON THE HIGH STREET	
liquor store	off license
newsstand	newsagent
notions	haberdashery
panties	knickers
panty hose	tights
raincoat	macintosh (or mac)/kagool
restroom	public convenience/loo/w.c./lavatory
sneakers	trainers or plimsolls
Scotch tape	cellotape
shorts (underwear)	pants
sweater	jumper
undershirt	vest
vest	waistcoat
IN SICKNESS AND IN HEALTH	
acetaminophen (Tylenol)	paracetamol
emergency room	casualty
Band-Aids	plasters
pimples	spots
rubbing alcohol	surgical spirit

PART TWO

PLANNING *your* VISIT

AIRLINE DEALS

British Airways (☎ 800-AIRWAYS, **www.britishairways.com**) and Virgin Atlantic Airways (☎ 800-862-8621, **www.virgin.com**) are the two largest transatlantic carriers in and out of London and are certainly the ones to check with first to get a baseline on a fare. They often engage in price wars, which means the other airlines will lower their prices too, or at least try to match the lowest rate.

Obviously, if you are collecting frequent flier miles with a particular carrier, that's the airline to use because you will accumulate a tidy sum of miles with a round-trip. With the recent difficulties in the airline industry, there is no predicting which airlines will have the best deals or the largest selection of flights to London, so you will need to call or surf around. Some of the United States–based, transatlantic airlines are American (☎ 800-433-7300, **www.aa.com**); Delta (☎ 800-241-4141, **www.delta.com**); and United (☎ 800-241-6522, **www.united.com**). They all fly into either Heathrow or Gatwick.

Consolidators buy up blocks of unsold seats from airlines and resell them to you. Some consolidators deal primarily with domestic tickets, and while they may get you a ticket to London, it might be the same price as the published fare from an airline, and more restrictions may apply. The Internet has made it so easy to shop for fares, but there is a here-today-gone-tomorrow quality of many of the Web sites, not to mention the gobbling-up of small sites by larger ones, such as the recent merger of Travelocity with the UK's Lastminute.com. Some of the so-called discount Web sites are actually owned by or partnered with various airlines and offer very little discount, if at all, and some are merely agencies to sell tickets. Before you start searching the Internet, call a couple of the big airlines to get

unofficial **TIP**
Flight consolidators are a good way to shop for the best deal, but be sure that the one you use books foreign travel.

an idea of what prices are available directly from them. Sometimes it helps to talk to a person; sometimes there are Web-only discounts from that airline, which they may tell you about. However, as far as discount shops go, the airlines maintain a dignified silence on the subject of bucket shops and flight consolidators: they would as soon tell you about these deals as Ticketmaster would direct you to a street scalper. Beware of prices that look too good to be true: They are probably the lowest-seasonal fare minus all those extra fees and taxes that can really add up. And forget about the last-minute concept—airlines will also wait till the last minute to see how full the flight will be before they start discounting tickets, and you probably won't get a better deal than you would have gotten by planning well ahead. In most cases, prices go up, not down, as the plane gets fuller—go and look what a ticket from New York to London costs for tomorrow on any airline Web site.

Check the back of the Sunday newspaper travel section for ads of consolidators, and make a few calls to them. You can often save money by taking a nondirect flight, changing planes in France or Germany or even Iceland, but this option requires the patience of Job and the resilience of a backpacker, turning a seven- to ten-hour flight into a (possibly overnight) marathon.

Here are a few tried-and-true Web sites (arranged alphabetically):

www.bestfares.com	Big database; lots of vacation options (cars, hotel rooms, packages)
www.cheapflights.com	Easy-to-use site with discount prices from airlines, agents, and discount specialists in the U.K. and the U.S.
www.cheaptickets.com	Finds cheapest Web fares available, and offers an affiliate program with travel rewards
www.expedia.com	Well-established Web site; always check prices against the airlines' Web sites before booking
www.goodfare.com	International travel discounts, including consolidator fares
www.priceline.com	Where you "bid" for a price, but rarely get it. (Best deals here are for the hotel rooms and some packages.)
www.orbitz.com	Good place to browse (thousands of fares); not always best prices
www.travelocity.com	Full-service everything; hotels, flights, rental cars, and tourist attraction ticket packages are decent, with a wide variety of hotels to choose from.

Winter is London's off-season, and that's when airlines and some hotels offer impressive packages. For information about finding and negotiating hotel deals, see page 72 in Part Three, Accommodations.

QUICK CHECK

TRAVEL INSURANCE Your own insurance company may offer travel insurance, so check first with them before buying any additional coverage. You can purchase insurance for canceled travel, lost luggage, and medical emergencies through Travel Guard International at ☎ 800-826-1300, **www.travelguard.com;** or Travel International, Inc., at ☎ 800-243-3174, **www.travelinsured.com.** While we're on the subject of emergencies, here's a Web site for worriers: **www.travel riskcenter.com.** With links to the U.S. State Department and the British Foreign and Commonwealth Office, it will apprise you of any health, political, or terrorist risks current in any location, and it has special reports on safety and security.

LUGGAGE Every airline has different rules, so call ahead to find out number of bags that can be checked, maximum weight, and size and weight of carry-ons. Virgin is very strict about carry-on luggage and will make you check even a backpack if it is too heavy. Rules also depend on the class in which you are traveling—if it's economy, don't try to bring all your luggage on board with you; it may not get by check-in, and if the flight is full, you will be depriving others of their fair share of space.

With the more stringent security enforced for carry-on luggage, you must be careful to put the following items in your checked luggage: scissors, nail files, nail clippers, penknives, razors or razor blades, knitting needles (some airlines allow these on board; call and ask if you want to knit on board), or any other sharp object that could conceivably be used as a weapon. Bottles of liquid and laptops and other electronic equipment may cause delays if you don't take them out of your luggage and put them in the plastic box provided, as you will usually be asked to do.

VALUABLES Valuables, such as cameras, jewelry, money, and anything particularly fragile or precious, including medication, should go on the plane with you. They may be able to send a man to the moon, but they can't always match up the luggage with the flight.

unofficial **TIP**
If you do lose your medication, it will help to know its generic name in order to get a new prescription.

MEDICATIONS You may want to bring an extra supply of any medicine you are taking, as well as a spare pair of eyeglasses. Prescriptions from a foreign doctor will usually be honored in England, so ask your doctor for a backup before you go. Wear a Medic Alert tag if you have a serious health condition.

PERSONAL ELECTRONICS Your laptop most likely has a built-in electrical transformer, and all you'll need to do is buy a plug adapter (or bring an extra battery). In London, the most common electrical plug is the large three-prong type, which is not the same as in the rest of Europe, where two round pins are used. RadioShack and Brookstone have foreign-plug adapter packages that cover pretty much any type of plug. Forget about hair dryers, electric toothbrushes, and other personal electronics; you will blow them up if you plug a 110-volt into the British 220-volt system without running it through an electrical converter, also known as a transformer. Your cell phone, unless it is one of the expensive tri-band world-wide-use models, will not work in England.

unofficial **TIP**
Many hotels have cell phones to rent, and you can pick up a pay-as-you-go U.K. cell phone for about £90, plus the cost of the talk minutes.

CAR RENTAL It's not a bad idea to reserve a rental car before you go to London; you can often get a better price from your country of origin. Check with your hotel to see if there is a nearby rental place, so you don't have to cross the entire city to pick up and drop off the car. You need to be over 25 years of age, have a license that's valid for two years, and, of course, a credit card.

BRITRAIL If you are going to travel around rural England by train, you can purchase a BritRail Pass before you leave and save a bundle. Call ☎ 888-BRITRAIL in the United States or ☎ 800-555-BRIT in Canada, or order the pass through **www.raileurope.com.** You can also order Travel Cards for the tubes and buses at that Web site, but there's no financial incentive, only convenience. You can buy Travel Cards when you get to London at any tube station or London Tourist Office.

MONEY There are ATMs with Cirrus, MAC, and credit card account systems all over London. You'll avoid many extra bank fees (and maybe get the VAT tax knocked off at some little shops) by paying cash—the credit card companies are ferocious in charging foreign currency conversion, which can really add up. If you need a cash advance from your credit card, remember that you can't access your credit card funds from an ATM without a PIN number, so make sure you have one before you go. If you don't have a credit card or ATM card, be sure to ask for traveler's checks in British pound sterling notes only.

▌ THE WEATHER

LONDON MEASURES ITS MILD WEATHER in degrees Celsius (centigrade) rather than Fahrenheit; zero Celsius is freezing, and anything over 30 Celsius is tropical. You can check out the weather from the United States before you go. Call ☎ 900-WEATHER and dial the first four letters of your destination city (LOND) for a recording of current temperatures, current weather conditions, and the forecast for the next few days. Go online to the Weather Channel Web site at **www.weather. com** or check CNN weather at **www.cnn.com.** You can also access London newspapers for local weather at **www.sunday-times.co.uk, www. guardian.co.uk,** or **www.telegraph.co.uk** for weather information.

Convert temperatures (approximately) from Celsius to Fahrenheit by doubling Celsius and adding 30. Here are some more exact numbers:

–3°C	=	26.7°F	15°C	=	59°F
–1°C	=	30.2°F	20°C	=	68°F
0°C	=	32°F (freezing)	25°C	=	77°F
1°C	=	33.8°F	30°C	=	86°F
5°C	=	41°F	37°C	=	98.6°F
10°C	=	50°F	(normal human body temperature)		

AVERAGE DAYTIME TEMPERATURES AND RAINFALL IN LONDON

MONTH	TEMPERATURE (°F/C)	RAINFALL (INCHES)
January	40° / 4	2.1"
February	40° / 4	1.6"
March	44° / 7	1.5"
April	49° / 9	1.5"
May	55° / 13	1.8"
June	61° / 16	1.8"
July	64° / 18	2.2"
August	64° / 18	2.3"
September	59° / 15	1.9"
October	52° / 11	2.2"
November	46° / 8	2.5"
December	42° / 6	1.9"

 # **WHAT** *to* **BRING**

WHAT TO BRING ON YOUR TRIP TO LONDON depends on the weather, which we've mapped out seasonally, but there are a few things that you might appreciate having handy at all times of the year:

- this book
- small map of central London and a portable street atlas, a small pocket-size book that has exhaustive maps of every neighborhood in London, which even the natives can't do without; *London A to Z, Collins,* or *Nicholsons London Street Atlas* are equally good

- £100, which you can buy from your bank at home, to pay for transportation from the airport in case the ATM at the airport is on the fritz, although you can alternatively ask the taxi driver to stop at a money machine. If you are taking the tube or the bus, you will only need about £10 per person.
- good backpack or shoulder bag
- small, collapsible umbrella
- rain poncho
- currency converter
- portable electrical transformer, if you can find one small enough and want to bring your own hair dryer or electric toothbrush (check amps to make sure it can handle your appliances—hair dryers are notorious ' for blowing out transformers); input from the wall outlet will be British 220 volts, which will be transformed into 110 volts for American electronics
- camera and lots of extra film (like everything else, film is expensive here)
- extra card for a digital camera, and either extra batteries or a recharger with electrical transformer that can be used on 220 volts
- sugar substitute (if you have a favorite brand)
- books on London that relate to your interests
- comfortable walking shoes
- passport-size photos for travel card (you can also get these done here easily)

CLOTHING

LONDON IS A CITY OF MANY ECONOMIC CLASSES and sartorial styles; there are lots of rich young things for whom dressing for dinner will mean a pair of £250 jeans, some fab shoes, and an outrageously expensive jacket, while the women of the WWII generation will wear skirts and sensible shoes on the street and into restaurants, still taking their fashion cues from their contemporary, the Queen. If you happen to come across a wedding, you'll see how seriously Londoners take their formal clothing— morning suits and eye-catching hats are de rigueur at most British nuptials, even at civil ceremonies at town hall. Harrods, which has a ridiculously high opinion of itself, actually has a dress code, as does the Ritz Hotel: No jeans or sneakers at the restaurant and bar of the Ritz Hotel; at Harrods it's completely and mysteriously up to their discretion. Generally speaking, however, globalization has ensured that the Western countries of the world all dress pretty much the same way (and in the very same designers), and except for very fancy and/or uptight places, there is no need to change the way you dress normally.

unofficial **TIP**
Theaters no longer require dressing up, thank goodness. We would urge you to dress in layers as it can get pretty warm in the middle of a sold-out play.

Bring one or two good comfortable outfits for stepping out to restaurants; smart casual is always safe. This is not Paris, where urban chic is the style on the street and the average human being can feel hopelessly dowdy in comparison. Although the elegance of Paris and Milan, as well as the exciting new British designers, exert a strong influence on the way London dresses, there's not a lot of snobbery about clothing. As a nation of grand old eccentrics, they are mostly unflappable when it comes to other people's personal styles. If you do end up at a restaurant with a tie-and-jacket code, they will likely be happy to lend you one.

WHEN *to* GO

THE BEST TIME TO GO TO LONDON IS WHENEVER it's possible for you. If you want more than anything to see this remarkable city but can't afford the high-season airfare, then by all means go in the winter, when the fares drop by as much as 75%—if you book sufficiently in advance and look around for·the good deals. Other considerations might include the special events you're eager to see—perhaps Wimbledon or the Chelsea Flower Show—or the attractions in which you're most interested. Some of your choices—stately homes, for example—are usually closed between October 31 and April 1. Although the winter is dark and dreary, it's free of the swarms of tourists that you find in the summer. Let's take it season by season:

SUMMER For many of us, summer is the only option because of our children's summer vacation and the slowdown in our work lives. Summer in London, though unpredictable, is often quite gorgeous. Henry James was probably thinking of England, his adopted home, when he declared the two most beautiful words in the English language to be "summer afternoon." One thing these summer afternoons can't promise, though, is consistent heat—three consecutive days of 75°F and sun is considered a heat wave. However, the global-warming trend is upsetting London's traditionally brisk summer, and the past few years have seen record-breaking high temperatures that upset both residents and visitors, as air-conditioning is relatively rare in shops, restaurants, and many hotels. The worst is that it's nonexistent in buses and trains, where the heat can get dangerously high—you'd be arrested for transporting animals in conditions similar to the tube in an August heat wave. The summer of 2003 broke all existing heat records with a high of 101°F during a long heat wave, and 2004 was almost as bad (Paris suffered more than London). Do check to make sure your hotel has air conditioning if you're coming in July or August; more and more hotels are taking the recent heat waves seriously and have added climate controls to their rooms. Nighttime temperatures, even on a hot day, do drop, and often a fan will suffice to cool a hotel room.

During each season in London, you should plan your clothing in layers, as the weather can change dramatically in one day. Don't pack only shorts and T-shirts, which you may not even get a chance to wear. Be sure to bring socks, a sweater, trousers ("pants" here are underpants, also known as knickers), a light jacket, and a rain poncho. The most crucial piece of clothing is a good pair of walking shoes, whichever shoes you personally find most comfortable.

In the summer you can count on all the museums and attractions being crowded. Busloads of tourists are constantly bearing down on the most popular attractions, and the decent hotels are often completely booked by April or May. Unless the global economy goes completely into the toilet (or the "loo," as it's called here), a summer visit to London can require nerves of steel and the planning capabilities of Admiral Nelson.

On the plus side, summer in London means that the parks are at their most fragrant and riotously floral and that all the stately homes and palaces are open. Buskers (street performers) are everywhere on the streets; there are carnivals, street fairs, and more outdoor dining than makes sense in a country with such variable weather. Private garden squares are open to the public on one Sunday in June; check **www.timeout.co.uk.** The Royal Parks have green-and-white-striped lawn chairs ready for hire, and stables lay on extra horses for rides in the parks. The locals take off on holiday, so the streets are relatively free to accommodate the stampede of visitors.

FALL I much prefer the autumn to the summer in London for many reasons, the most important being that the crowds simmer down. Also, there is something wonderfully atmospheric about London in the fall, with leaves starting to turn brown, and winds twisting them off the branches and twirling them along the streets. Because of London's mild climate, many flowers in the parks last all the way into November, and to see their radiance blending with the hues of the changing leaves is wonderful. The sunny days are mood lifting and the brisk air invigorating. The main thing to remember is that most of the stately homes and palaces close October 30, so come before then if these sights are at the top of your list. (Buckingham Palace closes at the end of September or in the first week of October.) November can get as cold as 40°F, but not usually much below that. Bring gloves and a hat for the windy days. The days get shorter and shorter.

WINTER There is a beautiful old English folk song heard at Christmas called "In the Bleak Midwinter" ("ground as hard as iron, water like a stone"), which plays in many Londoners' minds as they wake up to the darkness that returns around 4:30 p.m. The ancient trees in the parks have shed their leaves, standing like skeletons against a leaden sky. I personally don't mind the bleakness much, as it doesn't often include temperatures below freezing, and as the museums are so warm and inviting in the winter. The airline deals are fantastic, the hotels are cheaper, there aren't many visitors (just busloads of uniformed schoolchildren flooding the museums), and your choice of plays at the half-price ticket booths expands considerably. All in all, it's an economical time to make a cultural holiday. No one does Christmas quite like the English. They aren't constrained by the observation of Thanksgiving a month earlier, so they start their decorating and selling in the last weeks of October. There are the Oxford Street and Regent Street Christmas lighting ceremonies, and there's a small parade when Santa arrives at Harrods in early November. The decorations of Oxford and Regent streets are getting tackier and more commercial every year—go to Marylebone High Street, Bond Street, or St. Christopher's Place for more appealing Christmas lights. There are scores of wonderful candle-lit Christmas concerts at churches and cathedrals—check *Time Out* or *What's On* for where and when. What you won't find much of is snow, which may be a relief for some of you. But there is plenty of rain, and it's the cold, biting kind. The best news is that after December 21, the days start getting longer.

SPRING Spring starts early in London. Carpets of crocus cover Hyde Park as early as February, with daffodils not far behind. It's a fine time to visit; the stately homes reopen at the end of March or beginning of April, and the parks and gardens come into bloom. Early May is a time when Londoners fall in love all over again with their city, despite the pummeling from the pollen and the flying fluff from the flowering trees (the allergy-prone should pack plenty of meds). Lovely as it is, May can also be downright nippy, even though cafés start putting tables on the street in April. London starts coming back to its outdoor life, with the London Marathon, boat races on the Thames, and the Chelsea Flower Show. The weather can be fantastic with not as much rain as in winter, but no matter how cloudless the morning, only an optimist ventures into parks for long walks without an umbrella.

GATHERING INFORMATION

THE BRITISH TOURIST AUTHORITY IS READY to help with your vacation, with the following offices in the United States and a central toll-free number for information: ☎ 800-462-2748. (In London, call ☎ 0208-846-9000.) They have brochures, maps, and a booklet that they will be happy to give you. Make a point of calling, writing, or going in for these goodies.

IN CHICAGO No phone calls; write or walk in at 625 N. Michigan Avenue, Suite 1510, Chicago, IL 60611.

IN NEW YORK ☎ 212-986-2200 or 800-462-2748; 555 Fifth Avenue, Seventh Floor, New York, NY 10176. There is a bookstore next door to the office, which has many London-related items of interest.

IN AUSTRALIA ☎ 02-267-4555 or fax 02-267-4442; University Centre, Eighth Floor, 210 Clarence Street, Sydney NSW 2000

IN CANADA ☎ 800-847-4885; 111 Avenue Road, Suite 450, Toronto, Ontario M5R 3J8

IN NEW ZEALAND ☎ 09-303-1446 or fax 09-377-6965; Dilworth Building, Suite 305, Queen and Customs Streets, Auckland 1

WEB SITES

THERE ARE SO MANY WEB SITES ABOUT LONDON, it's hard to keep up with them. They are always being improved, or removed, and the addresses may change, but the following Web sites should provide you with enough links to keep you glued to your computer for weeks:

www.londontown.com	This is the London tourist board's Web site, with up-to-the-minute information on events, hotels, restaurants, sightseeing, exhibits, and more.
www.royal.gov.uk	Official Web site of the British monarchy, with information on royal palaces, castles, and museums
www.westminster.gov.uk	Links to London sites
www.cityoflondon.gov.uk	City government site
www.london.gov.uk	Another government site
www.24hourmuseum.org.uk	Information on museums, plus many London- and art-related links
www.timeout.co.uk	*Time Out's* online magazine, the city's best source for event listings
www.londonnet.co.uk	Magazine guide to events, plus articles, hotels, restaurants, entertainment
www.guardianco.uk	*The Guardian* and *The Observer* newspapers online
www.thisislondon.co.uk	Event listings and local news from the *Evening Standard*

▌SPECIAL CONSIDERATIONS

PASSPORT, VISAS, AND CUSTOMS

IF YOU'RE AMERICAN, CANADIAN, OR FROM New Zealand, all you need to enter England is a valid passport. Make sure your passport is up-to-date; you may not be allowed in if you have less than two months' validity remaining on it. Americans can find passport information, including forms to download, at the Department of State Bureau of Consular Affairs Web site, **www.travel.state.gov.** Alternatively, call the National Passport Information Center at ☎ 900-225-5674. You don't need a visa for a vacation; you will be allowed in for up to 90 days. Make two copies of the information page of your passport and give one to someone at home to keep. Put the other in your luggage to expedite replacement in case your passport gets lost or stolen.

WHAT YOU MAY AND MAY NOT BRING INTO THE UNITED KINGDOM

YOU CAN BRING IN, DUTY-FREE:

200 cigarettes, 100 cigarillos, 50 cigars, or 250 grams of tobacco

2 liters of table wine and 1 liter of alcohol over 22% by volume (most spirits) and either 2 liters of alcohol under 22% by volume (fortified or sparkling wine or liqueurs) or 2 more liters of table wine

50 milliliters of perfume

Other goods up to a value of £145 (about $250)

You may not bring in controlled drugs (any medication you take should be in its original bottle with your name on it), firearms and/or ammunition, plants and vegetables, fresh meats, or any kind of animals. Customs are currently somewhat relaxed about cigarettes—two or three cartons won't set off any alarms.

ELECTRICITY

THE ELECTRICITY SUPPLY IN THE UK IS 220 volts AC, which will blow out any American 110-volt appliance you may have. Electric lamps are the only items that don't require a transformer. Check to be sure your laptop computer has a built-in transformer; it's a standard feature. Razors, hair dryers, electric toothbrushes, as well as rechargers for cell phones, digital cameras, and music players—all most likely require a transformer. Leave them at home is our advice. Since the British outlets are made for large three-prong plugs, you will also need to get an adapter, available at any ironmonger (hardware store), chemists (drugstore), supermarket, or gadget store. Don't plug anything in until you've checked the voltage on the transformer! It should be set to "Input AC 220 volt, output AC 110 volt." You'll know by the pop, flash, and smoke if you got it wrong.

POUNDS, PENCE, AND TRAVELER'S CHECKS

THE BRITISH ARE GOING SLOWLY INTO THIS European Union business, taking a wait-and-see attitude toward the Euro Unit. At this writing, they are still using pounds (£), and the pound converts to about $1.80. In 2004 the pound cost a whopping $1.94, which made visiting London extremely painful to the pocketbook. Check any major newspaper's business section for current exchange rates, or go to **www.xe.com.** The pound is a unit divided into 100 pence, abbreviated "p." One p is called a penny; the plural is pence. Gone are the days of the shilling, the tuppence, and the farthing; what we lose in quaintness we make up for in manageability.

There are no longer any £1 notes. There are red 50s, purple 20s, brown 10s, and green 5s. Coins are divided into £2, £1, 50p, 20p, 10p, 5p, 2p, and 1p. Coins cannot be changed into foreign cash, so spend them while you're in London. Better still, donate them on your way home to the brilliant UNICEF Change Collection scheme that most airlines sponsor.

Go to your bank before you leave and buy about £100 worth of British pound sterling notes so you will have plenty on hand to pay for transportation from the airport and maybe even that first meal. Request 20s, as 50s can sometimes be hard to break.

See Part Four, Arriving and Getting Oriented for details on ATMs, changing money, and using your credit cards.

VALUE-ADDED TAX (VAT)

VAT IS ONE OF THE GREAT FRUSTRATIONS of shopping in London. It is a 17.5% "value-added tax" slapped on everything from hotel rooms to lipstick; the only exceptions are food, children's clothing, and books, yet these are still very expensive. There are ways to get this tax refunded, which we'll tell you about in Part Ten, Shopping. Almost everything has the VAT added into the sticker price, except for merchandise sold in some small shops, as well as various services. Before you book a hotel, check whether the quoted price includes VAT. It makes a huge difference in your bill, obviously.

EMBASSIES AND HIGH COMMISSIONS

United States

The American Embassy is housed in Mayfair at 24 Grosvenor Square, London, W1A1AE; ☎ 0207-499-9000 (tube: Bond Street). This is where you will go if your passport gets lost or stolen or if you have some emergency. The embassy's Web site is **www.usembassy.org.uk.** The hours are 8:30 a.m.–5:30 p.m. Passports are handled Monday through Friday, 8:30–11 a.m.; and Monday, Wednesday, and Friday, 2–4 p.m. The Passport Office is on 55 Upper Brook Street, around the corner from the main entrance (tube: Marble Arch or Bond Street).

Canada

The High Commission is at MacDonald House, 38 Grosvenor Square, W1; ☎ 0207-258-6600; **www.canadianembassy.co.uk** (tube: Bond Street). It is open Monday through Friday, 8–11 a.m.

Australia

The High Commission is at Australia House, Strand, WC2; ☎ 0207-379-4334; **www.australia.org.uk** (tube: Charing Cross) and is open Monday through Friday, 10 a.m.–4 p.m.

New Zealand

The High Commission is at New Zealand House, 80 Haymarket at Pall Mall, SW1; ☎ 0207-930-8422; **www.nzembassy.com** (tube: Charing Cross). It's open Monday through Friday, 9 a.m.–5 p.m.

Ireland

The Irish Embassy is at 17 Grosvenor Place, SW1; ☎ 0207-235-2171; **www.ireland.embassyhomepage.com** (tube: Hyde Park Corner). Hours are Monday through Friday, 10 a.m.–4 p.m.

TRAVELING WITH CHILDREN

IN PLANNING YOUR VACATION, REMEMBER that children get jet lag too, and plan your first day so you all can recover from it. We have a rating system in our attraction profiles that attempts to gauge suitability for children and adults of various ages, but bear in mind that all children have different interests and differing levels of tolerance for museums and attractions. See Part Seven, Children's London.

DISABLED ACCESS IN LONDON

LONDON MAY BE MORE WHEELCHAIR- AND disabled-access ready than many cities in Europe, but it still has some insurmountable problems in many of its attractions. In America you can count on wheelchair access and disabled restrooms in public buildings; in London you need to call ahead or use any of the following excellent references:

Access in London is the best book on the subject, researched by disabled people and updated regularly. It is published by the Access Project and is available at various bookstores and in the London Museum Giftshop; you can also call or write to order it: Access Project, 39 Bradley Gardens, London, W13 8HE; ☎ 0208-858-2375; **www.accessinlondon.org,** or you can also order from any online bookstore.

Access to the Underground is a brochure published by London Transport and is available at tube stations or by writing the London Transport Unit for Disabled Visitors, 172 Buckingham Palace Road, London, SW1 9TN.

Artslines is an organization that collects a number of sites and disability societies under one umbrella. They are at 54 Chalton Street, London, NW1 1HS; ☎ 0207-388-2227; **www.artsline.org.uk.**

Information for Wheelchair Users Visiting London is a pamphlet that you can find in any tourist office in London.

Holiday Care Service offers advice on disabled-friendly lodging; call ☎ 0845-124-9971 or visit **www.holidaycare.org.uk.**

Can Be Done is a tour operator specializing in London holidays and tours for disabled people; call ☎ 0208-907-2400 or visit **www.canbedone.co.uk.**

EASING JET LAG

JET LAG IS A VERY REAL PROBLEM, AS ANY long-distance traveler can tell you. The number of time zones passed through is directly proportional to how much jet lag you'll suffer; visitors from Los Angeles will feel worse than New Yorkers. The common wisdom is that you will have roughly one day of symptoms for each hour of time difference. Though some people don't experience jet lag at all, most of us do to varying degrees. The symptoms include fatigue, muscle aches and headaches, changes in appetite, sleep disturbances, irritability, forgetfulness, confusion, and dizziness. Of course, these symptoms could also describe middle age, but jet lag is much more pronounced, and eases up as the days go by. There are a number of confusing remedies—eating a certain kind and amount of food on either end of your trip, taking homeopathic remedies every hour on the plane, digesting a number of vitamins, and so on. For me, and I learned this through many painful flights between Hong Kong and New York, the best remedy is to try to reset your internal clock as soon as possible. The main thing to remember on the plane is to drink lots and lots of water, but no alcohol, and eat sparingly. Sleeping on the plane is not always an option, but do try. When you arrive, change your watch immediately and try to forget what time it is "for you." Your time is the time of wherever you are, and you've got to get on it as soon as possible. I advise my friends to use their first day to take an open-top bus tour, not just for the great introductory overview of the city but also for the generous helping of sunlight you (might) get. Exercise is also advised; a walk in the park helps stretch muscles that are achy from hours of immobilization on a plane.

unofficial **TIP**
The best way to reset your clock is to get as much sunlight as possible when you arrive—not always easy in London.

For those who can afford it, there are great benefits to be had from body massage in the treating of jet lag symptoms. It is not only a natural way to deal with it, but also so very pleasant. I know of a couple from Los Angeles who book a two-hour massage the minute they arrive at their hotel, and swear by it. **Body Tissue Service** (☎ 0793-913-2820 or 0870-382-1111; **www.bodytissue.com**) offers a reputable and convenient mobile massage therapy service, available from 8 a.m. to midnight seven days a week, and will come to your hotel room. Their prices will be better than any you would book through the hotel. I recently discovered the benefits of getting ten minutes on a sunbed: I know that skin cancer experts frown on the use of sunbeds, but one session proved to help me a lot with jet lag last time I flew from the States to London, especially since I couldn't rely on natural sunlight to help reset my biological clock. Another jet lag treatment is the hormone melatonin. It is a controversial supplement, and the strict scientific rules for its use are so complicated that only a trip of

12 time zones could really merit trying to follow them. Melatonin cannot be bought in England, but it is easily found in the United States in health-food stores, vitamin shops, and pharmacies. It is often used as a sleep aid, which can be helpful in the first few days of your trip, when your body clock tells you it's 7 p.m. but it's really after midnight and you have a full day of sightseeing planned for the next day. Take two to three milligrams for sleep—more than that will leave you groggy in the morning, and it can have a depressant effect. As with any drug, check with your physician before taking it.

HEALTH

YOU MAY WANT TO TAKE OUT MEDICAL INSURANCE before you leave—you won't be covered by the National Health Service, unless you're an EU citizen. You may be eligible for free emergency care, but anything else, including follow-up or specialist services, will be paid for out of your pocket. Check your existing policies to see if they cover medical services abroad. If they don't, try **Highway to Health Insurance,** which specializes in travel health and goods coverage (☎ 888-243-2358; **www.hthinsurance.com**). There is also **Health Insurance Finders** (☎ 800-259-0307; **www.healthinsurancefinders.com**). Both companies offer good temporary coverage at a good price.

PHARMACIES Pharmacies take turns being open 24 hours and on Sundays. Call your front desk or the local police station for a list. **Zafash Pharmacy** (233–235 Old Brompton Road, SW5; ☎ 0207-373-2798; tube: Earl's Court) is open 24 hours every day. **Bliss Chemist** (5 Marble Arch, W1; ☎ 0207-723-6116; tube: Marble Arch) is open from 9 a.m. until midnight every day.

DENTISTS For dental problems, call the **Dental Emergency Care Service** 24 hours a day at ☎ 0207-937-3951. They will give you the name of the nearest dental clinic.

DOCTORS The better hotels will have their own doctor on call. If not, contact **Doctors Direct** (☎ 0207-751-9701; **www.doctorsdirect.co.uk**). There's a private clinic in the famous Harley Street where you can seek medical help; contact **Medical Express** (117A Harley Street; ☎ 0207-486-0516; tube: Baker Street). It's open 9 a.m.–6 p.m. Monday through Friday.

In England the emergency room is called the **Casualty Department.** Call ☎ 999 or 112 for an ambulance. You'll be taken to the nearest hospital, or, if your symptoms are not life threatening, you'll be advised which is the closest hospital to you. The biggest difference between England and the States is that if you get in an accident, the emergency services are provided free. As one journalist noted in the aftermath of the 7/7 bombing, the victims were treated equally and professionally and did not have insult added to injury by being presented with a huge bill at the end of their hospital stay. Let's hope you don't ever have to experience the miracle of the National Health Service. I really don't think you'll get sick—London has good water and food. But you had better watch out for the cars. Americans and Europeans automatically look in the wrong direction when crossing the street, which is why you'll see directions ("Look Left") written on the street. Also keep a beady eye out for bicyclists and motorcyclists; they drive like maniacs here.

SELF-HELP

IF YOU'RE LOOKING FOR 12-STEP MEETINGS, there are plenty in London. Call for times and places.

ALCOHOLICS ANONYMOUS ☎ 0207-833-0022; **www.alcoholics-anonymous.org.uk**

NARCOTICS ANONYMOUS ☎ 0207-730-0009; **www.ukna.org**

OVEREATERS ANONYMOUS ☎ 0142-698-4674; **www.oagb.org.uk**

A CALENDAR *of* FESTIVALS *and* EVENTS

LONDON HAS A HUGE NUMBER OF TRADITIONAL and modern events each month, so many that we had to try to narrow them down to the most interesting and important. When you arrive in London, pick up a *Time Out* magazine for the full selection, dates, and times, or if you're the kind of person who likes to plan ahead, go to **www.timeout.com, www.visitbritain.com,** or to the London Tourist Board's Web site at **www.londontown.com.**

January

 NEW YEAR'S DAY LONDON PARADE January 1. A big, brash spectacle with giant balloons, marching bands, clowns, vintage cars, and more, much in the style of the big Fifth Avenue parades in the United States. Starting at Parliament Square at noon, the parade follows Whitehall, Trafalgar Square, Lower Regent, and Piccadilly, ending up at Green Park at 3 p.m. Lots of spillover fun can be had in Hyde Park later that day. ☎ 0208-566-8586; **www.londonparade.co.uk** (tube: for start of parade, Westminster; for middle, Charing Cross; for end, Green Park)

CHARLES I COMMEMORATION Last Sunday of January. The English Civil War Society, dressed in authentic 17th-century uniforms complete with arms, follows the route King Charles I took on January 30, 1649, before he lost his head. They march from St. James's Park at 11:30 a.m., down the mall, through the Horse Guards, to lay a wreath at the site of his execution in front of the Banqueting House. (tube: St. James's Park)

LONDON INTERNATIONAL BOAT SHOW The biggest boat and all-round water show in all of Europe, it takes place in mid-January and lasts about ten days. A must for even the most casual water bug. For tickets, call ☎ 0115-912-9190, or see **www.londonboatshow.com.** (tube: Earl's Court)

February

kids   **CHINESE NEW YEAR CELEBRATIONS** Chinese New Year changes every year but is always in either late January or early February. The celebration is usually on the first Sunday after the first day of the Chinese new year. London's Chinatown is located in Soho, around Garrard Street. It comes alive with bright decorations, red streamers, and the Lion Dance. Great food is everywhere. See **www.chinatownchinese.com** and click on London Chinatown. (tube: Piccadilly Circus)

GREAT SPITALFIELDS PANCAKE RACE Shrove Tuesday (changes yearly; check calendar—it can also fall in early March). Starts at noon near Brick Lane; starting place changes since it has been moved from Old Spitalfields Market. Here's fun: teams of people running around the East End flipping pancakes as they go, in the name of charity. If you want to join in, call a few days before—☎ 0207-375-0441; **www.alternativearts.co.uk.** (tube: Liverpool Street)

March

DAILY MAIL IDEAL HOME EXHIBITION Mid-March through April, Earl's Court Exhibition Centre 5. Enormous display of every possible gadget, knickknack, or consumer item one could attach to or use in a home. Call ☎ 0207-244-0371; **www.idealhomeshow.co.uk.** (tube: Earl's Court)

kids   **ST. PATRICK'S DAY CELEBRATIONS** Weekend nearest to March 17. With two-day celebrations in Trafalgar Square, Covent Garden, and South Bank, this has grown considerably in the past five years. Music, Irish produce stalls, entertainment, and a walloping big parade. See **www.timeout.co.uk** or **www.bbc.co.uk** for details. (tubes: Picadilly Circus, Covent Garden, Charing Cross)

HEAD OF THE RIVER BOAT RACE End of March (usually the Saturday before the Oxford vs. Cambridge Boat Race). Starting at Mortlake and ending at Putney, this is a smaller affair than the mighty Oxford and Cambridge race, but no less interesting to observe from the banks of the Thames. The Surrey Bank above Chiswick Bridge is a good viewing station, or you can park yourself in any of the riverside pubs along the way. Call ☎ 0193-222-0401 for date and starting time. (BritRail: Mortlake for start; tube: Hammersmith for midpoint, Putney Bridge for finish)

OXFORD VS. CAMBRIDGE BOAT RACE This takes place on a Saturday in late March or early April and is considered the big megillah, held since 1829. Teams of eight battle the current, rowing 6.8 kilometers upriver from Putney to Mortlake. Be prepared for crowds on the bridges, on banks, and in riverside pubs. Call ☎ 0207-379-3234 for information. (BritRail: Mortlake for finish; tube: Putney Bridge for start, Hammersmith for midpoint)

April

GUN SALUTE TO MARK THE QUEEN'S BIRTHDAY April 21. Features a 41-gun Royal Salute to Queen Elizabeth II, fired at noon by the King's Troop Royal House Artillery in Hyde Park, opposite Dorchester Hotel, then a 62-gun fiesta at the Tower of London at 1 p.m. Take your pick or enjoy both. Bring earplugs. If the date falls on a Sunday, the event will take place on the Monday that follows. (tube: Marble Arch for Hyde Park, Tower Hill for Tower of London)

kids **LONDON HARNESS HORSE PARADE** Easter Monday, Battersea Park. This competition of magnificent "working" horses drawing carriages and carts makes the parade a treat unlike any other. Battersea Park is a beautiful place in which to enjoy it. For information, call ☎ 0173-323-4451 or visit **www.eastofengland.org.uk** or **www. batterseapark.org.** (tube: Sloane Square, then bus to Battersea)

LONDON MARATHON Occurs on a Sunday in mid-April, starting at Greenwich Park and ending at Buckingham Palace. On average, 35,000 competitors participate, so if you want in, you'd better apply early. Entries close in October. Call ☎ 0207-620-4117 or check **www.londonmarathon.co.uk.** (BritRail: Blackheath or Greenwich for start; tube: Green Park for finish)

May

CHELSEA FLOWER SHOW Runs for five or so days in late May at the Chelsea Royal Hospital. This is the ne plus ultra of London's spring affairs, so you'd better get tickets in advance and prepare to be jostled. Go early in the morning to see the amazing flora and garden accoutrements, the great passion of even the city-dwelling English. The last day is a madhouse, as people buy up goods at bargain prices. For tickets call ☎ 0870-906-3781 or see **www.rhs.org.uk.** (tube: Sloane Square)

kids **MAY FAIR AND PUPPET FESTIVAL** Second Sunday at St. Paul's Church (not to be confused with St. Paul's Cathedral) Garden and Covent Garden. A procession, a service at St. Paul's, and then hours of Punch-and-Judy shows amount to family fun. Call Alternative Arts at ☎ 0207-375-0441 or go to **www. alternativearts.co.uk** for information. (tube: Covent Garden)

ROYAL WINDSOR HORSE SHOW Mid-May, Home Park, Windsor Castle. A wonderful day out for everyone, equestrian or not. Besides the jumping and showing competitions, there are amazing Pony Club games, booths galore, and a few carnival rides, all conducted under the impressive, hulking shadow of Windsor Castle. For information, call ☎ 0175-386-0633 or visit **www.royal-windsor-horse-show.co.uk.** (BritRail: Windsor)

June

BEATING RETREAT HOUSEHOLD DIVISION June 1 or 2, Whitehall Horse Guard's Parade. Part of the big celebration of the Queen's coronation anniversary, this is a spectacle of sound and sight, with troops in full regalia in the Horse Guard's Parade. To get your tickets call ☎ 0207-414-2479 or see **www.army.mod.uk.** (tube: Green Park)

TROOPING THE COLOUR June 1 and 2, Horse Guards Parade, Whitehall. Yes, the lucky queen gets two birthdays: April 21 when she was actually born, and June 2, the anniversary of her coronation, which is considered the "official" birthday. There's a procession to Buckingham Palace, where the air force flies overhead and a gun salute is fired. You can watch from the Mall, or try to get a ticket for a good view. Tickets are awarded by ballot; call ☎ 0207-414-2479 or see **www.army.mod.uk** for details. Check in Hyde Park during the preceding Saturdays—you may catch a full-dress rehearsal. (tube: Westminster)

KENWOOD LAKESIDE CONCERTS These are held at the beautiful Kenwood House grounds every Saturday night until September in Hampstead Heath, with headliners in jazz, classical, pop, and rock. A 50-year-old tradition, these open-air events also feature laser shows, fireworks displays, and the Heath at sundown—enchanting. For information, call ☎ 0207-973-3427 or see **www.picnicconcerts.com.** (tube: Archway, Golders Green, or Highgate, then bus 210)

ROYAL ACADEMY SUMMER EXHIBITION From early June to mid-August, the Royal Academy in Piccadilly. For over 200 years, the Royal Academy of Art has been showing the work of contemporary artists in its summer exhibitions, many of which have caused scandals in their day. You can browse or buy. Call ☎ 0207-300-8000 or see **www.royalacademy.org.uk.** (tube: Green Park or Piccadilly Circus)

ROYAL ASCOT Mid-June, Ascot Racecourse, Berkshire. Made famous to Americans by the scene in the movie *My Fair Lady,* Ascot brings out all of social London. It's almost more entertaining to dish the outfits and hats than to watch the races. For information, go to **www.royalascot.co.uk,** and for tickets call ☎ 0870-460-1238. (BritRail: Ascot)

WIMBLEDON LAWN TENNIS CHAMPIONSHIPS Late June to early July, Wimbledon, Southwest London. This is where all true tennis fans want to be, and everyone else loves the strawberries and cream. Demand for tickets always exceeds supply, so plan way in advance (at least three months). Queuing on the day is possible, but there's no guarantee you'll get in. Tickets for Centre and Number One Courts are awarded by ballot. Call ☎ 0208-971-2473 or see **www.wimbledon.org** for information. (tube: Wimbledon)

July

BBC HENRY WOOD PROMENADE CONCERTS (THE PROMS) Mid-July through September, Royal Albert Hall, Kensington Gore. Known affectionately as the "Proms," these eight weeks of a variety of orchestral concerts, from classical to contemporary, can be seen for a small fee (standing) or for significantly more (sitting), and can also be enjoyed on a blanket in Kensington Gardens, where the music is piped in. The last night is the big extravaganza, with fireworks. For tickets and information, see **www.bbc.co.uk/proms** or call the Royal Albert at ☎ 0207-589-8212. Tickets go on sale in mid-June. (tube: South Kensington or Gloucester Road)

August

OPENING OF BUCKINGHAM PALACE Early August through October. While the Queen's away, the tourists will play. Lines and lines of camera-laden hoi polloi wait to take the grand tour through Queen Elizabeth's pied-à-terre while she summers in Scotland. Tickets can be ordered in advance by calling ☎ 0207-766-7323, or you can buy them at the ticket booth in Green Park. Visit **www.the-royal-collection.com** for online booking and information. (tube: Green Park or St. James)

NOTTING HILL CARNIVAL End of August, Ladbroke Grove and Portobello Road. It's Europe's biggest street party, with a mad parade of floats and freaks, all dressed to the teeth in Caribbean queen costumes (male and female varieties); steel bands provide the beat, and West Indian food the aromas of the islands. The route of the parade is constantly being re-evaluated, with some sacrilegious proposals to move it to Hyde Park, but for now prepare to stand shoulder-to-shoulder in the midst of wild partying and (hopefully) sunny street fun. The best information is found at **www.bbc.co.uk/London/carnival.** (tube: Notting Hill)

September

GREAT RIVER RACE Mid-September, starting on the Thames at Richmond. You have never seen such a collection of boats. Over 200 traditional crafts—including such diverse specimens as whalers, Viking longboats, Chinese dragon boats, and canoes—race from Ham House in Richmond at 10:30 a.m., finishing at Island Gardens, across from Greenwich Pier, about three hours later. Call ☎ 0208-398-9057, or see **www.greatriverrce.co.uk.** (tube: Richmond for start; Docklands Light Rail: Island Gardens for finish)

OPEN HOUSE LONDON Mid-September. Finally, a chance to get in to look (for free!) inside more than 500 amazing houses and buildings usually off-limits to the likes of us commoners. Call ☎ 0207-267-7644 for information or visit **www.londonopenhouse.org.**

October

COSTERMONGERS PEARLY HARVEST FESTIVAL First Sunday in October, St. Martin-in-the Fields, Trafalgar Square. An old cockney tradition celebrating the apple (coster) harvest that starts with a service at the church and displays a Pearly King or Queen decked out in a costume bombarded with white buttons. Musical merrymakers are everywhere. Service starts at 3 p.m. Call ☎ 0207-930-0089 for details. (tube: Charing Cross)

TRAFALGAR DAY PARADE Third Sunday in October, Trafalgar Square. Big traditional, military-style parade commemorating Lord Nelson's sea victory at the Battle of Trafalgar in 1805. Marching bands, Sea Cadets. Call ☎ 0207-928-8978. (tube: Charing Cross)

November

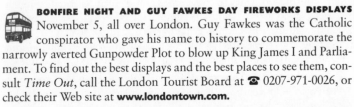 **BONFIRE NIGHT AND GUY FAWKES DAY FIREWORKS DISPLAYS** November 5, all over London. Guy Fawkes was the Catholic conspirator who gave his name to history to commemorate the narrowly averted Gunpowder Plot to blow up King James I and Parliament. To find out the best displays and the best places to see them, consult *Time Out*, call the London Tourist Board at ☎ 0207-971-0026, or check their Web site at **www.londontown.com.**

LONDON TO BRIGHTON VETERAN CAR RUN First Sunday of November. Come to Hyde Park to see the array of vintage cars that will drive to Brighton. Call ☎ 0175-368-1736 for time and exact place. (tube: Hyde Park Corner)

LORD MAYOR'S SHOW Mid-November. This is an event that goes back 700 years, old even by England's standards. The lord mayor rides through the city in a let-them-eat-cake-type gilded carriage (which can be seen at the Museum of London during the rest of the year), followed by a retinue of floats, bands, and military marchers. Call for details at ☎ 0207-606-3030, or see **www.lord mayorsshow.org.** (tube: Mansion House)

  REMEMBRANCE DAY November 11. At the 11th hour on the 11th day of the 11th month, all of England falls silent in remembrance of those who died in the two World Wars. Red poppies are bought and worn by a majority of Londoners to show respect for the soldiers who gave their lives for England. On the nearest Sunday to the 11th, there is a service for the war dead at the Cenotaph in Whitehall. Buy a poppy and wear it. For information about various Remembrance Day observations, see *Time Out*. (tube: Whitehall)

December

CHRISTMAS LIGHTS AND TREE Late November and December, central London. Various Christmas lighting ceremonies take place on Regent, Oxford, Bond, and Jermyn streets, among others. The switch is flipped by some flavor-of-the-month celebs who get a dollop of publicity in return. Check *Time Out*. The real fun is the tree-lighting ceremony in Trafalgar Square, which is followed by caroling around the tree each evening, between 4 and 10 p.m. Consult the London Tourist Board at **www.londontown.com** or try **www.timeout.com**.

OLYMPIA INTERNATIONAL SHOW JUMPING CHAMPIONS Mid-December, Grand Hall, Olympia. This is a fun-filled exhibition, rivaling even the Wembley Show for sheer excitement. Lots of trade booths provide plenty of Christmas-shopping opportunities for horse lovers. Call the box office for tickets at ☎ 0870-736-3105 (tube: Olympia)

PART THREE

ACCOMMODATIONS

SELECTING ACCOMMODATIONS

YOUR "HOME AWAY FROM HOME" IS CRUCIAL to the pleasure of your vacation or business trip. Traveling is stressful, touring around London is certainly tiring, and nothing takes the edge off exhaustion and jet lag like sinking into a warm, comfortable hotel room—that doesn't cost an arm and a leg—after a long day.

London hotels, like everything else here, are expensive, and it's important to try to strike deals, or take advantage of special offers, to whittle down the often breathtaking expense of even ordinary hotels (and naturally, the currency exchange rate is key to your budget). The standards for hotels are different from those for hotels in the United States: When you're paying a certain amount at a hotel in America, you can safely assume a variety of goods and services, such as bellhops, concierge, 24-hour room service, a health club, king-size beds, air-conditioning, full business facilities, minibar, satellite TV, and so on. Because many hotels in the States are part of a chain, they tend to have standardized properties with predictable amenities. Not so in London. You can go from crash pads to castles in one neighborhood, even on the same street, maybe even in the same hotel. In a typical converted town house hotel, you might have a room on the first floor with a balcony and French windows looking onto a garden square, and for the same price get a room on the top floor with small windows, a slanted ceiling, and a view of the brown-bricked backs of white-fronted houses. Even the chains that do operate here can have wildly varying properties with unvarying prices.

The aftermath of the terrorist strikes of September 11, the war in Iraq, and the occasional travel advisories from various state departments, as well as the inconvenient security measures at airports worldwide, all conspired to put a serious dent in London's tourist trade. The number of overseas visitors was climbing steadily to pre-9/11 numbers when London was hit with its own terrorist strikes in July 2005. Initially there was no sudden, dramatic drop in visitors, nor a rash of hotel cancellations, but the aftershocks will be felt for some time as, with the rumors of future attacks by home-grown British terrorists, people who had not already booked their travel may choose another city. As of this writing, I can confirm that the British Museum's halls do *not* have tumbleweeds rolling through them. Indeed, the attractions seem to be as crowded as ever, but the hotels are certainly to feel the pinch from the missing tourists and nervous out-of-towners. It's fair to say that hotels are ready to make a deal (except in June, when Wimbledon is on). They will do upgrades, discounts, and saver-rates without too much pushing, so don't neglect your homework: a phone call to the reservations manager is your best approach. Some of the bigger hotels that offer package tours may be filled, but the smaller boutique hotels may have empty rooms that they want to fill at any cost, and will charge the cost of discounts to the business of creating repeat customers. The very charming Franklin Hotel or the atmospheric Hazlitt's, to name just two, count heavily on the loyal custom of return visitors. London will no doubt rebound, as it has for two millennia after fire, flood, and wars, but as long as the tourist trade is in the doldrums, make a point of asking for a better rate than the one quoted. Although the prices given here are rack rate, don't let that scare you off: talk to the manager, or check out the Web site for promotions.

Although it may be somewhat cheeky for a guidebook to send you to the Internet (we're supposed to save you that effort, theoretically), one way of getting your vacation in order is to check into the travel shop Web sites that offer discount rooms or packages—you will often see as much as 50% off some of the nicer hotels, who need to push their product during slow times. I like **Travelocity.com, Expedia.com,** or **hotels oflondon.co.uk,** but I am leery of the many opportunistic Web sites that act primarily as an advertising outlet for hotels: you won't get deals, and you may not even get a shot at a reservation, as any time period you select will come up as "No rooms available for that day." Travelocity or Expedia may not get you any deep discounts, but they have a wide range of hotels, with photos, maps showing their locations, and they tell you the total amount for your entire stay. They also offer extras such as car rental, museum passes, or tourist bus tickets. That's a bit too much preplanning for me, but if you're juggling two or three kids, a full-time job, and inflexible vacation dates, it's nice to have all your confirmation numbers and directions in hand before going somewhere you've never been before. These two Web sites are a one-stop shop for everything from airport transfers to flights to hotel rooms and tourist attractions. All you need is a DSL line and a dream (and a credit card).

WHAT *to* EXPECT

HERE ARE SOME IMPORTANT FACTS TO remember and resign yourself to regarding London hotels:

1. Expect small rooms. A single room usually means a very small room, with one window and a single bed.

2. Certain amenities are not a given. Air-conditioning is not always available. Neither are minibars, safes, satellite TV, health facilities, or even private bathrooms (hostels and bed-and-breakfasts usually offer you the choice of private or shared bathrooms). We have listed some of the amenities, but call or check Web sites to be sure of what is offered—upgrading is common in newly popular or recently purchased establishments.

3. If the price is really low, say £25 a night, the likelihood is high that the hotel is going to be pretty funky, and you'll be sharing a bathroom. Budget hotels can be abysmal. I have included a few places that cost £60 and under that have proven to be clean and sometimes even charming.

4. When you're looking for a discount, you're better off calling a hotel directly and making a deal with the reservations manager than booking through a travel agent.

5. Take advantage of the weekend break rates at the five-star hotels, and spend the weekdays at a moderately priced one. Check Web prices against rack rates; they can often be discounted.

6. Don't expect the level of service you would get in a moderate-to-expensive hotel in the United States in comparable London hotels. It's pretty much only the five-star hotels here that have the customer-is-always-right-what-can-I-do-for-you-right-away-sir-yes-ma'am kind of service. However, there are some small, inexpensive hotels managed by their owners, who will make a point of providing friendly service with genuine concern for your well-being.

7. Always check to see if breakfast is included in your price. Also, it's very important to know if service and the 17.5% value-added tax (VAT) are included in the price. These two add-ons can amount to a considerable addition to your bill. In our listed prices, we have added the VAT where necessary. If you are talking directly to the hotel, be sure to ask if the VAT and/or service charges are part of the quoted price.

BEST OF BRITAIN

THE HOTELS LISTED HERE ARE THOSE THAT we think are very English, with the best kind of British atmosphere and charm. Of course, as London is arguably the most cosmopolitan capital in the world, cutting-edge design and ultramodern amenities abound in the world of hostelry—but usually at an ultrahigh price. With all due respect to lovers of the latest styles, and acknowledging the attractions of elegant minimalism, I prefer a more traditional English charm. Not necessarily the cabbage-rose-chinz and faux Victorianism of some "traditional" decor, but the kind of hotel that builds on the natural beauty of a Georgian terrace house, where architectural details and leafy gardens are a constant reminder of a more gracious era. We've included a few plain, chainlike, moderate hotels, as well as a couple of nice minimalist places, but we have concentrated on the ones that provide a sense of historical London. Many hotels in the city have pleasing sitting rooms with gas fires, antiques, and deep sofas, that serve an authentic cream tea and massive English breakfast—they simply must be experienced to get the full flavor of a certain ideal of London. Of course, some of the standard chain hotels might well have features that make the most sense for you, such as wheelchair access, fitness club, frequent-flier-mile tie-ins, good incentive packages, and the price and location you prefer. We have our own preferences as to neighborhoods, but they may not be yours.

NEIGHBORHOODS FOR HOTELS

THERE ARE A NUMBER OF EXCELLENT neighborhoods in which to stay. Here are our favorites:

SOUTH KENSINGTON If you stay in this neighborhood, you'll have an easy walk to Hyde Park and Kensington Gardens, three museums, Harrods, Albert Hall, Christies' Auction House, and Chelsea; three tube lines, many buses; French bakeries, restaurants for every budget; plus a small-town feeling in the big city. Filled with Georgian houses (often owned by one very wealthy family) and garden squares, South Kensington is a wonderful place to walk around in, with the Brompton Oratory church, the Victoria and Albert Museum, and the Natural History museum anchoring the area with their glorious facades and interior splendors. If you can find a reasonable rate in this neighborhood, go for it, especially if you're an avid museumgoer—all three museums (the above mentioned plus the Science Museum, which is just up Exhibition Road) are free, so if you're staying nearby, you can pop in and out to your heart's desire. I do love this London "village," and have since moving here in 1996. Sad to say (although you as visitors may not be bothered), grandiose plans for the area just south of the museums have started to change the local vibe and look. A property owner/developer has decided to call his little slice of ancestral South Ken pie (drum roll, please) "The Brompton Quarter." Small, long-established businesses crashed when rents were doubled and tripled, and the result is an ever-growing rash of hoardings, usually the harbinger of some chichi, useless shop or monotonous high street chain. We have seen this before, in Marylebone and east of Fulham, and the results are not altogether unpleasing, although I am dismayed by the homogenization of these once quirky London villages. The local council has come up with an excellent and long

*un*official **TIP**
Hotel prices in South Kensington are a bit expensive for smallish quarters, but there are still cheap, though not always cheerful, hotels around.

overdue plan to make Exhibition Road more pedestrian-friendly for the hordes of museumgoers who presently must inch along tiny sidewalks as they head for the tube after the museums close. With all this change in the air, odds are that hotel rooms here could become as impossibly expensive as those in posh Mayfair.

EARL'S COURT Further west, in Earl's Court, you can definitely get a better deal, and you're only a few bus or tube stops, a six-pound taxi ride, or a 15- to 20-minute walk to Hyde Park, Holland Park, and the Thames. There are lovely neighborhood squares, the atmospheric Brompton Cemetery, and a huge range of restaurants, pubs, and shops, including the only all-night pharmacy for miles around. It's got a less precious, more real-world vibe than the more expensive South Ken, and it's much more appropriate for young people, back-packers, and people allergic to pretentious redevelopment (although Earl's Court is bound to join in the trend one of these days). It's also got a lot of gay-friendly hotels and pubs, and the cemetery has a rep-utation as a hangout for gay guys. The Earl's Court Arena is right there; check to see what events or concerts they've got going. The downside is that it's well west of the central London attractions, and it's often dreadfully clogged with traffic. It's on the Piccadilly and District underground lines, which makes it a snap to get to and from Heathrow and central London.

KENSINGTON Above Earl's Court, across the ferociously busy six-lane Cromwell Road (I've avoided listing many otherwise decent hotels on Cromwell, as the noise from the street can be deafening), is the lower part of Kensington, an upscale area that nevertheless has a number of inexpensive hotels, small mum-and-pop shops, and lots of restau-rants. It is bounded by Kensington Gardens to the north and Holland Park to the northwest, with Gloucester Road running through the middle of it, leading up to Kensington High Street and Kensington Palace. I love the Gloucester Road area; it's got street after street of beautiful white stucco Georgian homes, a few garden squares, and some very charming rose-covered cottages tucked away in elegant lit-tle neighborhoods and mews. (Try to ignore the unattractive postwar replacements of blitzed buildings here and there.) There are very expensive hotels here as well as budget, which makes a nice mix of people on the street (although only the very rich or very old own homes here). Kensington High Street has every shop you could possi-bly want, with Marks and Spencers, Topshop, Barkers department store, and a good variety of cafés and eateries. There's a multiplex cinema at the western end, with Holland Park across the street. Buses and underground trains (Circle and District lines) can take you from here to just about anywhere in London with ease and dispatch.

MAYFAIR AND PICCADILLY Here you'll find Hyde Park, Green Park, St. James's Park, Bond Street shopping, art galleries everywhere, the Royal

Academy, an easy walk to the West End, and good transportation. No matter where you're staying, do have a stroll through the neighborhood, where you'll be enchanted by streets of mews houses, mansions, and cottages. You'll catch the scent of very old money, as well as the newer perfume of oil fortunes (the Saudi Embassy is gorgeous, and I'm told that the huge building across the street houses a single billionaire family). Indeed, this is one of London's most exclusive areas, and has been so for 300 years. Berkeley Square, Curzon Street, Charles Street, and the surrounding area have maintained a large number of quaint buildings, many of which missed being bombed in the Blitz by inches (as you can see from the sore thumbs of modernity sticking out here and there). The shopping of nearby Bond Street, Old and New, should not be approached without being fully armed with a platinum credit card, but anyone can window-shop or browse. Obviously there is a downside to this neighborhood, and it's a stubborn stumbling block to most mere mortals: the majority of the hotels are crushingly expensive. But you can always stop in at Claridges, Browns, or the Ritz for a drink or afternoon tea. You may find that even the snootiest grand hotel will have weekend package deals, or be amenable to striking a deal. It never hurts to ask.

unofficial **TIP**
Be sure to visit Shepherd's Market, a quiet little area that was once the shopping and gossiping center for the multitude of servants who maintained the grand houses around it.

SOHO AND THE WEST END This is where you'll strike the mother lode of entertainment: street musicians, nightclubs, theaters, cinemas, strip clubs, lap dancing, and every kind of shop imaginable (or unimaginable—you may want to cover your children's eyes as you pass some sex shops). Covent Garden, the Royal Opera House, Leicester Square, Soho Square, Piccadilly Circus, Regent Street, Trafalgar Square, Chinatown, the National Gallery, and Somerset House are some of the bigger attractions to be found here; the smaller seductions include street markets, Carnaby Street, the bookshops of Charing Cross, and St. Martins-in-the-Fields. There's a superabundance of inexpensive and not-too-grotty hotels, as well as some budget-busters, with the best people-watching and nightlife opportunities in London. This is where everyone comes out to play. The downside includes a lot of noise and traffic fumes, and it can get a bit dicey at night. When the bars close, the drunks and louts roar into the streets, sometimes heaving up their dinner onto the streets as they go (mind where you walk); and the after-midnight street dramas can hold their own against any of the stage action you may have seen earlier.

BLOOMSBURY This is a much quieter option, and yet still within walking distance of the nightlife of Soho and the West End. Its biggest attraction is of course the unparalleled British Museum, and if you look around at the blue plaques celebrating its literary inhabitants, you will get a feel for how bohemian and intellectual it used to be. It still has

unofficial **TIP**
Here is one neighbor-
hood that has not fully
succumbed to the
developers' greed.

interesting shops and a variety of restaurants; and best of all, there are so many budget hotels here that the competition between them all has kept the quality just a bit higher than in some of the other budget hotel areas. Bookstores that have been around forever still ply their trade, and there is an umbrella ("brolly") shop that has been there since before World War I. Some old-fashioned pubs maintain the etched glass privacy screens and elaborate mahogany bars of their Victorian youth. Downside: It can feel a little desolate here and there at night.

Cheap but Not Always Cheerful Hotel Neighborhoods

BAYSWATER, EARL'S COURT, AND VICTORIA This is not to say that these neighborhoods don't have some very attractive hotels at reasonable prices; it's just that they have a discouraging number of fleabags, so beware of low-priced hotels in these neighborhoods—you won't be able to know just how sleazy a place is by looking on the Internet.

Out There

There's something to be said for staying well out of central London, but not all of it is good. The public transportation can be dreadful and downright unapproachable at rush hours. Many of the outer areas of London do not offer a wide choice of amenities like restaurants, convenience stores, and entertainment. There are also parts of outer London that are aesthetically unpleasing, downright grotty, or dully suburban. Whatever hotels you may find may be less expensive, but may not offer the standard of service that the central London hotels will.

Having said that, there *are* good bed-and-breakfast deals in areas that are far from the sound and fury and pollution of London and are served by tube and rail services, which can get you into the middle of town in 30–40 minutes or less. People can get more space for their money out there, and so you may find a bed-and-breakfast with a garden, your own private entrance, perhaps a basement apartment or your own floor, cleanish air, and blessed quiet. The innkeepers probably will leave you quite alone, as personal reserve is still one of the great British traditions.

CALL FOR DEALS

AS STATED ABOVE, ALMOST EVERY HOTEL IN London, except for the already cut-rate ones, will have some kind of saver scheme, be it a weekend reduction, a package that includes breakfast and a free night, price reductions during the seasonal (January and August) sales held in London's big shops, a summer season, a low season, a Christmas season, a corporate rate, a half-price scheme, a desperate-for-business rate, a no-reason lowered rate, and so on. They want you to come to London, and they want you to stay in their hotel. There is also the possibility of a last-minute room, in which a hotel with an empty room will agree to a huge reduction just to fill it. This requires flexibility, but it can spell big savings.

Rule number one in making any of these deals is to talk to the reception manager—she or he is the only person who can agree to make deals. Chat with the manager and see what can be arranged— service is their business, and they do aim to please. But remember that some hotels don't need to make deals; check out the listings and see how many rooms a hotel has. Chances are that the more rooms there are, the more rooms will be empty. Often, the rooms that remain empty are the junior, executive, or superior suites. To get one of those for the price of a standard double is a worthy coup, and you will be very happy in such a room, especially in the grand hotels.

BED-AND-BREAKFASTS

BED-AND-BREAKFASTS ARE BIG IN BRITAIN, and in London there are some drop-dead gorgeous homes that are open to you through agencies. The price (with a few exceptions) includes breakfast and is per person per night, and offers you so much more than any hotel will, and at half the price. (You should take note that the majority of these don't have air-conditioning in the rooms, but they will always have fans available. Meteorologists claim that England's heat waves come every two years, the last being in 2003. Yet 2005 had only a couple of weeks with temperatures over 80 degrees in the day, and it cooled off at night. A fan has always sufficed for me for the last decade of living here, but who can say how high future summer temperatures will soar? Better safe than sweatily sorry.) Please note that some B&Bs require a two-night minimum stay. Most small establishments ask for a credit card deposit and a small booking fee, and then you'll pay your host the full cost of your stay in cash or by credit card upon arrival.

Some Excellent Companies

THE BULLDOG CLUB (☎ 0239-263-1714; fax 0870-622-0021; emma@ bulldogclub.com; **www.bulldogclub.com**) Only the crème de la crème of houses are included in this exclusive group, with grand homes in Mayfair, Belgravia, and Chelsea, as well as other beautiful neighborhoods. There are about 30 properties available. The criteria are that the guests have a separate area from the host family's quarters, the rooms are within a five-minute walk to public transportation, there are amenities such as bathrobes and tea- and coffee-making facilities, and that the home be of a high decorative standard. The hosts have usually been around the block, and they know what a five-star hotel is. You'll probably find high-quality bedding, chocolates on your pillow, organic food for breakfast, and fine china for your tea. The business was bought by Emma Webley in the summer of 2005, so look for a new Web site and a bigger selection of homes in the future. Prices start at £85 for a single and £115 for two people and include breakfast. You pay a fee of £25 to join the "club" for a three-year membership, which is the smartest money you'll spend in London. The prices have remained the same since I wrote the first edition of this book; expect a small—and fair—rise in prices in 2006 and 2007.

UPTOWN RESERVATIONS (☎ 0207-351-3445; fax 0207-351-9383; www.uptownres.co.uk) This is another very high-toned agency, with fine houses of high standard in good central neighborhoods as well as in outer London's leafy areas. Monica Barrington, a smart and energetic woman, will likely quiz you on your needs and style, and play wise matchmaker between you and a property. Singles are very reasonable at £72 a night, double or twin is £95, triple is £125, and a room for four is £135.

LONDON HOMESTEAD SERVICES (☎ 0207-286-5115; www.lhslondon. com) This service has about 200 homes in the London area, many of which you can see on the Web site. In fact, the Web site has invaluable information on the properties, categorized by budget, moderate, and premier. Prices range from £20 to £40 per person per night, which makes it one of the least expensive options in this category.

LONDON FIRST CHOICE APARTMENTS (☎ 0208-990-9033; fax 0208-754-1200; www.lfca.co.uk) LFCA has a large assortment of hotels, serviced and nonserviced apartments, and some bed-and-breakfasts. The prices may look at bit high, but if you get a place with a kitchen, you can save a bundle by staying away from restaurants for at least two meals a day. The prices quoted are per property, per night, and not per person, which makes them competitive with the above agencies. See the Web site for more information. Prices vary according to season, neighborhood, and type of accommodation, from £100 a night for a studio in Earl's Court to £3,400 per week for a three-bedroom apartment in Mayfair.

SERVICED AND SELF-SERVICED APARTMENTS

A SERVICED APARTMENT CAN BE A GOOD alternative to a hotel room, with commensurate prices and much more room—to be able to close a door on your traveling companion(s) once in a while can be a delightful luxury. The best ones will offer most of the services a hotel does; some even provide breakfast. You may get a 24-hour concierge, satellite TV, laundry, and daily maid service; you may even get a washer/dryer in the apartment, secretarial services, guest membership to a health club, a fully equipped kitchen, and more. When you factor in the costs of eating all your meals in restaurants, a hotel costs considerably more than its nightly rate; get an apartment and you can spend your restaurant budget on the less ephemeral pleasures of shopping sprees.

HOME FROM HOME (☎ 0207-233-8111; fax 0207-233-9101; www. homefromhome.co.uk) With over 200 properties in London, Home From Home can be dialed from America toll free at ☎ 800-748-9783 for a brochure, but its Web site suffices to show you what gorgeous houses and decent prices they offer: a one-bedroom starts at £575 per week.

CENTRAL LONDON APARTMENTS (☎ 0845-644-2714; fax 0845-644-2715; **www.central-london-apartments.com**) This firm specializes in short-term rental of hotel rooms and suites in every good neighborhood in London. The prices are guaranteed to be at least 30% less than hotel prices, and though the costs are high for a one- or two-bedroom suite, you can get a studio flat for as little as £69 a night. The properties are generally nicely appointed lodgings in desirable areas. Make sure the prices quoted include VAT, and negotiate a lower rate for stays of over a week.

LONDON'S LUXURY HOTELS

THE VARIOUS STAR RATINGS GIVEN BY Michelin and other authorities on hotels have placed the five-star hotel firmly at the top of the heap. In the *Unofficial Guide to London,* we have a similar star-rating system, ranging from five to one, five being the best. When we give a hotel a five-star rating, it is only in the **relative context of the hotels covered in this book,** and doesn't reflect the universally standard five-star rating of hugely expensive, world-class luxury hotels that we have listed below.

The reason these luxury hotels are listed separately is that some of them are classic London establishments, such as the Ritz or Claridges, and no book on London would be complete without them. But if you can afford the £250 to £500 plus a night that these hotels charge, you probably don't need recommendations from us. You will know that an expensive luxury hotel in London will have all the amenities and services found in the great hotels all around the world, many of which you will probably have stayed in, and presumably you will require all that these palaces have to offer.

However, a word of caution about the following hotels: the styles vary to a large degree, from the elegant minimalism of One Aldwych to the Georgian excesses of the Lanesborough or the art deco insouciance of Claridges. They also vary in size. Views are never a given, even when you're paying £350 a night; and business amenities are not always part of the package. In the converted–town house variety of hotel, the first-floor rooms (first above the ground floor, that is) are likely to have beautiful French windows with a balcony in front and garden views in back. The uppermost floors will probably have tiny windows and angled ceilings; while the below-ground rooms may make up in size what they lack in light and views, they may also have direct access to a patio or garden.

unofficial **TIP**
So buyer, beware: if you are splurging on a luxury hotel for a special occasion, question the reservations clerk closely as to what is offered, and make a point of requesting a good view, a spacious room, and a convenient yet quiet location on your floor—you don't want to be one thin wall away from the elevator.

The majority of the following hotels are in the Mayfair and Piccadilly areas. In the hotel-profile listing, you will find somewhat more moderately priced establishments in this area (except for the extended profile on Brown's), but the fact is that this is a very expensive hotel neighborhood, frequented by movie stars on studio tabs, assorted millionaires, and corporate bigwigs with unlimited expense accounts.

You can, however, call any of the following hotels and ask about discounts. There are a number of possibilities: low-season rates, applicable in January and February; summer discounts; promotions for the city-wide sale weeks in August and January; weekend break rates; upgrading to a bigger room; paying for your room in advance in dollars; executive discounts; and frequent-flier tie-ins. They say everything's negotiable, and certainly rack rates seem to reflect an ideal value, rather than the zero sum gain of letting hotel rooms stay empty. Call directly and talk to the reservations manager to see if you can work something out that you both can live with—many of the high-end hotels have toll-free numbers in the United States. There are also some Internet-only prices that you might check and then use as a challenge to the manager to sweeten the deal. A few of these luxury hotels are owned by chain groups, such as Savoy, Rocco Forte, Intercontinental, Maybourne, and Hilton. Chains may offer any number of promotional deals, from holiday discounts to packages that include breakfast or spa breaks. Some of these otherwise astronomically priced hotels have single rooms at not-too-shocking rates—the room may be small, but you'll have the best of comfort and service you can imagine. Reservation managers may upgrade you to a junior suite if there's one available. Remember that an empty hotel room is a perishable commodity, as hotels are well aware. All the prices quoted below are for **two people sharing a standard double room,** and we have calculated and included the 17.5% VAT (unless otherwise noted), which adds up to a sizable dollop on top of a sizable basic rack rate—many of the most expensive hotels just don't have the nerve to include it in quoted prices, and only mention this exclusion in small italics below the rates (they may also slip in a 3% to 5% service charge, which I haven't included in the price).

unofficial **TIP**
For many of us, the best way (the *only* way) to experience these hotels is to have tea, a cocktail, or a meal in one, and save your money on a less pricey pad. Rainy days notwithstanding, you haven't come to London to loll around in a deluxe hotel room with the meter running.

BAGLIONI HOTEL This new luxury hotel opened in 2004, after an extensive program of gutting and transforming an old budget hotel whose location was always its biggest asset: it is directly across the street from Kensington Palace, and just a few minutes from the heart of Kensington High Street. The Italian hotel group pulled out all the stops, turning the old building into a gracious, contemporary, Italian-style palace. They've got all the modern bells and whistles—interactive plasma screens, free broadband and wireless Internet access, a spa, espresso machines in every room, plus two presidential suites. In fact, of its 68 rooms, 50 are suites (which start at £425 plus VAT). A regular room (if any of the rooms could be called "regular") starts at £355. (60 Hyde Park Gate, SW7; ☎ 0207-368-5700; fax 0207-368-5701; **www.baglionihotellondon.com;** tube: Kensington High Street or South Kensington).

THE BERKELEY Right off Knightsbridge, west of Hyde Park Corner, this hotel has what's widely considered the best spa and gym in London; the highly rated Marcus Waring dining room, Petrus; and the equally impressive Boxwood Cafe. For cocktails, try the enchanting Blue Bar, which Madonna publicly declared her favorite bar in London. There are 214 serenely spacious rooms, starting at £269, with upgrades to deluxe king-size rooms and suites available at an extra £30-plus a night. (Wilton Place, SW1; ☎ 0207-235-6000; fax 0207-235-4330; **www.theberkeleyhotellondon.com;** tube: Knightsbridge or Hyde Park Corner).

BLAKES Utterly gorgeous and very intimate hotel in South Kensington, catering to rock stars, models, actors, and aristos. Although slightly less expensive than the others in this class, you can still fracture your credit card between the tariff and the extras, like the eponymous restaurant. The rooms are exuberantly and individually decorated in styles ranging from expensive bordello to country squire to Raj's field tent. Good value for a five-star hotel, even though some of the rooms are small. The restaurant serves a fantastic, untraditional afternoon tea, with sandwiches served in little glass boxes and the best tiny but tall homemade scones. There are 47 rooms, starting at £323 (33 Roland Gardens, SW7; ☎ 0207-370-6701; fax 0207-373-0442; **www.blakeshotel.com;** tube: South Kensington).

 BROWN'S HOTEL Victorian gentlemen's club atmosphere and beautiful antique furnishings; there's nothing ostentatious or over the top about this place except for its prices. Bought by the Rocco Forte group in July 2005, they've done a serious amount of upgrading, and have tried to modernize without sacrificing the traditional English charm. I do hope they will do something about the size of some of the rooms (especially on the top floor), which are not very commodious, albeit cozy. They serve an excellent afternoon tea from 2 to 6 p.m. in one of the three lovely sitting rooms. Don't try to eat it all. There are 117 rooms, starting at £325. See profile for more information (30–34 Albemarle Street, W1; ☎ 0207-493-6020; fax 0207-493-9381; **www.brownshotel.com;** tube: Green Park).

 CLARIDGES Bold decor evokes Jazz Age glamour and royal luxury. People of serious substance stay here—Mick Jagger reportedly rents a flat here, a wild extravagance for the

famously tight-fisted millionaire. They have a fantastic and fantasti-
cally expensive afternoon tea here, served in impressive surroundings.
On Saturdays, there's a good chance of seeing a society wedding, featuring women in charming chapeaus and men in morning coats. The
restaurant, Gordon Ramsey at Claridges, is one of London's best.
The art deco period details are deliciously evocative of the kind of
sophisticated mansions imagined in 1930s screwball-comedy flicks;
Jean Harlow or Mary Astor would look right at home, and Jay
Gatsby would have tried to buy it. There are 203 rooms starting at
£280. (Brook Street, W1; ☎ 0207-629-8860; fax 0207-499-2210;
www.theclaridgeshotellondon.com; tube: Bond Street).

THE CONNAUGHT Grand country house is the style here, and "perfect
service" the watchwords. It's been around since 1897; Charles de
Gaulle made it his wartime headquarters, and Cecil Beaton and
David Niven called it home. It attracts so many regulars that it's
almost a club; make reservations well in advance of your visit. There
are 92 rooms, starting at £280 plus service charge (16 Carlos Place,
W1; ☎ 0207-499-7070; fax 0207-495-3262; **www.theconnaughthotel
london.com;** tube: Bond Street).

THE DORCHESTER One of London's grandest establishments, this
hotel is right across from Hyde Park and walking distance to some of
the toniest shops in London. Restaurants and the health club are of
the highest standards, as are the rooms and the decor. You can see
where your money is going at this hotel. There are 244 rooms and
suites, starting at £475 (53 Park Lane, W1; ☎ 0207-629-8888; fax
0207-409-0114; **www.dorchesterhotel.com;** tube: Marble Arch).

THE FOUR SEASONS As part of the Four Seasons Group, this hotel
often offers promotional packages. The decor is opulent without
being overly ostentatious; naturally, they provide excellent service
and food. There are 220 rooms, starting at £405 (Hamilton Place in
Park Lane, W1; ☎ 0207-499-0888; fax 0207-493-6629; **www.four
seasons.com/london;** tube: Hyde Park Corner).

THE LANDMARK The Landmark gives good value for money because
it's out of the Mayfair-Piccadilly high-rent district, located in the
charming and convenient Marylebone village. There's an impressive
atrium for dining, a fitness center and pool, and good-size rooms.
Modern refurbishment in an old building. All 298 rooms are double
and start at £276 (222 Marylebone Road, NW1; ☎ 0207-631-8000;
fax 0207-631-8080; **www.landmarklondon.co.uk;** tube: Marylebone).

THE LANESBOROUGH You'd never guess to look at the elaborately
Georgian interior that gurneys used to be rolled around these floors
instead of room-service carts. This former hospital is now a formal
hotel, full of charm and mahogany-paneled splendor, which blends
interestingly well with the Asian decoration of the fine restaurant.
There's a butler call button in all the rooms; need we say more? There

are 95 rooms, starting at £345 for a standard double (Hyde Park Corner, SW1; ☎ 0207-259-5599; fax 0207-259-5606; **www.lanesborough.com;** tube: Hyde Park Corner).

MANDARIN ORIENTAL HOTEL A grand old hotel in a good location. There are only suites facing north with views of Hyde Park; the hotel also faces Knightsbridge, one of the noisiest streets in London, but it's a stone's throw from world-class shopping. There is a newly renovated restaurant on the first floor—much too modern for this elegant Edwardian building, but with a bit of a park view. There are 200 rooms; doubles start at £310 (66 Knightsbridge, SW1; ☎ 0207-235-2000; fax 0207-235-2001; **www.mandarinoriental.com;** tube: Knightsbridge).

THE METROPOLITAN Not only is this home to the esteemed and expensive sushi restaurant Nobu, but it also has the renowned Metropolitan Club, a private hot spot that was at the top of the social ladder when it opened in 1997, and is still formidable enough. Guests of the hotel have complimentary membership, a big plus for young social types. It has a state-of-the-art gym. The decor is all about cool beige, beech, and blank walls. There are 155 rooms, from £355 (Old Park Lane, W1; ☎ 0207-447-1000; fax 0207-447-1100; **www.metropolitan.co.uk;** tube: Hyde Park Corner).

ONE ALDWYCH Where to start? This elegant and modern hotel has so many amenities that I can only list the highlights: 56-foot pool in a magnificent spa; multimedia screening room with wide-body seats; 350 important works of art scattered throughout the rooms; three bars; a good restaurant; and a clientele that will have you itching to grab your camera. Doubles start at £255, with lower rates on weekends and in summer (1 Aldwych, WC2; ☎ 0207-300-1000; fax 0207-300-1001; **www.onealdwych.co.uk;** tube: Covent Garden or Charing Cross).

THE RITZ What can you say about the place that has given its name to the dictionary as a definition of luxury and extravagance? Before you think it's just plain out of the question, call and see what kind of deals they have: you might happen upon a weekend deal or discounted summer rate. The decor is Versailles on Piccadilly, and the comfort is sumptuousness itself. Individually decorated rooms, 131 in all, start at £390 and go up, up, up (150 Piccadilly, W1; ☎ 0207-300-2308; fax 0207-493-2687; toll free from U.S. ☎ 877-748-9536; **www.theritzlondon.com;** tube: Green Park).

SANDERSON This hotel, part of the Ian Schrager–owned Morgan Group, is favored by rich, high-profile media personalities, whose personal needs may be inferred by the excessive luxury offered here: 450-thread-count cotton, three phones with two private lines in each room, a private fitness area in some rooms, a yoga studio, and two-story holistic bathhouse. There's even the very rare feature of a children's play area—most luxury hotels hope that children will stay home. The decor is quirky, dreamy, Dali-esque, with eclectic furnishings in an array of colors and periods. Swathes of white muslin shroud mirrors, lights, and doorways, adding mystique to an already dreamlike interior. The rooms are stark yet chic, with chrome and white furnishings. All this makes up for the fact that Sanderson is housed in a charmless 1960s block building. There are 150 rooms, ranging from £255 upwards. Its sister hotel, St. Martin's Lane, is equally chic, hip, and trendy, but unfortunately, I have run into extreme forms of rudeness and slipshod service from its overly hip employees, and two people I know fled to another hotel after one night there (50 Berners Street, W1; ☎ 0207-300-1400; fax 0207-300-1401; **www.morganshotel group.com;** tube: Oxford Circus or Tottenham Court).

 THE SAVOY I don't think the Savoy has changed much since it was Frank Sinatra's favorite hotel in foggy London town. It is still a gorgeous place, and has done what's known as a sympathetic renovation recently: like Claridges, it maintains the decor of its salad days, and its service is impeccable. It's located right in the thick of things, perfect for theatergoers. Most interesting is that they host a writer-in-residence program, where an author gets to live there for a year—Fay Weldon never wanted to leave. Rooms, 161 in all, start at £270. The only rooms with a river view are the suites, which start at £780. I believe Old Blue Eyes took the penthouse. (1 Savoy Hill, Strand, WC2; ☎ 0207-950-5492; fax 0207-950-5482; toll-free in United States ☎ 800-637-2869; **www.savoy-group.co.uk;** tube: Charing Cross).

HOTEL RATINGS

OVERALL RATINGS We have distinguished the following properties according to relative quality, tastefulness, state of repair, cleanliness, and size of standard rooms, grouping them into classifications denoted by stars. Overall star ratings in this guide apply to London properties only and do not correspond to ratings awarded by the British Tourism Board, automobile clubs, or other travel critics. Overall ratings are presented to show the difference we perceive between one property and another. They are assigned without regard to location or to whether a property has restaurants, recreational facilities, entertainment, or other extras.

★★★★★	Superior	Tasteful and luxurious by any standard
★★★★	Extremely nice	Above average in appointments and design; very comfortable
★★★	Nice	Average but quite comfortable
★★	Adequate	Plain but meets all essential needs
★	Budget	Spartan, not aesthetically pleasing, but clean

QUALITY RATINGS In addition to overall ratings (which delineate broad categories), we also employ quality ratings. They apply to room quality only and describe the property's standard accommodations. In addition to standard accommodations, many hotels offer luxury rooms and special suites that are not rated in this guide. Our rating scale is ★–★★★★★, with ★★★★★ as the best possible rating and ★ as the worst.

VALUE RATINGS We also provide a value rating to give you some sense of the quality of a room in relation to its cost. As before, the ratings are based on the quality of room for the money and do not take into account location, services, or amenities.

Our scale is as follows:

★★★★★	An exceptional bargain
★★★★	A good deal
★★★	Fairly priced (you get exactly what you pay for)
★★	Somewhat overpriced
★	Significantly overpriced

A ★★½ room at £100 may have the same value rating as a ★★★★ room at £180, but that does not mean that the rooms will be of comparable quality. Regardless of whether it's a good deal or not, a ★★½ room is still a ★★½ room.

For each hotel we also provide the London neighborhood in which the property is located.

HOW THE HOTELS COMPARE

WHAT FOLLOWS IS A TABLE THAT CONTAINS the hotels we have researched and profiled organized by overall rating. To find a particular hotel listed in this table, look through the alphabetical section of profiles later in the chapter.

If you use subsequent editions of this guide, you will notice that many of the ratings and rankings change. In addition to the inclusion of new properties, these changes also reflect guest-room renovations or improved maintenance and housekeeping. A failure to properly maintain guest rooms or a lapse in housekeeping standards can negatively affect the ratings, or may result in deleting the hotel from the book altogether.

Finally, before you begin to shop for a hotel, take a hard look at this letter we received from a couple in Hot Springs, Arkansas:

We canceled our room reservations to follow the advice in your book [and reserved a hotel room highly ranked by the Unofficial Guide]. *We wanted inexpensive, but clean and cheerful. We got inexpensive, but [also] dirty, grim, and depressing. I really felt disappointed in your advice and the room. It was the pits. That was*

the one real piece of information I needed from your book!
The room spoiled the holiday for me aside from our touring.

Needless to say, this letter was as unsettling to us as the bad room was to our reader. Our integrity as travel journalists, after all, is based on the quality of the information we provide our readers. Even with the best of intentions and the most conscientious research, however, we cannot inspect every room in every hotel. What we do, in statistical terms, is take a sample: we check out several rooms selected at random in each hotel and base our ratings and rankings on those rooms. The inspections are conducted anonymously and without the knowledge of the management. Although unusual, it is certainly possible that the rooms we randomly inspect are not representative of the majority of rooms at a particular hotel. This is particularly true in the smaller London hotels that offer such a variety of room sizes and styles.

Another possibility is that the rooms we inspect in a given hotel are representative, but that by bad luck a reader is assigned a room that is inferior. When we rechecked the hotel our reader disliked, we discovered our rating was correctly representative, but that he and his wife had unfortunately been assigned to one of a small number of threadbare rooms scheduled for renovation.

The key to avoiding disappointment is to snoop around in advance. We recommend that you ask for a photo of a hotel's standard guest room before you book, or at least get a copy of the hotel's promotional brochure.

How the Hotels Compare

HOTEL	OVERALL QUALITY	ROOM QUALITY	VALUE QUALITY
Dukes Hotel	★★★★★	★★★★★	★★★
Brown's Hotel	★★★★★	★★★★★	★★
11 Cadogan Gardens	★★★★★	★★★★½	★★★
L'Hotel	★★★★★	★★★★	★★★★½
Thistle Hotel Victoria	★★★★★	★★★★	★★★★
Goring Hotel	★★★★★	★★★★	★★★
The Gore	★★★★½	★★★★½	★★★★
Threadneedles Hotel	★★★★½	★★★★½	★★★
The Draycott Hotel	★★★★	★★★★★	★★★
Covent Garden Hotel	★★★★	★★★★½	★★★
The Colonnade Hotel	★★★★	★★★★	★★★★
Hotel Russell	★★★★	★★★★	★★★★
The Zetter Restaurant & Rooms	★★★★	★★★★	★★★★

How the Hotels Compare (continued)

HOTEL	OVERALL QUALITY	ROOM QUALITY	VALUE QUALITY
Charlotte Street Hotel	★★★★	★★★★	★★★
London Marriot Hotel County Hall	★★★★	★★★★	★★★
The Montague on the Gardens	★★★★	★★★★	★★★
Great Eastern Hotel	★★★★	★★★★	★★½
Hazlitt's Hotel	★★★★	★★★★	★★½
Radisson Edwardian Hampshire	★★★★	★★★★	★★½
Franklin Hotel	★★★★	★★★★	★★
The Rookery	★★★★	★★★½	★★½
Miller's Residence	★★★★	★★★	★★★½
Abbey Court	★★★½	★★★★	★★★★½
Collingham Apartments	★★★½	★★★★	★★★½
Basil Street Hotel	★★★½	★★★★	★★★
The Portobello Hotel	★★★½	★★★★	★★★
Number Sixteen	★★★½	★★★★	★★½
Parkes Hotel	★★★½	★★★★	★★½
The Pelham	★★★½	★★★★	★★½
Lincoln House Hotel	★★★½	★★★½	★★★★½
Durrants	★★★½	★★★½	★★★½
Academy Bloomsbury Town House	★★★½	★★★½	★★★
Grange White Hall Hotel	★★★½	★★★½	★★★
Cadogan Hotel	★★★½	★★★½	★★
Pembridge Court Hotel	★★★½	★★★	★★½
The Gallery Hotel	★★★	★★★½	★★★½
The Claverley	★★★	★★★½	★★★
The Columbia Hotel	★★★	★★★	★★★★★
Five Sumner Place Hotel	★★★	★★★	★★★★½
The Rembrandt Hotel	★★★	★★★	★★★★½
The Gainsborough	★★★	★★★	★★★
Morgan Hotel	★★½	★★★	★★★★
Barkston Gardens	★★½	★★½	★★★★
Strand Palace Hotel	★★½	★★½	★★★
Holiday Inn Mayfair	★★½	★★	★★★
St. Margaret's Hotel	★★	★★½	★★★★★

How the Hotels Compare (continued)

HOTEL	OVERALL QUALITY	ROOM QUALITY	VALUE QUALITY
Quality Hotel	★★	★★½	★★★★
Comfort Inn Notting Hill	★½	★★½	★★★★½
Fielding Hotel	★½	★★	★★½
Edward Lear Hotel	★½	★½	★★★★
Ruskin Hotel	★	★★½	★★★★★
The Brompton Hotel	★	★	★★★
Royal Adlephi Hotel	★	★	★★★

Accommodations by Neighborhood

WEST END

Academy Bloomsbury Town House

Brown's Hotel

Charlotte Street Hotel

Covent Garden Hotel

Dukes Hotel

Fielding Hotel

Grange White Hall Hotel

Hazlitt's Hotel

Holiday Inn Mayfair

Hotel Russell

London Marriott Hotel County Hall

The Montague on the Gardens

Morgan Hotel

Radisson Edwardian Hampshire

Ruskin Hotel

St. Margaret's Hotel

Strand Palace Hotel

THE CITY

Great Eastern Hotel

The Rookery

Threadneedles Hotel

The Zetter Restaurant & Rooms

WESTMINSTER AND VICTORIA

Goring Hotel

Quality Hotel

Royal Adelphi Hotel

Thistle Hotel Victoria

KNIGHTSBRIDGE TO SOUTH KENSINGTON

Barkston Gardens

Basil Street Hotel

The Brompton Hotel

Cadogan Hotel

The Claverley

11 Cadogan Gardens

Collingham Apartments

The Draycott Hotel

Five Sumner Place Hotel

Franklin Hotel

The Gainsborough

The Gallery Hotel

The Gore

L'Hotel

Number Sixteen

KNIGHTSBRIDGE TO SOUTH KENSINGTON (CONTINUED)

Parkes Hotel

The Pelham

The Rembrandt Hotel

MARYLEBONE TO NOTTING HILL GATE

Abbey Court

The Colonnade Hotel

The Columbia Hotel

Comfort Inn Notting Hill

Durrants

Edward Lear Hotel

Lincoln House Hotel

Miller's Residence

Pembridge Court Hotel

The Portobello Hotel

HOTEL PROFILES

ALL PRICES INCLUDE THE 17.5% VALUE-ADDED TAX (VAT) and refer to the range of prices for a **double room for two people:** we are assuming that unless you're on business, you will be with a traveling companion. Some double rooms have only one rather smallish double bed; others have two single beds, or a king- or queen-size bed. In England, "king-size" is what Americans call a queen, and "super-king" is the U.K. equivalent of a U.S. king-size bed.

Obviously, a single room will be less expensive, but as noted in the reviews, the single rooms are often tiny and depressing, no matter how great the hotel is in general. I have suggested in some cases that even if you are alone, upgrade to a double room—the additional space is often worth the additional cost. In some B&Bs the total quoted price per night is for two people sharing a room, including breakfast for two. Other establishments may charge you for one room and two breakfasts; be clear what the *final* cost will be, and always check the fine print. We have added the VAT to all rates, so if you see a lower price on a Web site, you will probably see written in tiny italics somewhere on the page, "Rates are subject to 17.5% VAT," or "Rates are exclusive of VAT," or some variation thereof. I have not factored in the 3–5% charge some hotels add for service, because it differs from hotel to hotel; many hotels do not endorse this stealth surcharge and leave you to decide on tipping for service. What you want to see above or below the prices is "Rates include VAT, service charge, and breakfast." I admire a hotel that adds it all up and publishes the total on their rate cards or advertising. Prices for deluxe, executive, triple-occupancy, family rooms, and suites and rooms with special features (such as four-poster bed, fireplace, balcony, etc.) will be significantly higher. You will also notice that the least expensive places do not have air-conditioning, which is sometimes a problem. It

west end accommodations

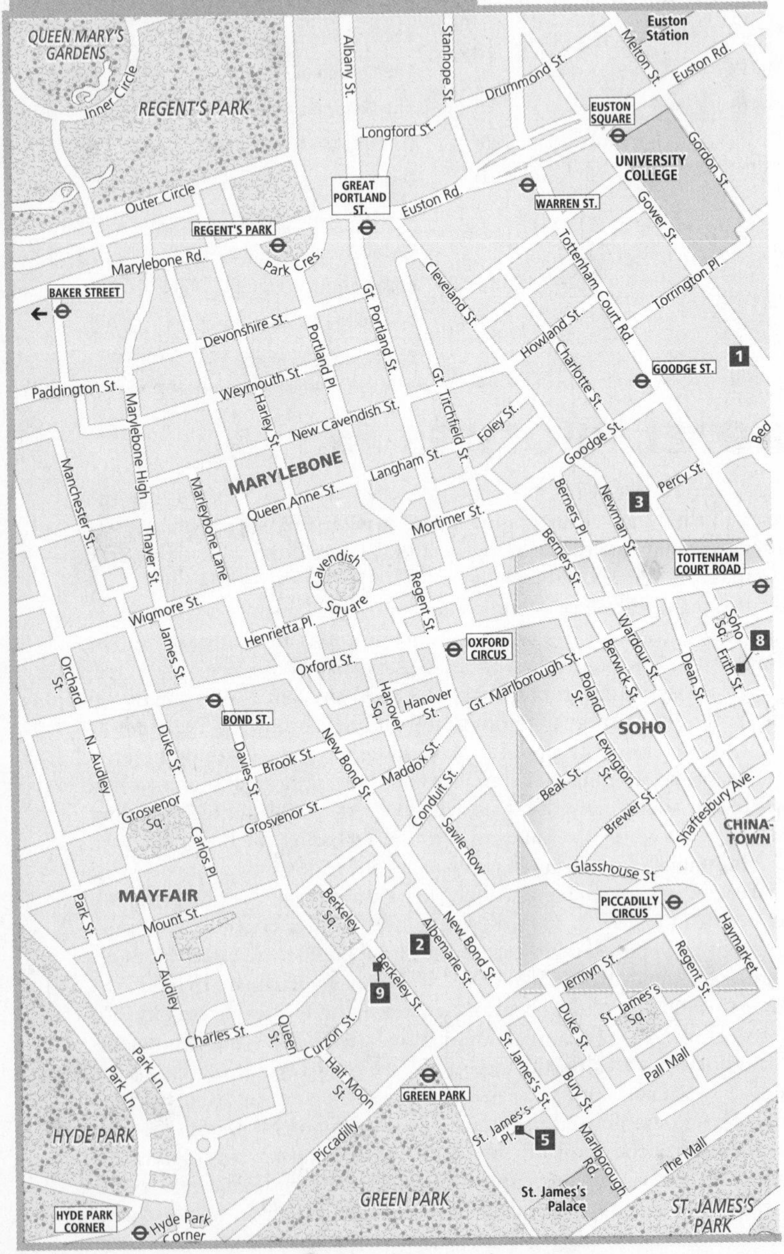

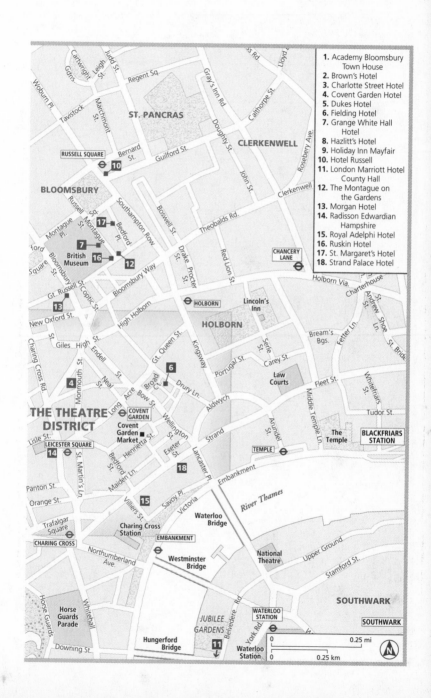

1. Academy Bloomsbury Town House
2. Brown's Hotel
3. Charlotte Street Hotel
4. Covent Garden Hotel
5. Dukes Hotel
6. Fielding Hotel
7. Grange White Hall Hotel
8. Hazlitt's Hotel
9. Holiday Inn Mayfair
10. Hotel Russell
11. London Marriott Hotel County Hall
12. The Montague on the Gardens
13. Morgan Hotel
14. Radisson Edwardian Hampshire
15. Royal Adelphi Hotel
16. Ruskin Hotel
17. St. Margaret's Hotel
18. Strand Palace Hotel

westminster and victoria accommodations and dining

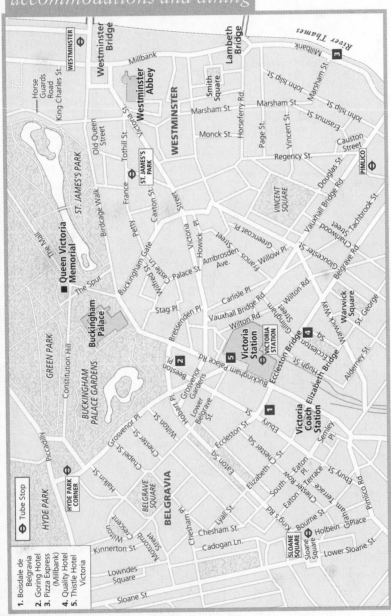

1. Boisdale de Belgravia
2. Goring Hotel
3. Pizza Express (Millbank)
4. Quality Hotel
5. Thistle Hotel Victoria

⊕ Tube Stop

"the city" accommodations

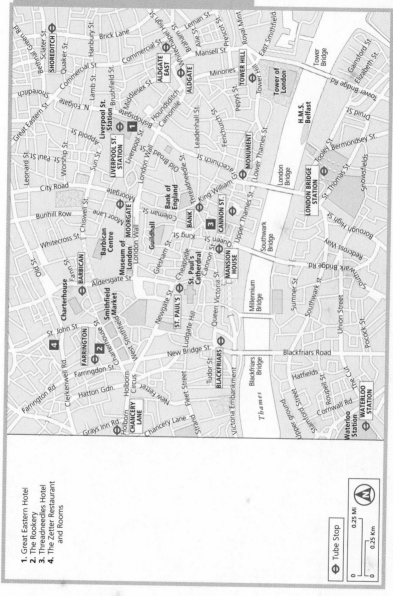

1. Great Eastern Hotel
2. The Rookery
3. Threadneedles Hotel
4. The Zetter Restaurant and Rooms

⊕ Tube Stop

0.25 Mi
0.25 Km

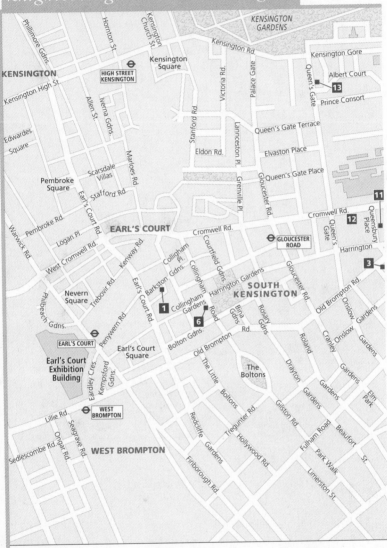

knightsbridge to south kensington

1. Barkston Gardens
2. Basil Street Hotel
3. The Brompton Hotel
4. Cadogan Hotel
5. The Claverley
6. Collingham Apartments
7. The Draycott Hotel
8. 11 Cadogan Gardens
9. Five Sumner Place Hotel
10. Franklin Hotel
11. The Gainsborough
12. The Gallery Hotel
13. The Gore
14. L'Hotel
15. Number Sixteen
16. Parkes Hotel
17. The Pelham
18. The Rembrandt Hotel

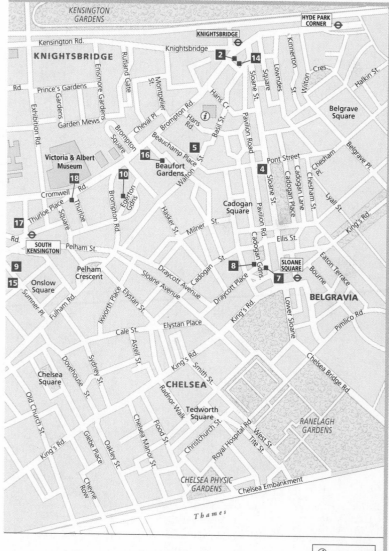

accommodations

KENSINGTON GARDENS

HYDE PARK CORNER

KNIGHTSBRIDGE

Kensington Rd.

KNIGHTSBRIDGE

Knightsbridge

2 · 14

Belgrave Square

Prince's Gardens

Rd.

Ennismore Gardens

Rutland Gate

Montpelier St.

Cheval Pl.

Brompton Rd.

Hans Rd.

Hans Cr.

Basil St.

Sloane St.

Square

Lowndes St.

Kinnerton St.

Wilton Cres.

Halkin St.

Exhibition Rd.

Garden Mews

Brompton Square

Beauchamp Place

Hans St.

Walton

Pavilion Road

Pont Street

Chesham Pl.

Belgrave Pl.

Garden Mews

i

5

Victoria & Albert Museum

16

Beaufort Gardens

18

10

Cromwell Rd.

Thurloe Place

Thurloe Square

Thurloe

Brompton Rd.

Egerton Gdns

Hasker St.

Milner St.

Cadogan

St.

4

Sloane St.

Pavilion Rd.

Cadogan Place

Cadogan Square

Cadogan Lane

Chesham St.

Lyall St.

King's Rd.

17

Rd.

SOUTH KENSINGTON

Pelham St.

Ellis St.

Eaton Terrace

9

15

Onslow Square

Summer Pl.

Fulham Rd.

Pelham Crescent

Ixworth Place

Elystan St.

Draycott Avenue

Sloane Avenue

Cadogan

Draycott Place

8 ·

7

SLOANE SQUARE

Cadogan Gdns

Lower Sloane

Bourne

BELGRAVIA

Cale St.

Elystan Place

Astell St.

King's Rd.

King's Rd.

Pimlico Rd.

Sydney St.

Chelsea Square

Dovehouse St.

Old Church St.

Smith St.

CHELSEA

Radnor Walk

Tedworth Square

Chelsea Bridge Rd.

RANELAGH GARDENS

King's Rd.

Glebe Place

Oakley St.

Chelsea Manor St.

Flood St.

Christchurch St.

Royal Hospital Rd.

West St.

Tite St.

Cheyne Row

CHELSEA PHYSIC GARDENS

Chelsea Embankment

Thames

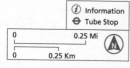

i Information

Tube Stop

| 0 | 0.25 Mi |
| 0 | 0.25 Km |

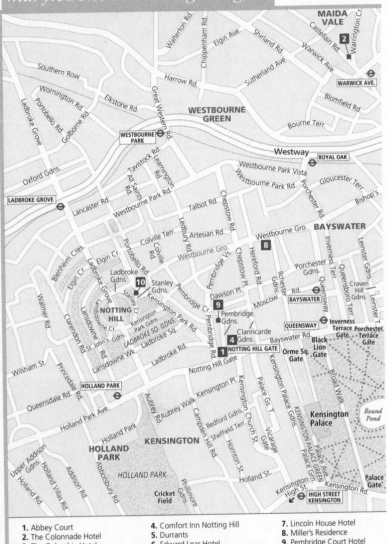

marylebone to notting hill gate

1. Abbey Court
2. The Colonnade Hotel
3. The Columbia Hotel
4. Comfort Inn Notting Hill
5. Durrants
6. Edward Lear Hotel
7. Lincoln House Hotel
8. Miller's Residence
9. Pembridge Court Hotel

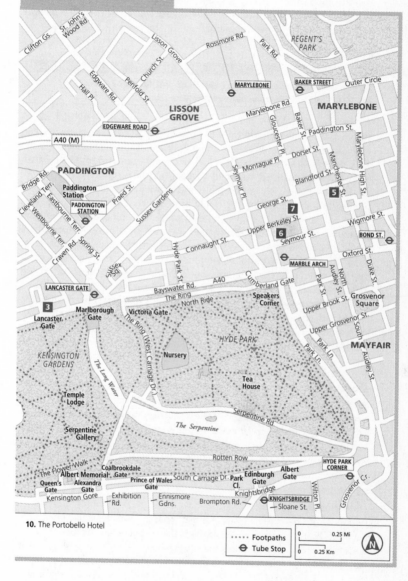

accommodations

10. The Portobello Hotel

····· Footpaths
⊖ Tube Stop

0   0.25 Mi
0   0.25 Km

seems that you get into deluxe prices when you stay in a hotel with air-conditioning, and in fact, some hotels have air-conditioning *only* in deluxe or better rooms; the others will have but a fan (which is usually sufficient at night). The following reviews are listed alphabetically.

Abbey Court

OVERALL ★★★½ QUALITY ★★★★ VALUE ★★★★½ PRICE RANGE £110–£175

20 Pembridge Gardens, Notting Hill Gate, W2; ☎ 0207-221-7518; fax 0207-792-0858; www.abbeycourthotel.co.uk

Abbey Court is a lovely old Victorian mansion, built in 1830, in a white-stucco-front neighborhood close to Portobello Road. It's a real beauty, and well priced, too. It's popular with antiques dealers, not only because they can walk to Kensington Church Street and all the antiques warrens along Portobello, but also because it has plenty of really fine old furniture, art, and decorations to admire. It's comfortable and homey, as well as elegant and serene—almost like visiting the home of a rich aunt with very good taste. There are plenty of old books on hand, some first editions, which you can (carefully) borrow to read. Downstairs there's a small conservatory where breakfast is served (continental breakfast is included), and an honor bar is set out all day. A tiny little patio off the conservatory has a small pool with goldfish. Newspapers are ordered for you free, and there are plenty of English magazines in each room. There are reductions for stays over a week; and you will find special deals or upgrades on the Web site. A total overhaul of the bathrooms, completed in 2003, has spruced up the loos, with off-white Italian marble and Jacuzzi jets in the tubs. The 14 rooms that were refurbished in the late 1990s have held up beautifully. John Galliano, the clothing designer, said that "The Abbey Court hotel truly understands the meaning of comfort and privacy," and that's high praise indeed from a guy who could stay just about anywhere in London. Please note that there is no elevator.

SETTINGS AND FACILITIES

Nearest tube station Notting Hill Gate. **Quietness rating** A in back, B+ in front (quiet street). **Dining** Small breakfast room. **Amenities** Newspapers, bathrobes, biscuits, and bottled water; high-speed Internet modems in rooms, computers for your use; associated with nearby health club; breakfast included, honor bar. **Services** Receptionist does work of concierge; multilingual staff; 24-hour room service, bellhop, laundry, and ticket procurement.

ACCOMMODATIONS

Rooms 22. All rooms Telephone, Internet modem, satellite TV, hair dryer, iron, bathrobe, heated towel racks, Jacuzzi bath. **Some rooms** Antique four-poster or brass beds, sitting areas. **Bed and bath** Italian marble bathrooms with tubs that have Jacuzzi jets, shower, and heated towel racks. Mattresses and sheets are of high quality. **Favorites** The four-poster rooms are the biggest and the nicest. **Comfort and decor** The decor is gorgeously traditional, with lovely antiques and prints all around, fantastic mirrors, and nice wallpaper. It's a pleasure to see how well appointed it is, and for me, that spells comfort. There's no elevator for the five floors, which may spell discomfort for many, but the stairway is beautiful.

Deposit Credit card; 48-hour cancellation policy. **Credit cards** All major. **Check-in/out** 3 p.m./11 a.m. **Pets** Not allowed. **Elevator** No. **Children** Yes. **Disabled access** No lift.

Academy Bloomsbury Town House

OVERALL ★★★½   QUALITY ★★★½   VALUE ★★★   PRICE RANGE £116–£160

21 Gower Street, Bloomsbury, WC1; ☎ 0207-631-4115; fax 0207-636-3442; www.theetoncollection.com

This is one of three perfectly beautiful hotels opened by The Eton Group in London in the past few years (see page 145 and page 105 for Thread-needles and The Colonnade Hotels). It's one of the nicest places to stay in the convenient Bloomsbury area, although Gower Street itself is not much to write home about. You're a short walk to the treasures of the British Museum, Oxford Street shopping, and the West End; University College London is right up the street. The hotel was created by linking five old town houses together, which gives it two private guest gardens in back, called the Conservatory and the Library, all abloom with flowers and statuary (there's even a third garden area attached to the Luxury Suite). The rack rate is £135 plus VAT (£158.60), but so certain am I that you will find a deal on the Web site for £99 plus VAT (£116.30), I have used that figure as the bottom of the price range. If you do pay the full freight, don't be afraid to ask for an upgrade, but only from the reservations manager. They have all the modern conveniences, like wireless broadband, air-conditioning, and satellite TV, but have retained the period details that make the hotel so charming and kind of quirky. The lounge areas have deep, comfy chairs, and there are lovely wrought-iron tables and chairs in the Conservatory Garden, where you can also have your breakfast, weather permitting. Certain rates include continental breakfast, but failing that, Bloomsbury is teeming with cafés, Starbucks, and breakfast joints. The downside, and it's a biggie if you're disabled or on the third floor, is that there's no elevator. Some of the grade-listed historic houses in London can't get permission to build one, so if you're loathe to climb stairs, get a ground floor room. The Academy is a good example of a modern hotel that feels like a private home, with homage paid to the traditions of England and the needs of the international traveler.

SETTINGS AND FACILITIES

Nearest tube station Goodge Street. **Quietness** A overlooking the gardens, C on the street. **Dining** Breakfast only. **Amenities** Newspapers, bathrobes, and bottled water; breakfast included with some rates, bar, 11 nonsmoking rooms. **Services** Concierge; 24-hour room service, bellhop, laundry.

ACCOMMODATIONS

Rooms 49. **All rooms** Telephone, wireless broadband, satellite TV, hair dryer, bathrobe. **Some rooms** Access to private garden; four-poster bed. **Bed and bath** Comfortable beds with fine cotton sheets, down pillows and duvet. Some doubles and all singles have shower only, the rest have full baths with designer toiletries.

Favorites Luxury suite with garden. **Comfort and decor** The high standards of the Eton Group have been adhered to at this more reasonably priced hotel, so you can expect Frette sheets, down pillows, elegant furnishings, and good service.

PAYMENT, RESERVATIONS, AND RESTRICTIONS

Deposit Credit card; 24-hour cancellation policy. **Credit cards** All major. **Check-in/out** 2 p.m./11 a.m. **Pets** Not allowed. **Elevator** No. **Children** Yes. **Disabled access** No.

 Barkston Gardens

OVERALL ★★½	QUALITY ★★½	VALUE ★★★★	PRICE RANGE £49–£120

34–44 Barkston Gardens, Earl's Court, SW5; ☎ 0207-373-7851; fax 0207-370-6570; www.barkstongardens.com

In an area known for its backpacker hostels and low-cost B&Bs, this is one of the best. Yes, some of the rooms are small, and the decor is just this side of mediocre, but it's clean, relatively well-run, convenient to transportation and shops, and good value for the money. Rooms for £45–£55 a night (these are the rates with Internet discount; rack rates are higher) are few and far between in a city like London, or at least they're hard to find if you have higher standards than a backpacking student. The nine family rooms are a good deal at £70. The Victorian red-brick town house has a charming exterior. The lobby has white marble floors and not a whole lot else, but what it lacks in sumptuousness it makes up for in convenience: it's a 15-minute walk to the museums and Hyde Park, and Earl's Court High Street, around the corner, has all the shops and pubs you could want (the tube station is yards from the hotel, and Earl's Court Arena is a block away). There are two eating venues in the hotel: Brewster's Bar, which serves sandwiches and spirits, and the Barkston Bistro, where you can eat breakfast and dinner. Some of the rates include continental breakfast; otherwise it costs a reasonable £6 for continental or £8 for full English breakfast. There is no air-conditioning, so bear that in mind if you're booking for summer—heat waves have become less of a rarity these days, even if they only last a week.

SETTINGS AND FACILITIES

Nearest tube station Earl's Court. **Quietness** A/B. **Dining** Yes, at Barkston Bistro or Brewster's Bar. **Amenities** Newspapers, Internet access in public area, breakfast and dinner. **Services** Concierge; limited room service.

ACCOMMODATIONS

Rooms 93. **All rooms** Telephone, TV, hair dryer, tea/coffee facility, trouser press, no air-conditioning. **Some rooms** View of gardens. **Bed and bath** Basic and functional. **Favorites** Family rooms; 1st floor rooms. **Comfort and decor** Although plain-jane, there are some period details in place that give it a more distinguished appearance than similarly priced hotels. Make sure you have a queen-size bed or twins for two; the doubles aren't big enough.

PAYMENT, RESERVATIONS, AND RESTRICTIONS

Deposit Credit card; 24-hour cancellation policy. **Credit cards** All major. **Check-

in/out 2 p.m./11:30 a.m. **Pets** Not allowed. **Elevator** Yes. **Children** Yes. **Disabled access** Limited.

The Basil Street Hotel

OVERALL ★★★½   QUALITY ★★★★   VALUE ★★★   PRICE RANGE £205–£246

**Basil Street, Knightsbridge, SW3; ☎ 0207-581-3311,
in U.S. ☎ 800-448-8355; fax 0207-581-3693; www.thebasil.com**

For over 85 years, The Basil Street Hotel has been attracting loyal customers with its homey comfort and unpretentious elegance. It's the kind of hotel you want to hang around in; there are a few common sitting areas that are so comfortable, so pleasing to the eye, and so well appointed that you may not be tempted outside to nearby Harrods, Hyde Park, the museums of South Kensington, Harvey Nichols, or the high-flying designer shops of Sloane Street. This is not an ostentatious hotel by any means, but if you look at the art on the wall—get a load of the glass-and-oil paintings in the dining room hallway—or the furniture, the carpets, and the bric-a-brac—you know some quiet care and expense has been lavished on the decor. The country-house feeling is maintained even against all the noise and hubbub of busy Sloane Street and Brompton Road. There are sitting alcoves looking out over the roofs of Knightsbridge that have desks supplied with writing paper, evoking a gentler time before e-mail. It's a feminine place in many ways, with white walls and oriental rugs that have the air of a serenely upper-class women's club from the 1920s, and indeed, you should see some of the very correct and British old-school dames who motor down from the country pile for a shot at the Harrods' sale. It's in no way frilly; compared to some of the faux olde-English-country-house decor in so many hotels in London, it's positively restrained—probably because it's the real thing. There has been a rumor afoot that the Basil may be sold in the not-too-distant future (she did have a good old run, after all), so get over at least for the afternoon tea, before someone gets out the wrecking ball and goes all minimalist on it.

SETTINGS AND FACILITIES

Nearest tube station Knightsbridge. **Quietness rating** C- on Brompton Road side, B+ on Basil Street. **Dining** Traditional sort of dining room, with Sunday roasts, and live classical music most nights. There's also a warm and comfy sitting room for excellent afternoon teas. **Amenities** Women's Club (The Parrot Club), into which men only can go if accompanied by a woman, and which provides office services for businesswomen; ironing rooms on each floor; parking spaces available at a reasonable charge; smoking and nonsmoking rooms. **Services** Concierge, bellhop, laundry.

ACCOMMODATIONS

Rooms 93. **All rooms** Telephone, modem, satellite TV, hair dryer, bathtub, writing desk, comfortable sitting chair. **Some rooms** Air-conditioning, bay windows, glass-fronted cabinets. **Bed and bath** Bathrooms range from irreproachable to irresistible: some spacious, some paneled in white painted pine wainscot. Beds are quite comfortable. **Favorites** Singles are among the largest in London (which isn't saying much, but still). Beautiful bay windows in some rooms. **Comfort and decor** Exquisite antiques and a huge collection of mezzotints, fine carpets, superior furniture, and fine porcelain and lamps. High ceilings, good closet space. Functional and roomy layout in all rooms (by London standards, anyway).

PAYMENT, RESERVATIONS, AND RESTRICTIONS
Deposit Credit card; 24-hour cancellation policy. **Credit cards** All major. **Check-in/out** Midday/noon. **Pets** Not allowed. **Elevator** Yes. **Children** Yes. **Disabled access** Limited.

The Brompton Hotel

OVERALL ★	QUALITY ★	VALUE ★★★	PRICE RANGE £70–£90

30 Old Brompton Road, South Kensington, SW7; ☎ **0870-742-3992; fax 0207-823-9936; www.bromhotel.com**

I hesitated to put this hotel in because of the previous letter about the budget hotel that the reader hated so much. I can only assume that when you go for a budget hotel, you *know* it ain't the Ritz. If you are dismayed by the hotel, ask to see other rooms or switch hotels. That's what I do, and I have been stuck in some dives in my day. This is one such nonritzy joint, and the prices (for this area, at least) reflect that. It has family rooms, connecting rooms, a modicum of comfort and not much more style, but offers very good rates for this convenient, up-scale location. You're near all the South Ken museums, you have all the public transportation you need to get everywhere (including Heathrow), and you are in the middle of a little town that features Christie's Auction House, great restaurants, and plenty of pubs and shops. OK, so it's a little outdated and Spartan, but that's the way it is in this city. You get what you pay for. Ask for rooms at the back, as the hotel fronts a very vehicle-heavy street. The Brompton offers wireless connection, a microwave and safe in the room, and continental breakfast is included in the price (it's brought to your room; no breakfast room). The attached Janet's Bar is a funky, down-home kind of place, where hotel guests get a 10% discount on food and drink. There's also a lounge, but you'll want to hit the streets instead and go to some of the many cafés all around you. You'll find a French flavor in the air, as the Lycee Charles de Gaulle is just around the corner. South Kensington is undergoing development pains, so it's possible that between the writing and the reading of this book, it may have been upgraded.

SETTINGS AND FACILITIES
Nearest tube station South Kensington. **Quietness** D in front; B in back rooms. **Dining** No. **Amenities** Continental breakfast included. **Services** 24-hour concierge, high-speed wireless access, secretarial services, laundry, safety deposit boxes, express checkout.

ACCOMMODATIONS
Rooms 25. **All rooms** Telephone, wireless Internet, TV, hair dryer, microwave, tea and coffee facilities. **Some rooms** Interconnected family rooms for 4 to 5 people. **Bed and bath** Some rooms have shower only, some have shower/tub combinations. **Favorites** Rooms on the lower floors—fewer steps to climb. **Comfort and decor** Very basic, very budget.

PAYMENT, RESERVATIONS, AND RESTRICTIONS
Deposit Credit card; 72-hour cancellation policy; 100% penalty. **Credit cards** All major. **Check-in/out** 1 p.m./10 a.m. **Pets** Not allowed. **Elevator** No. **Children** Yes. **Disabled access** No.

 ## Brown's Hotel

OVERALL ★★★★★   QUALITY ★★★★★   VALUE ★★   PRICE RANGE £325–£676

30–34 Albemarle Street, Mayfair, W1; ☎ 0207-493-6020; fax 0207-493-9381; www.brownshotel.com

This five-star hotel has something of a reputation among Americans as *the* English hotel to stay in, and it is indeed a venerable old London institution. Recently purchased by the Rocco Forte hotel group, it was closed for two months in summer 2005 for a major refurbishment. Assuming that they keep all the gorgeous period details, and don't start ripping out the wood panels or opening a pricey, modern, European cuisine bistro, it will maintain the dignified Britishness of its long-held character. The service is excellent and good-natured in that arch English way, and the food, though sky-high in price, is simple and well-prepared. Especially at teatime: the afternoon cream tea is excellent, and something of a tradition among many visitors to London, who don't mind the steep tariff for the pleasure of enjoying the gracious tea-time ambience of the sitting room. I do hope that the new management doesn't start monkeying around with the old style and add dried kiwifruit to the scones, or offer a thousand varieties of tea, or some such outrage. The history of Brown's is distinguished: Alexander Graham Bell made the first telephone call in Britain from here; Rudyard Kipling wrote books, poems, and articles in what is now the Kipling Suite (£2,900 a night); and Theodore Roosevelt got married while a guest at Brown's. Lord Byron's valet, James Brown, started the hotel in 1837. His wife, Sarah, and he had learned a thing or two from living in the "mad, bad, and dangerous to know" lordship's household, and the hotel was a success from the start. After the Browns sold it in 1859, the next owner made it the first hotel in London to have an elevator, telephone, and electricity. It grew from a single town house to 11, which is why you'll find the configurations of the rooms so completely unpredictable. Brown's is all about service: With 117 rooms, it has 160 in staff. The prices are astronomical, but you may be able to wheedle a deal out of the manager. .

SETTINGS AND FACILITIES

Nearest tube station Green Park. **Quietness rating** A. **Dining** Fine dining (and expensive, too) at award-winning 1837 Restaurant features English fare and one of the best wine lists in London. Breakfast in dining room, and afternoon teas in The Drawing Room. St. Georges' Bar for drinks and cigars. **Amenities** Fitness room, afternoon teas, business center. **Services** Concierge, 24-hour room service and valet, laundry, business support.

ACCOMMODATIONS

Rooms 117. **All rooms** Multiline telephone with voice mail, Internet access, mini-bar, sitting area, writing desk, satellite TV, air-conditioning. **Some rooms** Sitting areas with sofa, working fireplace, four-poster bed, French doors. **Bed and bath** Expect heated towel racks, Moulton Brown toiletries, bathrobe, and slippers. Queen- or king-size beds with top-of-the-line mattresses and bedclothes. **Favorites** Mayfair and Royal suites. First-floor rooms are the best, with high ceilings and big windows. Avoid the rooms at the top—they are low-ceilinged; some of the junior suites are small for the price. **Comfort and decor** You will find the comfort factor high, although some of the rooms are not as large as one would expect, and some are downright cramped. The decor is English country-house traditional, very comfy and unpretentious, with some fine pieces of furniture, carvings, and art here and there. There's an amazing and intricate carved wood fireplace in the reception; paneling, cut glass, and stained-glass windows in the stairwells and elsewhere. Again, I have no idea what the refurb will look like, but let's hope they don't make changes for the sake of change.

PAYMENT, RESERVATIONS, AND RESTRICTIONS

Deposit Credit card; 24-hour cancellation policy. **Credit cards** All major. **Check-in/out** 2 p.m./noon. **Pets** Not allowed. **Elevator** Yes. **Children** Yes. **Disabled access** Yes, though limited.

The Cadogan Hotel

OVERALL ★★★½   QUALITY ★★★½   VALUE ★★   PRICE RANGE £287–£352

75 Sloane Street, Knightsbridge, SW1; ☎ 0207-235-7141; fax 0207-245-0994; www.cadogan.com

In the last edition of this book, I wrote about the rumor that this historical hotel was up for sale, saying that I couldn't believe any new owner would tamper with the charming ambience of this London institution. It was bought by the Stein Group, which has luxury hotels all over the world, and I'm afraid they did tamper, a lot, though not to the extent of removing the wood paneling, the period moldings, or ripping out the fireplaces, thank goodness. The reception area is now something of a mystery, with a blank kind of modern rectangle dropped into the middle of this distinguished-looking wood-paneled and marble area. This first impression did not dispose me kindly to the refurbishment, and all I noticed at first was the absence of the old style—they chucked out the chintz in favor of anonymous earth tones that seem at odds with the Victorian bone structure of the old building. Sure, it's still nice enough, and if you aren't into faux-historical decor, you'll probably breathe easier, but I felt a little let down by the changes. Why take a place as historical as this and make it look like a million other hotels: it's like a bad face-lift on a beloved old granny. It doesn't work, and it looks like it's trying too hard to be hip. The building was constructed in 1887 along with the scores of red brick private homes in the exclusive development of Cadogan Gardens. It was here, in 1895, that Oscar Wilde (in room 118) was arrested for sodomy amidst great publicity and outrage. Lillie Langtry, popularly known as the "Jersey lily," was an actress and mistress of the prince of Wales (later King Edward VII). She lived in a house next door, which she sold to the hotel, and kept a bedroom suite here until 1897. These two artists represent a particular time and place in Victorian London that the Cadogan Hotel was part of; all Wilde devotees are certain to come have a look at this first station of his crucifixion. It used to be gratifying to walk in the door and see the faded roses of the fabrics, the William Morris–style wallpaper, and the stately and elegant drawing room. You could feel a real connection to Oscar and Lillie's era. Oh well. To give it it's due, the hotel is still smart and vital, with a restaurant that's become a destination for dedicated gourmets. The rooms are now a bit more on target for the steep rack rates—they've got all the modern toys and communication gear, and the spaciousness of many of the standard doubles may come as a pleasant surprise, especially if you've seen some of the old tiny single rooms. If you can get an upgrade to a luxury room, you'll be glad you did. Be sure to ask about the rooms on the first floor: they're likely to have bowfront windows, French doors, and an eye-level view of the leafy trees in Cadogan Square (hotel guests are given access to these gardens as well as to the tennis court within). The restaurant, Mes' Anges, is situated in what was the Miss Langtry's drawing room, and it's suitably impressive, with an excellent French menu. If you're put off by the prices of breakfasting at the hotel (£19 for a full English!), there are plenty of great cafés and restaurants within easy walking distance.

SETTINGS AND FACILITIES
Nearest tube station Knightsbridge or Sloane Square. **Quietness rating** A in the interior, C on Sloane Street, and B on Pont Street. **Dining** Mes' Ange for breakfast and dinner; afternoon tea served in bar or lounge (lounge is better). **Amenities** Health-club affiliation, access to gardens and tennis. **Services** Concierge, 24-hour room service, bellhop, laundry, touring suggestions and packages.

ACCOMMODATIONS
Rooms 65. **All rooms** Telephone, voice mail, Internet access, satellite TV, airconditioning, hair dryer, iron, writing desk. **Some rooms** Sitting room, 1 bedroom, 2 bathrooms, view of gardens. **Bed and bath** High standard of both. **Favorites** The Lillie Langtry room; any of luxury doubles on first floor. **Comfort and decor** All comfort is catered to, decor is restful and expensive-looking, but I miss the William Morris wallpaper in the hallways. **All rooms** are individually decorated and very comfortable.

PAYMENT, RESERVATIONS, AND RESTRICTIONS
Deposit Credit card; 24-hour cancellation policy. **Credit cards** All major. **Check-in/out** Noon/noon. **Pets** Small dogs allowed, and given a "designer pet bed." **Elevator** Yes. **Children** Yes. **Disabled access** Yes, though there are limits on wheelchair access.

The Charlotte Street Hotel

OVERALL ★★★★	QUALITY ★★★★	VALUE ★★★	PRICE RANGE £240–£334

15-17 Charlotte Street, Fitzrovia, W1; ☎ 0207-806-2000; fax 0207-806-2002; www.charlottestreethotel.com

The Charlotte Street Hotel is a small, luxurious hotel located in an area known to locals as Fitzrovia. The area is the epicenter of media activity and includes production houses, TV stations, and advertising agencies. It's a busy neighborhood, with plenty of restaurants and bars all up and down Charlotte Street. The hotel has been decorated and furnished in a fresh, modern

English style, with light wood paneling, wooden floors, plump, soft furnish-ings, and leather chairs. The large lobby area leads into the Oscar Bar & Restaurant, which serves modern European cuisine. The bar is popular with the local media lushes and bigshots. The drawing room and library just off the restaurant area are for guest use only and are ideal spots in which to don a smoking jacket, grab a stiff brandy, and puff on a large cigar in front of the open fireplace, while studying the original Bloomsbury-set artwork hanging on the walls. The bedrooms are individually decorated, with traditional British features such as floral curtains and floral wallpaper that somehow manage to avoid looking chintzy. The designer, Kit Kemp, is renowned for her trademark mannequin dummies that stand sentry style in every room (a quirky, superfluous detail, yet good for draping your jacket on). If it's within your budget, try staying in a loft suite; these rooms have stairs leading to the bedroom area on a mezzanine level and seem to be more like a doll's house than a hotel room. Although more useful for those attending a corporate event or for a local film director, another cool feature is the state-of-the-art screening room, which hosts the Sunday Film Club.

SETTINGS AND FACILITIES

Nearest tube station Tottenham Court Road/Goodge Street. **Quietness rating** A/C. All windows are double glazed, but street noise in front can be bothersome if you like to sleep with the window open. **Dining** Oscar Restaurant & Bar for breakfast, lunch, and dinner, and exotic cocktails. **Amenities** Restaurant, lounge areas, 24-hour gym, 2 meeting rooms, 1 screening room (67-seater mini cinema). **Services** Concierge, 24-hour room service, same-day laundry service, bellhop.

ACCOMMODATIONS

Rooms 52. **All rooms** Air-conditioning, en suite bathrooms, 2-line telephone with voice mail, Internet access, satellite TV, VCR/DVD and CD player, mini TV in bath-room, minibar, safe, movies and music to rent, hair dryer, writing desk. Fax machine, mobile phone, laptops available on request. **Some rooms** Walk-in shower and bidet. The more deluxe rooms have bigger beds (super-king-size, which is the U.S. king size), some four-poster beds. **Bed and bath** Bathrooms are in solid granite and oak, with a shower and tub, plus a mini TV. Regular rooms have big beds which can be split into twins. **Favorites** Room 108, one of the loft suites, is popular, as are the penthouse suites, which offer good views. **Comfort and decor** The rooms all have a sophisticated yet homey feel and are very comfortable.

PAYMENT, RESERVATIONS, AND RESTRICTIONS

Deposit Credit card; 24-hour cancellation policy. **Credit cards** All major, except DC. **Check-in/out** 1 p.m./11 a.m. **Pets** Not allowed. **Elevator** Yes. **Children** Yes. **Disabled access** Good general access (two modified rooms).

The Claverley

| OVERALL ★★★ | QUALITY ★★★½ | VALUE ★★★ | PRICE RANGE £149–£199 |

13–14 Beaufort Gardens, Knightsbridge, SW3; ☎ 0207-589-8541, in U.S. ☎ 800-747-0398; fax 0207-584-3410; www.claverleyhotel.co.uk

This inn is an award winner for Best Bed-and-Breakfast Hotel in Central and Greater London, although its value has dipped in the past few years as its rates have steadily risen. The majority of complaints about the size of the rooms come from those who stay in the monk's cell–like single rooms, which are nothing like the glorious suites and double deluxe rooms they advertise. My advice is to keep looking if they can't guarantee you a larger double for a good rate. Having said that, The Claverley is still a nice place to stay. It is clean, well decorated, has a charming breakfast room, and the selection of rooms ranges from serviceable to lovely. The single rooms all have large three-quarter beds. Smoking is not allowed in any of the rooms, which is good for nonsmokers, as tobacco smoke from the next room can be a ban to a good night's sleep. The breakfast (included in the price) is big and hearty; the location is pretty good. Harrods is around the corner, South Kensington museums and restaurants are a four-minute walk away, and Hyde Park can be accessed in minutes. The traditional English style of decor, the sunlight in the front rooms, and the relatively reasonable price (for the area) have made it a long-time popular destination for the discerning visitor.

SETTINGS AND FACILITIES

Nearest tube station Knightsbridge. **Quietness rating** A. **Dining** Breakfast in room or in breakfast room. **Amenities** Sitting room with carved fireplace and complimentary papers and magazines; breakfast room with waiter service and full English breakfast included in price. **Services** Concierge, bellhop, laundry.

ACCOMMODATIONS

Rooms 29. **All rooms** Telephone, Internet access, satellite TV, hair dryers. **Some rooms** Four-poster bed, balcony, pull-out sofa, writing desk, sitting area, walk-in closet. **Bed and bath** Beds are new. Bathtubs in 85% of rooms; the rest have shower stalls. All the bathrooms have been recently renovated and now sport power showers. **Favorites** Number 12 is the best junior suite, with balcony, French windows, and awesome four-poster bed. Junior suite number 33 has a walk-in closet. Single number 35, in the rear of the building, is pretty good, too, with a large bed and a charm not entirely defeated by the view of the brown brick backs of houses. **Comfort and decor** Individually decorated, each room is attractive and clean, and some are downright luxurious. The hotel has a great collection of portraits and drawings on the walls, with furniture and curtains in the traditional English style.

PAYMENT, RESERVATIONS, AND RESTRICTIONS

Deposit Credit card; 48-hour cancellation policy. **Credit cards** All major. **Check-in/out** 1 p.m./11:30 a.m. **Pets** Not allowed. **Elevator** Yes. **Children** Yes. **Disabled access** No wheelchair access.

 Collingham Apartments

OVERALL ★★★½   QUALITY ★★★★   VALUE ★★★½   PRICE RANGE £145–£195

26–27 Collingham Gardens, South Kensington, SW5; ☎ 0207-244-8677; fax 0207-244-7331; www.collinghamapartments.com

Here's a chance to stay at a serviced apartment in the leafy area west of South Kensington. At first glance the prices seem a tad high, but the savings in dining out make it a good, economical option: instead of dropping £10 per person for breakfast, buy a box of cereal or eggs and prepare breakfast in the kitchen. The area is great: you are about a 10-minute walk to Hyde Park, the museums of South Kensington; at Earl's Court underground station you can catch the Piccadilly, Circle, and District lines to get anywhere quickly. The neighborhood has rows of red brick early Victorian-style (from 1830) town houses, many of which have beautiful stained-glass windows in the doors, and white columns supporting an ornate entryway above which is a balcony. Collingham Apartments is made from two adjoining houses, and of the 25 rooms, there are ten one-bedroom/studios, ten two-bedrooms, three three-bedrooms, and two penthouses. Bought and upgraded in 1998, when London was on an economic upswing, the new owners spared no expense on the details, and they pretty much covered all the conveniences. The kitchens are all well furnished with quality appliances, and you won't find yourself hunting in vain for a frying pan or a spatula—everything you need has been provided, and what you don't have, the 24-hour concierge will be happy to provide. The apartments are nicely located across the street from the verdant greenery of Collingham Square, for which, sad to say, you don't have access, but you do have a pleasant view in the front rooms. The best thing about this establishment is the variety of rooms they have: it's perfect for a family with small children; you can close a door on them when they go to sleep. The two-bedrooms start at £280, and there's one unit that has two bedrooms and two bathrooms for £325, which sounds steep, but you could share the expense with one or two (very close) friends. The first-floor rooms have a cute little balcony and French doors, and the penthouses are stunning, with a terrace overlooking the gardens behind each house. The elevator is a crucial and excellent feature, tiny as it is. You'll be glad of it when you are struggling home from the nearby Sainsbury's or Waitrose supermarkets with bags of food to cook. Be very careful with your booking: you can only get a full refund if you cancel more than 28 days before arrival date.

SETTINGS AND FACILITIES

Nearest tube station Earl's Court or Gloucester Road. **Quietness** A in rear, B in front. **Dining** Self-service in kitchen or order takeaway. **Amenities** Bathrobes, hair dryer, stove, refrigerator, kitchen utensils, toiletries. **Services** Concierge, 24-hour reception and security porter, babysitting, bellhop, laundry facilities on site plus dry cleaning sent out, food delivery from local restaurants.

ACCOMMODATIONS

Rooms 25. **All rooms** Telephone with voice mail, high-speed Internet modem, satellite TV, modern full kitchen, air-conditioning, DVD player and DVD library, CD player, hair dryer, safe, bathrobes. **Some rooms** Balcony and terrace, 3 bedrooms. **Bed and bath** Well appointed bathrooms with tubs that have Jacuzzi jets, shower, and heated towel racks; big comfortable beds with good cotton sheets. **Favorites** Penthouses and front first-floor apartments. **Comfort and decor** Furnished to a high standard, with all considerations of comfort looked after. The decor is neutral, but pleasing.

PAYMENT, RESERVATIONS, AND RESTRICTIONS

Deposit Credit card; 28-day full-refund cancellation policy, 7-day partial refund. **Credit cards** All major. **Check-in/out** 2 p.m./noon. **Pets** Not allowed. **Elevator** Lift. **Children** Yes. **Disabled access** Six steps into buildings.

 **The Colonnade Hotel**

OVERALL ★★★★   **QUALITY** ★★★★   **VALUE** ★★★★   **PRICE RANGE £116–£160**

2 Warrington Crescent, Little Venice (Maida Vale), W9;
☎ 0207-286-1052; fax 0207-286-1057; www.theetoncollection.com

If your main concern is comfort and quiet, this elegant hotel in Maida Vale may be for you. It's one of the three boutique hotels that the Eton Group recently opened in London (see pages 95 and 145 for the Academy and Threadneedles hotels), and it shares the same dedication to pleasing surroundings and luxurious extras that those hotels are all about. The location may appear too far northwest of Central London for your touring plans, but it is an excellent introduction to the quiet joys of the Grand Union Canal, which you will enjoy walking along and looking into the colorful houseboats moored there. It's this once-busy canal that gave the area the nickname of Little Venice. You can walk to the waterbus dock and take a pretty canal trip to Regent's Park and the London Zoo, all of which will thrill the youngsters (you can purchase a boat ticket and London Zoo fast-track combination ticket to avoid queues at the zoo). Children under age 16 stay free, and the patio with tables outside is a safe place for them to burn off some energy so they don't endanger the antiques. There are a few adjoining rooms or suites that will do nicely for a family room. Cricket fans can take a 15-minute walk to see a game at Lord's Cricket Ground for only a fiver, and then wander around St. John's Wood, where tourists like to re-create the cover photo of the Beatle's *Abbey Road* album (the old Apple Studio building is just up the road). The hotel is made up of two imposing Victorian mansions built in 1865. There are suites named for John F. Kennedy and Sigmund Freud, who each stayed here briefly in 1962 and 1938, respectively (the bed built for President Kennedy's state visit is still there). It's a great hotel for those who prefer relatively fresh air and the Victorian vibe that the hotel has re-created so convincingly. The centerpiece is the museum-quality late-19th-century Wedgewood fireplace of some rarity, and the decor has wisely taken its cue from it. Heavy and elaborate drapes grace the windows without blocking the light, and the ambience is one of artful elegance and the graciousness of a bygone era. All the modern conveniences are firmly in place, with the concierge providing you with everything from walking directions to a holistic massage in your room given by a visiting professional. Thanks to its location on the outskirts, the prices here are reasonable for the luxury within, but you should still check into any promotions or Web site deals to whittle the cost down further—budget it's definitely not. Buses to all parts of London can be caught at the east end of the canal, on Maida Vale Road (which turns into Edgeware Road). Ask the concierge about the fabulous yoga studio around the corner on Randolph Avenue. If it's your first trip to London, you may want to be a little more central, and to be honest there are some unattractive areas around here, but if you've already had the experience of trying to sleep with the noise of London's traffic outside your window, check this little jewel out.

SETTINGS AND FACILITIES
Nearest tube station Maida Vale. **Quietness** A. **Dining** The E Bar serves authentic Spanish tapas for lunch and dinner and all-day snacks; nice breakfast room. **Amenities** Newspapers, bathrobes, breakfast included with some rates, bar. **Services** Concierge, 24-hour room service, bellhop, laundry, in-room spa treatments.

ACCOMMODATIONS
Rooms 43. **All rooms** Telephone, satellite TV, hair dryer, bathrobe, wireless broadband, air-conditioning, minibar. **Some rooms** Bowfront windows or French doors. **Bed and bath** Comfortable beds dressed in Frette linens, down pillows, and duvets; interesting and pleasing furnishings. Bathrooms are either shower-only or full bath with shower in tub; designer toiletries and heated towel rack. **Favorites** First-floor rooms. **Comfort and decor** Luxuriously comfortable in the traditional Victorian style; rich, dark fabrics for curtains and bed covers, comfortable chairs, and interesting, fine antique pieces and other period details.

PAYMENT, RESERVATIONS, AND RESTRICTIONS
Deposit Credit card; 24-hour cancellation policy. **Credit cards** All major. **Check-in/out** 2 p.m./11 a.m. **Pets** Not allowed. **Elevator** Yes. **Children** Yes (free under age 16). **Disabled access** Steps to entrance and steps from lift on third floor to fourth floor.

 The Columbia Hotel

OVERALL ★★★ **QUALITY** ★★★ **VALUE** ★★★★★ **PRICE RANGE** £86–£112

95–99 Lancaster Gate, Bayswater, W2; ☎ 0207-402-0021; fax 0207-706-4691; www.columbiahotel.co.uk

This is probably one of the better deals in the area—there are cheaper rooms to be had, but not with the amenities and friendliness of the Columbia. Created from five huge Victorian mansions put together, it fronts the busy Bayswater Road in an area that was the height of gentility for merchants and professionals in its heyday, with the abundance of space and the nearness of Hyde Park custom-made for their typically large families and army of servants. Those days are gone, as the roar of the traffic below reminds you constantly, but the riotous thoroughfare does afford easy access to public transportation (and I don't need to tell you how great Hyde Park is for a family with young kids). The rooms are in the standard hotel style, but they're clean and some are fairly roomy, with period details such as bay windows and fireplaces. Because of the layout of the hotel, or should I say the layout of the original buildings, there will be great disparity among the size and shape of the rooms, which were necessarily configured without tearing down weight-bearing walls. Unfortunately, the first floor, with its elegant high ceilings and huge windows, is mostly conference rooms, but there are many park-view rooms on the remaining floors. The only problem with having the beautiful park view is the noise of the traffic that comes with it, which includes hundreds of buses a day. This is a good, well-priced hotel, the chiefest of whose charms are the fact that it can nicely accommodate families, pets, and even automobiles (parking on a first-come, first-served basis). The higher price, £112, is actually for a triple room, but I would suggest that you spend the extra £16 a night for what is still a good deal to get a larger and possibly more interesting room (4-bed is £129, 5-bed is £146). Queensway, a few minutes' walk away, has lots of great restaurants (not to mention a skating rink and bowling alley). The staff is friendly and helpful. Breakfast is included.

SETTINGS AND FACILITIES

Nearest tube station Lancaster Gate. **Quietness rating** C- in front, A in back. **Dining** Breakfast included. **Amenities** Newspapers, lounge, maps, family rooms, crib rental, bar. **Services** 24-hour reception desk, laundry, overnight luggage storage.

ACCOMMODATIONS

Rooms 100. **All rooms** Shower and toilet, telephone, BBC TV, hair dryer. **Some rooms** View over park, connecting rooms, four beds in one room. **Bed and bath** Clean and satisfactory, mostly showers. **Favorites** Big rooms. **Comfort and decor** Very plain and simple.

PAYMENT, RESERVATIONS, AND RESTRICTIONS

Deposit Credit card; 24-hour cancellation policy. **Credit cards** All major, except DC. **Check-in/out** 2 p.m./11:30 a.m. **Pets** Allowed. **Elevator** Two. **Children** Yes. **Disabled access** One disabled room, and a bedroom for deaf or hearing impaired.

Comfort Inn Notting Hill

OVERALL ★½	QUALITY ★★½	VALUE ★★★★½	PRICE RANGE £75–£90

6–14 Pembridge Gardens, Notting Hill Gate, W2; ☎ 0207-221-3433; fax 0207-229-4808; www.ltf-hotels.com

Here's a budget hotel within a short walk of Portobello Road and Kensington Church Street—perfect for antiques hunters who want to spend all their money on treasures instead of hotels. It's also a short walk to Kensington Gardens and Hyde Park, and the tube is very near. Although the hotel is behind five connected Victorian beauties, inside it's a different story, with the kind of decor and ambience that you'd expect from a Comfort Inn, so caveat emptor. Pembridge Gardens, however, is full of charm, located on a nice side street off the busy Notting Hill Gate, the noise from which doesn't penetrate the hotel. Although undistinguished aesthetically (to put it nicely), it's clean and serviceable, with a couple of nice touches, like the huge chandelier. There are two video games and a chocolate vending machine in the honesty bar/lounge, which, along with the breakfast room, has piped-in pop music. Continental breakfast is included in the price. The breakfast room is a good size and pleasant enough. Good value for money here, with three- to five-bedded family rooms that can be comparatively spacious and suitable enough.

SETTINGS AND FACILITIES

Nearest tube station Notting Hill Gate. **Quietness rating** A in back, B in front. **Dining** Breakfast room, honor bar. **Amenities** Breakfast included, satellite TV in bar, video games, Laundromat, nonsmoking rooms, wireless access in lobby and on some floors. **Services** Reception acts as concierge, but you're basically on your own here.

ACCOMMODATIONS

Rooms 70. **All rooms** En suite shower/tub and toilet, telephone, BBC TV, hair dryer, ice machine, coffee machine, iron, safe. **Bed and bath** Utilitarian, clean, and serviceable. **Favorites** Take the double or twin room if you're alone, the twin if you're with a spouse (double beds are small), a family room if you require space. **Comfort and decor** Serviceable comfort, forgettable decor; like a college dorm.

PAYMENT, RESERVATIONS, AND RESTRICTIONS

Deposit Credit card; 48-hour cancellation policy. **Credit cards** All major. **Check-in/out** 2 p.m./10 a.m. **Pets** Not allowed. **Elevator** Two. **Children** Yes. **Disabled access** Steps outside, small lifts.

Covent Garden Hotel

OVERALL ★★★★   QUALITY ★★★★½   VALUE ★★★   PRICE RANGE £246–£358

10 Monmouth Street, Covent Garden, WC2; ☎ 0207-806-1000; fax 0207-806-1100; www.firmdale.com

Here's another fine hotel of the Firmdale group, which also owns the Pelham, Charlotte Street, Soho House, Number 16, and the Knightsbridge hotels (we have reviewed all but the Soho House, which is brand new and probably is as nice as the others). The Covent Garden is more spacious than other Firmdale Hotels, and offers more square footage, both in the size of the beds and the size of the rooms and hallways. It's such a great collection of hotels, I just wish they didn't have to charge so much, which lowers their value rating—but it's true that you get what you pay for. Look for summer and weekend promotion packages, which shave a bit off the overhead. Amenities offered include wireless access, laptop rental, cell phones, and in-room entertainment centers (DVD, VCR, CD). There is a fitness area, with treatment rooms for massage and beauty treatments. Brasserie Max has become a favorite London hangout for the young and famous, and why not: fine food, attractive surroundings, exotic cocktails, and a good-looking staff and clientele are a fantastic combo, especially if you're seated by a window for optimal people-watching. They've got two—count 'em—two big screening rooms that fit 56 and 100 people respectively, where first-run films can be viewed in comfort and style. But the outstanding thing about this hotel is the decor. It's just a place where all the taste and talents of the designer come together effortlessly and pleasingly. It is a superb location: Monmouth Street, on which the hotel is situated, is a relatively quiet street in Seven Dials, but is within skipping distance of Soho, Covent Garden, Bloomsbury, and the theaters of the West End.

SETTINGS AND FACILITIES

Nearest tube station Covent Garden. **Quietness rating** B normally, C– on weekend nights (all rooms are double-glazed and air-conditioned). **Dining** Brasserie Max is a modern-style dining room with good food. **Amenities** Two drawing rooms, one very large, with working fireplaces; restaurant; honor bar with snacks; personal safe; cell phone for rent; workout room; 2 screening rooms. **Services** Concierge, 24-hour room service, valet, bellhop, laundry.

ACCOMMODATIONS

Rooms 50. **All rooms** U.S.-size queen/king bed (even in singles), air-conditioning, telephone with extra line and voice mail, wireless access or high-speed modem points, satellite TV, DVD/VCR and movies to watch, CD player and CDs to borrow, writing desk, bathtub, umbrella. **Some rooms** Ornamental fireplace, four-poster bed, sofa and sitting area, roof terrace. **Bed and bath** Bathrooms are splendid, all gray marble and perfection. The beds are huge, outfitted in 100% cotton sheets and covered with the most beautiful duvets and pillows. **Favorites** Number 304 is a deluxe double with a blue theme, a gorgeous four-poster bed, and an ornamental fireplace with two big chairs in front of it. The terrace suite is preferred by the many movie stars who stay here; it has its own little terrace, a library, a sofa, and a sweetly appointed queen-size bed. The walls have been painstakingly painted with contrasting red sponge effect. **Comfort and decor** Comfort is of a very high standard, to a degree you probably don't have at home. The decor is sublime—Tim and Kit Kemp are geniuses at interior decoration, neatly blending traditional antiques with their own brand of quirky taste.

PAYMENT, RESERVATIONS, AND RESTRICTIONS

Deposit Credit card; 24-hour cancellation policy. **Credit cards** All major. **Check-in/out** 1 p.m./11 a.m. **Pets** Not allowed. **Elevator** Two. **Children** Yes. **Disabled access** Yes, big elevators and wide hallways.

 The Draycott Hotel

OVERALL ★★★★   QUALITY ★★★★★   VALUE ★★★   PRICE RANGE £229–£259

26 Cadogan Gardens, Knightsbridge/Chelsea, SW3; ☎ 0207-730-6466; in U.S. ☎ 800-747-4942; fax 0207-730-0236; www.draycotthotel.com

The Draycott is the new incarnation of the good old Cliveden Townhouse, bought in 2003 by the Mantis Collection. I am delighted to report that they haven't made any changes to the eccentric luxury of the hotel, which I loved (and at those prices, you'd better love it!). It is a wonderfully grand Victorian mansion, built in the 1890s, yet it isn't pretentious or stiff, but feels like a really beautiful home. The prevailing decor is of the sumptuous Edwardian period, and compared to the usual Victorian-era style, it is simple elegance itself (if perhaps a bit over-the-top for many of us). They've wisely kept the prevailing theme of the hotel, with rooms named after theatrical legends—Laurence Olivier, Edmund Kean, Edith Evans, George and Ira Gershwin, the Redgraves, Noël Coward, James Barrie, and so on. Each room is decorated with corresponding memorabilia, whose sepia tones nicely complement the wood paneling and leaded windows. The lovely drawing room has a welcoming, comfortable atmosphere and opens onto a nice-sized garden where you can relax with a book in good weather. As you walk in the door, two urns on either side are filled with apples, only the first of many appealing touches in this hotel town house. There are functioning gas fires in all but the single rooms, and air-conditioning in summer. A self-service tea is set out each day at 4 p.m., and a complimentary bottle of champagne is uncorked at 6 p.m. The single rooms are OK, but if you can afford it, step up to a double—even the standard doubles are quite big and have a fireplace and sofa. It's a short walk from Sloane Square and Knightsbridge, but you'd swear you were in the country when you're in a room with a bay window overlooking the garden. The only downside is that you may never want to leave the hotel.

SETTINGS AND FACILITIES

Nearest tube station Knightsbridge or Sloane Square. **Quietness rating** A. **Dining** Dinner on request, but no public dining room. Breakfast room is gorgeous and bright. **Amenities** Private dining room, drawing room, smoking room, afternoon tea, champagne at 6 p.m., honor bar, breakfast room, garden, public computer or wireless access. **Services** Concierge, complimentary chauffeur service into city each weekday, 24-hour room service, laundry, babysitting.

ACCOMMODATIONS

Rooms 35. **All rooms** Telephone, voice mail, fax and modem line, wireless connection, air-conditioning, satellite TV, DVD/VCR, stereo CD. **Some rooms** Garden view, fireplace. **Bed and bath** Excellent quality; bathrooms are superior as would be expected, and have some Edwardian period details, including some very big tubs. **Favorites** Any of the deluxe junior suites overlooking gardens; the doubles are quite fine, too. **Comfort and decor** Highest standard of comfort; the decor is delightful, sumptuous but not overbearing.

PAYMENT, RESERVATIONS, AND RESTRICTIONS

Deposit Credit card; Cancellation policy of 24 hours. **Credit cards** All major. **Check-in/out** 2 p.m./11 a.m. **Pets** Dogs allowed on ground floor rooms. **Elevator** Yes, two. **Children** Yes. **Disabled access** No, too many stairs.

Dukes Hotel

OVERALL ★★★★★   QUALITY ★★★★★   VALUE ★★★   PRICE RANGE £276–£400

35 St. James Place, St. James, SW1; ☎ 0207-491-4840,
in U.S. ☎ 800-381-4702; fax 0207-493-1264; www.dukeshotel.co.uk

Behind a charming courtyard, in one of the most appealing areas of central London is the deluxe Dukes Hotel. The neighborhood has been one of grandeur, populated by wealthy courtiers and aristocrats jousting to be near the power of St. James's Palace in the 18th century, and it continued its association with royalty when Buckingham House became another royal residence. "Ostentation" was the watchword then, as it has remained, although the majority of the chateau-like private homes have been turned into offices for institutions or flats for the very wealthy. Dukes Hotel has done a great job of updating this kind of antique luxury into a hotel of great charm with all the imaginable modern conveniences and comforts of today. You know you're in for a treat when you approach the hotel by night: authentic gas lamps light your way in. Inside, you'll find a sumptuous hotel that promises the highest standards in service and accommodation; it has won numerous awards for best luxury hotel, and even boasts a Zagat's Best Martini citation. It's terribly expensive of course, caters to the kind of clientele who likes amenities such as 100-year-old cognac, an elliptical cross-trainer in the gym, and who wouldn't flinch at the final bill's parade of zeros in front of the decimal point. It's an intimate, clubby kind of place, which is why it's in these reviews rather than with its high-priced brethren in the luxury section at the beginning of this chapter. Although it hardly needed it, it's been renovated and re-equipped in the past few years, dropping the smaller single rooms in favor of a double-size for a single guest; re-outfitting some rooms with Ralph Lauren fabrics, putting in wireless Internet access throughout the hotel, updating the fitness room, and refining the climate control and noise filters that you take for granted in a luxury hotel. The location is fantastic: besides all the bespoke shops and handy restaurants around the corner on Piccadilly, you also are within minutes of St. James's and Green parks, which is rather like having two magnificent backyard gardens. The weekend rates are reasonable(ish) at £193 per night, so it might be worth your while to splurge for a couple of nights and see how the other half lives. You couldn't ask for a more central yet still quiet spot to enjoy London. And if you're feeling flush, check out Penthouse One, with awesome views of all the glory that is London.

SETTINGS AND FACILITIES

Nearest tube station Green Park. **Quietness rating** A. **Dining** Private dining room can be booked. **Amenities** Bar with exceptional cognacs and wines; health club with massage and personal trainer available. **Services** Concierge, butler, valet, secretarial services, 24-hour room service.

ACCOMMODATIONS

Rooms 89. **All rooms** Telephone, satellite TV, air-conditioning, private bar, writing desks. **Some rooms** Oversize (7 feet square) "Emperor" bed; sitting rooms; views of Big Ben, Westminster Abbey, parks, and Parliament; exceptional amount of space (the penthouse is 700 square feet). **Bed and bath** Magnificent marble bathrooms with bathrobes and beds that you'd be proud to call your own. **Favorites** The penthouses are more like flats, huge and unimaginably luxurious, but even the standard doubles are very big by any hotel standard, much less London, averaging 190 square feet. You can't go wrong in any of the rooms here. **Comfort and decor** Highest standards of comfort and pleasing decor—not overdone, just serene and elegant.

PAYMENT, RESERVATIONS, AND RESTRICTIONS

Deposit Credit card. **Credit cards** All major. **Check-in/out** 2 p.m./noon. **Pets** Not allowed. **Elevator** Yes. **Children** No children under age five. **Disabled access** Limited.

Durrants

OVERALL ★★★½ **QUALITY** ★★★½ **VALUE** ★★★½ **PRICE RANGE £165–£180**

George Street, Marylebone, W1; ☎ **0207-935-8131; fax 0207-487-3510; www.durrantshotel.co.uk**

A hotel that has been run by the same family since 1921, Durrants has a lot going for it, not least of all its proximity to the Wallace Collection, Oxford Street, Marylebone High Street, and Regent's Park. The building has been there since 1790, and the decor is resolutely Regency, with authentic prints gracing the wall, and plenty of dark wood paneling that evokes the past nicely without overdoing it, or being too faux. But mainly, it's a hotel that gives good value for the money. The rooms are a wee bit bigger than comparably priced hotels, and they're also a lot nicer than most, furnished with some genuine antique pieces, as well as more standard, inoffensive gear, such as unexceptional wallpaper and fabrics. If your room is too small, ask for an upgrade or a change. The atmosphere in the public part of the hotel is that of a leather-chaired gentlemen's club, with oil paintings and gas fires. There's a tiny bar called The Pump Room, where once women were banned, apparently giving license for the proprietor to feature paintings of nudes on the walls. Breakfast (an expensive breakfast) is served by waiters in a very charming breakfast room, and the restaurant on the other side of the lobby is of a good quality. The hotel faces the back of the Wallace Collection, which you can explore for free as many times as you want. So, good location, historic building, nice atmosphere, summer rates of £130 for a double room—what's not to like? Some of you will be happy to know that around the corner on Hinde Street there's an AA meeting every weekday at 1 p.m.

SETTINGS AND FACILITIES

Nearest tube station Bakers Street or Bond Street. **Quietness rating** A. **Dining** The restaurant has the best booths I've seen, and decent British food besides. **Amenities** Air-conditioning in public area, on request when booking; Pump Room, lounges with fireplaces, bar downstairs. **Services** Concierge, 24-hour room service, bellhop, laundry, airport transfer, babysitting.

ACCOMMODATIONS

Rooms 92. **All rooms** Telephone, Internet access, satellite TV, hair dryer, iron, writing desks. **Some rooms** Air-conditioning, separate sitting rooms, minibars. **Bed and bath** All remodeled and upgraded in the past two years; beds are comfortable and bathrooms are attractive and relatively spacious. **Favorites** Suite number 305 is a two-room pleasure: The sitting room has lots of conversation areas and is beautifully decorated with old portraits. **Comfort and decor** Except for the lack of air-conditioning in some rooms (this feature is spreading slowly), it's a fine hotel. There's an effortlessness that is very appealing, and the comfort is part of this.

PAYMENT, RESERVATIONS, AND RESTRICTIONS

Deposit Credit card; must cancel by noon on the day before arrival hour. **Credit cards** All major, except DC. **Check-in/out** 2 p.m./noon. **Pets** Not allowed. **Elevator** 2. **Children** Yes; babysitting and cribs can be arranged. **Disabled access** Ground floor access rooms, but discuss when booking; call ahead.

Edward Lear Hotel

| OVERALL ★ ½ | QUALITY ★ ½ | VALUE ★★★★ | PRICE RANGE £74–£89 |

28–30 Seymour Street, Marble Arch, W1; ☎ 0207-402-5401; fax 0207-706-3766; www.edlear.com

The Edward Lear Hotel is a simple place, at a low price. Some rooms are dark and not extremely appealing, but the hotel does offer more amenities than comparative hotels, such as telephone, use of guest computer with free Internet access, and satellite TV. It's clean, well run, and provides a good breakfast in its price. Only 100 yards from Oxford Street and within a short walk of Hyde Park, the Edward Lear Hotel is popular among budget travelers, but not so attractive to those with a painful allergy to mediocre decor. There are some nice bits, such as charming drawings and limericks by the famous Victorian artist and poet Edward Lear, who once lived here. The exterior has greenery spilling from every window, which lends a nice homey touch.

SETTINGS AND FACILITIES

Nearest tube station Marble Arch. **Quietness rating** B in back, C in front. **Dining** Breakfast room. **Amenities** Full English breakfast, two lounges, one with free Internet access. **Services** Breakfast.

ACCOMMODATIONS

Rooms 30. **All rooms** Telephone, satellite TV, radio, tea and coffee. **Some rooms** Shower/toilet. **Bed and bath** Those rooms lacking an en suite bathroom are at least near a clean and functional shared bath (£47.50 for shared bath); beds are satisfactory. **Favorites** Triples with shower/toilet. **Comfort and decor** Plain, clean, and decorated with Edward Lear's marvelous drawings and nonsense poems and limericks. Small rooms.

PAYMENT, RESERVATIONS, AND RESTRICTIONS

Deposit Credit card; 24-hour cancellation policy. **Credit cards** MC, V. **Check-in/out** 1 p.m./11 a.m. **Pets** Not allowed. **Elevator** No. **Children** Yes. **Disabled access** No.

11 Cadogan Gardens

OVERALL ★★★★★ QUALITY ★★★★½ VALUE ★★★ PRICE RANGE £235–£285

11 Cadogan Gardens, Knightsbridge/Chelsea, SW3; ☎ 0207-730-7000; fax 0207-730-5217; www.number-eleven.co.uk

This is a delightful deluxe hotel tucked away behind Sloane Street in the expanses of redbrick Victorian town houses, the former private mansions of the lords and ladies whose descendants may still live in the neighborhood, but in relatively reduced circumstances. It was built as a private home in the 1860s, and it's been a hotel for 40 years, maintaining its quiet elegance and unostentatious luxury while updating with the times. It still feels more like a home, a very splendid home, than a hotel. The building has kept all of its oak-paneled walls, some of which have been brightened with ivory paint, which I thought looked excellent, despite my preference for natural wood. The molding and panels are perfectly set off by the William Morris hand-blocked wallpaper and tasteful Colefax & Fowler fabrics. The antiques are of high quality, and the walls are filled with fascinating portraits of people from the past few centuries—worthies on every wall. The drawing room has a genuine clubby atmosphere, and one could get extremely comfortable sitting before the fireplace with a book. Number 11 is popular for its brand of discreet, efficient service. The hotel has a decent gym room in the lower ground floor, with some good cardiovascular machines and weight equipment. All the rooms are different—in size, in decor, in views. The hotel is so impressive overall that any room will no doubt suit you just fine. Breakfast is not included in the price of the room and is quite expensive, but do try it one morning to enjoy the beautiful setting.

SETTINGS AND FACILITIES

Nearest tube station Sloane Square. **Quietness rating** A. **Dining** Food is available all day from the kitchen of the dining room, and is pricey but good. **Amenities** Drawing room, exercise room, aromatherapy, massage, wireless Internet access and modems. **Services** Concierge, 24-hour room service, bellhop, laundry.

ACCOMMODATIONS

Rooms 60. **All rooms** Telephone, Internet access, satellite TV, safe, hair dryer, excellent antiques. **Some rooms** Writing desk, views, air-conditioning. **Bed and bath** Bathrooms are marble, with an array of toiletries from The White Company; beds are comfortable; many single rooms have double beds. **Favorites** The ones with the view of the garden are nice, but the best is definitely the biggest suite in the hotel, which is more like a stately flat, with high ceilings, four-poster bed, limited kitchenette, big windows, and plenty of room for a family of four. **Comfort and decor** Exquisite decor suggesting a graceful bygone age; extremely comfortable.

PAYMENT, RESERVATIONS, AND RESTRICTIONS

Deposit Credit card; 24-hour cancellation policy. **Credit cards** All major. **Check-in/out** 1 p.m/noon. **Pets** Not allowed. **Elevator** Yes. **Children** Yes. **Disabled access** Will accommodate.

Fielding Hotel

OVERALL ★ ½	QUALITY ★ ★	VALUE ★ ★ ½	PRICE RANGE £100–£115

4 Broad Court at Bow Street, Covent Garden, WC2; ☎ 0207-836-8305; fax 0207-497-0064; www.the-fielding-hotel.co.uk

The Fielding is like a college dormitory: completely utilitarian and inoffensive. It even manages a small amount of charm; certainly the exterior is attractive, with its ivy-covered leaded windows, and you are free from traffic noise and fumes. It sits prettily on a pedestrian court with 19th-century lamps in the shadow of the Royal Opera House. The setting is unique and pleasant; you may hear glorious voices practicing arias day or night. It's all inexpensive pine and hard beds inside, but you don't have to share bathrooms, even at the cheapest rate, and everything is as clean and simple as you could ask for at the price. The proprietors and staff are friendly and helpful. They used to offer a good cheap breakfast, but they decided to withdraw that option, seeing as there are so very many cafés in every direction. This change has worked out fine for them—there's a lot less stress, as they tend to be booked solid. The superior double rooms in front are a bit nicer than the rest and are worth the extra dough. The Fielding is around the corner from Covent Garden and is within a healthy walking distance of the city, the British Museum, the Thames, and Piccadilly. It's a fabulous location at a very low price. No air-conditioning, but fans in each room.

SETTINGS AND FACILITIES

Nearest tube station Covent Garden. **Quietness rating** A/B. **Dining** No. **Amenities** Lounge, honor bar. **Services** Helpful reception desk.

ACCOMMODATIONS

Rooms 24. **All rooms** Telephone, five-channel TV, toilet. **Some rooms** Sitting area, writing desk. **Bed and bath** Hard beds, clean bathrooms with showers only. **Favorites** Superior doubles in the front of the building have the most space and light. **Comfort and decor** Somewhere between utilitarian and spartan.

PAYMENT, RESERVATIONS, AND RESTRICTIONS

Deposit One night's rate; 72-hour cancellation policy. **Credit cards** All major. **Check-in/out** Noon/11 a.m. **Pets** Not allowed. **Elevator** No. **Children** No children under age 13. **Disabled access** No (three floors).

Five Sumner Place Hotel

OVERALL ★★★   QUALITY ★★★   VALUE ★★★★½   PRICE RANGE £85–£130

5 Sumner Place, South Kensington, SW7; ☎ 0207-584-7586; fax 0207-823-9962; www.sumnerplace.com

Five Sumner Place has those most formidable of qualities: good value, good service, and good location. It's been honored over the years with many awards for best small hotel. And they aren't kidding about the small part, as you'd expect from a Victorian town house, but it makes much of its size, and the prices are good for this neighborhood (financier George Soros once owned a similar house up the street, so you know it's in an upmarket area). The South Kensington museums are a few minutes' walk away, and there are cafés, restaurants, and authentic French patisseries all around. The hotel is modest but comfortable and extremely clean and well kept. A couple of good rooms at the front have a scenic Mary Poppins–type view of a white row of town houses. Breakfast (included in the price) is served in the conservatory, which doubles as a sitting area. There are a lot of repeat customers, so book well ahead. You can get a 10% discount during January and February, and there are often online summer discounts.

SETTINGS AND FACILITIES

Nearest tube station South Kensington. **Quietness rating** A. **Dining** Breakfast; tons of restaurants and cafés, grocery nearby. **Amenities** Wireless access, daily newspapers, magazines, conservatory. **Services** Concierge services, laundry, bellhop, tea and coffee.

ACCOMMODATIONS

Rooms 13. **All rooms** Telephone, 5-channel TV, radio. **Some rooms** Refrigerator, balcony. **Bed and bath** Very good beds and showers, some bathtubs. **Favorites** Numbers 4 and 6 have balconies. Number 5 is a surprisingly spacious-feeling single. **Comfort and decor** It's not luxury, but it's not spartan either; in some rooms the decor is very comely, and in all rooms, clean and fresh. Some of the original moldings from 1848 have been beautifully preserved.

PAYMENT, RESERVATIONS, AND RESTRICTIONS

Deposit Credit card; 14-day cancellation policy. **Credit cards** All major, except DC. **Check-in/out** Noon/11 a.m. **Pets** Not allowed. **Elevator** Yes. **Children** No children under age 6. **Disabled access** Two ground-floor rooms, but steps leading to front door; no wheelchair access.

Franklin Hotel

OVERALL ★★★★   QUALITY ★★★★   VALUE ★★   PRICE RANGE £246–£293

28 Egerton Gardens, Knightsbridge, SW3; ☎ 0207-584-5533, in U.S. ☎ 800-473-9487; fax 0207-584-5449, in U.S. ☎ 800-473-9489; www.franklinhotel.co.uk

The Franklin Hotel is a small, elegant hotel situated on (and with access to) Egerton Gardens, which is a beautiful expanse of greenery wild with bright blooms in the spring. The hotel's almost sylvan peace is uncompromised by the fact that the bustling Brompton Road lies mere steps away. The magnificent Brompton Oratory, a Catholic Church, is a neighbor, and you can trot over to the Victoria and Albert Museum a few times a day. The atmosphere is serene, with antique furniture and art decorating the sitting rooms. The two lounges look onto the garden, and in winter a fire is kept blazing while you read the complimentary newspapers. There's an honor bar, and guests may congregate in the leather-chaired drinks room before dinner, or read the paper in one of the deep couches in the beautiful sitting rooms. This hotel, owned by the same people who gave us Dukes and the Egerton Garden Hotel (right down the street, but not as friendly as the Franklin) is a real favorite with Americans, who return again and again; the queen of Sweden also enjoys its comfort, decor, and excellent service. The hotel has a clean, elegant Georgian feel to it, and though the rooms may be on the small side, they are well-appointed. Check the Web site for special offers; or talk to the manager for upgrades or deals. They are very accommodating and amiable.

SETTINGS AND FACILITIES

Nearest tube station South Kensington or Knightsbridge. **Quietness rating** A in garden rooms, B- in front rooms. **Dining** Breakfast only. **Amenities** Honor bar, access to gardens, breakfast in breakfast room or bedroom, nonsmoking rooms, high-speed wireless access. **Services** Concierge, 24-hour room service, butler, valet.

ACCOMMODATIONS

Rooms 50. **All rooms** Direct-dial phones with data point and voice mail, wireless connection, satellite TV, minibar, hair dryer, iron, heated towel racks. **Some rooms** Garden view and entrance, four-poster bed, sitting area, two TVs, fax machine, bay window. **Bed and bath** Great beds with cotton sheets; all baths are marble and include power showers. **Favorites** There are two rooms that are split level and spacious, numbers 24 and 26. Number 1 has an entrance to the gardens and a four-poster. Number 3 is on the lower ground floor, but is very spacious yet cozy. Number 5 has a long view of the gardens; and number 19 has a dividing wall between the bedroom and the sitting room. **Comfort and decor** Excellent decor, homey feeling, extremely comfortable. More gracious than grand.

PAYMENT, RESERVATIONS, AND RESTRICTIONS

Deposit Credit card; 48-hour cancellation policy. **Credit cards** All major. **Check-in/out** 1 p.m./noon. **Pets** Not allowed. **Elevator** Yes. **Children** Yes. **Disabled access** Steps in front, but help can be arranged.

The Gainsborough

OVERALL ★★★   QUALITY ★★★   VALUE ★★★   PRICE RANGE £188–£211

7–11 Queensberry Place, South Kensington, SW7; ☎ 0207-838-1700, in U.S. ☎ 800-270-9206; fax 0207-970-1805; www.eeh.co.uk

Don't be put off by the high rack rates listed: there are *always* some kind of promotional discounts available that will lop off a third or more of that, both here and at its sister hotel across the street, The Gallery (or at The Willett Hotel in Sloane Square, which is not reviewed here). The Gainsborough is clearly the younger, less sophisticated sister of the two, in that there are no large sitting rooms, conference rooms, or fancifully dressed lounges, but it is still serviceable and well decorated. The smallish rooms are comfortable and tasteful; the staff is helpful and friendly. A hearty breakfast is included in the price, set out each day in the bright room off the lobby that becomes a tearoom/bar in the afternoon. Walk out of the hotel and you'll see the magnificent Alfred Waterston–designed Natural History Museum—one of three museums practically on your doorstep (the Victoria and Albert and the Science museums are the other two). The bus that goes past can be a problem for those in the front rooms.

SETTINGS AND FACILITIES

Nearest tube station South Kensington. **Quietness rating** B in back, D in front and on lower floors (the 74 bus goes past the hotel). **Dining** Breakfast, 24-hour room service. **Amenities** Breakfast room and bar, wired and wireless broadband, fax in lobby, discount at fitness club nearby. **Services** Concierge, room service, laundry, breakfast, bellhop.

ACCOMMODATIONS

Rooms 49. **All rooms** Telephone with modem and wireless access (charges apply), satellite TV, tea and coffee, safe, hair dryer, iron. **Some rooms** French windows, balcony, bigger TVs, air-conditioning. **Bed and bath** Beds are firm and comfortable. Singles all have showers only; doubles have shower/tub combinations; suites have spa baths. Nicely decorated bathrooms. **Favorites** Number 112 has a balcony and French windows and seems a little bigger than the others. **Comfort and decor** Rooms are small, but everything is clean and nicely presented. The decor is subdued, individual in each room, but homey.

PAYMENT, RESERVATIONS, AND RESTRICTIONS

Deposit Credit card; 24-hour cancellation policy. **Credit cards** All major. **Check-in/out** 1 p.m./noon. **Pets** Not allowed. **Elevator** Yes. **Children** Yes. **Disabled access** Call ahead to discuss wheelchair access.

The Gallery Hotel

OVERALL ★★★   QUALITY ★★★½   VALUE ★★★½   PRICE RANGE £188–£211

8–10 Queensberry Place, South Kensington, SW7; ☎ 0207-838-1700, in U.S. ☎ 800-270-9206; fax 0207-970-1805; www.eeh.co.uk

This is the above-mentioned sister of the Gainsborough Hotel, and you must forgive me for repeating myself by telling you that this is another good hotel in the heart of South Kensington, with the imposing Natural History Museum at the end of the street, the tube a two-minute walk away, and Kensington Gardens/Hyde Park a five-minute walk away. The rooms are not big, except for the fabulous suite (at £323), which has a private garden terrace. There is an attractive breakfast room (breakfast is included in some rates) with a well-stocked buffet. Upstairs you'll find a pleasant sitting room with a bar and a chessboard. Recently refurbished, the decor is attractive. Check the Web site for deals that can as much as halve the rack rates. Or ask for an upgrade to a suite. There is air-conditioning in the more expensive doubles or singles. The bus that goes past can be a problem for those in the front rooms.

SETTINGS AND FACILITIES

Nearest tube station South Kensington. **Quietness rating** A in back, D in front and on lower floors (the 74 bus goes past the hotel). **Dining** Breakfast room; 24-hour room service. **Amenities** Telephone with modem, wireless Internet (charges apply), minibars, satellite TV, iron, tea and coffee, safe, writing desk, fitness club nearby, music in bar on occasion, fax in lobby. **Services** Concierge, 24-hour room service.

ACCOMMODATIONS

Rooms 36. **All rooms** Telephone, high speed modem, wireless access, satellite TV, hair dryer, safe. **Some rooms** Air-conditioning, fax, couches, spa bathtubs. **Bed and bath** Excellent on both counts. Baths in doubles and suites, shower stalls in singles. **Favorites** Number 502 is a penthouse suite with a huge bed, a private garden terrace, a dining table, two couches, three phone lines, broadband and wireless Internet access. **Comfort and decor** Care has been taken to ensure all comforts, and the decor is individual and restful—a bit on the plain side, but clean and pleasing to the eye.

PAYMENT, RESERVATIONS, AND RESTRICTIONS

Deposit Credit card; 24-hour cancellation policy. **Credit cards** All major. **Check-in/out** 1 p.m./noon. **Pets** Not allowed. **Elevator** Yes. **Children** Yes. **Disabled access** No wheelchair access.

The Gore

OVERALL ★★★★½   QUALITY ★★★★½   VALUE ★★★★   PRICE RANGE £223–£246

189 Queen's Gate, South Kensington/Kensington, SW7;
☎ **0207-584-6601; fax 0207-589-8127; www.gorehotel.com**

I raved so much about this hotel in our first edition that visitors to the Gore were inevitably let down and unimpressed. There were complaints by three readers that The Gore did not live up to the glowing description in the book, and for that I am truly sorry. Hotels are only as good as the people who work there, and it takes only one or two bad apples to ruin the whole experience. To paraphrase Oscar Wilde, to have one disenchanted reader may be regarded as a misfortune, but to have three looks like carelessness. However, there's a new wind blowing at The Gore, and it's not just the air-conditioning that's been installed in all the rooms. The decoration has been freshened up with paint jobs, reframing the thousands of pictures, upgrading the baths, adding wireless access and high-speed modems to all the rooms, buying new mattresses and linens, and rearranging the public areas. The Gore was the brainstorm of two antiques dealers who started their hotel career with the wonderful Hazlitt's in Soho (see page 123), and who also own The Rookery (page 138). Their philosophy was to create hotels they would like to live in, decorated with authenticity and flair, a feast for the eyes. They bought this fine old mansion on Queen's Gate, steps from Kensington Garden, in which to hang 4,500 prints and paintings and house their serious collection of antiques. The Tudor Room could be part of a National Trust property, and its 16th-century bed could easily find a home in a museum. Even the single rooms are extraordinary, with beds and furnishings from the 19th century. The bathrooms are good, with attention paid to details. Bistro 190 offers great meals, from breakfast through dinner, and there is Bar 190 off the reception, which is a fabulous candlelit cocktail lounge that feels like a traditional men's club, with its wood paneling and leather couches. The Gore's location is good for lovers of Hyde Park and is also walking distance from South Kensington, the Albert Hall, and Kensington High Street. You can find weekend, package, and summer deals for about 50% off the rack rate.

SETTINGS AND FACILITIES

Nearest tube station Gloucester Road. **Quietness rating** A in back and top floors, B in lower front floors. **Dining** Bistro 190 for all meals. **Amenities** Use of two nearby fitness centers. **Services** Concierge, 24-hour room service, wireless Internet access, bellhop, laundry.

ACCOMMODATIONS

Rooms 48. **All rooms** Telephone with voice mail, high-speed broadband access, satellite TV, air-conditioning, minibar, antiques and art, genuine Victorian beds, fans, writing desks. **Some rooms** Stained-glass windows, French doors and balcony, sitting area, fireplace. **Bed and bath** The beds have been upgraded recently to accommodate people used to king-size modern hotel beds. Try the twin-bedded rooms if a double might be too small for you and your partner. The bathrooms are amazing: Many of them have the old-fashioned wooden loo chair above an antique Thomas Crapper porcelain toilet—a genuine "throne." Showerheads are big, tubs are deep. **Favorites** The Tudor is astonishing: a Victorian re-creation of an Eliza-bethan gallery, complete with huge stone fireplace (with gas flames) and stained glass of the queen herself. Carved lintels of heads and gargoyles are not for the faint of heart. Miss Ada's room (number 207) has a lovely Victorian theme; it's mascu-line and mahogany, with a very good double bed and a bust of Queen Victoria at the foot of it. In the Venus Room, a very feminine and well-named room, you can sleep in an antique rococo bed once owned by Judy Garland. The Dame Nelly suite is wonderful, and as for singles, although some are small, many have ornate beds and an airy atmosphere. **Comfort and decor** There is a sense of easy comfort throughout the hotel, and the decor is endlessly fascinating, although a minimalist would run screaming from its portals.

PAYMENT, RESERVATIONS, AND RESTRICTIONS

Deposit Credit card; 48-hour cancellation policy. **Credit cards** All major. **Check-in/out** 1 p.m./11:30 a.m. **Pets** Not allowed; exceptions made for guide dogs and perhaps well-behaved lap dogs. **Elevator** Yes. **Children** Yes. **Disabled access** No.

Goring Hotel

| OVERALL ★★★★★ | QUALITY ★★★★ | VALUE ★★★ | PRICE RANGE £311–£334 |

Beeston Place, Victoria, SW1; ☎ 0207-396-9000; fax 0207-834-4393; www.goringhotel.co.uk

The Goring is a gracious and lovely hotel, pure elegance and comfort a few steps from Victoria Station and within easy reach of the wonders of Westminster Abbey and Buckingham Palace. It has the great benefit of being on a tiny street where any traffic tends to be specifically for the hotel; in the back there's a lawn that is a real oasis of peace, even though you can only look but not frolic in it. Sometimes that's enough, especially when St. James's Park is so nearby. The hotel is justifiably proud of having remained in the same family since 1911, and it does indeed call to mind a fine country club of the early 1900s. It doesn't have any Victorian frippery, just a cool Edwardian elegance and comfort, from the bright yellow and marble of the beautiful lobby to the lounge tables that look like they've seen quite a few bridge games in their day. There's a finely carved fireplace and a wall of windows through which you can view the garden, and drinks and light food are served there all day. The dining room is of a high quality, as are the rooms themselves. Strangely but appealingly, there are adorable stuffed sheep in the rooms, which also have lovely furniture and excellent bathrooms outfitted with fine toiletries. The Goring plays to a lot of repeat customers—generations of them—and it's easy to see why. Special weekend rates are available, which is the only time we who are without a luxury hotel budget can afford to stay.

SETTINGS AND FACILITIES

Nearest tube station Victoria. **Quietness rating** A (double-glazed windows). **Dining** Beautiful dining room, plus garden bar and drawing room for teas and light meals. **Amenities** A very attractive and capacious drawing room and bar, a splendid expanse of lawn out back to admire, wireless Internet access, complimentary membership in nearby health club. **Services** Concierge, 24-hour room service, bellhop, laundry.

ACCOMMODATIONS

Rooms 75. **All rooms** Individual temperature control (including air-conditioning), telephone, high-speed modem, satellite TV, hair dryer, writing desk. **Some rooms** Balcony overlooking garden, fax. **Bed and bath** Beautiful wood-and-marble bathrooms and good-size beds in all the rooms. **Favorites** There are a few rooms with balconies that overlook the garden. These are fantastic and quite a rarity in London (or in any big city, for that matter). **Comfort and decor** The decor is extremely well done, suggesting a quite pleasing elegance and cheerfulness. All the common areas and the individual rooms are bright and warmly welcoming.

PAYMENT, RESERVATIONS, AND RESTRICTIONS

Deposit Credit card. **Credit cards** All major. **Check-in/out** Noon. **Pets** Dogs and birds not allowed (since 1911, when, judging from the posted restriction, apparently many people traveled with birds in hand). **Elevator** Yes. **Children** Yes. **Disabled access** Yes.

Grange White Hall Hotel

OVERALL ★★★½   QUALITY ★★★½   VALUE ★★★   PRICE RANGE £155–£164

**2–5 Montague Street, Bloomsbury, WC1; ☎ 0207-233-7888;
fax 0207-630-9897; www.grangehotels.com**

This is a pleasant and well-appointed hotel literally in the shadow of the British Museum (which just doesn't look quite as magnificent from the back—the red bricks are less impressive than the front's stone sheath). There's an exquisite, large garden with a glassed-in air-conditioned conservatory that can be used for afternoon teas or private functions. The rooms are as small as most London hotel rooms, but if you require space, ask for the lower ground (basement) rooms—some have more space for the same price as an upstairs room. The ambience is pleasing, and although the furniture is reproduction, the decor still has a certain flair and cleanliness. There are some really lovely touches, such as the elaborate molding in every room that has been painstakingly painted, the stencils on the walls, the glass and brass elevator, and the sumptuous curtains. There are a number of brilliant money-saving schemes—one of which is to book through the hotel's Web site, though you can also call and negotiate a deal.

SETTINGS AND FACILITIES

Nearest tube station Russell Square. **Quietness rating** A on garden in back, B+ in front (double glazing helps). **Dining** Breakfast, lunch, and dinner in the gorgeous English Garden Restaurant; The Museum Wine Bar is attached to the hotel, but with a separate entrance. **Amenities** Buffet breakfast, conservatory and garden, smoking and nonsmoking rooms, daily newspaper. **Services** Concierge, 24-hour room service, bellhop, laundry, fitness center two-minute walk away, business facilities.

ACCOMMODATIONS

Rooms 60. **All rooms** Telephone, high-speed modem, satellite TV, in-house movies, minibar, iron, tea and coffee, hair dryer, writing desk, computer modem. **Some rooms** Four-poster beds, balcony, garden view, French doors, sofa bed. **Bed and bath** Bathrooms are in perfect condition; beds are OK, and the four-posters are wonderful. **Favorites** Number 109 has a four-poster bed and a balcony on the garden; number 106 has an extra sofa bed and also a balcony on the garden. All the rooms on the first floor have high ceilings and French doors. **Comfort and decor** Decor is handsome. Care has clearly been taken to make this hotel visually gratifying, although it lacks a certain authenticity (not a lot of real antiques). It is comfortable enough, even though rooms are of the usual smallish variety.

PAYMENT, RESERVATIONS, AND RESTRICTIONS

Deposit Credit card; 24-hour cancellation policy. **Credit cards** All major. **Check-in/out** 2 p.m./11 a.m. **Pets** Not allowed. **Elevator** Yes. **Children** Yes. **Disabled access** Limited.

Great Eastern Hotel

OVERALL ★★★★   QUALITY ★★★★   VALUE ★★½   PRICE RANGE £225–£575

**Liverpool Street, by the City and East End, EC2; ☎ 0207-618-5000;
fax 0207-618-5000; www.great-eastern-hotel.com**

The Great Eastern Hotel is one of the better (as you can see from the above rack rates) full-service hotels in the Square Mile, as the financial center of the city is known. It's a great boon to business travelers, as well as for those who want to stay farther east than is common for the sightseeing visitor. Liverpool Street, a major transportation hub of London, is adjacent to the hotel, and while the neighborhood is not quite as appealing as many others in London, there is the ever-increasing trendiness of Hoxton Square and Spitalfields, once the center of French Huguenot weavers. The Great Eastern was one of the grand old Victorian terminus hotels, built in 1884 and expanded in 1901. A massive renovation, taking three years and millions of pounds, brought this old war horse into the 21st century with modern aplomb. The rooms are spare and minimalist, all sharp angles and fluffy pillows, attractive and functional, but a little too stark for my taste. They did take care to preserve some of the fine Victorian period elements, the best being the stained-glass dome in the restaurant Aurora, and much of the oak paneling and moldings. The hotel has everything a traveler could want, including a special jet-lag treatment and massage any time of the day or night. Attracting as they do a large number of well-traveled corporate types and big-name performers at the nearby Barbican Arts Centre, they know just what kind of sharp service is essential to their success, and they deliver: efficient room service, 24-hour business center, high-speed Internet access in every room, a top-shelf fitness room, and fine dining. All appetites are catered to: there's Myabi for Japanese, the Fishmarket for guess what, the George for olde England pub-style food, Aurora for fancy European dining under the glorious stained-glass dome, and Terminus for unfussy brasserie food, with artful desserts and a large menu. You'll never go hungry, day or night. Be skeptical of being urged to go to any of Sir Terence Conran's (the hotel's co-owner) many restaurants or to buy his book on London—it's clearly a bit of in-house publicity. They have weekend and special promotions, with rooms going for as little as £117.50 a night.

SETTINGS AND FACILITIES

Nearest tube station Liverpool Street or Bishopgate. **Quietness rating** B/C. **Dining** 5 restaurants, all pretty pricey but of good quality. **Amenities** Bars and lounges, newspapers, business center, health club with treatment facilities. **Services** Concierge, room service, same-day laundry, body treatments, mobile-phone rental, shoe shine, shops, valet parking.

ACCOMMODATIONS

Rooms 267, including 21 suites. **All rooms** Ergonomically designed workstation with two-line telephones, voice mail, high-speed modem and wireless access, fax, satellite TV with on-demand movies, hair dryer, minibar, safe, CD player, DVD player, and DVD library. **Some rooms** Fireplaces, high ceilings, big windows; others have more of a modern loft effect. **Bed and bath** Splendid, with Frette sheets and the latest bathroom fittings. **Favorites** I prefer the rooms on the lower floors of the east block because they have retained the most Victorian features; the higher floors are more modern. **Comfort and decor** As you'd expect from furniture magnate Terence Conran, the decor is modern, solid, and comfy, with clean lines and relaxing colors.

PAYMENT, RESERVATIONS, AND RESTRICTIONS
Deposit Credit card. **Credit cards** All major. **Check-in/out** 2 p.m./noon. **Pets** Not allowed. **Elevator** Yes. **Children** Yes. **Disabled access** Yes.

Hazlitt's Hotel

OVERALL ★★★★   QUALITY ★★★★   VALUE ★★½   PRICE RANGE £205–£299

6 Frith Street, Soho Square, W1; ☎ 0207-434-1771; fax 0207-439-1524; www.hazlittshotel.com

Hazlitt's Hotel was the first establishment of the creators of The Gore and The Rookery (see pages 118 and 138). Hazlitt's, which happens to be author Bill Bryson's favorite home away from home, is a perfect evocation of another time, with handsome antiques and decor in the Georgian style. For those allergic to Victorian fussiness, Hazlitt's is the perfect alternative to The Gore, and it's in the heart of Soho, where sleepy London tends to stay wide awake. It is a simple hotel, without an elevator and with only a tiny sitting room for communal lounging. Staying here is more like staying at a particularly well-appointed rooming house from days gone by. The house was built in 1718, and the floors sag and droop as you would, too, if you'd been trod on for close to 300 years. The rooms are luxuriously comfortable, with beautiful antique bedsteads and cotton sheets. Busts sculpted by one of the owner's relatives grace many of the bathrooms and rooms, and antique prints adorn the walls. The period verisimilitude is strict: the house of a writer like William Hazlitt would not have been overdone with gimcrackery or knickknackery. Hazlitt's attracts writers like honey draws flies, partly because of the respect they get here, and perhaps because they're the only people who know who Hazlitt was. In the sitting room is a bookcase with signed copies of books written by guests, and it's an impressive collection: Seamus Heaney, Ted Hughes, Vikram Seth, Jostein Gardner, Susan Sontag, Dava Sobel, and scores of others. Of course, the brilliant Bill Bryson's books are there; he sent the phones ringing off the hook when he mentioned his favorite hotel in his hilarious book on England, *Notes from a Small Island.* Hazlitt's attracts a loyalty—or eccentricity—hardly ever met with: one of the regulars paid for double glazing to be put on the windows of his favorite room. This is not to say that you will indubitably love Hazlitt's; it's for a particular type of person, one who likes the noise and action of the present-day West End as much as the atmosphere of long-ago Soho. Look for promotional deals on the Web site.

SETTINGS AND FACILITIES

Nearest tube station Tottenham Court. **Quietness rating** D/F in front on weekend nights, A/B in back at all times. **Dining** No. **Amenities** Writing desks and modems, cotton sheets, continental breakfast at extra charge. **Services** Receptionist, bellhop, laundry, 24-hour room service.

ACCOMMODATIONS

Rooms 23. **All rooms** Telephone, high-speed modem, satellite TV, bathtub, antiques, writing desk. **Some rooms** Ornamental fireplace, four-poster, high ceilings.

Bed and bath Superb on both counts. Victorian tubs, deep and delicious, with huge shower heads. Beds are comfortable, high off the ground, big, and cotton sheeted. **Favorites** The suite on the ground floor, the double-glazed Jonathan Swift room, and a small room in the back are best. Really, there are no rooms here that aren't charming and inviting; the higher ceilings are on the first and second floors. **Comfort and decor** Top-notch comfort (unless you require an elevator), and the decor is nourishing to the eye and soul.

PAYMENT, RESERVATIONS, AND RESTRICTIONS

Deposit Credit card; 48-hour cancellation policy. **Credit cards** All major. **Check-in/out** 2 p.m./noon. **Pets** Not allowed. **Elevator** No. **Children** Yes. **Disabled access** No.

Holiday Inn Mayfair

OVERALL ★★½   QUALITY ★★   VALUE ★★★   14-DAY ADVANCE PRICE £127–£150

3 Berkeley Street, Mayfair, W1; ☎ 0207-493-8282; fax 0207-629-2827; www.mayfair.holiday-inn.com

In the United States, the name Holiday Inn has the connotation of a budget-to-moderate kind of a place, which is why I had to gasp when I saw a Holiday Inn rack rate of £255! Well, I don't believe that *anyone* is paying rack rate here—even the advance flexible rate is £179 to £200 for two people in a double room. The smart money joins the Priority Club or takes advantage of any of the many packages and deals available on the Web site. The Holiday Inn Mayfair doesn't even have a tariff card to give out (nor will you get very far with them on the phone unless you have definite dates in mind), because there are so many possible combinations of discounts and promos—I practically had to wrestle that rack rate quote out of the front desk clerk. The neighborhood is excellent, and the rooms have pretty much everything you want. OK, the place is hardly dripping with charm, but it's attractive enough and clean as well. If you want to stay in a very high-class neighborhood at an affordable rate, you could do a lot worse than the good old Holiday Inn.

SETTINGS AND FACILITIES

Nearest tube station Green Park. **Quietness rating** A in back, B/C in front (double-glazed windows). **Dining** Nightingale's Restaurant serves international cuisine. **Amenities** Bar, very small fitness room. **Services** Concierge, 24-hour room service, bellhop, laundry.

ACCOMMODATIONS

Rooms 184. **All rooms** Telephone, modem lines and wireless, satellite TV, mini-bar, air-conditioning, hair dryer, iron, tea and coffee, in-house movies, writing desk. **Some rooms** Suites have two rooms, two bathrooms, two TVs. **Bed and bath** Bathrooms are fine; beds are comfortable. **Favorites** The suites and executive rooms have the most space. **Comfort and decor** Hotel style, but not drab; major refurbishment has been ongoing.

PAYMENT, RESERVATIONS, AND RESTRICTIONS

Deposit Credit card; cancellation by 6 p.m. on the day of arrival. **Credit cards** All major. **Check-in/out** 2 p.m./1 p.m. **Pets** Not allowed. **Elevator** Yes. **Children** Yes. **Disabled access** Two disabled rooms available.

Hotel Russell

OVERALL ★★★★   QUALITY ★★★★   VALUE ★★★★   PRICE RANGE £119–£260

**Russell Square, Bloomsbury, WC1; ☎ 0207-837-6470;
fax 0207-837-2857; www.principal-hotels.com**

This grand, old terra-cotta-faced edifice, built in 1898, changed hands recently, with Principal Hotels buying it from the Meridien group. The new owners can enjoy the fruits of the enormous renovation done by Meridien, and have even been able to lower the prices sensibly. I am happy to report that they haven't changed much at all, and why would they, since there are so many antique details that would be a shame to lose, such as the sweeping marble staircase. There are contemporary rooms, as well as a more classic style, air-conditioning in every room, and all the communications conveniences you could want. The hotel attracts a business crowd due to its conference facilities, and is accustomed to demanding customers. The restaurants are just OK, but quite convenient, and it's nice and close to the West End, the City, and the British Museum. It's a magnificent building—one of the great Victorian hotel palaces.

SETTINGS AND FACILITIES

Nearest tube station Russell Square. **Quietness rating** C in front (double glazing), B in back. **Dining** Fitzroy's Doll Bar-Restaurant serves European and British food; Virginia Woolf's Brasserie serves burgers, pastas, and so on. The King's Bar and Lounge has a club atmosphere, with fireplace, red leather couches, and drinks. **Amenities** Full business support, executive floor with lounge and continental breakfast gratis. **Services** Concierge, 24-hour room service, bellhop, laundry, conference ready.

ACCOMMODATIONS

Rooms 373. **All rooms** Telephone, modem, satellite TV, air-conditioning, hair dryer, iron, tea and coffee. **Some rooms** Minibar, writing desk, wide-screen plasma TV, bathrobes, balcony. **Bed and bath** Excellent; some bathrooms are quite big. **Favorites** A suite with a sitting room and French doors in both rooms looking out onto Russell Square. **Comfort and decor** It's got all the luxury trappings of a Meridien hotel, without paying Meridien prices: old-fashioned huge hallways, high ceilings, and big rooms. The common areas are appealing, with a grand staircase in the beautiful Victorian lobby.

PAYMENT, RESERVATIONS, AND RESTRICTIONS

Deposit Credit card; must cancel before 2 p.m. on day of arrival. **Credit cards** All major. **Check-in/out** 2 p.m./noon. **Pets** Not allowed. **Elevator** Yes, 3. **Children** Yes. **Disabled access** As a Grade II building, they can't alter structure for built-in ramps, but management can help a lot.

l'Hotel

OVERALL ★★★★   QUALITY ★★★★   VALUE ★★★★½   PRICE RANGE £182–£212

**28 Basil Street, Knightsbridge, SW3; ☎ 0207-589-6286, in U.S.
☎ 800-926-3199; fax 0207-823-7826; www.capital-london.net/lhotel**

This award-winning inn is next door to, and owned by, the five-star Capital Hotel. It has only 12 rooms, so speak up early if you want to book here—it's very popular among the cognoscente. The hotel is located 50 meters from Harrods and 250 from Hyde Park, with Sloane Street and its designer shops at the end of Basil Street. The rooms are all quiet and simple, in a French country style that may come as a relief to those who find the English traditional too floral and fussy. Pine furniture and neutral colors accented by elegant artwork and bibelots make it a restful and aesthetic experience. The staff is friendly and helpful—reception will act as concierge and help out wherever needed. Best of all, there are three rooms and one suite that come with gas fireplaces, and these are the rooms that require booking well ahead. The price, for the area and the quality, is good. All the rooms are double, with no extra charge for the second person. Le Metro is a bistro that serves great café food all day long, and if you're interested in a double-Michelin-starred French culinary mind- and budget-blower, the Capital Restaurant next door will have you drooling over their five-course, £68 tasting menu (£29.50 for three courses at lunch).

SETTINGS AND FACILITIES

Nearest tube station Knightsbridge. **Quietness rating** A (double glazing throughout). **Dining** Le Metro for breakfast, lunch, and dinner. **Amenities** Continental breakfast is included in price and can be served in room or at Le Metro; fax and iron on request. **Services** Concierge, breakfast room service only, laundry.

ACCOMMODATIONS

Rooms 12. **All rooms** Telephone, high-speed modems, minibar, satellite TV, in-house movies, hair dryer, tea and coffee, writing desk, ceiling fan. **Some rooms** Fireplace. **Bed and bath** Frette sheets and perfect bathrooms. **Favorites** Number 302, a room with a fireplace, and the suite. **Comfort and decor** Dedicated to comfort and simplicity of decor. A good feeling pervades, and the staff is friendly.

PAYMENT, RESERVATIONS, AND RESTRICTIONS

Deposit Credit card; 72-hour cancellation policy. **Credit cards** All major. **Check-in/out** 2 p.m./noon. **Pets** Not allowed. **Elevator** Yes. **Children** Yes. **Disabled access** One ground-floor room.

Lincoln House Hotel

OVERALL ★★★½   QUALITY ★★★½   VALUE ★★★★½   PRICE RANGE £69–£109

33 Gloucester Place, Marble Arch, W1; ☎ 0207-486-7630; fax 0207-486-0166; www.lincoln-house-hotel.co.uk

I have been meaning to put this lovely little B&B in this guide for ages, having heard so many good things about it from people who should know. Its reputation for friendliness and cleanliness is way up there, while the prices are way down. The neighborhood is north of Oxford Street and south of Regent's Park; transportation to everywhere is a short walk away, as are the conveniences of picturesque Marylebone. The proprietor, Joseph Sheriff, is a smart, well-traveled guy who takes great pride in knowing just what guests want, and he provides much more than you would find at a comparably priced hotel. The road it's on is a busy one, with buses going to and fro, but the rooms in the back are quieter, looking over the mews. You can be in Hyde Park in five or ten minutes from here, or you might prefer shopping in Selfridges, which is even closer. The rooms are, naturally, on the small side: big Americans may want to spring for the family room at £109. The prices include a good breakfast, served in the pleasant breakfast room or brought to your room, and offer both an English breakfast (eggs, bacon, sausage, toast, beans, tomatoes, and mushrooms) or a vegetarian version. Continental rolls and pastries are also available. This is a lovely old town house from the late 18th century, and many of the most charming period details have been lovingly restored.

SETTINGS AND FACILITIES

Nearest tube station Marble Arch. **Quietness** C in front rooms, B+ in rear. **Dining** Breakfast room. **Amenities** Breakfast (full English, vegetarian, or continental); rental of laptop, wireless Internet access, soft drink vending machine. **Services** Touring and ticket advice; breakfast brought to room free of charge; friendly, helpful staff.

ACCOMMODATIONS

Rooms 23. **All rooms** Telephone, satellite TV, hair dryer, trouser press, tea and coffee facilities, fan (no air-conditioning). **Some rooms** Minifridge; period details, high ceilings. **Bed and bath** Showers only. **Favorites** First-floor rooms with nice windows, or quieter rooms overlooking the mews. **Comfort and decor** Simple, clean, and pleasing, with some lovely Georgian architectural features. No air-conditioning, but fans in every room.

PAYMENT, RESERVATIONS, AND RESTRICTIONS

Deposit Credit card; 72-hour cancellation policy. **Credit cards** All major. **Check-in/out** 2 p.m./11:30 a.m. **Pets** Not allowed. **Elevator** No. **Children** Yes. **Disabled access** No.

London Marriott Hotel County Hall

OVERALL ★★★★   QUALITY ★★★★   VALUE ★★★   PRICE RANGE £292–£323

County Hall, South Bank, SE1; ☎ 0207-928-5200; toll free in U.S. ☎ 888-236-2427, toll free internationally ☎ 44-80-221-221, fax 0207-928-5300; www.marriotthotels.com

This hotel has the largest rooms of any Marriott in London, and it has all the amenities you'd expect from the chain, but with one major difference: it's located in the old County Hall building right on the Thames and has spectacular, postcard-perfect views of Parliament, Big Ben, the London Eye, and the tower of Westminster Abbey. You can stroll down the Thames Path, browsing at the secondhand book stalls, or popping in for a concert at the Royal Festival Hall, a play at the National Theater, or a late-night film at the cinema. In summer, all the world's a stage on the South Bank, even if there's not a whole lotta shakin' going on in the neighborhood to the south of the Marriot. Across the bridge is Westminster, which tends to roll up the sidewalks at night and on weekends. The hotel has a 25-meter pool and an excellent gym; beauty and health treatments are available. There are some delightful eating and lounging areas, which you should visit even if you don't stay here—the view is magnificent, especially at night. The library has been preserved from when it was part of the County Hall, and the books are all the original volumes. There are wood-paneled walls everywhere and all kinds of interesting architectural features in this historical, listed building. And the beds are huge. Ask for deals and promotions, as the rack rate is steep.

SETTINGS AND FACILITIES

Nearest tube station Westminster or Waterloo. **Quietness rating** A/B. **Dining** County Hall Restaurant has English cuisine and an oyster-and-seafood bar, plus great views of the Thames. Library Lounge has tea and snacks. There is also Leaders Cocktail Bar. **Amenities** Restaurant, lounge, bar, views of Parliament and Big Ben, health club with big pool, disabled rooms, valet parking. **Services** Concierge, 24-hour room service, valet parking, bellhop, laundry.

ACCOMMODATIONS

Rooms 186. **All rooms** Telephones, voicemail, high-speed modems, satellite TV, air-conditioning, minibar, hair dryer, tea and coffee, iron, safes. **Some rooms** Separate sitting rooms, river views. **Bed and bath** Excellent bathrooms; beds are queen- or king-size. **Favorites** Any of the rooms with a view of Parliament; inside rooms on courtyard are quiet. **Comfort and decor** Comfort is high, decor is high-standard hotel type, with some unfortunate choices in fabrics.

PAYMENT, RESERVATIONS, AND RESTRICTIONS

Deposit Credit card; must cancel by 4 p.m. on day of arrival. **Credit cards** All major. **Check-in/out** 2 p.m./noon. **Pets** Not allowed. **Elevator** Yes. **Children** Yes. **Disabled access** Six disabled rooms of a very high standard.

 Miller's Residence

OVERALL ★★★★ QUALITY ★★★ VALUE ★★★½ PRICE RANGE £176- £205

111A Westbourne Grove, Notting Hill Gate, W2 (entrance on southeast side of Hereford Road); ☎ 0207-243-1024; fax 0207-243-1064; www.millersuk.com

Miller's Residence has become one of London's worst-kept secrets; it opened in 1997 and has been quietly drawing strength from the numbers of people who love it and keep going back, as well as the numerous newspaper and magazine writers who keep writing about it. Martin Miller, of *Miller's Antique Guide,* and Kay Raveden have created an eccentric and beautiful "rooming house" in Notting Hill Gate, filled to bursting in the common areas with sublime antiques (there's a covered sedan chair in the front hall and an old sled on the wall, to name only two of the first things to hit your eyes). The drawing room is wonderful, with a fireplace that is stunningly carved, and still more antiques. The couple has clearly spent years successfully scavenging in markets like Portobello and Bermondsey and at many a country auction. The eight rooms (two are suites) are named after English Romantic poets and have lines from the poems of these masters on the back of each door. The Coleridge Room has an old model of the HMS *Bounty,* and the "Rime of the Ancient Mariner" is quoted on the door. This is the kind of quirky and interesting inn that appeals to a certain kind of sensibility or taste—if you're looking for a predictable hotel experience, this is not really the place, and it's probably not very relaxing if you have small children, who you'll have to keep a sharp eye on amidst the valuables on display here. But if you love antiques, and like to be in the very hip Westbourne Grove area, you will find this a delightful break from the usual hostelries. The house is on a busy stretch of Westbourne Grove full of restaurants and interesting shops; the health-food store Planet Organic down the street has a great juice bar. Guests who book long stays will get a discount. Book well in advance.

SETTINGS AND FACILITIES

Nearest tube station Bayswater. **Quietness rating** C/D. **Dining** Breakfast only. **Amenities** 24-hour computer access, exuberant drawing room with a fireplace, illuminated by candles at night, and another equally gorgeous lounge. **Services** Reception acts as concierge, limited room service (from local restaurants), laundry.

ACCOMMODATIONS

Rooms six; two apartment suites. **All rooms** Telephone, voice mail, satellite TV, wonderful antiques. **Some rooms** Four-poster, even more wonderful antiques. **Bed and bath** Good quality beds, and the bathrooms are of a high standard. **Favorites** All rooms are different and very cool. Try the red Coleridge Room or the lighter Tennyson Room. **Comfort and decor** Comfort is fine, except for the lack of a lift and the possibility of a hot day or two without air-conditioning. The decor has to be seen to be believed. The owners have spent their time amassing stunning antiques that they have spread wildly and well all over this wonderful rooming house.

PAYMENT, RESERVATIONS, AND RESTRICTIONS

Deposit Credit card; cancellation policy seven days prior to arrival. **Credit cards** All major. **Check-in/out** 2 p.m./12 a.m. **Pets** Not allowed. **Elevator** No. **Children** Yes. **Disabled access** No.

The Montague on the Gardens

OVERALL ★★★★   QUALITY ★★★★   VALUE ★★★   PRICE RANGE £185–£209

15 Montague Street, Bloomsbury, WC1; ☎ 0207-637-1001, in U.S. ☎ 800-424-2862; fax 0207-637-2516; www.montaguehotel.com

A deluxe hotel, The Montague on the Gardens features the type of sumptuous interior design that uses fabric as wallpaper and cleverly combines fine antiques with bold patterns and pleasing colors. It provides all the services one would expect of a deluxe hotel and then some. There's a garden in the back that you can enjoy while sitting on the patio off the Terrace Bar, and the restaurant is of good quality at reasonable (for London) prices. It's also across the street from the British Museum, and within walking distance of the West End. The delightful decor of the rooms can't conceal the small size of most, but it does tend to divert one's attention from it. The Montague is made from eight Grade II town houses strung together, so the rooms are all of different sizes and shapes. A recent renovation has turned some of the small single rooms into more spacious doubles, or a double into a suite. There are a couple of deluxe kings that are spacious (numbers 317 and 319). Ask about promotional deals. It's a bit pricey for the neighborhood—unless you simply *have* to be near the West End or the British Museum and want a full-service hotel.

SETTINGS AND FACILITIES
Nearest tube station Russell Square. **Quietness rating** A in garden rooms, B on street. **Dining** Blue Door Bistro is a three-star restaurant serving breakfast, lunch, and dinner, with a very pleasing and elegant interior. **Amenities** Smoking and nonsmoking rooms, bar, restaurant with piano music, bathrobes, in-room express checkout via TV system, executive room with business-related amenities, high-speed Internet access, mobile phones for rental, fax machines on request. Well-equipped fitness room. **Services** Concierge, 24-hour room service, bellhop, laundry, business support.

ACCOMMODATIONS
Rooms 99. **All rooms** Telephone, high-speed modem, voice mail, cable TV, in-house movies, air-conditioning, hair dryer, writing desk, iron, tea and coffee. **Some rooms** Minibars, fax lines, CD players and CD selection. **Bed and bath** Beautiful beds, most with elaborate canopies and handsome duvets and curtains. The bathrooms are first rate. **Favorites** Number 219, The Duchesse, is a fine suite that has a sky painted on the ceiling. **Comfort and decor** They aim to please here, so the comfort factor—even adjusting for the size of some rooms—is particularly high. The decor is impressive, if a bit over the top in places.

PAYMENT, RESERVATIONS, AND RESTRICTIONS
Deposit Credit card; 24-hour cancellation policy. **Credit cards** All major. **Check-in/out** 2 p.m./noon. **Pets** Large pets not allowed (small pets conditional). **Elevator** Yes. **Children** Yes. **Disabled access** Ramps for main stairs, and the people here are very helpful, but since it's a Grade II listed building, they can't create total wheelchair access.

Morgan Hotel

OVERALL ★★½	QUALITY ★★★	VALUE ★★★★	PRICE RANGE £95–£120

24 Bloomsbury Street, Bloomsbury, WC1; ☎ 0207-636-3735; fax 0207-636-3045

Make your reservation well in advance to get a room at this extremely popular family-run bed-and-breakfast/budget hotel. Practically on the doorstep of the British Museum and within walking distance of the West End, this is the place discerning cheapskates love to go. It's very old school—they don't even bother to have a Web site, much less high-speed modems in the rooms, which is kind of refreshing. They spruced the joint up in 2004 with new mattresses, carpets, and a paint job, all of which it frankly needed. It's an easy, informal sort of place, run by a cheerful family who seem to do absolutely everything themselves, and nicely, too. The breakfast room is the jewel here: it's done up in booths and decorated with an extraordinary collection of English ceramic Toby jugs, some very interesting pieces. Clearly, someone here has the taste to make a budget place look inviting and interesting, or maybe it's because they got started on decorating the place when they opened it over 25 years ago, back when you could still get a deal on Portobello Road. All the rooms have a private shower and toilet. Check out the hotel's annex of apartments, which have also had a recent spit and polish, and are great for families.

SETTINGS AND FACILITIES

Nearest tube station Tottenham Court. **Quietness rating** A in back, B+ in front (double-glazed windows). **Dining** Breakfast, which is included in price. **Amenities** Breakfast in delightful dining room, no-smoking floors. **Services** Bellhop.

ACCOMMODATIONS

Rooms 21 hotel rooms and 4 flats. **All rooms** Telephone, TV (BBC and CNN), hair dryer. **Some rooms** Tea and coffee, air-conditioning, writing desk, bath, TV and VCR in apartments. **Bed and bath** Highest cleanliness and comfort. **Favorites** Number 1 is a good size, with lots of drawers. Room B is a favorite; and Flat 1 is a nice apartment, with eat-in kitchen, pleasant decoration, and good space. **Comfort and decor** The decor is superior to most of the local B&Bs in this price range, with really interesting pictures on the walls and a fine collection of English porcelain. The family is well versed in making visitors comfortable.

PAYMENT, RESERVATIONS, AND RESTRICTIONS

Deposit Credit card; 72-hour cancellation policy. **Credit cards** Most major. **Check-in/out** Noon/10:30 a.m. **Pets** Not allowed. **Elevator** No. **Children** Yes. **Disabled access** No elevator.

Number Sixteen

OVERALL ★★★½   QUALITY ★★★★   VALUE ★★½   PRICE RANGE £200–£264

16 Sumner Place, South Kensington, SW7; ☎ 0207-589-5232, in U.S.
☎ 800-592-5387; fax 0207-584-8615; www.numbersixteenhotel.co.uk

This town-house hotel, an old favorite among visitors who love South Kensington, has been taken over by the Firmdale group (which owns the Pelham, Charlotte Street, Covent Garden, and other hotels) and has undergone a renovation that may have some of the former customers feeling a bit uncomfortable: gone is the chintz of yesteryear, as well as the old descriptive names of the rooms. It's now a modern, but not minimalist, boutique hotel, whose prices have also caught up to the present. There are quirky ethnic decorations around, huge birdcages, driftwood lamps, and the like, which work marvelously well in the formerly staid conservatory. The garden is as gorgeous as ever, and is often used for fashion shoots. The bathrooms have been seriously upgraded, with gray granite and power showers, and the bedrooms are all individually decorated. What they couldn't upgrade is the size of the rooms, which are pretty small, except for the superior deluxes. The lower ground floor has a few rooms with their own entrance to the garden, which is a big plus. There's no breakfast room, but food will be brought to your room, the conservatory, or one of the public sitting areas, 24 hours a day. Beds are big and draped in cotton sheets, which appeals to the 80% American clientele. Good service. Ask about promotional deals.

SETTINGS AND FACILITIES

Nearest tube station South Kensington. **Quietness rating** B. **Dining** 24-hour room service. **Amenities** Air-conditioning, voice mail, high-speed modem, satellite TV, DVD player (card to nearby video store), mobile phone rental, minibar, safe, access to health club nearby (for fee). **Services** Concierge, laundry.

ACCOMMODATIONS

Rooms 42. **All rooms** Air-conditioning, telephone with voice mail, modem point, minibar, DVD player, satellite TV, safe, hair dryer. **Some rooms** Balcony, French doors, access to garden. **Bed and bath** Of a very high standard; big beds, great bathrooms. **Favorites** Number 3 is on lower ground, but has space and a huge bed; 306 is red and elegant, if small; ask for rooms on the garden, as they're quieter. **Comfort and decor** Decor is eccentrically elegant, with faux stone painted walls and interesting artwork and knickknacks; comfort is top-notch.

PAYMENT, RESERVATIONS, AND RESTRICTIONS

Deposit Credit card; 48-hour cancellation policy. **Credit cards** All major. **Check-in/out** 3 p.m./noon. **Pets** Not allowed. **Elevator** Yes. **Children** Yes. **Disabled access** Four ground-floor rooms, three steps to front door.

Parkes Hotel

OVERALL ★★★½   QUALITY ★★★★   VALUE ★★½   PRICE RANGE £282–£340

41 Beaufort Gardens, Knightsbridge, SW3; ☎ 0207-581-9944; toll free in U.S. ☎ 800-306-5054; fax 0207-581-1999; www.parkeshotel.com

You'll find pristine English elegance at this luxury hotel, a mere stone's throw from Harrods on a tree-lined cul-de-sac off the busy Brompton Road. It's not at all stuffy, but it does has very high standards for decor and service, as it should for the price. There are plenty of maids and bellhops, and very friendly they are, too. There is no restaurant, but there is a breakfast room with a full English breakfast (not included), and you can get room service. But the best thing is that all the rooms have kitchens, so you can feast from Harrods Food Halls without any difficulty. Parkes had long prided itself on the fact that they offered no deals, but were always solidly booked; but in these strange times, even the Parkes Hotel needs to fill rooms and will offer upgrades or other money-saving deals.

SETTINGS AND FACILITIES

Nearest tube station Knightsbridge. **Quietness rating** B. **Dining** Breakfast room. **Amenities** Sitting room, complimentary newspaper, kitchens. **Services** Concierge, room service, bellhop, laundry, chauffeur service and airport transfer.

ACCOMMODATIONS

Rooms 35. **All rooms** Telephone, high-speed modem, satellite TV and in-house movies, kitchen, minibar, tea and coffee, hair dryer, iron, double bed, safe, bathtubs. **Some rooms** Fax, writing desk, sitting area, chandelier, fireplace. **Bed and bath** Excellent. **Favorites** The front-facing junior suite; one-bedroom suite with huge crystal chandeliers, high ceilings, and French windows in the bedroom and the sitting room. The doubles are a bit small, but the junior suites are a good size. **Comfort and decor** Pains have been taken to make the rooms comfortable, and the decor is well composed and attractive, even with its impersonal quality.

PAYMENT, RESERVATIONS, AND RESTRICTIONS

Deposit Credit card; 48-hour cancellation policy. **Credit cards** All major. **Check-in/out** 2 p.m./noon. **Pets** Allowed by arrangement. **Elevator** Yes. **Children** Yes. **Disabled access** No wheelchair access, lots of stairs and small hallways.

The Pelham

OVERALL ★★★½   QUALITY ★★★★   VALUE ★★½   PRICE RANGE £211–£229

15 Cromwell Place, South Kensington, SW7; ☎ 0207-589-8288, toll free in U.S. ☎ 800-553-6674; fax 0207-584-8444; www.firmdale.com

As with all the Firmdale establishments, the Pelham Hotel is visually arresting. Each room is unique and exquisitely decorated by the deft hand of the owner, and the hotel's size (46 bedrooms and suites) guarantees the guest the most punctilious and personal service. However, the size of many of the rooms leaves something to be desired, as with many period building conversions, but the decor lulls you into complacency. The atmosphere is that of a luxurious town house, with all the amenities you could desire. There are two sitting rooms with fireplaces, mahogany paneling, artfully arranged flowers, stunning furniture, and deep, comfy chairs and sofas. The views in the front are of the town of South Kensington, and there's not much to look at out of the rear windows except for the French Lycee playground (expect noise on school days). The location is excellent, with the museums of South Kensington just steps away, three tube lines across the street, buses that stop in front of the hotel (a big bother to noise phobics), and the shops of Knightsbridge a five-minute walk away. The staff is friendly, helpful, and knowledgeable. They can get you anything you need at any time—babysitter, massage therapist, tickets, tours, airport transfer. Call about the special deals they offer. Breakfast is included with some rooms.

SETTINGS AND FACILITIES

Nearest tube station South Kensington. **Quietness rating** B in rear, C in front (the front has *double* double-glazing, a real necessity). **Dining** Kemp's Restaurant has an excellent menu that changes every few weeks. The room is comfortable and relaxed. **Amenities** Sitting rooms with fireplaces, champagne and hors d'oeuvres on Wednesdays, honor bar and coffee and tea in back sitting room. **Services** 24-hour room service, concierge, laundry, anything you can think of.

ACCOMMODATIONS

Rooms 46. **All rooms** 2 telephones, voice mail, high-speed modem, satellite TV, mobile phone rental, minibar, sitting area. **Some rooms** DVD/VCR player, sofa, balcony, four-poster bed. **Bed and bath** Twin, double, king (which can be turned into twins) are all very comfortable; bathrooms have big tubs, good showers, granite and mahogany decor. **Favorites** Front-facing luxury double, with French doors leading to balcony; any of the deluxe doubles, the suite with the walk-in wardrobe, two sinks in bathroom, and shower cubicle as well as tub. **Comfort and decor** The comfort factor is what we'd all like to achieve in our own homes, and the decor is like stepping into the pages of *Architectural Digest*.

PAYMENT, RESERVATIONS, AND RESTRICTIONS

Deposit Credit card; 48-hour cancellation policy. **Credit cards** All major, except DC. **Check-in/out** 1 p.m./noon. **Pets** Not allowed. **Elevator** Yes. **Children** Yes. **Disabled access** Limited; steps into hotel must be negotiated with assistance.

Pembridge Court Hotel

OVERALL ★★★½   QUALITY ★★★   VALUE ★★½   PRICE RANGE £160–£195

34 Pembridge Gardens, Notting Hill Gate; ☎ 0207-229-9977, toll free in U.S. ☎ 800-709-9882; fax 0207-727-4982; www.pemct.co.uk

This is an excellent town-house hotel within easy reach of Portobello Road: you only need slip out the back of the house and through an alley, and you're there. The atmosphere of this Victorian house is bright and friendly, with a serene atmosphere abetted by the grace of the old Victorian building and neighborhood. The rooms are mostly a decent size—some bigger than others—and decorated in ingenious ways: antique gloves, dresses, belts, fans, and other accessories are beautifully framed and hung all around. There's a sitting room with a library and fireplace, as well as a smaller lounge to hang out in. A full English breakfast is included in the price, which is pretty good for this quiet and pleasant B&B. The breakfast room is probably the most ordinary element of the house, which has been recently refurbished with new rugs and fabrics. There's nothing precious or pretentious about this place; it's just relatively decent value and good vibrations in a convenient and charming setting.

SETTINGS AND FACILITIES

Nearest tube station Notting Hill Gate. **Quietness rating** A. **Dining** Breakfast room, and room service. **Amenities** Full English breakfast included, sitting room, arrangements with nearby health club, fax on request. **Services** 24-hour room service, limited menu, bellhop, laundry.

ACCOMMODATIONS

Rooms 20. **All rooms** Telephone, modem, satellite TV, desk, iron, air-conditioning. **Some rooms** Two telephones, DVD/VCR and CD players, sitting room. **Bed and bath** Bathtubs in all but four rooms (which have showers), Molton Brown toiletries, some four-poster beds. **Favorites** They're all different, but they're all nice. If you want a lot of space, look for the ground-floor room, or any of the suites. The rooms at front have marvelous large windows. **Comfort and decor** Very comfortable, colorful, and attractive.

PAYMENT, RESERVATIONS, AND RESTRICTIONS

Deposit Credit card; 48-hour cancellation policy. **Credit cards** All major. **Check-in/out** 2 p.m./noon. **Pets** Some small dogs allowed. **Elevator** Yes. **Children** Yes. **Disabled access** No, the front steps are an impediment to wheelchairs or cane users.

The Portobello Hotel

OVERALL ★★★½   QUALITY ★★★★   VALUE ★★★   PRICE RANGE £170–£190

22 Stanley Gardens, Notting Hill Gate, W11; ☎ 0207-727-2777; fax 0207-792-9641; www.portobello-hotel.co.uk

This is a trendy place with corporate accounts held by a number of modeling, music, and film agencies. Check out their roster of celebrity clients on the Web site—it's A-list all the way. It's in an old Victorian terrace house, and the rooms are completely different from one another, and admirably so. The rooms in the rear look out over a communal garden into which you may not go, but which provides a sublime view. The Portobello has a lot of charm, with whimsical, Asian-accented, and traditional decor blending nicely. There's a sitting room that looks out over the garden, where you may eat or have cocktails. Continental breakfast is included in the price and can be delivered to your room. The ambience is pleasant, especially if you get one of the larger rooms, but the singles are cell-like, despite the gracious decor, and there is no space to do anything other than sleep. The most imposing room, number 16, features a big round bed and a balcony overlooking the garden; there's a deep antique copper bathtub right in the room, a saucy invitation to romance. Number 13 has a huge, high four-poster bed that requires a footstool to mount. The hotel is within walking distance of Portobello Road, which makes it good for committed Portobello and Kensington Church Street shoppers, but it's not terribly well situated for general sightseeing due to its distance from public transportation. Of course, limo drivers know the address well, and the hotel can arrange transportation and any service you require.

SETTINGS AND FACILITIES

Nearest tube station Notting Hill Gate. **Quietness rating** A. **Dining** Very small breakfast room. **Amenities** Tiny basement restaurant with a few tables for breakfast and lunch; drawing room with fireplace and view of garden; health-club facilities are a four-minute walk away; computer in most rooms. **Services** Concierge, room service, continental breakfast sent to room, laundry, all business services.

ACCOMMODATIONS

Rooms 24. **All rooms** Telephone, high-speed modem, satellite TV. **Some rooms** Balcony, couches, minibar, air-conditioning, four-poster. **Bed and bath** Beds are comfy; baths range from a huge clawfoot tub to tiny shower stalls, but all are clean and user friendly. **Favorites** Number 16, with the balcony overlooking the garden and the big round bed, is everyone's favorite. I also like the garden-view Asian-style number 46. The single number 38 is very small, but has a good feeling to it. The first-floor rooms with the large French windows are spacious and fine. **Comfort and decor** The decoration here is extraordinary and includes a range of furnishings, from traditional English antiques to exotic Asian and Middle Eastern treasures. Comfort is as high a priority as style.

PAYMENT, RESERVATIONS, AND RESTRICTIONS

Deposit Credit card; 48-hour cancellation policy. **Credit cards** All major. **Check-in/out** After noon/noon. **Pets** Not allowed for a long stay, but they could hardly turn away the best friends of the rich and famous. **Elevator** Yes, but only to third floor. **Children** Yes. **Disabled access** No.

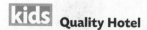 **Quality Hotel**

OVERALL ★★	QUALITY ★★½	VALUE ★★★★	PRICE RANGE £116–£132

82–83 Eccleston Square, Victoria, SW1; ☎ 0207-834-8042; fax 0207-630-8942; www.hotels-westminster.com

The hotel is standard, without even a whisper of charisma or glamour, but the rooms are tidy and reasonably sized, and it's got two big attractions for families: the garden square across the street and the Play Station in the room. There is a small restaurant and a self-service coffee area. There's a fax/Internet laptop in the lobby for your use, as well as wireless access for your own laptop, a sitting area, and a bar that opens at 5 p.m. Guests can request a key to the private Eccleston Square, a leafy garden with benches and flora across the street. You can also walk to many of the great sights of London, such as Westminster Abbey and Buckingham Palace. There are many promotional deals offered in conjunction with the Choice Hotels Europe Group, which has over 3,000 hotels worldwide.

SETTINGS AND FACILITIES

Nearest tube station Victoria. **Quietness rating** A/B. **Dining** Connaught's Brasserie serves breakfast, lunch, and dinner. **Amenities** Dining room, bar, airport transfer, key to private gardens across the street, nonsmoking rooms. **Services** Reception functions as concierge, limited room service, bellhop, laundry.

ACCOMMODATIONS

Rooms 107. **All rooms** Telephone, wireless access and modem, interactive satellite TV (with Play Station), ceiling fans, iron, tea and coffee, writing desk. **Some rooms** Minibar; some triples have two rooms. **Bed and bath** Standard middle-brow hotel style. **Favorites** Go for a premier double or triple. **Comfort and decor** Standard hotel style, inoffensive and clean.

PAYMENT, RESERVATIONS, AND RESTRICTIONS

Deposit Credit card. **Credit cards** All major. **Check-in/out** 2 p.m./noon. **Pets** Small pets allowed conditionally. **Elevator** Yes. **Children** Yes. **Disabled access** Steps outside, but people to help.

The Radisson Edwardian Hampshire

OVERALL ★★★★   QUALITY ★★★★   VALUE ★★½   PRICE RANGE £199–£234

31-36 Leicester Square, WC2; ☎ 0207-839-9399, toll free in U.S. ☎ 800-333-3333; fax 0207-930-8122; www.radissonedwardian.com

Housed in a magnificent building right on Leicester Square behind the half-price theater-ticket booth, The Hampshire is a four-star hotel run by the Radisson group. It has all the amenities you'd expect from a four-star inn, though, as with so many of London's hotels, not quite as much space in some of the standard rooms as you would want. The rooms are well appointed, and there's a kind of Asian theme to the decor. The lobby is gorgeous (check out the grandfather clock), with walnut paneling everywhere, offering a quiet sitting place far from the madding crowds of Leicester Square, yet with them still interestingly in view. There's a bar, a restaurant, and Oscar's Wine Bar with seating right on the square from which you can watch the milling crowds. There's a small fitness room with a few cardio-vascular machines and free weights. The four-poster bedrooms are beautiful, and all the junior suites are of a reasonable size, at an unreasonable price (£458!). Some of the rooms have views over Trafalgar Square in the back and Leicester Square in front. Leicester Square isn't for everyone; it's noisy and people packed, and the sleaze factor can be high on the weekends after the pubs close. Ask about Radisson-related deals, but forget the theater packages: you have the official London theater half-price ticket books (known as "tkts") outside your door. There are so many variables in price at the Radisson hotels, we hesitate to even list the costs. Call or visit the Web site to see what a wide array of prices they have.

SETTINGS AND FACILITIES

Nearest tube station Leicester Square. **Quietness rating** Triple glazing in the windows on the Leicester Square side makes those desirable rooms quiet, but beware of the occasional Carnival Fair in the square—you may want to hole up in the back. **Dining** Apex Bar & Restaurant, and Oscar's Wine Bar. **Amenities** Small fitness room, bathrobes, telephones in bathrooms, fully air-conditioned. **Services** Concierge, 24-hour room service, bellhop, laundry, business support, online check-in.

ACCOMMODATIONS

Rooms 124. **All rooms** Telephones, high-speed modems, minibar, satellite TV, in-house movies, air-conditioning, hair dryer, bathrobe, tea and coffee, iron, writing desk. **Some rooms** Four-posters, views, floor-to-ceiling windows. **Bed and bath** High quality. **Favorites** The four-poster suite with a view over Trafalgar Square. Junior suites are also great. **Comfort and decor** Five-star-hotel-style comforts and interesting decor, mixing 18th-century reproductions with Asian artwork.

PAYMENT, RESERVATIONS, AND RESTRICTIONS

Deposit Credit card; 24-hour cancellation policy. **Credit cards** All major. **Check-in/out** 2 p.m./11 a.m. **Pets** Not allowed. **Elevator** Yes. **Children** Yes. **Disabled access** Yes.

 The Rembrandt Hotel

OVERALL ★★★   **QUALITY** ★★★   **VALUE** ★★★★½   **PRICE RANGE £116–£215**

11 Thurloe Place, South Kensington, SW7; ☎ 0207-589-8100; fax 0207-225-3476; www.sarova.co.uk

The three main reasons to stay at the Rembrandt are location, location, location. It's across the street from the Victoria and Albert and a hop, skip, and jump from the Science Museum, the Natural History Museum, and Harrods. It is also a four-minute walk to the South Kensington tube station, where one can access the Piccadilly (which goes to Heathrow), Circle, and District lines. There are three useful buses within shouting distance, and taxis are a breeze to hail. The hotel has a pleasant feeling to it, with a big lobby that has a fireplace, bar service, and plenty of couches to go around. The rooms are nice enough, but without much character at all, and only the executive rooms have air-conditioning. Reservation clerks usually advise Americans to go for the double executive room since they're accustomed to lots of space. Breakfast may be included in your rate, and is always very hearty, served in the Masters Restaurant. On most Sundays, there's an antique fair in the rooms off the lobby, with everything from silverware to jewelry, and some interesting inexpensive bits and bobs. I never miss it (I live next door); look for an attractive woman named Kit who has the best deals there. The Aquilla is the attached health club, and they have a small and very warm pool that welcomes children most times of the day.

Kids will also like the nearness of the museums, especially on weekends when there are children's adventure activities on offer. The Rembrandt attracts a lot of business conferences, and is at the top of many package tours' hotel lists. Ask about upgrading rooms.

SETTINGS AND FACILITIES

Nearest tube station South Kensington. **Quietness rating** A rear and top floors; D/F front lower floors (double glazing is not 100% effective). **Dining** The Masters Restaurant serves traditional breakfast, lunch, and dinner. **Amenities** Lobby with bar and fireplace, big dining room and small conservatory, tour bus pick-up, health club with small pool (£7.50 charge, unless it's included in your rate), conference rooms, professional business services. **Services** Concierge, 24-hour room service, bellhop, laundry, fax and Internet in lobby, babysitting.

ACCOMMODATIONS

Rooms 195; two floors nonsmoking. **All rooms** Telephone, satellite TV, in-house movies, minibar on request, tea and coffee, hair dryer, writing desk. **Some rooms** Air-conditioning, high-speed modem, iron, bidet, sitting area. **Bed and bath** Beds are so-so; bathrooms are clean and good-sized by London standards. Jacuzzi on request for executive doubles. **Favorites** Executive-double front rooms on first floor facing Victoria and Albert Museum—you can admire the statues that you can't see so well from street level. The only drawbacks to these rooms are the roar of traffic and bus fumes. **Comfort and decor** The lobby is appealing, with a fireplace and plenty of seating, as well as a bar, but the rooms are dull and unremarkable. The decor could be described as unimaginative but safe.

PAYMENT, RESERVATIONS, AND RESTRICTIONS

Deposit Credit card; 48-hour cancellation policy. **Credit cards** All major. **Check-in/out** 2 p.m./noon; express checkout available. **Pets** Not allowed. **Elevator** Two. **Children** Yes. **Disabled access** Yes, but with three front stairs to be negotiated; doormen will gladly help.

The Rookery

OVERALL ★★★★   QUALITY ★★★½   VALUE ★★½   PRICE RANGE £264–£323

Peter's Lane, Cowcross Street, Clerkenwell, EC1; ☎ 0207-336-0931; fax 0207-336-0931; www.rookeryhotel.com

The Rookery is a charming hotel owned by the talented team of Peter McKay and Douglas Blain, who brought you the period authenticity of The Gore and Hazlitt's. Part of its authenticity is the absence of an elevator for the four floors. If it had an elevator, the value and quality ratings wouldn't be as low as they are, as I can't wrap my head around spending that kind of money if stairs were at all a problem for me. The hotel is in Clerkenwell, a short distance from the City, which makes it perfect for the businessperson. This is not the usual area where tourists stay, but it is definitely a viable choice, especially if you have an interest in the "real" historic London. Dr. Johnson would find himself completely lost in the postwar city of London, but you should be able to navigate from the hotel to St. Paul's Cathedral or the Old Bailey (both of which are visible from some of the hotel's windows). However, it is not only the neighborhood that lends appeal; the building itself is a conglomeration of restored 18th-century town houses that make for an intimate, delightful accommodation. All the modern conveniences are here, but they pale next to the glories of the past carefully culled from auction houses, flea markets, and antiques markets that litter the place. Like Hazlitt's, the exterior gives no hint of what wonders lie within: the old brick buildings are nondescript, located down a little lane and through an alley that cows used to cross making their fatal way to the Smithfield Meat Market. Look for lanterns and a discreet sign—no waving banners here. There are two common areas: a library and a conservatory that looks out onto a little garden. The rooms are of a decent size, and the bathrooms are unique. A great choice for the businessperson, the antiques freak, or one in search of a very good representation of old London. Weekend breaks are more affordable, as are some other deals; check the Web site or call.

SETTINGS AND FACILITIES

Nearest tube station Farringdon. **Quietness rating** A. **Dining** No. **Amenities** Conservatory, meeting rooms, personal safes in each room; you can take your breakfast in the lounge or in your room. **Services** Concierge, 18-hour room service, bellhop, laundry.

ACCOMMODATIONS

Rooms 33. **All rooms** Telephone, high-speed modem, satellite TV, fans on request, hair dryer, writing desk, personal safe. **Some rooms** Views, four-poster. **Bed and bath** Amazing. **Favorites** The Rook's Nest has a view of St. Paul's and the Old Bailey, and if you squint your eyes to remove the modern eyesores, you can really get the measure of Old London town. **Comfort and decor** Of the highest quality on both scores, except for the lack of an elevator.

PAYMENT, RESERVATIONS, AND RESTRICTIONS

Deposit Credit card; 48-hour cancellation policy. **Credit cards** All major. **Check-in/out** 1:30 p.m./11:30 a.m. **Pets** Not allowed. **Elevator** No. **Children** Yes. **Disabled access** No.

Royal Adelphi Hotel

OVERALL ★	QUALITY ★	VALUE ★★★	PRICE RANGE £68–£90

21 Villiers Street, Embankment, WC2; ☎ **0207-930-8764; fax 0207-930-8735; www.royaladelphi.co.uk**

This is a budget hotel that I think has enough going for it that people who are indifferent to their surroundings will find it a good deal in a great location. And by great location, I mean one in the throbbing center of London: there's a comedy club across the street, the famous club Heaven is on the same street, Trafalgar Square is a heartbeat away, and the distractions and attractions of South Bank are a quick walk across the bridge. If loud drunks at 3 a.m. are not your cup of tea, stop reading. If backpacker/college dorm is not your style, move on. If you're willing to share a bathroom for sixty-eight quid a night, or have your own private loo for £90, this is the place. You need to be strong enough and game enough to carry your own luggage up stairs (no lift); you're bound to get a fair amount of exercise here.

If you limit yourself to attractions in the West End, Soho, Covent Garden, Westminster, and South Bank, you will be kept completely entertained without having to spend money on transportation. OK, now that I've scared off the cream puffs, let me say that there's a nice, we're-all-in-it-together vibe at the Royal Adelphi, and you'll find strangers with backpacks comparing travelers' tall tales at the 24-hour bar (for hotel guests only) into the wee hours. Embankment Gardens just down the street are beautifully kept, with green deck chairs for rent, and lots of benches and green grass. It's perfect for a picnic of food-to-go picked up at any of the cheap and cheerful take-away shops and cafés that line this stretch of Villiers Street (there's a Starbucks at the foot of the street). At midday, the street and the park fill up with office workers having lunch or catching some rays. You may well ask if this hotel is so basic and borderline gritty, why does it cost twice as much as some of the other backpacker specials? I can answer that in those three magic words: location, location, location.

SETTINGS AND FACILITIES

Nearest tube station Embankment or Charing Cross. **Quietness** F in front, C in the back. **Dining** Breakfast only (included in price). **Amenities** Good location; cheap sleeps; 24-hour hotel guests–only bar; tiny lounge. **Services** Not much to speak of.

ACCOMMODATIONS

Rooms 47. **All rooms** Telephone, terrestrial TV, hair dryer, tea- and coffee-making facilities. **Some rooms** Very noisy, no windows. **Bed and bath** Spartan—bring your own sheets if you require cotton. **Favorites** On the lower floor, with a window. **Comfort and decor** Being improved all the time.

PAYMENT, RESERVATIONS, AND RESTRICTIONS

Deposit Credit card; 48-hour cancellation policy. **Credit cards** All major. **Check-in/out** 2 p.m./11 a.m. **Pets** Not allowed. **Elevator** No. **Children** Yes, but not if you have to carry them. **Disabled access** No.

Ruskin Hotel

OVERALL ★   QUALITY ★★½   VALUE ★★★★★   PRICE RANGE £62–£77

23–24 Montague Street, Bloomsbury, WC1; ☎ 0207-636-7388; fax 0207-323-1662; www.accomodata.co.uk

The Ruskin Hotel has been run by the same Spanish family for the past 22 years, and it has very much the feel of an inexpensive hotel in Barcelona. It also has the loyalty of many return customers. Unlike many of the budget bed-and-breakfasts in London, the Ruskin has an elevator to all floors, accepts all major credit cards, and is clean and friendly. The owner is not interested in customers who want to argue about services and room size, but is happy to house the kind of sensible souls who welcome a square deal that's across the street from the British Museum (the rooms in front have a view of the museum's side). The sitting room has a beautiful painting from 1801 by John Ward, a painter for the Duke of Bedford, whose estate still owns all the land around here. The house is quite old, having started out as a private residence before it served as a warren of offices where Sir Arthur Conan Doyle was reputed to have worked on his Sherlock Holmes stories. For a no-frills

B&B/budget hotel with breakfast included, the Ruskin is a good bet. The single rooms have no en suite toilets; you will need to get a double for that, and indeed at £62, you should (singles start at £43).

SETTINGS AND FACILITIES

Nearest tube station Russell Square. **Quietness rating** A in back, B in front (double-glazed windows help). **Dining** Breakfast room. **Amenities** Breakfast included; generous portions served by waiters in a nice breakfast room. **Services** *Se habla español;* they can manage a few other languages as well.

ACCOMMODATIONS

Rooms 33; 6 with shower and toilet. **All rooms** Telephone, hair dryer, tea and coffee. **Some rooms** Garden view, bathroom. **Bed and bath** Both communal and private bathrooms are in good shape; the beds are comfortable, though the doubles might be a squeeze for large Americans. **Favorites** Number 102 is a pleasant family room. **Comfort and decor** The exuberance of the many plants and flowers on the outside may betray the utilitarian decor within: strip lights over beds, Naugahyde, fake wood, and plastic furniture. Sensitive souls might shrivel at the decor, frankly, but if you can close your eyes to it, you might find time to admire certain features, like friezes and the sitting room mural.

PAYMENT, RESERVATIONS, AND RESTRICTIONS

Deposit One night nonrefundable, unless they can re-let room. **Credit cards** All major. **Check-in/out** 1 p.m./11:30 a.m. **Pets** Not allowed. **Elevator** Yes. **Children** Yes. **Disabled access** Yes.

kids St. Margaret's Hotel

OVERALL ★★   **QUALITY** ★★½   **VALUE** ★★★★★   **PRICE RANGE** £65.50–£97

26 Bedford Place, Russell Square, Bloomsbury, WC1; ☎ 0207-636-4277; fax 0207-323-3066; www.stmargaretshotel.co.uk

This is a place that you can't help but like, even if it has no frills. What it lacks in amenities and style, it more than makes up for in good intentions, friendliness, amazingly low prices, and a very fine dining room overlooking some lovely gardens, which you are welcome to enjoy at any time. It's an enormous old house, with staircases leading to unexpected areas, and the genial ambience of an old-school (and Anglicized) *penzione*, appropriately, as the owners are Italian. The senior Marazzis bought the house when they arrived in London after World War II, and their son and his bride took it over. Mrs. Marazzi's daughter has stepped into the ancestral business, which makes it a real family affair and a labor of love, which you can really feel. The place is informal and very clean, and although most of the single rooms don't have en suite bathrooms, the shared conveniences are spotless. It's got many rooms, which are renovated on a revolving basis, so there are always improvements being made. This is the kind of inexpensive hotel that people continue to come to time and time again for the feeling of community, the friendliness, the garden in back, the British Museum around the corner, the relative spaciousness of the rooms, and the sensible cost. Be warned, though, that this is a low-cost, bed-and-breakfast-type hotel—if you're looking for swanky decor and four- or five-star service, you need to pay a lot more than they're charging. However, they are amenable to helping you out with whatever you need, be it tourist tips, travel advisories, or electrical connections. Also be warned that there are lots of stairs and no elevator. Since all the rooms are so different, with different amenities, call or e-mail to discuss the options. Triples are £91.50–£108.50; singles are £53.50–£76.

SETTINGS AND FACILITIES

Nearest tube station Russell Square. **Quietness rating** A. **Dining** A bright and very pleasant dining room overlooking gardens (for breakfast only, which is included in the price). **Amenities** Breakfast in dining room, tea and coffee served anytime, safe in office, fax available for use. **Services** 24-hour receptionist.

ACCOMMODATIONS

Rooms 64; 12 with en suite bathrooms, more planned for future. Most singles have no toilet at present. **All rooms** Telephone (which you can use with a phone card to get your own dial-up Internet service for your laptop), BBC TV, sink. **Some rooms** En suite bathrooms, hair dryers, French doors and high ceilings, view of gardens. **Bed and bath** Beds are reasonably comfortable; baths are spotless in both communal and en suite bathrooms. **Favorites** Number 53 is a room that looks over the garden and features a glassed-in conservatory. Book this one well in advance, as it is the favorite of regulars. Number 40 is a fine family room with enough space for four to sleep comfortably, as is number 45. **Rooms** on the first floor all have high ceilings and tall French windows. **Comfort and decor** The decor is utilitarian and might offend very sensitive souls or those used to the Ritz. It feels like a place your sensible, thrifty grandma would have for a family haven.

PAYMENT, RESERVATIONS, AND RESTRICTIONS

Deposit One night's charge, £6 administration fee for cancellation at any time. **Credit cards** All major. **Check-in/out** Check in whenever room is available; out at noon. **Pets** Not allowed. **Elevator** No. **Children** Yes. **Disabled access** There are two rooms on ground floor, but there are steps to reception. Not good for wheelchairs, as there are no porters.

Strand Palace Hotel

OVERALL ★★½	QUALITY ★★½	VALUE ★★★	PRICE RANGE £110–£190

372 Strand, Covent Garden, WC2; ☎ 0207-836-8080; fax 0207-836-2077; www.strandpalacehotel.co.uk

The Strand Palace Hotel is smack in the middle of the Strand, directly in front of the delights of Covent Garden, a stone's throw from the National and the National Portrait Galleries, Trafalgar Square, St. Martins-in-the-Fields, Somerset House, three streets from the Thames (with only a river and a bridge between you and the fun of South Bank), and strolling distance to all the theaters of the West End (including two theaters you could do cartwheels to without getting out of breath). Besides all the culture, there's a heavy concentration of shops, banks, restaurants, historic pubs, and transportation links right outside your door. OK, so the location is great—what about the hotel? Well, charming it isn't. First of all, it's a megalith of a building, occupying about a block around, built back when

hotels were like small cities, making the most of the new miracle of elevators. It reminds me of the kind of hotel you would find in New York City or
Chicago in the 1940s and 50s, and is strangely comforting in its smooth
anonymity and abundance of rooms (783 rooms on 9 floors).

Unlike the popular boutique hotels (whose creation was in part a reaction
against these kinds of giants), there's no pretense here that it's some kind of
gentleman's club town house or family home; it's a big darn hotel, and that's
all it aims to be. Despite the great location and reasonable rates, there are
some justified complaints: It's certainly short on atmosphere; there's no air-
conditioning in most standard rooms; tiny single rooms should be avoided,
even if you're alone; there are five bars and restaurants, none of which are
that great; they haven't double-glazed all the windows, so it can be noisy (and
noisy from within—some walls are thinner than others); and check-in can be
as difficult as in the precomputer age. The biggest complaints about this hotel can be traced to its size: service is uneven, with too few workers to too
many guests; the occasional cold food from room service; and the nightmare
of tour buses checking in and out at all hours. Let's face it, if you really want
to stay in a smart London hotel in this area, you're going to have to fork over
the dough to stay at the Savoy across the street (rooms start at £270). But if
you love the neighborhood, or have business there, this is a plain-jane option
that always has deals and upgrades that might get you into one of the superior rooms that do have air-conditioning, Internet access, bearable decor, etc.
The recent renovation has helped a lot; while the rooms are still workmanlike
and basic at the standard level, the pricier rooms have a few more things going for them. The "Club" rooms offer a bit more than the standard rooms,
and you get access to a private lounge with wide-screen television and high-
speed modem access (the two don't seem to go together somehow). Superior Club rooms go much further with the amenities: in-room Internet access,
more space, and a free newspaper and pay-per-view movie each day. There
are a rash of chairs in the lobby (which looks like a *lobby*, not your Aunt
Matilda's drawing room) arranged strangely like a waiting room at an airport,
and the ambience is one of functionality. There are many interconnecting
rooms for families. The big advantage of a big hotel is that it has a lot of
rooms to fill, and you can always hit upon a deal or two. Read your bill carefully (don't get charged for a breakfast you didn't sign up for), and be sure to
bring your confirmation number if you book over the Internet or phone.

SETTINGS AND FACILITIES

Nearest tube station Charing Cross. **Quietness** C to D; rooms on the Strand are
the worst. **Dining** 372 The Strand: traditional English carvery buffet; Johnston's
Café & Bar; Biacones: Italian café and bar; Diva: coffee, snacks, and drinks; The
Mask Bar: cocktail bar; Hops! Bar; pub with music and a sports screen. **Amenities**
Breakfast included in some rates, minibars in some rooms. **Services** Concierge;
24-hour room service, bellhop, laundry.

ACCOMMODATIONS

Rooms 783. **All rooms** Telephone, TV, hair dryer, tea/coffee facilities. **Some
rooms** Air-conditioning, Internet access, a free newspaper and pay-per-view
movie each day. **Bed and bath** Standard hotel fare, nothing special, but clean and

functional. **Favorites** Superior Club rooms. **Comfort and decor**: Uninspiring decor, reasonable comfort.

PAYMENT, RESERVATIONS, AND RESTRICTIONS

Deposit Credit card; cancellation policy by 2 p.m. local time on day of booked arrival. **Credit cards** All major. **Check-in/out** 1 p.m./11:30 a.m. **Pets** Not allowed. **Elevator** Yes. **Children** Yes. **Disabled access** Yes.

Thistle Hotel Victoria

OVERALL ★★★★★   QUALITY ★★★★   VALUE ★★★★   PRICE RANGE £221–£232

Buckingham Palace Road, Victoria, SW1; ☎ 0207-834-9494; fax 0207-630-1978; www.thistlehotels.com

First of all, do not be afraid of the above rack rates; there's almost always a deal to be had. Most of you know that Thistle has frequent flier tie-ins, special rates and packages, and all manner of deals. You may also know that Thistle hotels run from the sublime to prison cell block, depending on the property they buy. Well, here they got lucky: this is one of those massive, grand Victorian terminus hotels that makes your eyes pop when you enter it, and by the time you reach the middle of the vast dome with the huge chandelier swinging from it, you've unconsciously straightened your posture. The hotel was built to accommodate the visitors coming to see the Great Exhibition of 1851, and it was built to impress, in the way Victorian England was so superior at pulling off (or so abhorred for, depending on your taste). There are stained-glass windows, wrought-iron staircases, columns, marble floors and walls, carved busts on stands or in alcoves outside and in, potted plants, and huge windows. The rooms are in excellent shape, the common areas are impressive, and the Galleria, which extends the already huge lobby to a second floor up, is one of the grandest hotel sitting areas in London. The hotel provides all the services one can expect from a hotel group with global standards: high-speed modems, fax on request, satellite TV, nonsmoking floors, complimentary newspapers, business support, and so on. It's near Victoria, Westminster Abbey, and Buckingham Palace—a central location that's noisy during the day. The rear rooms have unfortunate views over Victoria Station, but they are quiet. There are two sections: the "new" wing, built in the 1870s, has more standard-size rooms, whereas the old wing was built at a time when a guest required a couple of rooms plus one for the maid or valet, so this wing suffers from a rather knocked-together disparity of room size.

SETTINGS AND FACILITIES

Nearest tube station Victoria. **Quietness rating** A in back, C in front, D in lower floors with huge windows, but that doesn't stop people from requesting these rooms again and again. **Dining** Very stately dining room, big enough to seat the occupants of the whole hotel; Harvard Bar; Galleria and lounge for tea and meals. **Amenities** The above refreshment areas, modems, many different pillows available, newspaper. **Services** Concierge, 24-hour room service, bellhop, laundry.

ACCOMMODATIONS

Rooms 357. **All rooms** Telephone, high-speed modem, satellite TV, hair dryer, iron, tea and coffee, in-house movies, writing desk. **Some rooms** Minibar, four-poster and half-tester (half a four-poster, with canopy) beds, separate sitting room, huge windows, and high ceilings. **Bed and bath** 100% cotton sheets on the bed, and you can request special hypoallergenic, foam, or 100% down pillows. The bathrooms are good. **Favorites** The big rooms at the front in the old wing with the big windows—noisy, but gorgeous. **Comfort and decor** High quality; all rooms individually decorated in nice colors and furniture.

PAYMENT, RESERVATIONS, AND RESTRICTIONS
Deposit Credit card. **Credit cards** All major. **Check-in/out** 2 p.m./noon. **Pets** Dogs allowed conditionally. **Elevator** Yes. **Children** Yes. **Disabled access** No; many steps.

Threadneedles Hotel

OVERALL ★★★★½   **QUALITY** ★★★★½   **VALUE** ★★★   **PRICE RANGE** £193–£392

**5 Threadneedle Street, The City, EC2; ☎ 0207-657-8080;
fax 0207-657-8100; www.theetoncollection.com**

The City's financial square miles have long needed more hotels, or at least more charming hotels. This grand boutique hotel, the first luxury hotel in the City, fits the bill admirably, if expensively (with nonbusiness rates on weekends and some seasonal discounts for us noncorporate sponsees.) *Condé Nast Traveler* magazine called it the hottest hotel of 2003, and the praise went straight to the head of the Eton Group, who immediately opened two others in London, both equally boutique-y but less business-oriented (see page 105 and page 95 for The Colonnade and Academy Bloomsbury hotels). Once a grandiose bank built in 1856, its sympathetic renovation borders on code-pendence, so many magnificent period details have they kept: the colonnades at the base of the stained glass atrium, the wood paneling, and the strong scent of money. It's hardly a cheap hotel, as you can see by the prices, which reflect the big difference between weekend and weekday rates (rack rate for weekdays is £245 plus VAT) and may have been better placed in the luxury hotel section of this chapter, but the weekend rates make it a nice kind of outing, despite the quiet streets and closed businesses that are standard for the City on weekends. It's a three-minute walk from the Bank Tube, and within hailing distance of St. Paul's and other old churches, the Monument, the Barbicon, the Museum of London, and it is, of course, a neighbor of the august and imposing Bank of England. Although it has some weekday restrictions on hosting children, they are welcome on weekends, and they do have a couple of interconnecting rooms that will suit a family nicely. A recently built health spa/gym was added to their other amenities, such as the restaurant and top-of-the-line business/conference facilities. Bonds Restaurant & Bar has got the lion's share of the City's lunch and cocktail crowd of traders and bankers; hang out after bank hours and you might overhear some up-to-the-minute financial news. This is a top-grade hotel, with all the friendly service and efficient care for your comfort that you should expect from a luxury boutique hotel in the global financial center of England.

SETTINGS AND FACILITIES
Nearest tube station Bank. **Quietness** B, even in front thanks to double-glazed windows, C with windows open. **Dining** Bond's Restaurant & Bar for breakfast,

lunch, and dinner. **Amenities** Newspapers, bathrobes, safe, bottled water, break-fast included with some rates, fitness center, well-stocked minibar. **Services** concierge, 24-hour room service, bellhop, laundry, complimentary shoe shine, all business-center facilities and services.

ACCOMMODATIONS

Rooms 70. All rooms Telephone with voice mail, high-speed modem and wire-less Internet access, air-conditioning, satellite TV, CD player and music library, bathrobe and slippers, big desk. **Some rooms** Views of St. Paul's and the City. **Bed and bath** Frette bed linen, duck down pillows and duvet. Limestone bathrooms with chrome and glass features, bathtubs with Jacuzzi jets, upscale toiletries. **Favorites** Penthouse with great view of St Paul's. **Comfort and decor** Very high standards of excellence, with every comfort provided. But if you're looking for Jolly Olde England, you'd best keep moving: the decor is all about careful down-lighting, soothing hues, and no clutter; it's minimalist in its simplicity and elegance, but somehow warmer than you'd expect.

The Zetter Restaurant & Rooms

OVERALL ★★★★   QUALITY ★★★★   VALUE ★★★★   PRICE RANGE £130–£155

St. John's Square, 86–88 Clerkenwell Road, Clerkenwell, EC1;
☎ **0207-324-4444; fax 0207-324-4445; www.thezetter.com**

In the months following the opening of this hip new hotel in March 2004, major travel reviewers (*New York Times, Condé Nast Traveler, Elle Decoration, Time Out London,* and most of the local papers) went into paroxysms of praise for this delightful, quirky, trendy boutique hotel that doesn't cost the moon. The brain child of Mark Sainsbury (he of the supermarket dynasty) and Michael Benyan (hotshot London restaurateur), this hotel and restaurant have sealed Clerkenwell's recent reputation as a very hap-pening place. As one of the reviewers said, you would have to be a very grumpy person indeed not to be charmed by The Zetter. The pink neon "Z" outside announces its intention to amuse you with retro chic, and the Scandinavian purity of the decor tells you they won't waste your time on Olde English frippery. And the prices let you know they aren't going to mug you, no matter how popular or trendy the hotel may be: the founders' most important goal was "sensible prices."

A huge renovation was done on this old East End warehouse, carving a a five-story atrium into the heart of the building, with the rooms grouped around it; it lets in light that none of the former warehouse workers would have believed possible. The rooms are quite modern and sharp-edged, with vintage fabric swathes providing a splash of color and pattern for a calm focal point. This being London, the standard rooms (at £130) are small, or perhaps compact is a better description, because they aren't depressing. The beds are deluxe, as are the sheets and toiletries (from Bare-foot Botanicals). The products available in the tongue-in-cheek yet useful vending machines on each floor are top of the line: forget the pretzels, how about a disposable camera, a half bottle of champagne, gin and tonic, or the more standard toothbrushes and toothpaste? Zetter's Restaurant and

Bar occupies the ground floor and is bathed in light from the atrium by day, and at night flattering soft pink lighting makes everything—and everyone—look gorgeous (you can also switch the bedrooms' lights to pink, the advantage of which increases with age). The rooms all offer interactive TV with broadband Internet access, movies on demand, and other such modern conveniences that will keep you from feeling cramped or unhappy. The penthouses go way out on a limb, with wraparound floor-to-ceiling windows and terraces, plenty of amenities and lots of space. I love the Penguin Classic books on hand in each room, and the hot pink water bottles are a goof. You will feel as if you've stepped into an episode of *The Jetsons* or *Playboy After Dark* in the funny lounge with retro 1960s chairs. The whole establishment will make you smile, even if, like me, you are a devotee of a more bounteously cluttered, antique atmosphere.

SETTINGS AND FACILITIES

Nearest tube station Farringdon. **Quietness rating** B/D, quiet in rear rooms, noisy in front if windows are open; but double glazing helps a lot. **Dining** Zetter Restaurant, breakfast, lunch, afternoon tea, and dinner; mostly Italian menu. **Amenities** Newspapers; bathrobes; interactive TV with broadband access; movies on demand; 4,000 CD tracks to choose from; collection of Penguin Classics; associated with nearby health club; vending machines in halls with quality amenities; wheelchair access room on each floor. **Services** Concierge; room service, bellhop, laundry, business facilities, touring Clerkenwell packages, weekend packages.

ACCOMMODATIONS

Rooms 59. **All rooms** Telephone with voice mail, satellite and Internet-ready interactive TV, movies on demand, hair dryer, bathrobe, hot water bottle. **Some rooms** Terrace, minibar, bathtub with Jacuzzi jets. **Bed and bath** Sleek and modern, with bath products from Barefoot Botanicals; high-quality beds, good linen, down pillows and duvets. **Favorites** The penthouses. **Comfort and decor** Surprisingly comfortable for such a rigorously modern and iconoclastic place; the decor is amusingly eccentric.

PAYMENT, RESERVATIONS, AND RESTRICTIONS

Deposit Credit card; 24-hour cancellation policy. **Credit cards** All major. **Check-in/out** 2 p.m./noon. **Pets** Not allowed. **Elevator** Yes. **Children** Yes. **Disabled access** Full disabled access with one room on each floor for wheelchair users.

PART FOUR

ARRIVING *and* GETTING ORIENTED

ENTERING *the* COUNTRY

ARRIVAL CARDS MUST BE FILLED OUT BY those without an EU, Irish, or British passport, and each member of the family must complete one. You will be (or should have been) issued an arrival card by the cabin crew on the plane; make sure it has been filled out, and stick it in your passport. Immigration takes these cards seriously; be sure to give the complete address of where you'll be staying. If for some reason they don't give you the landing cards on board, you can get them at the counters or personnel at immigration. Don't wait till you reach the immigration desk; get it done before your turn. The walk from plane to immigration may be very long, so try to keep your carry-on luggage light and easy to handle.

IMMIGRATION

KEEP YOUR EYES ON THE SIGNS AND MAKE sure you are heading for the right immigration line. If you have been traveling in first or business class, you can usually head straight for the Fast Track line and show your Fast Track Pass or boarding ticket. Fast Tracks often close at night—check with the flight attendant so a closed Fast Track doesn't slow you down. There are two other lines: one for EU passport holders and one for all other nationalities. Have your passport and landing card ready, as the line can move pretty swiftly. You may be asked pointed questions about what you're doing here and where you're staying. Answer honestly and solemnly; immigration is a serious business in this country with national health service and other quality-of-life attractions, not to mention the threat of terrorism. Nationals from the United States, Canada, Australia, New Zealand, South Africa, Japan, or Switzerland can get in without a visa as long as they are on vacation. (If you are here on a job, you will need a work permit visa; students need a student visa. These visas must be obtained before arrival.) Other nationalities should check with the British consulate in their country before making plane reservations, or go to **www.britainusa.com** for visa information.

CUSTOMS

NEXT, YOU GO TO COLLECT YOUR BAGS. Grab a free trolley, and after you have retrieved your luggage, follow signs for customs. The Goods to Declare exit is red, the Nothing to Declare exit is green, and the European Union exit (for anyone arriving from the continent) is blue. For our readers who may be traveling abroad for the first time, you'll decide which exit to use based upon what you have brought along with you that was purchased outside England.

The guidelines for what you can bring into England are divided into two categories: one for goods bought within the European Union, and the other for items purchased outside the EU. The likelihood that you will bring large jewels or luxury goods to London is remote, but you may want to save some money by bringing in your own instruments of vice, bought for bargain-basement prices at the duty-free shop before leaving or on the plane during your flight. So, you may bring in, duty free:

- 200 cigarettes, 100 cigarillos, 50 cigars, or 250 grams of tobacco
- 2 liters of table wine and 1 liter of alcohol over 22% by volume (most spirits) and either 2 liters of alcohol under 22% by volume (fortified or sparkling wine or liqueurs) or 2 more liters of table wine
- 50 milliliters of perfume
- Other goods up to a value of £145 (about $250)

(In fact, these figures are the bottom line and the published official numbers. You will not be stopped and questioned if you happen to be carrying two or three cartons of cigs and a few bottles of vodka—they are reasonable people with grown-up attitudes here, and they can tell a big drinker or chain-smoker from a bootlegger or smuggler.) You may not bring in controlled drugs (any medication you have should be in its original bottle with your name on it), firearms and/or ammunition, obscene material, threats to public health and the environment, plants and vegetables, fresh meats, or any kind of animals.

unofficial **TIP**
If you have any questions about import and export issues, contact the Excise and Inland Customs Advice Centre (Her Majesty's Customs and Excise; ☎ 0845-010-9000, **www.hmce.gov.uk**).

If you have to pay duty, you can pay in pounds sterling or by MasterCard or Visa. You have rights, which Her Majesty's customs officers are supposed to make perfectly clear to you, such as receiving help in repacking bags if they make you unpack them, appealing on the spot to a senior officer against a proposed search, and claiming compensation if they have damaged any of your property. If you want to appeal a written tax or duty decision, let the officer know at the time. If you don't do so at the time, you must write to them within 45 days; they will give you a leaflet that explains how to appeal. If you have any complaints about how you were treated, you can get assistance from the Adjudicator's Office (Haymarket House, 28 Haymarket, London, SW1 4SP; ☎ 0207-930-2292; fax 0207-930-2298).

The customs hall is often unstaffed, or there will be only one or two people there. Assuming you have nothing to declare, march through the appropriate exit. There are large two-way mirrors in some of the airports here, and someone will definitely be watching. If you are stopped—occasionally random checks are carried out—*never* make jokes about the contents of your bags. You could be arrested, detained, and possibly deported. This is a nation that has had terrorist bombings for decades, and the officials are extremely and understandably jumpy. *Never* leave your bags unattended: especially these days, a left piece of luggage can result in the closure of the tube, the evacuation of an airport terminal or car park, and the controlled destruction of the left luggage.

If you don't have any English pounds to pay for your transportation from the airport, there are cash machines in all airports and train stations. They are known as "cashpoints" here, and they abound in London. Most of them are on the Cirrus or MacPlus system and will take money straight from your checking account at home. If you only have a credit card, make sure before you leave that you have a four-digit PIN for use in the cashpoints. There are seldom letters on the machines, so memorize your PIN numerically.

GETTING *into* LONDON

CAR RENTALS

CAR RENTAL COUNTERS ABOUND AT ALL the airports, with most of the major companies represented: Hertz, Avis, or Europcar. You can rent a car when you arrive if necessary, but it's best to reserve ahead. You must be over age 23 and have a valid license from your country. You will need to use a parking lot in London, as there are only metered spots and restricted parking on the streets. For reservations, visit **www.hertz.com, www.avis.com,** or **www.europcar.com.**

From Gatwick Airport (☎ 0870-000-2468)

IT'S A LONG DRIVE INTO LONDON FROM Gatwick, with a good chance of bad traffic. Taking a taxi to central London is not smart, as it can cost over £100, and can take well over an hour. By far the best way is the **Gatwick Express** (☎ 0845-850-1530, **www.gatwickexpress.co.uk**), which leaves every 15 minutes (between 5 a.m. and 1:35 a.m.) and takes you right to Victoria Station in half an hour, where you can catch a taxi, tube, or bus to your final destination. (After the trains stop running, you can catch a London-bound bus, which is also called a coach, outside the arrival hall.) Follow signs and take the escalator down to the platform. The Gatwick Express is clearly marked. You can pay on the train, where they take cash and most credit cards, or you can book a ticket ahead through the Web site; be sure to have your confirmation code. The fare is £12 one way, £23.50 round-trip, half price for children between the ages of 5 and 15, and free for children under age 5. Check the Web site for special offers, such as the four-for-two discount. Don't bother with first-class tickets; they're a rip-off.

South Eastern Trains (☎ 0845-000-2211, **www.setrains.co.uk**) has trains running every 15 minutes between Gatwick and Victoria, and although the trip takes slightly longer than the Gatwick Express, it costs less, at £8 one way, £15 round-trip during peak times; off-peak costs £8.30 round-trip (no one-way tickets sold).

Thameslink (☎ 0845-748-4950, **www.thames link.co.uk**) is another train line that has stops throughout the city: Blackfriars, City Thameslink, London Bridge, Farringdon, and King's Cross. Tickets are £10 single journey, £20 return. Tickets must be purchased at the ticket office, and the trains don't run as frequently as the Gatwick Express.

> *unofficial* **TIP**
> If you're staying in the east or north, Thameslink is a good choice.

Hotelink (☎ 0129-353-2244, **www.hotelink.co.uk**), at £18, is much cheaper than a taxi, and you'll be met at the plane and taken to your hotel, which is comforting after a long flight. You must book through the Web site, or ask your hotel to book it. They run about once an hour.

From Heathrow Airport (☎ 0870-000-0123, www.heathrow.co.uk)

BY TAXI Heathrow has a number of options for getting into London. The most expensive is the black-cab taxi, which can run from £45 for a no-traffic, west London drop off, to upward of £65 for a bad-traffic, central or north London destination. The best thing about the black cabs is that they are allowed to drive in the bus lanes, which saves time in rush hour. They are roomy enough for four people plus luggage, and they drop you at your doorstep.

> *unofficial* **TIP**
> Tipping is not expected, but a few extra pounds are much appreciated, especially if the driver helps you with your bags.

There are also car services known as "minicabs." They are normal-size cars, but the name differentiates them from the black cabs. They don't run on a meter; they are slightly cheaper than the black cabs, but they can be unreliable. Unless it's a reputable outfit like Addison Lee (☎ 0207-387-8888, **www.addisonlee.com**) that you must call in advance or book through the Internet, they will likely not know London as well as the black cabs, and they cannot drive in bus lanes. Take advantage of the safe and spacious black cabs, whose drivers have the "Knowledge" (a long and stringent study of London's 20,000-plus roads) to get you anywhere you want to go. Driving time varies with traffic, but it will generally take between 45 minutes and an hour to reach most central London locations.

BY BUS National Express (☎ 0870-580-8080, **www.nationalexpress. com**) has buses that run from Heathrow to Victoria Station from 6 a.m. to 9:30 p.m., and leave from all terminals at Heathrow about every half hour. It costs £10 one way and £15 round-trip, half price for children, and takes about 50 minutes to central London, depending on traffic.

BY UNDERGROUND (TUBE) (**www.londontransport.co.uk**) The Piccadilly line originates at Heathrow and is a fast and inexpensive way to get into the city, with convenient stops—Hammersmith, Earl's Court, South Kensington, Chelsea, Knightsbridge, Hyde Park Corner, Piccadilly, Leicester Square, Bloomsbury, King's Cross, Finsbury Park, and beyond to the northern suburbs. This is a great option if you aren't carrying a lot of baggage and it's not rush hour. Be careful about the train—there are some trains from which you have to get out and change trains at Acton Town—a pain that can add a sizable chunk of time to your trip. Buy the correct ticket—you'll be going to Zone One or Zone Two—and hold onto it. You need it when you leave the tube station. Tickets cost £4 one way, and can be purchased right outside the tube entrance. Look for signs to Underground. If you have the wrong ticket, you can be fined £10 on the other end. You can take the tube into town and then hail a taxi on the street to get to your hotel for a fraction of what a taxi would cost straight from the airport. Barring delays or train changes, it takes about an hour to get from Heathrow to Piccadilly Circus. The tube is the least expensive option and the best bet for large groups of travelers.

BY HEATHROW EXPRESS TRAIN (☎ 0845-600-1515; **www.heathrow express.co.uk**) Run and owned by British Airways, this train is the fastest way into London—at 100 miles an hour, it takes only 15 minutes, and it leaves every 15 minutes, from 5:10 a.m. to 11:10 p.m. The standard round-trip fare is £26; £14 for a one-way or single fare. The first-class price of £44 round-trip apparently makes it the most expensive public transport in the world per mile and minute traveled. Sadly, there are no longer any airline check-in desks at Paddington, another casualty of a changed world. Paddington's Underground station connects with four tube trains, as well as overland trains that go west.

*un*official **TIP**
There are plenty of taxis at Paddington Station; and they have recently instituted a taxi-share system which can save you time and money.

From Stansted Airport (☎ 0845-850-0150, www.stansted.co.uk)

This is a relatively new airport, and it functions quite smoothly. As it's 35 miles outside of London, a taxi is prohibitively expensive. Luckily, the Stansted Express train is very fast: you'll arrive at Liverpool Street Station in 45 minutes. Just follow airport signs down one floor to the train platform and catch the train to Liverpool Street, which is a major rail hub and Underground tube station. Journey time is 45 minutes, and the trains run from 5 a.m. to 11:30 p.m. The fare is £14.50 one way, and £24 round-trip. Trains run every 30 minutes. A taxi takes over an hour and costs more than £100. The Airbus A6 and A9 (☎ 0870-580-8080) takes more than an hour and a half and costs £10 one way, £15 round-trip; its only benefit over the train is that it runs 24 hours a day.

From Luton Airport (☎ 0158-240-5100, www.london-luton.co.uk)

Luton deals mostly with British charter flights or cut-rate budget airlines. Getting into London from Luton (which is about 30 miles north) by taxi can take more than 90 minutes in traffic and costs around £70 (they charge by the hour and there are a number of hidden fees; ☎ 0870-771-1711; **www.blueback.com**). It is, however, the best option for those in a hurry or with lots of baggage. There is a Luton Airport Parkway Station that is nearby, but not in the station, so you have to take the free shuttle bus to hook up with the Thameslink train, which takes about 45 minutes to King's Cross. It leaves every 20 minutes and costs £10 one way and £20 round-trip. The National Express (see information above) coach company runs a 24-hour bus service from Victoria to Luton, every 45 minutes for £8.50 one way, and from £9.40 return; children are half price. Greenline Bus 757 travels between Victoria Station in London and Luton for £9 one way, £12 round-trip. See **www.greenline.co.uk** or call ☎ 0870-608-7261 for times. Bus travel time is approximately an hour and 45 minutes.

From London City Airport (☎ 0207-646-0000, www.londoncityairport.com)

This is the closest airport to central London (nine miles east of Docklands), but it services only U.K. or European short hops. It is a good, well-run airport, and the transportation is convenient: A black-taxi ride to London runs about £25, and shuttle buses leave every 20 minutes or so for Canary Wharf (£3.50 one way) and Liverpool Street (£6.50).

By Eurostar (☎ 0123-361-7575, www.eurostar.com)

This high-speed train is a fast, though not necessarily cheap, way to get from the heart of Paris or Brussels to London's Waterloo Station. All leisure tickets are subject to availability, with the lowest price £59 (first-class £139) round-trip, for a nonrefundable, nonchangeable ticket, staying over one Saturday. To get these great fares, you must book at least two weeks in advance, and you should do so on the Web site in order to avoid a £3 per ticket handling fee. The Web site also gives you a chance to check out the various rates available. If you want to pop over for a one-night stand on the spur of the moment, there are a number of fares that can go as high as £298 for a fully refundable, fully negotiable ticket. Waterloo Station is on the south side of the Thames across from Westminster and is served by the tube's Northern line, buses, and taxis. The great advantage of the Eurostar over the plane or ferry is that it is absolutely the most convenient way to get to

unofficial **TIP**
You can sometimes get last-minute type deals on the Web site for first-class seats that will be cheaper than the standard coach fare, and I guarantee you will love the first-class service and ambience (even though it's not worth the normally extravagant first-class fares).

and from the continent—only two and a half hours from London to the Gare du Nord in Paris. (Don't forget to take your passport and fill out an arrival card for the British immigration checkpoint at the Gare du Nord.) The train travels at 185 miles per hour on French soil, but must slow down in England because the British don't have enough high-speed tracks yet. They are in the process of laying down the track, which will continue to cut travel times, and which will give the Eurostar access to and from St. Pancras Station, which is next to the King's Cross rail and tube station. By 2007 or 2008, all Eurostar trains will use *only* the St. Pancras Station, forsaking the more central Waterloo terminus. Given the many missed deadlines of construction projects in London, no one in London is holding his breath on that.

By Car from the Continent

Renting a car on the European continent to drive into Britain is expensive and a bit risky. There is compulsory insurance, and the European car will have the steering wheel on the "wrong" side of the car, which makes driving in England much more difficult. You will have to park in a lot in central London because most of London's parking is by meter or residential parking permit. There are car-rental companies at all the major ports, most of which will allow you to drop off at other locations, though there may be a small fee. It's important to buy a good road atlas of Great Britain if you plan to drive from any of the ports (Dover, Folkestone, Newhaven, Southampton, Harwich, or Ramsgate) into London. The signs are confusing at times, with more information on them than you may be able to take in at once, directing you off roundabouts. But this is the beauty of a roundabout: keep going around it until you're sure what direction to go.

By Ship from America

If you're phobic about air travel, have plenty of time and money, or want to see what a transatlantic crossing is like, you can call Cunard at 800-CUNARD, or look for fares and schedules on **www.cunard.com.** A round-trip from New York to London starts at $1,549. The crossing on the *Queen Elizabeth 2* takes six days. They also offer a one-way trip with a free economy air ticket for the return, starting at $1,900. Beware of the extra service charges and taxes, as well as the guaranteed weight gain from all the buffets on board.

GETTING ORIENTED *in* LONDON

POST CODES

AS WE EXPLAINED IN THE INTRODUCTION, London is divided into post codes, which instantly identify an area to those in the know. You'll see the post codes on maps, street signs, and addresses. These are not arbitrary; they represent compass directions: W1 is west and WC is west central, just as E1 is east and EC is east central. The closer an area is to central London, the lower the code number—all "1s" abut central London. These post codes can encompass more than one "village" and vice versa; SW1 includes Victoria, Pimlico, and Westminster, and Chelsea extends into districts SW3, SW7, and SW10. You'll quickly figure it out, and you'll have your own favorite post code before you know it.

GRASPING LONDON'S GEOGRAPHY The most important feature of London's geography is the rolling River Thames. It snakes through the city, bending around boroughs and post codes, and though it may not be the great and busy highway through London that it once was, it is still the major water artery and has been described as London's "liquid history." I predict that with public transportation as crowded as it has become, more and more river taxis will start plying the river, which would be a real boon to Canary Wharf commuters. (Most of the river's old tributaries have been filled in or covered over, and thank goodness for that: the Fleet and Tyburn rivers, for example, were fetid fluvial forms clogged with sewage and carrying cholera.) Starting in the east, the Thames slows down at the hairpin turn around the Isle of Dogs, with Greenwich on the south side of the river. There is a foot tunnel there that was built in Victorian times, when its snail-pace construction and unattractive plainess earned it the double-entendre nickname of "The Great Bore." Canary Wharf is on the Isle of Dogs, and at the next bend of the river is the East End. The river straightens out for the section that includes the Tower of London, Tower Bridge, and the City of London. To the south of this portion of the river is Southwark, turning into the South Bank to the west, with the Globe's thatched roof and the mighty London Eye Ferris wheel visible. On the northern side of the river is Somerset House, which was once approachable by boat until the Victoria Embankment was built to stay the ferocious destruction of the Thames' frequent floods (a thing of the past since the 20th-century construction of the Thames Barrier at the eastern mouth of the river). Along Victoria Embankment, you'll see the Temple, Cleopatra's Needle, Big Ben, the Houses of Parliament, and at Lambeth Bridge, on the opposite bank, is the medieval Lambeth Palace. Radiating north from this important stretch of the river is Covent Garden, Soho, then Bloomsbury, and slightly northwest is Regent's Park.

Come back down to the river and follow it past the grand Houses of Parliament at Westminster. The earliest incarnation of Westminster Abbey was located on a little island near the very spot on which it stands now. The river passes the Tate Britain museum at Pimlico on its way to Chelsea, where Sir Thomas More once had a grand riverside manor house, which Henry VIII liked so much that More (under pressure, no doubt) made him a gift of it. The Thames continues to flow west through Fulham, Hammersmith, and Chiswick, toward Richmond and Hampton Palace. North of Chelsea you'll find South Kensington, Hyde Park, Bayswater, and Marylebone, and run into Regent's Park again. North of that is Hampstead Heath.

Hyde Park (including the westernmost Kensington Gardens) is another landmark that helps visitors get a handle on London's geography. The park is surrounded by central London; to the north is Bayswater, to the east lie Marble Arch and Mayfair, to the southeast are Belgravia and Knightsbridge, to the southwest is South Kensington, and to the west are Kensington and Holland Park. To get from one place to the other via the parks green and pleasant pastures and walkways is a joy, if you care to make the effort.

London is a huge city, but it is divided into enough discrete areas that you can start to differentiate between parts of it rather easily, using the river and Hyde Park as baselines. Study the map of the whole city, seeing how the neighborhoods intersect; look at the tube map, bearing in mind that it's highly stylized, but it can help you get a grip on this vast metropolis. Look especially at the yellow Circle line, which orbits central London. The tube map was streamlined from a unreadable mess of meandering lines into what you see now. It works and it's readable, but it's not geographically exact. For instance, if you look at the tube map, the distance between Lancaster Gate to Paddington Station looks significant; in fact, it is only a four-minute walk. However, a walk from Marble Arch to Lancaster Gate looks pretty easy on the tube map, but it would take about 12 minutes.

*un*official **TIP**
Use the street map, not the tube map, to determine distance.

The *London A to Z Book,* pronounced "a to zed" by the British, is essential to you, as it is to any Londoner. There are other street atlases, by Collins and by Nicholson, which are also fine, but the *A to Z* is the most commonly used. It's not for tourists only. In fact, Londoners probably rely even more on these maps than tourists do, because they know how devilishly devious the streets here are. Not only are there streets of the same name in different post codes, but there are also major arteries that change names as they charge ahead through various areas. Thus the A4 from Heathrow becomes the Great West Road, then Talgarth Road, then Cromwell, Thurloe Place, Brompton Road, Knightsbridge, and Piccadilly, all without making a single turn.

The story of the *A to Z* book is typically English: Mrs. Phyllis Pearsall, one of those redoubtable, no-nonsense English women like Florence Nightingale, got so frustrated at being unable to find streets that she single-handedly walked and mapped the 23,000 streets of London in 1936. We salute her.

Some of the major thoroughfares in London are of rather ancient vintage—old commercial routes for horse-drawn carts, and all the streets, mews, alleys, dead ends, cul-de-sacs, terraces, and crescents that were often cowpaths, driveways, back passageways to a high street, or well-traveled footpaths between homes and pubs. This city was never brought to heel by planners in the way New York and parts of Paris were (although the Blitz certainly took care of many exotic East End warrens), which is what makes it so much fun to explore. For seeing the best of London by foot, there is nothing better than to just get lost. Indeed, it is highly unlikely that you won't do so unintentionally at least once when you're here. But as long as you carry an *A to Z* book and persist in one direction or another, you are bound to eventually hit some recognizable landmark . . . or a taxi.

In Covent Garden there's a fantastic shop called Stanford's (12–14 Long Acre; ☎ 0207-836-1321, **www.stanfords.co.uk;** tube: Covent Garden) that has every map known to London. Here you can find walking maps, cycling maps, subterranean maps, backstreet maps for avoiding the large thoroughfares, and maps of the old city. For your purposes, it is best to get the big picture with a fold-out map that is relatively simple, with a bird's-eye view of the cities' post codes, and keep the pocket street atlas for narrowing down your route.

THINGS *the* LOCALS *already* KNOW

GETTING THE LOWDOWN ON WHAT'S UP

FOR THE LATEST INFORMATION ON CURRENT plays, movies, art exhibits, clubs, fairs, museum tours, lectures, walking tours, or whatever, pick up a *Time Out* magazine. It's more thorough than its competitor, *What's On,* although *What's On* is a little simpler to read. On Thursday, the *Evening Standard* newspaper includes a magazine, *Metro Life,* which is the least expensive of the three and is very comprehensive.

If you want to get a copy of *Time Out* before you arrive, e-mail them at net@timeout.co.uk, or call their distribution department at ☎ 0207-813-6060. Or you can simply check out their Web site at **www.timeout.com,** a virtual magazine with some extras you won't find in the hard copy. If you're in a big city, try a newsstand that carries foreign newspapers and magazines; they might carry the weekly *Time Out London.*

TIPPING

IN MANY RESTAURANTS, THERE IS A SERVICE charge of between 12.5% and 15% added on; make sure you examine your menu and your bill to see if it has already been added. If it has, and you still get a credit card receipt with an empty gratuity line, just run a slash through it. If you pay with cash, you can leave some change from the bill if you feel like it. If service is not included, it will be mentioned in some obvious manner on the bill. Twelve to fifteen percent is appropriate for tipping in restaurants, twenty percent if the service was fantastic.

Taxi drivers do appreciate a tip and in many cases really earn it by helping with bags, taking a smart route, and giving information. Anything from 50p to £1 is usual in short-haul trips, and after £10, a tip of 10% to 15% is fine. You won't be abused for giving a lousy tip, and you may be warmly thanked for a good one. In the good hotels, you can tip the staff as you feel they deserve—£1 or £2 a bag for bell-hops, a fiver for the maid, whatever you think the concierge deserves for whatever service he or she provides. Check to see if service is added to your bill, in which case you may feel free to tip only those who have been especially helpful.

LONDON'S MEDIA

Newspapers

London has a huge selection of newspapers, from the solemn to the sleazy. Make a point of reading at least a couple of them while you're here.

The Times Now owned by media king Rupert Murdoch, it aspires to be a great newspaper, but falls short of the mark. The recent change to tabloid size has diminished it in more than size, but the tube riders like the convenience. It does have a big Sunday edition that has something for everyone.

The Independent A decent broadsheet with some good writing and a very good Sunday edition.

The Observer A Sunday-only paper with all the sections you'd expect; a fine read.

The Guardian A well-written liberal newspaper, recently reduced to tabloid size.

The Daily Telegraph Right-wing broadsheet with big Saturday and Sunday editions.

Financial Times Printed on pink paper; a must for the businessperson.

International Herald Tribune This is the fluff-free paper of choice for American expats—it features the best of the *New York Times* and has no advertising. Great editorial section with weekly contributions from America's favorite columnists, and Doonesbury, too.

Evening Standard Tabloid-size afternoon newspaper; a little light on news, but features good local stories and entertainment listings, plus the Metro Life entertainment supplement on Thursdays and the *Evening Standard Magazine* on Friday. It's handed out free once a week on busy streets, and there's a free morning edition, called the metro edition, which recaps yesterday's news.

Daily Mail Usually manages to have a star, a royal, or a socialite on the cover. Fairly good money section. Relatively free of hard news.

Daily Express Conservative middlebrow newspaper, not unlike the *Mail*.

The Sun Sleazy tabloid. This is the home of the famous Page Three Girl, the gratuitous photo of a topless woman placed on the third page. Its content is similarly absurd. Read it and laugh.

There are the other tabloids that you may not want to be caught dead reading, like *The Daily Star* or *The Sun*, full of the important news of women's breasts, murder, and sex scandals; and the *Sport*, which doesn't even bother to pretend it's anything but a titillation rag.

Magazines

The Big Issue You must buy this magazine. It provides the homeless with some income (feel free to give the vendor a tip when buying it), and it has some of the most interesting articles on London you can find. It's often guest-edited by some literary or media worthy.

The Economist Very serious and informative conservative mag on money and politics.

Harpers and *Queen* Glossy magazine devoted to the rich, famous, and beautiful; a bit like the *Tatler* in its social diary, but with more beauty articles.

Hello! Weekly rag that makes *People* look like *The New Yorker*. Lots of Hollywood celebs, minor royalty, gossip, puzzling media creations, and a weekly television and radio guide. *O.K.* is its closest competitor, and it's easy to get them mixed up; the same photos appear in both these weeklies.

The Literary Supplement Like the *New York Times Review of Books*, this is a ripping good intellectual read, with articles and book reviews written by some of the brightest people in the world of letters. After you've read a few pieces you'll wonder how you've lived without it.

Private Eye Funny political satire—it's the scourge of the establishment, any establishment. Might be obscure for nonresidents, but worth a try.

Punch Now owned by Mohammed Al Fayed, it's sold throughout Harrods and has certainly lost its punch. Don't bother, unless you happen across editions from the 19th century.

The Spectator Entertaining, with intelligent wit; politically to the right, which in England has no connection to religious fundamentalism, and is often intellectually rigorous.

Tatler House (or castle) organ of aristocrats, social climbers, and wanna-bes. Features such edifying articles as guides to eligible rich bachelors and bachelorettes. Endless pages of photos of dull social gatherings of marquises, dukes, and barons. Good information on how to spend all your money in one day.

Time Out The most comprehensive weekly magazine on what's going on in London.

W. H. Smith, the bookstore chain, has an enormous range of magazines and newspapers from all over the world, and there are press agents liberally scattered about that stock magazines from all over Europe in various languages. Pick up a Spanish ¡Hola! for that budding linguist back home.

Television

TV in England is paid for by subscription to the tune of £119 a year. This means that there are no commercials on BBC 1 and BBC 2, except for advertising for BBC's own shows and products. It's a lovely change of pace from American television. BBC 1 is the weakest of the British TV stations, with lots of cheaply produced cooking shows, talk shows, and animal programs. BBC 2 used to be very stuffy, but now regards itself as quite hip. It produces some decent dramas and reality shows, imports the occasional good movie, and has some good current-affairs shows. The independent station ITV is on channel 3 and currently produces the most expensive dramas seen on British TV. It's funded by commercials, which only appear (mercifully) every 15 minutes. Channel 4 is also a commercial station, but it's definitely the hippest. Conscientiously irreverent and edgy, it is where you'll find last year's season of favorite American TV fare, the good ones, usually. There's a movie channel on 5.

> *unofficial* **TIP**
> Do yourself a favor and watch some of the BBC— there are some truly wonderful shows on it, such as adaptations of Dickens or less recognized English authors, and quirky gardening or house-decorating programs that wouldn't last a minute on U.S. TV.

Cable, found in all the good hotels, provides Sky One, which has CNN, MTV, and plenty of movies and television programs from the United States.

Radio

The radio is mostly run by BBC, which has five national networks. The radio is in many ways quintessentially British: until the 1950s, BBC radio presenters were required to wear dinner jackets when reading the news. This Britishness is best heard on BBC Radio 3 and 4. Try to catch the shipping forecast at 6 p.m. daily on Radio 4. It is eccentric and incomprehensible to the layperson, and it articulates perfectly the voice of an old island culture.

The local listings in newspapers and magazines will tell you what is on when.

•	**Radio 1**	Pop music at 98.8 FM
•	**Radio 2**	Light entertainment at 89.2 FM
•	**Radio 3**	Classical music and related topics at 91.3 FM
•	**Radio 4**	The best thing in British media. Like National Public Radio, but much more, with short stories, serials, dramatizations, interviews, quizzes, comedies, and plays.

• **Capital FM**	Top-ten pop music on 95.8 FM and oldies on Capital Gold on 1548 kHz
• **Classic FM**	More classical music on 100.9 FM (an English friend told me that no Brit will ever complain about classical music played at ear-deafening decibels)
• **Jazz FM**	Great jazz and blues, at 102.2 FM
• **Newstalk**	All news all the time, with phone-in commentary that can be quite interesting, at 97.3 FM

Telephones

Criminally, some pinheads at British Telecom (BT) decided to remove and sell off the majority of the red phone boxes that were such a pleasing and distinctive hallmark of London. (Elton John has one in his gaden!) They have been kept in many of the tourist areas, but mostly you'll see soulless and ugly glass boxes with tons of sex-trade advertising (it's the specific job of one person to remove these cards each week, but they go back up immediately, as it is also the specific job of many people to make sure the cards are displayed). The public phone booths here take either coins or BT phone cards. Just to make things more confusing, there's a competitor, Mercury, which has its own phone booths and phone cards. Coins are your best bet, and you can make a very quick call for 10p. Some of the public phones in restaurants have a system in which you wait for the call to be answered before putting the money in—otherwise you lose it. Read the directions before using a pay phone.

unofficial **TIP**
Important: If you are calling England from overseas, you must drop the 0 at the beginning of the number. When in the country, you use the 0.

The telephone jacks in England will not fit an American modem cord, so if you have your laptop and want to get online, ask the hotel for an adapter or buy one at a department store (Harrods, John Lewis, Peter Jones, Dixons, and small electronics shops carry them).

International calls are made by dialing 00, then the country code, area code, and local number. To call through a long-distance service, dial their access lines and follow directions, using your credit-card number:

AT&T Direct ☎ 0800-890-011	**Australia** ☎ 0800-890-061
MCI World Com ☎ 0800-890-222	**New Zealand** ☎ 0800-890-064
Canada Direct ☎ 0800-890-016	

SOME IMPORTANT NUMBERS	
00	International dialing code; that is, if calling outside England, dial 00 + 1 for U.S. and Canada, 61 for Australia, 64 for New Zealand
100	General operator
112	Emergency for police, fire, or ambulance
153	International-directory inquiries
155	International operator
118118	U.K. directory inquiries
999	Emergency for police, fire, or ambulance

PUBLIC TOILETS

LONDON HAS EARNED THE ADMIRATION OF its tourists and the appreciation of its dwellers by its plentiful and clean public conveniences, also called WCs, laves, toilets, or loos. The secret may be that there's usually a small charge for their use, and people tend to be more respectful when they've invested some money. Twenty pence gets you 15 minutes in a free-standing cubicle, which is washed and sterilized automatically after each use. There always seems to be toilet paper in these loos as well as in the free lavatories found in the parks and in some tube stations and squares. Although we can't tell you it's OK to walk into a pub, hotel, or a restaurant and use the toilet if you aren't a customer, it is true that many people here aren't too uptight about that.

MAIL

GET YOUR STAMPS FOR POSTCARDS AND letters from a newsagent or a Mail Boxes shop. The post offices can be extremely crowded, as lots of people pay their bills there. If you want to get special-edition stamps, you will have to queue up at the post office. An overseas postcard stamp costs between 42p and 47p, and an overseas letter is 68p to 84p, depending on weight. Remember to put the air-mail sticker on your mail and don't forget to write "USA" or the name of the destination country at the bottom of the address. I once had a letter addressed to New York, New York, returned because I didn't write the country on it. Post offices are open Monday through Friday, 9 a.m.–5 p.m., and Saturday, 9 a.m.–12:30 p.m. With the cuts in services at the Royal Mail, getting your post twice a day is a thing of the past, and in order to save money, a post office will often be set up within the premises of a tourist bureau, a stationery store, or a press agent—there's even one in the lobby of the Science Museum! (**www.royalmail.com**).

STORE HOURS

THIS IS WHERE YOU GET TO REALLY APPRECIATE the American way: many retail shops here are on a rather old-fashioned schedule of 10 a.m.–6 p.m. and closed on Sundays. However, much to the dismay of the more traditional Londoners, stores, especially the clothing chains, are now open on Sundays. Some supermarkets and convenience stores have 24-hour opening times (though some close on Saturday at 10 p.m. and open at 8 a.m. Sunday in order to restock). Even the great holdouts—Harrods, John Lewis, and Peter Jones—are open later on Wednesdays and Thursdays. (Later only means until 7 or 8 p.m.)

unofficial **TIP**
Call and check before you take off for any shop, especially on a Saturday, when strange hours such as noon to 5 p.m. may be in effect.

CRIME

THERE'S A PERCEPTION OF LONDON AS one of the safest cities in the world, fostered by the fact that the bobbies (policemen) don't carry guns. Also, because of the strict gun laws in England, there just aren't the number of gunshot fatalities that plague the United States. Compared with other European cities, London is among the least violent, with one of the lowest homicide rates. But women take note: the statistics for rape are high. Try not to travel alone at night, and avoid minicabs.

There is definitely a disturbing trend on the streets of London toward the commission of crimes more violent than the usual purse snatchings. There have been a number of muggings involving knives and bodily harm. You hear of gangs of youths going on mugging or bodily-harm sprees. Shouting matches on the street are not an uncommon sight, and they frequently degenerate into fisticuffs. I lived in New York for many years, but I had to come to London to see grown men brawling in the street over a road rage incident. Rich neighborhoods are plagued by burglaries, car thefts, and highway robbery. As in all cities, there's a lot of stress, and bad behavior often follows on its heels. Do keep a sharp eye out, and try to avoid areas with a high concentration of pubs (Leicester Square, Soho) late at night. If you take a night bus, sit downstairs; the rowdies congregate on the upper deck. I don't wish to frighten anyone, but we need to be realistic about life in the big city. You may see big yellow signs asking for information on a crime that was committed at that spot. The police are reconsidering the usefulness of such public reminders of urban dangers as they tend to get people nervous, but for now, you don't need a newspaper to learn about local criminal activity.

Here are some safety tips, most of which are just common sense:

- Keep your pocketbook close at all times; sling it across your chest if possible, and don't leave it sitting unattended in public places—even on the back of a chair at a sidewalk café is a temptation to thieves.
- Don't put your wallet in a backpack unless it's in an inner zipped pocket.
- Put your wallet in a front pocket.

- Use a money belt when carrying large sums.
- Don't hang around counting your money after using an ATM.
- Watch your belongings on the tube and on buses.
- Don't wear flashy jewelry or an expensive wristwatch.
- Avoid buses after midnight; use a taxi or minicab instead. Women may be happier using the women's minicab company; call Lady Cabs (☎ 0207-254-3501) or, for a black taxi, try Dial a Cab (☎ 0208-253-5000) or Radio Taxis (☎ 0207-272- 0272). The car service Addison Lee is highly recommended (☎ 0207-387-8888).
- Never allow yourself to be picked up by a minicab on the street.
- Leave your passport in a safe at the hotel and carry a photocopy of the information page.
- Ignore any implausible story you might hear on the street; this town is full of talented con artists.
- Stay out of the parks after dark.
- Late at night, travel in groups, if possible.
- If you buy something at a very expensive store, get it back to your hotel or ask for a plain bag to carry it in.
- The emergency phone number is ☎ 999; *don't* use it unless it is truly an emergency. To report a crime, call ☎ 112 or directory assistance at ☎ 118118 for the number of the nearest police station.

THE HOMELESS AND BEGGARS

THE BEST WAY TO HELP THE HOMELESS is to buy *The Big Issue* magazine, which is sold on the street by licensed vendors. It's one of London's cleverest schemes, and the magazine is almost always fascinating, featuring guest editors and words and images by the homeless. Part of the money goes to the vendor, and you would be kind to also give the vendor a tip. They work hard in all weather for very little money. It's also an excellent magazine. There are an estimated 100,000 homeless persons on the streets of London, an enormous increase from only a few years ago. I'm happy to give money to the people sitting on sleeping bags asking for spare change, but many people are opposed to giving cash. Giving a sandwich or some food is a good alternative. As in many European cities, you will see many women in headscarves carrying sleeping babies and begging. These are highly organized groups, and if I thought the money would actually go to the mother and child, I'd be more than happy to give them money. But the word is that the women may "borrow" a child for more effective pathos, and it's been said that the babies are given sleeping drugs to keep them quiet.

RELIGION

BELOW ARE PHONE NUMBERS OF VARIOUS meeting places of the listed denominations to help you find a place to worship in your own way. If you're not picky, feel free to drop into any of the wonderful churches all over London for a bit of beauty and peace.

Anglican

St. Paul's Cathedral, ☎ 0207-236-4128, or
Westminster Abbey, ☎ 0207-222-5897

B'hai ☎ 0207-584-2566

Baptist ☎ 0207-221-7039

Buddhist ☎ 0207-834-5858

Catholic

Brompton Oratory, ☎ 0207-808-0900, or
Westminster Cathedral, ☎ 0207-798-9055

Christian Science ☎ 0207-499-1271

Evangelical ☎ 0207-207-2100

Greek Orthodox ☎ 0207-723-4787

Hindu ☎ 0208-961-5031

Islamic ☎ 0207-724-3363

Jewish

Liberal Jewish Synagogue, ☎ 0207-286-5181, or
United Synagogue, ☎ 0208-343-8989

Methodist ☎ 0207-222-8010

Pentacostal ☎ 0207-701-1658

Quaker ☎ 0207-387-3601

GAY LONDON

WHEN OSCAR WILDE WAS ARRESTED AT THE Cadogan Hotel in the last days of the 19th century on charges of homosexuality, that afternoon's boat to France was so crowded with single gentlemen that it almost sank. The law banning homosexuality was often enforced more for political reasons than anything else, but it made being a homosexual in England fraught with real danger. And it was all the more peculiar because of the tacit acceptance of homosexual dalliances in the male segregated school system of the upper classes. Homosexuality was seen by many as an adolescent phase that one outgrew. In 1967, the outdated law was finally changed, and London can now boast the most happening gay scene in Europe. There are gay hotels, bookshops, health clubs, religious groups, bars, night-clubs, cafés, travel agencies, publications, and even a taxi company. The best neighborhoods are in Soho (Old Compton Street in partic-ular) and Earl's Court. Clapham Common, Hampstead Heath, and the Brompton Cemetery are popular green spaces for hanging out and meeting people—and maybe doing a little cruising..

There is an excellent book by Graham Parker called *Gay & Lesbian London* (published by Metro Publications, P.O. Box 6336, London N1 6PY), which can be found in most bookstores and tourist centers. It lists and reviews every possible venue or service for the gay community in London.

Here are a few gay-friendly organizations and businesses:

Gay.com (www.gay.com) is a good place to start on the Internet. Go to the travel section and type in London. In the United States, call the International Gay Travel Association at ☎ 305-292-0217, or leave a message at ☎ 800-448-8550, for information about gay-friendly tours and services. Pick up or call for a copy of *Out and About,* a magazine that offers reviews of the best hotels, clubs, gyms, and so on in the world; call ☎ 800-929-2215.

London Lesbian and Gay Switchboard can be reached 24 hours a day, 365 days a year at ☎ 0207-837-7324 or www.llgs.org.uk. They can offer help, information, or counsel on any issues related to being gay in London.

Philbeach Hotel is a reasonably priced and fun exclusively gay hotel where a cross-dressing party erupts once a week. It is located at 30–31 Philbeach Gardens, Earl's Court, SW5 (☎ 0207-373-1244, www.philbeachhotel.freeserve.co.uk; tube: Earl's Court).

Gay's the Word is the oldest specifically gay and lesbian bookshop in the United Kingdom and can be visited at 66 Marchmont Street, Bloomsbury, (☎ 0207-278-7654; tube: Russell Square).

The **Clone Zone** has two conveniently located shops, one at 64 Old Compton Street (☎ 0207-287-3530; tube: Leicester Square) and one at 266 Old Brompton Road (☎ 0207-373-0598; tube: Earl's Court). You'll find books, cards, magazines, sex toys, clothes, and—most importantly—people to answer questions you may have about what's up in London.

Check out *Time Out* and the following Web sites to find gay-friendly and exclusively gay hotels, hostels, bars, restaurants, and so on: www.gaytravel.co.uk or www.pinkuk.co.uk will have hotel deals, information on special club nights and raves, and details about current cultural activities. Find out when the summer Gay Pride Day is held— it's one of the best parades in London and getting better every year.

LOST/STOLEN CREDIT CARDS

REPORT MISSING CREDIT CARDS TO BOTH the police and the 24-hour lost-or-stolen-card bureaus below:

American Express	☎ 0127-369-6933
Diners Club	☎ 0800-460-800
Mastercard/Eurocard	☎ 0800-964-767
Switch	☎ 0113-277-8899
Visa	☎ 0800-895-082

PART FIVE

GETTING AROUND

■ PUBLIC TRANSPORTATION

THE MOST IMPORTANT THING TO TAKE OUT with you in London is a good map and/or the pocket-size *London A to Z Book*—the map for the overall big picture and the *A to Z* for the small streets. You won't regret the extra weight in your bag. A camera is a must because you never know when you'll run into a horse-drawn carriage or a battery of the queen's guards outfitted in the kind of full regalia that really wouldn't work in battle: gold shields, plumed hats, silver swords, all manner of medals; loaded with significance and tradition. Strange details on buildings or gates will beg to be recorded, or juxtapositions of interest, such as a horse-drawn Harrod's carriage with a double-decker bus behind it, or a pigeon relaxing on the head of the lion in Trafalgar Square. Bring extra film or a second (or third) digital camera card. Also, be sure to carry a few 20p coins for the public toilets.

Like all big modern cities, London's biggest problem is transportation and traffic. The congestion charge initiated in February 2003 was an attempt to limit cars in a certain central area by charging drivers £5 a day to drive inside its perimeters. The idea was to get more people to leave their cars at home and use public transportation. The money generated by the congestion charge was to be used to improve underground and bus service. Now the charge has gone up to £8 a day, and the congestion area will likely soon encompass most of West London as well. The businesses are up in arms, the delivery people irate, and the traffic is still abysmal. The extra people using public transportation as a result of the congestion charge has made commuting in London just that much more hellish. There are constant delays and interruptions of service on the tube, and on the weekends repairs are made, which causes whole lines to be shut down. Buses, when not stuck in traffic, have an infuriating habit of arriving at long last in packs. But having said that, as visitors, you will be more tolerant than regular commuters, and will be

unofficial **TIP**
Just avoid public transport during rush hours, and resign yourself to taking a cab late at night.

able to travel during off-peak times. Eight times out of ten, the tube will get you wherever you're going quickly and efficiently, and the double-decker buses are a fun way to see London.

For any questions you might have regarding London travel information, call London Transport at ☎ 0207-222-1234, or visit the excellent Web site at **www.tfl.gov.uk.** You can get information on any facet of travel, including how everything (or *if* everything) is running, advice on the best discount fares, and apologia on why the tube has to stop at midnight (because, unlike modern undergrounds, London only has two tracks, and cannot simply divert trains onto other tracks for servicing).

TRAVEL ZONES

LONDON TRANSPORT HAS DIVIDED LONDON into six travel zones. Zone 1 is in the middle of central London, and the rest radiate outward in circles that end at zone 6 in the suburbs and at Heathrow in the west. Most of what you'll be doing in London will fall within zones 1 and 2. Bus and tube fares rise with zone numbers. For years, the transportation experts have discussed the possibility of simplifying fares by making one flat fee, but the size of London makes such a master stroke impractical.

OYSTER CARDS

WITH OYSTER CARDS, LONDON FINALLY CATCHES up to the rest of the world with the convenience of stored-value tickets that deduct your fare from a prepaid card, and which offer a slight discount and a reasonable cap on any travel. For £3, you purchase the card itself, and then you top up the value using cash or credit card at any tube or train station, usually putting ten or twenty pounds on it, depending on how much you'll use it. There are slight reductions on all bus and tube fares; plus the amount deducted from the card in one day will cap out at the cost of a one-day Travel Card. This is the easiest way to go, as one card will take care of all transportation. The only downside is that occasionally you'll find a bus whose Oyster machine is broken down. You touch the Oyster card to the reader and the cost of your trip—no matter how many zones you travel in—will be deducted.

TRAVEL CARDS

THE BEST ONE-OFF, ONE-DAY DEAL FOR TRAVELING on public transportation is the Travel Card, which gives you unlimited travel on the tube, buses, and most overland rail services in Greater London, including the Docklands Light Railway. A one-day off-peak Travel Card for zones 1 and 2 (bought after 9:30 a.m.) costs £4.70, which is the full-day cap on an Oyster card (which you can use at peak times). One-day peak travel cards cost £6. A single fare on the tube is £2, and buses charge £1.20. A weekly travel card costs £21.40; a 3-day travel card is £15.

The Family Travel Card is also a good deal: £3.10 per adult for London transport zones 1 and 2 on a one-day off-peak card and 80p per child. The family must consist of at least one adult and one child between the ages of 5 and 15; they need not be related. Family cards are valid only after 9:30 a.m. Monday–Friday and all day on weekends. For visitors, alas, there are no senior or student discounts; you have to be a London resident. Travel Cards can be bought at tube stations and also at certain newsagents. Travel Cards can be used on buses within the same travel zones.

kids **BUSES**

THERE IS NO BETTER VIEW IN THE WORLD than that of London from the top first-row seat of a double-decker bus. Many of the old buildings seem to have been designed expressly for the view from the top of the bus; the statues and gargoyles that decorate some of the fine architecture of the city are at eye level when you're riding up top. Kids love riding in them, and a short trip can calm the most fractious child. There are 17,000 bus stops all over London, so you should be able to get pretty close to whatever your destination may be. See pages 181–183 for some of the best London-viewing, double-decker public buses. The European Union forbids double-decker buses, and there is a threat that they may be removed from the London streets to comply with idiotic continental regulations. Let's hope the government keeps its head in this case and tells Brussels exactly what bus they can get on.

Types of Buses

ROUTEMASTER Sadly, by the time you read this, the old Routemasters will be a thing of the past. These are the wonderful buses that allow you to hop on at the rear of the bus and have conductors to take your fares. The goal is to get rid of all conductors, and at the time of writing, there are only a few Routemasters left.

DOUBLE-DECKER FRONT-ENTRY BUSES These are the new buses that will replace the old Routemasters. You get on in front, pay the driver, and take your seat. Try to have change for the sake of convenience. An Oyster or Travel Card makes paying much less of a hassle.

SINGLE-DECKER BUSES These tend to be for shorter journeys through London. Same price as the others, less room inside. Pay upon entering or use a transportation card—Oyster, Travel Card, or day bus pass.

NIGHT BUSES Night buses follow the same routes as the daytime buses, but run less often. They have an "N" before the route number, and run from around 11 p.m. to 6 a.m. They are the only

unofficial **TIP**
It is advised that you not sit alone on the top of a night bus late at night; there are many drunks and more sinister types out then, and there's no conductor to protect you.

all-night public transport, as the tube stops running around mid-night. Most night buses have a stop at Trafalgar Square.

Here's how the buses go 'round and 'round:

GET ON THE BUS Most bus-stop shelters have a big map of London displaying the bus routes. There is also a list of the stops of each number bus on the route. Be careful that you're standing at the correct bus stop—on Oxford Street or Hyde Park Corner, for example, there are many buses and many stops. If your bus number is not written on the red-and-white sign, it won't stop there. The bus stop with a red symbol on a white background indicates a compulsory stop, and the signs with a white symbol on a red background are known as request stops. Supposedly, a bus will always stop at a compulsory stop, but don't believe it. When you see your bus, wave your hand to flag it down, or it may just sail sedately by (if it's full, it will definitely sail by, so don't take it personally). When preparing to get out, press the red button on the yellow poles to stop the bus in advance of your stop. Ask for help if you're not sure where your stop is.

PAYING YOUR WAY The fares of the buses are determined by how far you travel, so you should know the name of your destination. The fares go up every year, but at time of publication, the fare for zone 1 was £1.20, for zones 2–4, £1.20, etc. You can buy a SaverTicket book of six bus tickets that cover all of London for £6, or a bus day pass for £3. They can be purchased at a Travel Information Center, Underground station, or newsagent. You can also use the tube Travel Card. Children under age 11 ride free; children ages 11–15 pay a child's fare of 40p in zones 1 and 2 until 10 p.m., after which they pay full fare. Fourteen- and fifteen-year-olds must carry child-rate photo cards, and if your child looks borderline you may be hassled by some persnickety conductors. Photo cards are available in any post office; take a passport-size photo and proof of age. Among the "improvements" being made to London Transport is the predominance of bus-ticket machines in most areas of Central London. You must have exact change (£1.20) to buy a bus ticket, and you show it to the driver when getting on. You can also get a day travel card for £3 from these machines. If there is no ticket machine at the bus stop, you can pay cash and get change. Try to have small coins on hand. Ticket machines are indicated by the route number at the bus stop displayed in yellow, and you won't be allowed to pay with cash at that stop (unbelievably, even if the machine is broken).

THE TUBE

THE FIRST TUBE LINE RAN IN 1863 AND CARRIED 40,000 people the first day. It now carries millions of passengers a day; at rush hour it feels as if there are millions in your train car alone. Avoid it at peak times if possible.

It is the best possible way to get around London, even with the breakdowns and delays. The streets are just so choked that buses are too iffy when you need to get somewhere quickly. The tube's most outstanding failing is that it doesn't run 24 hours a day. The last trains leave central London around midnight and begin again around 5:30 a.m. You pay according to transport zones, as outlined above. Zone 1 costs £2; zones 1–2 is £2.30; zones 1–3 £2.80; zones 1–4 £5.20. Your best bet is the Oyster or Travel Card as described above, or a ten-card "Carnet," for which you receive ten zone-1 tickets for £17 (£5 for kids). The ten tickets come in a handy holder with a tube map on it. *Beware:* If you are traveling with an invalid ticket (such as trying to leave a zone-3 station with a zone-1 ticket) you are liable to be fined £10 on the spot. You will certainly be asked to pay the difference. (You may not use the carnet tickets in conjunction with any other discount ticket, such the Travel Card or Oyster.) Look on one of the big maps posted near the vending machines and ticket windows—it will show you what stations fall in which zones.

TICKETS PLEASE Buy a ticket for your trip at the ticket window or use one of two machines. There is a big machine, which has in alphabetical order all the possible stations you might wish to go. You pick your station and the type of ticket you want (adult single journey, child single, adult return, and so on), and the machine will tell you how much money to insert; it takes credit cards and bills. The other, smaller machine is simpler, but assumes you know how much your ticket will cost and what travel zones you'll be in. You will most likely be buying the £2 ticket for zone 1. You can choose one way (single) or round-trip (return).

Put the ticket in the front of the turnstile, magnetic stripe down. It will come out at the top of the turnstile. Don't lose it; put it in a convenient pocket because you will need to put it into another turnstile as you exit your destination.

unofficial **TIP**
A lost ticket will cost you £10, so hold onto it.

READING THE MAP The tube map is an amazing feat of workmanship. Before it was standardized in 1931 by transport hero Harry Beck, it looked like an explosion in a string factory, with lines snaking all over central London. The map is not an accurate geographical representation of London, and much time and grief will be saved if you look at the *A to Z* first. Locate your destination and identify the color and/or pattern for each Underground line. Look for the key to the lines at the right bottom of the map. There are 12 tube London lines; to change lines, you must find the station connecting the lines, which are indicated by white circles outlined in black. The conductor may announce on board which lines you can catch at the next station, and newer tube trains have scrolling signs, but you're better off using your map and your head. If you get on a train and are totally confused, look at the map above the windows—it's a straight line of the stops on that particular train and is much easier to read than the big map.

WHICH WAY? Be aware of what direction you're traveling. Each platform has a sign indicating a compass direction. See where you are on your map and figure out which direction you want to go in and go to the correct platform. There are a few lines, as you will see on the map, that split off into different directions. Look at the map to see where your line terminates, and make sure you get on the train with that name; the final stop is posted on the front of the train.

unofficial **TIP**
Check the front of the train for its destination!

TUBE ETIQUETTE

A CARDINAL RULE IS TO ALWAYS STAND ON the right of the escalators to allow free passage to people who want to walk. Failure to observe this rule may be met with an impatient reprimand. As in any big city, rush hour is a nightmare, and it is best to try to avoid the tube at this time.

You must never leave a bag unattended on the tube, at a tube station, or on a bus. This is not so much an invitation to thieves (although it is certainly that) as it is an alarm to the commuters and underground staff who will treat it as a possible explosive device. In the week that followed the terrorist attack of 7/7/05, there were 110 left bags that caused tube shut-downs and interminable delays. And what's more, these bags were destroyed, so please, keep a hand on your bags at all times. There is no smoking allowed on the tube platforms or trains, this rule having been put in effect in 1984 when the combination of a smoker's lit match and the wooden escalator at Oxford Street made the ban advisable. Three years later, that same combination resulted in a much more horrific fire that led to the smoking ban being extended and the wooden escalators phased out.

TAXIS

THE FAMOUS BLACK TAXI CAB OF LONDON is not always black now—many are besmirched by advertising painted all over the body, a disturbing sight indeed. This is also now common on buses, too. As a symbol of London, the majestic black taxis are as recognizable as Tower Bridge. They are designed to specifications that echo their history: the high-ceilinged passenger compartment was meant to accommodate a gentleman's top hat, and the empty space in the front next to the driver was used for a bale of hay when the cabs were horse-drawn carriages, or cabriolets. Compared to New York City yellow taxis, or any of the small whizzing conveyances in the rest of Europe, the London black cab is king. Enjoy them while you can: they are very expensive to make, and the manufacturers would prefer to put a minivan-style taxi on the streets.

The taxis in London cruise the streets or line up in queues. If they are available, the light atop the car will be on, and you may wave them down. You can usually get a taxi on the opposite side of the road to stop for you, so don't despair if none are going your way. They are famous for being able to make U-turns on a dime—or on a 5p piece (in fact, the cars are specifically built for this flexibility).

unofficial **TIP**
If there are zigzagging lines running along the curb, the taxi cannot legally stop. Move to where those lines end to get picked up.

SEEKERS OF THE KNOWLEDGE As much a part of the London scene as their automobiles, the taxi drivers are a respected part of the work force. They have remarkable powers of navigation, of which they are justifiably proud. They train for three to five years, memorizing every street and landmark in London. You'll sometimes see people on mopeds, with maps clipped to the handlebars, looking around and making notes. These are student cab drivers. They have to learn, by heart, 60,000 routes across and around London. During their exams they have to recite these "runs" to their examiner, citing traffic lights, one-way systems, roundabouts, and landmarks. During this recital, the examiner will do everything he can to distract the student, often playing a difficult customer, hurling insults, singing, or arguing. Those who pass this stringent test are said to have "the Knowledge."

HOW TO TAKE A TAXI It may be because of the respect to which drivers feel entitled that the preferred etiquette is that you do not enter the cab until you have told the driver, from the curb through the passenger-side window, where you want to go. Do not ask if he knows the way; he's trained to know and what's more, he will not admit it if he doesn't (we say "he" because there are not so many women cab drivers at this time)—although to be fair, plenty of cabbies will gracefully turn to their oversize *A to Z* to check the route. When getting out of the cab, you are likewise expected to pay through the window, standing on the curb. This works to both your and the cabbie's advantage; you can get out and reach easily into your pocket or purse, and the driver doesn't have to turn around and reach through the partition. Smoking is prohibited in taxis, although if you see the driver light up, you can ask him if you might as well.

unofficial **TIP**
Don't eat or drink in a taxi. Many cabbies own their cars—which cost upward of £27,000—and are fiercely protective of their well-being.

In his hilarious, best-selling book about England, *Notes from a Small Island,* Bill Bryson observes that, although London taxi drivers are absolutely the most excellent in the world, they do have a couple of idiosyncrasies. One is that they are incapable of driving for any distance in a straight line: ". . . no matter where you are or what the driving conditions, every 200 feet a little bell goes off in their heads and they abruptly lunge down a side street." My own experience with London cabbies is that they are absolute geniuses at getting from point A to point B with the least amount of traffic and in the shortest amount of time. They know London better than anyone, and the more I get to know London, the more impressed I am with their ability to follow serpentine routes that lead you away from traffic and straight to the heart of where you're going.

WORTH (ALMOST) EVERY POUND I learn more about London and its roads when I take a cab, so much that I can justify the expense, which can be considerable. The surcharge on night rides has been dropped, while the rates have crept upward. A short trip will cost about £5; a trip from central London to, say, Hampstead, will be about £25 plus. Although, barring a breakdown, the tube is usually a quicker bet, it's always a pleasure to jump in a taxi and watch London go by from the dark comfort of the cab's very civilized interior. Sometimes you can also get a great conversation out of the deal.

Some drivers, on hearing an American voice, will want to tell you about their experiences in the United States or give you a heads-up as to what to expect in England. Cabbies are a talkative and opinionated lot, so much so that *Private Eye*, the satirical magazine, has run very funny op-ed pieces by "Lord Justice Cabdriver."

You can call a black taxi if you're staying in a place where they don't cruise regularly or if it's late at night. Some companies charge extra for booking over the phone or using a credit card—ask when you call.

Computer Cabs	☎ 0207-286-0286
Data Cab	☎ 0208-964-2123
Dial a Cab	☎ 0207-253-5000
Radio Taxis	☎ 0207-272-0272

MINICABS

MINICABS ARE A MUCH LESS RELIABLE OPTION than the black cabs, but they are cheaper and come in very handy in many instances, such as when you find yourself far from a tube stop in an outlying area or when you need to get back to your hotel very late at night and there's not a black cab in sight. There are a few reputable minicab companies, including some that have only women drivers. You must call to book a car; in that way you have some recourse should anything go wrong. Minicab drivers are not required to have "the Knowledge," which may be made abundantly clear by how lost they can get, but because there's a flat fee, there's at least no economical

unofficial **TIP**
You can't hail a minicab on the street; in fact, do *not* get into one that stops and offers you a ride. It's not at all kosher; there are a lot of scams and dicey drivers out there.

downside to this. Make sure you agree on a price when booking the cab, and confirm it with the driver when you get in. Tipping is normally between 10% and 15%. The cars are often two-door compacts—nowhere near as roomy as the black cabs—so if you have four large or five regular-size people, get a black cab, or ask if the minicab company has a people carrier (minivan). Addison Lee regularly uses them, which is one reason the company is so popular. Here are some good minicab companies:

A & A Chauffeurs Ltd.	☎ 0208-958-3344
Addison Lee	☎ 0207-387-8888
College Cars	☎ 0208-955-6666
Greater London Hire Ltd.	☎ 0208-444-2468
Lady Cabs	☎ 0207-254-3501

MOTORCYCLE TAXIS

MOTORCYCLE TAXIS ARE A NEW TRAVEL TWIST, currently also enjoying success in Paris, another clogged European city. The bike will get you through the worst possible traffic in a very short time, and the helmets are equipped with microphones so you can tell the driver to slow down. Not for the faint of heart. Call Addison Lee Taxybike (their motto: "Safe, Sedate, and You Won't Be Late") at ☎ 0207-387-8888, or visit **www.addisonlee.com.**

RAIL SERVICES AND DOCKLANDS LIGHT RAIL

TRAVEL CARDS CAN BE USED ON SOME OF the local commuter lines in London. The North London line is a good way to cross greater London as it cuts a swath from west (Richmond) to east (Woolwich); it stops at various train and some tube stations along the way. It's above ground, which is a nice change of pace from the mole tunneling of the tube. Call ☎ 0845-748-4950 for all train inquiries.

If you are using British Rail to get out of London, ask about the discounts it offers. There are a number of discount cards, which you may not think apply to you, as they are good for a year, but the savings can be enormous. Ask at any major rail station or travel agency. You can apply for the discount at the same time you buy your tickets.

The Docklands Light Rail (☎ 0207-363-9700) is clean, quiet, and rides above the ground. It services the East End, Canary Wharf, North Greenwich, the *Cutty Sark,* and ends in Lewisham. It is also becoming a tourist option, and special tickets combine rail travel with riverboat trips. These special trains leave from Tower Gateway and Bank every hour on the hour starting at 10 a.m., and you will hear interesting commentary from a guide as you ride.

GETTING AROUND
on YOUR OWN

RENTING A CAR AND DRIVING IN LONDON

IT'S NOT A GOOD IDEA TO RENT A CAR TO drive around London. London is a confusing, frustrating, and dangerous place to drive, even for those who are already used to driving on the left. Although you need only present a valid driver's license from any country or state to rent a car, traffic laws and driving customs are quite different from those of other countries. The driver's license here is the most difficult in the world to earn, with only Switzerland's test being harder. If you are driving out to the country and must rent a car, it might be best to take the tube out to Heathrow or Gatwick and rent a car from there to avoid the problems of central London's notorious traffic, and the pernicious congestion charge, which you will be responsible for.

If you do find yourself driving in England, here's a tip: the best way to remember which side of the road you're supposed to be on is to just keep yourself and your steering wheel (which is on the right side of the car) in the middle of the road, and not hugging the side of the road, and you'll always be in the right place. This is the same principle in countries that drive on the left—the driver is always in the middle of the road. As for traffic roundabouts, the saying is "right has might, left is bereft"; that is, yield to the person on the right.

unofficial **TIP**
Don't let the way the cars are parked throw you—you can park facing any old direction in England.

In London, the parking regulations are strict—look at lampposts to find signs outlining them. You can't park on a double yellow line ever; your car will be clamped or towed. If you're clamped, there will be a sticker telling you where to pay for its removal and the additional fine; if you're towed, call ☎ 0207-747-7474 to find out where your car was taken. The penalty is stiff: about £200, all told.

There are resident permits for parking in most neighborhoods, and you cannot park in these areas except at night, on bank holidays, and all day Sunday—Sundays you can park pretty much anywhere, on some red routes (red-lined avenues) and all single yellow lines. Read the signs carefully. There are meters and Pay and Display spaces for visitors to use. Pay and Display works like this: Park your car; find the ticket machine; pay the correct amount for the desired time; get your ticket and display it on your windshield or dashboard. There are a number of National Car Parks (signs say NCP) around central London: call ☎ 0870-606-7050, or go to their Web site at **www.ncp.co.uk** for locations.

The central numbers for the big rental companies (cars will cost about £65 plus a day) are as follows:

Alamo	☎ 0870-400-4508, www.alamo.com
Avis	☎ 0207-917-6700, www.avis.co.uk
Budget	☎ 0800-181-181, www.gobudget.com
Enterprise	☎ 0125-235-3620, www.enterprise.com
Europcar	☎ 0870-607-5000, www.europcar.co.uk
Hertz	☎ 0870-844-8844, www.hertz.co.uk

Expect to pay about £40 to fill up an economy car with gas, or petrol, as they call it here.

WALKING

PLEASE DO. YOU'LL BE SURPRISED AT HOW FAR you can go by foot—a lot faster at times than on the bus, and certainly more pleasantly than on the tube. You'll get to see small architectural curios, drop into inviting shops and restaurants, and find alleys and mews that you wouldn't see by cab. Keep your *A to Z* handy and go ahead and get lost. You'll thank yourself for it. Do keep an eye out for the maniac drivers, and be aware that your instincts when crossing the streets are all wrong. Take it slowly and *don't* try to outrun a walking light—the drivers will scare the devil out of you.

The zebra crossings, however, belong to the pedestrian. When you see a flashing yellow light and a cross path marked with white stripes, you are in the right of way—cars *must* stop for you. There may be one or two drivers who haven't quite got the hang of this system, so don't stride out without sensible caution.

Around big intersections such as Piccadilly Circus, Marble Arch, and Hyde Park Corner there are "subways," which are walkways beneath the street. They are well indicated with signposts, so you'll be able to know which way to go. Some are actually quite interesting—Hyde Park Corner has painted tiles giving you the goods on the duke of Wellington (whose house is right there) and the parks of London. Some of them use exit numbers and seem to go on forever. Avoid them late at night; some of the subways become little villages of sleeping homeless people.

> *un*official **TIP**
> Walking is the most interesting, healthy, revealing, ecologically sound, and inexpensive way to get around London; so bring the most comfortable shoes you have.

LOST AND FOUND

IF YOU HAVE LEFT SOMETHING IN ONE OF the above public conveyances, which is easily done when you're tired and jet-lagged, take heart: You just might get it back. For insurance claims you must inform the police of your loss. Do not call the emergency number; find the nearest police station by dialing ☎ 118118 information.

London Transport has a Web site that will help you to find your property—over 130,000 items are lost on buses, trains, and taxis a year. Go to **www.tfl.gov.uk/tfl/ph_lost.shtmlhttp,** and you can follow links to the appropriate office. Here are the numbers for lost property:

Buses	☎ 0207-486-2496
Black taxis	☎ 0207-918-2000
Train stations (railroad)	☎ 0870-000-5151
Tube trains	☎ 0207-486-2496

PART SIX

SIGHTSEEING, TOURS, *and* ATTRACTIONS

AN EMBARRASSMENT *of* RICHES

A TRIP TO LONDON SURELY MUST BE ON EVERY dedicated traveler's wish list. For the indefatigable sightseer, there is an endless itinerary to follow. For one in need of a little R and R, there are theaters to enjoy and parks to kick back in. For the scholar, there are museums, libraries, learned societies, free lectures, and landmarks. There's so much to see and do in London that you must try to restrict yourself to only that which you find fascinating, or you'll find yourself very, very tired. There are the obvious, must-see attractions—the Tower of London, the British Museum, the Victoria and Albert Museum, Westminster Abbey—and then there are the other bits that make London so wonderful: the parks, the themed walking tours, the obscure collections, and the marketplaces. Only you can determine what is most interesting to you and your companions, but we can help you to make your decisions.

DISSENSION IN THE RANKS

IN A PLACE LIKE LONDON, WITH SO MANY varied attractions, you can easily disagree with your traveling companions as to what are the most important sights. You may think that visiting the Globe Theatre without seeing a play is a yawn, and your spouse may be bored silly by the very idea of a design museum. There are two ways to go about solving these fundamental problems of taste, time, and touring. One is to compromise: You see one of mine, and I'll see one of yours. This at least addresses honestly the issue of not being keen on the attraction, instead of going along grudgingly and being resentfully uninterested. The other is to split up and go your own way. This has the great advantage of making it less likely that you will grow tired of each other's company, and ensures a ready store of dinner conversation as you each recount your adventures.

KNOW THY LIMITS

EVERYONE HAS A THRESHOLD AT WHICH sightseeing makes the transition from pleasure to torture. Your feet hurt, the lines are too long, the weather is appalling, you're hungry, jet lag has hit you hard. This threshold varies from person to person, but for the disabled, the elderly, and the very young, the passage over it can be risky as well as uncomfortable. There are a number of attractions in London without wheelchair access, or in which there are incredibly steep stairs, or where all the exhibits are too high for the young or a wheelchair user to see. You do not want to put yourself (or your companions if they are any of the above) in the position of finding out too late that the attraction just won't work. Although in our listings we try to judge whether a place is disabled- or child-friendly, it is always a good idea to call first and find out for sure. There are improvements being made all the time in the interests of easier access at most attractions, museums, churches, and stately homes, so check ahead. For children, you might want to find out if the museum you're visiting has any hands-on activities. The Victoria and Albert and the British Museum are just two of the "grown-up" museums that have plenty for children to see and do, with special childrens' activities available on weekends and school holidays (see Part Seven, Children's London, for more specifics about touring the city with children).

*un*official **TIP**
Also, there are some places that call themselves disabled friendly, but in reality have a limit on the number of wheelchairs allowed in at a time.

TOURIST INFORMATION CENTERS

THE FOLLOWING WEB SITES HAVE TONS OF up-to-the-minute information about attractions and sights.

www.visitbritain.com	Great Britain's official tourist Web site features lots of useful information and trip-planning advice.
www.londontown.com	The official London Tourist Board site offers specials on hotels, sells theater tickets, and offers news on the latest exhibitions.
www.visitlondon.com	London's official Web site features loads of information and lets you book hotels, buy discount passes, and more.

www.thisislondon.co.uk	The *Evening Standard*'s Web site is a good source for current entertainment and restaurant information.
www.timeout.com	The weekly magazine features cultural event listings, as well as information on entertainment, restaurants, and nightlife.

The biggest and most comprehensive walk-in tourist office is The **Britain and London Visitor Centre** (1 Regent Street, Mayfair, SW1; tube: Piccadilly Circus, open 9 a.m.–6:30 p.m. weekdays, 10 a.m.–4 p.m. weekends). You can pick up an armful of pamphlets, brochures, maps, and fliers, and reserve tickets, tours, and hotel rooms. You will also find it a one-stop shop for souvenirs and London-related books.

TOURING

JUMP ON THE BUS

THE BEST THING TO DO ON THE FIRST DAY in any city is to take advantage of a hop-on, hop-off bus tour. This gives you the lay of the land, and if the day is bright, the open top of a double-decker bus is the best place to get the sunlight that helps you get over jet lag. Just riding up high is a thrill to most kids, and the flexibility of the hopping on and off will keep them from getting restless. The buses make stops at most of the major attractions/intersections, such as the Tower of London, Madame Tussaud's, Green Park, Hyde Park Corner, Harrods, by the South Kensington Museums, Hyde Park, and so on. You can pick up a bus at almost any of the significant attractions; check with your hotel to determine the closest stop to you. Tickets can be bought on the bus or from the bus employees who stand at some of the bus stops. It is crucial that you get on the bus as early as possible to avoid the crushing traffic jams (congestion charging has only slightly eased them) that can make the tour a carbon monoxide-scented bummer. If you see traffic building up while you're touring, you can always hop off and continue your tour the next day or later in the afternoon, as the tour tickets are good for 24 hours, which is great—you can break up the tour nicely. You can also buy your tickets online, although that seems rather extreme preplanning to me, even with the £1 discount for online booking. Your move. Both companies offer fast-track attractions tickets to the more overcrowded spots, such as Madam Tussaud's and the Tower of London, which are well worth getting. Both of the following companies have basically the same routes and services.

   Big Bus Company (☎ 0207-233-9533; **www.bigbustours.com**) has a Red Tour that starts at Green Park and lasts approximately two hours, and a Blue Tour that commences at Marble Arch and goes for three hours. In the summer the buses run every 15 minutes or so; in winter they go about every half hour, stopping at all the major (and minor) attractions. Tickets are £20 for adults and £8 for children ages 5–15 (£2 discount for adults when buying online). The Big Bus Company also offers a number of walking tours (included in ticket price), such as Royal London, the Beatles' London, James Bond, ghosts, and famous movie locations. There are also river cruises and some out-of-town excursions. They won the 2004 London Sightseeing Tour of the Year.

The Original London Sightseeing Tour (☎ 0208-877-1722; **www.the originaltour.com**) offers tours in eight languages, fast-entry tickets, and four different touring options, including a river tour as part of the ticket price. Tickets range from £12 to £16, depending on the season, and from £7.50 to £10 for children ages 5–15. Tickets are good for 24 hours. The big advantage of this company (besides the more reasonable prices) is the wonderful Kid's Club, which provides lots of fun for the children, such as a kids' activity pack, games, quizzes, and Kid's Club commentary.

ON YOUR OWN

YOU DON'T HAVE TO SPEND ALL THAT MUCH to get a decent double-decker bus ride. There is the well-known **number 11** bus that takes you past many of the same sights the tourist buses pass, for a mere fraction of the cost. Pick it up at the King's Road at World's End or the Chelsea Town Hall stops, and you'll have a good look at that famous mod street, go through Victoria, past Westminster Abbey, Whitehall, Trafalgar Square, up the Strand to St. Paul's Cathedral, and finish in the East End at Liverpool Street. All this for only £2.

The **number 15** is also wonderful. I met a couple of elderly Londoner ladies on it once, and they told me they often get on it to take in the sights and visit with one another without having to spend money (British seniors, or old-age pensioners, as they're called, ride free). Pick up the 15 at Paddington and ride to Marble Arch, up Oxford Street, down Regent to Piccadilly Circus, down Haymarket to Trafalgar Square, up the Strand (which turns into Fleet Street), St. Paul's Cathedral, the Tower of London, and end up at Petticoat Lane (Middlesex Street), which has a market on Sunday mornings, as well as some stalls during the week.

The **number 14** goes from Tottenham Court Road (by the British Museum) over the Thames and west to Putney Heath, passing Piccadilly, Knightsbridge, the museums of South Kensington, and the shops of Fulham.

Bus **number 24** will take you north, from Victoria Station all the way to Hampstead Heath and Highgate, from which you can get an amazing view of London.

unofficial **TIP**
Get a bus map at any tourist center or hotel lobby and check out these routes and any others that look interesting to you. If, as you're traveling, you feel you are going too far afield, just get off and jump on a bus going in the opposite direction to get back to central London.

To get a look at some of South London, take the **number 2** bus from either Marylebone Station, Marble Arch, or Hyde Park Corner and ride across the Thames through Brixton, up Tulse Hill to Crystal Palace Park, where you can get out and look at the prehistoric creatures imagined and modeled by the Victorians.

PRIVATE TOURS

THE **Classic Coach Company** OFFERS A large taxi of classic design with room for 11 passengers, who are given a three-hour guided tour for £20 per person or £38.50 per person for a full-day tour. You can also hire the entire vehicle for £110 and up. The advantage to this coach tour is that, because it's smaller than the double-deckers, it can take you into small streets and squares that you couldn't see on other tours. And it's cool looking, with plenty of windows to gape from. Tours go daily at 8:30 a.m., 10 a.m., and 1 p.m. and feature stops and photo ops galore. Call ☎ 0208-390-0888, 24 hours a day; surf **www.classiclondontours.com**, or ask your hotel to book you a spot.

unofficial **TIP**
The great thing about Black Taxi Tours is that you can avoid traffic jams and get into the squares, mews, and backstreets that no tour bus can take you.

You can also hire a black cab to take you around London, creating your own tour, seeing only those sights that interest you most. Call **Black Taxi Tours of London** at ☎ 0207-935-9363, or visit their Web site at **www.blacktaxitours.co.uk.** A two-hour tour will cost about £80 for a taxi, which holds a maximum of five people.

SEEING THE HIGHLIGHTS

THE DOUBLE-DECKER BUS TOURS ARE DESIGNED for seeing the sights of London in a general way. You can see where everything is in relation to everything else, perhaps find out how long the lines are for certain attractions, figure out what can be done in a day or a week, and determine which areas seem most intriguing. Taking a general tour first thing will help you make plans more efficiently for the days ahead. You'll learn that you won't be able to do the Tower of London on the same day you take a walk in Hampstead Heath, which is so far away that it's off any standard London tour itinerary. Or you will note that a trip to the National Gallery can be combined with a visit to any or all of the following: the adjacent National Portrait Galley, St. Martin-in-the-Fields, Trafalgar Square, Leicester Square, Covent Garden, and Somerset House, topped off by a half-price ticket for an evening show at the theater.

SIGHTSEEING COMPANIES

THERE ARE A LOT OF TOUR COMPANIES IN London doing very similar out-of-town and London tours for roughly the same prices. You can find their brochures in any hotel lobby. A word of caution: they have many courtesy hotel pick-up points in London, which sounds very convenient—who doesn't want to fall out of their hotel room into a waiting coach at 8 a.m.? But yours may just be the first of 15 stops, and if you get stuck in the normal London traffic, you can be on the bus for an hour before you actually get started on the tour. You'll probably find it less annoying to meet your bus at the final departure point. When you reserve your seat, find out where the bus will actually leave for the tour, then take the tube or a taxi to get there. The downside to this evasive action is that you may not get the seat you want on the bus. The best seats are clearly the top-floor front row.

The tour companies offer half-day, morning, night, full-day, or two-day tours of London, plus tours to such places as Windsor and Leeds Castles, Eton, Hampton Court, Stonehenge, Bath, Stratford-upon-Avon, Oxford, Cambridge, Salisbury, Brighton, Dover, Canterbury, York, Chester, Warwick Castle, the Lake District, Scotland, and even Paris and Amsterdam. They will provide bus, train, or boat transport depending on the destination. The price of the tour almost always includes entrance fees for the attractions and the cost of meals, and in the case of the overnight trips, the cost of accommodations.

Here are some of the tour companies; do take a look at their Web sites:

Astral Travels (☎ 0700-078-1016 or 0870-902-0908; fax 0707-071-2035; www.astraltravels.co.uk) escorts small groups on mini coach day tours, as well as extended 3- to 14-day all-over tours. The range of interests catered to on their specialized one-day tours is most impressive.

Evan Evans (☎ 0207-950-1777; fax 0207-950-1771; www.evanevans.co.uk)

Frames Rickards (☎ 0207-828-9720; www.framesrickards.co.uk)

Golden Tours Deluxe (☎ 0207-233-7030; toll free ☎ 800-456-6303 in U.S.; www.goldentours.co.uk)

Visitors Sightseeing (☎ 0207-636-7175; fax 0207-636-3310; www.visitorsightseeing.co.uk)

For tours along the river, call **Catamaran Cruisers** (☎ 0207-987-1185; www.catamarancruisers.co.uk) or **City Cruises** (☎ 0207-740-0400; www.citycruises.com).

For boat rides along the canals of Little Venice and Camden Lock, call **London Waterbus Company** (☎ 0207-482-2550 or 0207-482 2660; www.londonwaterbus.com).

OUTSIDE LONDON

ALTHOUGH JUST GETTING A TASTE OF LONDON'S richness can take all of even a long vacation, it may be a great change of pace to get out into the famous English countryside. There are so many delightful medieval towns and inspiring cathedrals to see. The above tour companies conduct such trips conveniently and hassle free, although you may not fancy joining a tour group.

unofficial **TIP**
Astral Tours is an especially good option if you're not fond of big buses with lots of people.

You may want to rent a car to do your sightseeing, but sometimes it's just easier to let others do the driving. Taking a train will work for going to Bath, Oxford, Salisbury, Cambridge, or Stratford-upon-Avon, where you can get a hotel room and walk around town, but for trips to Stonehenge or to places such as the town of Laycock or Warwick Castle, you are better off going with a tour. Visit any of the above companies' Web sites to decide where you want to go. Ask how many people have already booked—perhaps you can find a day when it will only be a handful of people.

SOME GOOD SIDE TRIPS

NOTE: ALL THE TRAVEL TIMES GIVEN BELOW are for British Rail train service.

BATH is about one-and-a-half hours from Paddington Station (170 miles) and is a gorgeous Georgian town with Roman relics, famous for its historic buildings and Sally Lunn cakes. Jane Austen once lived there, in its heyday as a fashionable spa town.

kids **BRIGHTON** is one hour from Victoria Station (53 miles). Brighton makes for jolly seaside fun, with kid-friendly rides and games on the pier, little shopping streets and alleys, and the Brighton Pavilion, an amazing Oriental-fantasy retreat of George IV.

CAMBRIDGE is one hour from King's Cross Station (85 miles). Cambridge is a quiet university town, with beautiful river views and significant buildings, such as the early-Tudor King's College Chapel.

CANTERBURY is 80 minutes from Victoria Station (50 miles). The old pilgrimages used to come to the cathedral, in which Saint Augustine converted King Ethelbert in 597, and Thomas à Becket was murdered.

HATFIELD HOUSE is 20 minutes from King's Cross Station (20 miles). This is where Queen Elizabeth I spent her childhood.

OXFORD is one hour from Paddington Station (56 miles). Oxford is the university city of "dreaming spires" and a good jumping-off place for the Cotswolds.

ST. ALBANS is 30 minutes from King's Cross Station (25 miles). St. Albans is an old Roman stronghold, with ruins and rose gardens.

SALISBURY is one-and-a-half hours from Waterloo Station (84 miles), with a magnificent cathedral, military museum, and beautiful flower-filled neighborhoods around the cathedral. Stonehenge is a short drive away.

STRATFORD-UPON-AVON Paddington Station to Stratford takes about three hours (91 miles). This is Shakespeare's town—he was born, married, and buried there—and the town is devoted to him, but it has other attractions as well. See a play by the Bard while you're there; they have matinees on most days as well as evening performances, and the town is just charming, with canal boats and markets.

WINDSOR is 30 minutes from Waterloo Station (20 miles), and you can see the storybook castle by the Thames, plus a fine old town with good pubs. The playing fields of Eton are nearby, and there are lovely little shops and restaurants all around.

NOT TO BE MISSED IN LONDON: A HIGHLY SUBJECTIVE LIST

- The British Airways London Eye (see page 210)
- The British Museum (see page 212)
- Hampton Court Palace (see page 223)
- Museum of London (see page 238)
- The National Portrait Gallery (see page 242)
- St. Paul's Cathedral (see page 245)
- The Science Museum (see page 251)
- The Tate Modern (see page 256)
- The Tower of London (see page 258)
- Victoria and Albert Museum (see page 260)
- Westminster Abbey (see page 263)
- The Globe Theatre (see page 221)
- Hyde Park on Sunday (see page 269)
- St. James's Park (see page 273)
- A street market on the weekend (see page 000)

ROMANTIC LONDON

ONE REALLY DOESN'T ASSOCIATE ROMANCE WITH London in the way one does with Paris or Venice, but that's not to say there aren't some romantic places to seek out with your beloved. Judging by the snogging (kissing) that goes on in Hyde Park, we'd have to say that taking a blanket, a jug of wine, and your special someone to the park for a lie around in the sun is one of London's favorite pastimes for couples, and it's free. If you need exercise, get in a paddleboat built for two and tool around the Sepentine. Take a night cruise along the

Thames, or sit on a bench at sunset on the Thames at the end of Oakley Street, watch the birds circling overhead, and wait for the lights to illuminate the spectacular Albert Bridge. The ongoing rejuvenation of the South Bank makes it a midsummernight's dream in warm weather, as you stroll along and watch the boats pass by the twinkling lights of London. My favorite evening out is a concert at the Royal Festival Hall or a play at the National, then a walk along the river and over any of the bridges for a view of the London Eye and a long stare into the fast-flowing Thames.

A romantic restaurant would be **Momo** (25 Heddon Street, off Regent Street, Mayfair, W1; ☎ 0207-434-4040; tube: Oxford Circus); it's a Middle Eastern restaurant done exquisitely in *Arabian Nights* fantasy style. The quite expensive **Pont de la Tour** (Butler's Wharf, 36D Shad Thames, SE1; ☎ 0207-403-8403; tube: London Bridge or Tower Hill) has good food and wonderful views of Tower Bridge, which can be pretty romantic, unless you truly only have eyes for each other.

The most romantic hotels are **The Portobello** (ask for the room with the round bed); the **Covent Garden Hotel** (wonderful amenities, which mean you never have to leave the premises), and **The Gore** (request The Venus, the Tudor, or the Miss Ada suite). And, of course, you can't go wrong at the **Ritz** for romance—check out the weekend break prices and tell them you want a honeymoon-type room or, better still, a suite (see Part Three, Accommodations, for more information).

Agent Provocateur (16 Pont Street, Belgravia, SW1; ☎ 0207-235-0229; **www.agentprovocateur.com;** tube: Knightsbridge) sells *very* sexy underwear that's erotic and sophisticated at the same time. And for chocolate massage-oil bars and bath salts for two, go to **Lush** in Covent Garden (Unit 11, Central Piazza, WC2; ☎ 0207-240-4570; **www.lush.co.uk;** tube: Covent Garden) or in Chelsea (123 King's Road, SW3; ☎ 0207-376-8348; tube: Sloane Square). Then there is the popular **Myla,** an exotic and erotic shop that has not just seductive clothing and sexy what-nots, it also has a bra-fitter on staff (4 Burlington Gardens, Mayfair, W1, ☎ 0207-491-8548; **www.myla.com;** tube: Green Park or Piccadilly.

OH, SUCH *a* PERFECT DAY

WHAT CONSTITUTES A PERFECT DAY IN LONDON will naturally depend on who's in your party and what your keenest interests are. One person's poison is another one's mead, as they say. But if I were to try to conjure up a day that would hit as many of my personal favorite high notes as possible, it would go something like this:

I would want to start my day with the best cappuccino in London, which would be near my hotel in the Knightsbridge or South Kensington area: Orsini's Café (8a Thurloe Place, SW7; ☎ 0207-581-5553; tube:

South Kensington) is across the street from the Victoria and Albert Museum and just east of the Rembrandt Hotel. It's a friendly family-run café that feels like a little slice of Italy in London. I love having a cappuccino and toasted bread at a pavement table even with the roar of traffic. If you require a more hearty breakfast, go up the street to Patisserie Valerie—the croissants are unlike those anywhere else, and they serve a large selection of hot breakfasts (215 Brompton Road, SW3; ☎ 0207-823-9971; tube: Knightsbridge). Another option is to go around the corner to the Brompton Cross, where La Brasserie serves perfect continental breakfasts as well as eggs in an authentically Parisien atmosphere—which includes sidewalk tables and brusque waiters (272 Brompton Road, SW3; ☎ 0207-584-1668; tube: South Kensington). If you prefer a less smoky atmosphere, the no-smoking Aubaine restaurant-and-bakery, right next door, serves a great continental breakfast.

After breakfast, go look at the Brompton Oratory Church (1 Thurloe Place; tube: South Kensington). It's an amazing edifice, with small chapels lining the enormous hall, and a rotunda to rival St. Paul's. Go through the churchyard and out to Ennismore Gardens, which you'll take up to Hyde Park, a couple of blocks away. Amble around the park, and go to the riding ring and see if any of the queen's guards are exercising their horses or rehearsing any ceremonies. Go feed a duck or two at the Serpentine, and check out the problem-plagued Princess Diana Memorial (it has had to be closed for repairs and rethinks numerous times since its opening in July 2004).

Exit the park at Exhibition Road (have a quick look at the Albert Memorial on your right: you might want to stop for a photo-op) and head for the Victoria and Albert Museum down the street (opens at 10 a.m.). Wander around the Fakes and Forgeries Statue Court and go admire the William Morris tearoom. The British Galleries are very interesting and charming; it's one of the finest examples of modern curating in London. The outside courtyard has been redone in a pleasing style, though I miss the old fountain. If the weather is fine, have a rest and a cup of coffee there. Then walk through South Kensington (or take a taxi or the 49 bus from outside the South Ken tube station) up Sydney Street to the Chelsea Town Hall. Across from the hall is the Bourbon-Handy Antiques Centre for browsing or buying; next to it is Daisy and Tom's, a wonderful place to buy British books for your little friends. And then, if the weather's warm, have lunch outside at one of the restaurants at the Chelsea Marketplace; if it's cold or rainy, try Dan's Restaurant (119 Sydney Street, SW3; ☎ 0207-352-2718; tube: South Kensington or Sloane Square), or have a less expensive ploughman's lunch at the pub next to the neo-Gothic St. Luke's Church (where Dickens got married). Within the marketplace is a good health-food store, called Here; Neal's Yard Remedies shop; and the truly marvelous Chelsea Gardener center. You'll be sorry you can't take home some of the plants and flowering trees sold there.

unofficial **TIP**
Although you might not find tickets for your desired play on sale at the half-price kiosk, there's always something great to see, and the price is right. You may even get to watch some American screen or TV star strut their stuff in a West End play.

Stroll down the King's Road toward Sloane Square, maybe do a little window-shopping, and catch the 11 bus wherever possible. Take the 11 past all the great sights: Westminster Abbey, Big Ben, Whitehall, Trafalgar Square, up Fleet Street, to St. Paul's. If you have the energy, climb up to the top of St. Paul's and enjoy the view. If not, just have a seat in the church and admire the craftsmanship that went into this magnificent building, or perhaps rest in the courtyard of the church and watch the tourists. Catch a bus toward Trafalgar Square and go to Leicester Square to buy half-price theater tickets at the Tkts kiosk there for that evening. There's no saying what plays will be available, but it's always great to see an Oscar Wilde or Noël Coward play if possible: so very, very English. Check to see what stars are performing: you may get the pleasure of seeing Judi Dench, one of the Redgraves, or Maggie Smith tread the boards.

Then, depending on the time, your next move would be a toss-up between having tea at Browns Hotel or Fortnam and Masons (more economical). If you're still full from lunch, skip tea and go try the brass-rubbing in the crypt at St. Martin-in-the-Fields. It's a real treat. You pick out one of the many medieval brass plates with engraved images, get a piece of paper and a selection of colored wax, and tease out the design by rubbing the wax stick over the plate; artistic talent not required. Take your time with the rubbing, enjoying the atmosphere and the pastime. Buy some gifts in the wonderful shops (one at the brass-rubbing area and one in the other part of the crypt). Then walk over to Covent Garden and watch the buskers (street entertainers) at work. Dinner at last. For the atmosphere and the Yorkshire pudding, try Rules, the oldest surviving restaurant in London (35 Maiden Lane, WC2; ☎ 0207-836-5314; tube: Charing Cross). Yes, it's a tourist trap, but it is also redolent of a long-gone era, with the photos and cartoons on the wall charting its history since it opened in 1798. And where else can you get grouse, woodcock, and partridge?

You will most likely love the play, especially because you will have paid half price for some perfectly decent seats, and the theater itself may be an architectural gem. You will love how they sell delicious ice cream right in the theater at the intermission (or, as they call it, "the interval"), and you will be proud of yourself for already ordering your refreshments before the play started and finding them waiting for you at the bar at intermission. When the play gets out at 10:30 or 11 p.m., walk over to Ronnie Scott's (47 Frith Street, W1; ☎ 0207-439-0747; tube: Tottenham Court Road) and listen to jazz until it's time to call it a day and go back to your hotel.

WALKING IN *and* AROUND LONDON

WALKING IS BY FAR THE BEST WAY TO EXPERIENCE London. Grab a map and your camera, select a starting point, and just begin to explore. You never know what you may find once you move off of London's bustling main thoroughfares: a cobbled alleyway with a quaint café, a medieval church, or even a dreamy view across the river. Below are a number of suggested walks covering a diverse range of areas. Many cross the paths of some great London attractions and can create an entire day's worth of wandering if you decide to stop off and visit some of the sights along the way.

You might also want to try out **The Original London Walks** (☎ 0207-624-3978; **www.walks.com**), which offers 120 weekly themed walks dedicated to Jack the Ripper, ghosts of London, lost palaces, The Beatles, rock and roll, literary London, the swinging 1960s, Princess Diana, Charles Dickens, and so many more. Pick up a leaflet at any hotel or check for daily events in *Time Out*. Another option is to enjoy the encyclopedic knowledge of Diane Burstein of **Secret London Walks** (☎ 0208-881-2933; **www.secretlondonwalks.co.uk**). You can choose from a variety of themed walks, or you might prefer to arrange a private tour dedicated to your own personal interests.

WALKING ON YOUR OWN

IF YOU PREFER TO WALK AT YOUR OWN PACE, try the strolls we've outlined here.

City of London: Through the Centuries

TIME TO ALLOW 3–4 hours depending on indoor visits.

DISTANCE Approximately 1.5 miles.

TUBE St. Paul's or Barbican.

SIGHTS Museum of London; St. Botolph, Aldersgate; Postman's Park; St. Bartholomew-the-Great Church; National Postal Museum; Christ Church, Greyfriars; St. Paul's Cathedral; Guildhall (including Guildhall Clock Museum and Guildhall Art Gallery); St. Lawrence Jewry.

This walk gives just a glimpse of the vast array of architecture that has evolved in London over the centuries, from the ancient Roman wall that once enclosed the fourth-century city of Londinium, to the skyscrapers of the modern financial district. Begin your wanderings at the Museum of London, looking out from the museum's terrace, where you are surrounded by concrete and glass. This is 20th-century London, with heavy traffic and office buildings. However, if you know where to look, you will glimpse bits of old—the London of

medieval peasants, Renaissance grandeur, and Victorian sentimental-
ity. A stop at the museum is great for getting your bearings on
London's diverse historical eras.

After enjoying an engaging hour or two of well-curated history,
head across the traffic circle to Aldersgate. Locate Little Britain
Street on the right; St. Botolph Church is on the corner. The church's
classical Georgian interior is a glorious contrast to its bland and
unassuming exterior. Turn right as you exit the church and enter
Postman's Park. This hidden churchyard was dedicated by the Victorians in 1900 as a memorial to "heroes of everyday life" who died in
acts of selfless bravery (it forms an important plot twist to the 2004
movie *Closer,* with Jude Law and Natalie Portman, a great movie for
London-location viewing). In the center of the intimate park, you
will find the protected wall of memorials. One epitaph reads, "Saved
a lunatic woman from suicide at Woolwich Arsenal, but was himself
run over by the train." Exiting the park on the opposite side, turn
right onto King Edward Street, then follow Little Britain around to
the left to where it deposits you in Smithfield Square.

In medieval times, the marketplace of Smithfield Green was thriving with merchants, peddlers, peasants, and livestock. Jousts,
tournaments, horse fairs, and hangings have all been held here. To
your left is St. Bartholomew's Hospital. Begun in 1123 as a priory and
hospice, it is London's oldest hospital. Out front is a memorial to Sir
William Wallace, known as Braveheart, the Scot who defied a king
and was torn in quarters by four horses for the crime of treason. If
you venture inside the hospital's main entrance, you will find the small
hospital church of St. Bartholomew-the-Less and an 18th-century
courtyard. Back out on the square and to your right you will see a
half-timbered Tudor gatehouse. Through here is a gem of medieval
London, the Priory Church of St. Bartholomew-the-Great, also dating back to 1123. Don't miss the opportunity to take a look at this
breathtaking example of original 12th-century Norman architecture.

Making your way back to Little Britain, turn right onto King Edward Street, using the dome of St. Paul's Cathedral before you as a
guide. Past Postman's Park and the National Postal Museum, at the end
of Little Britain, are the remains of Christopher Wren's Christ Church,
Greyfriars. Originally built in 1691, it was destroyed during air raids in
World War II. Today, the tower and walls enclose a lovely trellised garden marking the original location of the church columns and center
aisle. Cross Newgate Street and turn left. Beyond the tube station entrance is the churchyard of St. Paul's Cathedral. Vastly different from
medieval St. Bart's, Christopher Wren's Renaissance masterpiece is the
second largest cathedral in the world. Stop here to see the glorious interior or perhaps climb the dome for unparalleled city views.

Wandering back through the churchyard, turn right and head east
on Cheapside. Cross over and make a left on Wood Street and then fol-

low Milk Street as it bears to the right. This area was another of London's medieval marketplaces, although the only remnants are the street names—Bread Street, Milk Street, Honey Lane—to remind you of its past. Just ahead is the entrance to Guildhall, the headquarters for the Corporation of London. Behind the bleak 20th-century facade lies the impressive Great Hall, open 10 a.m.–4:30 p.m. Monday through Friday. Next door, the Guildhall Library houses a clock museum (open 9:30 a.m.–4:30 p.m., Monday through Friday) and a remarkable art collection. Also, if you can catch it open, be sure to stop in and see the spectacular interior of the Church of St. Lawrence Jewry located on the main road. The name is derived from its location on the site of London's early Jewish ghetto. Finally, follow King Street south to Victoria Street. Turn right and end your walk at Mansion House tube station.

Old Hampstead Village

TIME TO ALLOW 2 hours.

DISTANCE Approximately 1.5–2 miles.

ALSO NEARBY Freud Museum, Kenwood House.

TUBE Hampstead.

SIGHTS Church Row, St. John's-at-Hampstead, Fenton House, Admiral's House, Burgh House, Flask Walk and Well Walk, Downshire Hill, Keats House, Hampstead Heath, Hampstead High Street.

The history of Hampstead has always been tied closely to its hill, its heath, and its healthy environment, and in the early 1700s, Hampstead became a booming spa town. The area's iron-rich water was said to cure all manner of ailments, and you could purchase flasks of the vile-tasting stuff for 3p a bottle or bathe in it at one of the local bathhouses. Today, narrow streets lined with lovingly restored 18th-century homes help the village retain much of its charming Georgian atmosphere.

Arriving in Hampstead via the underground, you come up London's deepest elevator shaft near the top of Hampstead Hill in the village center. Heath Street and Hampstead High Street stretch before you, lined with shops, cafés, and restaurants—definitely a great area in which to stop for tea at the end of your walk. Exiting the tube station, cross over and turn left on Heath Street, then right on Church Row, one of the best-preserved streets in London. Notice the grand wrought-iron work, the remains of early 18th-century oil lampstands, and the intricately detailed windows over many of the homes' main entrances. These fanlights, illuminated from behind by candles, helped identify one's home after dark in the days before street lighting. Famous residents here included George du Maurier and H. G. Wells. At the end of the line of trees sits St. John's-at-Hampstead, consecrated in 1747. Take some time to wander the graveyard and church, then head up Holly Walk.

At the top of the hill on the right, St. Mary's Church is nestled among a row of homes. One of London's oldest Roman Catholic churches, its discreet location is due to its existence before religious tolerance was granted in 1829. Make a right and follow Mount Vernon down to where it meets up with Hampstead Grove. Turn left. Another worthwhile stop is Fenton House on the right. This wonderfully preserved 17th-century home today houses an exquisite collection of Asian, European, and English china, needlework, and furniture, but its finest attraction is its unique collection of early musical instruments, including Handel's harpsichord. Beyond Fenton House, turn left onto Admiral's Walk. Look carefully at the house and you will see the nautical alterations made by Lt. Fountain North in 1775. North adapted the roof to resemble the deck of a ship, complete with flagstaff and cannon, which were fired to celebrate naval victories. P. L. Travers and Walt Disney fans should find this all vaguely familiar; the character and home of Admiral Boom in *Mary Poppins* was based on this eccentric individual.

At the end of Hampstead Grove, where it runs into the main thoroughfare of Heath Street, you will find a small reservoir on your left. Whitstone Pond, built in 1856, allowed Londoners who had successfully navigated the steep muddy roads to the hilltop to clean their carriages by walking their horses down the ramps and through the pond. Crossing Heath Street, begin your journey down the hill and alongside Hampstead Heath, turning right at Squire's Mount and passing some lovely cottages, which date to 1704. Continue on Cannon Lane, turning left on Well Road, so named for the spring that gave the town its reputation for health. Famous residents here included D. H. Lawrence, J. B. Priestly, and John Constable. Turning left on New End Square brings you past Burgh House, the 1703 home of Hampstead Spa's physician, William Gibbons. Today the building is a local museum, meeting place, and exhibition space. There is a small tearoom downstairs if you need a snack or rest. To your left is Well Walk and to your right, Flask Walk. Just up Flask Walk on your right is a bathhouse that was actually in use by some locals until the late 1960s. Cross Well Walk and enjoy a downhill stroll on Willow Road. At the bottom, turn right on Downshire Hill.

This is another picturesque street lined with 19th-century homes and gardens; its centerpiece is St. John's-at-Hampstead Church, opened in 1823. If open, it is worth taking a quick peek inside. Turning left on Keats Grove brings you to our last stop. John Keats lived in Hampstead from 1818 to 1820, and it is here that he produced many of his most famous works. The home is carefully restored and decorated as Keats would have known it, and the intimate museum is a wonderful tribute to his short, tragic life. Upon leaving Keats House, turn left and head back up Keats Grove, then left again on Downshire Hill. Make a right on Rosslyn Hill and enjoy some window-shopping or stop in one of the many cafés on your way back toward the Hampstead tube station, just a five-minute walk up the road.

Royal London: From Palace to Parliament

TIME TO ALLOW 3–4 hours.

DISTANCE Approximately 2.5 miles.

TUBE Victoria.

SIGHTS Royal Mews, Queen's Gallery, Buckingham Palace, St. James's Park, Cabinet War Rooms, Admiralty Arch, Trafalgar Square, National Gallery, National Portrait Gallery, St. Martin-in-the-Fields Church, Royal Horse Guards, Banqueting House, 10 Downing Street, Cenotaph, Houses of Parliament, St. Margaret's Church, Westminster Abbey.

This walk takes you past many of London's most popular sights. London's history, royalty, and fabulous architecture are thoroughly represented as we travel throughout Westminster, home to London's monarchy and Parliament. The walk affords plenty of opportunities to stop along the way, so the length of the walk depends entirely on your stamina.

Begin your walk at Victoria tube station. Turn right on Buckingham Palace Road, following signs for the palace. Just beyond Lower Grosvenor Place you will find the entrance for the Royal Mews on the left. Housed here in the palace stables is an impressive display of royal carriages; the oldest, made in 1762 for George III, is still used for coronations. Just past the Royal Mews is the Queen's Gallery, recently renovated and upgraded to display even more of the royal monarch's incredible collection of privately owned works of art. Continuing, you will soon arrive in the palace forecourt.

Buckingham Palace has been the official London residence of the sovereign since George III bought the place from Lord Buckingham in 1762. The palace is home and office for Her Majesty, and its elaborately decorated rooms are in continuous use for state affairs, official receptions, ceremonial occasions, and Parliamentary meetings. See the attractions listing for opening times; it is currently open to the public only from August through October. North of the palace is Green Park, but you need to locate St. James's Park, to the right of The Mall, as that is our next area to explore.

Enter the park by Birdcage Walk, and wander east along the pond's edge. St. James's is the oldest of London's parks. It started life as part of the private grounds of St. James's Palace, but was opened to the public during the reign of the Stuart monarchs. Cross over the bridge, stopping to take in the stunning views of the palace to the west and the Horse Guards Parade to the east. As you continue to walk along the path beside the lake, the London Eye Ferris wheel, Westminster Abbey, and St. Stephen's Clock Tower can be seen through the trees, wildlife skitter past or glide by on the water, and if you're lucky, the sun will shine a few rays through the clouds above. Charles II, Samuel Pepys, and John Milton have all enjoyed similar views (except for that of the London Eye, of course, which has a modern elegance I'm sure they would have loved). The most famous residents of the park are the pelicans, who have delighted visitors there since the 17th century. Every afternoon they parade across the lawn on Duck Island to receive their daily fish dinner, and they thoroughly enjoy the sanctuary provided here, along with the 20 or more other species of duck and goose that call St. James's home.

As you reach the other side of the park, cross Horse Guards Road. Just in front of you, King Charles Street ends at a stairway, and to the right of this is the entrance to the Cabinet War Rooms, a fascinating museum that now has its own restaurant. Winston Churchill and his cabinet carried out operations here during World War II. From the War Rooms, turn right on Horse Guards Road, passing the Horse Guards Parade, where the Changing of the Guard occurs daily at 11:30 a.m. (Sunday at 10 a.m.). Never take the daily changing of the guard as a given: It is frequently canceled (call 0906-866-3344 for recorded information). Turn right on The Mall and walk under Admiralty Arch and into Trafalgar Square. In the center stands Nelson's Column, the memorial to Britain's best-loved national hero, Admiral Lord Horatio Nelson, who defeated Napoléon at the Battle of Trafalgar in 1806. The square is the location for frequent political demonstrations, London's annual Christmas tree lighting, and New Year's countdowns. The famous feeding of pigeons was outlawed a few years ago to the relief of the cleaning crew and the disappointment of the ornithologically courageous. Behind is the National Gallery, where you could spend hours enjoying one of the world's greatest art collections. To the right is the 18th-century church of St. Martin-in-the-Fields, definitely worth a stop. Its simple but elegant interior offers free lunchtime concerts. Downstairs, the church's Café-in-the-Crypt provides soups and sandwiches.

Leaving Trafalgar Square, walk down Whitehall (the street directly opposite the National Gallery). You will pass the front of the Horse Guards Building, with its guards at attention, and almost directly opposite is the Banqueting House, the only intact remains of the great palace at Whitehall, which burned to the ground in 1698. Prior to this loss, the palace was the site of numerous historical events, such as the marriage of Henry VIII to Anne Boleyn and the execution of Charles I during the English Civil War. Others who have lived here include Cardinal Wolsey, Oliver Cromwell, Charles II, and William III and Mary II. It's a quick hit kind of place, but well worth a stop, as the Rubens ceiling celebrating the Stuart kings has a lot to do with why they lopped Charles I's head off: he truly believed in the divine right of kings, as the Rubens ceiling so absurdly demonstrates.

Farther along Whitehall on the right is 10 Downing Street, home of Britain's prime minister, although you are not likely to see much, because the street is guarded and gated and crawling with police. The Cenotaph, in the middle of Whitehall, is Britain's memorial to those who died in World War I. It is the focal point of the country's Remembrance Day ceremonies, which include two minutes of silence throughout the entire country on the 11th minute of the 11th hour of the 11th day of the 11th month each year.

Not far ahead, you will begin to see the buildings of Westminster coming into view. Once you have arrived in Parliament Square, you have a number of choices before you. You can wander out onto Westminster Bridge for the best views of Westminster Abby, Parliament, and St. Stephen's Tower, and have a look at the wonderful statue of the warrior Queen Boadica on her horse-drawn chariot, at the foot of the bridge. You can sit in on debates in the Houses of Parliament or explore the 16th-century St. Margaret's Church (where Sir Walter Raleigh is laid to rest). And take the opportunity at walk's end to enjoy inspiring hymns sung by the Westminster Boys Choir during the daily choral evensong at Westminster Abbey, possibly the most visited tourist sight and certainly one of the most beautiful churches in London.

█ FOR MUSEUM LOVERS

IF YOU LOVE GOING TO MUSEUMS, YOU ALREADY have a lot in common with typical Londoners. London is crammed with wonderful museums, many of which are free of charge.

There's a remarkable Web site that details current and upcoming exhibitions at 2,000 museums in London and across the country; it also offers virtual tours of the permanent collections of the museums featured. It's a great way to see some of the smaller, harder-to-visit museums without leaving your desk. The Web site's goal is to represent Britain's entire cultural history—no small undertaking. Visit it at **www.24hourmuseum.org.uk.**

Saving Money on Museum Admissions

There are ways to save on the admission fees of museums, attractions, and galleries. However, let me point out that the British, Victoria and Albert, Science, Natural History, both Tates, and many other smaller museums are free of charge, except for special exhibitions. So if you really want to do London on the cheap, you could skip the high ticket prices of the Tower of London, the London Eye, the Saatchi Gallery, Madame Tussauds and others, and you will still have so much to do you may not fit it all in. If you want it all, as well as additional deal sweeteners, try the Londonpass, a program launched by the London Tourist Board in 1999. This pass affords fast-track, reduced, or free entry into more than 50 fee-charging attractions, free travel on tubes, trains, and buses; discounts at a number of restaurants; free phone rental; discounts on film developing; free walking tours; and a plethora of other incentives to buy. They had to pull out all the stops to make the Londonpass attractive since so many museums dropped their entrance fees in late 2001. It's not exactly inexpensive, with a one-day pass starting at £27 (without transport or the 17.5 percent VAT) for adults and £18 for children; rising to £32 for adults and £20 for children with transport. The price goes incrementally higher per day, with a 6-day-plus-transport pass costing £110 for adults and £61 for children ages 5–15 (a no-transport 6-day pass is either £72 or £48. OK, now only you can make the call if it's worth it or not. The more days you stay the higher the savings, but you may want to go out of London for a day or two, or simply rest in the hotel or at a park some days. However, if you're one of those very organized and energetic types determined to drink the last drop of honey from London's bounteous cup, it will definitely save you plenty. For example, if you are planning to go to, say, the Tower of London, at £14.50 for adults and £9.50 for children, and then want to take a river cruise to Hampton Court or see the Tower Bridge Experience, it may be worth it, especially with all the extras, such as free skating or bowling at Firstbowl Queensway, or £4.50 worth of free brass rubbing at St. Martins. Passes can be purchased (for a £1 discount) online at **www.londonpass.com** or at the British Visitor Centre (1 Regent Street, south of Piccadilly Circus). Just remember that getting to and from attractions in London can take a big bite out of your day and may make seeing more than two attractions per day difficult.

London Attractions by Neighborhood

ATTRACTION NAME/ LOCATION	DESCRIPTION	AUTHOR'S RATING
WEST END		
British Museum	Among the most famous museums in the world	★★★★★
Dickens House	Historic home and museum	★
London Transport Museum	Interactive museum of trams, buses, and trains	★★★★
National Gallery	Art gallery	★★★★★
National Portrait Gallery	Famous faces of England	★★★★
Royal Academy of Arts	Museum and exhibition venue	★★★★
Sir John Soane's Museum	Historic home and museum	★★★★
Somerset House	Historic home and art galleries	★★★★★

ATTRACTION NAME/ LOCATION	DESCRIPTION	AUTHOR'S RATING
THE CITY, EAST END, AND SOUTH LONDON		
Bank of England Museum	Museum of money and banking	★★
The British Airways London Eye	Observation wheel	★★★★★
Clink Exhibition	Re-creation of a medieval prison	★★★
Dali Universe	Surrealist master's works	★★★★
Design Museum	Changing exhibits of exemplars of design	★★
Dr. Johnson's House	Historic home and museum	★★
The Globe Theatre	Reconstructed Shakespearean theater	★★★★
Guildhall	Corporate headquarters for the City of London	★★
HMS *Belfast*	Royal Navy battleship from WWII	★★
Imperial War Museum	British military experience	★★
London Aquarium	Wonderland of fish	★★★★
London Dungeon	Horror attraction	★★★
Millennium Bridge	Footbridge across the Thames	★★★
The Monument	Commemorating the Great Fire of 1666	★★★
Museum of Childhood at Bethnal Green	Large museum of toys	★★★
Museum of London	Museum of the city's history	★★★★★
Old Bailey	London's central criminal courts	★★
Old Operating Theatre, Museum, and Herb Garret	Museum of old medical equipment	★★★★
Saatchi Gallery	Best of young British modern art	★★★
Southwark Cathedral	Small medieval church	★★★
St. Paul's Cathedral	London's most prominent cathedral	★★★
Tate Modern	Museum of international modern art	★★★★
Tower Bridge Experience	Offers terrific views	★★
The Tower of London	Ancient fortress	★★★★★
Windsor Castle	Queen's country house in Hertfordshire	★★★★
WESTMINSTER AND VICTORIA		
Big Ben Clock Tower	Monument	Not rated
Buckingham Palace	Stately home of the queen	★★★
The Cabinet War Rooms and Churchill Museum	Secret WWII headquarters	★★★

London Attractions by Neighborhood *(continued)*

ATTRACTION NAME/ LOCATION	DESCRIPTION	AUTHOR'S RATING
WESTMINSTER AND VICTORIA (CONTINUED)		
Changing of the Guard	Grand old tradition	★★
Houses of Parliament	Britain's working chambers of government	★★★
Queen's Gallery, Buckingham Palace	Art gallery	★★★
Royal Mews, Buckingham Palace	Where royal carriages and queen's horses are kept	★★★
Tate Britain	Museum of English painters	★★★★
Westminster Abbey	Historically important church	★★★★
KNIGHTSBRIDGE TO SOUTH KENSINGTON		
Apsley House (The Wellington Museum)	Historic home and museum	★★★
Carlyle's House	Historic home and museum	★★★
Natural History Museum	Old and modern exhibits	★★★
The Science Museum	Huge, excellent museum	★★★★
Victoria and Albert Museum	Museum of decorative arts	★★★★★
The Wellington Arch	Small, specialty museum of architecture	★★
MARYLEBONE TO NOTTING HILL GATE, KENSINGTON		
Albert Memorial	Outdoor memorial	★★
Kensington Palace State Rooms	Stately home of Kensington Gardens	★★★★
Leighton House Museum and Art Gallery	Historic home	★★
Linley Sambourne House	Historic home	★★★
Madame Tussaud's Waxworks and the London Planetarium	World-famous wax museum	★
Sherlock Holmes Museum	Museum	★★★
Wallace Collection	Private collection of 19th-century Anglo-French art	★★★
NORTH LONDON		
British Library at St. Pancras	Multidisciplinary cultural collection	★★★★

ATTRACTION NAME/ LOCATION	DESCRIPTION	AUTHOR'S RATING
NORTH LONDON (CONTINUED)		
Burgh House and Hampstead Museum	Museum with exhibition and concert space	★★
Freud Museum	Historic home and museum	★★
Kenwood House (The Iveagh Bequest)	Georgian villa and art gallery	★★★★
London Zoo	Modernized old zoo	★★★★
GREENWICH AND DOCKLANDS		
Cutty Sark	Restored sailing clipper ship	★★★
National Maritime Museum and Queen's House	Largest maritime museum in the world	★★★★
Royal Greenwich Observatory	Location of world's prime meridian	★★★
WEST LONDON		
Chiswick House	Stately home and gardens	★★★
Hampton Court Palace	Royal palace and gardens	★★★★★
Hogarth's House	Historic home	★★

MUSEUMS *and* ATTRACTIONS

For a look into London's parks and green spaces, see "Green and Pleasant Lands: Parks of London" on page 266. Also, at the end of this chapter is a profile of Greenwich.

unofficial **TIP**
Please be sure to call the following places before you go; opening times can be subject to change without notice.

Albert Memorial

APPEAL BY AGE	PRESCHOOL ★★	GRADE SCHOOL ★★	TEENS ★★
YOUNG ADULTS ★★		OVER 30 ★★	SENIORS ★★

Kensington Gardens, west of Exhibition Road, Kensington, SW7; tube: High Street Kensington

Type of attraction Outdoor memorial to a beloved prince consort. **Admission** Free. **Hours** Daily, dawn to dusk. **When to go** A sunny day, or at night when the floodlights are on. **Special comments** Bring binoculars so you can see the amazing detail of the high parts of the memorial. **Author's rating** ★★. **How much time to allow** 15 minutes, plus time to hang around on the steps. It's a good people-watching place, right near Kensington Palace.

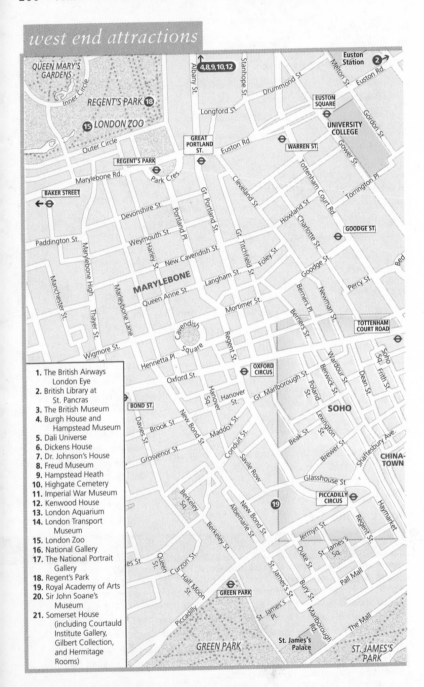

west end attractions

1. The British Airways London Eye
2. British Library at St. Pancras
3. The British Museum
4. Burgh House and Hampstead Museum
5. Dali Universe
6. Dickens House
7. Dr. Johnson's House
8. Freud Museum
9. Hampstead Heath
10. Highgate Cemetery
11. Imperial War Museum
12. Kenwood House
13. London Aquarium
14. London Transport Museum
15. London Zoo
16. National Gallery
17. The National Portrait Gallery
18. Regent's Park
19. Royal Academy of Arts
20. Sir John Soane's Museum
21. Somerset House (including Courtauld Institute Gallery, Gilbert Collection, and Hermitage Rooms)

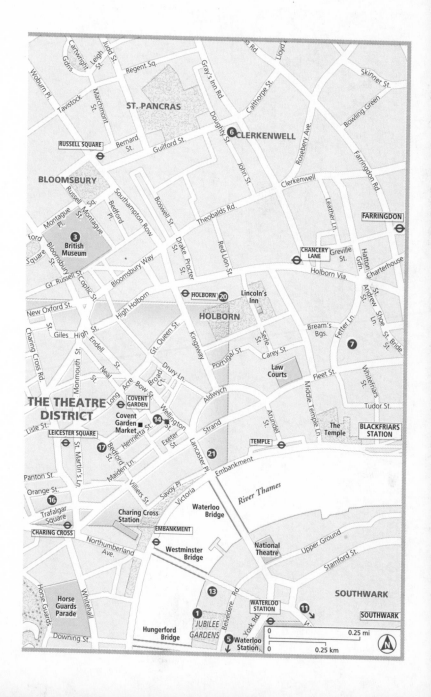

westminster and victoria attractions

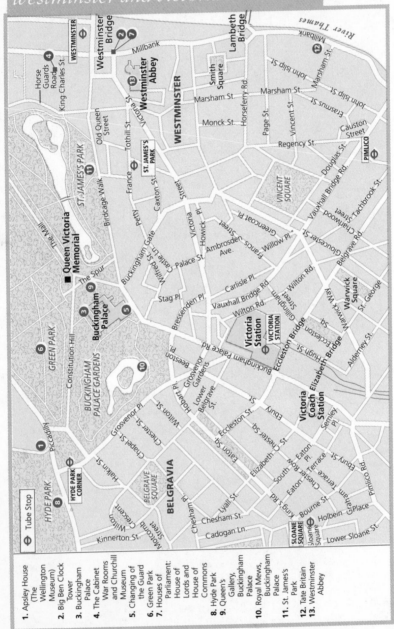

Tube Stop ⊕

1. Apsley House (The Wellington Museum)
2. Big Ben Clock Tower
3. Buckingham Palace
4. The Cabinet War Rooms and Churchill Museum
5. Changing of the Guard
6. Green Park
7. Houses of Parliament: House of Lords and House of Commons
8. Hyde Park
9. Queen's Gallery, Buckingham Palace
10. Royal Mews, Buckingham Palace
11. St. James's Park
12. Tate Britain
13. Westminster Abbey

"the city" attractions

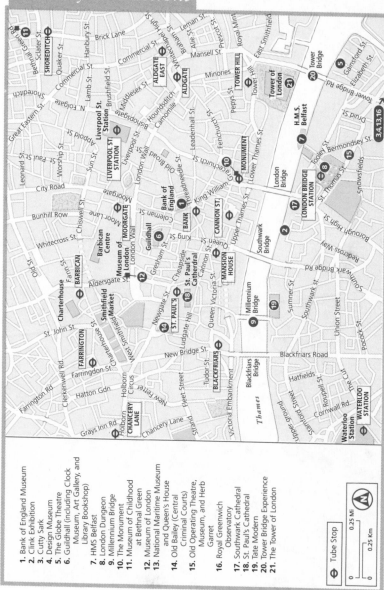

1. Bank of England Museum
2. Clink Exhibition
3. Cutty Sark
4. Design Museum
5. The Globe Theatre
6. Guildhall (including Clock Museum, Art Gallery, and Library Bookshop)
7. HMS Belfast
8. London Dungeon
9. Millennium Bridge
10. The Monument
11. Museum of Childhood at Bethnal Green
12. Museum of London
13. National Maritime Museum and Queen's House
14. Old Bailey (Central Criminal Courts)
15. Old Operating Theatre, Museum, and Herb Garret
16. Royal Greenwich Observatory
17. Southwark Cathedral
18. St. Paul's Cathedral
19. Tate Modern
20. Tower Bridge Experience
21. The Tower of London

Ⓗ Tube Stop

0   0.25 Mi
0   0.25 Km

knightsbridge to south kensington

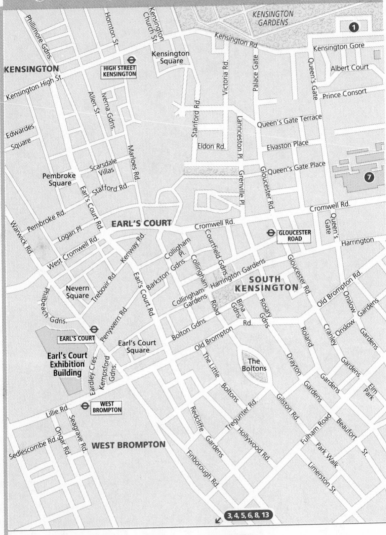

1. Albert Memorial
2. Carlyle's House
3. Chiswick House
4. Hampton Court Palace
5. Hogarth's House
6. Kew Gardens
7. Natural History Museum
8. Richmond Park
9. Saatchi Gallery
10. The Science Museum
11. Victoria and Albert Museum
12. The Wellington Arch
13. Windsor Castle

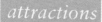

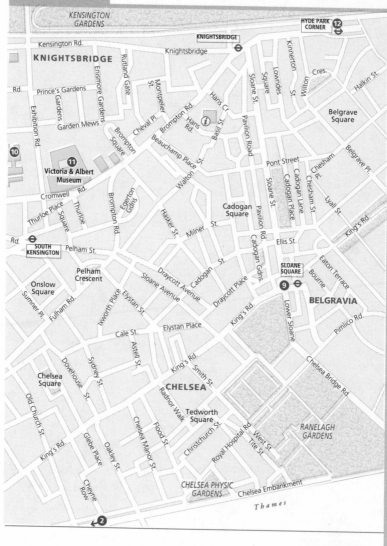

Information

Tube Stop

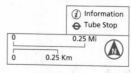

marylebone to notting hill gate

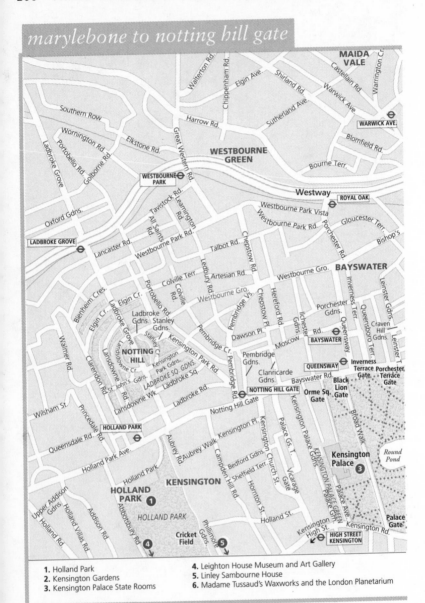

1. Holland Park
2. Kensington Gardens
3. Kensington Palace State Rooms
4. Leighton House Museum and Art Gallery
5. Linley Sambourne House
6. Madame Tussaud's Waxworks and the London Planetarium

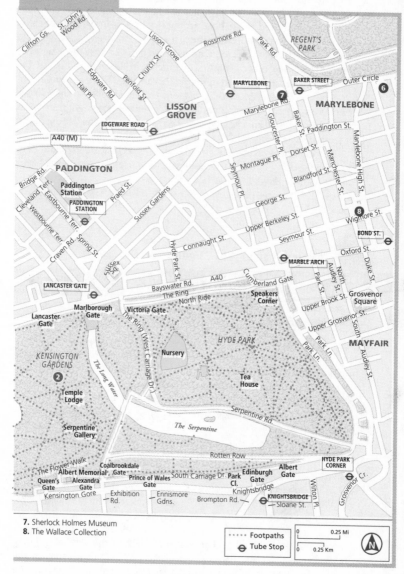

attractions

7. Sherlock Holmes Museum
8. The Wallace Collection

····· Footpaths
⊖ Tube Stop

0   0.25 Mi

0   0.25 Km

DESCRIPTION AND COMMENTS This memorial, built by a grieving Queen Victoria after her husband's death from typhoid at the age of 42, is no small thrill to see, as it had been covered in plastic and scaffolding for over a decade while being restored. It had been stripped of its gold in 1915, so we are in the privileged position of being the first generation in almost a century to see it in all its exuberant neo-Gothic gilded glory (it cost three times as much to build as one of the finest churches in Kensington built at the same time, and it caused an uproar in Parliament). There are some Londoners who find the entire thing hideous and are appalled at the millions of pounds spent for its conservation. But whatever one might think of its artistry, it is a visual knockout. Check it out at night with the floodlights on it to appreciate a view the Victorians were denied.

The memorial can be seen from many angles in Hyde Park and Kensington Gardens, but don't imagine you have experienced its full flavor until you have looked the buffalo square in the eye.

TOURING TIPS Make this part of your Kensington Palace/Gardens and Hyde Park day.

 ## Apsley House (The Wellington Museum)

APPEAL BY AGE	PRESCHOOL ★	GRADE SCHOOL ★★	TEENS ★★
YOUNG ADULTS ★★★		OVER 30 ★★★	SENIORS ★★★

149 Piccadilly, W1; ☎ 0207-499-5676;
www.english-heritage.org.uk/apsleyhouse; tube: Hyde Park Corner

Type of attraction Former home of the duke of Wellington. **Admission** £4.95 for adults, £2.50 children under age of 16, £3.70 seniors. **Hours** Tuesday–Sunday, 10 a.m.–5 p.m., March–October; closes at 4 p.m. October–March; last entry half-hour before closing. **When to go** Anytime. **Special comments** There is no wheelchair access, and there are multiple steps into the house and between the floors. If you walk along the pedestrian subway below Hyde Park Corner, you can see the story of Apsley House and the duke of Wellington rendered on the tiles on the wall, a good way to prepare for the visit to the house. **Author's rating** ★★★. **How much time to allow** 45 minutes to an hour; more if you really love old masters.

DESCRIPTION AND COMMENTS This grand house was built between 1771 and 1778 by Robert Adams, and was purchased and upgraded by the duke of Wellington in 1817, after his military successes in the Napoléonic Wars. There's an incongruously huge, naked (with fig leaf, of course) statue of the petite Napoléon in a stairwell, and an outrageously detailed silver centerpiece that runs the length of the very long dining table. While the Hyde Park Corner traffic circle whirls in front of the house, the windows in the back of Apsley House look out onto a serene vista of Hyde Park, the rose gardens, and the occasional horseback riders. Apsley House is of great interest to art lovers as its gallery is filled with old masters such as Velázquez, Goya, and Rubens, along with some lesser luminaries. The house is lovingly kept in good repair after being recently handed over to English Heritage by the Victoria and Albert

Museum, and it gives one an invaluable education in the decoration of great houses of the day. The basement houses a collection of political cartoons that will teach you about the duke—one of the towering public figures of his day—and his times.

TOURING TIPS This is a small, quick-hit kind of place, and it fits in well with a walk through Hyde Park and a visit to the Wellington Arch, before moving on through Green and St. James's parks.

Bank of England Museum

APPEAL BY AGE	PRESCHOOL —	GRADE SCHOOL ★★	TEENS ★★
YOUNG ADULTS ★★		OVER 30 ★★	SENIORS ★★

Threadneedle Street, The City, EC2 (museum entrance on Bartholomew Lane); ☎ 0207-601-5545; www.bankofengland.co.uk; tube: Bank

Type of attraction Historical displays tracing the rise of banking and the use of currency. **Admission** Free. **Hours** Monday–Friday, 10 a.m.–5 p.m.; closed weekends and bank holidays. **When to go** Anytime. **Special comments** Disabled friendly, with portable ramps available on request. **Author's rating** ★★. **How much time to allow** 1 hour.

DESCRIPTION AND COMMENTS This is the only part of the massive fortress that is the Bank of England, known as The Old Lady of Threadneedle Street, that mere mortals can enter. One display shows the evolution of the banknote from 1694—when the bank was formed to lend money to the government to pay for King James II's war against France—to the present; much of the currency used over time can be viewed here. Another display is modeled after the first bank and includes mannequins of wigged clerks and a huge fireplace behind mahogany counters. A video shows real footage from the building of the present bank in the 1930s, and there are interactive computer screens that provide a lot of information. Be warned: The displays require quite a bit of reading, as well as a particular interest in money and banking.

Big Ben Clock Tower

Parliament Square, Westminster, SW1; www.londontouristboard.com; tube: Westminster

Type of attraction Look-only clock tower; enduring symbol of London. **Admission** One cannot enter the tower. **Hours** 24 hours a day. **When to go** When you're in the area.

DESCRIPTION AND COMMENTS Big Ben is not an attraction per se, but it is a beautiful piece of architecture that you can set your watch to. It is the most recognizable symbol of the city, and replicas of Big Ben are at the top of most visitors' must-have souvenir list. The bells play an instantly recognizable tune on the hour, followed by a wonderful tolling of the time.

In 1834, the old Palace of Westminster burned to the ground, and Parliament decided to build itself a Gothic-style replacement—neo-Gothic was all the rage in those days, as the ugliness of the industrial present bathed the past in a nostalgic glow. The clock tower was part of the grand plan, but due to its exacting specifications, construction took some time and was beset by difficulties. Big Ben refers in fact to the actual bell that chimes, and it was Big Trouble from the start. The first bell cast cracked almost immediately—probably from the weight of the clapper—and had to be recast in a smaller format. The clock's hands were too heavy to move, and also had to be replaced. The bell cracked again, and was silent for three years, until a solution was found in 1862. Big Ben has been ringing out the famous Westminster chimes ever since.

  ## The British Airways London Eye

APPEAL BY AGE PRESCHOOL ★ ★ ★ ★   GRADE SCHOOL ★ ★ ★ ★ ★   TEENS ★ ★ ★ ★ ★
YOUNG ADULTS ★ ★ ★ ★ ★   OVER 30 ★ ★ ★ ★ ★   SENIORS ★ ★ ★ ★ ★

In Jubilee Gardens, next to County Hall by Westminster Bridge, on the south bank of the Thames; ☎ 0870-500-0600; www.londoneye.com; tube: Westminster or Waterloo

Type of attraction The world's biggest observation wheel. **Admission** £13 for adults, £10 for seniors and the disabled, £6.50 for children ages 5–16, free for kids under age 5; 10% discount for parties of 10 or more or by booking online. **Hours** May–June, daily, 9:30 a.m.–8 p.m., weekends till 9 p.m.; July–September, daily, 9:30 a.m.–10 p.m.; October–December, 9:30 a.m.–8 p.m.; closed for 3 weeks in January. **When to go** Best on a sunny day or clear night; avoid these glassed-in pods on very hot days. **Special comments** This is not for those suffering from vertigo; it is very high and can make one feel quite exposed. It is disabled friendly. No baby stroller unless it folds up small; they can loan you a baby carrier. **Author's rating** ★ ★ ★ ★ ★. **How much time to allow** If you haven't ordered tickets ahead of time, you may have to wait in line, depending on the season and the weather. If you have reserved tickets (by phone or Web site), you can pick them up easily, and then you must wait about a half hour for boarding. The rotation takes 30 minutes.

DESCRIPTION AND COMMENTS Definitely London's most successful attraction designed to celebrate the new millennium, the London Eye is a colossal (450 feet high) silver wheel sprouting clear pods that hang off the frame. Originally planned to last for a five-year period, its wild popularity has ensured it a place among the most traditional of London's attractions. There have been constant improvements in the running of it, and now it boasts a gift shop, a free guidebook, and a much more efficient system of ticket buying and boarding. You can pay extra to have a private pod, which comes with a guide, and they have special champagne "flights" (British Air uses aeronautical terms rather endearingly). Each of the 32 pods carries about 25 people, with benches for those who wish to sit. The design and the effect are surprisingly elegant and graceful; the wheel soars above the old buildings of Westminster and the South Bank. It moves slowly and majestically up, until its zenith of 450 feet, at which point passengers can see a good 25 miles away on a clear day. It's an amazing view of London. Most Londoners have taken the arching view of the wheel to heart, and rank it as a graceful addition to the skyline. An uproar in 2005 over price gouging on the lease of the land on which it sits was settled amicably, but the skirmish revealed just how much the locals value this attraction.

TOURING TIPS If you order tickets ahead of time on the Web site or by telephone, you choose the day and the time you wish to "board"; then you show up with your credit card and retrieve your tickets from the center in the City Hall Building—follow the signs to it. A word of caution: The glass pods can be hot on sunny summer days. Combine your visit with a trip to the aquarium (especially if traveling with children), Dali's Universe, or lunch at the Marriott Hotel's dining room with the river view.

British Library at St. Pancras

APPEAL BY AGE	PRESCHOOL –	GRADE SCHOOL ★★	TEENS ★★
YOUNG ADULTS ★★★	OVER 30 ★★★		SENIORS ★★★★

96 Euston Road, North London, NW1; ☎ 0207-412-7000; www.bl.uk; tube: King's Cross

Type of attraction New location of reading rooms (manuscript-archive collections) formerly housed in the British Museum (see profile below). **Admission** Free. **Hours** Daily: general admission, 10 a.m.–5 p.m.; special exhibition times vary. **When to go** Anytime. **Special comments** Full wheelchair/disabled access. **Author's rating ★★★★. How much time to allow** 1–2 hours.

DESCRIPTION AND COMMENTS The embattled (and expensive: £500 million!) project to move the reading rooms from their beautiful, longtime niche at the British Museum was one of those necessary concessions to age that no one really wanted to make. However, since the opening, visitors and readers have grudgingly admitted that it is a vast improvement over the cramped old quarters. Even Prince Charles, who scorned the exterior as "a collection of brick sheds groping for significance," was impressed with the interior. The fact is that, however lacking in aesthetics the place may be, it's still a veritable Aladdin's cave of treasures, and a much improved one at that. Manuscripts such as the Lindisfarne Gospels from the tenth century, James Joyce's first draft of *Finnegan's Wake*, a copy of the Magna Carta from 1215, the Gutenberg Bible, and plenty of documents related to the greatest English writer of all, Shakespeare, are only some of the magnificent materials on view here.

The library offers to the public a fine bookstore, a café, and three exhibition galleries. There's the John Riblat Gallery, in which are displayed some of the library's most ancient and valuable manuscripts and maps. There's a wondrous room called "Turning the Page" in which a computer allows you to virtually flip through four gloriously illuminated texts: the Lindisfarne Gospels, the Diamond Sutra, da Vinci's notebooks, and the Sforza Hours. You can listen to James Joyce and other authors reading from their work, and to music of all types, too. In the Pearson Gallery of Living Words are educational exhibits, one of which explores the history of writing; another is a reading area, with a good display of children's literature. There are a few interactive, fun things to do, such as design a book or check out the evolution of recorded music.

TOURING TIPS This is not really a tourist attraction; it is for people who love and respect books, so take care who you take along with you. Sign up for a guided tour to see the parts of the library not open to the public.

 ## The British Museum

APPEAL BY AGE   PRESCHOOL ★★★★   GRADE SCHOOL ★★★★   TEENS ★★★★★
YOUNG ADULTS ★★★★★   OVER 30 ★★★★★   SENIORS ★★★★★

Great Russell Street, Bloomsbury, WC1; ☎ 0207-636-1555; www.britishmuseum.ac.uk; tube: Tottenham Court Road

Type of attraction Colossal museum housing treasures of the British empire. **Admission** Free. **Hours** Saturday–Wednesday, 10 a.m.–5:30 p.m.; Thursday–Friday, 10 a.m.–8:30 p.m. (selected galleries only open after 5:30 p.m.). **When to go** Early mornings. **Special comments** Obtain a leaflet from the information desk for details about wheelchair accessibility; wheelchairs are also available to borrow. Queen Elizabeth II Great Court opened in December 2000 and has improved the museum immensely. **Author's rating** ★★★★★. **How much time to allow** 2–4 hours.

DESCRIPTION AND COMMENTS This venerable old institution houses more than 50,000 items in 100 galleries, and receives upward of 7 million visitors a year. It all began when Sir Hans Sloane bequeathed his remarkable collection of art and artifacts to the state in 1753, and the earl of Oxford's rare manuscripts were added to the mix. The collection grew rapidly, as it became the scholarly and patriotic thing to do to leave one's finest possessions to the museum, and the museum repeatedly benefited from England's greatest empire-booty-looting years. Even the stolen goods from Napoléon's own prodigious empire-building campaigns were placed here after the British defeated the French at Alexandria during the Napoléonic Wars.

At the British Museum, you can travel to the ends of the globe, throughout centuries of humankind's time on earth, and see just about every little thing that our ancestors thought up along the way: mummies, pottery, clocks, painting, tools for war and peace, sculpture, personal decoration, household goods, treasures of gold and precious stones, and far more. Not only are there artifacts from practically every civilization throughout time, but they are of the greatest significance. The Rosetta Stone, the Lindow Man, the Egyptian mummies, and prehistoric pieces are just a few of the finds that have literally changed history and now reside here.

The building itself contributes to the museum's appeal. Recently remodeled, it features at its center the Queen Elizabeth II Great Court, which is the largest covered square in Europe, with over 3,000 panes of glass sheltering an area the size of a soccer field. This courtyard has not always been accessible, because it was gradually filled with the materials of the round, domed Reading Room of the British Library. When the library was removed to St. Pancras in 1997 (see preceding profile), the courtyard space was reclaimed.

The museum also offers numerous gift shops, many benches and tables on which to rest your tired bones, and a restaurant at the top of the courtyard that lends wonderful views of the courtyard and the Reading Room below. There are children's activities available on weekends, and occasional workshops for them during the week. It's lovely on a sunny day, and quite atmospheric during more typical gray and rainy English weather. To make the most of your visit, do study the Web site, which has the hours of all the shops, cafés, restaurants, exhibitions, and special lectures.

TOURING TIPS It's far too big to try to cover in one visit, so consult the map and the interests of your group before heading to the galleries, and use the compass multimedia system in the Reading Room to help plan your tour. There's a good guidebook sold in the excellent bookstore. And as with most museums, getting there before the school buses arrive is key. It is hard to gaze with the proper wonder at the Rosetta Stone when you're being jostled by an army of uniformed schoolchildren.

Buckingham Palace
(see profiles for Queen's Gallery and Royal Mews, both on premises)

APPEAL BY AGE	PRESCHOOL ★	GRADE SCHOOL ★★	TEENS ★★
YOUNG ADULTS ★★★		OVER 30 ★★★	SENIORS ★★★

Buckingham Palace Road, Victoria, SW1; ☎ 0207-766-7300;
www.royalcollection.org.uk; tube: Green Park

Type of attraction Stately home of the queen. **Admission** £13.50 for adults, £7 for children ages 5–16, free for children under age 5, £11.50 for seniors and students, £34 for a family ticket (£1 service charge for booking over the phone or Web site). **Hours** August–September, daily, 9:30 a.m.–4:30 p.m. **When to go** If you purchase tickets from the ticket office in Green Park, go at 9 a.m. The queues can be murder. **Special comments** Wheelchair users are required to arrange a visit in advance. I personally wouldn't inflict this tour on a preschooler, although they assure me that the young ones seem to love it. **Author's rating ★★★. How much time to allow** The better part of a morning, between the queues and the tour, which is about an hour.

DESCRIPTION AND COMMENTS Buckingham House was purchased by King George III in 1761 from the duke of Buckingham. Like most real estate, it's three most attractive features were location, location, location. Situated between St. James's and Hyde parks, with a tree-lined avenue affording views of Westminster and even St. Paul's Dome, it was like a country estate in the city (or near the city, as west of the house was still country). It was a private residence, the official court remaining—as it does to this day, if only in name—that of St. James's, and no doubt one of its attractions was that it was within easy walking distance of St James's Palace. When George IV ascended the throne, he had his favorite architect, John Nash, remodel it in the grandiose style you see today.

There are only two months in one year when you can view the state rooms at Buckingham Palace, so plan accordingly. In 1996, Queen Elizabeth II decided to open part of the palace to the public to pay for the restoration of Windsor Castle, which was severely damaged by a fire in 1992. By now, they've probably covered the cost several times over.

It's an amazing spectacle, even more so when you ponder that for all the years of the palace's existence, most loyal subjects of the Crown never had a prayer of setting foot in these august precincts, and now they're letting in the likes of you and me to eyeball the queen's goods. And what goods they are: treasures of painting, sculpture, furniture, and decoration beyond description, so I won't even try. (Neither do they. You have to buy the official guidebook to know what you are looking at; there are no signs anywhere.) I will say that after a while, I felt rather unsettled, if not revolutionary, by the endless, priceless display that must lie useless under dust clothes for much of the year. And there are hundreds of other rooms you're not allowed to see. The views through the numerous French doors are magnificent; you can look out at the back garden, a piece of ye olde English countryside within earshot of the roar of Hyde Park Corner.

Warning: This is not an attraction for everyone, not least because of the ridiculous lines you have to wait in; even the timed tickets haven't eliminated the queues. It's a lot of money and a lot of effort for what is essentially an inert stately home. You could feel equally, if not more, satisfied with a good book on the palace.

TOURING TIPS Don't bring in any bags, so you can avoid the baggage security check. Before your tour time, do go buy the official guide from the gift shop next to the palace at the Queen's Gallery—you'll save yourself a wait on the way into the palace. I repeat: It's important to get this book if you want to know what is what, because just as in your own home, there are no labels on the goods. The guides are there to answer questions, and they're very knowledgeable. There's no guided tour per se; you just go in and follow the group. The time designated for your entry will be printed on your ticket; don't bother lining up until about 15 minutes beforehand. You might wander around the gift shop or St. James's Park in the meantime.

Burgh House and Hampstead Museum

APPEAL BY AGE	PRESCHOOL ★	GRADE SCHOOL ★	TEENS ★
YOUNG ADULTS ★★		OVER 30 ★★	SENIORS ★★

New End Square, Hampstead, NW3; ☎ 0207-431-0144; www.burghhouse.org.uk; tube: Hampstead

Type of attraction Lovely period home and arts center providing exhibitions, concerts, and lectures. **Admission** Free. **Hours** Wednesday–Sunday, noon–5 p.m.; bank holidays, 2–5 p.m. **When to go** Anytime. **Author's rating** ★★. **How much time to allow** 1 hour to see Hampstead Museum exhibit; other times depend on lecture or concert lengths.

DESCRIPTION AND COMMENTS The meandering streets of Flask Walk and Well Walk are picturesque reminders of when Hampstead was a thriving spa village. To step out of the sometimes brisk Hampstead breeze, you might stop at this well-maintained Queen Anne home, where a modest museum of local history along with other, changing exhibitions are housed. The house is more well known among the locals for its ongoing series of concerts, including opera, chamber music, and jazz. (Call for a current schedule.) There is also a charming tearoom called The Buttery (☎ 0207-482-0869 for reservations) downstairs.

TOURING TIPS See our walking tour of Old Hampstead Village (pages 191–193) for other sights worth visiting in the area.

kids The Cabinet War Rooms and Churchill Museum

APPEAL BY AGE	PRESCHOOL ★	GRADE SCHOOL ★★	TEENS ★★★
YOUNG ADULTS ★★★		OVER 30 ★★★★	SENIORS ★★★★

Clive Steps, King Charles Street, Whitehall, SW1; ☎ 0207-930-6961;
www.iwm.org.uk, click on Cabinet War Rooms;
tube: Westminster or St. James's Park

Type of attraction World War II shelter for Churchill and his cabinet, now includes a museum devoted to the former prime minister. **Admission** £10 for adults, free for children under age 16, £8 for seniors and students; admission includes audio guide. **Hours** April–September, daily; 9:30 a.m.–6 p.m. **When to go** Anytime. **Special comments** Good disabled access, including wheelchairs on loan and accessible toilets. **Author's rating** ★★★. **How much time to allow** 1–2 hours.

DESCRIPTION AND COMMENTS This is the shelter in which Winston Churchill met with his staff, heads of state, and military personnel during the six years of World War II, when Hitler's bombs rained with grim regularity on London. Churchill's historic broadcasts to buck up the public were made from this site, and desperate decisions that could have turned the war against the Allies were strategized in these rooms. From the sandbags that line the front of the shelter to the old telephones and notepaper on Churchill's desk, this is an unusually close encounter with the reality of the war in London. When the war ended, the lights were turned off and the door shut, and the rooms remained exactly as they were left until the 1980s, when they were opened to the public. In 2003, the Churchill suite was opened to the public; this was where Winston and his wife, Clementine, slept, dined, and entertained during the long nights of the Blitz. The recent Churchill Project has sunk 13.5 million pounds into upgrading the existing structure and into the opening of the first museum dedicated exclusively to the indomitable Prime Minister. Children will be better catered to, with planned interactive exhibits, although the nature of the place will take their fancy no matter what "games" they offer. A place for refreshments, the Switchroom cafeteria, was opened in 2005, and is decorated with photographic artifacts. This attraction offers a good audio tour, or you can get a booklet with which to go through the rooms. This is a must for the WWII veteran or buff.

TOURING TIPS Combine with a visit to St. James's Park.

Carlyle's House

APPEAL BY AGE	PRESCHOOL ★	GRADE SCHOOL ★★	TEENS ★★
YOUNG ADULTS ★★★		OVER 30 ★★★	SENIORS ★★★

24 Cheyne Row, Chelsea, SW3; ☎ 0207-352-7087; www.nationaltrust.org.uk; tube: Sloane Square

Type of attraction Queen Anne home of the sage of Chelsea. **Admission** £4 for adults, £2 for children under age 16. **Hours** April–October, Wednesday–Sunday and bank holidays, 11 a.m.–5 p.m.; November–March, 2 p.m.–5 p.m., Wednesday–Sunday. **When to go** Anytime it's open. **Special comments** It's an old house with steep stairs; no wheelchair access. **Author's rating** ★★★. **How much time to allow** 1 hour.

DESCRIPTION AND COMMENTS It's likely that the name Thomas Carlyle may not mean anything to most people these days; he was a great essayist and historian in his own time (1795–1881), known and admired by all the Victorian literati. His house was a salon of luminaries such as Charles Dickens, George Eliot, Alfred Lord Tennyson, and Frederic Chopin, drawn as much by the sage of Chelsea's wisdom as by the famous wit of his wife, Jane. His impecunious one-time neighbors, artist Frederick Leighton and his wife, were in and out of the house constantly, borrowing everything from money to teacups to a fire screen, much to Jane's bemused annoyance. Leighton later made enough money to create a beautiful home in Kensington, now a museum (see page 230). What is marvelous about this house, in the absence of any great feeling for its former owners, is that it was made a museum not too long after Carlyle's death, and so has an abundance of authentic minutiae—a hat hung on a hook, clothing in a drawer—that is lacking in most literary shrines of this sort. There's a wonderful garden reflecting the Victorian reverence for controlled nature. All the furnishings are authentic, and the atmosphere is beyond the wildest dreams of a Victorianaphile.

TOURING TIPS Be sure to look at all the blue plaques around here to see the kind of neighbors Carlyle enjoyed.

 ## Changing of the Guard

APPEAL BY AGE	PRESCHOOL ★	GRADE SCHOOL ★★	TEENS ★★
YOUNG ADULTS ★★		OVER 30 ★★	SENIORS ★★

In the forecourt of Buckingham Palace, at the end of Pall Mall, SW1; ☎ 0906-866-3344; www.royal.gov.uk; tube: Green Park, then walk directly through the park to the palace

Type of attraction A grand old London tradition. **Admission** Free. **Hours** April–July, daily at 11:30 a.m.; August–March, every other day at 11:30 a.m.; be

sure to call or check Web site for information. **When to go** Arrive by 10:30 a.m.
to get a good place by the forecourt railings or on the statue of Victoria, especially
in the summer on a nice day. **Special comments** The pageant is canceled in very
wet weather. **Author's rating** ★★. **How much time to allow** The actual ceremony lasts 40 minutes, but you should show up an hour earlier for a better view.

DESCRIPTION AND COMMENTS The Queen's Guard, often accompanied by a band,
leaves Wellington Barracks at 11:27 a.m. and marches along Birdcage
Walk to the Palace, where they . . . well, change. One shift of guards
goes on duty, and one goes off, amidst all this fanfare. I'm not crazy
about this attraction even though I love horses and history. There's
something so annoying about the hordes of people standing around,
very few of whom can get a good look at the ceremony, and even the
ones pressed up against the railings look miserable for all the waiting
they've had to do. That said, I can recommend the statue of Victoria for
a vantage point that isn't quite as desperate and uncomfortable as the
scene around the palace railings. (I'm talking about the summer
months; in the winter, it's not quite so bad.) If it's too crowded for you
around the palace, go to the Horse Guards Parade on Horse Guards
Parade Road, which is on the far eastern perimeter of St. James's Park
(tube: Embankment or Charing Cross). There is a less elaborate ceremony
at 11 a.m. Monday–Saturday and at 10 a.m. on Sunday. The Queen's Life
Guards leave the Hyde Park Barracks at 10:30 a.m. Monday–Saturday and
at 9:30 a.m. on Sunday, and march most impressively through Hyde Park
Corner, Constitution Hill, and The Mall.

TOURING TIPS If it's too crowded one day and you can't get a good view,
save it for the next. There's a small Guard's Museum at the Wellington
Barracks on Birdcage Walk that is open daily from 10 a.m. to 4 p.m.;
entrance fee £2; ☎ 0207-414-3271; **www.armymuseums.org.uk.** It
may be of interest to military enthusiasts and many young boys, and it
has a decent gift shop of Guards' memorabilia.

Chiswick House

APPEAL BY AGE	PRESCHOOL ★	GRADE SCHOOL ★	TEENS ★
YOUNG ADULTS ★★		OVER 30 ★★	SENIORS ★★

Burlington Lane, West London, W4; ☎ **0208-995-0508;**
www.english-heritage.org.uk; tube: Turnham Green, or Chiswick by rail

Type of attraction Stately home with major gardens. **Admission** £3.50 for adults,
£2 for children under age 16. **Hours** April–October, Wednesday–Saturday, 10
a.m.–5 p.m.; November–March by appointment only. **When to go** In good
weather; the garden is splendid. **Special comments** Limited disabled access; call
for details. **Author's rating** ★★★. **How much time to allow** 1 hour.

DESCRIPTION AND COMMENTS It's a bit of a hike from either the train station in
Chiswick or the tube at Turnham Green, but for anyone interested in Palladian design and 18th-century, over-the-top splendor, this is the place.
Built in 1725 by Lord Burlington and William Kent, it has at its heart an oc-
tagonal room with a classically symmetrical dome. Its original purpose

was more to show off Burlington's extensive art collection than to live in, but alas, most of those treasures have long since been retired to museums. However, the decoration, carvings, and statuary that remain are magnificent, and the William Kent ceilings are as sumptuous as those he painted at Kensington Palace. In summer, the gardens are spectacular, filled with wonderful follies—mock ruins that were all the rage in the 18th and 19th centuries, ponds, statues, benches, and formal gardens.

TOURING TIPS This can be combined with a trip to Hogarth's House.

Clink Exhibition

APPEAL BY AGE	PRESCHOOL †	GRADE SCHOOL ★	TEENS ★
YOUNG ADULTS ★		OVER 30 ★	SENIORS ★

† Too creepy for preschoolers

1 Clink Street, South London, SE1; ☎ 0207-403-0900; www.clink.co.uk; tube: London Bridge

Type of attraction Re-creation and exhibition of a medieval prison. **Admission** £5 for adults; £3.50 for seniors, students, and children under 16; £12 family. **Hours** Daily, 10 a.m.–9 p.m.; in winter months it closes at 7 p.m. **When to go** Anytime. **Special comments** This attraction is not accessible to those in wheelchairs or baby strollers, as the entrance to the basement site is down a rather dark flight of stairs, and the exhibit itself includes a number of narrow doorways that must be stepped over. **Author's rating ★★★. How much time to allow** 30 minutes.

DESCRIPTION AND COMMENTS Be warned: There's much less to this attraction than meets the eye, despite recent efforts to upgrade the entertainment value, and I would advise you give it a pass unless you are deeply interested in the history of everything. The Clink began as a dungeon for disobedient clerics, debtors, and prostitutes. The exhibition presents itself as a re-created medieval dungeon and includes some dismal cell re-creations, diagrams of medieval torture devices, and fact boards on some of the prison's prior inhabitants. Though one might think that the ghoulish subject matter would be of high interest to grade-school kids and teens, most of the information must be read from the mounted displays, something most kids grow weary of too quickly.

TOURING TIPS If you do decide to explore this area, be sure to include a stop at Southwark Cathedral and Shakespeare's Globe Theatre, both within only a few minutes' walk of the Clink Exhibition.

kids *Cutty Sark*

APPEAL BY AGE	PRESCHOOL ★★	GRADE SCHOOL ★★★★	TEENS ★★★
YOUNG ADULTS ★★★		OVER 30 ★★★	SENIORS ★★★

Greenwich Pier; ☎ 0208-858-3445; www.cuttysark.org.uk; Docklands Light Railway: Greenwich

Type of attraction Last of the great sailing clipper ships, restored. **Admission** £4.50 for adults, £3.20 for children, £3.75 students and seniors, £12 for family. **Hours** Daily, 10 a.m.–5 p.m.; last admission at 4:30 p.m. **When to go** Anytime.

Special comments Access for the disabled is limited to the entrance level of the ship, as the ship contains stairways that may prove difficult for some to maneuver. **Author's rating** ★★★. **How much time to allow** 45–90 minutes.

DESCRIPTION AND COMMENTS First launched in 1869, the *Cutty Sark* spent seven years in the China tea trade, but actually became famous as a wool-merchant ship in the years that followed, able to sail from England to Australia in only 72 days—mighty speedy for those days. The ship's main hold contains a history of this well-known tea clipper (there's a small gift shop there, too), but it is the lower hold that most impresses with the largest collection of merchant-ship figureheads in Britain. Captain John Cumbers of Gravesend, better known as Long John Silver, amassed the colorful display. Tours of the ship can be arranged at no additional charge simply by asking. Children love to explore the restored ship's cabins, which give an alarming indication of the appalling inequity between captain and crew.

TOURING TIPS From the *Cutty Sark's* bow you can also see the much smaller *Gipsy Moth IV*, in which Francis Chichester first sailed solo around the world.

Dali Universe

APPEAL BY AGE	PRESCHOOL ★★★		GRADE SCHOOL ★★★		TEENS ★★★★
YOUNG ADULTS ★★★★		OVER 30 ★★★★		SENIORS ★★★★	

County Hall Gallery, Riverside Building, South Bank; ☎ **0207-620-2720; www.daliuniverse.com; tube: Westminster or Waterloo**

Type of attraction Restrospective of surrealist master, plus related exhibits. **Admission** May–September, £9.75 for adults; £6.25 for children ages 8–16; 4 for children aged 7–7; concessions £7.50; family £29. October–April, adults £8.75; children ages 8–16 £5.50; concessions £7; family £25. **Hours** Daily, 10 a.m.–6:30 p.m. **When to go** Anytime. **Special comments** Wheelchair access available at entrance along Queens Walk. **Author's rating** ★★★★. **How much time to allow** 1 hour.

DESCRIPTION AND COMMENTS This is a wonderful gallery honoring the surrealist master Salvador Dali. While certainly not as impressive as the Dali Museum in Figueres, Spain, it is certainly as, if not more, comprehensive as the one in Paris. Over 500 of his works include the famous red-lips sofa, the lobster telephone, and many of his best-known and -loved canvases, along with some personal artifacts. Dali Universe contains the largest collection of his sculptures from the years between 1935 and 1984, and the gift shop sells copies of many of them, almost impossible to resist. It is an intelligently and creatively curated exhibit, making the most of lighting and backgrounds to create a temple that Dali would most likely have approved. Look for temporary exhibitions (at a separate cost) such as the 2005 Picasso display.

TOURING TIPS Combine with visits to any of the South Bank attractions, such as the London Aquarium, the London Eye, or the Saatchi Gallery.

Design Museum

APPEAL BY AGE	PRESCHOOL ★	GRADE SCHOOL ★	TEENS ★
YOUNG ADULTS ★★	OVER 30 ★★★		SENIORS ★★

28 Shad Thames, Butler's Wharf, SE1; ☎ 0207-378-6055; www.designmuseum.org; tube: Tower Hill or London Bridge

Type of attraction Four floors featuring the design of everyday items. **Admission** £6 for adults, £4 for students and seniors, children under 12 free. **Hours** Daily, 10 a.m.–5:45 p.m.; Friday, open till 9 p.m. **When to go** Anytime. **Special comments** Wheelchair/disabled accessible. **Author's rating** ★★. **How much time to allow** 60–90 minutes.

DESCRIPTION AND COMMENTS The Design Museum strongly features changing exhibits of design from all possible areas of life. One of the most popular was a recent show of Manolo Blahnik's shoe designs, which highlighted his cunning skill and artistry.

The museum is well attended and appreciated by Londoners and tourists, who flock here to look at the mass-produced designs of the 20th century that we've lived with, perhaps without even noticing what they really looked like. One need only look at the collection of evolving TV sets to see that our household items have their own histories, which are inextricably linked to our domestic memories. Cars, office furniture, radios, and household utensils are all part of a permanent collection, which is added to regularly. New ideas and design breakthroughs are highlighted here. The Design Museum was created by restaurant and furniture king Terence Conran, on the south bank of the Thames by Tower Bridge. The Blue Print café and restaurant have splendid views and decent food; in fact it's a destination restaurant for many.

TOURING TIPS Walk around the Thames waterfront; it's an interesting and vibrant part of London.

Dickens House

APPEAL BY AGE	PRESCHOOL ★	GRADE SCHOOL ★	TEENS ★
YOUNG ADULTS ★	OVER 30 ★★		SENIORS ★★

48 Doughty Street, Bloomsbury, WC1; ☎ 0207-405-2127; www.dickensmuseum.com; tube: Russell Square

Type of attraction Literary shrine to the great Charles Dickens. **Admission** £5 for adults, £4 for students and seniors, £3 for children. **Hours** Monday–Saturday, 10 a.m.–5 p.m.; Sunday, 11 a.m.–5 p.m. **When to go** Anytime. **Special comments** The house contains numerous steps and no wheelchair access. **Author's rating** ★. **How much time to allow** 40 minutes.

DESCRIPTION AND COMMENTS I am a big Dickens fan, and I was hoping for more from this museum; it is sad that London, the city that Dickens made real for so many readers, doesn't have a better temple to honor him. Dickens actually only lived in this house for two years, so his spirit certainly does not walk these floors the way you sense Carlyle's does in his house. There are manuscript pages that are exciting to see, lots of wonderful illustrations from his books and portraits of the writer, and these make it worth the trip. The gift shop sells some fine old and new editions of Dickens and some of his contemporaries. Watch the video in the basement first; it's very good. Also, check the Web site to see what kind of events and special exhibits are on, which include dramatic readings and displays related to all things Dickens.

TOURING TIPS If you happen to be visiting between May and September, go on Wednesday evening for the so-called "longest-running one-man show," "Sparkler of Albion," which starts at 7:30 p.m. and costs £16 per ticket; come at 6 p.m. for a free glass of wine.

Freud Museum

APPEAL BY AGE	PRESCHOOL ★	GRADE SCHOOL ★★	TEENS ★
YOUNG ADULTS ★★	OVER 30 ★★		SENIORS ★★

20 Maresfield Gardens, South Hampstead, NW1; ☎ 0207-435-2002; www.freud.org.uk; tube: Finchley Road

Type of attraction English home of famous psychoanalyst Sigmund Freud. **Admission** £5 for adults, £2 concessions, children under 12 free. **Hours** Wednesday–Sunday, noon–5 p.m. **When to go** Anytime. **Special comments** Limited access for disabled; no lift to upper floor. **Author's rating** ★★. **How much time to allow** 2 hours.

DESCRIPTION AND COMMENTS The house at 20 Maresfield Gardens, Hampstead, was the home of Dr. Sigmund Freud, the father of psychoanalysis, for the last year of his life, after he fled the Nazis in Vienna in 1938. It continued to be home to his daughter, Anna, until her death in 1982, and on her request, it now celebrates the life and work of her father. Inside, each room is carefully decorated as it had been in 1938, and the museum contains all of the possessions from Freud's former home in Vienna in which he had lived for over 47 years. The exhibition's centerpiece is Freud's library and study, including his famous analytic couch and numerous antiquities.

TOURING TIPS A wonderfully informative video is available for viewing upstairs. The 45-minute film, partially narrated by Anna Freud, contains silent black-and-white footage of Freud at home in Vienna as well as a description of the family's harrowing escape in 1938.

(Shakespeare's) Globe Theatre

APPEAL BY AGE	PRESCHOOL ★	GRADE SCHOOL ★★	TEENS ★★
YOUNG ADULTS ★★★	OVER 30 ★★★★		SENIORS ★★★★

21 New Globe Walk, Bankside, SE1; ☎ 0207-401-9919; www.shakespeares-globe.org; tube: Mansion House or Blackfriars

Type of attraction Magnificently reconstructed Shakespearean theater. **Admission** The Globe Exhibition and guided tour cost £9 for adults, £7.50 for seniors and students, £6.50 for children ages 6–15, and are free for children under age 5; a family ticket is £25; tours run every half-hour. **Prices** for performances run from £5 (standing room) to £29 (tiered seating). **Hours** Daily, 10 a.m.–5 p.m.; check with the box office for performance times and dates. **When to go** Anytime. **Special comments** The exhibition is easily accessible for individuals in wheelchairs. **Author's rating** ★★★★. **How much time to allow** 1–2 hours for museum and tour.

DESCRIPTION AND COMMENTS Brilliantly reconstructed as an almost exact replica of its former self (and founded by the late American actor and director Sam Wanamaker), The Globe officially opened in 1998 and is a delightful place to learn about the world's greatest playwright, William Shakespeare. In his day, Shakespeare's plays were also performed at The Rose and occasionally The Swan, but it was at The Globe that Shakespeare made his literary name. The tour of the theater, often led by actors and very well done, provides marvelous details about Elizabethan theater and the notoriously debauched Bankside area. Performances run in the summer months, and are held outdoors under natural light, as they used to be. The Globe Exhibition was opened in 2000 and is located beneath the theater. The exhibit is a fact-filled museum on the life and times of the Bard, and includes some of the impressive reproductions of medieval tools that were actually used in the building of the theater. It focuses as well on the actors and the audiences who have made Shakespeare's plays so enduring. The complex also contains a café, as well as a more upscale restaurant with a view of the river and the city.

TOURING TIPS The box office says that the best seats for performances are not seats at all but the standing area in front of the stage, where the "groundlings" stand; the actors may mingle, and the rain may pour (don't worry; they sell rain ponchos). Personally, I prefer the seats, which are authentic and not all that comfy, but you get a strong sense of what theatergoing was like in the old days (it feels very convivial and festive).

Guildhall (including Clock Museum, Art Gallery, and Library Bookshop)

APPEAL BY AGE	PRESCHOOL ★	GRADE SCHOOL ★★	TEENS ★★
YOUNG ADULTS ★★		OVER 30 ★★	SENIORS ★★

Gresham Street, The City, EC4; ☎ 0207-332-1456; www.cityoflondon.gov.uk; tube: St. Paul's, Mansion House, or Bank

Type of attraction Corporate headquarters for the City of London. **Admission** Free. **Hours** Guildhall: Monday–Friday, 10 a.m.–5 p.m.; Guildhall Clock Museum and Library Bookshop: Monday–Saturday, 10 a.m.–5 p.m., Sunday, noon–4 p.m. **When to go** Anytime. **Special comments** Partial access for disabled. **Author's rating** ★★. **How much time to allow** 1–1½ hours.

DESCRIPTION AND COMMENTS Guildhall has witnessed traitors' trials and heroes' welcomes, freedom ceremonies and glittering state occasions. The seat of London's municipal government for over 800 years, it is still used for official ceremonies, state banquets, and the annual installation of the lord mayor of London (it was the venue for my daughter's high school graduation!). Although surrounded by 20th-century government offices and largely reconstructed after a World War II bombing, the Great Hall still impresses. Its walls are original and date to the 15th century. An array of monuments lines the hall in honor of national figures from the past three centuries, and banners of the 12 Great Livery Companies hang from above. The complex itself also houses over 700 examples of timekeeping in its rather small Clock Museum; its Art Gallery houses the Corporation of London's impressive collection of works depicting London life from the 15th century to the present.

TOURING TIPS The 15th-century crypt and 19th-century Old Library are generally off-limits to the public, but it is well worth asking to see them. Guided tours include these spots.

kids HMS *Belfast*

APPEAL BY AGE	PRESCHOOL ★★	GRADE SCHOOL ★★★	TEENS ★★★
YOUNG ADULTS ★★		OVER 30 ★★	SENIORS ★★

Morgans Lane, Tooley Street, South London, SE1; ☎ 0207-940-6328; www.iwm.org.uk; tube: London Bridge

Type of attraction Perfectly preserved Royal Navy battleship from World War II permanently moored in the Thames. **Admission** £8 for adults, £5 for seniors and students, free for children under age 16. **Hours** March–October, daily, 10 a.m.–6 p.m.; November–February, daily, 10 a.m.–5 p.m. **When to go** Weekdays; call to see if any class trips are scheduled. **Special comments** Ship accessible to disabled, but there are many areas that are impassable for wheelchairs. **Author's rating** ★★. **How much time to allow** 90 minutes.

DESCRIPTION AND COMMENTS A bit of floating history, the HMS *Belfast* was built in 1938 and pressed into service at the D-day landings. Decommissioned in the 1960s, the HMS *Belfast* is run by the Imperial War Museum. It's a popular tourist attraction, although its appeal is not universal. You can explore all seven levels of this huge battleship and check out the boiler room, the cabins, and the gun turrets, as well as exhibitions and videos about life on board in 1943 and the history of the Royal Navy. Children of all ages tend to love this ship, and those very interested in World War II may find it an enlightening experience.

Hampton Court Palace

APPEAL BY AGE	PRESCHOOL ★★	GRADE SCHOOL ★★★	TEENS ★★★★
YOUNG ADULTS ★★★★★		OVER 30 ★★★★★	SENIORS ★★★★★

East Molesey, Surrey, approximately 12 miles outside of central London; ☎ 0208-781-9500; www.hrp.org.uk; tube: Richmond, then R68 bus; British Rail (accessible from Waterloo Station): Hampton Court

Type of attraction London's most impressive royal palace. **Admission** £12 for adults, £7.80 seniors and students, £7.80 for children ages 5–15, £35 for families; prices include admission to the gardens and maze. **Hours** March 25–October 27, daily, 10 a.m.–6 p.m.; October 28–March 24, the palace closes at 4:30 p.m. **When to go** Anytime. **Special comments** Disabled access, including ramps to the Tudor kitchens, access to some areas of the gardens, lifts to the first floor, and equipped toilets. **Author's rating** ★★★★★. **How much time to allow** Head out early to give yourself the full day to enjoy Hampton Court and time to arrive back in London for dinner or perhaps a trip to the theater.

DESCRIPTION AND COMMENTS One of the nicest things about Hampton Court Palace is its location. If you have been running all over the city of London, deciphering bus schedules and tube maps, a trip to the outskirts of the metropolis is a relaxing treat.

The powerful and influential lord chancellor to Henry VIII, Cardinal Wolsey, built Hampton Court Palace in 1516 and proceeded to live lavishly there. In 1528, after Henry commented sourly on the extravagance of such a home for a member of the clergy, Cardinal Wolsey offered it to the king. After Wolsey failed to secure from the pope Henry's much-desired annulment from Catherine of Aragon in 1529, Henry accepted his offer, no doubt with malicious glee. Henry created the enormous Tudor kitchens and redesigned the chapel. Alterations were also made in the following century by the great architect Christopher Wren, under the direction of William and Mary, and further changes were instigated by Queen Anne. The result allows palace visitors to clearly distinguish some of the most important design styles in England's history.

The palace is organized into six walking tours, and then there are also the gardens and maze in which to wander. With all this to see, your best bet is to decide whether you want to start inside or out. I usually find that after an hour or two inside the vast halls I need to get outside for a bit and can then return to more fully enjoy the rest of the palace. Costumed guides offer tours of Henry VIII's apartments, the King's rooms, and, in summer, the Queen's apartments at no additional charge. Taking one or more of these tours is always a good way to start your visit, as the fascinating story of Hampton Court is vividly brought to life by these experienced historians. If you prefer to head out on your own, audio guides of Henry's apartments and the Tudor kitchens are also available at no additional cost.

Of significant interest in Henry's Great Hall are the hammer-beam ceiling and stunning medieval tapestries. The rather plain hallway leading to the king's chapel is the Haunted Gallery, said to be the restless wandering ground for the ghost of Henry's fifth wife, Catherine Howard, who had run down this hall shrieking for her husband to save her fom her order of execution by decapitation. (Henry's second wife, Anne Boleyn was beheaded at the Tower of London, and her unhappy ghost apparently appears regularly there.)

Outside, you have a wide choice of garden styles to match the rooms they surround. The grandest of these is William III's Fountain Garden; on the south side is the Privy Garden. Beyond this are the sunken Pond Gardens and Tudor-style Knot and Herb Gardens, while on the opposite side of the palace you can venture into the less manicured Wilderness with its evergreens and the ever-popular maze, beloved by children who couldn't care less about the palace. It was originally laid out in 1714.

TOURING TIPS A sunny day makes Hampton Court's ornate gardens a fantastic picnic spot for families. Alternately, you might head to the Tiltyard Tearoom for an enjoyable light meal, or wander beyond the Lion Gates for a number of cozy pubs, all serving some traditional lunchtime fare. Hampton Court is easily reached by train from Waterloo or Wimbledon Stations, but if you have time, the best way to approach the palace is by water. Boat tours up the Thames run in the summer months from Richmond (for a half-hour ride) or Westminster (for an hour-long excursion). Approaching the palace in this manner affords an unequaled view of the majestic King's Apartments, the magnificently cultivated Privy Gardens, and the vast park areas that once served as Henry's private hunting grounds. For river-tour schedules and pricing information, call ☎ 0207-930-4721.

Hogarth's House

APPEAL BY AGE	PRESCHOOL ★	GRADE SCHOOL ★	TEENS ★★
YOUNG ADULTS ★★		OVER 30 ★★	SENIORS ★★

Hogarth Lane, Great West Road, West London, W4; ☎ 0208-994-6757; tube: Turnham Green or British Rail to Chiswick

Type of attraction The satirist and painter's summer home filled with memorabilia, fine art, and the artist's engravings. **Admission** Free. **Hours** April–October, Tuesday–Friday, 1–5 p.m., Saturday and Sunday, 1–6 p.m.; November–March, Tuesday–Friday, 1–4 p.m., Saturday and Sunday, 1–5 p.m. Closed Monday and the month of January. **When to go** As part of a day in Chiswick (Chiswick House is a short walk away). **Special comments** Disabled accessible. **Author's rating** ★★. **How much time to allow** 1 hour.

DESCRIPTION AND COMMENTS If you go to Chiswick House in the morning, you might want to visit Hogarth's House in the afternoon. It used to be a quiet country retreat for the brilliant painter and satirist William Hogarth, but is now located on a particularly busy section of the A4 motorway, known as the Hogarth roundabout. More than 200 of Hogarth's most famous prints are here, including *Marriage à la Mode, A Rake's Progress,* and *A Harlot's Progress.* It's quite delightful to take your time looking at these witty prints in this setting that the master called home for 15 years, until his death in 1764 (his grave is a short walk away, if you're so inclined). It is a beautiful house with a fine garden, and boasts the largest collection of Hogarthiana in the world.

TOURING TIPS Make this visit part of your trip to Chiswick House.

Houses of Parliament: House of Lords and House of Commons

APPEAL BY AGE	PRESCHOOL †	GRADE SCHOOL †	TEENS ★★
YOUNG ADULTS ★★		OVER 30 ★★★	SENIORS ★★★

† Not appropriate for young children.
Parliament Square, SW1; Commons information ☎ 0207-219-4272; Lords information ☎ 0207-219 3107; www.parliament.uk (go to index and click on Visiting Parliament); tube: Westminster

Type of attraction Britain's working chambers of government. **Admission** Free, except for prebooked tours. **Hours** House of Lords: the public is admitted to the Strangers' Gallery Monday–Wednesday, beginning at 2:30 p.m., Thursday beginning at 3 p.m., and occasionally on Friday, beginning at 11 a.m. To the House of Commons, Monday–Wednesday, 2:30–10:30 p.m., Thursday, 11:30 a.m.–7:30 p.m., and Friday, 9:30 a.m.–3 p.m. Check whether the House is in session by calling ☎ 0207-219-4272. Question Time (accessible by special prebooked tickets) takes place Monday–Wednesday, 2:30–3:30 p.m., and Thursday, 11:30 a.m.–12:30 p.m. The prime minister answers questions 3–3:30 p.m. Summer Opening: This is a new opportunity for overseas visitors to take tours during August and September; Monday, Tuesday, Friday, and Saturday, 9:15 a.m–4:40 p.m.; Wednesday and Thursday, 1:15–4:40 p.m.; £7 adults, £5 students, seniors, and children under age 16; £22 family ticket. **When to go** Summer Opening or whenever you can get in. The 2005 terrorist attacks have had security officials weighing the dangers of allowing public access to the Houses of Parliament against the long-held democratic belief that government must be transparent. Do go to the Web site to see what kind of changes may be made to the visting schedule. **Special comments** Security is very tight. Allow plenty of time to clear security checks. Do not bring food, drinks, mobile phones, or pagers. They will allow you in with a camera as long as it stays in your bag; absolutely no photography is permitted. **Author's rating** ★★★. **How much time to allow** 1–2 hours, depending on how long you'd like to observe the debates (allowing at least 30 minutes to clear security).

DESCRIPTION AND COMMENTS The first Parliament was convened in 1254 and consisted of lords, bishops, abbots, knights, and local citizens. Today's Parliament, closely based on its predecessors, includes the sovereign, the House of Lords (which used to consist of hereditary peers, but is now made up of members who've been elected or appointed to their positions) and the House of Commons (members elected from their respective English, Welsh, Scottish, and Northern Irish communities). The current buildings in which they meet, built between 1840 and 1860, have become the most recognized trademarks of London. Parliament burned down in the mid-19th century, and was rebuilt in its present neo-Gothic splendor by architect Sir Charles Barry and his assistant Augustus Pugin, who was responsible for much of the intricate decoration. Pugin went mad after years of working on what must have been an exhausting project—just look at all the details of the exterior. You can see Parliament in session on CSPAN and certain BBC channels, and it is a most refreshing sight: The Prime Minister will be questioned, chastised, or challenged directly by the ministers in often rowdy sessions that seem much more of an exercise of democracy than the carefully controlled press conferences of the American president.

TOURING TIPS Do use the Web site to plan your visit, because admission policies are currently being updated and the place may be temporarily closed to visitors, or call to get the latest information. If you want to do more than witness debates, you can arrange to receive permits that allow you unchaperoned access as you follow a printed guide through splendidly decorated lobbies, corridors, the grand Westminster Hall, and the two Houses. When the Houses are in recess, tours take place Monday–Saturday, 9:15 a.m.–4:30 p.m. When the Houses are in session, tours will be scheduled only for Friday (you can also pay £25 for a personal guide). For tours when the Houses are in session, you must write a few months in advance to: Parliamentary Education Unit, Norman Shaw Boulevard (North), London SWIA 2TT. Be sure to include the exact dates of your visit, the total number in your party (not to exceed 16 people), your home address, and your London address and telephone. Permits will be mailed, so be sure to allow enough time.

If you can't get into the Houses of Parliament for any reason, visit Jewel Tower (Abingdon Street, by Westminster Abbey; ☎ 0207-222-2219), where you can see, for a small fee, an interactive virtual reality tour of both Houses. It's open 10 a.m.–4 p.m. in winter and 10 a.m.–6 p.m. in summer.

Imperial War Museum

APPEAL BY AGE	PRESCHOOL ★	GRADE SCHOOL ★	TEENS ★★
YOUNG ADULTS ★★		OVER 30 ★★	SENIORS ★★

Lambeth Road, South London, SE1; ☎ 0207-416-5320; www.iwm.org.uk; tube: Elephant and Castle or Lambeth North

Type of attraction Highlights 20th-century British military actions. **Admission** Free. **Hours** Daily, 10 a.m.–6 p.m. **When to go** Anytime. **Special comments** Limited access for disabled; wheelchairs can be booked by calling ☎ 0207-416-5397. **Author's rating** ★★. **How much time to allow** 1 hour.

DESCRIPTION AND COMMENTS Housed in the famous former lunatic asylum known as Bedlam, the Imperial War Museum is an oddly appropriate present tenant, dedicated to the madness that is war. It is a sobering museum, especially the section on the liberation of Belsen, part of the permanent exhibit on the Holocaust completed in 2000. Overall, it can be hard not to be upset by the blithe displays of the awful hardware of destruction: guns, tanks, zeppelins, V2 rockets, bombers. You are given insight into the horror of war by the re-creation of the sights and sounds and smells of the Blitz, a clock counting down the numbers of war deaths in this century, and the nightmare of life in a World War I trench, but then it seems you are invited to appreciate the machinery of it.

TOURING TIPS After experiencing war, go bask in the Peace Garden (dedicated by the Dalai Lama in May 1999), which shares the grounds with the Imperial War Museum.

Dr. Johnson's House

APPEAL BY AGE	PRESCHOOL ★★	GRADE SCHOOL ★★	TEENS ★★
YOUNG ADULTS ★★		OVER 30 ★★	SENIORS ★★

17 Gough Square, The City, EC4; ☎ 0207-353-3745; www.drjohnsonshouse.org; tube: Blackfriars

Type of attraction Literary attraction in historic house. **Admission** £4 for adults, £3 for children ages 10–16, free for children under age 10, £9 for families. **Hours**

May–September, Monday–Saturday, 11 a.m.–5:30 p.m.; October–April, Monday–Saturday, 11 a.m.–5 p.m. **When to go** Anytime. **Special comments** No wheelchair access; steep stairs. **Author's rating** ★★. **How much time to allow** 27 minutes for video, 10–15 minutes for the house.

DESCRIPTION AND COMMENTS I like Samuel Johnson more than the average bloke on the block, but even I wasn't overly impressed by this house, the only surviving London domicile of the 17 he lived in. I might have felt differently had the admission been free; however, I do respect and applaud the fact that this house on prime property has managed to avoid the wrecking ball for 250 years. This alone makes it worth the visit and the price. Dr. Johnson spent 11 years in this house working on his famous dictionary, as well as bopping around London with his biographer Boswell at his heels, dropping bons mots and shillings in the coffeehouses and taverns of his beloved London. The collection of mezzotints and books on Johnson are impressive. You must watch the video, very well done and interesting, which does make the remarkable Johnson, and Boswell, come to life.

If you are a true Dr. Johnson buff, consider taking a train to Lichfield, in Staffordshire, to see the Dr. Johnson Museum there. It is the very house in which he was born, and where his father ran a bookstore on the ground floor. It has more Johnsonalia on its five floors than the London house, and is located in a town famous for its grand cathedral and village charm. Go to **www.lichfield.gov.uk/sjmuseum** for more information; and see the entry for "Stained Glass" in the shopping chapter (p. 419) for additional fun in Lichfield.

 ## Kensington Palace State Rooms

APPEAL BY AGE	PRESCHOOL ★★	GRADE SCHOOL ★★	TEENS ★★★★
YOUNG ADULTS ★★★★	OVER 30 ★★★★		SENIORS ★★★★

Kensington Gardens, Broad Walk; ☎ 0207-937-9561; www.hrp.org.uk; tube: High Street Kensington

Type of attraction Stately home in the middle of Kensington Gardens. **Admission** £11 for adults, £7.20 for children ages 5–16, free for children under age 5, £32 for families. **Hours** April–September, daily, 10 a.m.–6 p.m.; October–March, daily, 10 a.m.–5 p.m. **When to go** Mornings in summer; anytime in winter. **Special comments** There are wheelchair-accessible toilets and a ramp to Orangery, but many steps inside the palace. Upstairs is inaccessible. **Author's rating** ★★★★. **How much time to allow** 1½ hours.

DESCRIPTION AND COMMENTS Kensington Palace is the former home of Princess Diana, and the place where Princess Victoria was told that she had become queen. It's not a grandiose palace like Buckingham, which makes it in many ways more interesting. It was built in 1605 and sold to King William and Queen Mary in 1689 as a country escape from the noxious fumes of Whitehall, which were aggravating the king's asthma. The monarchs immediately hired Christopher Wren and Nicholas

Hawksmoor to improve the house. Queen Anne later added more improvements, such as the Orangery, which was her "summer supper house," and acres of gardens (which are now the surrounding Kensington Gardens). George I turned what was essentially a country estate into a palace, and it's fascinating to note the difference between the homey oak-paneled dining room of William and Mary and the over-the-top décor of William Kent's innovations, which may be more a function of the style of the period, or, as I like to think, a reflection of the personalities of those monarchs. King George II and Queen Caroline made extensive additions to the gardens that can be enjoyed today, such as Broad Walk, the Round Pond, and the Serpentine. In 1841, the gardens were opened to the public, when the palace became a source of "grace and favour," apartments for offshoots of the royal family, such as the late Princess Margaret, the newly divorced Princess Diana, the Duke and Duchess of Kent, and the very old Princess Alice, aunt to the Queen, who died in 2004 at the age of 104, and who lived through the bombardments of both WWI and WWII.

You can see the bedroom in which Princess Victoria lived with her mother, the duchess of Kent, until she was made queen at 18. There are fine examples of furniture and brilliant trompe l'oeil ceiling paintings and murals by William Kent. Two oddities that must be seen are the wind-dial by which King William III could tell how fast his ships might be approaching, and the massive clock in the Cupola Room that used to play tunes by Handel, Corelli, and Geminiani, and which, even minus this feature as it is now, represents a marvelous marriage of 16th-century technology and art.

TOURING TIPS Make this part of a day in the park. Early birds get the worm here, but it's also nice to come later in the day and follow up your visit with tea at the Orangery next door. Be sure to take advantage of the audio tour, as it's very thorough and interesting.

Kenwood House (The Iveagh Bequest)

APPEAL BY AGE	PRESCHOOL ★	GRADE SCHOOL ★ ★ ★	TEENS ★ ★ ★
YOUNG ADULTS ★ ★ ★		OVER 30 ★ ★ ★	SENIORS ★ ★ ★

Hampstead Lane, Hampstead Heath, NW3; ☎ 0208-348-1286; www.english-heritage.org.uk; tube: Archway or Golders Green

Type of attraction World-class art gallery in an elegant Georgian villa. **Admission** Free. **Hours** April–October, daily, 10 a.m.–5 p.m.; November–March, daily, 10 a.m.–4 p.m. **When to go** Anytime, but preferably on weekdays and in good weather so you can enjoy the heath. **Special comments** Limited wheelchair access for ground floor only. **Author's rating** ★ ★ ★ ★. **How much time to allow** 2 hours in the house, plus time for tea or a walk around the grounds and on the heath. It's a great day out in good weather, not so fab in the rain.

DESCRIPTION AND COMMENTS Kenwood is the most elegant exponent of architect Robert Adams's early Georgian design. He was commissioned by Lord Mansfield to turn the original 1700 brick house into what you see today, and it took from 1764 till 1779 to get it just right. It is gorgeous, with

Adams and Chippendale furniture and decoration, the stunning master-pieces on the walls, and exceptional views all year long.

After passing from one Lord Mansfield to the next, by 1923 it was ownerless and being eyed by developers, who would have made a right mess of the wondrous surrounding heath. Saved from the wrecking ball or worse by brewery magnate Edward Guinness, earl of Iveagh, he filled it with his extensive collection of 17th-century Dutch and Flemish and late 18th-century British paintings, including works by Sir Joshua Reynolds, George Romney, J. M. W. Turner, Gainsborough, and Raeburn. His bequest of the house and its contents was a great act of patronage: there are quite a few absolutely unmissable old masterpieces here, such as Rembrandt's *Self-Portrait* and Vermeer's *The Guitar Player.* As an art gallery, it is right up there in the top ten of London. A number of somewhat quirky displays of miniature portraits, jewelry, ceramics, and 1,300 Georgian shoe buckles have also been donated by a variety of collectors.

TOURING TIPS Combine this visit with a trip to Hampstead Village and the heath. If you're visiting in the summer, combine it with the weekend classical concerts. Bring a blanket and food, or stop into the excellent café, which serves hot and cold food in a charming, floral courtyard.

Leighton House Museum and Art Gallery

APPEAL BY AGE	PRESCHOOL ★	GRADE SCHOOL ★	TEENS ★★
YOUNG ADULTS ★★		OVER 30 ★★	SENIORS ★★

12 Holland Park Road, Kensington, WI4; ☎ 0207-602-3316; www.rbkc.gov.uk/leightonhousemuseum; tube: High Street Kensington, then bus 9, 10, 27, 33, or 49 to Odeon Cinema, then walk through Holland Park

Type of attraction House of pre-Raphaelite painter Lord Frederick Leighton. **Admission** £3 adults, £1 children and concessions, £6 family ticket. **Hours** Monday–Saturday, 11 a.m.–5 p.m.; closed Tuesday. **When to go** Anytime. **Special comments** Not wheelchair accessible; many steps to top floor. **Author's rating** ★★. **How much time to allow** 30 minutes.

DESCRIPTION AND COMMENTS If you are a true lover of the pre-Raphaelites (Edward Burne-Jones, John Millais, Frederick Leighton, and others) this is a must-see. Lord Leighton, whose magnificent painted hallway can be seen in the Victoria and Albert Museum, dedicated his home as "a private palace devoted to art." The main attraction is the Arab Hall, which is a Victorian fantasy of the Middle East, with Isniuk tiles, elaborately carved and gilded woodwork, and the mosaic frieze. There is a wonderful sunken fountain in the middle of the room, which furthers the impression of a courtyard straight out of the pages of *The Arabian Nights.* The top floor is Leighton's old studio, and the huge windows, skylights, and dome were clearly the heart's desire of any 19th-century painter. There's a good collection of Victorian paintings on the lower floor, including Leighton's *Roman Mother;* upstairs you can see temporary exhibits of a widely varied nature. The house is sadly lacking in furniture and knickknacks, and despite the stuffed peacock in the hall, one wishes for more of the decorative exuberance that must have resided when Leighton lived his often messy and hectic life here.

TOURING TIPS Combine this with a trip to Holland Park and the Linley Sambourne House (tickets to the Sambourne House are available only at Leighton House).

Linley Sambourne House

APPEAL BY AGE	PRESCHOOL ★	GRADE SCHOOL ★★	TEENS ★★
YOUNG ADULTS ★★★		OVER 30 ★★★	SENIORS ★★★

18 Stafford Terrace, Kensington, W8; ☎ 0207-602-3316; www.rbkc.gov.uk/linleysambournehouse; tube: High Street Kensington

Type of attraction Perfectly preserved home of Victorian punch cartoonist. **Admission** £6 for adults, £4 for concessions, £1 for children. **Hours** Daily, 11 a.m.–5:30 p.m.; closed Tuesday. **When to go** Weekends for costumed tours. **Special comments** Lots of stairs and no wheelchair access. **Author's rating ★★★. How much time to allow** 1–2 hours.

DESCRIPTION AND COMMENTS This place is a veritable time machine, plunking one smack down in the middle of the late Victorian–early Edwardian era, with the sumptuous clutter that incited the backlash of modernism. William Morris designs adorn both walls and floors, and there are a few stained-glass windows to admire. A predominant thought on seeing the vast collection of clocks, vases, gimcracks, and knickknacks was of pity for the poor servant in charge of dusting. The immense aesthetic weight of all the pretty possessions can be a bit tiring, but it is an amazing piece of preservation, and the tours conducted by guides in period costume are fun. On the last Thursday of every month, £20 will buy you tickets to either the 6 p.m. or 8 p.m. performance promoted as "A Victorian twilight encounter." It's based on family diaries that reveal the scandals and secrets of life in the house in 1899.

TOURING TIPS The weekend tours are your best bet, conducted as they are by actors in costume. Combine with a trip to Holland Park and/or to the Leighton House Museum, which is where you get tickets for the Sambourne House.

kids London Aquarium

APPEAL BY AGE	PRESCHOOL ★★★★	GRADE SCHOOL ★★★★	TEENS ★★★
YOUNG ADULTS ★★★		OVER 30 ★★★	SENIORS ★★★

County Hall, Riverside Building, Westminster Bridge Road, SE1; ☎ 0207-967-8000; www.londonaquarium.co.uk; tube: Westminster or Waterloo

Type of attraction Wonderland of fish on the bank of the Thames. **Admission** £9.75 for adults, £7.50 seniors and students, £6.25 for children ages 3–14, free for children under age 3, £29 for families. (These are the peak prices, which go for mid-March–September 30, as well as for school holidays in February, October, and December. Off-peak prices are only slightly less.) **Hours** Daily, 10 a.m.–6 p.m. (last entry at 5 p.m.). **When to go** Avoid weekends and school holidays if possible; go early. **Special comments** Fully accessible for disabled persons. To avoid steps, go around building to Belvedere Road to reach entrance. Picnic area available. **Author's rating** ★★★★. **How much time to allow** 2–3 hours.

DESCRIPTION AND COMMENTS In a most unlikely conversion, a portion of London's County Hall (also the former home of the Greater London Council) has become three dimly-lit and atmospheric floors of enormous tanks filled with sea life and freshwater fish of every kind. The Atlantic tank holds 800,000 liters of water and tons of sharks, eels, and stingrays. It's most impressive, although I felt badly for the magnificent sharks whose snouts have been damaged by hitting the glass walls. There's a petting pool for kids to stroke manta rays, who actually seem to invite these caresses. In the Pacific tank, even bigger than the Atlantic, reside more sharks, rays, groupers, and smaller fish. The piranha tank is interesting, especially at dinnertime, when you get to see what a real-life feeding frenzy looks like (call ahead to find out feeding times for various fish). There are new octopus, jellyfish, and European freshwater fish displays, which are wonderful; and Friday nights in summer the aquarium offers activities for the young.

This is not the most amazing aquarium in the world by a long shot, even if their claim is true that you would have to cover 38,337 miles (how do they arrive at that number?) to see all these fish in their natural habitat. If you have access to a good aquarium where you live, you might as well leave this off your list, but it has been proven to me time and again that, when it comes to taming small children, fish take the cake. Plus the surrounding area is a blast, with the London Eye and all the wonders of the South Bank and Thames at your disposal.

TOURING TIPS There's a McDonald's next door, with its own entrance to the aquarium. There's also a wonderful gift shop for every budget.

London Dungeon

APPEAL BY AGE	PRESCHOOL †	GRADE SCHOOL ★★	TEENS ★★★★
YOUNG ADULTS ★★		OVER 30 ★★	SENIORS ★

† *Too scary for preschoolers.*
28–34 Tooley Street, South Bank, SE1; ☎ 0207-403-7221; www.thedungeons.com; tube: London Bridge

Type of attraction Over-the-top yuck-fest with historical pretensions. **Admission** £15.50 for adults, £12.25 for seniors and students, £10.95 for children ages 5–14, free (though not advisable) for kids under 5. **Hours** July–August, daily, 10 a.m.–6 p.m.; September–June, daily, 10:30 a.m.–5 p.m. **When to go** Weekdays as soon as it opens; it gets pretty crowded midday, and weekends are tough. **Special comments** Wheelchair access; don't bring small children. **Author's rating** ★★★. **How much time to allow** 90 minutes.

DESCRIPTION AND COMMENTS I am the first one to line up for the weird and horrible—the only thing I didn't yawn over at Madame Tussaud's was the Chamber of Horrors—but this place hit me the wrong way. The relentless gore without context was disturbing, and the "Jack the Ripper Experience" was just plain offensive. The hordes of French teenage boys who were there during my visit seemed to find it hilarious. They cheered wildly when we saw a dummy guillotined—as their ancestors must have done. There's a little boat ride that takes you on a trip to Traitor's Gate, which at least gets you off your feet for a bit. The best part was the gift shop, where I picked up a life-size skull candle and some fun Halloween stuff. If you want to get a sense of just what this place is about, call the phone number and listen to the hilariously bad "scary" recorded greeting voice.

TOURING TIPS   Drop off the tweenies and teens here and go wait for them in one of the restaurants in the area, or take a look at nearby Southwark Cathedral while the kids do their thing. For about £2 more per ticket, you can get the "queue-busting" online tickets; just print out the confirmation and hand to the ticket taker.

kids London Transport Museum

APPEAL BY AGE	PRESCHOOL ★★★★	GRADE SCHOOL ★★★★	TEENS ★★★
YOUNG ADULTS ★★★		OVER 30 ★★★	SENIORS ★★★

39 Wellington Street, off Covent Garden Piazza, WC2; ☎ 0207-565-7299; www.ltmuseum.co.uk; tube: Covent Garden, Leicester Square

Type of attraction A fun, interactive museum of trams, buses, and trains of old and new London. **Admission** £5.95 for adults, £4.50 for seniors and students, free for accompanied children under age 16. **Hours** Daily, 10 a.m.–6 p.m.; opens at 11 a.m. on Friday. **When to go** Anytime. **Special comments** Wheelchair and stroller access; café and gift shop. **Author's rating** ★★★★. **How much time to allow** 1 hour.

DESCRIPTION AND COMMENTS   This is one of the best venues for kids in London, and adults love it, too. Although many might yawn at the idea of a museum dedicated to that most prosaic feature of urban life, public transportation, this museum is so cleverly and earnestly organized that it's impossible not to get swept up in the fun of it. From horse-drawn stagecoaches and omnibuses, to buses that you can pretend to drive and underground switches you can pretend to throw, this is a reasonably interactive museum that most kids will love. You're given a ticket to be stamped at each of the numbered sites until you've filled up your card and seen all there is to see. There are videos of old-time trams and buses and a wonderful short film on the touching last trip of the last tram in London, with everyone singing "Auld Lang Syne." There's so much for adults to learn here, too, such as why the fares on buses and trains in London have to be so complicated; and that 40,000 people took the first underground line on its first day. (Alas, we don't find out why you can wait forever for your bus and then three will come all at once.)

The gift shop has a huge selection of great postcards and underground posters and a wealth of books about London's transport. You can get just about anything with the London Underground map on it, even slippers.

TOURING TIPS Buy the museum guide if you have children under age 12—there's a fun pull-out section with games and educational pursuits in it. Combine this trip with a visit to Covent Garden, also fun for the kids, especially on weekends. Call or visit their Web site to check for lectures, tours, films, and family activities.

kids London Zoo

APPEAL BY AGE	PRESCHOOL ★★★★	GRADE SCHOOL ★★★★	TEENS ★★★
YOUNG ADULTS ★★★		OVER 30 ★★★	SENIORS ★★★

Regent's Park; ☎ 0207-722-3333; www.londonzoo.co.uk; tube: Camden Town

Type of attraction Modernized old zoo set at the edge of Regent's Park. **Admission** £14 for adults, £10.75 for children ages 3–15, £12 seniors and students. **Hours** Daily in summer, 10 a.m.–5:30 p.m.; closes at 4:30 p.m. in winter. **When to go** When it's warm and not raining. **Special comments** Wheelchair access. **Author's rating** ★★★★. **How much time to allow** 2 hours.

DESCRIPTION AND COMMENTS The London Zoo has had some financial headaches for some time now, as there are no significant subsidies from the government to help it operate. It is trying its best, and the education that it provides on endangered species is invaluable, as is the experience of seeing Asian lions, lemurs, and rhinos in the flesh; it makes the possible loss of these animals to extinction all the more horrific. The zoo has tried hard to be the best it can be and has created a small but full environment of hooved, winged, and four-legged friends, and was voted best attraction in London by a reader's poll in *Time Out*. The argument against the confinement of beasts rages on, but it has been shown that without zoos such as this, even more creatures would be extinct. Certainly many naturalists, conservationists, and environmentalists have been inspired in their choice of career by a childhood visit to a zoo. It may well be that when people actually see the magnificence of these endangered species, they may be moved to do something about the problem, or at least to not participate in the sale or trade of ivory, animal skins, or exotic food. Certainly the London Zoo has done a lot to make a more natural habitat for their animals, unlike some of the egregious zoos of some developing countries, even though English climate bears no relation to the climate of some of these creatures' birthplace. Opened in 1828, the zoo has clearly evolved from the old animals-in-cages standard, but it can't be all things to all animals, as is clear from the Bactrian camel, used to the torrid aridity of the Gobi Desert, standing listlessly in the chilly, damp air of London or from the gorilla rocking back and forth, giving his viewers reproachful looks. On a brighter note, the reptile house—which appeared in the first Harry Potter book, when he discovered he could speak "parsel," the language of snakes—is magnificent, with cobras, pythons, and even alligators in nicely designed environments, plus a teaching center with snakeskins and things made from the hides of unfortunate animals. The aquarium is also quite comprehensive and well housed. There are a lot of monkeys and a petting zoo for children. The shop is fantastic and will fulfill all your animal-paraphernalia needs, with books, stuffed animals, knick-knacks, gimcracks, and geegaws.

Madame Tussaud's Waxworks and the London Planetarium

APPEAL BY AGE	PRESCHOOL ★★	GRADE SCHOOL ★★	TEENS ★★
YOUNG ADULTS ★★		OVER 30 ★★	SENIORS ★★

Marylebone Road, Marylebone, NW1; ☎ 0870-400-3000 to book tickets in advance and avoid the queue (for £1 extra on each ticket) or ☎ 0870-400-3000; www.madame-tussauds.com; tube: Baker Street

Type of attraction World-famous display of wax dummies, chosen most arbitrarily. **Admission** £22.99 for adults, £18.99 for children under age 16, £19.99 for seniors, free for children age 4 and under. Family tickets only available with pre-booking. This breathtaking entry fee includes tickets to the London Planetarium and the Chamber Live, the newly renamed Chamber of Horrors, which now features "live" serial killers (£2 less for no Chamber Live; discounted tickets between 5 and 5:30 p.m.; £1 less on weekends). **Hours** Daily, 9 a.m.–5:30 p.m. Opens at 9:30 a.m. on weekends, bank holidays, and summer weekdays. **When to go** They advise that you go in the afternoon, but there always seems to be a line there, no matter what the time, even a half hour before it opens. Go a day before or book over the phone or online to get a fast-track, timed ticket. Weekends are unpredictable: sometimes more and sometimes less crowded. **Special comments** Limited wheelchair access: call in advance ☎ 0870-400 3000. **Author's rating** ★. **How much time to allow** 2 hours.

DESCRIPTION AND COMMENTS I am not the one to talk to about Madame Tussaud's, because I found it ridiculous—I might have been more pleased with it if it were not for the lines, the price, and the milling hordes inside. I also think that it may have been more interesting in the days before film, when one really didn't know what the great personages of the day looked like. However, I have many friends who love it, so I decided to give it the benefit of the doubt. It's certainly one of London's most visited attractions. I liked the section on the history of the waxworks, where you got to see the unfortunates who'd been decommissioned and decapitated and ended up with their heads on the shelf: Liza Minelli, Nikita Krushchev, Sammy Davis Jr., and W. C. Fields were but a few. Some of the newer dummies are frighteningly real, down to the gleam in the eye. One can't say for sure about the verisimilitude of the old ones, like Voltaire, but I must say that Princess Diana's is a pretty good imitation. I loved the surreal display of the duke of Wellington staring down at the wax effigy of his old nemesis, Napoléon, an event that actually transpired.

There is a pretty silly ride in a miniature black taxi that rushes you through the history of London (from Elizabeth I till now) at a breakneck pace. All you can do is giggle as you fly along. The renamed Chamber of

Horrors, now the Chamber Live, is entered through a gate with the Dante inscription "All Hope Abandon, Ye Who Enter Here!"—a sentiment perhaps more fitting for the end of the queue outside. It is a sobering and disturbing exhibit, which manages to even approximate the smell of unwashed bodies and despair (also reminiscent of the queue outside) in the prison section. They have tried to jazz it up a lot with actors playing serial killers, which is pretty creepy. But of all the horrors, murderers, and bloodiness, there is surely nothing more chilling than the display of Madame Tussaud herself, lantern held aloft, searching a mountain of decapitated bodies for the head of her former employer, Marie Antoinette. I think they should dump the celebrities and make the museum all about the madame: the young Marie Grosholtz Tussaud started out in the late 1700s assisting a doctor who specialized in making wax anatomy forms. Her talent for portraiture was so extraordinary that she was hired to teach art to the children of the doomed king and queen of France. When the French Revolution came, she was imprisoned (rooming with the future Josephine Bonaparte) and marked for the guillotine. Marie was saved by those who wanted her to remain alive long enough to make death masks of the aristocrats, many of whom she had known personally. She spent many a night poking through the bloody corpses for the heads she was commissioned to work on. What a way to make a living.

TOURING TIPS Book a ticket in advance by phone or in person, so that you can avoid the lines, or at least minimize waiting time.

Millennium Bridge

APPEAL BY AGE	PRESCHOOL ★★★	GRADE SCHOOL ★★★★	TEENS ★★★
YOUNG ADULTS ★★★		OVER 30 ★★★	SENIORS ★★★

Upper Thames Street on north bank of river; Bankside on south side of river; phone the Tourist Board for information, ☎ 0207-932-2000; www.londontouristboard.com; tube: Mansion on north, London Bridge on south London

Type of attraction A footbridge across the Thames linking the Tate Modern with St. Paul's Cathedral. **Admission** Free. **Hours** 24/7. **When to go** Anytime, but sunny days are best. **Special comments** Wheelchair accessible. **Author's rating** ★★★. **How much time to allow** 15 minutes to cross it very slowly.

DESCRIPTION AND COMMENTS The Millennium Bridge opened to great fanfare in 2000, but when the people spilled over its shimmering expanse, it started swaying dangerously, throwing some people to the ground, and it had to be closed for reengineering. It's the first new bridge to be built over the Thames since 1894, and it's closed to motor vehicles. The original cost of £16 million kept going up as the engineers and architects tried to address its instability. It was amusing to watch the architect blame the engineers and the engineers blame the architect when the bridge started swinging to and fro. Now that it's stable, it certainly is pleasing, forming what architect Lord Norman Foster envisioned as a "blade of light," and providing great views as well as an efficient way to cross the Thames.

Millennium Dome

The Millennium Dome exhibition has come and gone, and the fate of the bulbous growth has yet to be determined—maybe sports arena, visitors center, or technology park; we shall see. With the Olympics lined up for 2012, smart money says it will form an important venue for sports, and an integral part of the Olympic village. Which is great, as this thing has just sat there doing nothing for ages.

kids The Monument

APPEAL BY AGE	PRESCHOOL —	GRADE SCHOOL ★★	TEENS ★★★
YOUNG ADULTS ★★★		OVER 30 ★★★	SENIORS VARIES

Monument Street, The City, EC3; ☎ 0207-626-2717; www.towerbridge.org.uk (scroll down and click on The Monument link); tube: Monument

Type of attraction Tower commemorating the Great Fire of 1666. **Admission** £2 for adults, £1 for children under age 16. Joint ticket with Tower Bridge Experience: £6.50 for adults, £4.50 for children under age 15, seniors, and students. **Hours** Daily, 9:30 a.m.–5:30 p.m. (last admission at 5 p.m.). **When to go** Any time you feel perky enough to climb the stairs. **Special comments** Not for claustrophobes, acrophobes, or the infirm. **Author's rating** ★★★. **How much time to allow** 20 minutes.

DESCRIPTION AND COMMENTS At 202 feet high, the Monument was once as visible as St. Paul's Dome, which was certainly no coincidence, as Christopher Wren designed both (aided, in the case of the Monument, by Dr. Robert Hooke). It was built in 1677 to commemorate the Great Fire of 1666, which was actually responsible for making Wren, King Charles II's chief surveyor, one of London's most prolific architects. If laid down on its side, the Monument would reach directly to the spot on Pudding Lane where the fire started. It also has a precise linear relationship to St. Paul's, no doubt a touch that Wren relished.

The 311 steps to the top take about five minutes to walk, though it seems much longer. The stairs are pie shaped, which makes passing on them a little delicate. There is no stated etiquette for who takes which part of the steps as the climbers and descendants squeeze by each other, but the guard assured me that good manners and awareness are all that's necessary to negotiate the pass. There are three or four window seats on which to take a breather while ascending. The view is quite fine—spectacular, in fact—and the best possible place from which to see Tower Bridge, whose managers recently took stewardship of the Monument. Sadly, the views of the Tower of London and the whole of St. Paul's have been severely compromised by newer buildings. I was assured by a taxi driver that the view used to be much more amazing. He also told me that his four-year-old son was completely freaked out by the height, although older kids love the challenge of the climb and the view. Look down the stairwell when you get to the top—it's like an Escher drawing or something out of Alfred Hitchcock's *Vertigo*.

TOURING TIPS Bring a camera, and don't forget to pick up your "I-climbed-the-Monument" certificate as you leave.

kids Museum of Childhood at Bethnal Green

APPEAL BY AGE	PRESCHOOL ★★★★	GRADE SCHOOL ★★★★	TEENS ★★★
YOUNG ADULTS ★★★		OVER 30 ★★★	SENIORS ★★★

Cambridge Heath Road, East End, E2; ☎ 0208-980-2415; www.vam.org.uk; tube: Bethnal Green

Type of attraction Largest museum of toys in the world. **Admission** Free. **Hours** Daily, 10 a.m.–5:50 p.m.; closed Friday. **When to go** Anytime. **Special comments** The museum is being closed for a year for a very considerable upgrade, to re-open in October 2006. **Author's rating** ★★★. **How much time to allow** Depends on what activities your children engage in.

DESCRIPTION AND COMMENTS Housed in a building directly across the street from the Bethnal Green tube station, the Museum of Childhood is part of the Victoria and Albert Museum, which over the years has contributed thousands of items from its vast stores to make this museum, which opened in 1872. The building itself is based on the iron framework of a temporary museum created for the Great Exhibition of 1851, which stood on the Victoria and Albert Museum's current site. It may be of interest that the mosaic floor was constructed by the labor of women prisoners from Woking Gaol. It has an unparalleled collection of children's toys and accessories from the 16th century to the present. There are amazing old dollhouses, model trains, hobby horses, old mechanical games and toys, dolls of every possible kind, teddy bears, and even old-fashioned prams and nursery furniture. Not surprisingly, the children seem to prefer pumping the mechanical toys full of coins to admiring the antiques behind glass, which is why the museum has been steadily expanding the fun interactive stuff for kids. The closing of the museum from October 2005 to October 2006 makes it hard to discuss it in any great detail, but if you've been there before, you will probably not recognize the upgraded visitor facilities, the wider range of activities for small people, and the many hands-on exhibits that were sorely needed at this museum. My educated guess is that you should prepare to be dazzled, even if you're not, nor have, a child.

kids Museum of London

APPEAL BY AGE	PRESCHOOL ★★★	GRADE SCHOOL ★★★★	TEENS ★★★
YOUNG ADULTS ★★★		OVER 30 ★★★★	SENIORS ★★★

London Wall and Aldersgate, The City, EC2; ☎ 0207-600-3699 or 0207-600-0870; www.museumoflondon.org.uk; tube: St. Paul's or Barbican

Type of attraction Museum covering thousands of years of London history. **Admission** Free; fee for special exhibits. **Hours** Monday–Saturday, 10 a.m.–5:50 p.m., Sunday, noon–5:50 p.m. **When to go** Anytime, although you may be navigating around large groups of schoolchildren if you go too early on weekdays while school is in session; after 2:30 p.m., they're gone. **Special comments** Good handicapped accessibility with a number of ramps and lifts for all floors. **Author's rating** ★★★★★. **How much time to allow** 2–3 hours.

DESCRIPTION AND COMMENTS   The Museum of London tells the story of London from its first settlers back in 4,000 B.C. to the present, using a variety of eye-catching displays and fascinating reconstructions. Its chronologically themed tour route allows visitors to explore more closely the time periods each finds most intriguing. This museum is extremely kid friendly, with some interactive or tactile displays. A few not-to-be-missed exhibits include a large section of London's fourth-century town wall, located outside but incorporated into the museum's Roman London exhibition through a window overlook, the 1757 gilded Lord Mayor's Coach, and re-created 19th-century street scenes and shops.

There are exhibits here that can be quite fascinating—my favorite had to do with Londoners' bodies over the centuries and displayed skeletons, corsets, and bones ravaged by such diseases as rickets and syphilis. It is a very well-presented museum, and it manages to make London's history feel quite intimate. There's a real cell from Newgate Prison that is perfectly chilling, and the Victorian shops give one the strangest, most impossible sense of déjà vu. The displays about the years of the Blitz are riveting. If you are even slightly interested in London's history, this museum is a must-see; if you're not, you will be after a visit. The gift shop has a huge assortment of wonderful books—including the best collection of historical fiction around, as well as nonfiction about London and English history for all ages. There's a good café, too.

TOURING TIPS   For an introduction to many of the exhibitions and information on current exhibits, check out the museum's Web site. Also, call ahead to find out how many schools are booked on the day of your visit—if there are a lot, come after 2:30 p.m.

National Gallery

APPEAL BY AGE	PRESCHOOL ★	GRADE SCHOOL ★★★	TEENS ★★★
YOUNG ADULTS ★★★★★	OVER 30 ★★★★★		SENIORS ★★★★★

**Trafalgar Square, West End, WC2; ☎ 0207-839-3321;
www.nationalgallery.org.uk; tube: Leicester Square or Charing Cross**

Type of attraction Splendid art gallery of 700 years of European painting. **Admission** Free, though there is a charge for special exhibits. **Hours** Daily, 10 a.m.–6 p.m.; late view, Wednesday till 9 p.m. **When to go** The quietest times are weekday mornings and Wednesday late view. Avoid major exhibits on weekends. **Special comments** Wheelchair accessible. **Author's rating** ★★★★★. **How much time to allow** As much as you can physically handle.

DESCRIPTION AND COMMENTS   This is one of those amazing art museums, like The Louvre, in which you get to see the original of some utterly familiar image—Holbein's *The Ambassadors,* Van Gogh's *Sunflowers,* or Monet's *Water Lily Pond*—practically every time you turn around. It is the repository of about 2,300 works from 700 years of European art; you can spend hours gazing at paintings by Titian, Rembrandt, Caravaggio, Vermeer, Velazquez, Michelangelo, da Vinci, Van Eyck, and other old masters too numerous to mention. As if that weren't enough, the East Wing is filled with Impressionists, featuring some 50 paintings on a sort of permanent loan from the Tate Gallery. You'll see Seurat, Pissarro, Gauguin, Degas, Corot, and others. The collection is laid out quite methodically, and excellent inscriptions accompany each painting. The special exhibits are always worth the fee, and do get yourself a headset to listen to the tour.

The National Gallery was founded in 1824 under King George IV, when the government purchased 38 important paintings—from artists such as Raphael, Van Dyck, and Rembrandt—from the estate of banker John Julius Angerstein. The building was commissioned with a few strange requirements, such as the cupola crowning the front portico, initially ridiculed as a mustard pot, with the two bell towers on either side looking like salt-and-pepper shakers. The architect, William Wilkens, was also asked to use a portion of a former royal palace in his design, so the slightly ungainly appearance may be due to these arbitrary requirements.`

The modern Sainsbury's Wing houses the oldest paintings, dating from 1260 to 1510. Don't miss Jan Van Eyck's *Arnolfini Marriage,* and look for the artist reflected in the mirror. The West Wing has paintings dating from 1510 to 1600, including Tintoretto's *St. George and the Dragon.* The North Wing (paintings from 1600 to 1700) is filled with works by Rembrandt and other 17th-century geniuses whose paintings have an almost supernatural power that no reproduction can capture. The East Wing takes us from 1700 up to 1920, with Canaletto and Turner's land- and seascapes giving way to the English portraits and social scenes of Gainsborough, Reynolds, and the prodigious Hogarth, whose series *Marriage à la Mode* can be seen here. The Impressionist rooms are always crowded with fans admiring Rousseau's *Tropical Storm with Tiger,* Renoir's *Umbrellas,* Van Gogh's *Chair,* and so many more. Picasso is represented in the East Wing as well, though there are no really major items here, except for *Minotauromachia.*

There's a food shop in the basement with excellent sandwiches and salads, and in the Sainsbury Wing is a more upscale restaurant serving decent food. The gift shops are filled with the most wonderful collection of books, postcards, and calendars, and must be visited. Try to get your hands on the National Gallery Advent calendar, which conceals masterpieces under each day's tear-off flap. And if there's a sale on, be smart and stock up on gift goods for the future. One of the most fabulous recent additions to the gift shop is the reproduction service, located at the rear of the store. Here you can get any number of sizes, from postcard up to poster, of just about anything from the magnificent collection. Besides the computer database that you can use for searches, there is also a huge volumn handy with which you can look up pictures in the old style. It's an exhaustive index that allows you to search for, say, paintings of dogs, or seascapes, as well as by artist or period. There are plenty of postcards and posters already there, but for the more obscure work, this service is a dream come true.

TOURING TIPS Take advantage of the lectures and recorded tours available here; they are great aids. There is also a computer in the Micro Gallery, where you can look up and print out information about the art and artists. Also, when looking at the collection, keep an eye out for that special piece of art that sings to you, and have it reproduced at the gift shop to bring home with you. It's money well spent.

National Maritime Museum and Queen's House
(see also profile for Royal Greenwich Observatory)

APPEAL BY AGE	PRESCHOOL ★★★	GRADE SCHOOL ★★★★	TEENS ★★★
YOUNG ADULTS ★★★★		OVER 30 ★★★★	SENIORS ★★★★

Romney Road, Greenwich, SE10; ☎ 0208-312-6565; www.nmm.ac.uk; take Docklands Light Railway: Greenwich

Type of attraction Largest maritime museum in the world. **Admission** Free; fee for special events and exhibits. **Hours** Daily, 10 a.m.–5 p.m.; until 6 p.m. in summer. **When to go** Anytime on weekdays; early in the day on weekends. **Special comments** It's a steep walk up the hill to the museums, but once you get there it is accessible with lifts for disabled, touch-talks for visually impaired, and sign-interpreted talks. Call for details. **Author's rating** ★★★★. **How much time to allow** 2–3 hours for the museum and 1–2 hours for Queen's House.

DESCRIPTION AND COMMENTS The National Maritime Museum was restructured and revitalized just in time for the new millennium, and it now fashions itself as part of the larger "Maritime Greenwich World Heritage Site," which includes the Queen's House and the Royal Observatory. Its new galleries, courtesy of a £20 million face-lift, include lots of interactive displays exploring the impact of the oceans on our daily lives, as well as our destructive impact on the seas. Exhibitions include the re-creations of steerage and first-class cabins and deck sections from an ocean liner, thousands of ship models, hundreds of navigational instruments, and galleries devoted to the history of British naval conquests and accomplishment. Of particular interest to adults is the elaborate Horatio Nelson exhibition, which pays homage to the famous admiral who defeated Napoléon at the Battle of Trafalgar, and the very uniform in which he was killed is one of the most priceless items there. Kids will have to be dragged out of the All-Hands Gallery, a fascinating interactive collection of exhibits, tools, and experiments of nautical principles. The fun includes raising and lowering signal flags, working a crane to load a ship's cargo, or attempting some deep-sea engineering.

The Queen's House, adjacent to the museum, has undergone major refurbishment and presents an architectural triumph of 17th-century architect Inigo Jones. It is said to be England's first home built in the classical style. The Queen's House is now a venue for the appreciation of maritime-related artwork, with exhibits regularly mounted, such as the comprehensive exhibition on Queen Elizabeth I, friend to sailors and pirates alike. The interior of the house has been restored to the days of Charles II, and the Royal Apartments on the upper floor are especially dazzling.

TOURING TIPS The museum offers a wide range of children's educational workshops and activities, many free of charge. For details and a full schedule of planned events, check the excellent Web site.

The National Portrait Gallery

| APPEAL BY AGE | PRESCHOOL ★ | GRADE SCHOOL ★ ★ | TEENS ★ ★ ★ |
| YOUNG ADULTS ★ ★ ★ ★ | | OVER 30 ★ ★ ★ ★ | SENIORS ★ ★ ★ ★ |

2 St. Martin's Place, West End, W2; adjacent to the National Gallery;
☎ 0207-306-0055; www.npg.org.uk;
tube: Leicester Square or Charing Cross

Type of attraction Collection of the most famous faces in British history. Admission Free; £4–£8 for special exhibits. Hours Monday–Wednesday and Saturday–Sunday, 10 a.m.–6 p.m.; Thursday and Friday, 10 a.m.–9 p.m. When to go Anytime. Special comments Very accessible to disabled individuals. Author's rating ★ ★ ★ ★. How much time to allow 2–3 hours.

DESCRIPTION AND COMMENTS Of all the museums that London has to offer, the National Portrait Gallery holds particular appeal, as it's compact and people-oriented, as well as being in the middle of a very interesting area. It's across the street from St. Martin-in-the-Fields Church, and sits next to the National Gallery, just off Trafalgar Square. It's quite manageable in a couple of hours, unlike the eight miles of the Victoria and Albert or the endless rooms of the National Gallery. Its size allows for relaxed browsing without the feeling that you must rush or you won't see everything. The NPG gives the casual student of England a direct line to its history through the faces of its most interesting and important people. It's a veritable Who's Who of England that includes the lean faces of the early medieval kings; the Tudors, with Holbein's images of Henry VIII and his many wives; the Stuarts in the 17th century; the 19th-century Victorians; and, finally, portraits and photos of the current royal family. As you take this visual voyage through the ages, notice the changing styles of portraiture and what kinds of people each age deemed worthy of portraiture. You will see people from various disciplines—science, literature, politics, art, and entertainment—whose contributions to English life reached far beyond this small island. With the help of the NPG sound guides, the amount of history you absorb will change how you perceive London's most famous sights. There's a good restaurant on the top floor offering glorious views over Trafalgar Square and beyond.

TOURING TIPS In addition to the more pricey roof restaurant, there is also the Portrait Café in the basement. Combine your visit with a trip to the National Gallery next door.

kids Natural History Museum

APPEAL BY AGE   PRESCHOOL ★★★   GRADE SCHOOL ★★★★   TEENS ★★★
YOUNG   ADULTS   ★★★   OVER 30   ★★★   SENIORS   ★★★

Cromwell Road, South Kensington, SW7; ☎ 0207-942-5000;
www.nhm.ac.uk; tube: South Kensington

Type of attraction Exhibits on the history of the natural world. **Admission** Free.
Hours Monday–Saturday, 10 a.m.–5:50 p.m.; Sunday, 11 a.m.–5:50 p.m. **When to
go** Weekends can be quite crowded, so go early. **Special comments** Complete disabled access. **Author's rating** ★★★. **How much time to allow** 2 hours or more.

DESCRIPTION AND COMMENTS   As part of the South Kensington cultural revolution of the 19th century, the Natural History Museum was formed by
the British Library's collections of Sir Hans Sloane, which were divvied
up and sent to South Ken in the 1860s. It's a grand old institution,
housed in a majestic building that, in itself, makes the visit worthwhile.
Notice the animal statues on the outside, and the terra-cotta monkeys
and other beasts climbing on stone vines in the lobby. It has all the hallmarks of a Gothic cathedral, an impression that architect Alfred
Waterhouse intended, to inspire the proper reverence for nature. It is a
huge place, full of many surprises and some really fine examples of educational curation, such as the Ecology Gallery, in which you walk
through a rain forest, and the new Darwin Centre with 22 million specimens of everything from amoebas to monkeys. It has plenty of
interactive, permanent displays and temporary exhibits, some of which
have been very good, such as the one on human biology. The Earth Galleries (entrance on Exhibition Road) are entered via a long escalator
that goes through a model of the earth and features a re-creation of a
convenience store in the Kobe earthquake. The Earth Galleries are full
of see-and-touch educational exhibits, which is fine with kids, but perhaps not so wondrous for adults. I am much more impressed with some
of the older artifacts: dioramas of exotic animals, including the extinct
dodo bird, and cabinets full of butterflies, all the bounty brought back
from the far-flung reaches of the empire, much of which is utterly irreplaceable and of great scientific importance. The dinosaur exhibit is
wonderful, and of interest to old and young alike, and if you're lucky,
they will still have the motion-sensor roaring dinosaur that has kids
both terrified and delighted. The dinosaur area is set out in such a way
that one follows along paths and climbs up stairs, which keeps the kids
active and happy, while the parents can take the time to read the information posted there. The gift shops are excellent for children's
educational toys and books, as well as geological booty.

TOURING TIPS   Be sure to look at the entire front of the building on Cromwell
Road: in a witty reflection of the statues of artists that adorn the front of
the neighboring Victoria and Albert Museum, the Natural History Museum has statues of animals on its facade. If the line at the Cromwell Road
entrance is long, enter at the Earth Galleries on Exhibition Road.

Old Bailey (Central Criminal Courts)

APPEAL BY AGE	PRESCHOOL †	GRADE SCHOOL †	TEENS ★★
YOUNG ADULTS ★★	OVER 30 ★★★		SENIORS ★★★

† Not appropriate for children

Old Bailey Street, The City, EC4; ☎ 0207-248-3277; ask for List Office; www.courts-service.gov.uk; tube: St. Paul's

Type of attraction London's court of justice. **Admission** Free; children under age 14 not admitted. **Hours** Monday–Friday, 10:30 a.m.–4:30 p.m.; closed for lunch from 1–2 p.m. **When to go** Arrive for the times given. The public gallery in each courtroom has a limited number of seats, and bailiffs may not allow access once court is in session. **Special comments** Security searches are routine. Do not bring backpacks, cameras, food, cell phones, or pagers. These items are prohibited, and there is no cloak room for storing them. **Author's rating ★★**. **How much time to allow** As much time as your interest in the proceedings dictates.

DESCRIPTION AND COMMENTS Although most interesting to those with a background in law, the cases held in London's Old Bailey are criminal cases, and just about anyone will find both the content of the cases and the etiquette of the British courtroom intriguing for some length of time. Wigged and traditionally robed barristers address each other as "friend" and the judge as "milord," and politely assert their cases while the defendant sits at the rear of the courtroom, visibly separated from the "gentlemen's proceedings" going on in front of him. Be warned, you are not likely to see some kind of dramatic *Law and Order*–style court case.

The Old Bailey was built on the site of Newgate Prison, the noxious and notorious prison that held criminals and public executions from the twelfth century until it was destroyed in 1902. Not the best feng shui for a court, one might say, with God only knows how many desperate ghosts hanging around. This court saw the spectacle of Oscar Wilde's trial—"the butterfly broken on a wheel"—as well as those of the Yorkshire Ripper and the wife-killer, Dr. Crippen. Public hangings took place often in the 18th and 19th centuries, with people paying dearly for a "good" view of the proceedings, a lucrative business for people in the neighborhood whose windows looked into the courtyard. In 1787, transportation to Australia became common for felons, reducing the number of hangings. In the mid-to-late 20th century, capital punishment was eschewed, and finally outlawed in the UK.

TOURING TIPS The entrance to the public galleries is off Newgate Street and down Old Bailey, past the original courts building and its contemporary addition, to Warwick Passage on the left. Call ahead to find out what cases are currently on the docket and at what point in the proceedings they are. Dial the number above and ask for the List Office, or check online at the above Web site. For a good background on the history of the Old Bailey, go to www.oldbaileyonline.org.

Old Operating Theatre, Museum, and Herb Garret

APPEAL BY AGE	PRESCHOOL †	GRADE SCHOOL ★	TEENS ★★
YOUNG ADULTS ★★★	OVER 30 ★★★		SENIORS ★★★

† Not appropriate for preschoolers.
9A St. Thomas's Street, South Bank, SE1; ☎ 0207-955-4791; www.thegarret.org.uk; tube: London Bridge

Type of attraction Haunting museum of old medical equipment and an early Victorian operating theater. **Admission** £4.75 for adults, £3.75 for seniors and students, £2.75 for children under age 16, £12 for a family. **Hours** Daily, 10:30 a.m.–5 p.m. **When to go** Anytime. **Special comments** The stairs in this old house are very, very steep. There is no wheelchair access. **Author's rating** ★★★★. **How much time to allow** 1 hour.

DESCRIPTION AND COMMENTS In a tiny old house in a street by London Bridge is one of the most fascinating medical museums in London. You must climb up some rather treacherous steps to reach the musty old attic in which you'll find displayed many of the gruesome medical instruments used before the days of anesthesia. Around the room are sheaths of herbs—comfrey for healing bones, pennyroyal for nausea, willow bark from which aspirin was derived, and elderflowers for what ails you.

The centerpiece of the museum is the operating theater from the early 19th century, a case study for postoperative infection from the days before Dr. Lister figured out the germ theory. The table is made of wood, and under it is a box of sawdust, which the surgeon would kick into place around the table to catch the blood; there's a small wash-basin in which hands were washed *after* the operation. The room is ringed by semicircular levels of observation areas into which medical students would be crammed like sardines to stand and watch. The gift shop is packed with interesting books on herbal remedies.

TOURING TIPS Take your time and read the descriptions of everything. You'll be glad you live in the modern world. Not for the queasy or sensitive.

Queen's Gallery, Buckingham Palace

APPEAL BY AGE	PRESCHOOL ★	GRADE SCHOOL ★	TEENS ★★
YOUNG ADULTS ★★★	OVER 30 ★★★		SENIORS ★★

Buckingham Palace, SW1; ☎ 0207-766-7301; www.royal.gov.uk; tube: Victoria, Green Park, or St. James's Park

Type of attraction Rotating exhibition of a fraction of the queen's treasures. **Admission** £7.50 for adults, £4 for children, £6 seniors and students, £19 family ticket (you can save £1 on all tickets by booking online). **Hours** Daily, 10 a.m.–5:30 p.m.; occasionally closed between exhibitions, so call ahead. **When to go** Anytime, but it can be very crowded in summer. **Special comments** A new wing offering three and a half more times display space opened in spring 2002 to celebrate the Queen's Golden Jubilee and is disabled friendly. **Author's rating** ★★★. **How much time to allow** 1 hour.

DESCRIPTION AND COMMENTS The new Queen's Gallery is an impressive piece of renovation and curating. New rooms have been built in the grand style of the Buckingham Palace state rooms, and are completely modern and practical. Total wheelchair access has been added, which is impossible to do in many renovations of old buildings. It is certainly a triumph. There are sketches by da Vinci and paintings by old masters. There is extraordinary furniture—don't miss the silver table and mirror if they are still there; understandably, not much silver furniture has made it intact through the ages. There are gold table services, sculpture, porcelain, and treasures from every corner of the empire. Unlike Buckingham Palace, this gallery has comprehensive explanatory signs describing the marvels, and it would appear that the bulk of the current exhibits were accumulated under Charles II and mad George III, whom you would think certainly had other things on their minds besides bibelots and art. You will always be impressed by whatever the Queen's Gallery is showing because there is such bounty in her treasure vaults to choose from: 20,000 drawings by old masters, such as Holbein, Canaletto, da Vinci, Michelangelo, Carracci, and more; 10,000 old masters' paintings, including such artists as Rembrandt, Vermeer, Holbein, Brueghel, Van Dyck, and Rubens; royal portraits by Gainsborough, Reynolds, and Wilkie, as well as George Stubbs's magnificent equine portraits; 30,000 English watercolors, a possible half-a-million prints, and countless sculptures, glass and porcelain works, books, and Fabergé trinkets. There is an excellent gift shop on the site with lots of royal memorabilia.

TOURING TIPS Leave your backpacks and pocketbooks at the hotel: there is a very slow security drill in place in which your bags are examined and you must check them into the coatroom. The gallery is great, but nothing is worth that length of time and that kind of hassle to enter.

 ## Royal Academy of Arts

APPEAL BY AGE	PRESCHOOL ★	GRADE SCHOOL ★	TEENS ★★
YOUNG ADULTS ★★★★		OVER 30 ★★★★	SENIORS ★★★★

Burlington House, Piccadilly, W1; ☎ 0207-300-5760 or 0207-300-5761; www.royalacademy.org.uk; tube: Piccadilly Circus, Green Park

Type of attraction Venue for the world-famous Summer Exhibition of contemporary artists, record-breaking exhibitions of major artists and art themes, and a small but fine permanent collection of past academicians. **Admission** Prices vary with each exhibition but run about £7 for adults, £6 for seniors, £5 for students, £3 for children ages 12–18, £2 for children ages 8–11, children under age 7 are free. **Hours** Daily, 10 a.m.–6 p.m.; open until 10 p.m. on Friday. **When to go** The largest crowds will be when there's a very popular exhibition; weekends are normally crowded. Go in the morning if possible. **Special comments** Wheelchair access. **Author's rating** ★★★★. **How much time to allow** It depends on the exhibit, but 2 hours is a good estimate.

DESCRIPTION AND COMMENTS The academy is housed in the beautiful old Burlington House, off Piccadilly. The courtyard usually features some exhibit of sculptures, often marvelously at odds with the Palladian grandeur of these last few surviving 18th-century palazzos. This was England's first art school, founded by Gainsborough and Reynolds, among others, in 1768. To be counted among the academicians was the highest mark of success. Today, it continues its tradition as a venue for new artists by hosting the 200-year-old Summer Exhibition, in which painters and sculptors compete for the honor of displaying their work to an appreciative audience, many of whom come to buy. It's a bit of a hodgepodge and scorned by many of the chattering classes (critics and journalists) and most of the artists who don't get in the exhibit. But everyone keeps trying to win a place on the wall.

The exhibits are usually excellent. One record-breaking exhibit was the Monet show in which people had to be let in on a timed basis, and for the last couple of days, they had to keep the academy open for 24 hours. A less popular but no less interesting show was of the whimsical Victorian paintings of fairies. A permanent collection includes work from past academicians, as well as its most significant treasure, Michelangelo's marble frieze of Madonna and child.

TOURING TIPS For £58, you can become a Friend of the Royal Academy, which allows you use of the very pleasant Friends' Room, free admission plus a guest, and, most importantly, you can jump the queue for the blockbuster exhibitions. You also get to feel quite virtuous as a much-needed patron of the arts. Call the academy ahead of time, or just come to the Friends' Desk and sign up. Of course, this may be a bit more than you would want to commit, given you are on holiday, but this institution does need support.

kids Royal Greenwich Observatory

APPEAL BY AGE	PRESCHOOL ★	GRADE SCHOOL ★★★	TEENS ★★★
YOUNG ADULTS ★★★		OVER 30 ★★★	SENIORS ★★★

Blackheath Avenue, hilltop of Greenwich Park; ☎ 0208-312-6565; www.nmm.ac.uk; Docklands Light Railway: Greenwich

Type of attraction Location of the world's prime meridian (0 degrees longitude). **Admission** Free; fee for special events, exhibits, and planetarium shows. **Hours** Daily, 10 a.m.–5 p.m. **When to go** Anytime. **Special comments** Not all observatory buildings are fully accessible. **Author's rating** ★★★. **How much time to allow** 1–2 hours, or a full day's outing to see the adjacent Queen's House, the National Maritime Museum, and the *Cutty Sark* at the dock.

DESCRIPTION AND COMMENTS In 1675, Charles II appointed John Flamsteed his Astronomer Royal, with the specific mandate to create better navigational maps for the British Empire. Christopher Wren then designed and built an observatory for him on the highest point of the king's royal hunting grounds in Greenwich. Today, this small complex of buildings is a popular museum. You can place yourself in two hemispheres at the same time as you straddle the prime meridian, a favorite photo-op for visitors who line up to take their turn. Inquisitive children are riveted by all the important-looking equipment and love the gift shop, too The museum's oldest part, Flamsteed House, is the restored home of the first Astronomer Royal. Its main galleries tell a variety of the bizarre methods once used to help ships' captains determine their location at sea and the increasingly important race to discover longitude. The remaining buildings contain a number of astronomical tools and telescopes, including Britain's largest, in the impressive Telescope Dome. The ongoing renovations may result in some wings being closed at any given time; check by phone or on the Web site.

TOURING TIPS Go on a nice day and enjoy walking around Greenwich. Picnic in the surrounding park; and be sure to get a gander at the view of London from the top of the hill.

kids Royal Mews, Buckingham Palace

APPEAL BY AGE	PRESCHOOL ★★	GRADE SCHOOL ★★★	TEENS ★★
YOUNG ADULTS ★★		OVER 30 ★★	SENIORS ★★

Buckingham Palace Road, SW1; ☎ 0207-766-7302; www.royal.gov.uk (click on Queen's Gallery); tube: St. James's Park or Victoria

Type of attraction Where the royal carriages and queen's horses are kept. **Admission** £6 for adults, £5 for seniors, £3 for children under age 17, £15.50 for family. **Hours** Daily (but closed on Friday October through the end of July), 11 a.m.–6 p.m. During Palace State **Rooms** opening in August and September, daily, 10 a.m.–7 p.m. Subject to sudden closures, so be sure to call first. **When to go** See hours above. **Special comments** Disabled are free, and there is good wheelchair access. **Author's rating ★★★. How much time to allow** 40 minutes.

DESCRIPTION AND COMMENTS It's a small attraction and of limited appeal to many, but I urge any horse-and-carriage fancier to go take a look, if only to see the most elegant, cleanest stables in the entire world. Designed by John Nash, the stables retain a Georgian perfection, with freshly painted stalls of a pale yellow and lovely wrought-iron lamps. The horses are just as magnificent as you would expect: strong, well-bred, and glossy. How they handle the oddly narrow riding ring is anyone's guess, but what the ring lacks in practicality, it makes up for in beauty. The royal coaches and automobiles are just mind-boggling, especially the gold state coach built for George II in 1761, which is still in use. There's a room with some of the most admirable tack and saddles ever made, with sketches and photos of royal public occasions also on display.

TOURING TIPS Try to make this part of your trip to Buckingham Palace and/or the Queen's Gallery. I guarantee that out of the three, this will be the kids' favorite attraction.

Saatchi Gallery

APPEAL BY AGE	PRESCHOOL ★	GRADE SCHOOL ★★	TEENS ★★★★
YOUNG ADULTS ★★★		OVER 30 ★★★	SENIORS ★★★

**County Hall, South Bank, SE1; ☎ 0207-823-2363;
www.saatchi-gallery.co.uk; tube: Waterloo or Westminster**

Type of attraction Collection of young British artists. **Admission** £9, £6.75 seniors and students, £26 family ticket. **Hours** Daily, 10 a.m.–6 p.m.; Friday and Saturday, open until 10 p.m. **When to go** Anytime, although weekend days can be crowded. **Special comments** Complete disabled access; entrance at Belvedere Road. **Author's rating** ★★★. **How much time to allow** 2 hours.

DESCRIPTION AND COMMENTS   It's not just the well-done renovation of 40,000 square feet of the old County Hall that makes one favorably disposed toward this gallery; nor is it only its opening celebration attended by the city's leading citizens that featured a performance-art piece of 200 naked people happily mingling with the celebs that make one feel like cheering modern art. It's more a combination of the above and the long-term speculation about the wisdom of the Young British Artists' patron Charles Saatchi plunking down thousands of pounds for artworks such as Damien Hirst's shark in formaldehyde and Tracey Emin's unmade bed being somewhat resolved by the robust attendance at this new gallery, opened in June 2003. One goes along to this gallery with a sense of humor, and one is not disappointed. There is plenty to be amused by here, and the cheekiness of the young (or rather, now aging) British artists known as the Britpack exhibited in some of these pieces can only be admired. The first exhibit featured Damien Hirst, whose animal cadavers caused such a hue and cry in the 1990s. Although Charles Saatchi's collection is heavy with such contemporary British artists, his intention for his new gallery is to make it a center for modern art that may—depending on its exhibitions—rival the Tate Modern. It is a good opportunity to make up your own mind about the art that the media has been tut-tutting about for the past ten years, and to realize how powerful some of these pieces are. The current exhibit is called The Triumph of Painting, with some excellent and noncontroversial oils and drawings to admire; but stay tuned: Saatchi has a lot of unusual modern art up his sleeve.

TOURING TIPS   Combine a visit with any of the other South Bank attractions, such as the London Eye, Dali Universe, or the London Aquarium. Friday and Saturday late nights are good times to enjoy the night lights of Westminster's sights from a good vantage point outside County Hall.

 ## St. Paul's Cathedral

APPEAL BY AGE	PRESCHOOL ★	GRADE SCHOOL ★★	TEENS ★★
YOUNG ADULTS ★★★		OVER 30 ★★★	SENIORS ★★★

**Ludgate Hill, The City, EC4; ☎ 0207-236-4128; www.stpauls.co.uk;
tube: St. Paul's or Mansion House**

Type of attraction London's most prominent cathedral. **Admission** Cathedral, galleries, and crypt entry: £8 for adults, £7 for seniors and students, children under age 16 free, £19.50 family ticket. Self-guided tours (with cassette) and guided tours are available for an extra fee. **Hours** Visitors to cathedral: Monday–Saturday, 8:30 a.m.–4:30 p.m.; galleries open at 9:30 a.m.; choral evensong occurs weekdays at 5 p.m. and Sunday at 3:15 p.m. Call the cathedral for other mass times, and for information on closures due to weddings or baptisms. **When to go** Early in the day on weekdays to avoid the crowds and catch the best chances for clear-sky views from the dome. **Special comments** Good disabled access to cathedral's nave and crypt, but there is no lift access to the galleries. **Author's rating** ★★★. **How much time to allow** 1–3 hours, depending on whether you plan to climb to the top of the dome, and see every nook and cranny.

DESCRIPTION AND COMMENTS There was once a Roman temple to the goddess Diana on the site of the present St. Paul's, but even such ancient sanctity did not put the succeeding buildings out of harm's way; the first church was destroyed by fire around 660. The second was demolished by Vikings. A huge wooden cross was struck by lightning in 1382, and in 1561 a spire was also toppled by lightning. During Henry VIII's reformation, the church turned into a kind of public marketplace. A bishop described the nave in 1560: "The south side for Popery and Usury; the north for Simony (buying and selling pardons); and the horse-fair in the middle for all kinds of bargains, meetings, brawlings, murders, conspiracies; and the font for ordinary payments of money." The Great Fire of 1666 destroyed the third incarnation of St. Paul's Cathedral, along with four-fifths of the city. King Charles II's surveyor-general, Christopher Wren, became responsible for designing its replacement, and this became his masterpiece. The cathedral was finished in the course of 35 years (the first cathedral to be completed by a single architect), and its stone English baroque style, despite being dwarfed by the encroachments of skyscrapers, still dominates the neighborhood. At 360 feet, the dome is one of the highest in the world and second in size only to St. Peter's Basilica in Rome. Its lantern weighs a massive 850 tons.

Inside the cathedral, there are mosaics and frescoes, the *Light of the World* by Holman Hunt, Jean Tijou's grand sanctuary gates, and the intricate choir-stall carvings designed by the most skilled woodcraftsman of the day, Grinling Gibbons. The crypt is the resting place of—among other notables—Lord Admiral Horatio Nelson, the duke of Wellington, and Wren himself, whose son composed the Latin inscription on his tomb that translates: "Reader, if you seek his monument, look around." Also in the crypt are the cathedral shop and a small café.

The 530 steps that take you to the top of St. Paul's are worth the effort, especially if you are lucky enough to have a clear, or even sunny, day. It is an easy walk to the Whispering Gallery, the first of the three levels, where words whispered on one side of the gallery can be clearly heard on the other. On the second level, the external Stone Gallery provides telescopes and benches, but it is the uppermost Golden Gallery that offers the most spectacular views of London. To see them, however, you must submit to considerably more nerve-racking climbing.

TOURING TIPS If your interest in Christopher Wren is inspired by St. Paul's, there are a number of other charming examples of his 17th-century work, many of which are just around the corner. Some of those closest to the cathedral include St. Mary-le-Bow (Cheapside), St. Bride's (Fleet Street), and Christ Church (Newgate Street), that has only its tower remaining. A lovely garden now fills what was once the nave. Also visit St. Bartholomew the Great, in Little Britain Street; it's London's oldest monastic church (☎ 0207-606-5171).

kids The Science Museum

APPEAL BY AGE	PRESCHOOL ★★★★	GRADE SCHOOL ★★★★	TEENS ★★★★
YOUNG ADULTS ★★★★		OVER 30 ★★★★	SENIORS ★★★★

Exhibition Road, South Kensington, SW7; ☎ 0207-942-4000; www.sciencemuseum.org.uk; tube: South Kensington

Type of attraction Abundant collection of scientific/technological odds and ends that add up to a fascinating experience. **Admission** Free; charge for IMAX and special exhibits. **Hours** Daily, 10 a.m.–6 p.m. **When to go** Avoid school holidays and weekends, unless you're there at 10 a.m. It's one of London's most popular museums, so go early or on weekdays. **Special comments** Wheelchair access and facilities. **Author's rating** ★★★★. **How much time to allow** As much as you can spare—you could easily spend all day here, there's so much to see. If you're with children who want to play in the interactive areas, plan to spend at least 2 hours.

DESCRIPTION AND COMMENTS You don't need any particular interest in things scientific to love this most comprehensive collection displaying the progress of technology and science from the dawn of time to today. It is dauntingly large and there is a lot to read, but it allows you to travel, from an early hourglass in the time gallery to the *Apollo 10* Command Module in the exploration-of-space exhibit. Moving exhibits include a miniaturized field with examples of plowing carried out by a number of small tractors, and a stupendously huge mill engine in the middle of the East Hall. You can watch Foucault's pendulum swinging away in the staircase by the East Hall, or check out a replica of a turn-of-the-century pharmacy in the area that focuses on the art of medicine. The supermarket Sainsbury's has contributed a "Food for Thought" exhibit that examines every aspect of nutrition, the strangest being the mannequins of a young man and a young woman, showing what food they consumed in a month, how much sweat, feces, and urine they excreted, and how much their hair and nails grew.

Downstairs in the basement is a wonderful place to bring the young children: There's a hands-on gallery where children between ages 3 and 6 can splash around (hands only) in a water sluice and build things with giant LEGOS, to name only two of its many attractions. You'll never get them out of there, which may be why the museum suggests starting at the top and moving downward.

TOURING TIPS If you arrive and find a line, go across the street to the Natural History Museum, and come back late in the afternoon when the families have taken their tired kids home.

Sherlock Holmes Museum

APPEAL BY AGE	PRESCHOOL ★	GRADE SCHOOL ★	TEENS ★★★
YOUNG ADULTS ★★★	OVER 30 ★★★		SENIORS ★★★

221B Baker Street, Marylebone, NW1; ☎ 0207-935-8866; www.sherlock-holmes.co.uk; tube: Baker Street

Type of attraction Re-creation of fictional Victorian bachelor's house. **Admission** £6 for adults, £4 for children under age 16, free for children under age 7. **Hours** Daily, 9:30 a.m.–6 p.m. **When to go** Anytime, especially if you're waiting for Madame Tussaud's to open or are on your way to the London Zoo. **Special comments** No wheelchair access; numerous, steep stairs. **Author's rating** ★★★. **How much time to allow** 30–40 minutes.

DESCRIPTION AND COMMENTS I am a Sherlock Holmes fan, and I am also a sucker for anything from the 19th century. But even if you are neither of the above, I think you'll find this a charming, if expensive, little stop. The self-guided (and short) tour through the little house is like stepping back in time: there are fires laid in all the rooms, which are bursting with curios and furniture, much in the way described in the stories by Sir Arthur Conan Doyle, who at the end of his life felt strangled by his own creation, and created an uproar when he killed him off (and was forced to bring him back). It is a funny experience, seeing this fictional place brought to life; by the time you leave you may think there really was a Sherlock Holmes. The decor is wonderful. There's the violin he so famously played close at hand in the study, leg irons on the bed by a valise half packed, a medical corner for Dr. Watson, a remarkable early typewriter, and a turn-of-the-century telephone. Even the attic is perfect, stuffed with leather goods, hatboxes, and other household items we're all too young to remember. Props from the stories are displayed with appropriate quotes from the books, and there's an extraordinary chess set in gold and silver with characters from the books as the pieces.

TOURING TIPS Time your visit so you can have a traditional tea in the charming Hudson's Victorian Dining Room on the ground floor of the museum.

Sir John Soane's Museum

APPEAL BY AGE	PRESCHOOL †	GRADE SCHOOL ★	TEENS ★★★
YOUNG ADULTS ★★★★	OVER 30 ★★★★		SENIORS ★★★★

† *Not appropriate for young children.*

13 Lincoln's Inn Fields, Holborn, WC2; ☎ 0207-440-4263; www.soane.org; tube: Holborn, Central and Piccadilly lines

Type of attraction Fascinating, eccentric collection of sculpture, art, and antiquities belonging to neoclassical architect Sir John Soane. **Admission** Free. **Hours** Tuesday–Saturday, 10 a.m.–5 p.m.; open the first Tuesday of each month 6–9 p.m., with some of the rooms lighted by candles. **When to go** Anytime, although there is an excellent tour of the museum on Saturday at 2:30 p.m., which is limited to 20 people and costs £3. **Special comments** The museum is not handicapped accessible, because it was formerly the private home of Sir John Soane and was directed to be left as he had it. You will even be asked to leave backpacks at the front desk so there is less chance of knocking over any of the hundreds of items that can be seen in each room. This attraction is not recommended for very young children with the tendency to touch everything. **Author's rating ★★★★. How much time to allow** 1½–2½ hours.

DESCRIPTION AND COMMENTS   Many Londoners consider this their favorite museum. As small as it is, there are treasures in every conceivable cranny. You can visit this residence over and over and still find new things in this wonderous collection. Situated just a stone's throw from one of the early Inns of Court, Sir John Soane bought and reconstructed the Georgian homes at 12, 13, and 14 Lincoln's Inn Fields and began filling them with a rather eccentric collection of art and antiquities. His architectural talent is seen in the unique floor plan of number 13, which includes a glass-domed roof and central atrium that lights three floors as well as in the Soanes' dining room and breakfast parlor, both of which incorporate an unusual display of mirrors that reflect light and add illusions of space.

Other remarkable aspects of the collection include the series of paintings by William Hogarth, entitled the *Rake's Progress* and *Election,* in an impressive picture gallery of false and hidden walls; a mock medieval monk's parlor containing gloomy casts and gargoyles; and the sarcophagus of Seti I surrounded by rows of antique statuary. Saturday's hour-long tour takes you through all of this and into number 12 as well, where you can see Soane's enormous research library, complete with Soane's architectural plans for the Bank of England, Whitehall, and parts of the treasury, along with numerous models of Pompeiian temples.

TOURING TIPS   If you can't manage the Saturday tour, definitely strike up a conversation with any of the museum curators. They are very friendly and love to talk about the plethora of items acquired by Sir John Soane. It is the only way to really appreciate the amount and variety of items you see housed in this small town house. Call about the candlelit late opening (which doesn't really work in the height of the long summer days).

 Somerset House (including Courtauld Institute Gallery, Gilbert Collection, and Hermitage Rooms)

APPEAL BY AGE	PRESCHOOL ★★★	GRADE SCHOOL ★★★	TEENS ★★★
YOUNG ADULTS ★★★★	OVER 30 ★★★★		SENIORS ★★★★

Strand, West End, WC2; Somerset: ☎ 0207-845-4600;
Courtauld: ☎ 0207-848-2526; Gilbert: ☎ 0207-420-9400;
Hermitage: ☎ 0207-845-4630; www.somerset-house.org.uk;
www.courtauld.ac.uk; www.gilbert-collection.org.uk; www.hermitage
rooms.com; tube: Covent Garden, Holborn, Temple (except on Sunday).

Type of attraction Magnificent edifice with river views, a classical courtyard, a river terrace, and three separate art galleries. **Admission** Free for Somerset House and grounds. Courtauld Institute Gallery: £5 for adults, £4 for seniors; admission is free on Monday between 10 a.m. and 2 p.m. Gilbert Collection: £5 for adults, free for children under age 18 and full-time UK students (an audio guide and magnifying glass are included in the price). Combined-admission adult tickets for the Courtauld Gallery and Gilbert Collection are £8. Hermitage Rooms: Prices depend on the current exhibit and will range from free to £8 for adults. Children under age 18 are admitted free of charge to all galleries. **Hours** Somerset House and all galleries are open daily, 10 a.m. to 6 p.m., and on Sunday from noon to 6 p.m. During the summer, the house itself, its terrace and courtyard stay open on Friday till 10 p.m. **When to go** The courtyard and terrace of the house are splendid on a sunny day; inside galleries are great anytime, but see special comments about the Hermitage Rooms. **Special comments** The house and the galleries are all wheelchair accessible. Special sign-language talks are also offered occasionally; call ☎ 0207-848-2549 for details. Because the Hermitage Rooms are small, the tickets are sold for timed slots, on the hour and on the half hour; about 60 at a time can go in. Also, check the Hermitage Web site to be sure they are not in the middle of staging a new exhibit; the exhibits are shown in ten-month cycles. **Author's rating ★★★★★. How much time to allow** This depends on whether you go to any or all of the art galleries and on how long you stroll around or linger in the cafés or on the terrace. You could spend the day here.

DESCRIPTION AND COMMENTS Somerset House is one of the great jewels in London's architectural and historical crown. It was opened to the public in 2000, after a lengthy and expensive renovation that included adding the Gilbert Collection and the Hermitage Rooms to its long-standing Courtauld Gallery Institute. The site of Somerset House has a long history, going back to 1547. In addition to the galleries, it now houses a fair number of cafés, gift shops, and places to sit and watch the Thames flow by. The onsite Admiralty Restaurant is very upscale, and a destination restaurant on its own. In winter, the courtyard fountain is turned into a skating rink.

The Courtauld Gallery is an integral part of the Courtauld Institute of Art. The gallery originated with textile magnate Samuel Courtauld's private collection from the 1930s, but has grown considerably since then. It is most famous for its priceless Impressionist works, which include Van Gogh's *Self-Portrait with Bandaged Ear,* Degas's *Two Dancers,* Renoir's *La Loge,* and Manet's *Déjeuner sur l'herbe.* The medieval and early Renaissance works in galleries 1 and 2 are also quite impressive, with paintings by Brueghel, Bellini, and Rubens.

The Gilbert Collection is a museum of decorative arts, housing Sir Arthur Gilbert's mammoth collection of gold, silver, and mosaics. There are silver items here to rival the Victoria and Albert's collection, and I don't know where in the world there could be more "micro-mosaic" tables, artwork, and snuff boxes. A staggering amount of work went

into these pieces, and I would advise that you take the offered magnifying glass to fully appreciate what's here.

In the Hermitage Rooms are exhibited selections from the great
Hermitage Museum of St. Petersburg, Russia. If you are a museum lover,
this is a must-go; it's a long way to St. Petersburg.

TOURING TIPS The Courtauld offers a fantastic educational booklet called
"Courtauld Gallery Trail," available at the admissions desk, that
instructs children (ages 5–12) in the study of the gallery's fine-art collection by asking practical questions about how to look at and learn
from the paintings.

Southwark Cathedral

APPEAL BY AGE	PRESCHOOL ★ ★	GRADE SCHOOL ★ ★ ★		TEENS ★ ★
YOUNG ADULTS ★ ★ ★		OVER 30 ★ ★ ★		SENIORS ★ ★ ★

**Montague Close, Southwark, SE1; ☎ 0207-367-6700; www.dswark.org;
tube: London Bridge**

Type of attraction Small medieval cathedral with famous literary ties. **Admission** Combined exhibition and audio tour: £6 for adults; £2 for children under age
12. Otherwise admission is free, although they do suggest a donation of £5.
Hours Monday–Saturday, 10 a.m.–6 p.m.; Sunday, 11 a.m.–5 p.m. **When to go**
Anytime. **Special comments** Disabled access; permits must be obtained from welcome desk for photography or videotaping. **Author's rating** ★ ★ ★. **How much
time to allow** 1–2 hours.

DESCRIPTION AND COMMENTS Although it has been a cathedral since 1905,
parts of this building date back to the twelfth century, when it was the
Augustinian priory church of St. Mary Overie. In the time span
between, the cathedral was frequented by many notables of their day.
William Shakespeare attended mass here regularly, and his brother,
Edward, is interred in the choir aisle. A chapel is dedicated to the
founder of Harvard University, John Harvard, who was born in Southwark and baptized in the church in 1607. In addition, there is the tomb
of poet John Gower, a contemporary of Chaucer, and a memorial to
Shakespeare that includes a glorious 20th-century stained-glass window depicting almost two dozen of Shakespeare's most famous
characters.

As part of the £10.9 million Southwark Cathedral Millennium Project, there is a new exhibition using technology such as computers to
look at artifacts and films, interactive cameras contrasting today's view
from the top of the cathedral tower with views since the 16th century,
and an amazing 24-hour time-lapse 360-degree view from London
Bridge. There's also a shop and a restaurant.

TOURING TIPS Southwark Cathedral makes a nice stop if you are wandering
around the Southwark area, especially if you have already been to
Shakespeare's Globe Theatre.

Tate Britain

| APPEAL BY AGE | PRESCHOOL ★ | GRADE SCHOOL ★★ | TEENS ★★★ |
| YOUNG ADULTS ★★★★ | | OVER 30 ★★★★ | SENIORS ★★★★ |

Millbank, on Thames, SW1; ☎ 0207-887-8008; www.tate.org.uk; tube: Pimlico

Type of attraction Museum of English painters. **Admission** Free, though donations are eagerly accepted; there's a charge for special exhibits. **Hours** Daily, 10 a.m.–5:50 p.m. **When to go** Anytime, but avoid midday if there's a big exhibition. **Special comments** Access-for-disabled leaflet is available at information desks. Parking spaces and wheelchairs are available, but must be booked in advance. **Author's rating ★★★★. How much time to allow** 2 hours or more.

DESCRIPTION AND COMMENTS   The old Tate Gallery was morphed into the Tate Britain in the spring of 2000, when the international modern art was moved across the river to the new Tate Modern (see separate profile) at the Bankside Power Station. This left a completely marvelous collection of English painters and sculptors from the 16th to the early 20th century here at Tate Britain. The building itself is quite impressive, one of London's greatest exteriors in my opinion. Look for Poseidon situated between a lion and a unicorn on the roof, stately columns adorning the entrance, and halls of beautiful marble and design. In October 2001, a new extension opened five new galleries, another entrance and shop, and better visitor facilities. There are plenty of benches from which to enjoy the paintings and the ambience. All the great British artists are here: Hogarth, Stubbs, Reynolds, Blake, Burne-Jones, Constable, and even an honorary Englishman, the American expat James Whistler. The pride of the collection is J. M. W. Turner, whose paintings and memorabilia fill the Clore Gallery. The gift shop has an excellent selection of books, gifts, and postcards, and the café and more formal dining room are top-notch—remember that spending money at this gallery helps support this excellent free art gallery and its sister gallery across the river, the Tate Modern. There's a ferry service across the street from the museum that will take you to the London Eye and then on to the Tate Modern. The pier was designed by the same people who gave us the London Eye, and the boat itself was decorated with the help of artist Damian Hirst.

Tate Modern

| APPEAL BY AGE | PRESCHOOL — | GRADE SCHOOL ★★ | TEENS ★★★★ |
| YOUNG ADULTS ★★★★ | | OVER 30 ★★★★ | SENIORS ★★★★ |

25 Sumner Street, Bankside, SE1; ☎ 0207-887-8008; www.tate.org.uk; tube: Southwark or Blackfriars

Type of attraction Museum of international modern art. **Admission** Free, except for special exhibitions, lectures, and films. **Hours** Sunday–Thursday, 10 a.m.–6 p.m.; Friday–Saturday, 10 a.m.–10 p.m. **When to go** Anytime. **Special comments**

Individuals with wheelchairs or strollers should use the north entrance from river walkway or the west entrance on Holland Street. To reserve a parking space or wheelchair, call ☎ 0207-887-8888. **Author's rating ★★★★. How much time to allow** 1–2 hours.

DESCRIPTION AND COMMENTS Housed in the old Bankside Power Station, the Tate Modern opened to loud acclaim in 2000. This national museum's nucleus was formed from the old Tate Gallerys (now called the Tate Britain) modern art collection, from 1900 to the present day. The work of Dali, Picasso, Matisse, Duchamp, Warhol, and Rothko are here, among many other names prominent in modern art. This former utility megalith has been put to good use, housing enormous art installations and sculptures, and the views across the Thames are wonderful, taking in the Millennium Bridge and St. Paul's. There are good exhibits here, two cafés and an espresso bar, a large shop by Turbine Hall, and an over-all interesting architectural conversion from power station to art gallery. The cavernous Turbine Hall has been home to enormous stat-ues and light-inspired art installations that are really impressive. My favorite artwork is by Sam Taylor-Wood called *Still Life*. It's a framed video of a bowl of fruit going through the changes of a month in a mat-ter of seconds—you see the fruit at the height of its freshness, then it quickly shrinks and withers, then flies come into the picture, then a big blob of mold is left. It's near another of my favorite things: a display of all the items dredged up from the Thames when the building was con-structed—a visual history of the discarded and lost.

TOURING TIPS Walk across the Millennium Bridge to St. Paul's for a nice con-trast between centuries. Or else jump on the ferry that goes to the London Eye and the Tate Britain. Be prepared to spend a lot of time hanging out here—the people-watching possibilities are wonderful.

Tower Bridge Experience

APPEAL BY AGE	PRESCHOOL ★	GRADE SCHOOL ★	TEENS ★
YOUNG ADULTS ★★	OVER 30 ★★		SENIORS ★★

Tower Bridge, Tower Hill (The City), SE1; ☎ 0207-403-3761; www.towerbridge.org.uk; tube: Tower Hill or London Bridge

Type of attraction History of the bridge and a walk across the top of it. **Admis-sion** £5.50 for adults, £3 for children ages 5–15, £4.25 for seniors and students, £14 for family tickets. You can get joint tickets here for the Tower Bridge Experi-ence and The Monument. **Hours** April–September, daily, 10 a.m.–6:30 p.m.; November–March, daily, 9:30 a.m.–6 p.m. (last admission is 75 minutes before closing). **When to go** Early morning or around 4 p.m. **Special comments** Disabled access; call for details and to make plans. **Author's rating ★★. How much time to allow** 90 minutes.

DESCRIPTION AND COMMENTS This is the bridge that everyone thinks is London Bridge, and allegedly what the American investors thought they were getting when they bought London Bridge in the 1970s to put up in the Arizona desert. They must have been quite disappointed to get the real, boring London Bridge (though they hotly deny that they didn't know what they were doing). Tower Bridge was built in 1894 and remains a beautiful piece of architecture, as well as a marvel of engineering. It is adequately appreciated from the ground, and I don't really think all that much is gained by waiting in interminable lines to go in it, but if you can get in without waiting for more than half an hour, it's worth a look. They seem to be straining to provide a tour of some length, with a kind of corny multimedia trip through time to the bridge's inception, but the old films are fun to watch, and the history of how they ended up using this design is interesting, but probably not to children. However, once you are on the walkway high above the Thames, with views everywhere, you can't help but be glad you visited.

TOURING TIPS If there's a huge line—one that reaches out onto the bridge— go enjoy the south riverside cafés and stores or go to the Tower of London and return when the line has shortened (to just inside the ticket area), which is, according to the staff, usually around 4:15 p.m. Combine this with a visit to the nearby Monument—they sell combined and Monument-only tickets here.

  The Tower of London

APPEAL BY AGE	PRESCHOOL ★★★	GRADE SCHOOL ★★★★	TEENS ★★★★
YOUNG ADULTS ★★★★★	OVER 30 ★★★★★	SENIORS ★★★★★	

Tower Hill, Tower Hill (The City), EC3; ☎ 0870-756-6060; www.hrp.org.uk; tube: Tower Hill

Type of attraction Ancient, history-rich fortress on the banks of the Thames. **Admission** £14.50 for adults, £11 for seniors and students, £9.50 for children ages 5–16, free for children under age 5, £42 for family tickets. **Hours** March–October, Monday–Saturday, 9 a.m.–5 p.m., Sunday, 10 a.m.–5 p.m.; November–February, Sunday and Monday, 10 a.m.–4 p.m. and Tuesday–Saturday, 9 a.m.–4 p.m. **When to go** The lines get pretty ferocious in the summer; line up early or go later in the day. **Special comments** Lots of difficult stairs and passageways. A limited number of wheelchairs are available; ask at the group ticket office. **Author's rating** ★★★★★. **How much time to allow** 3 hours or more.

DESCRIPTION AND COMMENTS OK, I admit it: this is in many people's minds one of the biggest tourist traps in London. But methinks they just don't appreciate the genuine historical importance of this place, and can't see the castle for the tourists and gift shops. The first time I entered the Tower of London through the Middle Tower, I literally went weak in the knees. To an American with more than a passing interest in English history, a trip to the tower is a transcendent experience. Yes, it is undeniably tourist-ridden, but I have never found that to be a mitigating factor in my awe and appreciation of it. Yes, it is usually packed with howling schoolchildren and grumpy parents; yes, there are gift shops and snack bars all over the place; and yes, some of the attempts at historical verisimilitude are corny. But this is still one of the most important sites in all of England and was the scene of dramas beyond counting. Numerous guidebooks will tell you that it's hard to feel the essential grimness of the place with all the happy sightseers around, but I say that with a little imagination and focus, you can sense the ghosts that plague this place of imprisonment, torture, and death.

As anyone who is near there after dark can tell you, the place is lousy with ghosts, and not the happy kind. Macaulay, the 19th-century historian, wrote of the small burial ground by the Chapel of St. Peter Ad Vincula: "In truth, there is no sadder spot on earth as this little cemetery. Death is there associated, not, as in Westminster Abbey and St Paul's, with genius and virtue, but with whatever is darkest in human nature and in human destiny, with the savage triumph of implacable enemies, with the inconstancy, the ingratitude, the cowardice of friends, with all the miseries of fallen greatness and of blighted fame." It does make you shiver when you hear the roll call of the imprisoned and beheaded: Thomas More, Anne Boleyn, Lady Jane Grey and her husband, Queen Catherine Howard, a host of lords and ladies whose only crime was to end up on the wrong side of the monarch. There were also kings of Scotland and France, William Wallace (alias Braveheart), King Henry VI, the two little princes murdered in their sleep (allegedly by their uncle, Richard III), Sir Walter Raleigh, and countless victims of religious persecutions. It is, for all its present serenity and beauty, a place soaked in centuries of blood and cruel injustice.

The tower was started as a simple fortification on the Thames in 1066 by William the Conqueror, and grew over the years to include 13 different towers, numerous houses, walks, armories, barracks, and greens, all surrounded by a moat. The moat was drained in 1843 due to the mephitic stink of it, but there are plans afoot to fill it in again, which would be quite pleasing to the eye. The Yeoman Warders, also known as Beefeaters, have been at the tower since the 1300s and are now an invaluable source of information about the tower. They are happy to answer questions, and you may attach yourself to any group that is being entertained and enlightened by a Beefeater. There are Yeoman Warder talks and free tours daily; the Lanthorn Tower and the Middle Tower have information boards outlining the day's talks, tours, and events. There are also actors in period costumes wandering about, striking up conversations in character; children get a huge kick out of this, as they tend to be unembarrassed about chatting up these funny folk. (Kids also go mad for the gift shops, or as my nephew called them when I took him there, the "gift flops.") You'll see the famous ravens there. They are a very important part of the tower, and have been kept here with wings clipped for over 600 years. The legend is that if the ravens should ever leave, the tower will fall and England will be in great danger. If you have a chance to speak to the Raven Master, ask him about the bird named Thor, who could imitate human speech.

One of the most famous sights at the tower is the Crown Jewels. I was not all that interested in them—the line can be awfully long, and while the crowns and scepters are interesting as historic emblems, they are strangely lifeless. Seeing them was not nearly as gratifying as reading the scratched graffiti—in English and Latin—of the unfortunate prisoners in Beauchamp Tower, or sitting under a tree in one of the greens absorbing the atmosphere. It's a good place to hang around, so take your time. The audio tours are great and can be done at your own pace, and the guidebook is an excellent investment.

TOURING TIPS There is a security check that slows down the entrance; if possible, leave your knapsack or bag at home when you visit. Check out the Web site, **www.tower-of-london.com**, to get a preview of many of the strange tales about the Tower of London, complete with atmospheric music, and little-known facts about the traditions of the tower-keepers.

  Victoria and Albert Museum

APPEAL BY AGE	PRESCHOOL ★★	GRADE SCHOOL ★★★	TEENS ★★★★
YOUNG ADULTS ★★★★		OVER 30 ★★★★★	SENIORS ★★★★★

Cromwell Road (second entrance on Exhibition Road), South Kensington, SW7; ☎ 0207-942-2000; www.vam.ac.uk; tube: South Kensington

Type of attraction Breathtaking collection of decorative arts and design displayed in 8 miles of galleries. **Admission** Free; charge for special exhibits. **Hours** Daily, 10 a.m.–5:45 p.m.; Wednesdays and last Friday of the month selected galleries are open until 10 p.m., and food, live music, and the gift shop are available. **When to go** Anytime. **Special comments** Wheelchair access is from the Exhibition Road entrance; there are ramps over most of the many small sets of steps. **Author's rating** ★★★★★. **How much time to allow** As much as possible.

DESCRIPTION AND COMMENTS The Victoria and Albert Museum houses the most engaging assortment of treasures in London, and although it has been criticized for not having a strict enough focus, that is precisely its charm. It could be the enormous attic of some mad uncle, wealthy beyond all measure, indiscriminately collecting anything and everything of interest that might make his home more beautiful. You have an endless choice of things to see: armor, religious artifacts, stained glass, sculptures, wood carvings, jewelry, musical instruments, ironwork, furniture, glasswork, clothing, paintings, photographs, and whatever special exhibit is being held at the time, always very well mounted. It is difficult to be specific about what galleries to see, as there has been an ongoing renovation for the past few years that will continue into the next decade. This means that every time I visit (which I do often, as I live across the street from it) some of my favorite treasures have been removed to some other place, or there are hoardings covering entire halls. But if the relatively new British Galleries are anything to go by, the changes are sure to be well thought out and pleasing. The old Pirelli Courtyard was just reopened after a total overhaul, and while I was deeply attached to the old fountain and trees, the new big oval of a water feature and the neat lines of box-light planters and English garden borders are undeniably elegant.

The original V&A was part of Prince Albert's grand scheme to make South Kensington a center for arts, science, and learning. When it opened in 1852, funded by the Great Exhibition of 1851, Prince Albert envisioned the South Kensington Museum, as it was known then, to be a repository of applied arts—items that happily married beauty and utility, a school of thought championed by William Morris. Such restrictions were hopeless from the start, as treasures started arriving from all over the empire and with thousands of legacies. As you wander around the museum—and I believe that's the best way to go, although many would guide you toward the introductory tours that occur daily—you might bear in mind the fact that there are millions more objets d'art, paintings, photographs, clothing, textiles, and so on stored away in the basement.

By 1899, the old housing for the collection was clearly unfit, and work was begun on the present building, named by Queen Victoria, who never neglected an opportunity to honor her long-departed husband. She didn't live to see it completed ten years later, but she presides over its Cromwell Road entrance like a secular version of the Virgin Mary, who tops the Brompton Oratory Church next door. There has been talk about finding a more appropriately descriptive name for this wonderful museum, but I think that evoking the quintessential couple of that inquisitive, acquisitive 19th-century British Empire is perfect. The building is a real beauty, inside and out, and any visit to the museum should always include a few moments to appreciate the grace of the main entrance dome, with its fantastic glass chandelier by Dale Chiluly, the Fakes and Forgeries' immense halls and skylights, the Garden Courtyard, and especially the areas that, in a less populated age, served as the museum's main eateries: the Poynter, Gamble, and Morris Rooms. These rooms are simply magnificent. The British Galleries are a must-see, as are Raphael's cartoons, the Beasts of Dacre, the dress collection, and the stained glass.

TOURING TIPS On Wednesday (depending on the season, call ☎ 0207-942-2209 to make sure it's on), there's a Late View, with a limited number of galleries open, a lecture in the beautiful old lecture hall past the Silver Galleries, and a gallery talk. The restaurant is open and has candles on the table, and live music is played there as well as in the front hall. It's a wonderful way to pass a Wednesday evening. The weekends feature a Family Cart, with wonderful activities for children. It's extremely entertaining and educational for kids of every age.

The Wallace Collection

APPEAL BY AGE	PRESCHOOL ★	GRADE SCHOOL ★	TEENS ★★
YOUNG ADULTS ★★★		OVER 30 ★★★	SENIORS ★★★

Hertford House, Manchester Square, Marylebone, W1; ☎ 0207-935-0687; www.the-wallace-collection.org.uk; tube: Bond Street

Type of attraction Collection of 19th-century Anglo-French art. **Admission** Free. **Hours** Monday–Saturday, 10 a.m.–5 p.m.; Sunday, noon–5 p.m. **When to go** Anytime. **Special comments** Good disabled access including an outdoor ramp, lifts to the upper floors, and mostly uncluttered rooms in which it is easy to maneuver. **Author's rating** ★★★. **How much time to allow** 1–3 hours.

DESCRIPTION AND COMMENTS The Wallace Collection is tucked away in a lovely Georgian square between Regent's and Hyde Parks. The second marquess of Hertford leased the home, now Hertford House, in 1797, for the excellent duck shooting for which the area was well-known. Today, Hertford House holds the combined acquisitions of five generations of marquesses and marchionesses of Hertford. Between 1750 and 1880, this family formed an impressive collection to decorate their impressive home.

The collection is displayed throughout this French chateau's two main floors, and some areas are worthy of special note. Galleries 2, 3, and 4 contain some fabulous pieces of Louis XIV furniture and art. A remarkable European Renaissance armory is housed in Galleries 8, 9, and 10; and Gallery 11 is devoted to Asian arms, armor, and art. Hertford House's largest room, Gallery 22, offers one of the finest displays of European paintings to be seen anywhere in the world. This impressive gallery, formerly called "The Long Picture Gallery," houses works by such masters as Titian, Fragonard, Poussin, Rembrandt, Rubens, Van Dyck, and Velázquez. Yet even if the house were empty of art, it would still be worth visiting to see the carved mantelpieces and elegant design of this architectural paragon of a bygone era.

Temporary exhibits, educational facilities, expanded galleries, and a restaurant, along with certain engineering reconstructions, were part of an intensive Centenary Project in 2000 that cost over £10 million. It was money well and wisely spent, making this good small museum a great small museum.

TOURING TIPS Free public lectures and tours on various aspects of the collection are given on weekdays and weekends. Tours usually last about 45 minutes and give good insight into the styles and history of the artists and their times. If you are on a tight schedule, call for touring times, or just arrive and wander on your own until a tour begins.

The Wellington Arch

| APPEAL BY AGE | PRESCHOOL — | GRADE SCHOOL ★ | TEENS ★ |
| YOUNG ADULTS ★ | OVER 30 ★★ | | SENIORS ★★ |

In the middle of Hyde Park Corner roundabout, SW1; ☎ 0207-973-3494; www.english-heritage.org.uk; tube: Hyde Park Corner

Type of attraction Architectural- and London-related items in the arch. **Admission** £3 for adults, £1.50 for children, £2.30 for seniors and students. **Hours** Wednesay–Sunday 10 a.m.–5 p.m.; November–March, closes an hour earlier at 4 p.m. **When to go** On a sunny day. **Special comments** The entrance is on the south side inside the arch, a small doorway with no banners or big signs announcing its position. You reach the island either through the subways or at the street crossing in front of the Lanesborough Hotel. **Author's rating** ★★. **How much time to allow** Depending upon your interest, 30 minutes to an hour.

DESCRIPTION AND COMMENTS This is one of those specialty museums for either architectural historians or London-obsessed cranks. It was designed in the 1820s by Decimus Burton to commemorate England's victory over Napoléon, and was originally located at Buckingham Palace. It's our good fortune that the statue of Wellington that once topped the arch was replaced by the magnificent *Peace Descending on the Quadringa of War,* which gives Hyde Park Corner such a stunning aspect. It's worth a go, as it's relatively inexpensive, and if you combine it with a visit to Apsley House across the way, it will leave you feeling as if you know all there is to know about that corner of London. There are a couple of films running in loops that have wonderful old shots of Hyde Park Corner from the horse-and-cart era to the present; and the molds from the magnificent statue on top of the arch are most inspiring. But the best thing about it is the views to be had from the observation platforms. The look in at the tennis courts in the "backyard" of Buckingham Palace was a first for me; and the views of the London Eye and Westminster are nice, too. A photo display of Londoners' snapshots of their city is riveting.

TOURING TIPS If you walk from Apsley House to the Arch via the below-ground subway path (follow signs for Green Park), you get the story of the duke of Wellington recapitulated in tile on the walls, as well as an hour-to-hour description of the battle of Waterloo.

 ## Westminster Abbey

APPEAL BY AGE	PRESCHOOL ★	GRADE SCHOOL ★★★	TEENS ★★★★
YOUNG ADULTS ★★★★		OVER 30 ★★★★	SENIORS ★★★★

20 Dean's Yard, just off Parliament Square, Westminster, SW1;
☎ **0207-222-5152; www.westminster-abbey.org;**
tube: St. James's Park or Westminster

Type of attraction England's historically most important church. **Admission** Free admission for services or to visit the nave and cloisters; royal chapels and tombs: £8 for adults; £6 for students, seniors, and children ages 11–16; £18 for family. Entry fee includes visit to the Westminster Abbey Museum. **Hours** Royal chapels are open Monday–Friday, 9:30 a.m.–3:45 p.m.; Saturday, 9:30 a.m.–1:45 p.m. (Closing times given are for last admission.) Museum hours are Monday–Saturday, 10 a.m.–3:30 p.m. The abbey is closed before special services, on Sunday (except for services), December 24–28, Good Friday, and on Commonwealth Observance Day. **When to go** Early mornings on weekdays, especially during the busy summer months. If you really hate crowds in close spaces, make a quick call to be sure you aren't arriving at the same time as three tour groups. **Special comments** Audio guides are available in 7 languages for £3, Monday–Friday, 9:30 a.m.–3 p.m. and Saturday, 9:30 a.m.–1 p.m. Guided tours cost £4 plus entry fee. **Author's rating** ★★★★. **Additional tips** My favorite way to experience Westminster Abbey is to arrive around 3:30 p.m. and then wander the cloisters (especially the lovely Little Cloister) before returning to the nave to wait for the 5 p.m. evensong. It is worth waiting at the head of the line (which starts to form at about 4:15 p.m.), as the first evensong attendees are seated in the stately choir stalls where the atmosphere and view of the Westminster Boys Choir is the best. **How much time to allow** 1½–2 hours for audio guides; evensong is about 45 minutes.

DESCRIPTION AND COMMENTS Since the 900-year-old Abbey is one of the most popular tourist sights in London, the key here is to avoid touring when it is mobbed. When you are moving in a sluggish single-file line through the chapels, you lose sight of the beauty of the interiors (displaying at least four different eras of architecture), the sheer numbers of people buried here (over 3,000), and the incredible amount of history that this building has seen. Instead, try to start off your day with a visit or end your day with one.

Since 1998, the primary entrance to the abbey has been through the North Transept, which gives a rather disjointed image of the abbey on first glance. I suggest that you immediately head back toward the West Front entrance so that you can see the abbey as it was meant to be viewed. From this perspective you can clearly see the majesty of the tallest nave in England (at 102 feet). In front of you is the Tomb of the Unknown Soldier, and to your right is a 14th-century portrait of Richard II, the oldest known image of a monarch painted from life. As you head back toward the North Transept, also called Statesmen's Aisle, you pass through Musician's Aisle and end up back near the admissions and information desks. From here you can enter the smaller chapels of Elizabeth I and Innocents Corner and head toward the fantastic display of English perpendicular architecture that makes up the Henry VII Chapel. The elaborately carved choir stalls here are dedicated to the Knights of the Order of the Bath, whose banners and helmets decorate the stalls. Among the notable names buried in this chapel alone are Henry VII and his wife; King George II and Queen Caroline; Henry VIII's only son, Edward VI; and James I and his lover, George Villiers, the first nonroyal to be buried in this part of the abbey.

As you head along the south aisle of Henry VII's chapel, you can see the tombs of Mary Queen of Scots (reburied in the Abbey by her son, James I, and in unfortunate proximity to the tomb of her enemy, Queen Elizabeth I, who ordered her execution; Lady Margaret Beaufort, Henry VII's mother; as well as William and Mary, Queen Anne, and Charles II. Walking back toward the nave, you pass the oak throne dating back to 1300 called the Coronation Chair, which has been used in every royal coronation since then. For 700 years, the Stone of Scone, or the Stone of Destiny, was tucked under it, a prize stolen from Scotland and triumphantly displayed, but in 1996, it made the historic trip home, to Edinburgh Castle. Just beyond this point, tombs and gatework hide much of the abbey's most famous tomb, the shrine of St. Edward the Confessor. Unfortunately, this tomb, although recently restored, remains closed to the public. The South Transept of Poet's Corner, however, continues to be a favorite of visitors and contains the grave slabs of, among many others, Geoffrey Chaucer, Robert Browning, Alfred Lord Tennyson, Charles Dickens, Rudyard Kipling, and Thomas Hardy, as well as impressive memorials to William Shakespeare and George Frideric Handel. The last person to have been buried here was Sir Laurence Olivier, who died in 1989.

After exploring the abbey's interior, be sure you find your way out to the cloisters, where the monks worked, studied, and lived. Visiting on a cold day gives you insight into the hearty constitution these early scholars must have had. Today, the cloisters contain a small shop and café. English Heritage also runs a small area just off the east cloisters. This includes the Chapter House, which was the original meeting place of the House of Commons until the time of Henry VIII, and the now-closed-to-the-public Pyx Chamber, which served as the sacristy and royal treasury of the earliest church.

TOURING TIPS Before you enter Westminster Abbey, take the time to enjoy its lesser-known neighbor. Many people head straight for the entrance and fail to even notice St. Margaret's Church, which shares the churchyard. Built in 1523, this tiny church's simple and uncluttered interior contrasts sharply with the abbey's appearance as an overflowing mausoleum.

Photography is not permitted in any part of the abbey at any time. Leave the camera and knapsack home, as the security checks will slow you down.

Windsor Castle

APPEAL BY AGE	PRESCHOOL ★	GRADE SCHOOL ★★	TEENS ★★★
YOUNG ADULTS ★★★★		OVER 30 ★★★★	SENIORS ★★★★

Windsor, Hertsfordshire, outside London; ☎ 0207-766-7304; www.royal.gov.uk; British Rail: Waterloo Station to Windsor Riverside

Type of attraction The queen's country house, a mighty fine old castle. **Admission** £12.50 for adults, £10.50 for seniors and students, £6.50 for children ages 5–16, free for children under age 5, £31.50 for a family ticket. **Hours** March–October, daily, 9:45 a.m.–5:15 p.m., last admission at 4 p.m.; November–February, daily, 9:45 a.m.–4:15 p.m., last admission at 3 p.m.; St. George's Chapel closed Sunday. **When to go** Always call first! Windsor Castle is subject to regular, annual, and sudden closures due to various royal ceremonies and events. The month of June is particularly susceptible to this sort of thing. Otherwise, go anytime, but show up early before the tour groups. **Special comments** Limited wheelchair access, lots of walking. **Author's rating** ★★★★. **How much time to allow** Half a day, plus time to wander in Windsor.

DESCRIPTION AND COMMENTS In November 1992, the world saw film footage of Windsor Castle with smoke and flames pouring out from behind its distinctive crenelated keep and foremen running to and fro with priceless paintings and furniture. The fire destroyed over 100 rooms, and it took five years to repair the terrible damage done to the ancient castle. Even if you don't normally like gaping at castles, you might make an exception of Windsor, for the restoration of the gutted and devastated castle—burnt to its medieval stone walls, with roofs collapsed—is a marvel in itself, and the exhibition that describes the process is remarkable.

William the Conqueror, who also built the Tower of London, chose this site in Windsor for a fortress to protect London from Western invaders. The castle has been continually inhabited for the past 900 years, and many additions and deletions—many due to fire—have been made over those years.

It is presently a place of overwhelming splendor and tremendous riches, which might be best summed up by the awesome Queen Mary's Dolls' House. This is big luxury on a small scale: Sir Edward Luytens designed the multistory dollhouse in the 1920s, and it took three years and a thousand craftsmen and artists to complete it. It has running water, electric lights, a working elevator, actual miniature books, fine art, gorgeous furniture, every kind of servant all dressed in livery, carpet cleaners, tiny bottles filled with real wine, and even two tiny thrones with crowns on them.

Another attraction at Windsor is St. George's Chapel, started in 1475; it's a stunning example of great medieval architecture, with stained-glass windows of unparalleled beauty. Ten monarchs are buried within its precincts, and there are some stupendously crafted sarcophagi. The crests and banners of the Knights of the Order of the Garter are all there, and you get a feel for the ritual and pageantry that have propped up the ruling classes of England for centuries. A new garden, the first one planted since 1820, was designed to celebrate the Queen's Golden Jubilee, and features a bandstand on which Her Majesty's various military bands perform.

TOURING TIPS Be sure to make time to wander around the pleasant town of Windsor.

GREEN *and* PLEASANT LANDS: PARKS *of* LONDON

ON THE WEEKENDS, WHEN THE MUSEUMS and tourist attractions are packed, go to the parks and enjoy the fruits of England's mania for nature tame and wild. Part of London's appeal as a city is its careful conservation of greenery—whether in its many squares or its enormous parks. For more information, contact The Royal Parks Agency at ☎ 0207-298-2000 or go to **www.royalparks.gov.uk.**

PARKS	DESCRIPTION
Green Park	Between Hyde Park and St. James's Park (Mayfair)
Hampstead Heath	Enormous expanse of country (North London)
Highgate Cemetery	Atmospheric Victorian graveyard (North London)

PARKS	DESCRIPTION
Holland Park	54-acre landscaped park (West London)
Hyde Park	350-acre people's park (Knightsbridge to Bayswater)
Kensington Gardens	Gardens, walkways, fountains, palace (Kensington to Notting Hill)
Kew Gardens (The Royal Botanic Gardens)	Botanical extravaganza (West London)
Regent's Park	490-acre elegant park (North London)
Richmond Park	London's largest park (West London)
St. James's Park	Oldest royal park in London (Whitehall to Victoria)

Green Park
Between Piccadilly and Constitution Hill (between Hyde Park and St. James's Park); enter at Hyde Park Corner; tube: Green Park

Type of park Expanse of green lawn and old trees. **Admission** Free. **Hours** Daily, 5 a.m.–midnight. **When to go** Anytime; summer is especially pleasant, with deck chairs for rent and the local workers enjoying lunch in the sun.

DESCRIPTION AND COMMENTS   Like St. James's Park, Green Park was also reclaimed from the marshy meadows that surrounded the Tyburn River as it made its way south to the Thames. Originally purchased by Henry VIII for enclosed grazing and hunting, the land was made into a formal park in 1667. It became a favorite place for duels and highwaymen, military parades, ballooning, and people-watching. Green Park was opened to the public in 1826, and since then people have loved strolling along the east end of the park, admiring the fine mansions there, ending up at Buckingham Palace and St. James's Park. There are no flower beds in Green Park (allegedly removed by order of King Charles II's queen, in a jealous fury over some flower-related indiscretion of her philandering husband), but the crocuses in spring more than make up for that lack, and the 950 magnificent plane, oak, poplar, chestnut, and other varieties of trees to be seen there are completely pleasing. You may rent chairs in the spring, summer, and fall, which makes a nice break from shopping or sightseeing in the Piccadilly area. A refreshment stand is available at the Buckingham Palace end of the park, and toilets can be found by the Green Park tube station.

Hampstead Heath
Hampstead; tube: Highgate, then take 210 bus to West Gate

Type of park Enormous expanse of country in Greater London area. **Admission** Free. **Hours** Daily, 8 a.m.–dusk. **When to go** Anytime; and be sure to check out Kenwood House.

DESCRIPTION AND COMMENTS   Though Hampstead Heath is not actually a park per se, it is a most remarkable place, covering a staggering 1,600 acres of undeveloped land and offering stunning views over London. There are hills, lakes, wild woods, and landscaped gardens. Hampstead Heath has so much to offer, not the least of which is Kenwood House, a stately home and fine art museum at the northernmost top of the heath. There are outdoor concerts in the summer on Saturday nights, which are followed by displays of fireworks. People bring blankets and picnic hampers and sit on a hill outside, while those who pay for tickets hunker down a little closer to the music. The Men's and Ladies' Ponds for swimming in the summer are part of a set of lakes along the Highgate border of the heath. There's also a pond for model boats and one for bird-watching. Parliament Hill, across the bicycle track that cuts through the heath, is the best place in London for viewing the Guy Fawkes Day fireworks, and in all seasons has spectacular views of London. You can hardly believe you are even near an urban area in many parts of the heath, where mansions on hills look like castles and conspire to make you feel you are in a storybook. You can get a good lunch at the Kenwood House outdoor café in the summer, or stay inside the cozy retreat in winter.

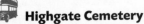 **Highgate Cemetery**

Located on either side of Swains Lane in Highgate, adjacent to Waterlow Park; ☎ 0208-340-1834; www.highgate-cemetery.org; tube: Archway (Northern line)

Type of park Wildly overgrown Victorian graveyard. **Admission** West Cemetery (access is as part of guided tours only) £3; East Cemetery £2; £1 photo permit (£3 for guided tour on weekends). **Hours** West Cemetery, April to September: tours are given Monday–Friday at 2 p.m.; Saturday and Sunday, 11 a.m.–4 p.m. hourly. October to March: tours are given on weekends only, hourly, 11 a.m.–3 p.m. East Cemetery, April to September: daily, 10 a.m.–5 p.m. October to March: daily, 10 a.m.–4 p.m. **When to go** Anytime, although they only allow 20 people on each weekend hourly tour, so if you arrive late you may find yourself wandering the East Cemetery for an hour. Also, the cemetery closes for funerals, so call to check before setting out.

DESCRIPTION AND COMMENTS Opened in 1839, Highgate Cemetery became "the" place to be buried for London's wealthy Victorian families, intellectuals, and artists. One of seven cemeteries designed and opened during this time of continued population explosion, it remains one of the most elaborate and stirring examples of Victorian statuary excess. Overgrown and badly vandalized, the West Cemetery was closed in 1975 and is now diligently cared for by the Friends of Highgate Cemetery. Lush vegetation fills what was once an open, rolling hillside, and volunteers continue to clear overgrown pathways and graves. This extensive foliage creates eerie shadows; this, combined with the cracked and toppled grave markers everywhere, gives the cemetery its fabulously gothic atmosphere, which makes it a favorite subject for black-and-white photographers. Tour guides are well versed on the many famous residents of the cemetery, as well as having a number of fascinating anecdotes that explain the elaborate and symbolic Victorian statuary. The cemetery's creepiest section includes the Egyptian Avenue and the Terrace Catacombs. Buried here are Karl Marx, Christina Rossetti, George Eliot, and others, all watched over by magnificent angels of stone.

You can wander on your own in the East Cemetery, but it holds a less eerie charm. Still, it is nice to be able to linger where you will and get up close to the graves, some of which contain the most interesting epitaphs. There is a £1 "camera permit fee" for those interested in capturing the morose views. It's best to go early in the day, hopefully on a day with some sun, as the shadowy effects can create fantastic photographic images.

kids Holland Park

Holland Park, between Kensington and Shepherd's Bush; tube: Holland Park Avenue (then a 10-minute walk to park) or Kensington High Street and take westbound bus 9, 10, 27, 28, 31, or 49

Type of park 54-acre landscaped park with a Japanese garden. **Admission** Free. **Hours** Daily, 7:30 a.m.–dusk. **When to go** Anytime; there are camellias, roses, irises, and other blossoms in spring; dahlias in summer; and autumn leaves.

DESCRIPTION AND COMMENTS Holland Park once housed the magnificent Holland House, more castle than mansion, where the literati of the early 19th century flocked to mix with politicians and aristocrats. The house was bombed during World War II, but what remains are fascinating monuments to the past: the surviving wings of Holland House, one of which houses a youth hostel; the wrought-iron gates that formed the entrance to the estate; the Orangery; the Ice House from the 1770s; the summer ballroom that is now a fancy restaurant, called The Belvedere; the old stables; and the many walks and enclosures that make up Holland Park.

There is a wonderful variety of flora and fauna here, thanks to Lord Holland—a venerable Victorian gentleman—and his great interest in planting and wildlife. He can be seen in the National Potrait Gallery, as styled by his good friend sculptor G. F. Watts, surveying his land, occasionally providing a roosting place for some of the 60 wild bird species that have been spotted in the park. One feature he never saw, which was created in 1991, is the Kyoto Garden, a perfect Japanese garden. The peacocks gather in the Yucca Lawn, along with numerous rabbits. There is an over-the-top adventure playground in the park that is a must-do for families with young children.

kids Hyde Park

Bordered by Park Lane, Knightsbridge, and Bayswater Road; tube: Hyde Park Corner

Type of park 350-acre park with expansive lawns. **Admission** Free. **Hours** Daily, dawn to dusk. **When to go** Anytime; there are roses in summer, crocuses and daffodils in spring, fall foliage in autumn, and atmospheric bare trees in winter.

DESCRIPTION AND COMMENTS During the dissolution of the monasteries in 1536, Henry VIII grabbed a hunk of land from the manor of Hyde and enclosed it for his hunting pleasure. James I opened the park to aristocrats, who took the air daily, a habit that persisted into the early 20th century with Rotten Row—originally Route du Roi, King's Road—resounding with the beating of hooves and the chatter of the idle class. Once, Kensington Gardens was part of Hyde Park—and is still separated only by a roadway—but in the mid-1700s, Queen Caroline appropriated 200 acres to make suitable gardens for Kensington Palace.

Hyde Park today is a wonderful escape from the high-decibel traffic noise of its bordering streets Park Lane, Knightsbridge, and Bayswater. You enter the park from any of those streets; and within minutes of walking toward the Serpentine, the watery heart of the park, a delightful quiet descends. There's so much to do in Hyde Park: Besides the very good playground for kids that is conveniently located next to an exercise ring for the queen's guards, there are biking and inline skating paths through and around the edge of the park (do not bicycle on any paths not marked with the outline of a bike); there are cricket and soccer pitches; there are tennis courts, paddle- and rowboats; and one can even ride along Rotten Row on horseback. During the warm months, there are numerous places to rent lawn chairs, and you can get a bite to eat at the Lido or the cafeteria at the east end of the Serpentine. The Rose Walk by Hyde Park Corner is magnificent in June, and the Italian Piazza, with fountains and statues, is wonderful at all times. Speaker's Corner, at the northeast end of the park, is hopping on Sunday, often featuring born-again Christians yelling at us to repent, no longer on soapboxes, but on little stepladders or overturned buckets. The queen's guards exercise their horses and rehearse their ceremonies in Hyde Park, on the south by Prince's Gate. It's an astonishing thing to be walking through the park and suddenly be set upon by a regiment of sword-waving, plume-hatted horsemen.

By the Serpentine, you will find the problem-plagued memorial fountain to Princess Diana. It is a round oval that is in the form of a ditch filled with running water that was intended to be a place where children could splash and play. It was closed a week after the opening because leaves were clogging it, and then children started slipping on the algae on the bottom, and before you knew it, there was a fence and guards all around trying to prevent lawsuits. There is also a touching Holocaust Memorial in Hyde Park, and numerous statues and gardens and nooks—it's a great place to explore. Hyde Park in sunlight is the best place to be in London. They have something called the Liberty Drive for the disabled to enjoy a tour through the park. They pick up passengers at clearly marked spots on the park's perimeters. To book, call ☎ 046-749-8096.

If you want to get from South Kensington to Piccadilly, or from Knightsbridge to Marble Arch, do yourself a favor and walk through Hyde Park.

kids Kensington Gardens
Kensington Gore; tube: Kensington High Street

Type of park Gardens, walkways, fountains, statues, and a palace. **Admission** Free. **Hours** Daily, dawn to dusk. **When to go** Anytime, especially when Kensington Palace and the Orangery are open. In spring and summer there is the flower walk and great foliage in fall.

DESCRIPTION AND COMMENTS Kensington Palace will probably be forever associated with the extraordinary event of public mourning for Princess Diana in 1997, when in the days after her death in Paris, people arrived and laid flowers in front of the palace that was her home. By week's end there was a sea of blooms and cellophane in front of the gates, and the trees nearby were festooned with pictures, poems, and flowers, and candles stood burning everywhere. A permanent tribute to the "People's Princess" is the Princess Diana Memorial Playground in the northwest corner of the park, a state-of-the-art playground with a pirate's ship to climb on, that is always filled to capacity with happy children. Her monument is by the Serpentine in Hyde Park (see above).

By the side of the palace is a lovely sunken garden that can be looked at, but not entered. In front of the Orangery, which is a good place for tea, are topiary trees that recall the Restoration; and the Round Pond on which children have sailed toy boats for generations brings *Mary Poppins* vividly to mind. There is also a fanciful statue of Peter Pan; author J. M. Barrie lived right by the park, and the island in the middle of the lake is clearly the model for the Island of the Lost Boys.

The Broad Walk is good for inline skating, as is the area in front of the Albert Memorial. And if you're in the mood for modern art, the Serpentine Gallery has changing exhibits, a good bookshop, and a café.

Kew Gardens (The Royal Botanic Gardens)
Southwest London on the Thames; tube: Kew Gardens

Type of park Botanical extravaganza with 30,000 species of plants and flowers planted over 300 acres; follies, water features, and conservatories. **Admission** £10 for adults, £7 for seniors and students, free for children under age 16. **Hours** Daily, 9:30 a.m.–4:14 p.m. in winter; open later in spring and summer. **When to go** Any time of the year, although summer is the best time to get your money's worth.

DESCRIPTION AND COMMENTS The Royal Botanical Gardens at Kew were begun in the 18th century, when wealthy and royal folks began to keep rustic retreats on the outskirts of smelly, polluted, crowded London. The Botanical Gardens, originally developed for the pleasure of the royal family, intersected nicely with the global travels of adventurers such as Captain Cook, who brought home never-before-seen specimens of plant life, such as the geranium. The gardens have gone from strength to strength since then as one of the world's most remarkable and serious centers of botanical research.

The enormous glass Palm House is a treasure trove of exotic tropical plants, with two levels on which to wander through the huge fronds and steamy atmosphere. There's a tropical aquarium in the basement that furthers the impression of being in a foreign clime. The Water Lily House is also interesting, and a testament to the wide-ranging journeys of the English explorers. The Temperate House is an even more impressive structure than the Palm House, twice as large, and containing plants from each and every continent, some of which were planted at Kew in the middle of the 19th century.

There are identifying plaques on the trees and signs on the flower beds, so that a visit to Kew can be a real education in botany. Two art galleries, Kew Palace, a Japanese pagoda, and numerous follies and conservatories make Kew an outing at which you can easily spend the whole day. There are a few cafés to choose from, and believe me, you'll need refreshment after a long day of plant viewing. It's a shame that Kew is right in the path of Heathrow airport traffic—the impression of stepping back in time is continually spoiled by the noise of overhead jets.

  Regent's Park

At end of Baker Street; for south entrance, take the tube to Regent's Park or Baker Street

Type of park Playground of 490 acres with 6,000 trees. **Admission** Free. **Hours** Daily, 5 a.m.–dusk. **When to go** Anytime; there are flower gardens in spring and summer, autumn leaves.

DESCRIPTION AND COMMENTS Named for George IV, when he was mad King George's understudy monarch, or acting regent, Regent's Park was designed by John Nash as part of the grand plan for a garden city of terraced mansions with countrylike views. Started in 1811, the scheme ultimately failed, with only a portion of the terrace houses sold (and those were said to be of substandard quality). However, in 1835, the park was flourishing and was opened to the public. Although the neighborhood may not have turned out exactly as Nash planned, it's still gorgeous, and few can resist the grace and beauty of the classically inspired white mansions of Cumberland Terrace that look out on the magnificent landscape.

Within the park you will find the home of the American ambassador, donated by the heiress Barbara Hutton and suitably fenced and secured; a boating lake with ornamental bridges and an island; a lake by Queen Mary's Rose Gardens, which are quite extraordinary and include a waterfall and an open-air theater; a number of lodges; a mosque; Regent's Canal; and of course, the London Zoo, which no child can resist. In the summer there are concerts on the Bandstand and plays at the theater, bird-watching walks, puppet shows, and outdoor refreshments. The Royal Horse Artillery can be seen occasionally on Cumberland Green.

Richmond Park
Southwest London;
tube: Richmond Station, then take bus 72, 265, 371, or 415

Type of park London's largest park, featuring deer and ancient oak trees. **Admission** Free. **Hours** Daily, 7 a.m.–dusk. **When to go** Anytime, though winter is cold.

DESCRIPTION AND COMMENTS   Richmond Park is a gargantuan 2,470-acre preserve in which 400 fallow deer and 250 red deer live and graze. It is an extraordinary place, a piece of rolling countryside a stone's thrown (seven miles from Charing Cross) from the center of a major metropolitan city, with wildlife still roaming freely. Richmond had its first royal connection with King Edward in the 13th century; Henry VII also took refuge there, and during his reign its name was changed from Sheen to Richmond. In 1625, surrounding lands were seized and walled to give King Charles I a country asylum from the plague. His wall created much ill will among the neighbors, who had been used to grazing their animals on the land and using the common roads. The king tried to compensate by allowing foot traffic through the park and permitting the local poor to gather deadwood for their hearth fires. After the Civil War in the 1650s, the House of Commons voted to leave the park as undeveloped land, and so it has remained ever since. There were various skirmishes between the royals and the public over right of access, which were put to rest on the death of the last royal ranger, Edward VII, in 1910. Today, Richmond Park is a testament to the admirable environmental protectionism of the British and provides for the visitor a wonderfully unchanged picture of a medieval hunting ground.

Be aware that the deer are not completely harmless and can be aggressive if they are bothered while tending young or during rutting season. There are refreshments found in the Pembroke Lodge Cafeteria from April through October, from 10 a.m. to 5:30 p.m. (7 p.m. on weekends). White Lodge houses the Royal Ballet School. There are many seasonal events that take place in Richmond Park—check a newspaper or *Time Out* to see when, what, and where. Pembroke Lodge often stages lunchtime concerts. It's a bit of a hike from central London, so you may need to budget a whole day for the outing. It's not fun for unwilling walkers.

 St. James's Park

East of Buckingham Palace gates; tube: St. James's Park

Type of park Oldest royal park in London. **Admission** Free. **Hours** Daily, 5 a.m.–midnight. **When to go** Any time is excellent, but in summer it is the most floral, and there are concerts on the bandstand between May and August.

DESCRIPTION AND COMMENTS   St. James's is certainly London's most royal of all parks, lying as it does between Buckingham and St. James's Palaces. There is a view from Buckingham Palace and from the bridge in the middle of the lake that is just magical—it looks like our fondest fantasy of an enchanted fairy-tale kingdom, with the turrets and steeples of Whitehall in the distance. St. James's is the place to see birds; the famous pelicans are there, as well as a huge assortment of other unusual feathered friends.

Kids have a great time spotting the birds, and it's educational and fun for them. A leper hospital, called St. James, was erected here in the 1400s. The Tyburn River flowed through this area, so the land was marshy and unsuitable for much more than hunting until King James I drained and planted the area as a pleasure garden, filling it with pelicans and other rara avises. He also had an exotic menagerie there, with crocodiles and elephants, for his court's entertainment. When Charles II returned from exile in France, he redesigned the park in a more formal, French manner, and opened St. James's Park to the public. It was embraced enthusiastically and began its long life as a favorite spot for Londoners to meet and stroll—although it did have its darker days when people hung laundry there, muggers prowled the bushes, and prostitutes conducted business. Its appeal was upgraded when George IV rebuilt Buckingham House as a royal palace and had John Nash make the park a more beautiful and natural-looking place. The Ornithological Society of London donated exotic birds to the open-air aviary in 1837.

There is a children's playground on the southwest corner of the park, and at the recently opened refreshment establishment, Inn the Park, you can either sit down for a table-service lunch, or save some money and go for the cafeteria option next door (same food, big difference in price). There are concerts at the bandstand in summer, and the birds are there all year to be admired. Green-and-white-striped deck chairs can be rented on an hourly basis between April and September.

GREENWICH

IN 1863, AMERICAN AUTHOR NATHANIEL Hawthorne described the quiet town of Greenwich as "beautiful,—a spot where the art of man has conspired with Nature." No doubt he was thinking about how the rolling hills of Greenwich Park create a glorious backdrop for Christopher Wren's splendid Royal Naval College and Inigo Jones's equally noble Queen's House, while Wren's other Greenwich project, the Royal Observatory, sits serenely on the park's highest hill. Greenwich has undergone a recent renaissance, as rising rents have pushed businesses and Londoners further from the center of the city. The streets of Greenwich are good for strolling; whether you are wandering down historic Croom's Hill or over past St. Alfrege's near the town center, the area has retained much of its cozy village atmosphere. Weekends bring craft and antiques lovers of all kinds converging on the busy Greenwich Market.

Greenwich is steeped in royal history. The park dates from 1433, and the Palace of Placentia once graced the riverside where the Royal Naval College now stands. Henry VIII and all three of his children, Mary I, Elizabeth I, and Edward IV were born here. In 1616, Jones began building the Queen's House as a Palladian country home at the bottom of the park for Charles II's wife, Henrietta Maria; Wren followed this project with the hilltop Observatory and the Naval College, which elegantly frames the Queen's House today. Walk the Greenwich foot tunnel under the Thames (takes about 5–10 minutes) for a perfect view of it. You can catch the Docklands Light Railway (DLR) from the Island Gardens station nearby. Just north of the town's center, the colossal Millennium Dome sits in anticipation of its next incarnation as an arena for sports and entertainment, and its future as a site for the 2012 Olympic games.

GETTING THERE

LOCATED A FEW MILES DOWNRIVER FROM London, Greenwich is relatively easy to reach and makes a delightful day trip for visitors. The town center provides a wide variety of book, art, and nautical shops as well as a diverse selection of restaurants from Vietnamese to Mexican to good old English pub food. On weekends, the Greenwich Market offers craft stalls and, combined with the nearby flea market and secondhand book market, can allow for hours of browsing.

To get to Greenwich, catch Docklands Light Railway, a fully automated and electric overland tram car type of transport that leaves from Bank Street or Tower Hill. The trip takes about 20 minutes from either station and in the summer includes a recording that guides you through the wharfs and docks of London's East End, leaving you at the Greenwich Pier or the *Cutty Sark*. Alternatively, catch the Jubilee Live and get off at the *Cutty Sark* station. Another, more leisurely and entertaining travel option, is the guided riverboat ride along the Thames, past views of St. Paul's Cathedral, Tower Bridge, and Docklands. Boats leave from Westminster, Charing Cross, and Tower Pier for Greenwich approximately every 45 minutes and take 40 minutes to an hour, depending on where you embark. Inquiries can be made by calling ☎ 0207-930-4097 or 0207-987-1185.

Finally, you can call the Greenwich Tourist Information Center at ☎ 0208-858-6376, visit the official Web site at **www.greenwich. gov.uk,** or stop by their location at 46 Greenwich Church Street, London, SE10 9BL, for information on guided tours in Greenwich, special events, or any additional information you may need.

PART SEVEN

CHILDREN'S LONDON

LONDON *with* CHILDREN

LONDON IS A WONDERFUL CITY FOR CHILDREN, even jet-lagged ones who can't quite figure out when to go to sleep. Before you go to London, get out some English nursery rhymes or Dickens (depending on the age of your children) and introduce them to the wonders of London in letters. It will make it that much more exciting when you get here. Rent some classic London movies for kids to introduce them to the city and get them in the mood for their visit: *101 Dalmatians* (*not* the animated one), *Oliver!* (*not* the dark Roman Polanski film of 2005, unless they are over age 12), *Mary Poppins, A Little Princess* (Shirley Temple version), *The Prince and the Pauper, A Christmas Carol* (the Muppets version is less scary than the old Alistair Syms one), *The Princess Carabou*, and for over-eights, the fog-filled back-streets and the spooky Tower in *The Adventures of Sherlock Holmes*. There's a brilliant Web site by the London Tourist Board at **www.londontown. com** that provides a kid's-eye view of London and its attractions. We strongly recommend that grade-school children visit it. When you arrive in London, try any central bookshop (Waterstone's Books on Trafalgar Square or Piccadilly) for activity books, sticker books, or story books on London. A great resource for these is Bookends in South Kensington (see page 290).

London has an enormous selection of attractions for children of all ages. The museums are getting more interactive and attention-grabbing all the time. Even the staid old Victoria and Albert features a fun cart on weekends, a family program, and trail kits to keep the kids busy, entertained, and actually learning something about the wonderful collection. Parents will enjoy the kids' attractions as much as the children will. Just maybe, if you give the kids a chance, they will find something great in the places that cater to a more mature palate, such as the National Portrait Gallery or the Globe Theatre. But don't count on it with the really little ones. They're more into playgrounds and riding on the fun double-decker buses, although there are some museums that can keep their little hands and minds busy.

A "LONDON BOOK"

A GREAT IDEA TO REALLY GET THE KIDS PAYING attention and having fun is to start a "London book" before you even leave. Pick out a blank book big enough to paste lots of things in (but not so huge as to waste pages, as often happens), and write down the itinerary; paste in pictures of planes, get the airline cabin crew to sign it, and so on. Then, everywhere you go, collect stubs and pamphlets and take plenty of photos. Get film developed at one-hour labs (or for digital at any Boots Chemists), and spend the evening helping with the scrapbook. Drawings, poems, thoughts, a leaf from Holland Park, a feather from the Serpentine—all these things can make a beautiful scrapbook that children will always love to look through. Get a disposable camera for your child to use to take his or her own photos; you'll be surprised at how much more they'll go in for sightseeing when it has such a personal creative purpose.

PLANNING *and* TOURING TIPS

HERE ARE A FEW IDEAS TO BEAR IN MIND when planning a vacation with the little and not-so-little ones:

AGE Although the wonderful park playgrounds and some tourist attractions of London have much to offer toddlers and preschoolers, the bulk of London's attractions is generally oriented to older kids and adults. Children should be a fairly mature 5 years old to get the most out of popular attractions such as the London Eye, the HMS *Belfast*, possibly even the Tower of London, and a year or two older to enjoy the art museums, cathedrals, and palaces that London has in such grand abundance.

TIME OF YEAR TO VISIT If there is any way to swing it, avoid the crowded summer months. Try to go between late September and November or between early April and mid-June. If you have children of varying ages and your school-age kids are good students, consider taking the older ones out of school so you can visit during the less expensive, less congested off-season. Arrange special study assignments relating to the many educational aspects of London.

unofficial **TIP**
If your school-age children cannot afford to miss any school, take your vacation as soon as the school year ends in June, or before school starts in September.

BUILDING NAPS AND REST INTO YOUR ITINERARY London offers more attractions than you can possibly see in a whole week, so don't try to see too much in one day. Tour in the early morning and return to your hotel midday for lunch and possibly a lie-down. Kids need time to just chill or they can become recalcitrant. Go back and visit more attractions in the late afternoon, or go to a park or The London Eye, which stays open till dusk in the summer; or else take a bus tour that is easier on the legs. Don't pooh-pooh jet lag; children seem to suffer from it less than the adults, but they are definitely thrown off-kilter by the time change. Try to get them adjusted to the time by exposing them to plenty of sunlight and not letting them nap too long during the day.

unofficial **TIP**
Neglecting to relax and unwind is the best way to get the whole family in a snit and ruin the day.

WHERE TO STAY The best area to stay when you're carting kids around is near a park—Hyde, Holland, and Kensington Gardens are good. Kids who will complain about tired feet and hunger in a museum will perk up amazingly when they see a swing set, have some room to kick a soccer ball around, or can watch horses ride by. It's important to get small children off the tourist trail for some rest and recuperation.

With small children, you will be glad to have planned ahead. Make sure you get a hotel within a few minutes' walk to a tube station. Naps and relief from the frenetic pace of touring London are indispensable. Even if you do get some good downtime in a park, for the little ones there is no true substitute for returning to the familiarity and security of your own hotel. Children too large to sleep in a stroller will relax and revive better if you get them back to your room.

unofficial **TIP**
The health club attached to the Rembrandt Hotel (see page 137) has a perfect pool for children, as well as special times for them. It's pricey, but happiness can be costly.

You may want to choose a hotel that has a swimming pool. A lot of visitors to London assume that, like those in so many American destinations, the big London hotels automatically come with a pool. Nothing could be further from the truth. There are a few expensive ones that do; more to the point, there are many hotels that can steer you to a public pool or that have some arrangement with a health club. Call ahead to find out if there are any age restrictions on swimming. A swimming pool can be a lifesaver for both you and your kids, keeping you all happily busy and healthily exercising in between the sightseeing.

GETTING AROUND Getting around can be a bit of a hassle because of traffic congestion, hence decisions about how to get around and how much time to allow need to be made. Probably the most fun way is to take a double-decker bus. Sitting on the top deck of a double-decker is a great way to see London, as there are plenty of sights and weird people for the kids to goggle at. The problem with buses is that you might get stuck in traffic, and the old-fashioned double-decker buses are not stroller-friendly, unlike the newer single-decker buses, which you can usually board without having to collapse your stroller. Fine if you have eight arms to struggle with the bags, baby, and other bits and pieces! However, since Ken Livingstone became Mayor, the dedicated "bus lanes" are ubiquitous, making bus travel a lot quicker, and there are now plenty of wheelchair- and stroller-friendly single-decker buses in the center of the city.

The quicker way to get around is via the tube. However, the system is neither disabled- nor stroller-friendly. Strollers can be negotiated on the escalators, but there are a lot of stairs to deal with when changing trains. This is fine if there are two or more adults in your group, but if you're alone, you could be left struggling, scooping up the whole stroller with baby inside, to get up and down the stairs. You'd be surprised how many other passengers are quick to push or scurry by, rather than offer a helping hand. If you are expecting a baby, don't expect people to surrender their seats for you.

unofficial **TIP**
It is worth noting that there is priority seating on the bus and tube trains clearly indicated for the elderly, the handicapped, or those with small children. So, if no one has offered and you're feeling bold, you have every right to ask someone to move.

For short hops with the kids, a black cab might be the best idea (if walking is not an option, of course). Children love the jump seats. Do be warned, though, that the traffic can be bad in the central areas during the day (Oxford Street, Marble Arch, Piccadilly, Bayswater, Knightsbridge, Chelsea, and Kensington), and taxis are not cheap.

STAY LOOSE As every parent has discovered by day three of their first baby's life, flexibility is everything in parenting, and that goes double for sightseeing with children. Remember that having fun is not necessarily the same as seeing everything. Trust your instincts. What would really feel best right now? Another museum, a snack break, or going back to the room for a nap or quiet time? The way to have a great vacation is to put the emphasis on being happy and having a good time, whatever that takes. You do not have to meet a quota for experiencing every museum or attraction, seeing every neighborhood and monument, or following every suggestion in the book. London has been here for a long time, and it's not going anywhere. Your kids' childhood, on the other hand, is a flash of lightning. Make sure their memories of London are happy ones, and they'll want to come back when they're grown up.

unofficial **TIP**
When you and your children start getting tired and irritable, call a time-out and regroup.

ALL FOR ONE AND ONE FOR ALL When you're traveling *en famille,* you are a moving unit made up of many differing tastes, abilities, and interests. Accept that energy levels vary among individuals, and be prepared to respond to small children or other members of your group who poop out. Try not to let your own disappointment hurt the tired one's feelings. Maybe you can take turns with the other grown-up, if there is one with you, in taking the walking wounded back to the hotel, so that one of you can continue sightseeing.

SETTING LIMITS AND MAKING PLANS The best way to avoid arguments and disappointments is to develop a (very flexible) game plan before you go. Establish some general guidelines for each day and try to get everybody excited about the plans. Be sure to include:

1. Wake-up time and breakfast plans.

2. Departure time for the part of London you plan to explore.

3. Necessary items to take.

4. A policy for splitting the group up or for staying together.

5. A clearly understood strategy for what to do if the group gets separated or someone is lost.

6. Estimate of morning touring time and what you want to see, including fallback plans in case an attraction is too crowded or unexpectedly closed.

7. A policy on what you can afford for snacks, lunch, and refreshments. This is very important in this very expensive city.

8. A target time for returning to your hotel for a rest.

9. If you rest, a target time for returning to the touring and for how late you will stay out.

10. Plans for dinner.

11. A policy for shopping and buying souvenirs, including who pays (parents or kids). Be prepared to go over your original budget.

BE FLEXIBLE Having a game plan does not mean forgoing spontaneity or sticking rigidly to the itinerary. Once again, listen to your intuition. Alter the plan if the situation warrants. Be prepared to roll with the punches.

unofficial **TIP**
The best and lightest protection is a plastic rain poncho; you can carry a few and not have as much weight or bulk as with a couple of umbrellas.

RAIN, SUNBURN, AND DEHYDRATION London's weather is changeable. Although it's not often terribly hot, it can get quite warm in the sun, and you can get a beauty of a sunburn. Carry a small bottle of sunscreen, or smear it on before you go out. Remember to take a bottle of water to rehydrate the happy campers. Rain is the biggest surprise in London; you never know when it's going to come, but chances are it will, if only for a sprinkle.

BLISTERS Blisters and sore feet are common for visitors of all ages, so wear comfortable, well-broken-in shoes. If you or your children are unusually susceptible to blisters, carry some precut moleskin bandages; they offer the best possible protection and won't sweat off. When you feel a hot spot, stop, air out your foot, and place a moleskin over the area before a blister forms. You'll probably find some in London in a pharmacy under a Dr. Scholl's display, but bring some with you just in case. Sometimes small children won't tell their parents about a developing blister until it's too late. Check out your preschooler's feet a couple of times a day—this penny's worth of prevention will be worth many pounds of cure to you and them.

HEALTH AND MEDICAL CARE If you have a child who requires medication, pack plenty and bring it on the plane in a carry-on bag. A bottle of liquid Dramamine will come in handy to fight off motion sickness, which can affect kids who are normally fine in a car but may get sick in a plane, train, or boat.

A small first-aid kit, available at most pharmacies, will handle most minor cuts, scrapes, and splinters, and is easy to pack. Grown-up and children's strength aspirin or Tylenol, a thermometer, cough syrup, baby wipes, a plastic spoon, a battery-powered night-light, and pacifiers will round out a small kit of health-related items for people traveling with children or infants. The most popular acetaminophen (Tylenol) elixir for infants is called Calpol or Panadol Junior and is sold everywhere.

IF YOU BECOME SEPARATED Before venturing out of your hotel room, sit down with your kids and discuss what they should do if they get separated from you while touring a museum or attraction. Tell them to find a uniformed guard and ask for help. Point out that the main entrance of most London attractions has an information desk where they should go if they temporarily get separated.

It's not a bad idea to dress the smaller kids in distinctive colors so you can find them with a quick scanning. It is also considered prudent to sew a label into each child's shirt indicating his or her name, your name, and the name of your hotel. The same thing can be accomplished less elegantly by writing the information on a strip of masking tape. Hotel security professionals suggest that the information be printed in small letters and that the tape be affixed to the outside of the child's shirt five inches or so below the armpit.

RAINY DAYS As you know, London is a pretty rainy place—certainly not as bad as its reputation (Rome actually has more inches per year), but it does come down. Museums and galleries are obvious solutions to the rainy-day blues; that old stand-by, the movies, is a good place to kick back, but finding kids' movies is easier said than done. Look in the *Evening Standard* for IMAX movies—there's the big London IMAX at Waterloo and another inside the Science Museum. Leisure Box in Queensway has an indoor ice-skating rink and bowling alley, and there are a few paint-your-own-pottery places that kids just love—see "Activities" below for names and numbers. You have to wait a day or two to pick up your finished pieces, so ask ahead how long it will take to fire your kids' work. There's also brass rubbing at St. Martin-in-the-Fields, a cheaper option, and the kids can take their rubbings with them when leaving the church.

unofficial **TIP**
Look in *Time Out* under children's events; there may be a puppet show or story-time reading where you can stay dry.

RECOMMENDED ATTRACTIONS
and ITINERARIES

THE LISTS BELOW INCLUDE ONLY A LOOSE age guide, since obviously some kids will enjoy certain attractions more than others. We've left out some of the activities that one can do in any city, such as visiting arcades and amusement parks.

THE TOP 10 MOST POPULAR SIGHTS FOR CHILDREN

1. The British Airways London Eye (all ages; 45 minute "flights")
2. Science Museum (all ages; go to the basement with under-fives)
3. London Aquarium (toddlers and preschoolers are very entertained here; older ones might prefer something more *Londonesque*)
4. Museum of London (grade-school age)
5. Victoria and Albert Museum (over-fives)
6. Tower of London (over-fives)
7. Natural History Museum (all ages)
8. London Transport Museum (all ages, even teens)
9. London Zoo (all ages)
10. Boys: HMS *Belfast* (over-fives, although toddlers treat it as an adventure!); Girls: Museum of Childhood, Bethnal Green (under-tens)

ALSO SEE

1. Royal Mews (all ages)
2. Theatre Museum (over-fives)
3. British Museum (over-fives)
4. London Bridge Experience
5. London Dungeon (for gore-loving adolescents)
6. All the military museums for children of that bent: Cabinet War Rooms, Imperial War Museum, Guards Museum, National Army Museum (mostly over-fives, although the Imperial War Museum allows tiny ones running-around space and buttons to press at random)
7. South Bank Center (all ages; see Good Days Out, below)
8. Look out for the reopening of the much-loved Pollock's Toy Museum (**www.pollocksmuseum.co.uk**), which lost its lease in Scala Street and is looking for new premises.
9. Shakespeare's Globe Theatre
10. The Royal Observatory (over 5s)

THE TOP 10 LEAST POPULAR SIGHTS FOR CHILDREN

1. Queen's Gallery	6. Florence Nightingale Museum
2. Leighton House	7. Carlyle's House
3. Dickens House	8. Sir John Soane's Museum
4. British Library	9. Design Museum
5. Royal Academy of Arts	10. Courtauld Institute

BEST DAY OUT FOR ALL THE FAMILY
The South Bank

This stretch of the south bank of the Thames provides something for the whole family: traffic-free outdoor and indoor space for children to run around in; film, theater, music; an art gallery; street artists; restaurants; a beautiful and unique view of the river and the buildings that line its banks; the London Eye; Shakespeare's Globe; and much, much more.

BEFORE YOU LEAVE If you're in London during the summer, phone ahead and plan your visit to coincide with a free outdoor theater event in the National Theatre Square behind the National Theatre building (☎ 0207-452-3400); you can also prebook tickets for the London Eye online or by calling ☎ 0870-500-0600.

GETTING THERE Take the underground/overground train to Waterloo and follow the exit signs to the South Bank.

CHOOSE TWO OR THREE ACTIVITIES—NO MORE!

- Head straight for the **London Eye,** and you'll find yourselves on the river. If you've booked a ride on the Eye, or the queues don't look too long, this could be a good time to take your unmissable "flight." The **London Aquarium** is to your left if you're facing the river, and so too is the Saatchi Gallery, which is well worth a visit but is rarely suitable for children younger than teenage.

- Heading east along the river bank, there are often street artists and stalls lining the **pedestrian river path.** You'll enjoy the riverside views, and it's only a few minutes before you come across the Brutalist sixties architecture for which the South Bank Centre is famous. Throughout the year the **Royal Festival Hall** has free lunchtime foyer music (12:30 p.m. to 2 p.m.), ranging from solo recitals to jazz bands, in a large, open space in which children can move and even run around. This way adults get to snatch a bit of culture (with a glass of wine/bowl of pasta from the rather good café or bar), and yet the children aren't rebelling at being forced to sit completely still. If you have to leave because of the little ones, at least you haven't wasted the price of a concert ticket. Lots of parents take advantage of this arrangement, so you don't feel embarrassed at having a noisy or restless child in tow.

- Have a look at the **second-hand book stalls** under the bridge in front of the National Film Theatre. The food in the NFT café is reasonable, and with outdoor seating this can be an ideal place for a snack.
- Next is the National Theatre, and on your right is **National Theatre Square,** where free outdoor performances take place in the summer months. This is perfect for families, since behind the seating is an installation that looks like a group of rocks, that children love to climb on. However, if you have under-threes with you it's best to skip this and move on along the river.
- **Gabriel's Wharf** is a row of old buildings that have been turned into an arty space for tourists. It's a wonderful place for families, because it's a fairly enclosed space and feels very child-friendly, has arty shops sporting handmade clothes, paintings, and jewelry, and a choice of three restaurants for lunch. There's a wood-carving shop called Noah's Ark that leaves its creations out in the middle of the square, and toddlers love to climb and ride on them, which is allowed. The pizza restaurant has high chairs, and the staff in all three restaurants are very used to children.
- Next to Gabriel's Wharf is a small grassed area used for the annual **Coin Street Festival,** a culturally themed series of free events taking place throughout the summer, involving music, dance, street theater, fairground rides, and food (☎ 0207-401-2255).
- Then comes the **Oxo Tower:** take the lift to the eighth floor, turn right out of the lift and then right immediately again passing through the back of the restaurant, and onto the viewing gallery with breathtaking views over London. The Oxo Tower was originally a power station built at the turn of the century. It now houses art galleries, shops, and retail studio space where the public can watch designers at work.
- Should you make your way further east along the South Bank, you'll come across **Shakespeare's Globe Theatre,** which offers tours; **The Tate Modern,** which offers children's activities and a huge space to run around in, and is situated on the south side of the **Millennium Foot Bridge,** which is a wonderful way of getting views up and down the river, and leads to **St. Paul's Cathedral.** However, be warned, by this time small legs will be aching and there's still the walk back to Waterloo Station, unless you want to continue to London Bridge and hail a taxicab.

SERVICES *for* FAMILIES

RENTAL EQUIPMENT AND CHILD CARE

Chelsea Baby Hire (☎ 0208-789-9673; **www.chelseababyhire.co.uk**) and **Nappy Express** (☎ 0208-361-4040; **www.nappyexpress.co.uk**) rent cribs, high chairs, double strollers (or buggies, as they're known here), along with toys, household products, and more. For child care, consider

Childminders (evening bookings ☎ 0207-935-3000; day bookings ☎ 0207-935-2049; **www.babysitter.co.uk**). You'll pay a joining fee of £59, and the hourly fee starts at £5.20. **Universal Aunts** (☎ 0207-738-8937) can deal with any domestic need or crisis, like a good auntie should, including short-term babysitting. **Hopes and Dreams Montessori Nursery School** (☎ 0207-833-9388; **www.hopesanddreams.co.uk**) is a babysitting and nanny agency, as well as a day nursery for kids, complete with organic food and big fun. Day rates (8 a.m. to 6 p.m.) are from £60, plus registration fee. **Pippa Pop-Ins Excursions and Activities** (☎ 0207-385-2438; **www.pippapopins.com**) is another good day nursery that's been around for years, based in Fulham. Call to check for available space; £75 for full day (8:15 a.m. to 6 p.m.). You can also e-mail me at LesleyLogan@aol.com—I may be able to help you find less expensive sitters.

ACTIVITIES

PAINT YOUR OWN POTTERY

COLOUR ME MINE (4 Chiswick High School Road, Chiswick (West London), W11; ☎ 0208-994-4100; **www.colourmemine.com;** tube: Chiswick Park Station) This studio offers ceramics, mosaics, glass-painting, and even bead stringing. Drop in with your kids (it entertains them right up to adolescence and even beyond) or bring your tiny child to get a foot or hand impression done.

POTTERY CAFÉ (735 Fulham Road, Fulham (West London), SW6; ☎ 0207-736-2157; **www.pottery-cafe.com**; number 14 bus toward Fulham, or tube: Fulham Broadway) They have a good selection of ceramic items to paint and fire, and you can also decorate drinking glasses or glass vases. Cream teas are served in the courtyard. There is another branch in Richmond.

BRASS RUBBINGS

BRASS RUBBING CENTRE (Trafalgar Square, WC2; ☎ 0207-930-9306; tube: Leicester Square) in the crypt of St. Martin-in-the-Fields offers a wonderful treat for kids age 6 and up. They can make their own souvenirs by rubbing a waxy color stick over paper to reveal the beautiful carved brasses with medieval motifs such as knights, dragons, crests, etc. **All-Hallows-By-The-Tower** (Byward Street, EC3; ☎ 0207-481-2928; tube: Tower Hill) is another option. The church, which was built in A.D. 675, has an interesting history. John Quincy Adams, the sixth president of the United States, was married here, and William Penn, founder of Pennsylvania, was baptized here. Check out the museum (with an audio tour available); it's good for kids, because it covers all sorts of exciting historical events, including the Great Fire of London (1666), complete with sound effects. Brass rubbing is done 11 a.m.–4 p.m., but call first to be sure it's open.

SKATING

QUEEN'S ICE-SKATING RINK (17 Queensway, Bayswater, W2; ☎ 0207-229-0172; tube: Queensway or Bayswater) is a big rink that is part of a fun complex that also has bowling. Children should be able to fit into a children's size 6 boot. (For a full description of sports and exercise venues, see Part 11, Excercise and Recreation.)

BOOKSTORES

CALL THE FOLLOWING TO CHECK ON CHILDREN'S summertime activities and storytelling: **Books Etc.** (Whiteleys Center, Bayswater, W2; ☎ 0207-229-3865; tube: Queensway or Bayswater) and **Children's Book Centre** (237 Kensington High Street, Kensington, W8; ☎ 0207-937-7497; tube: High Street Kensington). Also see **Daisy & Tom's** under "Shopping for Children" below. They have a huge, wonderful selection of children's books, as well as a puppet theater show.

PLAYGROUNDS

BATTERSEA PARK (Albert Bridge Road, Battersea, SW11; tube: Sloane Square, then bus 19 or 137) has a boating lake, adventure playground, a small art gallery, plus a children's zoo (which is newly refurbished with animals well cared for and some new ones your kids can pet).

CORAM FIELDS (93 Guildford Street, Bloomsbury, WC1; ☎ 0207-837-6138; tube: Russell Square) is a famous playground that only allows adults with an accompanying child—and they mean it. It was built in 1936 on the site of the old foundling hospital. It's got a wide variety of play equipment to suit all ages. Animals are on view, and it's open 9 a.m. to dusk.

HOLLAND PARK (tube: Holland Park) has peacocks and an impressive multilevel adventure playground, with an area for kids under age 8.

HYDE PARK (tube: High Street Kensington) There's a good playground on the south side of the park, near the riding ring where you may see the Queen's Horse Guards exercise their steeds (not to mention the regular traffic of folks on horseback). Weekends there are soccer games for the young footie fan to watch. There are ducks and paddleboats on the Serpentine and a lido (☎ 0207-706-3422) with a kids' pool in summer, and Peter Pan's statue all year.

KENSINGTON GARDENS (tube: High Street Kensington) has the Princess Diana Memorial Playground at the north end of Broad Walk (only adults accompanied by a child will be admitted; a huge wooden ship is spectacularly popular with the kids); remote-control model boats to watch in the Round Pond.

REGENT'S PARK (tube: Regent's Park) has three playgrounds and two boating lakes, one of which is expressly for children.

ST. JAMES'S PARK (tube: Green Park) has a smallish playground by Birdcage Walk and plenty of pelicans and other birds to watch. The 3 p.m. feeding of pelicans is very popular.

SYON PARK AND LONDON BUTTERFLY HOUSE (tube: Gunnersbury or Kew Bridge rail, then bus 267 or 237) is an estate open daily, 10 a.m. to 5:30 p.m. Older kids might appreciate the Butterfly House, but the younger ones will appreciate the **Aquatic Experience** (☎ 0208-847-4730), which features fish, reptiles, amphibians, and other small animals in their natural habitats. There's also **Snakes &** **Ladders** (☎ 0208-847-0946), an adventure playground. Check out the miniature steam train in the gardens. Call ☎ 0208-560-0881 for Syon Park information and ☎ 0208-560-0378 for Butterfly House information.

unofficial **TIP**
Two caveats: This attraction is not easy to get to without a car, and the planes overhead landing or taking off from Heathrow are most annoying. Otherwise it's got enough activities to easily fill a day.

THEATERS

LITTLE ANGEL THEATRE (14 Dagmar Passage, off Cross Street, Islington, N1; ☎ 0207-226-1787; **www.littleangeltheatre.com;** tube: Angel or Highbury & Islington) The city's only permanent puppet theater, which has been running for 40 years, is a delightful venue with a 100-seat auditorium. Weekend shows by the resident or visiting puppet companies are offered, as well as shows during Christmas and half-term holidays.

NATIONAL FILM THEATRE (South Bank, SE1; ☎ 0207-928-3535; **www.bfi.org.uk;** tube: Waterloo or Embankment) runs Movie Magic matinee screenings of perennial movie favorites for kids every weekend day from 3 to 4 p.m., and some weekdays during school holidays.

POLKA THEATRE FOR CHILDREN (240 The Broadway, Wimbledon, SW19; ☎ 0208-543-4888; **www.polkatheatre.com;** tube: Wimbledon or British Rail to South Wimbledon) seats 300 and also has an 80-seat adventure room for children under age 5, a small but unusual playground, a café, and a gift shop; excellent disability access.

PUPPET THEATRE BARGE (Blomfield Road [opposite #35], Maidavale, W9; ☎ 0207-249-6876; **www.puppetbarge.com;** tube: Warwick Avenue) is a traveling puppet barge featuring wonderful string marionettes. It is moored in Little Venice, Maida Vale, from November to May. Shows run on weekends and during school holidays, beginning at 3 p.m. From July to October, the theater travels on the Thames River, with shows at Henley-on-Thames, Marlow, and Richmond. Call or look on the Web site to find out where and when. Advance reservations are recommended.

TRANSPORTATION

TRAVEL IS FREE FOR CHILDREN AGES 5 YEARS and under on all buses, tubes, and local trains. Under-sixteens pay child's fares until 10 p.m., after which they pay adult fares. Because of the difficulty of identifying an adolescent's age, 14- and 15-year-olds are required to produce proof of age (a passport or copy of one), or a Child Photocard, which can be obtained from any post office. Bring a passport-size photo and proof of age, and you'll be good to go. Unfortunately, many conductors on buses will not take your word for your teen's age.

WHERE to EAT

KIDS NEED A BIT OF ENTERTAINING TO KEEP them happy in a restaurant, and they generally require something fried and finger-fed. Most kids will be happy as clams at the outdoor cafés in the parks, or with a picnic of sandwiches from one of the "sarnie" shops such as Pret à Manger (the best quality in take-away sandwiches and they're all over town). The chains of Boots, Waitrose, Sainsbury's, and Starbucks all sell ready-made sandwiches and drinks—buy a bagful, some crisps, drinks, and Bob's your uncle, as they say here. If you require a sit-down out of the weather, here are some kid-friendly places to eat, none of which are at the top of any serious gourmand's list, but they'll serve your children with a smile:

BIG EASY (332–334 King's Road, Chelsea, SW3; ☎ 0207-352-4071; tube: Sloane Square) is geared up for kids; there's a special menu, plus crayons to keep those hands busy. Kids' prices are £4.95–£8.95 and include unlimited soft drinks and some chocolate gooey thing.

HARD ROCK CAFÉ (150 Old Park Lane, Mayfair, W1; ☎ 0207-629-0382; www.hardrock.com; tube: Green Park or Hyde Park Center) has lots of loud music and rock memorabilia festooning every available surface. It may not be suitable for very young children, as the music rocks hard, as you would imagine. There is a special kids' menu for £5.95 and crayons to distract them.

MAXWELLS (8–9 James Street, West End, WC2; ☎ 0207-395-5804; tube: Covent Garden) is in a great location, near the Covent Garden piazza, and has a special kids' menu, crayons, balloons, and more. During some holidays, they decorate the restaurant and provide seasonally festive menus.

MILDREDS (45 Lexington Street, Soho, W1; ☎ 0207-494-1634; www.mildreds.co.uk; tube: Piccadilly Circus) For vegetarians or people with special diets, this is the place to come. There's everything from freshly squeezed juice (with blue-green algae), burgers, stir-fries, special vegan/wheat-free/milk-free dishes to mouth watering puddings you'll want to come back for again and again. And there *is* a bar, so adults can have a glass of wine, too!

RAINFOREST CAFÉ (20 Shaftsbury Avenue, Soho, WC2; ☎ 0207-434-3111; **www.therainforestcafe.co.uk;** tube: Piccadilly Circus), an American import, is a great place for kids, with its children's menu (burgers, ribs, sandwiches) and special treats for parties (face painting, goodie bags, and more), all in a jungle-esque setting with a rumbling faux volcano that erupts intermittently. If you're on a budget, try to keep them out of the gift shop.

STICKY FINGERS (1A Phillimore Gardens, Kensington, W8; ☎ 0207-395-5805; **www.stickyfingers.co.uk;** tube: High Street Kensington) is owned by Bill Wyman (ex–Rolling Stones member) and offers a kids' menu for £4.95 that includes burgers, ribs, chicken, and more. Sundays are best, with face painting, balloons, and a generally fun atmosphere.

SMOLLENSKY'S (105 The Strand, West End, WC2; ☎ 0207-497-2101; **www.smollenskys.co.uk;** tube: Charing Cross) This is the perfect place for kids, especially for Saturday and Sunday lunch. There's a play area, a crèche for the really young ones, and endless entertainment, including magicians, clowns, face painting, computer games, and more.

TGI FRIDAY'S (6 Bedford Street, West End, WC2; ☎ 0207-379-0585; **www.tgifridays.co.uk;** tube: Covent Garden or Charing Cross), another American import that's family friendly, offers balloons, crayons, and children's menus, including a Sesame Street one that comes with a free toy. On weekends, there is face painting and a magician on Sunday. They offer free organic baby food.

TEXAS EMBASSY CANTINA (1 Cockspur Street, West End, SW1; ☎ 0207-925-0077; **www.texasembassy.com;** tube: Charing Cross) This is an authentic Tex-Mex place, situated in the building that housed the embassy of the short-lived nation of Texas. It's near the National Gallery and Trafalgar Square. Lots of room for big parties, plus outdoor seating (watch the buses inch along). Very cool decor that will make an American feel right at home, and children most welcome.

TOOTSIES (120 Holland Park Avenue, Kensington, W11; ☎ 0207-229-8567; **www.tootsiesrestaurants.co.uk;** tube: Holland Park) A really great place for upscale diner-type food, with a huge menu that includes burgers of every description, all-day breakfasts, and lots of salads. Very child-friendly and relaxed. There are branches in South Kensington (107 Old Brompton Road, SW7; ☎ 0207-581-8942; tube: South Kensington); and in Marylebone (35 James Street, W1; ☎ 0207-486-1611; tube: Marble Arch or Bond Street).

SHOPPING *for* CHILDREN

TOYS

Daisy & Tom's (81 King's Road, Chelsea, SW3; ☎ 0207-352-5000; tube: Sloane Square) is a great kids' store with toys, books, nursery furniture, a carousel, and a very cool, very fun hair-cutting salon. **Davenport's Magic Shop** (7 Charing Cross Underground Concourse, Strand, WC2; ☎ 0207-836-0408; tube: Charing Cross) is still going strong after 100 years of selling magic. **Hamleys** (188–196 Regent Street, West End, W1; ☎ 0207-734-3161; **www.hamleys.com**; tube: Oxford Street or Piccadilly Circus), with its seven floors, is said to be the largest toy store in the world; and kids instinctively seem to know this, going bonkers with toy-lust. Consider yourself warned. **Harrods** (87 Brompton Road, Knightsbridge, SW1; ☎ 0207-730-1234; **www.harrods.com**; tube: Knightsbridge) has a remarkable selection of dolls, games, and action toys, but watch that wallet: they also feature miniature automobiles. **Tridias** (25 Bute Street, South Kensington, SW7; ☎ 0207-584-2330; tube: South Kensington) sells lots of interesting European toys and small, inexpensive gimcracks.

BOOKS

ALTHOUGH ALL THE BIG BOOK SHOPS HAVE great children's sections (Harrods also has a particularly good kid's section), my favorite for all ages (that includes you) is **Bookends** (25–28 Thurloe Place, South Kensington, SW7; ☎ 0207-589-2285; tube: South Kensington) where you'll find lots of London-related books and art, as well as wonderful coloring books of stained glass, medieval art, historical costumes, sticker books of various subjects, and art projects. It has everything you need for busy little hands and minds—there's also an art store downstairs. Bring your children here after a trip to the nearby Victoria and Albert and let them make their own masterpieces.

CLOTHING

THESE STORES TEND TO BE LIKE INFANTS AND young children themselves—here one minute, gone the next. Most of the clothes stores listed in our first and second editions have gone belly-up, so it's wise to call before you venture to the following stores. Most of the stores listed are included not so much because they represent good deals (the prices can be as breathtaking as the clothes in some of the stores, and unless you're loaded or plan to hand-me-down to a large brood, these are strictly luxury purchases) but because they have interesting and distinctive European selections from Petit Bateau, Petite Ourse, Laura Ashley, and other British or French designers.

BRORA (344 King's Road, Chelsea, SW3; ☎ 0207-352-3697; **www.brora.co.uk**; tube: Sloane Square) specializes in cashmere and woolen clothes for newborns and young children, along with their established adult line. Multiple branches.

CARAMEL (291 Brompton Road, South Kensington, SW3; ☎ 0207-589-7001; tube: South Kensington) offers lots of cute and trendy gear for children up to approximately 8 years of age. They have a little sale box, which, depending on your luck, can yield a treasure or two.

CLEMENTINE (73 Ledbury Road, Nottng Hill, W11; ☎ 0207-243-6331; tube: Notting Hill Gate or Westbourne Park) specializes in French and Italian clothes for children of all ages.

CATIMINI (52 South Molton Street, Mayfair, W1; ☎ 0207-629-8099; **www.catimini.fr;** tube: Bond Street) has cute clothes with unusual details, such as pockets that resemble dolls' faces and candy-shaped buttons. It carries clothing for children up to about 14 years of age.

DAISY & TOM'S (181–183 King's Road, Chelsea, SW3; ☎ 0207-352-5000; tube: Sloane Square) is a great kids' shop with designer labels such as Petit Bateau, Miniman, and Damask. While you shop, kids can ride the carousel or get a haircut. Clothes are for children up to 10 years old.

JIGSAW JUNIOR (190 Westbourne Grove, Notting Hill, W11; ☎ 0207-727-0322; **www.jigsaw-online.com;** tube: Notting Hill) offers simple clothes from the successful Jigsaw chain of fashion stores; for girls only. There are plenty of playthings in the store to keep young shoppers happy. Clothes are for children up to 13 years of age. Multiple branches.

MOTHERCARE WORLD (461 Oxford Street, West End, W1; ☎ 0207-629-6621; **www.mothercare.com;** tube: Marble Arch or Bond Street) Although a chain store, this is a great place to snap up affordable home-brand basics and clothing featuring licensed characters such as Barbie, Action Man, and Winnie the Pooh. Additional branches abound. The shop also carries baby products (see "Baby Goods").

OILILY (9 Sloane Street, Knightsbridge, SW1; ☎ 0207-823-2505; **www.oilily.nl;** tube: Knightsbridge) Oilily is a bright and cheerful collection from a popular Dutch design team. It's very 1960s in a pop-art way, featuring beautiful patterns and well-decorated basics. There are one-of-a-kind knit sweaters and gorgeous baby blankets, cool shoes, affordable hats, and baby bags.

PETIT BATEAU (103 Kings Road, Chelsea, SW3; ☎ 0207-838-0818; tube: Sloane Square) This venerable French company has been dressing European infants in its luxurious cotton onesies and sweet fashions for years, and now the teenagers have rediscovered the label, making the PB T-shirts a must-have fashion.

PLEASE MUM (85 Knightsbridge, Knightsbridge, SW1; ☎ 0207-486-1380; **www.pleasemumlondon.com;** tube: Knightsbridge) specializes in Italian designers, from Moschino to Versace, plus the Please Mum home-brand collection. Frilly, old-fashioned children's ball gowns are a unique offering. Clothes are for children up to 14 years of age.

PAUL SMITH FOR CHILDREN (40–44 Floral Street, West End, WC2; ☎ 0207-379-7133; **www.paulsmith.co.uk;** tube: Covent Garden) features this world-famous designer's funky collection, including bold duck, helicopter, and airplane prints, which really do look cool. Shoes are also available. Clothes are for children up to 16 years of age.

TARTINE ET CHOCOLAT (66 South Molton Street, Mayfair, W1; ☎ 0207-629-7233; tube: Bond Street) is the place to go if you're looking for more conservative outfits. You'll find double-breasted coats, velvet dresses, lots of blues for baby boys, and lots of pinks for baby girls at this Parisian boutique.

SHOES

BUCKLE MY SHOE (Harvey Nichols, Buckle My Shoe Department 2nd Floor, 67 Brompton Road, Knightsbridge, SW1; ☎ 0207-235-5000; **www.bucklemyshoe.com;** tube: Knightsbridge) has more cute delights for those tiny feet—funky animal-print slippers, glittery sandals. Not cheap, but so cute!

INSTEP (45 St. John's Wood High Street, North London, NW8; ☎ 0207-722-7634; **www.instepshoes.co.uk;** tube: St. John's Wood) They design their own shoes here and have them made in Italy. They have gorgeous decorative footwear for those babies who have yet to put a foot down, good learning-to-walk shoes, and plenty for older kids to choose from.

LOOK WHO'S WALKING (78 Heath Street, North London, NW3; ☎ 0207-433-3855; tube: Hampstead) Love the name, love the store. Very small store with very big taste: Dolce & Gabbana, Pom d'Api, Naturino make beautiful shoes for kids to quickly grow out of. Plus the store has designer clothes for up to age 12.

BABY GOODS

MOTHERCARE WORLD IS ALWAYS HEAVING WITH expectant and established parents, stocking up on cribs, bedding, strollers, high chairs, bottles, diapers, toys, and more. Particularly handy are the bathroom stalls (big enough to push strollers into), a feeding area with bottle warmers, and a special room for nursing mothers complete with rocking chairs and a water dispenser. (See the entry in the "Clothing" section, above, for location information.)

Nursery Window (83 Walton Street, Chelsea, SW3; ☎ 0207-581-3358; **www.nurserywindow.co.uk;** tube: South Kensington), which is not too pricey, specializes in nursery furnishings: cribs, bedding, curtains, and even wallpaper. All fabrics are designed and printed in the United Kingdom. There's also a mail-order service.

PART EIGHT

DINING *and*
RESTAURANTS

THERE'S AN OLD JOKE ABOUT WHAT awaits Europeans in Heaven: The police are English, the chefs are French, the mechanics are German, the lovers are Italian, and everything is organized by the Swiss. In Hell, the police are German, the chefs are British, the mechanics are French, and everything is organized by the Italians. Well, that old saw has become as outdated as *lederhosen*. There were more than a few tears shed into a soufflé or two in Paris when *Restaurant Magazine* named London as the new food capital of the world in 2005. The winner of the survey is the triple-Michelin-starred The Fat Duck, an hour outside of London (High Street, Bray, Berkshire, ☎ 0162-858-0333, **www.fatduck.co.uk**), where the chef is celebrated for unusual combinations (anyone for snail porridge?) and his revolutionary kitchen methods, called "molecular cooking." With ten other restaurants in the Best 50 list, London alone has edged out the whole of France, building on its winning streak that started in the "foodie" revolution of the 1990s. I'm certain that Heaven would happily claim for its own any of the British celebrity chefs: Gordon Ramsey, Jamie Oliver, Marco Pierre White, Angela Harnett, Richard Lindsey, the Roux brothers, and the team from the River Café. And there are so many more big names, there wouldn't be room at the celestial stove.

For centuries, food in London, and in all of the United Kingdom, was famous for its brutally unyielding awfulness: great lumps of indifferently prepared beef, vegetables boiled beyond all recognition, potatoes whose only concession to taste was being drowned in butter (or worse, in oily margarine) and salted to within an inch of its life. The best that could be said about British food back then was that they had wonderful names: toad-in-the-hole, bubble and squeak, spotted dick, bangers and mash, apricot fool, ploughman's sandwich, bacon buttie, and Poor Knights. Good comfort food (especially the Sunday roasts with Yorkshire pudding), but as Shakespeare said, a rose by any other name would smell as sweet; and these colorful names didn't change the meat-and-potatos workmanlike nature of these dishes. Most of the great restaurants in London earned their stripes on a Gallic menu, with chefs strictly trained in classical French cuisine. However, *Restaurant* magazine's top 50 include the Asian restaurants Hakkasan, Nobu (see page 339), and Yauatcha (see page 355). Asian and South Asian cuisines have always been a strong point in London, and they remain so—but they're even better now, especially Indian cooking. There's a bigger range than ever before, with more regional variety and a general emphasis on fresh ingredients cooked to order. The same can be said of Chinese food, another traditional area of strength. It's true also of French and Italian cooking. Even old-fashioned British food is taken with the greatest seriousness, again at every price level, with handmade specialty sausages and garlic potato puree putting a new shine on the old bangers and mash.

It's all about a relatively recent phenomenon that's called modern British, or (the term used here) modern European cooking. Nearly everyone who pays attention to gastronomic trends will use some version of this term. Defining it precisely . . . well, that's another matter. But here's a rough working definition: classic European techniques (especially French and Italian) applied to top-quality ingredients that may—but don't necessarily—come from any corner of the globe.

London is well suited to the development of this kind of eclecti-cism in cooking. The ingredients are there because of the city's location within Europe and its long-time connections with Asia. In addition, a widely traveled customer base provides a serious demand for good cooking. Some of the best chefs exploit these elements with amazing results. Some borrow widely from Asia and the Americas, with the results bordering on so-called fusion cooking. Some remain deliberately French and Italian in orientation, whereas others emphasize the British source of ingredients and inspirations.

unofficial **TIP**
Modern European is the most interesting food being cooked in London now, and restaurants of this type feature promi-nently in these listings.

If eating out in London is better than ever, you should also be warned of the downside: It's often bruisingly expensive—even for Lon-doners, and especially for traveling Americans, with the dollar so terri-bly weak against the pound sterling. It is nearly impossible to find an outstanding three-course meal with a bottle of wine for under £35 a head outside Asian restaurants, and even fairly basic restaurants have an annoying tendency to cost twice that amount if you drink more than the house wine. We wish it weren't so, but the high cost of eating in London, combined with dreadful exchange rates, shows no sign of abating. But if you're after a cheap meal in an interesting part of town, look no further than Brick Lane (tube: Aldgate East). Very much like what Sixth Street used to be like in New York City, this is a long street filled with balti houses, Indian restaurants from every state in India, and very good deals. On weekends you'll be accosted every few steps by some cheerful fellow pressing you to eat at this or that restaurant, offering discounts of anywhere from 10 to 40% off the bill. I am skeptical about these deals, but the fact is that you can feed a group of four for under £10 a person. Walk the entire expanse before settling on any one restaurant; the touts are always good for a quick, friendly conversation and a card for their restaurant.

In the meantime, those who seek high quality at low prices should pay special attention to the list of gastro-pubs in the "More Recommendations" section. These are old-fashioned pubs, refurbished in a simple style, that place the greatest emphasis on good food rather than beer and crisps (potato chips). The top gastro-pubs are usually off the beaten track (one reason they can charge lower prices), but you should seek them out if you don't mind a bit of extra traveling.

unofficial **TIP**
Gastro-pubs are some of London's best bets for budget eating in totally relaxed surroundings.

At the other restaurants, there are ways to cut costs. Lunch is likely to be considerably cheaper than dinner, and some places have pre- or post-theater offers with limited choice and lower prices. With drinks making up a large part of many bills, look for house wines or order by the glass if that's all you want. And don't feel obliged to order a bottle of water (almost always marked up heavily) if tap water will please you just as well: London's water is perfectly potable. You may feel subtly pressured to buy a bottle of mineral water (some restaurants have an annoying habit of asking "still or sparkling" when you order H_2O, so be firm in specifying tap water). If you're traveling with children but don't see a children's menu, ask if a child-size portion can be prepared, as many good restaurants will oblige.

The other big complaint about London restaurants is the quality of service, and there's a lot of merit in the complaint. The cafés and restaurants here are flooded with young people from all over the EU, looking to improve (or learn) the English language, and snap-to-it professionalism is not always part of the package. You may find yourself waiting a long time for your order to be taken, and getting a bill may require an absurd amount of effort. I have often left restaurants in annoyance after waiting 15 minutes without even being acknowledged, only to find the same problem at the next one. Cooking skills have certainly improved, but the perennial shortage of well-trained, conscientious waiters and slipshod service can ruin even the best-tasting meal. At expensive restaurants this should not (in theory) be a problem, but in others—well, you may be lucky and you may not. Complain if you feel it's warranted, but don't expect much in the way of compensation. And if you get poor service at high prices, complain even more vociferously. It shouldn't happen, but it does.

One final word is in order here. There's almost nonstop change in the London restaurant world. Restaurants accept reservations one day and announce their closure the next. Chefs move around at an unprecedented rate. Menus are changed fundamentally. New management moves in on well-established operations. The pace of change from week to week makes it inevitable that further change will have occurred by the time you hold this book in your hands—some months after the section was written. Needless to say, this is out of our control.

THE RESTAURANTS

RATING OUR FAVORITE LONDON RESTAURANTS

WE HAVE DEVELOPED DETAILED PROFILES for the best and most interesting (in our opinion) restaurants in town. Each profile features an easily scanned heading that allows you, in just a second, to check out the restaurant's name, cuisine, star rating, cost, quality rating, and value rating.

CUISINE This is actually less straightforward than it sounds. A couple of years ago, for example, "pan-Asian" restaurants in Washington, D.C., were serving what was then generally described as "fusion" food—Asian ingredients with European techniques, or vice versa. Since then, there has been a pan-Asian explosion, but nearly all specialize in what would be street food back home: noodles, skewers, dumplings, and soups. Occasionally, you'll find bizarre combinations of dishes that resemble something from the United Nations cafeteria: Cuban, Chinese, Spanish, American, Middle Eastern, and more all making an appearance on the menu. This is usually not a good sign: Who could do justice to all these cuisines in one kitchen? Once-general categories have become subdivided—French into bistro fare and even Provençal, "new continental" into regional American and "eclectic"—while others have broadened and fused: Middle Eastern and Provençal into Mediterranean, Spanish and South American into nuevo Latino, and so on. In some cases, we have used the broader terms (e.g., "French") but added descriptions to give a clearer idea of the fare. Again, though, experimentation and "fusion" are ever more common, so don't hold us, or the chefs, to too strict a style.

OVERALL RATING The overall rating is a rating that encompasses the entire dining experience, including style, service, and ambience, in addition to the taste, presentation, and quality of the food. Five stars is the highest rating possible and connotes the best of everything. Four-star restaurants are exceptional, and three-star restaurants are well above average. Two-star restaurants are good. One star is used to indicate an average restaurant that demonstrates an unusual capability in some area of specialization—for example, an otherwise unmemorable place that has great barbecued chicken.

COST Our expense description provides a comparative sense of how much a complete meal will cost. A complete meal for our purposes consists of an appetizer, entree, and dessert. Drinks and tips are excluded.

Inexpensive	Less than £20 per person
Moderate	£20–£50 per person
Expensive	More than £50 per person

QUALITY RATING The food quality is rated on a scale of one to five stars, five being the best rating attainable. The quality rating is based expressly on the taste, freshness of ingredients, preparation, presentation, and creativity of food served. There is no consideration of price. If you are a person who wants the best food available and cost is not an issue, you need look no further than the quality ratings.

VALUE RATING If, on the other hand, you are looking for both quality and value, then you should check the value rating. The value ratings are defined as follows:

★★★★★	Exceptional value; a real bargain
★★★★	Good value
★★★	Fair value; you get exactly what you pay for
★★	Somewhat overpriced
★	Significantly overpriced

PAYMENT We've listed the type of payment accepted at each restaurant using the following codes: AE equals American Express (Optima), CB equals Carte Blanche, D equals Discover, DC equals Diners Club, JCB equals Japan Credit Bureau, MC equals Master-Card, and V equals VISA. Despite the increasing globalization of commerce, the acceptance of American Express, Carte Blanc, Diners Club, and JCB should not be taken for granted: the high fees charged by AE, and the relative rarity of the others, means that some restaurants may have abandoned one or more of them, so be sure to call for an update.

WHO'S INCLUDED Restaurants in London change owners at an alarming rate. So, for the most part, we have tried to confine our list to establishments with a proven track record over a fairly long period of time. The exceptions here are the newer offspring of the demigods of the culinary world—these places are destined to last, at least until our next update. Also, the list is highly selective; there are so many restaurants in this sprawling metropolis. Noninclusion of a particular place does not necessarily indicate that the restaurant is not good, only that either we did not feel it ranked among the best in its genre, or that we have not visited it enough to make a fair assessment. Detailed profiles of individual restaurants follow in alphabetical order at the end of this chapter.

London Restaurants by Cuisine

NAME/CUISINE	OVERALL RATING	PRICE	QUALITY RATING	VALUE RATING
AMERICAN				
Joe Allen	★★½	Inexp/Mod	★★½	★★½
Arkansas Café	★★	Inexp	★★★	★★★★
ASIAN				
E & O	★★★★	Mod/Exp	★★★★	★★
Wagamama	★★	Inexp	★★	★★★★
BELGIAN				
Belgo Centraal	★	Inexp/Mod	★★	★★★
BRITISH				
Fifteen	★★★★★	Exp	★★★★★	★★★★
Richard Corrigan at Lindsay House	★★★★	Mod/Exp	★★★★½	★★½
The Tea Palace	★★★½	Exp	★★★	★★
Rules	★★★	Mod/Exp	★★★	★★★
Boisdale of Belgravia	★★½	Mod	★★★	★★★
CARIBBEAN				
Cuba	★★½	Mod	★★★	★★
CHINESE				
Yautcha	★★★★½	Exp	★★★★½	★★★
Mr. Kong	★★★½	Inexp/Mod	★★★½	★★★★
Royal China	★★★	Inexp	★★★	★★★★
Chinese Experience	★★★	Inexp	★★★	★★★
FRENCH				
Le Gavroche	★★★★½	Exp	★★★★½	★★★
Nathalie's	★★★★	Mod	★★★★	★★★★★
Angela Hartnett at the Connaught	★★★★	Exp	★★★★	★★★
Brasserie St. Quentin	★★★★	Mod/Exp	★★★½	★★★★
Crêperie d'Hampstead	★★★	Inexp/Mod	★★★	★★★
Chez Gérard at the Opera Terrace	★★	Inexp/Mod	★★★	★★★
Aubaine	★★	Mod	★★★	★

NAME/CUISINE	OVERALL RATING	PRICE	QUALITY RATING	VALUE RATING
FUSION				
Providores and Tapa Room	★★★★	Mod/Exp	★★★★½	★★★★
INDIAN				
Café Spice Namaste	★★★★	Mod	★★★★	★★★★
Rasa	★★★½	Mod	★★★½	★★★★
Tamarind	★★★½	Mod	★★★½	★★★
La Porte des Indes	★★★½	Exp	★★★	★★★
Veeraswamy	★★★	Mod	★★★	★★★½
Masala Zone	★★	Inexp/Mod	★★★½	★★★★
ITALIAN				
The River Café	★★★★½	Exp	★★★★	★
Orsini's Café	★★★½	Mod	★★★★	★★★
Strada	★★★½	Inexp	★★★½	★★★★½
Café Carluccio's	★★★	Mod	★★★	★★★★
JAPANESE				
Nobu	★★★★	Exp	★★★★	★★
Matsuri	★★★½	Mod/Exp	★★★½	★★
MODERN EUROPEAN				
Orrery	★★★★½	Exp	★★★★½	★★★
Clarke's	★★★★	Exp	★★★★	★★★
The Ivy	★★★★	Mod	★★★★	★★★
The Wolseley	★★★★	Mod/Exp	★★★★	★★★
Bibendum	★★★★	Exp	★★★★	★★
Blueprint Café	★★★	Mod	★★★★½	★★★
Dan's	★★★	Exp	★★★★	★★★
Bank Aldwych	★★★	Mod	★★★½	★★★
Le Caprice	★★★	Mod	★★★½	★★★
Cantina Vinopolis	★★½	Mod	★★½	★★★★
Mash	★★	Inexp/Mod	★★★½	★★★
Corney and Barrow	★★	Mod	★★★	★★★
PIZZA				
Pizza Express	★	Inexp	★★	★★★★

London Restaurants by Cuisine (continued)

POLISH				
Baltic	★★½	Mod	★★★	★★★
SANDWICHES				
Café Primo	★★★★	Inexp	★★★★	★★★★★
Pret à Manger	★	Inexp	★★	★★★★
SEAFOOD				
fish!	★★	Inexp/Mod	★★½	★★★½
North Sea Fish Restaurant	★½	Inexp	★★½	★★★★★
SPANISH				
Moro	★★★★	Mod	★★★★	★★★★
Cambio de Tercio	★★★	Mod	★★★	★★★
TEX MEX				
Navajo Joe's	★★½	Mod	★★★	★★★
Texas Embassy Cantina	★★½	Mod	★★★	★★★
VEGETARIAN				
Food for Thought	★★★½	Inexp	★★★★	★★★★★
World Food Café	★★★	Inexp	★★★	★★★★

London Restaurants by Neighborhood

WEST END
Angela Hartnett at the Connaught
Belgo Centraal
Chez Gérard at the Opera Terrace
Chinese Experience
fish!
The Ivy
Joe Allen
Le Caprice
Le Gavroche
Masala Zone
Mash
Mr. Kong
Nobu
North Sea Fish Restaurant
Rasa
Richard Corrigan at Lindsay House
Rules
Strada
Tamarind
Veeraswamy
Wagamama

THE CITY AND SOUTH THAMES
Arkansas Café
Baltic
Bank Aldwych
Blueprint Café
Café Spice Namaste
Cantina Vinopolis
Corney and Barrow

**THE CITY AND SOUTH THAMES
(CONTINUED)**
Moro
Pret à Manger

WESTMINSTER AND VICTORIA
Boisdale of Belgravia
Le Caprice
Matsuri

**KNIGHTSBRIDGE TO
SOUTH KENSINGTON**
Aubaine
Bibendum
Boisdale of Belgravia
Brasserie St. Quentin

Café Primo
Cambio de Tercio
Dan's
Orsini's Café
Nathalie's

**MARYLEBONE TO
NOTTING HILL GATE**
Caffé Carluccio's
Clarke's
Orrery
Pied à Terre
Providores and Tapa Room
Royal China

NORTH LONDON
Pizza Express

MORE RECOMMENDATIONS
Chinese

- **Fung Shing** (15 Lisle Street, West End, WC2;
  ☎ 0207-437-1539; tube: Piccadilly)
  Features cooking similar in ambition to Mr. Kong (see page 337) and is
  capable of producing memorable dishes.
- **Good Earth** (233 Brompton Road, Knightsbridge, SW3;
  ☎ 0207-584-3658; tube: South Kensington or Knightsbridge)
  Located in expensive Knightsbridge, and the prices and the ambience
  are upscale, but the food is quite good, as is the service.
- **Harbour City** (46 Gerrard Street, West End, WC2;
  ☎ 0207-439-7120; tube: Piccadilly)
  Serves superb dim sum and is good in the evenings as well. This place
  is very popular with the local Chinese community.
- **Hunan** (51 Pimlico Road, Pimlico, SW1;
  ☎ 0207-730-5712; tube: Sloane Square)
  One of London's few Hunan specialists; essential for devotees of that
  spicy cuisine.

Indian

- **Benares** (12 Berkeley Square, Mayfair, W1;
  ☎ 0207-629-8886; tube: Green Park)
  The creation of Atul Kochhar, formerly of Tamarind (see page 349)
  and universally regarded as one of London's greatest Indian chefs;
  swanky setting and location that serves staggeringly good food.

- **Star of India** (South Kensington, SW5; ☎ 0207-351-3594;
tube: Gloucester Road)
Though unpredictable, when on form the food is wonderful and the
ambience is kind of shabby-elegant.
- **Shezan** (Knightsbridge, SW7; ☎ 0207-584-9316;
tube: Knightsbridge)
A bit pricey, but it serves only halal meat and has a traditional menu
based on its 40 years in business—none of those new-fangled "modern
Indian" dishes. Good mulligatawny soup and curries.

Fish, and Fish and Chips

- **Back to Basics** (21A Foley Street, West End, W1;
☎ 0207-436-2181; tube: Goodge Street)
A small, buzzy place that has been packing in locals for sensationally
good, and sometimes very innovative, fish cooking; very reasonable
prices, too.
- **Geales** (2 Farmer Street, Notting Hill, W8;
☎ 0207-727-7969; tube: Notting Hill)
Long established and consistently good. This popular spot in fashionable Notting Hill is almost always crowded.
- **Poissonerie de l'avenue** (82 Sloane Avenue, South Kensington, SW3;
☎ 0207-589-2457; tube: South Kensington)
A lovely restaurant specializing in fish (there is a fish market next
door) done in modern English and French style. Very elegant.

French

- **Mon Plaisir** (21 Monmouth Street, West End, WC2;
☎ 0207-836-7243; tube: Covent Garden)
Ranks among London's longest-established French restaurants. This is
simple bistro fare, centering on steak and frites (French fries); decent
prices and generally very sound quality.
- **Racine** (239 Brompton Road, South Kensington, SW3;
☎ 0207-584-4477; tube: Knightsbridge)
A lovely place serving bistro food of the highest quality, and at reasonably fair prices. The chef is Henry Harris, who formerly worked at
Bibendum (see page 316).
- **1 Lombard Street** (1 Lombard Street, The City, EC3;
☎ 0207-929-6611; tube: Bank)
A big brasserie and a smaller, pricier dining room in a building that
began life as a bank; the cooking can be sensational, and the location
is good if you're exploring the City (London's financial district).
- **Gordon Ramsay** (68–69 Royal Hospital Road, Chelsea, SW3;
☎ 0207-352-4441; tube: Sloane Square)
Boasts three Michelin stars, an extraordinarily talented—and now very
famous—chef, and a small space that means tables are hard to come
by. You have to reserve tables a month in advance. But it's probably

the best restaurant in London, so if the dizzying prices (outside the set lunch) don't scare you, it's worth a last-minute call to see if they've had a cancellation.

- **The Square** (6–10 Bruton Street, Mayfair, W1;
  ☎ 0207-495-7100; tube: Green Park or Bond Street)
  Some people consider the modern European cooking here among the best in London, and their views are legitimate. Only the pricey wine list and occasional wobbles of service excluded it from the main entries, but it should be a top choice for a special, expensive meal.

Gastro-pubs and Wine Bars

- **Cork & Bottle Wine Bar** (44–46 Cranbourn Street, West End, WC2;
  ☎ 0207-734-7807; tube: Leicester Square)
  The food is nothing special, but the wine list is amazing, and the Leicester Square location is as central as you can get. This is why the cramped basement rooms are always packed. It's good for a light bite and a drink before or after a movie or play.

- **The Cow** (89 Westbourne Park Road, Notting Hill, W11;
  ☎ 0207-221-0021; tube: Ladbroke Grove)
  Prices are not especially low, but quality is especially high at this popular place near Notting Hill.

- **The Eagle** (159 Farringdon Road, The City, EC1;
  ☎ 0207-837-1353; tube: Farringdon)
  The first of the gastro-pubs and still one of the best, though its immense popularity means space is hard to come by; if you're nearby, pop in for classy Italian/French cooking.

- **The Havelock Tavern** (57 Masbro Road, Shepherds Bush, W14;
  ☎ 0207-603-5374; tube: Shepherds Bush)
  A popular local pub in a nice residential area; it has great atmosphere and great food.

Greek

- **Café Corfu** (7–9 Pratt Street, Camden Town, NW1;
  ☎ 0207-267-8088; tube: Camden Town)
  London was once famous for its Greek restaurants, but most are a shadow of their former glory. This is one of the exceptions, featuring innovative cooking in a trendy setting.

- **Halepi Restaurant** (18 Leinster Terrace, Bayswater, W2;
  ☎ 0207-262-1070; tube: Bayswater or Queensway)
  This is a down-home kind of a family place, with excellent Greek dishes and a few Middle Eastern touches, such as the incomparable baklava, possibly the best in London.

Italian and Pizza

- **Condotti** (4 Mill Street, Mayfair, W1; ☎ 0207-499-1308; tube: Green Park)
  In an expensive area, this is a cheap source of good pizza in an attractive

space; the proprietor was one of the founders of Pizza Express (see page 343).

- **Locanda Locatelli** (8 Seymour Street, Marylebone, Wl; ☎ 0207-935-9088; tube: Marble Arch)
  One of London's very best Italian restaurants. Fairly pricey, and incredibly difficult to get a table, but it's worth a try if you want spectacular cooking in attractive surroundings.

- **Riva** (169 Church Road, Barnes, SW13; ☎ 0208-748-0434; tube: Hammersmith)
  Way, way out in quasisuburban Barnes, but if you really love the finest Italian food and feel like a walk around one of London's loveliest neighborhoods, consider it a top destination.

Japanese

- **Kulu Kulu** (76 Brewer Street, Soho, W1; ☎ 0207-734-7316; tube: Regent's Park)
  The first and best of London's kaiten sushi restaurants—where dishes are circulated on a conveyor belt and you pick what you want as it goes around. Some of the best sushi in town, and cheap, too.

- **Misato** (11 Wardour Street, West End, W1; ☎ 0207-734-0808; tube: Piccadilly)
  A small, simple place in Chinatown for a quick meal; don't expect anything astounding, but quality is good and prices are low.

- **Itsu** (103 Wardour Street, West End, W1; ☎ 0207-479-4790; tube: Piccadilly)
  Another kaiten sushi restaurant, this one with a European spin on the sushi dishes; trendy, attractive, and very popular with local office workers. There's also one in South Kensington at the corner of Draycott and Walton Streets.

Middle Eastern and Turkish

- **Al Hamra** (31–33 Shepherd Market, Mayfair, W1; ☎ 0207-493-1954; tube: Green Park)
  Popular with tourists and locals alike. This Middle Eastern restaurant specializes in meze (assorted small dishes); it sometimes disappoints, but when it's good, it's very good. And the neighborhood is charming.

- **Fakhredine** (85 Piccadilly, Mayfair, W1; ☎ 0207-493-3424; tube: Green Park)
  Has the great advantage of a beautiful view over Green Park, and a 2003 renovation gave it a much-needed face-lift. Great mezza and Sunday brunch.

- **Patogh** (8 Crawford Place, Marylebone, W1; ☎ 0207-262-4015; tube: Marble Arch or Edgeware Road)
  Simple in decor but with exceptionally fine cooking, Patogh is one of the better Middle Eastern restaurants in an area that's crowded with them. There's no license to serve alcohol, but you can bring your own.

- **Ranoush Juice Bar** (43 Edgware Road, Bayswater, W2;
  ☎ 0207-723-5929; tube: Edgware Road)
  This is London's first juice bar and still a source of excellent sandwiches, kebabs, and desserts, as well as a lovely range of delicious fruity drinks; great budget food.

Thai

- **Nahm** (The Halkin Hotel, Halkin Street, Belgravia, SW1;
  ☎ 0207-333-1234; tube: Hyde Park Corner)
  Easily London's best Thai restaurant—and its most expensive by a long shot. Lunch is the affordable time to go; dinner is only for people who really love Thai cooking and are willing to pay around £50 a head before drinks.
- **Patara** (181 Fulham Road, South Kensington, SW3;
  ☎ 0207-351-5692; tube: South Kensington)
  Located on the increasingly swanky stretch of Fulham Road at Sydney Street, this Thai restaurant is a solid choice. Good service, fine food, and not so hard on the wallet.
- **Sri Siam** (16 Old Compton Street, Soho, W1;
  ☎ 0207-434-3544; tube: Piccadilly)
  This old warhorse is very central, very popular, and still capable of doing good things when everything's working well; the £7.95 "lunch box" is a bargain.

▌ RESTAURANT PROFILES

Angela Hartnett at the Connaught ★ ★ ★ ★

FRENCH AND ITALIAN (HAUTE CUISINE) EXPENSIVE   QUALITY ★ ★ ★ ★   VALUE ★ ★ ★

**Carlos Place, Mayfair, W1; ☎ 0207-592-1222;
www.the-connaught.co.uk; tube: Green Park**

Customers Hotel guests, tourists, and locals. **Reservations** Essential. **When to go** Lunch or dinner. **Entree range** Lunch menu £30–£55 for 3 courses, dinner menu £55–£70 for 3 courses (Menu and the Grill). **Payment** AE, CB, D, DC, MC, V. **Service rating** ★ ★ ★ ★. **Friendliness rating** ★ ★ ★½. **Bar** Yes. **Wine selection** Excellent. **Dress** Smart casual. **Disabled access** Limited. **Hours** Monday–Friday, noon–3 p.m. and 5:45–11 p.m.; Saturday, noon–3:30 p.m. and 5:45–11 p.m.; Sunday, noon–3:30 p.m. and 6–10:30 p.m.

SETTING AND ATMOSPHERE Grand, old-fashioned room with modern touches in lighting, decoration, and furniture; formal but not intimidating, with a nonsmoking policy in the dining room.

HOUSE SPECIALTIES Duck breast with caramelized onions.

OTHER RECOMMENDATIONS Roasted tomato soup; roast lamb.

SUMMARY AND COMMENTS The old Grill Room at the Connaught was a bastion of men's-club civility and upper-class tradition: the old menu even had a special symbol for dishes created by long-serving chef Michel Bourdin for

"the city" dining and nightlife

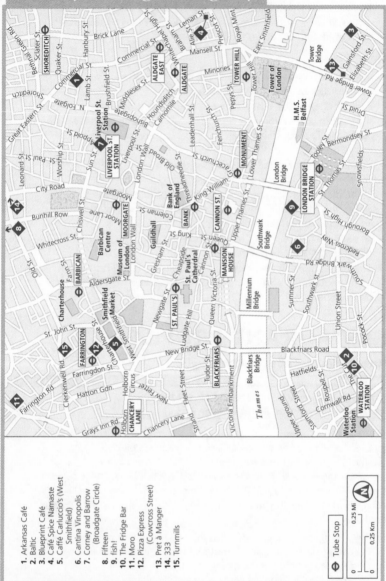

1. Arkansas Café
2. Baltic
3. Blueprint Café
4. Café Spice Namaste
5. Caffé Carluccio's (West Smithfield)
6. Cantina Vinopolis
7. Corney and Barrow (Broadgate Circle)
8. Fifteen
9. fish!
10. The Fridge Bar
11. Moro
12. Pizza Express (Cowcross Street)
13. Pret à Manger
14. 333
15. Turnmills

Tube Stop

0   0.25 Mi
0   0.25 Km

the Queen's Silver Jubilee in 1977. In 2003, when it was announced that the venerable restaurants at the Connaught hotel were being closed down and taken over by Gordon Ramsay, there were anguished wails of horror from all over London. Ramsay announced his intention of discarding the old restaurant, putting in charge one of his best protegées, Angela Hartnett, and switching to an Italian-oriented menu, with a decided French twist. The results have been mixed, with the old guard dubious about the new restaurant, but with acclaim from other circles, including the Michelin Guide, which awarded it one star. You will find very fine cooking, good service, and a much livelier atmosphere, it has to be admitted, than the old regime. There are two principal restaurants, Menu and the Grill, that serve the same food. Menu features the old mahogany panels, and the Grill, decorated by Nina Campbell, is more understated. The old place was one of a kind not just in London but in the world. Its successor is not unique, but it is very good—if expensive, as you would expect in these surroundings.

Arkansas Café ★ ★

AMERICAN	INEXPENSIVE	QUALITY ★ ★ ★	VALUE ★ ★ ★ ★

**Spitalfields Market, East End, E1; ☎ 0207-377-6999;
tube: Liverpool Street**

Customers Locals and American business community. **Reservations** Not necessary. **When to go** Lunch. **Entree range** £3.50–£14.50. **Payment** MC, V. **Service rating** ★ ★ ★. **Friendliness rating** ★ ★ ★ ★½. **Bar** Yes. **Wine selection** Minimal but inexpensive. **Dress** Shirt and shoes mandatory. **Disabled access** Main dining room only. **Hours** Monday–Friday, noon–2:30 p.m.; Sunday, noon–4 p.m.

SETTING AND ATMOSPHERE Roadhouse barbecue joint.

HOUSE SPECIALTIES Barbecued ribs, brisket, sliced pork, chicken, burgers.

ENTERTAINMENT AND AMENITIES Two-man rockabilly band, on occasion.

SUMMARY AND COMMENTS If you are suffering withdrawal symptoms for top-quality American barbecue, come to the Arkansas. The proprietor is a prizewinning barbecue chef from Maryland, and his specially imported pit barbecues turn out the best ribs in town. You get the meat cooked right in front of you, and the smells and sizzles will transport you to a Fourth of July small-town, down-home cookout. The success of this small venue has encouraged other barbecue joints to give London a taste of the colonies, but Arkansas got here first, and has a devoted clientele. The totally laid-back atmosphere will make you feel at home, and your kids will find this a welcoming place where they can be themselves. Vegetarians won't have much fun; everyone else will have loads of it.

Aubaine ★ ★

FRENCH (BISTRO)	MODERATE	QUALITY ★ ★ ★	VALUE ★

**260–262 Brompton Road, South Kensington, SW7; ☎ 0207-052-0100;
www.aubaine.co.uk; tube: South Kensington**

west end dining

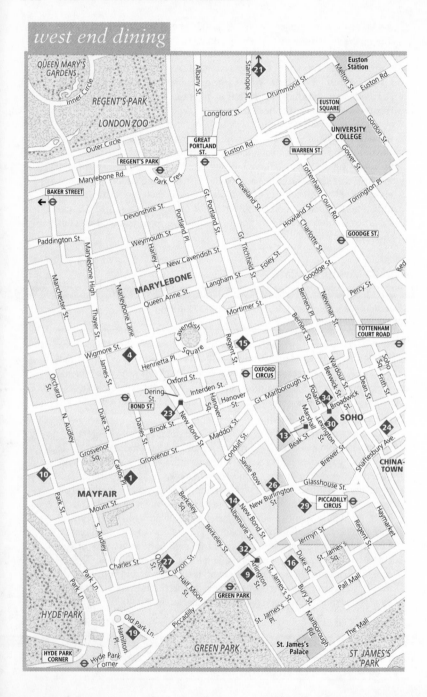

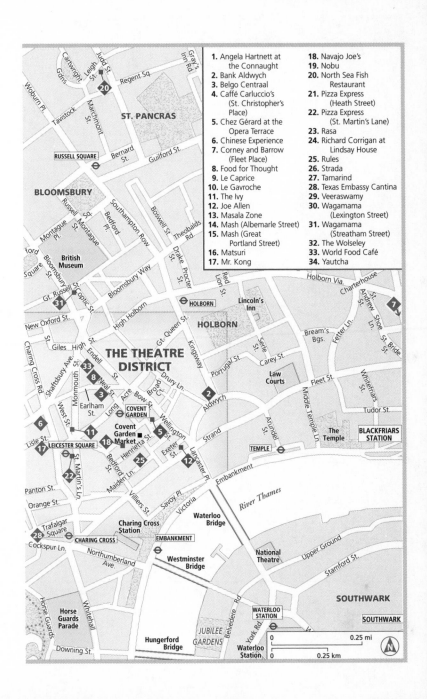

1. Angela Hartnett at the Connaught
2. Bank Aldwych
3. Belgo Centraal
4. Caffé Carluccio's (St. Christopher's Place)
5. Chez Gérard at the Opera Terrace
6. Chinese Experience
7. Corney and Barrow (Fleet Place)
8. Food for Thought
9. Le Caprice
10. Le Gavroche
11. The Ivy
12. Joe Allen
13. Masala Zone
14. Mash (Albemarle Street)
15. Mash (Great Portland Street)
16. Matsuri
17. Mr. Kong
18. Navajo Joe's
19. Nobu
20. North Sea Fish Restaurant
21. Pizza Express (Heath Street)
22. Pizza Express (St. Martin's Lane)
23. Rasa
24. Richard Corrigan at Lindsay House
25. Rules
26. Strada
27. Tamarind
28. Texas Embassy Cantina
29. Veeraswamy
30. Wagamama (Lexington Street)
31. Wagamama (Streatham Street)
32. The Wolseley
33. World Food Café
34. Yautcha

knightsbridge to south kensington

1. Aubaine
2. Bibendum
3. Brasserie St. Quentin
4. Caffé Carluccio's
   (Old Brompton Road)
5. Cambio de Tercio
6. Chutney Mary

7. Crêperie d'Hampstead
8. Cuba
9. Dan's
10. Embargo
11. Nathalie's
12. Orsini's Café
13. Pizza Express (Kings Road)

14. The River Café
15. 606 Club

dining and nightlife

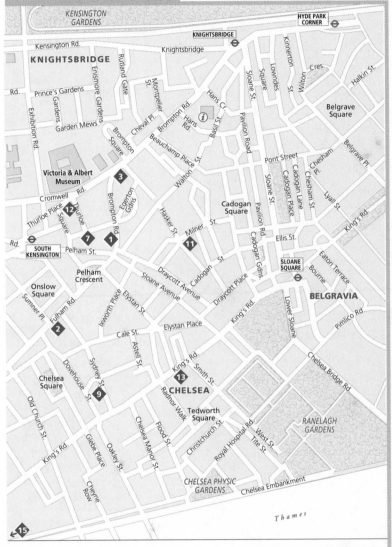

KENSINGTON GARDENS

HYDE PARK CORNER

KNIGHTSBRIDGE

Kensington Rd.

Knightsbridge

KNIGHTSBRIDGE

Kinnerton St.

Lowndes Square

Sloane St.

Wilton Cres.

Halkin St.

Prince's Gardens

Ennismore Gardens

Rutland Gate

Montpelier St.

Hans Cr.

Pavilion Road

Belgrave Square

Rd.

Exhibition Rd.

Gardens

Garden Mews

Cheval Pl.

Brompton Rd.

Hans Rd.

Basil St.

Brompton Square

Beauchamp Place

Pont Street

Chesham Pl.

Belgrave Pl.

Victoria & Albert Museum

3

Cromwell Rd.

Thurloe Place

12

Thurloe Square

Brompton Rd.

Egerton Gdns

Walton St.

Cadogan Square

Sloane St.

Cadogan St.

Chesham St.

Lyall St.

King's Rd.

Rd.

SOUTH KENSINGTON

7

1

Pelham St.

Hasker St.

Milner St.

11

Pavilion Rd.

Cadogan Gdns

Ellis St.

Eaton Terrace

Pelham Crescent

Onslow Square

Sumner Pl.

Fulham Rd.

Ixworth Place

Elystan St.

Draycott Avenue

Sloane Avenue

Cadogan St.

Draycott Place

SLOANE SQUARE

Bourne

BELGRAVIA

2

Cale St.

Astell St.

Elystan Place

King's Rd.

Lower Sloane

Pimlico Rd.

Dovehouse St.

Sydney St.

9

King's Rd.

Smith St.

13

CHELSEA

Chelsea Bridge Rd.

Chelsea Square

Old Church St.

King's Rd.

Glebe Place

Oakley St.

Chelsea Manor St.

Radnor Walk

Flood St.

Tedworth Square

Christchurch St.

Royal Hospital Rd.

West St.

Title St.

RANELAGH GARDENS

Cheyne Row

CHELSEA PHYSIC GARDENS

Chelsea Embankment

Thames

15

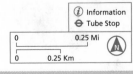

ⓘ Information

⊖ Tube Stop

| 0 | 0.25 Mi |
| 0 | 0.25 Km |

N

marylebone to notting hill gate

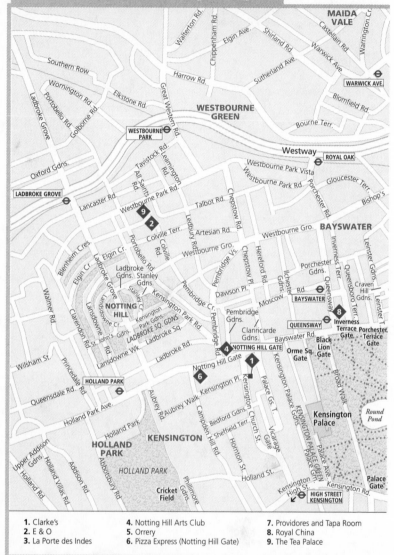

1. Clarke's
2. E & O
3. La Porte des Indes
4. Notting Hill Arts Club
5. Orrery
6. Pizza Express (Notting Hill Gate)
7. Providores and Tapa Room
8. Royal China
9. The Tea Palace

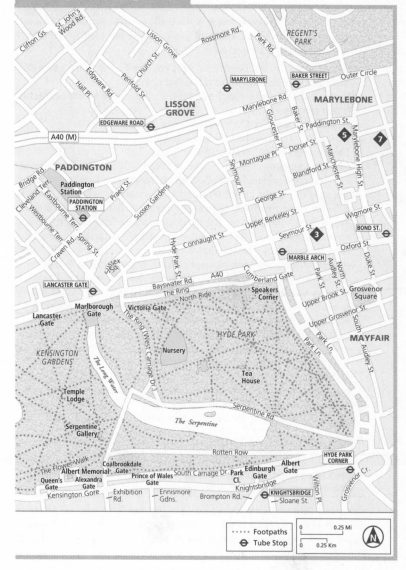

dining and nightlife

Customers Local French or Francophiles, nonsmokers, bread addicts, and ladies who lunch. **Reservations** Recommended, except for breakfast. **When to go** Breakfast, lunch, or dinner. **Entree range** £7.75–£19.50. **Payment** AE, MC, V. **Service rating** ★★★. **Friendliness rating** ★★. **Bar** No. **Wine selection** Excellent for such a small place. **Dress** Casual. **Disabled access** Yes. **Hours** Monday–Saturday, 8 a.m.–11 p.m; Sunday, 9 a.m.–10 p.m.

SETTING AND ATMOSPHERE Bright and light country French, with an on-the-ball staff; very popular at both lunch and dinner.

HOUSE SPECIALTIES Exquisite variety of French bread and patisserie; filet de boeuf tartare.

OTHER RECOMMENDATIONS Club Aubaine steak tartine.

ENTERTAINMENT AND AMENITIES Sidewalk tables in good weather, take-out bakery, and various condiments for sale.

SUMMARY AND COMMENTS Aubaine opened in early 2005, and it has been quietly gaining in popularity among the locals who were accustomed to frequenting the nearby Le Brasserie and Patisserie Valerie when they wanted a French bistro meal or croissant. The attraction has a lot to do with the superb bread, the good service, the decent range of choices, and the nonsmoking dining room (in summer you can smoke outside). Although it is hard to forgive the loss of the marvelous Italian tiled walls of the old restaurant that had been here for so long, the new decor is bright and countrified, redolent of an old-fashioned Provencal restaurant. The menu relies on time-honored French favorites such as *coquilles St Jacques* and *coq au vin.* There is a nice collection of *tartines,* open-faced sandwiches with a variety of toppings, such as smoked salmon with cucumber salad or brie with walnuts and honey. The breakfasts are excellent: eggs Benedict, granola, omelets, *croque-monsieur,* and of course, the classic continental breakfast of breads and jam, croissant, and coffee. The prices reflect the chichi neighborhood, and one may balk at spending £9.75 for a wild mushroom and Gruyère cheese sandwich with just the one slice of bread, but it appears that a lot of people are willing to spend that extra pence (£16.25 for the boeuf tartare) to eat raw steak in England.

Baltic   ★ ★ ½

POLISH	MODERATE	QUALITY ★★★	VALUE ★★★

74 Blackfriars Road, South London, SE1; ☎ 0207-928-1111; www.balticrestaurant.co.uk; tube: Southwark or Waterloo

Customers Diverse, mostly young locals. **Reservations** Recommended. **When to go** Lunch or dinner. **Entree range** £12.50–£15.50. **Payment** AE, DC, MC, V. **Service rating** ★★★. **Friendliness rating** ★★★★½. **Bar** Yes. **Wine selection** Small but good and very reasonable. **Dress** Casual. **Disabled access** Yes. **Hours** Monday–Friday, 12:30–2:30 p.m. and 7–11:15 p.m.; Saturday and Sunday, 7–11:15 p.m.

SETTING AND ATMOSPHERE Small rooms and plain decor; popular at both lunch and dinner, and very welcoming.

HOUSE SPECIALTIES Traditional Polish dishes such as blinis, dumplings, and herring; extensive vodka list.

OTHER RECOMMENDATIONS Vodka.

ENTERTAINMENT AND AMENITIES Jazz Sunday evenings, 7–11 p.m.

SUMMARY AND COMMENTS London has a long tradition of hosting emigrés from Eastern and Central Europe, who have brought with them the richness of their national cuisines. Baltic is part of that tradition, but it is not a traditional restaurant: the setting is very contemporary, and so is the food, despite paying due respect to classic Polish fare. This gives a meal at Baltic a welcome element of surprise, and it also means you can eat more lightly here than at many restaurants serving this type of cuisine, some of which seem to specialize mainly in heavy cooking oil. For many customers, however, Baltic, like its sister restaurant Wodka in Kensington, is preeminently a vodka bar: aficionados can choose from around 30, including vodkas flavored on the premises (such as vanilla or pear). There's a good wine list, however, and beers as well. For interesting, flexible eating with a different twist, Baltic is a great spot—and justly popular.

Bank Aldwych ★ ★ ★

MODERN EUROPEAN	MODERATE	QUALITY ★ ★ ★ ½	VALUE ★ ★ ★

1 Kingsway, The City, WC2; ☎ 0207-379-9797;
www.bankrestaurants.com; tube: Covent Garden or Holborn

Customers Mostly locals. **Reservations** Recommended. **When to go** Lunch or dinner. **Entree range** £9.95–£20.50. **Payment** AE, CB, D, DC, MC, V. **Service rating** ★ ★ ★ ½. **Friendliness rating** ★ ★ ★ ½. **Bar** Yes. **Wine selection** Good. **Dress** No code. **Disabled access** Yes. **Hours** Monday–Friday, 7:30–10:30 a.m., noon–3 p.m., and 5:30–11 p.m.; Saturday, 7–10:30 a.m., 11:30 a.m.–3 p.m., and 5:30–11 p.m. Restaurant is closed Sunday, but bar is open from noon–5 p.m.

SETTING AND ATMOSPHERE The big, ultramodern room is almost always packed in the evening, both at the bar and in the restaurant.

HOUSE SPECIALTIES Baltic herring, new potatoes, and Swedish mustard dressing; peppered foie gras parfait, apple and pear chutney, toasted brioche; shellfish (lobster, crab, oysters); fish and chips; pan-roasted venison; beet marmalade; and sautéed potato Lyonnaise.

OTHER RECOMMENDATIONS Pretheater set menu, breakfast, steak and chips, desserts.

SUMMARY AND COMMENTS Bank is one of London's big restaurants, occupying a huge site that was formerly a branch of one of the national banks. Despite its size, it manages to wear a human face, and its central location and extensive opening hours make it a very useful place to know about, especially if you want a good breakfast before 8 a.m. Though the chef is French, the food takes on Italian, Asian, and ultratraditional British cooking—what's more, everything is done with consistent skill. Due to its size, Bank is not necessarily a place to linger, though you can if you want to. The low-cost prix fixe menu (available at lunch and in the evening until 7 p.m.) offers two courses for just £13.50 and three for £16. The wine list offers ample choices under £20, service is friendly, and the bar would not be out of place in any big American city. If you like buzz and bustle, chances are you'll like Bank, and if you do like it, there's another branch in Westminster between St. James's Park and Buckingham Palace: 45 Buckingham Gate, SW1E; ☎ 0207-379-9797.

 Belgo Centraal ★

BELGIAN	INEXPENSIVE/MODERATE	QUALITY ★★	VALUE ★★★

50 Earlham Street, West End, WC2; ☎ 0207-813-2233; www.belgo-restaurants.com; tube: Covent Garden

Customers Locals and tourists. **Reservations** Recommended. **When to go** Lunch or dinner. **Entree range** £8.95–£16. **Payment** AE, CB, D, DC, MC, V. **Service rating** ★★. **Friendliness rating** ★★½. **Bar** No. **Wine selection** Adequate; beers are outstanding. **Dress** Casual. **Disabled access** Yes. **Hours** Monday–Thursday, noon–11:30 p.m.; Friday and Saturday, noon–midnight; Sunday, noon–10:30 p.m.

SETTING AND ATMOSPHERE Big, high-ceilinged subterranean room with a view of the kitchen and a deliberately encouraged air of conviviality.

HOUSE SPECIALTIES Croquettes de fromage; salade Liègoise; chateaubriand for two; Belgian braised meats; mussels in all guises; Belgian crêpes and waffles.

OTHER RECOMMENDATIONS The beer list.

SUMMARY AND COMMENTS Belgo is a success story with a simple formula: sell Belgian food and drink at low prices—with a helpful array of special offers to keep them even lower—and get the waiters to dress in monks' robes. Not everyone's a fan, and the food (especially more complicated dishes) can be of variable quality. But the simpler mussel dishes are usually just fine. What's more, you can wash them down with a truly stunning array of the great beers of Belgium, one of the world's great beer producers. Belgo is not the great bargain it once was, and the novelty value has long since worn off; moreover, the business has had its ups and downs. But with a lunchtime deal of £5.95, Belgo Centraal (and its other branch, Belgo Noord; 72 Chalk Farm Road, NW1; ☎ 0207-267-0718) continues to offer reasonable food at fairly reasonable prices.

 Bibendum ★★★★

MODERN	EXPENSIVE	QUALITY ★★★★	VALUE ★★

Michelin House, 81 Fulham Road, South Kensington, SW3; ☎ 0207-581-5817; www.bibendum.co.uk; tube: South Kensington

Customers Locals, tourists, and gastronomes. **Reservations** Recommended. **When to go** Lunch for the cheapest option; dinner for that special occasion. **Entree range** Lunch £28.50 for 3-course set lunch; dinner main entrees £16.50–£27.50. **Payment** AE, D, DC, MC, V. **Service rating** ★★★★. **Friendliness rating** ★★★★. **Bar** No. **Wine selection** Excellent but expensive. **Dress** Smart casual. **Disabled access** Yes. **Hours** Monday–Friday, noon–2:30 p.m. and 7–11:30 p.m.; Saturday, 12:30–3 p.m. and 7–11:30 p.m.; Sunday, 12:30–3 p.m. and 7–10:30 p.m.

SETTING AND ATMOSPHERE A large, wonderfully high-ceilinged art deco room in what was formerly the headquarters of the Michelin Tire Company. The decor is simple and contemporary, but the setting is dominated by huge stained-glass windows, which let in a shower of light by day and offer a fine view. (Check out the *belle époque* painted tiles on the east side of the building.)

HOUSE SPECIALTIES Escargots de Bourgogne; sauté foie gras with Armanac jelly; lobster and fennel salad; roast quail; grilled calves liver; fish and chips; grilled wild salmon with artichoke puree; warm salad of calves brains with cucumber; sauté foie gras; poulet de Bresse à l'estragon.

OTHER RECOMMENDATIONS Set lunch (£28.50 for three courses), French and Italian desserts.

SUMMARY AND COMMENTS Bibendum was the first restaurant in Sir Terence Conran's soon-to-be empire, and it remains one of the best exponents of modern cooking in London. You can come here for lunch or dinner knowing that you'll get superbly cooked food from ingredients of the highest quality, served with consummate professionalism that still manages to be friendly. As you can see from the dishes listed above, the orientation is French and classic, but Asian influences appear as well, as does solid Britishness (the fish and chips are probably the best in London, and are the least expensive main course on the menu). This is what has brought London food fanatics back to Bibendum for years. There are sometimes complaints about service, though not enough to keep the place from being enduringly popular. The real complaint: cost. They're not ripping anyone off with the food prices (attention to detail is expensive, especially when success depends heavily on top-quality ingredients), but wine is marked up without mercy, making an evening meal here a very costly exercise. Is it worth it? Yes, for a rare and very special treat in exquisite surroundings—or for the much more affordable set lunch. There is also a small oyster bar and a separate café (both downstairs) where you can eat quickly and lightly without doing violent damage to your budget.

 Blueprint Café ★ ★ ★

MODERN EUROPEAN	MODERATE	QUALITY ★★★★½	VALUE ★★★

Design Museum, 28 Shad Thames, South London, SE1; ☎ 0207-378-7031; www.blueprintcafé.co.uk; tube: London Bridge or Tower Bridge

Customers Mostly locals. **Reservations** Recommended. **When to go** Lunch or dinner. **Entree range** £12.50–£19.50; set lunch: 2 courses £19.50, 3 courses £29.50. **Payment** AE, D, DC, JCB, MC, V. **Service rating** ★★★. **Friendliness rating** ★★★★. **Bar** Yes. **Wine selection** Very good. **Dress** Informal. **Disabled access** Yes. **Hours** Monday–Saturday, noon–3 p.m. and 6–11 p.m.; Sunday, noon–3 p.m.

SETTING AND ATMOSPHERE This attractive, modern room with big windows overlooking the Thames hosts a trendy clientele.

HOUSE SPECIALTIES Polenta, grilled bream, razor clams with a parsley crust.

OTHER RECOMMENDATIONS Pork with fennel.

SUMMARY AND COMMENTS The Blueprint is one of many restaurants in the Shad Thames area, and one of several in the empire of Sir Terence Conran (see Bibendum, page 316). It is also one of several with a sweeping view of the Thames, and for this reason alone it is worth a visit. The food is more or less consistently good, year after year: modern in style and with heavy emphasis on the Mediterranean, especially Italy. The seasons and the market are king here, so the menu changes twice daily to reflect what's available. Fish, pasta, and home-curing are strong points. The wine list is not huge but is carefully chosen and easily accommodates diners on a budget. In warm weather, beg for a table on the terrace.

Boisdale of Belgravia ★ ★ ½

BRITISH	MODERATE	QUALITY ★★★	VALUE ★★★

15 Eccleston Street, Belgravia, SW1; ☎ 0207-730-6922; www.boisdale.co.uk; tube: Victoria

Customers Tourists and usually affluent locals. **Reservations** Recommended. **When to go** Lunch or dinner. **Entree range** £13.50–£25. **Payment** AE, CB, D, DC, MC, V. **Service rating** ★★★½. **Friendliness rating** ★★★½. **Bar** Yes. **Wine selection** Good. **Dress** Smart casual. **Disabled access** No. **Hours** Monday–Saturday, noon–2:30 p.m. and 7–midnight.

SETTING AND ATMOSPHERE Dark wood and red paneling, clublike ambience, garden at rear open in warm weather.

HOUSE SPECIALTIES Anything with a Scottish element, such as smoked salmon, smoked grouse, venison, Highland lamb, Aberdeen Angus beef.

OTHER RECOMMENDATIONS Set menus.

ENTERTAINMENT AND AMENITIES Late jazz bar, live music.

SUMMARY AND COMMENTS Boisdale has established itself as London's most serious champion of the food and drink of Scotland. The emphasis is on getting great ingredients, whether raw or cured, and presenting them to their best advantage. You can go for the simplicity of an Aberdeen Angus steak (with sizes ranging from small to gargantuan), grilled and served with béarnaise or Bloody Mary sauce, or venture into more modern territory if you're feeling adventurous. The kitchen does well with both approaches, and the cozy atmosphere makes a warmly attractive setting. If you're game enough to try haggis, one of Scotland's national dishes, this is probably the place to do it. Whiskey lovers should note that Boisdale's Back Bar, open throughout the day, has London's largest selection of single-malt scotch; the selection of cigars is also notable.

Brasserie St. Quentin ★ ★ ★ ★

FRENCH MODERATE/EXPENSIVE	QUALITY ★★★½	VALUE ★★★★

243 Brompton Road, South Kensington, SW3; ☎ 0207-589-8005; www.brasseriestquentin.co.uk; tube: South Kensington or Knightsbridge

Customers Locals, businesspeople, gastronomes, old conservatives. **Reservations** Yes for dinner, not for lunch. **When to go** Anytime, but set lunch is a good deal. **Entree range £11.50–£20.50. **Payment** AE, MC, V. **Service rating** ★★★★. **Friendliness rating** ★★★★½. **Bar** Yes, but just for waiting for tables. **Wine selection** Excellent. **Dress** Casual. **Disabled access** Yes. **Hours** Daily, noon–2:30 p.m.; 6:30–10 p.m.

SETTING AND ATMOSPHERE A very Parisian interior, with red leather banquettes lining the room, and smoked glass mirrors; it's a quiet sort of place with unpretentious classiness.

HOUSE SPECIALTIES Escalope of Cranborne pork with Parmesan crust and a fried egg; roast Lough Neagh eel with horseradish cream and lambs lettuce; sautéed scallops with pancetta, green beans and sesame dressing; Morecambe Bay shrimps, salt marsh lamb from Holker in Cumbria.

OTHER RECOMMENDATIONS Hot chocolate fondant with burnt orange ice cream; Raspberry brulee; Mille feuille of fruits with citrus sabayon; set menus (or *table d'hote,* as they call it).

ENTERTAINMENT AND AMENITIES Private room downstairs; full range of wines and liqueurs.

SUMMARY AND COMMENTS The St. Quentin celebrated its 25th anniversary in 2005, and after a certain lull in the early 1990s, its back on form and always a pleasure. Sold to the Savoy group in 1989 (which is when it went downhill) it was repurchased by Lord Rathcavan and friends in 2002. The Marquess of Salisbury is one of the shareholders, whose estates in Dorset supply St. Quentin with traditional breed pork products, roe deer, and other game. The cooking is of a high caliber, and it always puzzles me why so many people flock to the other French restaurant next door, rather than head straight for this, superior in many ways, brasserie. They have lunch set menus that are a great deal: £15.50 for 2 courses, £17.50 for 3 courses. My favorite St. Quentin story is that once, when Mrs. Thatcher had dinner there a few years back, the other diners rose to their feet in silent homage as she was leaving. It's that kind of place.

kids Café Primo ★★★★

SANDWICH/BREAKFAST	INEXPENSIVE	QUALITY ★★★★	VALUE ★★★★★

10–12 Old Brompton Road, South Kensington, SW7; ☎ 0207-589-3555; tube: South Kensington

Customers French locals, businesspeople, tourists, and students. **Reservations** No. **When to go** Anytime. **Entree range** £1.80 for egg salad sandwich to pasta specials for £4.20. **Payment** AE, V. **Service rating** ★★★★. **Friendliness rating** ★★★★★. **Bar** None. **Wine selection** None. **Dress** Casual. **Disabled access** Steps outside and to toilets. **Hours** Daily, 7 a.m.–11 p.m.

SETTING AND ATMOSPHERE Bright wall of windows looks out at Kensington and the flower stall across the street. Chairs are uncommonly comfortable, and the atmosphere is relaxed—you can linger for hours, as I do.

HOUSE SPECIALTIES Sandwiches and breakfast.

OTHER RECOMMENDATIONS Spanish omlette, pastries, cappucino.

SUMMARY AND COMMENTS When you're good and tired of spending a forune on breakfast and lunch in South Kensington, you cannot do better than to drop in at the new Café Primo in the center of town. Opened in 2005 by retired businessman Walid Khatib, it is managed beautifully by his daughter Reem. Both are longtime expats from Toronto. The cafe mixes the best of North American diner integrity with a touch of European and Middle Eastern taste (try the labneh yogurt sandwich on pita bread). Prices are exquisitely inexpensive, the service is friendly and efficient, and the food is unfussy and fresh. The cafe is a retirement project whose guiding ethos is to provide good-quality food in a bright and pleasant environment at excellent prices. It's great!

Café Spice Namaste ★ ★ ★ ★

INDIAN	MODERATE	QUALITY ★ ★ ★ ★	VALUE ★ ★ ★ ★

**16 Prescott Street, The City, E1; ☎ 0207-488-9242;
www.cafespice.co.uk; tube: Tower Hill or Tower Gateway**

Customers Mostly locals, especially businesspeople and aficionados. **Reservations** Recommended. **When to go** Lunch or dinner. **Entree range** £8.25–£18 **Payment** AE, CB, D, DC, JCB, MC, V. **Service rating** ★ ★ ★. **Friendliness rating** ★ ★ ★ ★. **Bar** Yes. **Wine selection** Good. **Dress** Casual. **Disabled access** Yes. **Hours** Monday–Friday, noon–3 p.m. and 6:30–10:30 p.m.; Saturday, 6:30–10:30 p.m.

SETTING AND ATMOSPHERE A nicely redecorated, high-ceilinged room in a 19th-century building.

HOUSE SPECIALTIES Unusual curries from various Indian regions; tandoori dishes; breads; vegetarian dishes.

OTHER RECOMMENDATIONS Weekly changing specialty menus.

SUMMARY AND COMMENTS Since 1995, chef Cyrus Todiwala (known as the "Svengali of Spice") has made Café Spice Namaste one of London's best places to find really serious Indian food. Indeed, he is one of the prime "modernizers" of this favorite British cuisine, raising standards in every aspect over the nondescript "curry houses" of the bad old days. The dishes on the regular menu cover nearly every area of the Indian subcontinent and are distinguished for their subtle, complex spicing and relative rarity on British menus. There is a weekly specialty menu as well, featuring a particular region, and the wine list is notable for its serious attention to matching every style of food on the menu. There are only two minor negative points to bear in mind. One is the out-of-the-way location. The other is an occasional problem with rowdy (affluent) clients, given the restaurant's proximity to London's financial center. Apart from that, there's no way to recommend Café Spice Namaste too highly.

Café Carluccio's ★ ★ ★

ITALIAN	MODERATE	QUALITY ★ ★ ★	VALUE ★ ★ ★ ★

**St. Christopher's Place, Marylebone, W1; ☎ 0207-935-5927;
www.carluccios.com; tube: Bond Street.
Other of the dozen branches include: 12 West Smithfield, EC1;
☎ 0207-329-5903; tube: Farringdon; 1–7 Old Brompton Road, SW7;
☎ 0207-581-8101; tube: South Kensington**

Customers Locals. **Reservations** Recommended. **When to go** Lunch or dinner. **Entree range** £4.95–£10.95 . **Payment** AE, MC, V. **Service rating** ★★★½. **Friendliness rating** ★★★★½. **Bar** No. **Wine selection** Small and inexpensive. **Dress** Casual. **Disabled access** No. **Hours** Monday–Friday, 8 a.m.–11 p.m.; Saturday, 9 a.m.–11 p.m.; Sunday, 10 a.m.–10:30 p.m. (All Central London branches adhere approximately to this schedule.)

SETTING AND ATMOSPHERE Simply decorated deli-style rooms, bustling all hours of the day, friendly and informal.

HOUSE SPECIALTIES Breads, antipasti, pasta, salad, simple meat and fish dishes.

SUMMARY AND COMMENTS The 12 branches of this incredibly—and justly—successful chain are nearly always full to bursting. The formula works and the reason is simple and obvious: this is top-quality, mostly very simple food served in pleasant (if somewhat noisy) surroundings and with an absolute minimum of fuss. Cheerful waiting staff may want to place you at one of the long, cafeteria-style tables, and if there's nothing else available you won't mind a bit. Pasta is a particularly strong point, as you would expect, and you can eat lightly on just an antipasto such as bruschetta served with roasted or grilled vegetables (£3.95). Being open all day is another major attraction, especially because the baked goods and the coffee are of exceptional quality. There is also a deli counter where you can get takeout, as well as baked goods, ground espresso, olive oils, and anything Italian you can think of. And if you're eating in, try to leave some room for delicious desserts; a real star of the current catering scene.

Cambio de Tercio ★ ★ ★

SPANISH	MODERATE	QUALITY ★ ★ ★	VALUE ★ ★ ★

163 Old Brompton Road, South Kensington, SW5; ☎ 0207-244-8970; tube: Gloucester Road

Customers Locals. **Reservations** Recommended. **When to go** Lunch or dinner. **Entree range** Lunch £13.50–£15.50. **Payment** AE, MC, V. **Service rating** ★★★★. **Friendliness rating** ★★★★. **Bar** No. **Wine selection** Excellent, mostly Spanish. **Dress** Casual. **Disabled access** Restaurant only. **Hours** Monday–Saturday, 12:30–2:30 p.m. and 7–11:30 p.m.; Sunday, 7–11 p.m.

SETTING AND ATMOSPHERE A crowded yet cozy basement room decorated with bullfighting motifs.

HOUSE SPECIALTIES Oxtail, hake, suckling pig, tapas.

SUMMARY AND COMMENTS Cambio is one of London's best Spanish restaurants. The kitchen is equally adept at staple dishes, using the best and most authentic imported ingredients, and at reinterpreting classics with a modern slant. Lovers of tapas, the "little dishes" with which Spanish people love to begin an evening's festivities, should note that the selection and quality here are excellent—and the choice of sherries, the perfect partner for this kind of eating, is similarly broad. There have been a few personnel changes in the kitchen in recent years, but standards seem to have remained high. And though there have been loud grumbles about service from some quarters, they are neither numerous nor serious enough to keep Cambio off your list of possibilities. Dessert lovers should note that while Spain does not always excel in that department, Cambio de Tercio almost always does.

Cantina Vinopolis ★ ★ ½

MODERN EUROPEAN   MODERATE   QUALITY ★ ★ ½   VALUE ★ ★ ★ ★

1 Bank End, South London, SE1; ☎ 0207-940-8333; www.cantinavinopolis.co.uk; tube: London Bridge

Customers Mostly locals. **When to go** Lunch or dinner. **Entree range** £11.50–£16.95. **Payment** AE, DC, MC, V. **Service rating** ★★. **Friendliness rating** ★★★. **Bar** Yes. **Wine selection** Enormous. **Dress** Casual. **Disabled access** Yes. **Hours** Monday–Saturday, noon–2:45 p.m. and 6–10:15 p.m.; Sunday, noon–3:45 p.m.

SETTING AND ATMOSPHERE Plain but comfortable decor in a converted industrial space with yellow brick walls and high, vaulted ceilings.

HOUSE SPECIALTIES Calves liver with bacon and spinach, spring onion pancakes filled with mushrooms and other vegetables.

OTHER RECOMMENDATIONS Artichoke stuffed with Camembert, pine nuts, and sun-dried tomato; chicken breast with polenta and pesto.

SUMMARY AND COMMENTS Vinopolis is London's "wine museum," and this is part of it (though run by an outside company). The museum has had a hard time commercially, but its catering side is a great success. Unsurprisingly, the wine list is huge—and all are sold by the glass. That would be reason enough to come here, since the location is good for the ever-increasing attractions of the Bankside area. The food supplies the rest of the reason for coming along: it can be really excellent with good ingredients treated with care, flair, and respect. French and Italian dominate, but there are a lot of New World features as well, and the prices are exceptionally reasonable. And with all those wines by the glass, this can be one of the most reasonable high-quality meals in the area. One thing not to expect, however, is atmosphere: this is a big, bustling place with few frills.

Le Caprice ★ ★ ★

MODERN   MODERATE   QUALITY ★ ★ ★ ½   VALUE ★ ★ ★

Arlington Street, Mayfair, SW1; ☎ 0207-629-2239; www.caprice-holdings.co.uk; tube: Green Park

Customers Celebrities, affluent locals. **Reservations** Recommended. **When to go** Dinner or Sunday brunch. **Entree range** £13.50–£24.75. **Payment** AE, D, DC, MC, V. **Service rating** ★★★. **Friendliness rating** ★★★. **Bar** Yes. **Wine selection** Short but good. **Dress** No code. **Disabled access** Yes, but not to toilets. **Hours** Monday–Saturday, noon–3 p.m. and 5:30 p.m.–midnight; Sunday, noon–3:15 p.m. and 6 p.m.–midnight.

SETTING AND ATMOSPHERE Lively but low-key, modern room that is pleasant but of no great distinction.

HOUSE SPECIALTIES Nearly everything on the menu; especially simple dishes such as fish and chips, salmon cakes, gnocchi pomodoro, and eggs Benedict.

SUMMARY AND COMMENTS Le Caprice has a well-deserved reputation for serving food that reaches a high standard pretty consistently. But that is not the main reason that Londoners come here, even if it helps. Le Caprice is a supremely fashionable restaurant in a low-key, understated kind of way. It's the kind of place where no one raises an eyebrow if the next table is occupied by a princess, two movie stars, and a Nobel Prize–winning novelist—well, anyway, not in a way that you would notice. This is surely one of the reasons why the rich, fashionable, and celebrated love the place so much, just as they love its sister restaurant, The Ivy (see page 333). For us mortals, the possibility of stargazing might be a bonus. But I have paid three visits with not a star in sight and have loved the place anyway. It is comfortable and well run, and the food can be outstanding. And when it isn't outstanding, it's still very good. Dinners are buzzy, while Sunday brunch is more laid-back.

 Chez Gérard at the Opera Terrace ★★

| FRENCH (BISTRO) | INEXPENSIVE/MODERATE | QUALITY ★★★ | VALUE ★★★ |

The Market, The Piazza, West End, WC2; ☎ 0207-379-0666; www.chezgerard.com; tube: Covent Garden

Customers Locals and tourists. **Reservations** Recommended. **When to go** Lunch or dinner (restaurant); for an early pretheater dinner. **Entree range** £8.25–£15.85. Good set menu prices: £13.50 for 2 courses, £16.75 for 3. **Payment** AE, CB, D, DC, MC, V. **Service rating** ★★½. **Friendliness rating** ★★★½. **Bar** Yes. **Wine selection** Good. **Dress** Casual. **Disabled access** No. **Hours** Monday–Saturday, noon–3 p.m. and 5:30–11:30 p.m.; Sunday, noon–3:30 p.m. and 5:30–10:30 p.m.

SETTING AND ATMOSPHERE Conservatory overlooking Covent Garden market with an open-air terrace in warm weather.

HOUSE SPECIALTIES Steak, especially Châteaubriand and onglet (hanger steak), served with pommes frites.

OTHER RECOMMENDATIONS Simple bistro-style dishes such as oysters, fish soup, snails, and Bayonne ham with pickles.

SUMMARY AND COMMENTS Groupe Chez Gérard, which has ten other branches in addition to this one, has a very simple formula: French-style steak, French-style pommes frites (better known as French fries), and French-style service. They usually do it very well, though there are variations from branch to branch, and prices are kept low enough to keep most people happy even if they run into occasional problems with cooking or service. Fish eaters will always find at least one dish aimed at them, as will vegetarians, but these are the most variable options in terms of quality, and they are not—let's be frank—what Chez Gérard is about. Don't come here expecting the meal of a lifetime (although the Gatwick and Heathrow branches are your best bet for airport eating), but if you're a steak lover, this will be your home away from home.

Chinese Experience ★ ★ ★

| CHINESE | INEXPENSIVE | QUALITY ★ ★ ★ | VALUE ★ ★ ★ |

118 Shaftesbury Avenue, West End, W1; ☎ 0207-437-0377; www.chineseexperience.com; tube: Piccadilly

Customers Locals, visitors, London Chinese. **Reservations** Not necessary. **When to go** Before a play, or anytime. **Entree range** £7–£18 (average is about £9). **Payment** AE, DC, MC, V. **Service rating** ★★★★. **Friendliness rating** ★★★. **Bar** Drinks available. **Wine selection** Ordinary. **Dress** Casual. **Disabled access** Yes. **Hours** Daily, 10 a.m.–10 p.m.

SETTING AND ATMOSPHERE Simple but very attractive, none of that tired old Chinese restaurant red-lantern decor; extremely friendly and professional servers. Always filled with Chinese diners.

HOUSE SPECIALTIES Sweet and savory dim sum; vegetarian and set meals.

OTHER RECOMMENDATIONS Fried noodles with vegetables.

SUMMARY AND COMMENTS This is a new restaurant in Chinatown, and it was recommended highly by friends from Shanghai. It's got a winning formula: well-made food at affordable prices in an appealing, unfussily decorated dining room. You may end up sharing long six-person tables, but only in a big rush—there are plenty of tables for two and four. The menu is wide and various, and the dim sum is fabulous. Sweet and sour pork with guava is a nice twist to an old favorite; and bean curd mock "chicken" is a delightful vegetarian option. The crunchy fried noodles with vegetables in a light sauce are just like the ones I loved when I lived in Hong Kong and have never been able to find until I went here. They also do the wonderfully sugary toffee bananas and apples for dessert. Best of all, you can easily get filled up here for ten pounds a person.

Clarke's ★ ★ ★ ★

| MODERN EUROPEAN | EXPENSIVE | QUALITY ★ ★ ★ ★ | VALUE ★ ★ ★ |

124 Kensington Church Street, Kensington, W8; ☎ 0207-221-9225; tube: Notting Hill Gate

Customers Mostly locals. **Reservations** Essential. **When to go** Lunch or dinner. **Entree range** Lunch from £16 ; dinner set menu £49 for 4 courses. **Payment** AE, D, DC, MC, V. **Service rating** ★★★★½. **Friendliness rating** ★★★★½ **Bar** No. **Wine selection** Outstanding. **Dress** Casual. **Disabled access** Restaurant yes, toilets no. **Hours** Monday, 12:30–2 p.m.; Tuesday–Friday, 12:30–2 p.m. and 7–10 p.m.; Saturday brunch, 11 a.m.–2 p.m. At present Monday is open for lunch only. Closed Sunday.

SETTING AND ATMOSPHERE Upstairs room is tiny and intimate; downstairs is big and bustling, with a view of the kitchen.

HOUSE SPECIALTIES Menu changes daily.

SUMMARY AND COMMENTS No one in Britain understands Californian cooking better than Sally Clarke, who worked there years ago (at Chez Panisse and elsewhere) before moving back to London and opening her own place. She bases her cooking on the seasons and on what's available in the market on a given day. Thus, menus change every day (and reservations are accepted 24 hours in advance, so she knows how much to buy), with a short carte at lunchtime and fixed menus (following the example of Chez Panisse) at dinner. The cooking is strong in baking (including some of the best bread in London, which you can now buy at the bakery next door), roasting, and char-grilling. Combinations are often simple, but they never fail to impress, partly because the execution is so skilled and especially because the ingredients are as good as money can buy. The lack of choice at dinner may be somewhat irritating. Phone in advance to find out what's on the menu; however, given enough warning they will happily provide alternatives if possible. The wine list is superb and not especially high priced. Clarke's is not at all cheap, but at its price level it is one of the best restaurants in London.

Corney and Barrow ★ ★

MODERN EUROPEAN	MODERATE	QUALITY ★ ★ ★	VALUE ★ ★ ★

19 Broadgate Circle, Broadgate, EC2; ☎ 0207-628-1251; tube: Liverpool Street. 3 Fleet Place, The City, EC4; ☎ 0207-329-3141; tube: Mansion House; www.corney-barrow.co.uk

Customers Mostly locals, especially businesspeople. **Reservations** Not necessary. **When to go** Lunch or dinner. **Entree range** £7–£14.50 (lunch), £5–£12.95 (evening). **Payment** AE, CB, DC, MC, V. **Service rating** ★★½. **Friendliness rating** ★★★. **Bar** Yes. **Wine selection** Excellent. **Dress** Casual. **Disabled access** No. **Hours** Monday–Friday, 7:30 a.m.–11 p.m. Closed Saturday and Sunday.

SETTING AND ATMOSPHERE Three separate bar areas, some open-air seating under heated canopies, comfortable and lively contemporary feel.

HOUSE SPECIALTIES Bar bites are great for snacking while drinking: tempura prawns, chick tikka skewers, and Cumberland sausages. Breakfasts are good: Full-English-or-museli type menu.

OTHER RECOMMENDATIONS Over-the-top heart-stopper burger with three cheeses, bacon, and a fried egg if you want.

SUMMARY AND COMMENTS Corney and Barrow has established itself as a high-class group of wine bars, mostly now concentrated in the EC postal codes and especially popular with a young, local office-based crowd. The group is backed up by a retail and wholesale wine merchant of great distinction, so the wine list is predictably strong: plenty of choices under £20, a rarity for London, and interesting bottles from all over. But the food is taken seriously, too, and being open all day it allows you to eat and drink—whether a snack or a full meal—whenever you want. Note: each bar has its own menu, and there are 12 other branches in addition to the 2 listed above. Worth bearing in mind when you're doing the sights in the City. Also bear in mind that, as with many City restaurants, most of these joints are closed on the weekend.

Crêperie d'Hampstead (or Hampstead Crêperie) ★ ★ ★

FRENCH CREPERIE **INEXPENSIVE/MODERATE** **QUALITY ★ ★ ★** **VALUE ★ ★ ★**

2 Exhibition Road, South Kensington, SW7; ☎ 0207-589-8947; tube: South Kensington

Customers Tourists, French people, locals. **Reservations** No. **When to go** On a sunny day to sit outside, or anytime but lunch. **Entree range** £4–£10. **Payment** AE, MC, V. **Service rating** ★ ★ ★. **Friendliness rating** ★ ★ ½. **Bar** None. **Wine selection** None. **Dress** Casual. **Disabled access** Yes. **Hours** Daily, 9 a.m.–9 p.m.

SETTING AND ATMOSPHERE No-frills French crêpe joint; small dining room, a few tables outside.

HOUSE SPECIALTIES Galettes with any filling you want, sweet crêpes.

OTHER RECOMMENDATIONS Crêpe with almonds, cream, and real maple syrup. Get one to go if there is no table available.

ENTERTAINMENT AND AMENITIES Watching the chef make the crêpes; non-smoking interior.

SUMMARY AND COMMENTS From a crêpe cart outside a pub in West Hampstead, the owners of this authentically French crêperie took their rollicking success and opened a little shop in South Kensington (plus another in Fulham). The name is misleading, but we who trekked up to Hampstead just to eat their crepes on the street knew exactly who they were, and we were thrilled when they ventured south. If you've ever traveled through France, you will know the genre: menu of savory galettes, which are made with a darker flour, and white flour, sugary sweet crêpes. They also have desserts, salad, and sandwiches, but none are much to write home about. What you want from this quick-hit place is, say, a ham and cheese galette followed by any of the sweet ones: chocolate with chantilly cream (whipped cream), nuts and honey, syrup and butter, or the simple perfection of a *crêpe sucre*, with no more than fine sugar sprinkled on it. They do the wrapped-up to go crêpes, or you can sit and watch the museumgoers pass before you (it's a stone's throw from the Natural History, Science, and Victoria and Albert museums). I have seen many young picky eaters transformed into Francophiles at their first taste of one of these sweet crêpes.

 ### Cuba ★ ★ ½

CUBAN **MODERATE** **QUALITY ★ ★ ★** **VALUE ★ ★**

11–13 Kensington High Street, Kensington, W8; ☎ 0207-938-4137; www.fiestahavana.com; tube: Kensington High Street

Customers Latinos, locals, salsa lovers. **Reservations** Not necessary **When to go** Anytime; but Saturdays nights are most fun. **Entree range** £7.95–£12.95. **Payment** AE, V. **Service rating** ★ ★ ★. **Friendliness rating** ★ ★ ★ ★. **Bar** Great old bar to hang out at after you eat. **Wine selection** Nothing special. **Dress** Casual. **Disabled access** Only to bar area. **Hours** Sunday–Thursday,

5 p.m.–midnight; Friday and Saturday, noon–2 a.m.; Sunday 5 p.m.–midnight (dinner only on Sunday–Thursday).

SETTING AND ATMOSPHERE Funky wooden bar with a dining room up a few stairs, under a huge skylight; old historic photos of Fidel Castro, Che Guevara, and other Cuban subjects on wall. Atmosphere is laid-back and very cool Latin.

HOUSE SPECIALTIES Grilled rib-eye steak, topped with king prawns in garlic; roasted corn; nacho tortilla chips with all the fixings; selection of Spanish cured meats, olives, warm breads, Manchego and blue cheeses; spicy chorizo or chicken on skewers; burgers.

OTHER RECOMMENDATIONS Surprisingly interesting desserts, such as cinnamon waffles with a chocolate fudge brownie, served with vanilla ice cream; Latin cinnamon doughnut served with caramelized banana and drizzled with chocolate sauce.

ENTERTAINMENT AND AMENITIES Free salsa lessons from 7:30–9:30 p.m. on Saturdays; live music on some weekends. Happy hour at 5 p.m.

SUMMARY AND COMMENTS If you're looking for a fun, meat-eating, party-time Caribbean restaurant, Cuba is a good bet. In fact, it's more like the kind of hip ethnic restaurants you'd find in Camden Town or Soho, but a little more customer-oriented. I was very impressed by the efforts of the bartender to make a virgin piña colada despite not having it on the menu (and it was perfect). The nachos are great, the fajitas closer to the kind I love than any other place in London, and the desserts are typically fattening. The music—live and taped—is strictly Latin, both the upbeat kind and the very soulful. Most of the dining room is on the conservatory level with a sky light, which makes lunches on weekends a bright and sunny affair, and the bar is suitably dark and sexy. It's a good place for a Caribbean meal, even if the food does not stand out hugely. The price is reasonable, and the atmosphere is fun.

Dan's ★★★

| MODERN BRITISH | EXPENSIVE | QUALITY ★★★★ | VALUE ★★★ |

119 Sydney Street, Chelsea, SW3; ☎ 0207-352-2718; tube: South Kensington or Sloane Square

Customers Well-heeled Chelsea types and businessmen. **Reservations** Recommended. **When to go** Lunch on a warm day for a garden table. **Entree range** £12–£20. **Payment** AE, MC, V. **Service rating** ★★★★. **Friendliness rating** ★★★★. **Bar** Yes. **Wine** Excellent. **Dress** Casual. **Disabled access** None to garden; one step outside. **Hours** Monday–Sunday, 12:15–2:30 p.m. and 7–10:30 p.m.

SETTING AND ATMOSPHERE Lovely little restaurant with Stubbs-like prints of animals on the walls; beautiful garden; very efficient and rather French.

HOUSE SPECIALTIES Grilled meats, fish and potatoes; sautéed *foie gras* with mango chutney.

OTHER RECOMMENDATIONS Desserts, especially the passion fruit crème brûlée.

ENTERTAINMENT AND AMENITIES Able to cater to big parties in separate dining room downstairs.

SUMMARY AND COMMENTS I've walked past this place for over a decade and recently became aware of an enticing buzz about it. Opened in 1980, this French-accented, unpretentious restaurant has been the serene secret of the older, chic Chelsea set and local businesspeople. Run with perfect efficiency and even grace, the ambience is warm and convivial, and there's certainly none of the waiting around for your drink order to be taken that is so disgracefully common in London. The kitchen operates with similar dispatch and turns out perfectly cooked meat and fish accompanied by fresh and tasty vegetables. The roasted potatoes are artful and satisfying, and whatever sauce accompanies your choice is sure to be an excellent complement to the dish. Though originally skeptical about the passion fruit crème brûlée (I can't bear it when people mess with this supremely rich and simple dessert), by the second spoonful I was a convert: it has a perfume of the fruit and is lighter than most that I've tasted. The only drawback here is the prices, which are slightly higher than seems strictly necessary, but you are definitely paying for the service and the guarantee of a satisfying eating experience.

E&O ★★★★

ASIAN FUSION	MODERATE/EXPENSIVE	QUALITY ★★★★	VALUE ★★

14 Blenheim Crescent, Notting Hill, W11; ☎ 0207-229-5454; www.eando.nu; tube: Notting Hill or Ladbroke Grove

Customers Elegant Notting Hillbillies. **Reservations** Recommended. **When to go** Dinner for a look at the beautiful people. **Entree range** £9–£28 (for lobster); dim sum £3–£8. **Payment** AE, DC, MC, V. **Service rating** ★★★. **Friendliness rating** ★★★. **Bar** Yes. **Wine selection** Good. **Dress** Casual. **Disabled access** Yes. **Hours** Monday–Friday, 12:15–2:45 p.m. and 6:15–10:45 p.m.; Saturday, noon–3:45 p.m. and 6:15–10:45 p.m.; Sunday, 1–3:45 p.m. and 6:15–10:15 p.m.

SETTING AND ATMOSPHERE Very cool Zen-like simplicity, with linen-tablecloth elegance.

HOUSE SPECIALTIES Edamame, soy and mirin dim sum; duck with watermelon and cashew, pad thai.

OTHER RECOMMENDATIONS Vegetarian dishes, such as avocado, aubergine, and sweetcorn tempura, wrapped in Chinese paper.

ENTERTAINMENT AND AMENITIES Watch the beautiful people on diets actually eat the local and delicious food.

SUMMARY AND COMMENTS E & O is one of the four restaurants dreamed up by Aussie Will Ricker, whose success in London's cut-throat restaurant scene has been impressive (see below for names and addresses of the other eateries). Notting Hill has flocked to the E&O like lemmings, making this one of the trendy media folk's favorite joints, not least because of the painstaking presentation of the often carb-free, wheat-free, and dairy-free—but never taste-free—dishes. It's a pan-Asian menu featuring unusual combinations in dim sum, such as water chestnut and date gyosa, as well as the old standbys of baby pork or chicken with coriander. The main dishes should be ordered with abandon and shared by the table; try the duck with watermelon and cashews, and any of the vegetarian fare (E&O was awarded the 2003 *Time Out* Best Vegetarian Restaurant, despite the meat that is on the menu). The desserts are inventive: chocolate and honeycomb mochi, or mango sashimi, lemongrass and lime leaf granite, and make sure at least one of you orders the special chocolate pudding (tell the waiter early on, as it takes 20 minutes to prepare). Curries, sashimi, tempura, and Oriental salads are all artfully placed on the plates and are a real treat for the palate. Other restaurants are Eight Over Eight (with a more Chinese menu), 392 Kings Road, Chelsea, SW3, ☎ 0207-349-9934; Great Eastern Dining Room, 54–56 Great Eastern Street, The City, ☎ 0207-613-4545; Cicada, 132–136 St. John's Street, The City, EC1, ☎ 0207-608-1550.

 Fifteen ★ ★ ★ ★ ★

MODERN BRITISH	EXPENSIVE	QUALITY ★ ★ ★ ★ ★	VALUE ★ ★ ★ ★

**13 Westland Place, East End, N1; ☎ 0871-330-1515;
www.fifteenrestaurant.com; tube: Old Street (exit 1)**

Customers Everyone and anyone. **Reservations** No reservations for the Trattoria, 1 week's advance reservation for dinner at Fifteen. **When to go** Whenever you can. **Entree range** Trattoria £5.50–£20.95, fifteen set menus, lunch, £22 for 2 courses, £25 for 3 courses; dinner tasting menu (6 courses), £60 (vegetarian £40–£50). **Payment** AE, MC, V. **Service rating** ★ ★ ★ ★. **Friendliness rating** ★ ★ ★ ★ ½. **Bar** No. **Wine selection** Excellent wine, some sold by the glass. **Dress** Casual. **Disabled access** Trattoria yes, downstairs no. **Hours** Trattoria: Monday–Saturday, 8:30 a.m.–11 p.m.; Sunday, noon–5 p.m. (lunch only). Fifteen: Monday–Saturday, noon–3 p.m. and 6–10 p.m.

SETTING AND ATMOSPHERE Nonsmoking in both dining rooms. Cheerful, warm trattoria that's great for breakfast; downstairs dining room is very cool and funky, with distressed wooden floors, hot pink banquettes, and modern molded-plastic chairs. Uniforms are courtesy of the popular and hip Topshop.

HOUSE SPECIALTIES Scallop crudo, which is raw scallops cured in Japanese yuzu lime with ginger, coconut, coriander and strawberries. It's their signature dish and is more delicious than it might sound.

OTHER RECOMMENDATIONS Roast loin of pork stuffed with peaches and mint; scallops, red mullet, and salmon with fried zucchini, chili and mint sauce; raspberry crème brûlèe tart with raspberry sorbet. They also, amazingly, have a vegetarian tasting menu. Choose any of the set menus at lunch or dinner.

SUMMARY AND COMMENTS You have got to love Jamie Oliver, the puckish young chef who became famous with his cookbooks and the reality show, *Jamie's Kitchen,* where viewers got to see the sweaty drama of the kitchen (Gordon Ramsey's similar show is much less fun, as it consists of him having tantrums, and making C-list celebrities cry). Jamie's (we all call him Jamie) dream was to take a number of disadvantaged kids, either homeless or in foster care, and train them to be great chefs. Two dozen kids (at last count) have graduated from this hands-on, frying-pan-into-the-fire school and gone on to find full-time jobs at some of the best restaurants in the world. Jamie's activism in improving school lunches is equally impressive, with his saving-the-world-one-meal-at-a-time philosophy showing hard, practical results. His work in the cafeterias of state-funded schools proved, in a matter of weeks, that eating fresh and healthy meals on a regular basis can improve a child's attendance, attention, behavior, and grades (see **www.feedmebetter.com** for more information on this program). Jamie has thrust the fire of his crusading spirit into the face of the public, and we all love him for it. It also means that eating at Fifteen is not merely a selfish gastronomic pleasure, but a donation toward his admirable projects, with all profits going to the Fifteen Foundation (a new Fifteen opened in Amsterdam in 2004, giving more kids a head start). If you know anything about Jamie Oliver, you know that the market determines the menu, with only the freshest ingredients making it onto his cutting boards. There's a trattoria on the ground floor for breakfast, lunch, and dinner, with à la carte selections that change daily. In the basement is the more formal dining room, with exquisite tasting menus, set lunches, and dinners. The food can best be described as Modern British with a Mediterranean slant, probably best summed up in the ravioli stuffed with chicken "label anglais," mascarpone, and roast garlic, or the indescribably fluffy potato gnocchi with Scottish mushrooms. Do make a reservation and prepare for an admittedly expensive, but oh so virtuous, delicious meal.

 fish! ★★

FISH AND SHELLFISH   INEXPENSIVE/MODERATE   QUALITY ★★½   VALUE ★★★½

Cathedral Street, London Bridge, SE1; ☎ 0207-407-3803; www.fishdiner.co.uk; tube: London Bridge

Customers Locals and tourists, many families. **Reservations** Recommended. **When to go** Lunch or dinner. **Entree range** £10.95–£16.95. **Payment** AE, D, DC, JCB, MC, V. **Service rating** ★★★. **Friendliness rating** ★★★½. **Bar** In some branches, but designed for customers waiting for tables. **Wine selection** Small, adequate, inexpensive. **Dress** Smart casual. **Disabled access** Yes. **Hours** Monday–Saturday, 11:30 a.m–11 p.m.; Sunday, noon–10:30 p.m.

SETTING AND ATMOSPHERE Informal, modern dining rooms with a view of the kitchen.

HOUSE SPECIALTIES Fresh fish, plainly cooked.

ENTERTAINMENT AND AMENITIES Watching the chefs at work.

SUMMARY AND COMMENTS There were six fish! restaurants in London and four more in other towns and cities a while ago; the empire has shrunk considerably, so now there is just the one left in Central London, (although they are expanding their Jarvis Fish Shop to add a new fish! in late 2005 in Kingston-Upon-Thames). Quality and consistency have suffered somewhat as the group's troubles bit, but this is still a useful place to know about. The emphasis is on buying top-quality fish, offering it steamed or grilled, and allowing customers to choose the sauce (e.g., salsa, hollandaise, herb and garlic butter, and so on). There are a few appetizers, too, along the lines of rock oysters, prawn (shrimp) cocktail, and smoked salmon; and there are a few concessions to meat lovers among the main courses, as well as a few slightly more complicated fishy main courses. But the core concept is by far the best way to be sure of success. The restaurant is specifically designed with children in mind, and they make it possible to eat quickly if that's what you're after—the Spartan decor won't make you want to linger endlessly, though of course no one will kick you out. These are just good, reliable restaurants that won't break the bank. Though it should be noted that bills can rise quickly if you eat a full meal with extra options such as side orders.

Food for Thought ★ ★ ★ ½

VEGETARIAN	INEXPENSIVE	QUALITY ★★★★	VALUE ★★★★★

31 Neal Street, Covent Garden, WC2; ☎ 0207-836-0239; tube: Covent Garden

Customers Local vegetarians and vegans. **Reservations** No. **When to go** Avoid the heart of lunch hour; arrive at the stroke of noon or after 2 p.m. as it gets very crowded, with people waiting on the rickety steps to the basement dining room. **Entree range** £4.20–£6.30. **Payment** Cash, no credit cards. **Service rating ★★★**. **Friendliness rating ★★★½. Bar** No. **Wine selection** BYOB. **Dress** Casual. **Disabled access** No. **Hours** Monday–Saturday, noon–8:30 p.m.; Sunday, noon–5 p.m.

SETTING AND ATMOSPHERE Spartan, yet pleasant withal; wooden tables, nonsmoking and air-conditioning in summer. A very bohemian, student-like vibe.

HOUSE SPECIALTIES Stir-fried vegetable with tofu and brown rice; vegan and wheat-free cakes; vegetable stews and casseroles.

OTHER RECOMMENDATIONS Salad with tahini dressing.

SUMMARY AND COMMENTS This is another one of those time capsules, like the World Food Café (see page 354), that reminds me of some of the great natural foods restaurants in San Francisco, back when meat-free, wheat-free, or no-dairy diets were somewhat exotic. The food is served up cafeteria style; you may have to stand in a queue that often goes all the way up the stairs (the dining room is in the basement of an old Georgian building) and out the front door. Indeed, it opened in 1974, when Neal Street and the surrounding area was full of head shops and store-front mystics (there's still a crystal shop and an astrology shop there), and it answered the needs of chronically broke students, artists, and rebels with its dirt cheap, delicious, and filling vegan and vegetarian dishes: stir-fries, brown rice, pasties, and salads, served in a mellow atmosphere. With vegetarianism more mainstream than ever, this restaurant has managed to hold on to its lease in the ever-rising rents of the area around Seven Dials by sticking to their tried and true methods: they use good local produce, change the menu each day (except for the brown rice and stir-fried vegetable option), and give you good value for your money. If I am having a large dinner party with a few vegans present, I let Food for Thought do the cooking—they always get it right. For a healthy and inexpensive pretheater meal within easy walking of most of the West End playhouses, this is the place.

 Le Gavroche ★ ★ ★ ★ ½

| FRENCH (HAUTE CUISINE) | EXPENSIVE | QUALITY ★★★★½ | VALUE ★★★ |

43 Upper Brook Street, Mayfair, W1; ☎ 0207-408-0881; www.le-gavroche.co.uk; tube: Marble Arch

Customers Wealthy locals, serious gourmets, and tourists. **Reservations** Essential. **When to go** Lunch or dinner. **Entree range** £26.80–£38.80. **Payment** AE, CB, DC, MC, V. **Service rating** ★★★★★. **Friendliness rating** ★★★★. **Bar** Yes, for diners only. **Wine selection** Excellent. **Dress** Smart casual, jackets for men. **Disabled access** No. **Hours** Monday–Friday, noon–2 p.m. and 7–11 p.m. Saturday, 7–11 p.m. Closed Sunday.

SETTING AND ATMOSPHERE This downstairs room offers intimate comfort at both lunch and dinner; it's indisputably grand, and you will unconsciously sit up straighter as you are eased smoothly into your seat. It's got that old-world gracious elegance that tells you straight off you are in for an extraordinary dining experience.

HOUSE SPECIALTIES Soufflé Suissesse (Gruyère cheese soufflé; agneau de lait roti (roast lamb); le demi homard roti aux cepes et romarin (half lobster roasted with wild mushroom and rosemary); tartare de thon et saumon marine au caviar (raw tuna and salmon marinated in caviar); raviolis tiedes aux pruneaux et armagnac, glace a la vanilla (small warm prune tarts with cognac and vanilla ice cream); stunningly perfect crème brûlée.

OTHER RECOMMENDATIONS Set lunch.

SUMMARY AND COMMENTS Le Gavroche is one of London's most famous and most expensive restaurants. It is classic in every sense, even though the menu has been "modernized" in recent years. The service is among the best in London, priding itself on knowing what customers want before they themselves know they want it, and the care taken with every detail is astonishing. There are menus without prices given to those who are obviously guests of someone; plates of tiny but elaborate *amuse bouches* (hors d'oeuvres) are laid at your table; a palate-clearing sorbet is often served between courses; and the painstaking desserts alone would justify a visit. All this comes at a truly frightening price outside the set lunch, which at £44 per person includes three courses, half a bottle of wine, water and coffee, and service. Sure, that's pretty expensive, too. But with main courses alone costing £30 on average, lunch is the only way most people can afford Le Gavroche. It's worth that one splash-out, because this is a great restaurant of the old-fashioned, perfectionist kind. Bread, ice creams and sorbets, premeal tidbits—they're all outstanding. And the all-French cheese board is probably the best in London. Come here if you want to treat yourself. And if you're feeling particularly flush (and very hungry) there is a perfectly amazing tasting menu for £86.

 The Ivy ★ ★ ★ ★

MODERN EUROPEAN | **MODERATE** | **QUALITY ★ ★ ★ ★** | **VALUE ★ ★ ★**

1 West Street, West End, WC2; ☎ 0207-836-4751; www.caprice-holdings.co.uk; tube: Leicester Square

Customers Mostly locals, which include the theater folk after 10 p.m. **Reservations** Essential. **When to go** Lunch or dinner. **Entree range** £8.25–£29.75. **Payment** AE, D, DC, JCB, MC, V. **Service rating ★ ★ ★ ★. Friendliness rating ★ ★ ★.** **Bar** For diners only. **Wine selection** Good. **Dress** No dress code. **Disabled access** Restaurant only. **Hours** Monday–Saturday, noon–3 p.m. and 5:30 p.m.–midnight; Sunday, noon–3:30 p.m. and 5:30 p.m.–midnight.

SETTING AND ATMOSPHERE Exceptionally comfortable wood-paneled room with stained-glass windows, discreet and refined.

HOUSE SPECIALTIES Simple classics such as steak tartare, calf's liver, smoked salmon with scrambled eggs, shepherd's pie, eggs Benedict, grilled or fried fish.

OTHER RECOMMENDATIONS Salads, desserts, Asian dishes; set lunch (Saturday and Sunday), £21.50 for three courses.

SUMMARY AND COMMENTS Let's get the bad news out of the way first. Getting a table at The Ivy is famously difficult, due to it being one of London's favorite restaurants, and rich hunting grounds for the paparazzi. If you're planning a trip and are dying to eat here, it's advisable to reserve at least a few weeks in advance. Why should this be? Here's the good news: The Ivy is a supremely wonderful place. The food is mostly simple but always executed with skill, and the prices are not at all astronomical (which works for the underpaid theater crews who pop in after the performance). Service is mostly professional and efficient, though there are sometimes complaints about off handedness. But The Ivy isn't just a place to eat and drink. It is also, for most people, a spot to do a bit of stargazing. The rich and famous love it, and chances are reasonable that you'll spot a familiar face while enjoying your eggs Benedict or fish and chips. But don't stare, please. That wouldn't be in keeping with Ivy etiquette.

Joe Allen ★ ★ ½

AMERICAN | **INEXPENSIVE/MODERATE** | **QUALITY ★ ★ ½** | **VALUE ★ ★ ½**

13 Exeter Street, West End, WC2; ☎ 0207-836-0651; www.joeallenrestaurant.com; tube: Covent Garden

Customers Varied, locals and tourists. **Reservations** Recommended. **When to go** Anytime. **Entree range** Lunch £6.50–£14.50. **Payment** AE, MC, V. **Service rating ★ ★ ★ ½. Friendliness rating ★ ★ ★ ★.** **Bar** Yes. **Wine selection** Small but good. **Dress** Casual. **Disabled access** No. **Hours** Monday–Friday, noon–1 a.m.; Saturday, 11:30 a.m.–1 a.m.; Sunday, 11:30 a.m.–midnight.

SETTING AND ATMOSPHERE Think of your favorite local bar/restaurant—the kind of place you go for a cheerful, noisy night out with friends—and you have it.

HOUSE SPECIALTIES Black-bean soup; chopped chicken liver; chili con carne; Caesar salad; eggs Benedict or eggs Joe Allen; grilled sirloin steak with steak fries; brownies; cheesecake.

OTHER RECOMMENDATIONS Anything cooked simply (which means just about everything on the menu), especially hamburgers, sandwiches, and salads.

ENTERTAINMENT AND AMENITIES Piano player Monday–Saturday, 9 p.m.–1 a.m.; jazz Sunday, 8 p.m.–1 a.m.

SUMMARY AND COMMENTS Like its other branches in Paris and the United States, the London Joe Allen is a place to go for unpretentious American-style food in a lively atmosphere. It's set in the heart of theaterland, and its theatrical connections are firmly cemented in the cheap pretheater menus (£15 for two courses, £17 for three courses) and the late opening hour. Actors come in from the nearby theaters after their performance, and if you're lucky you may find yourself eating Caesar salad next to someone you watched on stage an hour earlier. It's the spirited buzz that brings Londoners in rather than any fancy fireworks in the food; and there are sometimes complaints about brusque and unhelpful service. But the food itself is solid, rarely disappointing those who like simple classics done well, and the drinks list, though short, is enticing at every level.

La Porte des Indes ★ ★ ★ ½

| INDIAN | EXPENSIVE | QUALITY ★ ★ ★ | VALUE ★ ★ ★ |

32 Bryanston Street, Marylebone, W1; ☎ 0207-224-0055; www.blueelephant.com; tube: Marble Arch

Customers Celebrants, romantic couples, tourists. **Reservations** Yes, but not essential. **When to go** Anytime. **Entree range** £9.50–£19.50, menu Maison £33; vegetarian menu £31. **Payment** AE, DC, MC, V. **Service rating** ★ ★ ★. **Friendliness rating** ★ ★ ★ ½. **Bar** Yes. **Wine selection** Good. **Dress** Casual. **Disabled access** Limited. **Hours** Monday–Friday, noon–2.30 p.m. and 6–11.30 p.m.; Saturday, 6–11.30 p.m.; Sunday, noon–3 p.m. and 6–10:30 p.m.

SETTING AND ATMOSPHERE Decadent Raj splendor, with waterfall, many different dining rooms, all beautifully appointed, and skylights.

HOUSE SPECIALTIES Shrimp, mangoes, green chilies, ginger and poppy seeds in coconut curry; grilled lamb chops marinated in "aphrodisiac" spices; crab Malabar; makal palak pakora (fritters of chickpea flour, leaf spinach, and corn).

OTHER RECOMMENDATIONS Grilled lobster anarkali; gulab jamun (deep-fried milk curd nuggets in cinnamon and rose syrup).

ENTERTAINMENT AND AMENITIES Private rooms; a variety of beautiful vistas within the main dining rooms; occasionally they have live jazz on Sundays.

SUMMARY AND COMMENTS Let it be said straight away that one first comes for the decor, and comes back for the food. I first read of this restaurant in the *Evening Standard,* who sent a couple there on a blind date. Intrigued by this (the *Standard* occasionally gets it right on all things London), I went for lunch to see the 40-foot waterfall, and the skylights, and the general exuberance of the decor. Yes, it is beautiful, yes it makes you feel as if you're on a film set of a Bollywood extravaganza, and yes, it is a bit pricey. But for great food for a large party, La Port des Indes is a wonderful setting, and as the name implies, it's a strongly French-influenced Indian place—no curry in a hurry here. The food focuses on the former French colonies of India, and there are eight specialist chefs in the kitchen to make sure each of the regional cuisines ring true. They are very accommodating about the degree of spiciness in the dishes, but Western palates should take care with the vindaloos and other hot dishes. The service is good and the wine respectable, and the set menus are a good way to try everything, although it's probably less expensive to share a few à la carte dishes. It's owned by Blue Elephant International, who seem to have perfect pitch interpreting Eastern food for Western gastronomes; and whoever does their decorating should win an award. Check out the elaborate ceiling in the Shamiana room.

Masala Zone ★★

INDIAN	INEXPENSIVE/MODERATE	QUALITY ★★★½	VALUE ★★★★

9 Marshall Street, Marylebone, W1; ☎ 0207-287-9966; www.realindianfood.com; tube: Oxford Circus

Customers Locals, mostly office workers at lunch. **Reservations** Not accepted. **When to go** Anytime. **Entree range** £5–£9.50, thalis £8–£12. **Payment** MC, V. **Service rating** ★★★. **Friendliness rating** ★★★★. **Bar** No. **Wine selection** Cheap and good. **Dress** Casual. **Disabled access** Yes. **Hours** Monday–Friday, noon–2:45 p.m. and 5:30–11 p.m.; Saturday, 12:30–11 p.m.; Sunday, 6–10:30 p.m.

SETTING AND ATMOSPHERE Open-plan cafeteria-style, modern and light decor.

HOUSE SPECIALTIES Thalis, snacks, mango lassi, and Indian lemonade.

SUMMARY AND COMMENTS Masala Zone is part of the group that owns Veeraswamy (see page 351), Chutney Mary's, and Amaya (which are also worth a visit). It opened in 2001 with a very novel approach: high-quality, adventurous, and sometimes unorthodox Indian-style food at very low prices. It has gone from strength to strength, never wavering in its commitment to quality, freshness, and precise, friendly service. One of the best things about it is the flexibility of the food: you can have a full meal or a "light bite" if your appetite is small. There's a grilled club sandwich—chicken, bacon, egg, cheese, and mayo—if that's all you want, and filling noodle bowls (for under £6!) for a heartier meal. Because of the no-reservations policy you may have trouble getting a table—and sometimes there's a long line both at lunch and dinner. But sometimes there is no wait at all. If you like Indian food and don't want to spend a fortune for it, Masala Zone is well worth seeking out.

And its central location, close to theaterland, makes it all the more attractive.

Mash ★★

MODERN EUROPEAN	INEXP/MODERATE	QUALITY ★★★½	VALUE ★★★

19–21 Great Portland Street, Marylebone, W1; ☎ 0207-637-5555;
tube: Oxford Circus. 26B Albemarle Street, Mayfair, W1;
☎ 0207-495-5999; tube: Green Park

Customers Mostly young locals. **When to go** Lunch or dinner, weekend brunch, late night. **Entree range** £7–£14.50. **Payment** AE, D, DC, MC, V. **Service rating** ★★½. **Friendliness rating** ★★★½. **Bar** Yes. **Wine selection** Very good. **Dress** Smart casual but relaxed. **Disabled access** Ground floor only. **Hours** Monday–Friday, noon–3 p.m. and 6–11:30 p.m.; Saturday and Sunday, 6–11 p.m.

SETTING AND ATMOSPHERE Futuristic, modern decor with high ceilings and a microbrewery in the ground-floor bar; fairly noisy when crowded.

HOUSE SPECIALTIES Fresh fruit drinks, microbrewed beer.

ENTERTAINMENT AND AMENITIES DJ Thursday through Saturday nights.

SUMMARY AND COMMENTS Mash is lively, boisterous, ultracool, and very popular with a mostly young clientele, who crowd into the ground-floor bar and upstairs restaurant by day and night. Some come for the excellent beers brewed on premises, and you can join a lunchtime tour on Saturday (12:30 p.m.) for a tour, tasting, and two-course lunch. Or you can just come in to eat and drink without the educational angle. Grilling over wood and pizzas baked in a wood oven are strong points of the hip, usually well-judged cooking, from a short menu that does pretty well by vegetarians. The bar is a good place for a quick lunch, and there's also a deli counter where you can get meals to take out. Noisephobics should avoid the restaurant in the evening, but everyone else will enjoy the good buzz and decent food.

Matsuri ★★★½

JAPANESE	MODERATE/EXPENSIVE	QUALITY ★★★½	VALUE ★★

15 Bury Street, Mayfair, SW1; ☎ 0207-839-1101;
www.matsuri-restaurant.com; tube: Green Park

Customers Locals and tourists. **Reservations** Recommended. **When to go** Lunch or dinner. **Entree range** £15–£33. **Payment** AE, CB, DC, MC, V. **Service rating** ★★★½. **Friendliness rating** ★★★½. **Bar** Yes. **Wine selection** Adequate; beer and sake better. **Dress** Casual. **Disabled access** Yes, for diners only. **Hours** Daily, noon–2:30 p.m. and 6–10:30 p.m.

SETTING AND ATMOSPHERE Big, spacious main dining room and smaller sushi bar; elegant but relaxed.

HOUSE SPECIALTIES Sushi and teppanyaki.

SUMMARY AND COMMENTS London has its full share of big Japanese restaurants catering to businesspeople with expense accounts as big as the Grand Canyon. You'll find a few of them in the "More Recommendations" section, along with some smaller places at significantly lower prices. This is a big place, but the prices are relatively reasonable (£6.50–£12.50 for a daily special set lunch) and the quality is high. Sushi and sashimi are expertly prepared and can be ordered either à la carte at the bar or in various permutations of a set meal. Most of the space is given over to teppanyaki tables, where your choice of fish, meat, and vegetables is prepared and cooked for you on a sizzling hot plate; very theatrical, but also good food. There's even a nod toward fusion cooking, in the form of tuna tartare, foie gras "Japanese," and little dishes such as deep-fried chicken. The list of specialty-brand sakes is intriguing, though not cheap. But, then, top-quality Japanese never comes cheap.

Moro ★★★★

SPANISH/MIDDLE EASTERN   **MODERATE**   **QUALITY ★★★★**   **VALUE ★★★★**

34–36 Exmouth Market, The City, EC1; ☎ 0207-833-8336; www.moro.co.uk; tube: Farringdon or Angel

Customers Locals, both young and old. **Reservations** Recommended. **When to go** Anytime. **Entree range** £13.50–£17.50. **Payment** AE, D, MC, V. **Service rating** ★★★. **Friendliness rating** ★★★½. **Bar** Yes, with tapas menu. **Wine selection** Very good. **Dress** Casual. **Disabled access** Yes. **Hours** Monday–Friday, 12:30–2:30 p.m. and 7–10:30 p.m.; Saturday, 1–3:30 p.m. and 7–10:30 p.m.; closed Sunday.

SETTING AND ATMOSPHERE   Casual and lively; high-ceilinged room with simple decor.

HOUSE SPECIALTIES   Everything cooked in the wood-fired oven, such as cod with saffron rice, caramelized onions, and tahini; charcoal-grilled dishes like lamb kebab with egg and mint salad and bulgur; homemade breads and yogurt; tarts and other desserts.

OTHER RECOMMENDATIONS   Vegetarian dishes, well-chosen Spanish cheeses, braised dishes.

SUMMARY AND COMMENTS   Since opening in 1998, Moro has become one of the most popular restaurants in London. The area is off the beaten track as far as sightseeing is concerned, but the area is also increasingly trendy in a bohemian way. Moro has played a part in this. It is a destination restaurant because the food is really outstanding: if anyone has ever had a bad time there, we haven't heard about it. The prices are very reasonable for cooking of this quality. Based on the cuisine and culture of Moorish Spain, when the country was under Islamic rule, the food has big, bold flavors and generous spicing. You can never tell what you'll find at Moro, because the menu changes weekly. Everything's delicious. This is not a place for a quiet evening, but definitely a place for a memorable meal that shows why people enthuse about London's gastronomic renaissance.

Mr. Kong ★★★½

CHINESE   **INEXPENSIVE/MODERATE**   **QUALITY ★★★½**   **VALUE ★★★★**

21 Lisle Street, West End, WC2; ☎ 0207-437-7341; tube: Leicester Square

Customers Mostly locals. **Reservations** Recommended. **When to go** Lunch or dinner. **Entree range** Lunch £6–£26. **Payment** AE, CB, D, DC, MC, V. **Service rating**

★★★. **Friendliness rating** ★★½. **Bar** No. **Wine selection** Adequate. **Dress** Casual. **Disabled access** Restaurant. **Hours** Daily, noon–2:45 a.m.

SETTING AND ATMOSPHERE Unexceptional if well-appointed Chinese decor; usually very busy.

HOUSE SPECIALTIES Chef's specials, especially shellfish and hot-pot dishes.

OTHER RECOMMENDATIONS Standard Cantonese dishes.

SUMMARY AND COMMENTS In an area crowded with Chinese restaurants, Mr. Kong stands out by virtue of its interesting and innovative cooking. The menu is long, but you don't need to look any further than the Chef's Special page—over 50 dishes, some of them found nowhere else. They seldom climb beyond the £14 mark, and there's enough to keep you happy for a good half-dozen mealtimes. Adventurous eaters can sample baked frogs' legs, jellyfish, or pig's head or intestines; seafood fans should have soft-shell crabs (an occasional special), clams in various guises, or steamed crab with rice wine. Even if you stick with more conventional dishes, you will be well fed. Though Mr. Kong is somewhat more expensive than most restaurants in the area, it's worth the money. And you know it's good food because it's usually filled with Chinese locals.

Nathalie's ★★★★

FRENCH	MODERATE	QUALITY ★★★★	VALUE ★★★★★

3 Milner Street, Chelsea, SW3; ☎ 0207-581-2848; www.nathalie-restaurant.co.uk; tube: South Kensington

Customers Locals and Francophiles. **Reservations** Recommended for dinner. **When to go** Lunch will get you your best deal; dinner is a bit more elegant. **Entree range** £15–£23. **Payment** AE, MC, V. **Service rating** ★★★★★. **Friendliness rating** ★★★★★. **Bar** Drinks served. **Wine selection** Excellent. **Dress** Casual. **Disabled access** 3 steps into restaurant. **Hours** Tuesday–Saturday, noon–2 p.m. and 7–10 p.m.

SETTING AND ATMOSPHERE A simple dining room nicely lit, in contemporary simplicity, with big windows opening to a quiet street.

HOUSE SPECIALTIES Lunch is a "French Bento box," a selection of small dishes served at once. Lots of great food, and plenty of it.

OTHER RECOMMENDATIONS Grilled filet of beef with dauphinois potatoes; steamed sea bream.

SUMMARY AND COMMENTS Opened in 2003 by Frenchman Eric Chatroux, who trained at La Tante Claire as well as in Paris, this is a wonderful secret place that deserves a wider audience. Tucked away behind posh Walton Street, it is a charming little dining room with a seriously French cuisine adapted to today's healthier diet. Chatroux, who lives upstairs with his family, is a friendly and knowledgeable presence in the dining room and in the kitchen. His guiding philosophy is superb French food at reasonable (for what you get) prices in an atmosphere much less stuffy than the other cathedrals of haute cuisine. The most interesting lunch is served there: in order to accommodate people's lunch hour, he places succulent delights, six courses in all, on one lacquered tray which you can enjoy in the order you wish. At a prix fixe of £14.50, you simply cannot go wrong. In summer he serves an amazingly light and flavorful gazpacho made of watermelon, vegetables, and tomatoes. His sauces are divine, and the desserts alone worth the trip.

kids

Navajo Joe's ★ ★ ½

UPSCALE TEX-MEX	MODERATE	QUALITY ★ ★ ★	VALUE ★ ★ ★

34 Kings Street, West End, WC2; ☎ 0207-240-4008; www.navajojoe.com tube: Covent Garden

Customers Locals, business lunchers, after-work partyers, tourists. **Reservations** Not necessary. **When to go** Anytime. **Entree range** £10–£20. **Payment** AE, DC, MC, V. **Service rating** ★ ★ ★. **Friendliness rating** ★ ★ ★ ★. **Bar** Fabulously well-stocked with good munchies available. **Wine selection** Decent. **Dress** Casual. **Disabled access** Yes. **Hours** Daily, noon–midnight; open until 11:30 p.m. on Sunday.

SETTING AND ATMOSPHERE Western-accented, with wooden tables and a warm glow, helped along by the enormous candle "sculptures" on the bar, made by the dripping wax of hundreds of burning candles over the years.

HOUSE SPECIALTIES Lobster and mango nachos, barbecue glazed ribs, spicy chicken wings, asparagus and mushroom enchilada, fajitas.

OTHER RECOMMENDATIONS Rib-eye steak with béarnaise sauce; baked vanilla bean cheesecake.

ENTERTAINMENT AND AMENITIES Lots of camaraderie in the early evening, as workers from Covent Garden pile up at the bar. Music a little American-centric, circa 1960s and 1970s.

SUMMARY AND COMMENTS There are so many restaurants to choose from in the Covent Garden area, sometimes you just have to give up and go for an American meal. And they do it pretty well here, better than their sister restaurant Cactus Blue in Chelsea in my opinion, although the menus are very similar. The restaurant occupies a big, high ceilings store front that looks over Covent Garden, with a loft upstairs, a big bar in the front, and tables sprinkled around in such a way to give a sense of intimacy. The food is a strange sort of combination of old Tex-Mex standbys with new twists, such as pulled duck nachos with plum salsa, or tequila lime chicken chimichanga; and a kind of no-man's-land cuisine of mushroom and mascarpone ravioli, or sea bass served on a banana leaf with green curry and rice. They have something you don't see in a lot of British restaurants, which is a classic surf 'n' turf of roasted whole lobster and grilled 12 oz. steak (for two, at £32). The vanilla bean cheesecake is probably the best I've had in London, resembling the Junior's cheesecakes in the Bronx that always set the standard for me. You can also have what they call "Amusements" anytime, or small noshes such as steak teriyaki, spring rolls, or spicy meat balls, and so on, for £10 for a selection of three, or two for £7.

Nobu ★ ★ ★ ★

"NEW-STYLE" JAPANESE	EXPENSIVE	QUALITY ★ ★ ★ ★	VALUE ★ ★

**19 Old Park Lane, Mayfair, W1; ☎ 0207-447-4747;
www.noburestaurants.com; tube: Hyde Park Corner**

Customers Businesspeople, tourists, the occasional celebrity. **Reservations** Essential. **When to go** Lunch or dinner. **Entree range** £6.50–£27.50. **Payment** AE, CB, DC, MC, V. **Service rating** ★★★½. **Friendliness rating** ★★★. **Bar** Yes. **Wine selection** Very good. **Dress** Fashionable. **Disabled access** Yes. **Hours** Monday–Friday, noon–2:15 p.m. and 6–10:15 p.m.; Saturday, 6–11 p.m.; Sunday, 6–9:30 p.m.

SETTING AND ATMOSPHERE Ultraminimalist decor for an ultrachic clientele.

HOUSE SPECIALTIES Special appetizers such as yellowtail sashimi with jalapeño and tomato rock shrimp sceviche; all traditional sushi and sashimi.

OTHER RECOMMENDATIONS Special dishes such as black cod with miso and Inaniwa pasta salad with lobster.

SUMMARY AND COMMENTS Nobu is a one-of-a-kind restaurant, with eight worldwide restaurants and two new branches opening soon in London and New York. If you've ever been to a Nobu in Milan, Beverly Hills, Miami, Dallas, or Las Vegas, you are aware of Matsuhisu Nobuyuki's extraordinary reworking of Japanese cuisine (and the extraordinary prices, as well). There are three things that come to mind, and the most important is startling innovation that almost invariably sends diners into raptures. This is like no other Japanese food, taking in influences from every corner of the globe, especially South America. But it's innovation that works, which is what counts. The second thing is chic: Nobu attracts entertainment people, and you may get to see one or two when you eat here. The third thing is the daunting expense. If you order a full meal, it's hard to come away without spending £60 or more on food alone, and that won't even fill you up. This means Nobu doesn't rate well for value. In fact, in a newspaper's celebrity questionnaire, called My London, Nobu is invariably the response to "What was your most expensive meal in London?" But it is an amazing place, and everyone should visit once. Consider going for a sushi lunch, which shouldn't set you back more than £25 a head as long as you avoid alcohol.

 kids **North Sea Fish Restaurant** ★ ½

FISH AND CHIPS	INEXPENSIVE	QUALITY ★★½	VALUE ★★★★★

**7–8 Leigh Street, North London, WC1; ☎ 0207-387-5892;
tube: Holborn or King's Cross**

Customers Mostly locals. **Reservations** Not necessary. **When to go** Lunch or dinner. **Entree range** £8–£16.95. **Payment** AE, MC, V. **Service rating** ★★★. **Friendliness rating** ★★★★. **Bar** Yes. **Wine selection** Adequate. **Dress** Casual. **Disabled access** Limited. **Hours** Monday–Saturday, noon–2:30 p.m. and 5:30–10:30 p.m.

SETTING AND ATMOSPHERE Cheap and sort of cheerful old-fashioned room with wooden beams and a lively buzz.

HOUSE SPECIALTIES Fish and chips, avocado prawn, seafood platter, scampi, salmon, Dover sole.

OTHER RECOMMENDATIONS Traditional desserts.

SUMMARY AND COMMENTS Everyone visiting London should eat fish and chips at least once. And if you eat it here, you'll see why it's one of the national dishes. To succeed, a cook needs top-quality fish and potatoes, good batter and oil, and an intimate knowledge of the art of deep-frying. At North Sea, they have all the requirements. You can have your choice of fish either fried in batter or matzo meal, or plainly grilled. Don't be put off by the fear of frying (even if it's supposedly "bad for you"). Batter-fried cod at the North Sea is absolutely delicious, not leaden or greasy like some fried foods. If you want to be authentic, have a side order of pickled onion to go with it. Service is decorous and efficient, the wine list is short but good, and the homemade desserts are wonderful. If you have room for them, that is.

Orrery ★ ★ ★ ★ ½

MODERN EUROPEAN	EXPENSIVE	QUALITY ★ ★ ★ ★ ½	VALUE ★ ★ ★

55 Marylebone High Street, Marylebone, W1; ☎ 0207-616-8000; www.conran-restaurants.co.uk; tube: Baker Street

Customers Affluent locals from all over London. **When to go** Lunch or dinner. **Entree range** £14.50–£29. **Payment** AE, D, DC, JCB, MC, V. **Service rating** ★★★★★. **Friendliness rating** ★★★★★. **Bar** Yes. **Wine selection** Outstanding but expensive. **Dress** Smart. **Disabled access** Yes. **Hours** Monday–Saturday, noon–3 p.m. and 7–11 p.m.; Sunday, 7–10:30 p.m.

SETTING AND ATMOSPHERE Long, narrow second-floor room with skylight; small adjacent bar; open-air terrace in good weather, nice view of the churchyard opposite.

HOUSE SPECIALTIES Somerset lamb with aubergine cannelloni; oven-roasted foie gras with pickled vegetables and lemon syrup; sea bass semolina gnocchi, pot-roast lamb; sweetcorn raviolis with cauliflower beignets.

OTHER RECOMMENDATIONS Light dinner menu on the terrace, weather permitting (summer only); set lunch and Sunday set dinner menus (£25–£75); menu gourmand (£55).

SUMMARY AND COMMENTS Orrery is part of the large Conran group and is universally regarded as the best of its restaurants for those seeking high-quality cooking in more intimate surroundings. The restaurant is small by Conran standards; the emphasis here is on the food rather than the buzz. And the kitchen consistently meets the high standards it sets itself: the cooking here is among the best in London, and sometimes reaches dazzling heights in inventiveness, seasoning, and presentation. It has a Michelin star, but probably deserves two. On the other hand, the prices are as dazzling as the food. It is alarmingly easy to spend £75 a head for a full meal with wine, and if you take on the five-star reaches of the fine but costly wine list, you can go a lot higher than that. But they also have many wines by the glass, and the set lunch (£25 for three courses) is a bargain by anyone's standards.

A small *epicerie* (grocer in French) opened downstairs in 2003 and serves café food, breakfast, and meals at a long communal table. They sell deli-type prepared food, which you can buy for a dinner party and claim credit, as well as spices, wine, and pantry items.

With service that combines military precision with a genuinely warm welcome, Orrery is one of London's top stars.

kids Orsini's Café ★ ★ ★ ½

ITALIAN CAFÉ	MODERATE	QUALITY ★ ★ ★ ★	VALUE ★ ★ ★

8A Thurloe Place, South Kensington, SW7; ☎ 0207-581-5553; tube: South Kensington

Customers Locals and museumgoers. **Reservations** No **When to Go** Breakfast, lunch, or afternoon coffee. **Entree range** Lunch £4.50–£10 . **Payment** AE, MC, V. **Service rating** ★ ★ **Friendliness rating** ★ ★ ★ ★ ★ **Bar** Basic mixed drinks, Italian liquors, beer, and wine. **Wine selection** Italian table red or white, specials weekly. **Dress** No dress code. **Disabled access** For downstairs nonsmoking area or outdoor tables only. **Hours** Daily, 8 a.m.–10 p.m.

SETTING AND ATMOSPHERE Temporary art exhibits decorate the walls; wooden tables and chairs on two floors. Casual, very Italian.

HOUSE SPECIALTIES Daily pasta and meat specials using fresh, organic products, such as mozzarella and aubergine fettuccini; homemade soups, panini, breaded chicken (or grilled) cutlets with salad; great cappuccino, fresh-squeezed orange juice.

OTHER RECOMMENDATIONS Homemade desserts.

SUMMARY AND COMMENTS Located across the street from the Victoria and Albert Museum on a leafy stretch of road, Orsini's Café is a family-run eatery that provides good, homemade food and the authenticity of a café in Naples. It's run by Antonella Orsini, baking is done by her talented mother Anna, and the good cheer is provided by father Salvatore. Even in the face of astronomical rent and service hikes through the neighborhood, it has managed to hang in there. It's a favorite with the locals, museumgoers, and visitors staying at the nearby Rembrandt Hotel. The chef, Mario, is extremely inventive and unfailingly great; the daily specials are always a treat, made with the best fresh produce of the day, chosen with care: porcini mushrooms, clams, artichokes make their sporadic appearance in unique dishes. The friendly service, provided by good-looking young Europeans, can be a bit unpredictable, but the sense of Mediterranean relaxation is part of the charm. In the best tradition of Italy, children are more than welcome, strollers and all. The breaded chicken cutlets are my favorite dish, and always done to perfection; the pasta cooked just right, with creative sauces. They have added eggs and other hot breakfast dishes to the menu, which pleases those of us who love a good morning cappuccino. The prices reflect the high rents of the area, but it's still a good value, and no one raises an eyebrow if you linger over an espresso for hours. There's a smoking section upstairs, which leaves the nonsmokers run of a fume-free ground floor. I'm keeping fingers crossed that the current appalling rash of small-business closures doesn't run Orsini's out of SW7, as it has so many of the long-term, useful shops of the neighborhood.

 Pizza Express ★

PIZZA	INEXPENSIVE	QUALITY ★★	VALUE ★★★★

80–81 St. Martin's Lane, West End, WC2; ☎ **0207-836-8001;**
tube: Charing Cross.
26 Cowcross Street, West End, EC1; ☎ **0207-490-8025; tube: Farringdon.**
25 Millbank, Pimlico, SW1; ☎ **0207-976-6214; tube: Millbank.**
The Pheasantry, 152 Kings Road, Chelsea, SW3; ☎ **0207-351-5031;**
tube: Sloane Square.
137 Notting Hill Gate, Notting Hill, W11; ☎ **0207-229-6000;**
tube: Notting Hill Gate.
70 Heath Street, North London, NW3; ☎ **0207-433-1600;**
tube: Hampstead; www.pizzaexpress.co.uk

Customers Locals and tourists. **Reservations** Not necessary. **When to go** Anytime. **Entree range** £4.95–£7.95. **Payment** AE, DC, MC, V. **Service rating** ★★★. **Friendliness rating** ★★★½. **Bar** In some, not in others. **Wine selection** Minimal. **Dress** Casual. **Disabled access** Yes. **Hours** Daily, 11 a.m.–midnight.

SETTING AND ATMOSPHERE Relaxed, unpretentious, and notably child-friendly.

SUMMARY AND COMMENTS I have given specific information for branches in several neighborhoods, but trust me when I say that no matter where you are, there is a Pizza Express nearby—they are as ubiquitous as Starbucks, and offer the same kind of quality-controlled, predictable fare. Its formula is very simple. There are 16 types of pizza, a couple of baked pasta dishes and salads, and a few side dishes. The thin-crust pizzas are smallish by American standards but reliably good; the pasta dishes are acceptable but not really what you should go here for; the salads are not at all bad, if a little skimpy, and come with pizza dough balls. In short, not a place to come for a special meal but when you want something cheap and fast. It is especially good for children, who are always made welcome. Art lovers should note that they contribute 25p to the Veneziana Fund, formerly Venice in Peril, whenever they order a Veneziana pizza (onions, capers, olives, pine nuts, sultanas, mozzarella, tomato, £5.55). Pizza Express is listed here because it's everywhere and it promises decent quality; for something better in the pizza field, see Strada (page 349).

 Pret à Manger ★

SANDWICHES, ETC.	INEXPENSIVE	QUALITY ★★	VALUE ★★★★

1 Great Tower Street, The City, EC3; ☎ **0207-932-5265; www.pret.com;**
tube: Tower Hill or Monument

Customers Locals and tourists. **Reservations** Not necessary. **When to go** Breakfast, lunch, or snack. **Entree range** £1.50–£4.99 (children's sandwiches are around £1.50). **Payment** AE, CB, D, MC, V. **Service rating** ★★★. **Friendliness**

rating ★★★½. **Bar** No. **Wine selection** None. **Dress** Casual. **Disabled access** Yes. **Hours** Daily, 8:30 a.m.–6 p.m.

SETTING AND ATMOSPHERE Sandwich shop.

SUMMARY AND COMMENTS Pret à Manger isn't a restaurant but an outlet for fast food, mostly sandwiches, and part of a chain of 150 in the capital (and many more outside London and overseas). Sandwiches range from ultrasimple egg salad (called "egg mayonnaise" in Britain) to wraps filled with hummus and red pepper salad, or avocado and pine nuts; they also do a great vegetarian sushi or deluxe sushi. The menu tries to stay up-to-the-minute with current diet fads, and now offer such noshes as no-bread poached salmon and egg, and a no-bread mozzarella (which may not help calorie-counters: there's not much in the way of lo-cal sandwiches). The salads, while small by Yankee standards, are varied and yummy, and you can put your own dressing on most of them. Cakes and desserts are decent; coffee is of high quality. Pret is good, it's cheap, it's quick, and it's everywhere. If you just want a light, quick refueling session, this is one place to get it.

Providores and Tapa Room ★★★★

FUSION	MODERATE/EXPENSIVE	QUALITY ★★★★½	VALUE ★★★★

109 Marylebone High Street, Marylebone, W1; ☎ 0207-935-6175; www.theprovidores.co.uk; tube: Bond Street

Customers Mostly locals. **Reservations** Essential. **When to go** Lunch or dinner. **Entree range** Tapa Room, £4–£12; Providores, £10–£24. **Payment** AE, MC, V. **Service rating** ★★★★½. **Friendliness rating** ★★★★★. **Bar** "People can come and just drink but they cannot sit or stand at the bar." **Wine selection** Excellent. **Dress** Smart casual. **Disabled access** Yes. **Hours** Tapa Room, Monday–Friday, 9 a.m.–11:30 p.m.; Saturday, 10 a.m.–10:30 p.m.; Sunday, 10 a.m.–10 p.m. Providores, Monday–Friday, noon–3 p.m. and 6–10:30 p.m.; Saturday and Sunday, noon–3 p.m. and 6–10 p.m.

SETTING AND ATMOSPHERE Beautiful modern decor, warm minimalism with a New Zealand theme.

HOUSE SPECIALTIES Varying menu might offer sweet potato, feta, and caramelized red onion tortilla with smoked tomato vanilla relish; baked goat's cheese ricotta with grilled asparagus; five-spiced roast Barbary duck breast; Berbere spiced kangaroo filet on a shitake, basil and haloumi fritter tahini and yogurt; roast monkfish on chorizo mash with artichoke and bean salsa.

SUMMARY AND COMMENTS Just looking at the list of specialties may tell you you're on unfamiliar territory. But while the dishes sound strange, the genius of chefs Peter Gordon and Anna Hansen ensures that even the strangest-sounding combinations work beautifully on the plate. They really know their stuff, regardless of where the ingredients and methods come from. Asian influences are effortlessly and expertly absorbed into their own highly individualist cooking. And one of the nicest things here is the plentiful plateful of dining possibilities. You can go in for breakfast, brunch, a light snack in the Tapa Room, or a full meal in the main restaurant. Prices are not ultralow, even in the Tapa Room, a mellow kind of eatery with a great breakfast menu (including the surprisingly delicious sweet brown rice and apple porridge), and all-day tapas such as shitake and haloumi fritters with pomegranate cumin yogurt. The higher prices upstairs are not out of line for restaurants of this quality. And the quality—even while challenging every known rule of modern cooking—is truly exceptional. If you have a sense of culinary adventure, head straight for Providores.

Rasa ★ ★ ★ ½

INDIAN	MODERATE	QUALITY ★ ★ ★ ½	VALUE ★ ★ ★ ★

6 Dering Street, West End, W1; ☎ 0207-629-1346; www.rasarestaurants.com; tube: Oxford Circus

Customers Locals and aficionados. **Reservations** Recommended. **When to go** Lunch or dinner. **Entree range** £6.25–£10.95. **Payment** AE, CB, D, MC, V. **Service rating** ★ ★ ★ ½. **Friendliness rating** ★ ★ ★. **Bar** Yes. **Wine selection** Small but good. **Dress** Casual. **Disabled access** Restaurant only. **Hours** Monday–Saturday, noon–3 p.m. and 6–11 p.m.

SETTING AND ATMOSPHERE Pleasant modern interior, simply decorated, friendly and informal.

HOUSE SPECIALTIES Southern Indian vegetarian dishes.

OTHER RECOMMENDATIONS Breads, pickles, and chutneys.

SUMMARY AND COMMENTS The original Rasa, in out-of-the-way Stoke Newington, has educated thousands of Londoners about the beauties of Keralan (Southern Indian) cuisine. The second branch, in W1, more centrally located, deserves a visit if you have the slightest interest in Indian food. Once a strictly vegetarian restaurant, their success has persuaded them to add Northern Keralan meat and seafood dishes to the menu. You can ask them to put together a Kerala feast, which will give a good balance and range of dishes featuring different flavors and textures. Or choose for yourself among the dosas (filled pancakes), curries, and side dishes of rice, vegetables, and exquisite bread. The food is filling but not stodgy, and no one who eats it comes away unimpressed. Besides the two new Rasa Express take-away shops they've opened, they also have a branch called Rasa Samudra (5 Charlotte Street, W1; ☎ 0207-637 0222; tube: Goodge Street).

Richard Corrigan at Lindsay House ★ ★ ★ ★

BRITISH	MODERATE/EXPENSIVE	QUALITY ★ ★ ★ ★ ½	VALUE ★ ★ ½

21 Romilly Street, West End, W1; # 0207-439-0450; www.lindsayhouse.co.uk; tube: Leicester Square or Piccadilly Circus

Customers Mostly locals. **Reservations** Recommended. **When to go** Lunch or dinner; à la carte lunch only, £14 for starters, £26 for main course, £8 for dessert; set menus £25 (lunch), £48 (dinner). Pretheater dinner is £25 for 3 courses. **Payment**

AE, CB, D, MC, V. **Service rating** ★★★★. **Friendliness rating** ★★★★. **Bar** No. **Wine selection** Excellent but expensive. **Dress** Smart casual. **Disabled access** No. **Hours** Monday–Friday, noon–2:30 p.m. and 6–11 p.m.; Saturday, 6–11 p.m.

SETTING AND ATMOSPHERE Two stories of a town house decorated with quiet elegance; cozy and subdued but not stuffy.

HOUSE SPECIALTIES An ever-changing menu offers such dishes as monkfish *en croute* with béarnaise sauce; caramelized veal sweetbreads; braised pig's cheek with pork belly and pineapple; gnocchi with fontina and wild mushrooms; steamed fillets of sole with beurre fondue, salsify, and brown shrimp; roasted scallops with spiced chicken and pea shoots. Desserts may include sauté of seasonal fruits with cinnamon brioche; cinnamon rice pudding with poached pear; sour apple sabayon; and lime soufflé with coconut sorbet.

SUMMARY AND COMMENTS Richard Corrigan, the chef at Lindsay House, has long had devoted followers for his robust, sophisticated approach to modern cooking. After moving around a slew of London restaurants, he seems to have settled into this beautiful, slightly eccentric Georgian town house, giving his fans the kind of hearty and exciting food that they've come to expect from him. Corrigan is Irish, and his native tradition shows in a love of pork, offal, and Irish ingredients such as black pudding. But his cooking is also based in French classicism, and it is both refined and adventurous, with unusual combinations of foods and tastes adding up to a sublime experience. Desserts are a strong point. Prices are not low on the menu or (especially) the wine list; this is a restaurant for a special occasion. But if you like hearty cooking raised to the level of culinary art, chances are you'll love the Lindsay House. They'll cook specially for vegetarians if asked.

 The River Cafe ★ ★ ★ ★ ½

| TUSCAN ITALIAN | EXPENSIVE | QUALITY ★★★★ | VALUE ★ |

Thames Wharf, Rainville Road, Hammersmith, W6; ☎ 0207-386-4200; www.rivercafe.co.uk; tube: Hammersmith

Customers People with very deep pockets or on expense accounts, celebs, local worthies, foodies. **Reservations** Essential; weeks in advance usually. **When to go** Anytime; try for a table outside. **Entree range** £26–£28; starters £11–13. **Payment** AE, DC, MC, V. **Service rating** ★★★★. **Friendliness rating** ★★★★. **Bar** For waiting diners. **Wine selection** Good, but like everything, expensive. **Dress** Smart casual. **Disabled access** Yes. **Hours** Daily, 12:30–3:30 p.m. and 7–11 p.m. (last booking at 9 p.m.).

SETTING AND ATMOSPHERE There's a wall of floor-to-ceiling windows on one side of the long, narrow dining room, and on the other side is the busy kitchen, a kind of short-order diner-looking affair. The general tone is unpretentious and functional. Seats in the garden are coveted on warm days.

HOUSE SPECIALTIES Changing menu reflects seasonal freshness of produce.

OTHER RECOMMENDATIONS Risotto, pasta of the day, any of the fish (John Dory filet wood-roasted with olives, or chargrilled Scottish salmon with artichoke fritti); the desserts.

ENTERTAINMENT AND AMENITIES Outside, there's the Thames, inside there's the cooking going on behind the counter. They sell olive oil and cookbooks. Parking valet service.

SUMMARY AND COMMENTS Having heard so much about the River Café for so long, I finally got a chance to try it, at the urging of an out-of-town friend who footed the bill (thank goodness). It's hard to get reservations, but if you book enough in advance it's possible (just don't try changing it—we were unable to change the booking from two people to three, even a week ahead). Opened in 1987 by Rose Grey and Ruth Rogers, in a building next to Richard Roger's architectural firm, and on the banks of the Thames. Thanks to training at Chez Panisse, the women's idea was to cook simple dishes of the Tuscan variety with perfectly fresh and seasonal produce. Their success was extraordinary, and the River Café cookbooks became the bible of many a foodie. The dishes are sensationally excellent, although not grand or showy in the French style. The specials of the day are always good: I shared a grilled scallop with anchovies and lentils appetizer that, despite my general avoidance of anchovies, was superb, awakening taste buds I didn't know I had. However, the prices are truly astronomical for what is essentially an upgrade of typical Tuscan peasant fare. A three-course meal with dessert (and without wine) can easily cost £65 before the 12.5% service charge is added. It's safe to say that the bill can kill the overall pleasure of the meal, as one reflects on the small portions and the general workaday ambience. However, for true seekers of good cooking, or anyone whose rich uncle wants to buy them a meal, the River Café is a must-try: since it opened in 1987, its simple, healthy philosophy has had a huge influence on the revolution in modern British eating habits.

Royal China ★ ★ ★

CHINESE	INEXPENSIVE	QUALITY ★ ★ ★	VALUE ★ ★ ★ ★

13 Queensway, Bayswater, W2; ☎ 0207-221-2535; www.royalchinagroup.co.uk; tube: Bayswater or Queensway

Customers Locals and tourists, many Chinese. **Reservations** Not necessary. **When to go** Weekend lunch or dinner. **Entree range** £7–£24; as much as £50 for abalone, and £36 for set meals. **Payment** AE, D, MC, V. **Service rating** ★ ★. **Friendliness rating** ★ ★ ½. **Bar** Yes. **Wine selection** Excellent for a Chinese restaurant. **Dress** Casual. **Disabled access** Restaurant only. **Hours** Monday–Thursday, noon–11 p.m.; Friday and Saturday, noon–11:30 p.m.; Sunday, 11 a.m.–10 p.m.

SETTING AND ATMOSPHERE Plush Chinese decor with lots of black lacquer and gold, comfortable seating; can be quite hectic when there's a crowd.

HOUSE SPECIALTIES All shellfish, especially lobster (cooked in six different ways), scallops, and prawns; dim sum.

OTHER RECOMMENDATIONS Chicken with cashews; sautéed chicken with black beans and chili; fillet steak with black pepper; hot and spicy veal; Royal China Dover sole; Royal China lotus leaf rice; chilled mango pudding.

SUMMARY AND COMMENTS Probably the very best restaurant in this Chinese restaurant–crowded street, Royal China is also a cut above in comfort, and care has been taken with the decor, even if it is not to everyone's taste. But the food is to everyone's taste, as you'll see if you go along for dim sum. There are the usual dumplings and rolls, as well as special dishes rarely found elsewhere, and the quality is exceptional. The only problem is the crowds, which on weekends (especially Sunday) can lead to enormous lines outside. Go during the week for a more leisurely affair, and for dinner as well as lunch. Seafood is exquisite, and even the set meals (normally a no-go area) are good. Service can be a little abrupt, but it is better than at many comparable places. And the wine list is a surprise, as good as some upper-echelon European restaurants—and much cheaper!

 Rules ★★★

BRITISH	MODERATE/EXPENSIVE	QUALITY ★★★	VALUE ★★★

35 Maiden Lane, West End, WC2; ☎ 0207-836-5314; www.rules.co.uk; tube: Covent Garden or Charing Cross

Customers More tourists than locals. **Reservations** Recommended. **When to go** Dinner is best. **Entree range** £15.95–£19.95. Post-theatre 2-course meal at 10 p.m. for £18.95. **Payment** AE, DC, JCB, MC, V. **Service rating** ★★★. **Friendliness rating** ★★★. **Bar** No. **Wine selection** Small but good. **Dress** Casual. **Disabled access** Yes. **Hours** Monday–Saturday, noon–11:30 p.m.; Sunday, noon–10:30 p.m.

SETTING AND ATMOSPHERE Ornate old-fashioned decor with prints and statues, but modern lively bustle at busy times.

HOUSE SPECIALTIES Game dishes, Aberdeen Angus beef.

OTHER RECOMMENDATIONS Chateaubriand, béarnaise sauce, and asparagus; Scottish salmon with cauliflower, pea shoots, and shallot puree; grilled calves liver; steak, kidney, and oyster pudding; rib of beef, Yorkshire pudding; warm chocolate pudding with rose petal and pistachio ice cream cornet; sticky date and toffee pudding.

SUMMARY AND COMMENTS Rules has been serving food from this location since 1798. That by itself is not a reason to recommend it, and for years the restaurant served indifferently cooked game and beef to tourists seeking a taste of tradition. But for some years now it has had a French-trained chef who combines classic game and meat cookery with up-to-the-minute modern touches. The menu doesn't stand still, which is a good sign. There is less unusual experimentation than before, and fish lovers will find more choice. But many will choose the appetizing selection of meat and game. The selection of "feathered and furred game" (some from their estate in Scotland, which also occasionally supplies beef and pork) is as good as you'll find anywhere in London. Vegetarians should probably go elsewhere. If you want to try a classic, old-fashioned rib of beef, or steak and kidney pie (with or without oysters), Rules is one of your best bets.

 Strada ★ ★ ★ ½

| ITALIAN | INEXPENSIVE | QUALITY ★★★½ | VALUE ★★★★½ |

15–16 New Burlington Street, Mayfair, W1; ☎ 0207-287-5967; www.strada.co.uk; tube: Oxford Circus

Customers Local office workers, families, tourists. **When to go** Lunch or dinner. **Entree range** £6.50–£14.50 . **Payment** AE, MC, V. **Service rating** ★★★. **Friendliness rating** ★★★. **Bar** No. **Wine selection** Adequate. **Dress** Casual. **Disabled access** Yes. **Hours** Monday–Friday, noon–2:30 p.m. and 6:30–10:45 p.m.; Saturday, 6:30–10:45 p.m.; Sunday, noon–2:45 p.m.

SETTING AND ATMOSPHERE Casual, informal Italian.

HOUSE SPECIALTIES Pasta and pizza.

OTHER RECOMMENDATIONS Salads, soups, simple appetizers, risotto.

SUMMARY AND COMMENTS Pizza Express (see page 343) may have more branches and a higher public profile, but everyone in the know will assure you that Strada is the better bet. Their menus feature a range of dishes, with good choice at every course, and the pizza is cooked in a wood stove, with a delicious thin crust. The level of cooking is generally very sound. But most people who come to Strada come for pizza or pasta, served in friendly, lively surroundings by a young (usually) Italian waitstaff. Prices are low by London standards, and ingredients really taste of Italy. Moreover, they positively adore children in true Italian fashion. Don't expect fireworks, but do expect to be well fed and well looked after. And note that there are 20 other locations at the time of writing.

Tamarind ★ ★ ★ ½

| INDIAN | MODERATE | QUALITY ★★★½ | VALUE ★★★ |

20 Queen Street, Mayfair, W1; ☎ 0207-629-3561; www.tamarindrestaurant.com; tube: Green Park

Customers Locals and tourists. **Reservations** Recommended. **When to go** Lunch or dinner. **Entree range** £12.95–£24. **Payment** AE, CB, D, DC, MC, V. **Service rating** ★★★. **Friendliness rating** ★★★. **Bar** Yes. **Wine selection** Very good. **Dress** Smart. **Disabled access** No. **Hours** Monday–Friday, noon–2:45 p.m. and 6–11:30 p.m.; Saturday, 6–11:30 p.m.; Sunday, 6–10:30 p.m.

SETTING AND ATMOSPHERE Chic, stylish decor sets the tone.

HOUSE SPECIALTIES Venison with turnips; roast duck breast; salad of tandoori chicken and grilled paneer in a honey-lemon marinade with chilies and avocado; carrot fudge with melon seeds and raisins served with vanilla ice cream.

OTHER RECOMMENDATIONS Pretheater set menu, from 6 to 7 p.m.; set lunch, based on seasonal produce, £16.95 for two courses, £18.95 for three; an amazing tasting menu at £48.

SUMMARY AND COMMENTS Tamarind's immensely gifted founding chef, Atul Kochhar, left the restaurant in 2003 to set up his own Benares. But thanks to the talented new chef, Alfred Prasad, things have remained steady here, despite the new competition. Tamarind has always produced excellence in every department, from chutneys and pickles (available for sale) to breads and rice, and on to the meat, fish, and vegetable dishes that make this one of the best Indian eateries in London. (Vegetarians could do very well just ordering rice, bread, and a selection of side dishes.) Mind you, it's also one of the most expensive. A three-course meal with all the right side dishes can easily cost £45 before drinks. Part of that is paying for the setting, for a large and polished team of waiters, and for rent in one of London's most exclusive areas. But it's also paying for the best ingredients, cooked with exceptional skill and attention. And I defy you to find a better set-lunch deal at any of the other one-Michelin-starred fancy restaurants in town. If you want to find out how good Indian restaurant cooking can be and don't mind paying "European" prices for the pleasure, this is one of the three or four best places to do it.

 The Tea Palace ★ ★ ★ ½

BRITISH MODERN	MODERATE	QUALITY ★ ★ ★	VALUE ★ ★

175 Westbourne Grove, Notting Hill, W11; ☎ 0207-727-2600; www.teapalace.co.uk; tube: Notting Hill Gate

Customers Chic mothers (called "yummy mummys" here), Notting Hillbillies, tea fanciers. **Reservations** No. **When to go** Breakfast, lunch, or tea time. **Entree range** Breakfast £4–£8.50; lunch £6.75–£13.75; afternoon tea from £12. **Payment** MC, V. **Service rating** ★ ★ ★. **Friendliness rating** ★ ★ ★ ½. **Bar** No. **Wine selection** Not big, but good champagne. **Dress** Casual. **Disabled access** Yes. **Hours** Daily, 10 a.m.–7 p.m.

SETTING AND ATMOSPHERE Crisp, clean, old-fashioned tea shop atmosphere, with linen tablecloths and the occasional celeb sightings.

HOUSE SPECIALTIES Every kind of tea known to mankind; homemade scones, and healthy, fresh food on the local side.

OTHER RECOMMENDATIONS Homemade crumpets served with a honeycomb; cold avocado and yogurt soup; warm chicken salad; buttermilk pancakes. Afternoon tea is classically English, and beautifully served.

ENTERTAINMENT AND AMENITIES Within the café, there is a Tea Emporium, with shelves of exotic or everyday teas reaching to the ceiling. They are very knowledgeable about tea, so do have a chat with the clerk.

SUMMARY AND COMMENTS This tea shop/café opened in 2005, and has fit in seamlessly with the varied group of specialty food shops, good restaurants, and take-away delis on the stretch of Westbourne Grove just northeast of Portobello Road. It's popular with the locals, and many people are making the trip from afar to get their hands on the finest, most unusual teas imported these days. There's a health consciousness to the menu, as befits the neighborhood, where probably ever third woman is on some kind of ferocious diet. The fact that breakfast is served at 10 a.m. gives you an idea of who goes there: no builder's breakfasts of bacon butties here. The menu is small, but elegant, and the food is bought (heavy on the organic) and prepared with care. Afternoon tea is very good, if a bit steep in price, but it has all the yum yums you want: homemade scones, with or without raisins (sultanas), clotted cream, homemade jams, little tea sandwiches, and a selection of pastries. They also offer champagne for tea time so dieters can drink their refreshments.

 Texas Embassy Cantina ★ ★ ½

TEX-MEX	MODERATE	QUALITY ★★★	VALUE ★★★

2 Cockspur Lane, West End, SW1; ☎ 0207-925-0077; www.texasembassy.com; tube: Charing Cross

Customers Tourists, teenaged Londoners, expat Americans. **Reservations** For large parties. **When to go** Anytime. **Entree range** £6.50–£12. **Payment** AE, DC, MC, V. **Service rating** ★★★. **Friendliness rating** ★★. **Bar** Yes. **Wine selection** Wines from California and parts of Latin American. **Dress** Casual. **Disabled access** Yes. **Hours** Daily, noon–midnight.

SETTING AND ATMOSPHERE Faux wild west, with weird stuff on the walls and floors; old American license plates, painted footsteps that you follow to the bathroom, gaily lit strings of lights all over, and western music blaring.
HOUSE SPECIALTIES Fajitas, nachos, chimichangas, burritos, and so on, with Texas-sized portions. Ribs, steaks, and chicken, cooked in Tex-Mex style.
OTHER RECOMMENDATIONS Frozen margaritas, Jose Cuervo and other tequila-based crazy cocktails.
ENTERTAINMENT AND AMENITIES Gift shop selling items that you don't need.
SUMMARY AND COMMENTS OK, so it's not *entirely* believable Tex-Mex food, but they do give it their best shot, and do it better than most in London. And the drinks are pretty great, as are the nachos. What I like about it best are the appetizers and the whole Texas/USA vibe it's got; it's a little taste of home for me. With the walls covered in oddities and mad decorations, coming in here lifts your mood a bit, and it's a big hit with children. There's a kids' menu, which, considering the size of the regular portions, is a dang good idea. The building once housed the White Star Shipping Line (the company that launched the *Titanic*) and is not actually the site of the real Texas Embassy, which was in St. James nearby. Another draw is that this eatery is near Trafalgar Square and convenient to everything. In the summer they put lots of tables out, and the liquor and laughs flow freely.

Veeraswamy ★ ★ ★

INDIAN	MODERATE	QUALITY ★★★	VALUE ★★★½

Mezzanine Floor, Victory House, 99 Regent Street, Piccadilly, W1; ☎ 0207-734-1401; www.veeraswamy.com; tube: Piccadilly Circus Chutney Mary, 535 King's Road, Chelsea, SW10; ☎ 0207-351-3113; www.chutneymary.com; tube: Fulham Broadway

Customers Mostly locals. **Reservations** Recommended. **When to go** Lunch or dinner. **Entree range** £9–£14 . **Payment** AE, CB, DC, MC, V. **Service rating** ★★★★.

Friendliness rating ★★★★. **Bar** No. **Wine selection** Very good. **Dress** No dress code. **Disabled access** Restaurant only, not restrooms. **Hours** Monday–Friday, noon–2:30 p.m. and 5:30–11:30 p.m.; Saturday, 12:30–3 p.m. and 5:30–11:30 p.m.; Sunday, 12:30–3 p.m. and 5:30–10:30 p.m.

SETTING AND ATMOSPHERE Stylish, colorful room overlooking Regent Street; mostly young, fashionable crowd.

HOUSE SPECIALTIES Mussels in coconut and ginger sauce; supreme of chicken with sesame; Malabar lobster curry with fresh turmeric and raw mango; chicken curry with saffron and Himalayan screw pine essence; tandoori chicken tikka sautéed in a sauce of tomato and onion; green chili and cheese naan.

OTHER RECOMMENDATIONS Breads, condiments, set lunch (in addition to à la carte menu), Monday to Saturday: £13.50 for two courses, £15.50 for three courses; Sunday, lunch of Indian favorites is £16 for three courses and £8 for kids. Also there's a pretheater dinner, £16 for three courses.

SUMMARY AND COMMENTS Veeraswamy, Britain's first Indian restaurant, has been on this site for decades, but the quality-conscious Chutney Mary group took over and revamped it in 1998. They modernized everything from decor to menu to wine list, and the result is one of London's better Indian restaurants. (And for those of you who are interested in tradition, there are fascinating sepia photos on the wall of how it used to be.) The attractively modern room has contrasting pale wood with deep, well-chosen color, and is a far cry from the decor of most Indian restaurants in London. Service is from a young, multiethnic crew, and the kitchen specialists prepare dishes of their own region. This means that each dish is likely authentic, whatever part of India it represents. Vegetable and fish/meat/chicken dishes are given equal prominence and cooked with equal care, making Veeraswamy a particularly good place to come with a mixed group of vegetarians and meat eaters. Prices are fair, compared with other Indian restaurants at this level, and set-price offerings make them even better. If your time is limited and you can eat only at one Indian place, you can't go wrong here or at its sister restaurant, Chutney Mary (whose atmosphere I prefer, but it's more hassle to get to than Veereswamy's prime location on a funny little street between Regent Street and Piccadilly).

Wagamama ★★

ASIAN	INEXPENSIVE	QUALITY ★★	VALUE ★★★★

4A Streatham Street, Bloomsbury, WC1; ☎ **0207-323-9223;**
www.wagamama.com; tube: Tottenham Court Road
10A Lexington Street, West End, W1; ☎ **0207-292-0990;**
tube: Oxford Circus or Piccadilly Circus

Customers Mostly locals. **Reservations** Not accepted. **When to go** Anytime. **Entree range** £5.25–£9.50. **Payment** AE, D, JCB, MC, V. **Service rating** ★. **Friendliness rating** ★★. **Bar** No. **Wine selection** Minimal. **Dress** Casual. **Disabled access** No, but see below. **Hours** Monday–Saturday, noon–11 p.m.; Sunday, 12:30–10:30 p.m.

SETTING AND ATMOSPHERE Spartan room with communal seating at long tables.

HOUSE SPECIALTIES Soup noodles, fried noodles, dumplings.

SUMMARY AND COMMENTS Wagamama has spoken to the zeitgeist of London, growing from the original restaurant on Streatham Street to 19 others, and several outside London as well. The expansion tells the story of a phenomenal success based on a simple idea. Produce a menu that focuses on just a few things, make them consistently well, and cut out all the frills so you can sell them cheap. The focus is on noodles, mostly Japanese varieties such as ramen and udon, although each year the menu grows longer, with deep-fried katsu of all kinds, salads, curry, fried rice, raw salad, gyoza—all sorts of good solid pan-Asian dishes, and lots of fruit/vegetable juice combos. The frills that disappear are personal space (you sit at long tables with other diners) and flexibility. You're in a machine at Wagamama, and it's not a place to dawdle. But the meals are cheap, well made and filling, and you can be in and out very quickly when you're on the go. Complaints almost always deal with service, which has little to do with personalized attention and much more with keeping the machine working smoothly. The places can't be ignored for their quality and speed; just don't expect to feel pampered. Kids like the informality of the place, and recognizing this, they now offer a kids' menu with non-yucky food they might like (breaded chicken or noodles), at prices you will like (£2.75–£3.95). *Note:* Some other branches have disabled access.

The Wolseley ★ ★ ★ ★

MODERN BRITISH	MODERATE/EXPENSIVE	QUALITY ★ ★ ★ ★	VALUE ★ ★ ★

160 Piccadilly, West End, W1; ☎ 0207-499-6996; www.thewolseley.com; tube: Green Park

Customers Variety of celebs, ladies who lunch, local businesspeople. **Reservations** Essential. **When to go** Morning, noon, or night, though breakfast is the least expensive. **Entree range** £6.50–£27.50. **Payment** AE, DC, MC, V. **Service rating** ★ ★ ★ ★. **Friendliness rating** ★ ★ ★ ½. **Bar** Yes, and very attractive it is. **Wine selection** Excellent. **Dress** Smart casual. **Disabled access** Yes. **Hours** Monday–Friday, 7 a.m.–midnight; Saturday, 9 a.m.–midnight; Sunday, 9 a.m.–11 p.m.

SETTING AND ATMOSPHERE Gorgeous, if a bit cavernous, sharing a lovely stretch of Piccadilly with the Ritz.

HOUSE SPECIALTIES Oysters, crab hash with lemon aioli; steak frites.

OTHER RECOMMENDATIONS Any of the plats du jour; wiener schnitzel; pan-fried gnocchi; desserts.

SUMMARY AND COMMENTS This grand café on Piccadilly opened in 2003 and hasn't had a slow day since. It's the place of the moment but not because it's trendy, but because it has so much to offer. The owners, also responsible for the success of La Caprice, The Ivy, and J. Sheeky, named this eatery after the company that commissioned the 1921 building as a car showroom, before it became a Barclay's Bank. It's filled with A-, B-, and C-list celebrities, some of whom rate the small dining room up the staircase at the back. It's distinguished without being intimidating, and the prices of the well-prepared dishes are not ridiculously out of this world—you can order a hamburger for £9.50 without inviting a sneer from the waiter. The pan-fried gnocchi with pesto and spring vegetables is so delicious I tried to make it myself, but there is no way a home-cooked job will measure up. The efficient service and attention of the waiters, and the buzzy energy in the dining room, definitely add to the enjoyment of its reliably great food. You'll need to reserve a table well in advance of your visit, so make the call—they don't take e-mail reservations. If you can't get in for lunch or dinner, I urge you to check out the fine breakfast, served from 7a.m.; the post-lunch all-day menu; or a late afternoon tea that costs about 10 quid less than the same thing at the many fancy hotels in the area.

World Food Café ★ ★ ★

INTERNATIONAL VEGETARIAN   INEXPENSIVE   QUALITY ★ ★ ★   VALUE ★ ★ ★ ★

14 Neal's Yard, upstairs, West End, WC2; ☎ 0207-379-0298; tube: Covent Garden

Customers Healthy locals and vegetarians. **Reservations** No. **When to go** Lunch. **Entree range** £4.85–£7.95. **Payment** Cash only, no credit cards. **Service rating** ★ ★ ★. **Friendliness rating** ★ ★ ★ ★½. **Bar** No. **Wine** BYOB. **Dress** Casual. **Disabled access** No. **Hours** Monday–Saturday, noon–7 p.m.

SETTING AND ATMOSPHERE Funky cafeteria-type place overlooking Neal's Yard.

HOUSE SPECIALTIES Anything on the blackboard list of dishes, be it Korean, African, or Mexican.

OTHER RECOMMENDATIONS Desserts are good and even healthy-ish.

ENTERTAINMENT AND AMENITIES Watching the cooks work from your perch on a counter stool; the loo is interestingly decorated.

SUMMARY AND COMMENTS Although this is basically a self-service restaurant (you order at the till, pay, sit down, and they bring your food), it is one of my favorite places to eat when I am in Covent Garden. You can always be sure of some complex and fresh vegetarian fare made up of dishes from around the world. Couscous, guacamole, African stew, Greek salads, and more, are all inexpensive and filling. There's a remarkable serenity about the people who work together in the middle of the lunch counter, a graceful ballet of putting food on plates that is hypnotizing. It has a great kind of 1960s Haight-Ashbury vibe that is enhanced by the photos of exotic places taken by the owners, who seem to have made all the stops on the hippie trail. There's no smoking, free water, and almost always a seat, which is more than one can say about Food for Thought (see page 331) another excellent, inexpensive vegetarian restaurant nearby.

Yautcha ★ ★ ★ ★ ½

| CHINESE AND DIM SUM | EXPENSIVE | QUALITY ★★★★½ | VALUE ★★★ |

**15–17 Broadwick Street, Soho, W1; ☎ 0207-494-8888;
tube: Oxford Circus**

Customers Expense accounters, Soho businesspeople, trendies. **Reservations** Yes.
When to go Anytime. **Entree range** Dim sum dishes, £3.20–£20. **Payment** AE, DC,
MC, V. **Service rating** ★★★★. **Friendliness rating** ★★. **Bar** Tearoom to wait for
table. **Wine selection** Excellent. **Dress** Casual. **Disabled access** No. **Hours** Tearoom, Monday–Saturday, 10 a.m.–11 p.m.; dining room, Monday–Saturday, 11
a.m.–11 p.m.; Sunday, 11 a.m.–10 p.m.

SETTING AND ATMOSPHERE Extraordinary modern, almost sci-fi decor, with
enormous fish tanks and moody lighting.

HOUSE SPECIALTIES Dim sum and plenty of it; mango spring roll; chicken feet
in chili black-bean sauce; crispy duck roll; crystal buns; shumai.

OTHER RECOMMENDATIONS Desserts.

ENTERTAINMENT AND AMENITIES People watching, fish-tank gazing, and
unusual restrooms.

SUMMARY AND COMMENTS Alan Lau is a well-known restaurateur in London,
having founded the successful Wagamama (see page 352), as well as the
only Chinese restaurant in Britain to win a Michelin star, the very expensive and innovative Hakkasan (8 Hanway Place, Soho, W1; ☎ 0207-
927-7000). Yautcha is his latest venture, an achingly hip spot that cost
£4.5 million to decorate (you may find yourself wondering where the
money went; except for the fish tanks, it's very minimalist). It certainly is
dramatic, and interesting, and edgy, but the real star here is the dim sum,
translated from Yau's native Hong Kong into a vernacular that is
authentic yet updated. Cheong Wah Soon, the former chef at Hakkasan
has brought his Michelin-honored talents to the kitchen, with predictably excellent results. The dishes themselves are not expensive, but
watch what you order, as the bill can climb very steeply, very easily. The
dim sum is not served on the old traditional trolley, but on bamboo
trays by elegantly attired waitstaff (their uniforms were created by the
costume designer for the film *Crouching Tiger, Hidden Dragon.*) You'd be
forgiven for thinking the waiters, regardless of their clothes, could be a
bit friendlier and less abrupt, but if you've ever eaten in Hong Kong,
you'd know that's the norm there: get 'em in, feed 'em up, get 'em out.
There was originally a 90-minute maximum for eating, and you'd be
told you couldn't have dessert if your time was up. But thanks to the
patronage of the Beautiful People, that rule's less rigid these days; the
idea of some crouching tiger waiter telling the dragon-like Naomi
Campbell to vacate her table *now* is hilariously unlikely.

PART NINE

ENTERTAINMENT
and NIGHTLIFE

 THE LONDON SCENE

NO OTHER METROPOLIS CAN RIVAL LONDON for the overall quality and quantity of its theaters, opera, ballet, concert halls, jazz venues, art galleries, antiques fairs, auctions, exhibitions, cinemas, cabarets, comedy clubs, television, historic buildings, historic walks, private clubs, nightclubs, pubs, shops, and restaurants. A huge number of books and magazine titles are published in the United Kingdom (including the Harry Potter global phenomenon), and Londoners enjoy four quality national newspapers in addition to a rash of bumptious tabloids. The U.K. gives the U.S. market a run for its money in its wealth of silly celeb-worshipping mags (*Heat, Now, Closer, Hello, OK,* to name just a few), and they don't even bother, as *People* magazine does, to pretend to care about ordinary folks—its just all about paparazzi pix and captions. In fact *Heat* magazine has a two-page section on what celebs were spotted where doing what ("Victoria Beckham was seen getting into a limo on Bond Street," that sort of thing), as well as intensive coverage of the 15-minutes-of-famers from the wildly popular *Big Brother* reality show.

It's a bit of a schizophrenic culture, where BBC productions of classic, quality literature share the same airwaves as people eating spiders on *I'm a Celebrity, Get Me Out of Here.* The art scene, too, ranges from the sublime to the ridiculous, where an unmade bed of Tracy Emin commands higher prices than a David Hockney or Lucian Freud portrait. This all-encompassing embrace of the cutting-edge and the kooky, with the traditional and classic, is probably what makes London's culture so utterly incomparable; where the 2005 production of Shakespeare's *Henry IV* packed in as many eager viewers as did magician David Blaine's 2004 stunt of living in a transparent box above the Thames.

This enthusiasm for wildly diverse entertainment may lay in the diversity of London's population. Although the city remains English in character, it has, since World War II, become a microcosm of the defunct British Empire, with one person in five now hailing from an ethnic minority. The Indian, Asian, and Afro-Caribbean influences on the London scene have helped make it as vibrantly international as New York. And London's got a few liberal features that New York doesn't, such as the freedom to smoke in bars and pubs, a liberal language policy on BBC and ITV, and a wide variety of casinos and betting parlors.

As any James Bond expert is aware, gambling has long been legal in Britain. Along with the high-class and the seedy casinos, most high streets (the main shopping street of an area) have an easily recognizable Ladbrokes betting shop, where one might place a wager on the horses, cricket results, snow at Christmas, or even on who will win the latest series of reality/humiliation TV contests, which England has so taken to heart.

Soho is the epicenter of London's nightlife. Here's where you'll find the theaters, cinemas, pubs, clubs, and restaurants that have made London famous. But London's culture and night fun is not limited to this neighborhood by any means. Pick up copies of *Time Out, What's On,* or the Thursday supplement of *The Evening Standard, Metro Life,* to see what's going on where and when.

unofficial **TIP**
You can check out **www.timeout.com** in the weeks prior to your visit to hone your list of what to do in London.

THEATER

LONDON THEATER COMES IN THREE CATEGORIES: the West End, London's equivalent to New York City's Broadway; off–West End, ditto; and fringe, which is roughly similar to New York's off-Broadway.

THE WEST END

ALTHOUGH "THE WEST END" REFERS TO AN area of central London, it also indicates cultural status and encompasses the **National Theatre,** which is located south of the Thames. West End theaters are famous for their musicals and mainstream productions, but drama in the West End is of variable quality, ranging from the sublime to the overtly commercial.

However, the theaters of London's West End enjoy such renown that Hollywood actors able to command millions of dollars per film clamor to appear in the theaters for a relative pittance and, more often than not, to mixed reviews. Nicole Kidman, Daryl Hannah, Jerry Hall, Kevin Spacey, Madonna, Matthew Perry, David Schwimmer, and Ellen Burstyn are just a few of the Yankee stars who have lit up the West End in recent years, and there are always more waiting at the gate for this supreme thespian challenge.

Try **www.officiallondontheatre.co.uk** for a listing of current plays, plus reviews, phone numbers, and tips. Choose the production venue, and then click on a seating plan of the theater, which is very useful when ordering tickets. The stalls are the seats on the same level as the stage; dress circle is the first balcony, and upper circle is the second balcony, also known as the nose-bleed seats, even though in many theaters a front row upper circle ticket is even better than a rear row stalls seat.

Don't be tempted to buy a ticket from a tout (essentially, a scalper type), because he or she will charge an unfair price for it, compared to the legitimate half-price tickets found in the discount ticket booth, called **tkts,** a little house located on the south side of the grassy part of Leicester Square (tube: Leicester Square). It is a tan building with a clock on top of it. You can also identify it by the lines forming on either side of it. The west side is for night performances; the east side sells matinee tickets. They charge £2.50 per ticket for a service fee, they accept cash or credit cards (no traveler's checks), and limit each customer to four tickets. The booth is open Monday through Saturday from 10 a.m. to 7 p.m., Sunday from noon to 3:30 p.m. (for matinees only). Tickets for the big West End shows are expensive, ranging in price from £19 to £50 (and even beyond). If it's a hot production you want to see, such as the current *Guys and Dolls* at the Piccadilly Theatre, starring Ewan MacGregor and Jane Krawkoski (who played Elaine on *Ally McBeal*), you aren't likely to find half-price tickets available. In the case of the blockbuster West End play, you will need to book tickets through **Ticketmaster** (☎ 0207-344-4444; **www.ticketmaster.co.uk**) or **Firstcall** (☎ 0207-420-0000; **www.firstcalltickets.com**), or call the box office directly. However, booking fees add around 10% (and can soar to a punishing 20% in some cases) to the price of a ticket, and many theaters charge a telephone booking fee. The least expensive way to acquire a ticket is to turn up at the box office in person, hoping for a ticket return.

unofficial **TIP**
Be sure you go to the tkts booth only and not one of the many shop fronts around Leicester Square that call themselves discount or half price, but actually offer no deals at all.

Many theaters offer half-price tickets on Mondays and for dress rehearsals. Some also grant concessions to students and seniors. Queuing for return tickets (or standby tickets) before a performance can also sometimes yield a discount. London recognizes the need to make cultural events affordable: in 2003 the National Theatre, with the financial sponsorship of Travelex, launched a £10 ticket scheme that will fill the seats and please the pockets. The London Symphony Orchestra has also reduced prices and has introduced a £5 concert ticket. West End/Broadway impresario Cameron Mackintosh has even reduced some of the ticket prices for the massive musicals he produces (although you can still get skinned for as much as £50 for a good seat on a Saturday night). So some things actually do go down in price in London—and it all seemed to start with the handful of big museums eliminating entrance fees in December 2001. Interestingly, these adjustments have nothing to do with getting more government subsidies, which in fact continue to drop shamefully.

The **National Theatre** (South Bank, SE1; box office ☎ 0207-452-3000; information ☎ 0207-452-3400; **www.national theatre.org.uk;** tube: Waterloo) has three theaters (Cottesloe, Lyttelton, Olivier) presenting plays in repertory, as well as special events with live music or dance DJs. In 2003 Trevor Nunn yielded his position as director to Nicholas Hytner, whose first change was to drop the politically loaded "royal" from the theater's title to the approbation of many traditionalists (no word on what the Queen thought). The quality of the theatrical presentations continues from strength to strength, encompassing classical as well as new and neglected plays from the whole of world drama. On the lighter side, the National also offers musicals and even productions for children, six days a week throughout the year. The box office is open Monday through Saturday, 10 a.m.–8 p.m. Prices range from £10–£35.

unofficial **TIP**
Go for the standby tickets a half hour before the performance.

Royal Court Theatre (Sloane Square, SW1; ☎ 0207-565-5000; **www.royalcourttheatre.com;** tube: Sloane Square) re-opened in 2001 after an extensive and expensive refurbishment. The Royal Court has long been the most important venue for new writers of every nationality; the *New York Times* called it "the most important theatre in Europe." The "Royal Court Young Writers Programme" has exchange residencies with other countries, and also stages new productions in many cities around the world. It opened in 1956 with John Osborne's *Look Back in Anger,* which is considered ground zero of the "Angry Young Men" generation of playwrights, novelists, and filmmakers. The Royal Court also had the distinction of staging international plays by Bertolt Brecht, Eugene Ionesco, Samuel Beckett, and Jean-Paul Sartre. At the Royal Court, you could witness the debut of a new Vaclav Havel, Caryl Churchill, or David Hare. There are two theaters: the Downstairs main theater and the Upstairs studio. Performances are held Monday–Saturday at 7:30 p.m., and the Saturday matinee is held at 3:30 p.m. Tickets are £9–£27.50 Tuesday–Saturday; £9–£15 on Friday and for previews and matinees; and £7.50 on Monday (£9 if you book in advance).

unofficial **TIP**
The Royal Court is a great alternative to the West End theaters, and it's cheaper, too.

The authentic re-creation of **Shakespeare's Globe Theatre** (New Globe Walk, SE1; ☎ 0207-401-9919; **www.shakespeares-globe. org;** tube: Blackfriars), close to its original site, is the achievement of American expat actor Sam Wannamaker. Sadly, Wannamaker died shortly before the completion of the restoration. It is an extraordinary accomplishment and as fascinating to the student of historical architecture as it is to Bard buffs. It was made using only the tools

unofficial **TIP**
Most restaurants in the West End, even the upscale ones, offer pre-show menus at reduced prices. The three theaters described here have decent restaurants on site offering good deals on pretheater dinners.

available to the original builders: imagine dovetailing joints without electricity! Although the basement museum remains open year-round to provide the world's largest exhibition devoted to Shakespeare and the theater of his time, the roofless Globe's theatrical season is limited to April through October. The box office is open Tuesday–Saturday, 10 a.m.–6 p.m. Matinees are Saturday at 2 p.m. and Sunday at 1 p.m. or 6:30 p.m. (times alternate each week). Tickets are £5–£29. The cheap tickets are for standing in the yard in front of the stage, not a viable option for many people, but a lot of fun for those with stamina (and a rain poncho).

OFF–WEST END

OFF–WEST END THEATERS OFTEN PROVIDE THE most outstanding productions in terms of creativity because they offer writers, directors, and actors an artistic freedom that can be lacking in the more commercially motivated organizations. With emphasis firmly on the modern and avant-garde, the **Almeida** (Almeida Street, N1; ☎ 0207-359-4404; **www.almeida.co.uk;** tube: Angel) features cerebral drama from top writers and actors, and came under the direction of former Royal Shakespeare Company head Michael Attenborough when it reopened in spring 2003. Tickets are £6–£30. The intimate 105-seat **Bush Theatre** (Shepherd's Bush Green, W12; ☎ 0207-610-4224; **www.bushtheatre.co.uk;** tube: Shepherd's Bush or Goldhawk Road) is considered the next most important spot (after the Royal Court theater) for productions by new writers, many of whom have gone on to greater successes. Tickets are £6–£14. The **Donmar Warehouse** (41 Earlham Street, WC2; ☎ 0207-369-1732; **www.donmarwarehouse. com;** tube: Covent Garden) became an exciting venue in the late 1990s under the artistic direction of Sam Mendes, who was followed in early 2003 by Michael Grandage, who continues to provide provocative drama. Tickets are £12–£29. Home to gay and lesbian productions, the **Drill Hall** (16 Chenies Street, WC1; ☎ 0207-307-5060; **www.drillhall.co.uk;** tube: Goodge Street) welcomes everyone. The atmosphere of this intimate theater is brilliant. Monday evenings are for women only. Tickets are £10–£16. A small theater located above a pub, **The Gate** (The Prince Albert, 11 Pembridge Road, W11; ☎ 0207-229-0706; tube: Notting Hill Gate) has a fine reputation for its low-budget yet high-quality drama from all over the world. Budding actors and directors relish the opportunity to work here and will happily do so for free, so great are the kudos. Performances run Monday through Saturday. Tickets are £10–£20. **The King's Head** (115 Upper Street, N1; ☎ 0207-226-1916; tube: Angel) is London's most venerable pub theater and frequently puts on top-quality, small-scale plays, revues, and musicals. It's a fine pub as well.

Sadly, its founder and guiding spirit Dan Crawford died in 2005, but the shows, as usual, will undoubtedly go on. Tickets are £10.50–£22.50. **Regent's Park Open Air Theatre** (Regent's Park, NW1; ☎ 0207-486-2431; **www. openairtheatre.org.uk;** tube: Baker Street) provides for those who like their theater alfresco. Set in the middle of the eponymous park and furnished with a bar and snacking facilities, this charming summer theater is an ideal venue in which to see the company's vastly entertaining version of *A Midsummer Night's Dream*. The season kicks off on June 4, and tickets are £12–£30.

unofficial **TIP**
Be prepared for the vagaries of British weather. Performances will be canceled in torrential rain, but they will soldier on in the usual drizzle; bring a rain poncho.

   Riverside Studios (Crisp Road, W6; ☎ 0208-237-1111; **www.river sidestudios.co.uk;** tube: Hammersmith) overlooks the river Thames near Hammersmith Bridge. There are three studio spaces: one seats 400, another seats 150, and the third is in permanent use for a TV show. In addition to the theatrical and dance productions, there is also a repertory cinema, a gallery, and a café overlooking the river. The **Soho Theatre** (21 Dean Street, Soho, W1; ☎ 0207-478-0100; **www.sohotheatre.com;** tube: Tottenham Court Road) has been happily at home in this modern and well-appointed space for the last few years, producing topical new plays, as well as occasional stand-up comedy, and readings by authors. Standing in the shadows of the Old Vic theater, **YoungVic** (66 The Cut, SE1; ☎ 0207-928-6363; **www.youngvic.org;** tube: Southwark) has become a successful venue, attracting big-name actors and touring companies such as the Royal Shakespeare Company. Shows run Monday through Saturday. Tickets are £15–£40.

FRINGE

FRINGE THEATER CAN BE FOUND THROUGHOUT London, but like British weather, is variable and generally of patchy quality. Still, the following theaters do provide the occasional ray of histrionic sunshine:

   The small **Chelsea Theatre** (King's Road, SW10; ☎ 0207-352-1967; **www.chelseatheatre.co.uk;** tube: Sloane Square, then bus 211, 319, 19, 22; or South Kensington, then bus 49, 45) focuses on exciting new plays, which run seven to eight weeks at a time. Performances are held Monday–Saturday, at 8 p.m. Tickets are £8–£12. **The Finborough** (Finborough Arms, Finborough Road, SW10; ☎ 0207-373-3842; **www.finboroughtheatre.itgo.com;** tube: Earl's Court) is a small pub venue that hosts new writers, some of whom have ended up in the West End or on Broadway. Performances are Tuesday–Saturday, at 7:30 p.m.; Sunday matinees occur at 3:30 p.m. Tickets are £12. For previews and Tuesday performances, all seats are £8. Credit cards are *not* accepted. Being so close to Piccadilly, **Jermyn Street Theatre** (16b Jermyn Street, SW1; ☎ 0207-287-2875; **www.jermynstreettheatre. co.uk;** tube: Piccadilly Circus) is a great alternative to a big West End

unofficial **TIP**
Although a tuxedo is no longer requisite attire when attending the theater, the British middle class still appears to dress with care for certain events, and black tie remains mandatory for any gala charity night where royals may be present. Certainly suits and smart dresses are often seen in West End and off–West End theaters, but you will not feel out of place in the egalitarian sneakers, baseball cap, and jeans.

production. This intimate 70-seater venue hosts a mixture of shows, but musicals are the main feature. Performances are daily at 7:30 p.m.; Sunday matinees are at 3 p.m. Tickets are £12–£18. The **New End Theatre** (27 New End, NW3; ☎ 0207-794-0022; **www.newendtheatre.co.uk;** tube: Hampstead) is a venue with reliably interesting productions, situated in lovely Hampstead. Tickets range from £15–£18. New writing and a thriving bar can be found in plentiful supply at the legendary **Old Red Lion** (416 St. John Street, EC1; ☎ 0207-837-7816; **www.oldredliontheatre.co.uk;** tube: Angel). Tickets are around £10.

LAUGHS *in* LONDON

THE BRITISH FREQUENTLY CONGRATULATE themselves on their ironic sense of humor, and justly so; surely no other country has produced so many comic novelists of the caliber of Henry Fielding, William Makepeace Thackeray, Jane Austen, E. F. Benson, George Meredith, Anthony Trollope, Jerome K. Jerome, Evelyn Waugh, Tom Sharpe, Kingsley Amis, and, of course, the divine P. G. Wodehouse, to name only a few.

British humor extends even to politicians, some of whom are given to entertaining quips (intentional and not) that would soon see them hounded out of office in less tolerant societies. Winston Churchill was undoubtedly the wittiest of leaders and is eminently quotable; no prime minister has since lived up to his standards.

Although British sitcoms are currently in the doldrums, the BBC has an unrivaled roster of past triumphs. If you are staying in one evening, try renting videos of *Fawlty Towers, Black Adder, Yes Prime Minister, Jeeves and Wooster, Drop the Dead Donkey, Alan Partridge, Rising Damp, Only Fools and Horses, French and Saunders, The Comic Strip, The Fast Show, Slap the Pony, Absolutely Fabulous, Stella Street,* and *The Office.* (Keep your eye peeled for Ricky Gervais's follow-up to *The Office,* called *Extras,* a comedy that trains a jaundiced eye on the low end of the film business, with outrageous cameos by big-name actors mocking themselves). Although most English-born and expats find most of the above seriously funny, it's hard to gauge how well they travel—some foreigners are mystified by them, as comedy tends to be culture specific.

London has more comedy outlets than most cosmopolitan cities. The humor on display varies in quality and includes traditional improvisation and physical, surreal, and observational comedy. Most venues provide food and drink, both of which help if the acts are dreadful. There's a **London Comedy Festival** in May (☎ 0870-011-9611; **www.londoncomedy festival.com**) that tee-hee aficionados will like.

Amused Moose Soho (Barcode, 3–4 Archer Street, W1; ☎ 0208-341-1341; **www.amusedmoose.co.uk;** tube: Piccadilly Circus) Shows are at 8:30 p.m. on Monday, Wednesday, and Thursday; and 8 p.m. on Saturday and Sunday. Tickets are quite reasonably priced from £4–£10.

unofficial **TIP**
They boast that their comedians are "first-date friendly," which presumably means you won't be hounded or humiliated as part of the act.

Comedy Café (66 Rivington Street, EC2; ☎ 0207-739-5706; **www. comedycafe.fsnet.co.uk;** tube: Old Street) is one of the handful of clubs in London devoted entirely to comedy and takes the generous precaution of granting free admission on Wednesday, when new acts make their debuts. Comedy Café is open Wednesday through Sunday. Tickets are £5 on Thursday, £10 on Friday, £14 on Saturday. They offer a "party package" that rather endearingly includes party hats, as well as entrance cost, 3-course dinner, and entrance to weekend disco; packages cost £14.50 on Wednesday, £21.50 on Thursday, £26.50 on Friday, £29.50 on Saturday.

Comedy Store at Haymarket House (1A Oxedon Street, SW1; ☎ 0207-344-0234; **www.thecomedystore.co.uk**; tube: Piccadilly Circus) is the venue from which alternative comedy exploded onto British television screens. Such stars as Jennifer Saunders (of *French and Saunders* and *Absolutely Fabulous*), Keith Alan, Ben Elton, and Ric Mayall began their careers here. It's still the best club on the circuit; open Tuesday through Sunday. Tickets range from £13–£15; Monday the cost is only £5 for the King Gong show. **Jongleurs** (The Cornet, 49 Lavender Gardens, SW11; ☎ 0207-564-2500; **www.jongleurs.com;** tube: Clapham Junction) is as popular as the Comedy Store, with an impressive lineup of performances that aren't all stand-up comedy. Shows are on Friday at 8:45 p.m., followed by a disco and late bar until 1 a.m. Saturday performances start at 7:15 p.m. with a late show at 11:15 p.m. There's another branch in North London, **Jongleurs Camden Lock** (Dingwalls, Middle Yard, Camden Lock, Camden High Street, NW1; ☎ 0207-564-2500; **www.jongleurs.com;** tube: Camden Town or Chalk Farm) that is comfortable and busy, so book in advance. Shows on Friday start at 8:45 p.m., followed by a disco; on Saturday, performances start at 7:15 p.m. and 11:15 p.m. Tickets are £11–£15 on Friday and £15–£20 on Saturday.

▌ CLASSICAL MUSIC

LONDON, ARGUABLY THE MUSIC CAPITAL of the world, is endowed with four highly regarded orchestras, two internationally renowned arts establishments, numerous ensembles, and a correspondingly wide range of concerts.

Although the Barbican's London Symphony Orchestra remains the capital's leading ensemble, with the London Philharmonic only just behind, the South Bank Centre's London Philharmonic Orchestra has been gaining in strength. Then, too, the Royal Philharmonic Orchestra enjoys a distinguished history, despite having to get by without public funding. Many of the world's leading musicians flock to London stages, often for the city's frequent music festivals, especially the Henry Wood Promenade Concerts (more affectionately known as The Proms), held each year from July to September at the **Royal Albert Hall** (Kensington Gore, SW7; ☎ 0207-589-3203 or 589-8212; **www.royalalberthall.com;** tube: Gloucester Road or South Kensington). The Albert is a prodigious Victorian building that hosts pop gigs, opera, ballet, the *Cirque du Soleil,* and even wrestling bouts. Tickets are from £6 right up to £80. An impressive exterior restoration opened up the original entrance on the opposite side of Kensington Gore; the sweeping steps afford a view of the friezes and other details that define Victorian grandeur.

The refurbished **Royal Opera House** (Covent Garden, WC2; recorded information ☎ 0207-304-4000 or box office ☎ 0207-240-1200; **www.royalopera.org;** tube: Covent Garden) is worth a visit just to see the beautiful building, and in fact they do offer tours of the House. They have classical productions of operas and ballets, and the price of the tickets is wonderfully varied: from £4–£180.

Wigmore Hall (36 Wigmore Street, W1; ☎ 0207-935-2141; **www.wigmore-hall.org.uk;** tube: Bond Street) is the best place in town to hear piano recitals and chamber groups. Although the hall was revamped not long ago, Wigmore continues to serve up a largely traditional fare. Tickets are £5–£40.

You might care to attend a lunchtime concert held every second Thursday in the converted church of **St. John's Smith Square** (Smith Square, SW1; ☎ 0207-222-1061; **www.sjss.org.uk;** tube: Westminster). St. John's, near the Houses of Parliament, is nestled in an area of antique civility, and the church is possessed of a magical ambience. Tickets are £10–£15; £5 for students.

It is easy to lose one's way down the labyrinthine corridors of that monster of modernism, the **Barbican Centre** (Silk Street; ☎ 0207-638-8891 or 0207-638-4141; **www.barbican.org.uk;** tube: Barbican). Still, the fact that the Barbican has superb acoustics, is home to the London Symphony Orchestra, and hosts the "Great Orchestras of the World" makes it worth a music lover's effort. Other great orchestras that perform a wide range of classical music at the Barbican are the BBC Symphony Orchestra, the City of London Simfonia, and the English Chamber Orchestra. Tickets start at £6.50.

Perched just above the Thames next to Waterloo Bridge is the **South Bank Centre** (Belvedere Road, South Bank, SE1; box office ☎ 0207-960-4242; recorded information ☎ 0207-633-

0932; **www.sbc.org.uk;** tube: Waterloo). Its Royal Festival Hall (RFH1) is the main auditorium for symphony concerts; the smaller Queen Elizabeth Hall (RFH2) puts on semi-stage operas and chamber groups; and recitals as well as ensembles are performed in the intimate setting of the adjacent Purcell Room (RFH3). The South Bank Centre comes complete with restaurants, cafés, bars, and book and record shops. Ticket prices vary from £6–£80.

Weather permitting, there is nothing more English or more delicious than listening to classical music outdoors in the summer air, beside a great castle or on the grounds of a fragrant park. The **Hampton Court Palace Festival** (Hampton Court, East Molesey, Surrey; ☎ 0207-344-4444; **www.hamptoncourtfestival.com**) is held in June. British Rails, Hampton Court riverboat from Westminster, or Richmond to Hampton Court Pier (April–October). Tickets are £15–£85.

unofficial **TIP**
The impressive historic palace lawns beside the Thames make a perfect picnic ground.

The Holland Park Theatre (Holland Park, Kensington High Street, W8; box office ☎ 0207-602-7856; information ☎ 0207-603-1123; **www.operahollandpark.com;** tube: High Street Kensington or Holland Park) stages an array of music, theater, and dance performances in one of London's loveliest parks. Guests are sheltered from the harmful effects of storm and sun by an enveloping canopy. The Holland Park Theatre is open June–August. Tickets are £21, £38, and £43.

Kenwood Lakeside Concerts (Kenwood House, Hampstead Lane, NW3; ☎ 0208-233-7435; **www.picnicconcerts.com;** tube: Golders Green or East Finchley to courtesy bus on concert nights) are best enjoyed on the nights when they punctuate the concert with fireworks. Held during July and August on the grounds of Kenwood House in Hampstead Heath, this is one of London's most delightful events. Tickets vary from £17–£26, and seating is either in deck chairs or on the grass (bring a blanket and a picnic).

DANCE *and* BALLET

WHEN ONE THINKS OF DANCE IN London, a flood of terpsichorean images come pirouetting to mind: *The Red Shoes,* Fontaine and Nureyev, Fred and Adele Astaire, Sadler's Wells, The Royal Ballet, Covent Garden, and the wonderful movie *Billy Elliot,* which was reinvented for stage in 2005, becoming the biggest smash hit of the year in the West End.

Dance grew steadily in popularity throughout the 1990s, abetted by several festivals. **Dance Umbrella** (☎ 0208-741-5881; **www.dance umbrella.co.uk**) features contemporary dance from all over the world and normally runs during September and October for six weeks. The events are hosted at various venues across London, and the ticket prices vary according to the venue.

kids   **The Place Theatre** (17 Duke's Road WC1; ☎ 0207-387-0031; **www.theplace.org.uk;** tube: Euston, Euston Square, or British Rail: Euston) hosts over 32 dance events annually, featuring British and international contemporary dance companies, with a platform for new and emerging choreographers. The 300-seat theater also features a special children's season; tickets run from £5–£15.

Two of the largest and most active dance venues are the **Barbican Centre** and the **South Bank Centre** (see "Classical Music," above, for contact information).

The **Royal Ballet** hosts productions in the main theater of the **Royal Opera House** (see entries for the venue in the "Classical Music" and "Opera" sections). One can expect to see performances of such classics as *Don Quixote, The Nutcracker, La Bayadere, Giselle,* and *Romeo and Juliet.* Tickets are £4–£180.

The refurbishment of **Sadler's Wells** (Rosebury Avenue, EC1; ☎ 0207-863-8000; tube: Chancery Lane) has been completed at last, and the more intimate and central **Peacock Theatre** (Portugal Street, off Kingsway, WC2; ☎ 0207-314-8800; **www.sadlers-wells.com;** tube: Holborn), which served as the interim house during the refurbishment, is now a permanent branch of Sadler's Wells. The revamped Sadler's Wells has extensive bars, state-of-the-art flying and lighting equipment, an ultraflexible stage—twice its original size—and an 80-seat orchestra pit, among other attractions. Tickets are £10–£38.

unofficial **TIP**
Peacock and Sadler's Wells tend to feature more contemporary ballet performances.

Vast in scale, yet graceful in outline, the **London Coliseum** (St. Martin's Lane, WC2; ☎ 0207-632-8300; **www.eno.org;** tube: Charing Cross) is the home of the **English National Opera** (ENO) for most of the year, and also presents such leading dance companies as the English National Ballet and The Royal Ballet during its Christmas and summer seasons. Christmastime will feature *The Nutcracker.* See separate listing in "Opera," below.

◼ OPERA

THE **Royal Opera House's** (SEE "CLASSICAL MUSIC," above, for contact information) main theater is home to the **Royal Ballet,** but within the Royal Opera House there are two more intimate venues for opera and dance: the **Linbury Studio Theater** with 420 seats, and the **Clore Studios,** a 200-seater space, which is ideal for workshops and performances. At these smaller theaters one can see opera stripped to its essentials and for a more affordable price than the great productions in the main theater. Disability access has also improved. There is also the enticing Amphitheatre Bar and Restaurant, whose terrace overlooks Covent Garden. Ticket prices range from £5 for lunchtime performances and some severely restricted views of evening performances to £180 for the best seats. Go to **www.royalopera.org** for the latest information.

Home to the English National Opera, the **London Coliseum** (St. Martin's Lane, WC2; ☎ 0207-632-8300, **www.eno.org;** tube: Charing Cross) is a grand venue that tries to promote a populist image—with affordable ticket prices and challenging productions. Here, the operas are sung in English. Please note that the English Ballet takes over the Coliseum mid-December through mid-January. Tickets run from £10–£74.

LIVE JAZZ, POP, *and* ROCK

LONDON IS A MATRIX OF PERFORMING talent, and on any given Saturday night there will be well over 100 gigs being played throughout the city. Tickets vary in price from a fiver or less for pop gigs to more than £100 for a top pop attraction.

The thriving London jazz scene has, over the years, given the world such international luminaries as John McLauglin, George Shearing, and Dave Holland, which is indicative of the talent found here. Numerous restaurants, bars, pubs, and cafés continue to pleasantly enhance their atmosphere with live jazz music; see *Time Out* and the *Evening Standard's Metro Life* magazine for details. Among the leading jazz venues for largely local talent (all of which are profiled in the following club section) are **Ronnie Scott's, The 606 Club, Jazz Café,** and **Pizza Express.**

unofficial **TIP**
As with the theater, you must never buy tickets from scalpers, because the practice is illegal and their merchandise is probably forged. It is always best to purchase tickets from the concert venue itself. You will usually not be charged a booking fee if you pay with cash.

The Barbican and South Bank Centre often present top international stars, and two big jazz festivals are held in the autumn: the **Soho Jazz Festival** and the **Oris London Jazz Festival.**

The **Notting Hill Carnival,** held in late August, is Europe's largest street festival and features huge sound systems pumping out reggae, rap, and drum bass. Be warned, though: this event is not for the agoraphobic or timid—there are entirely too many muggers, pick-pockets, and deranged people pumped full of alcohol for it to suit every sensibility.

Gargantuan rock structures include the spectacularly renovated 11,000-seat **Wembley Arena** (Empire Way, Wembley, Middlesex; ☎ 0208-902-8833 or 0870-739-0739; **www.wembley.co.uk** or **www. whatsonwembley.com;** tube: Wembley Park); the 20,000-seat **Earl's Court Exhibition Centre** (Warwick Road, SW5; ☎ 0207-385-1200; **www.eco.co.uk;** tube: Earl's Court); and the 12,000-capacity **London Arena** (Limeharbour, Isle of Dogs, E14; ☎ 0207-538-1212; **www. londonarena.co.uk;** tube: take Jubilee to Canary Wharf, change to

Docklands Light Rail south to Crossharbour and London Arena). Of course, the sheer vastness of these coliseums tends to undermine the sonic and visual aspects of performance, and refreshments are overpriced. Still, if you want to catch the monsters of rock and pop, you'll probably have to go to these places; Coldplay, Madonna, and Paul McCartney have all chosen Earl's Court for their London gigs.

Smaller-scale venues are preferable in every way. The midsize **Shepherd's Bush Empire** (Shepherd's Bush Green; W12; ☎ 0207-771-2000; **www.shepherds-bush-empire.co.uk;** tube: Shepherd's Bush) had previously been the BBC Television Theatre before developing into a top popular music spot with an excellent sound system. The Empire has a three-tiered seating arrangement, and the first balcony has better views than the ground floor. Expect to pay about £10–£30 for tickets.

unofficial **TIP**
Brixton Academy lies within one of London's more dodgy areas, so use common sense and don't go wandering around after the gig.

The **Brixton Academy** (211 Stockwell Road, SW9; ☎ 0207-924-9999; **www.brixton-academy. co.uk;** tube: Brixton) has a 4,300-person capacity with a seated balcony and standing room at ground level. Many popular bands perform here, and the place has a good atmosphere. Tickets vary from £10–£26.

DANCE CLUBS

LONDON HAS THE REPUTATION OF BEING the dance-club capital of Europe, an assertion that's hard to refute when you get a load of its huge range of nightclubs, offering everything from hard-core techno to smooth jazz to tabletop dancers. London's clubs generally provide excellent quality. There are also many clubs who seek to filter out the riffraff and stay open very late by incorporating itself as a "members' club." One-off admissions depend on the club's popularity, clientele, and exclusivity—sometimes all it takes is a registration fee and the booking of a table to get in; call the club and check. However, many hot clubs will operate a rigorous suitability scan by some petty tyrant of a doorman, whose decisions as to who gets in and who doesn't are as mysterious as they are final.

unofficial **TIP**
Many clubs offer reduced admission rates before 10:30 p.m., and it is easier to gain admittance at that hour. A club that is quiet at 11 p.m. can often be packed to the rafters by midnight.

Therefore, it may be a good idea not to set your heart on one club when there are so many to choose from. Only do make an early start— before 11 p.m.—then, should the doorman prove intractable, you have the option—indeed, satisfaction—of repairing to a rival club.

Some clubs in London start late and carry on until 6 a.m., with their busiest period between 11:30 p.m. and 2 a.m. If you intend to dine at the club, we recommend you book a table for 10 p.m., after which you will be permitted to stay on for the dancing. Not all clubs serve dinner; call for information.

The following clubs (all profiled in the following section) are reliably fun, and have managed to withstand the violent winds of change that constantly blow through the club scene: **Embargo, Hanover Grand, Ministry of Sound,** and **Café de Paris.** Most venues have a rotation of club nights, with musical themes such as techno, blues, ska, trance, house and garage, rhumba, salsa, or disco. Some have school-night parties where you have to wear a school uniform to get in. Best to check in *Time Out, What's On,* or Thursday's *Metro Life* magazine section of the *Evening Standard* newspaper to see what is offered at which club so you aren't turned away for not wearing your sexiest old school uniform. A blazer and tie should do it for the guys; girls can throw on a very short kilt and an abbreviated top.

▌ BARS *and* PUBS

THE BRITISH ARE, GENERALLY SPEAKING, formidable drinkers, with the pub having stood since time immemorial as the central institution in the British experience. Sadly, pubs have been closing in droves in the last decade, victims of high rents, gentrification, and changing fashions. Many of the old stalwarts (and by old I mean going back to Tudor times) have been folded under the umbrellas of a few megalithic pub chains whose menus and prices are all pretty much the same. What used to be a quiet neighborhood place for the local working man to get quietly inebriated with his friends has had to change with the times by offering entertainment, upgrading its menu (there are more than a few Thai-food pubs in London), charging extortionate prices for a pint, or coming up with some hook to get the punters in. A favorite tradition of some bars and pubs is the Quiz/Trivia Night, which provides great entertainment—and education—while you drink.

Keeping pace with the British as they effortlessly knock back pint after pint is not an easy task for the uninitiated. Still, accomplished boozers, after putting in an appropriate amount of time and practice, should be able to hold up their end of the proceedings. If, however, you have inadvertently permeated the wall of British reserve to strike up an acquaintance with some friendly natives in a pub, and it is your turn to spring for a round but you haven't finished your pint, it is better to swallow one's pride rather than keep everyone waiting, and head over to the bar, cash in hand.

It's no surprise that the British lead the world at the sport of drinking pints of beer. Their superb beer comes in a variety of appealing guises, including lager (light continental beer), bitter (rightly named Anglo-Saxon ale), mild (concocted with chocolate malt), cider (fermented apple juice), and shandy (half lager, half lemonade). Best of all are real ales, the boozy equivalent of organic whole-meal bread.

Pub food also can be surprisingly good, depending on the overall quality of the pub itself. Most pubs are strongly historical in ambience, with walls festooned with attractive 18th- and 19th-century bric-a-brac, etched-glass privacy screens, flagstone floors, and deliriously over-carved mahogany or oak bars. In winter, many pubs have a roaring fire, and in summer, a beer garden.

Although bars with a special-hours certificate may remain open until 3 a.m., pubs tend to close at 11 p.m. on weekdays and at midnight on weekends. Britain, however, is forging ever closer ties with Europe, and British licensing laws are expected to soon be extended to match those of other EU member states. One of the most contentious proposals of the government is the almost Orwellian plan to curb public drunkenness by keeping pubs and drinking holes open 24 hours a day. The "thinking" behind this absurd concept is that if people don't feel the pressure to pack in as many drinks as possible before the closing gong at 11, there would be fewer drunks roaming the street in a stupor at 11:05. My belief is that only problem drinkers would feel compelled to down twelve-for-the-road; giving them full-time access to binge drinking isn't doing anyone any favors, least of all the public. We shall be keeping an eye on this as it develops.

If you wish to include a visit to an archetypal old-world inn on your agenda, you could not do better than the **Prospect of Whitby** (57 Wapping Wall, E1; ☎ 0207-481-1095; tube: Wapping). Whitby dates back to 1520 and is mentioned in Pepys's diary. The pub is renowned for its Elizabethan pewter bar, flagstone floors, cast-iron hearths, and small round windows. It is open daily, 11:30 a.m.–3 p.m. and 5:30–11 p.m.

 A haven for journalists and scribblers of all types since before 1666, when it was singed by the Great Fire, **Ye Old Cheshire Cheese** (145 Fleet Street, EC4; ☎ 0207-353-6170; tube: Blackfriars) is a storybook tavern replete with blazing fires, nooks and crannies, wooden floors, sundry bars, and dining sections often populated by tour bus habitués. And well they might have a visit: it is a must-see even for teetotalers; mind your head as you walk through the low ceilings of the little warrens. During your visit to Old Cheesy, you may as well raise a glass to previous regulars Thackeray, Johnson, Voltaire, Pope, and Tennyson. It's open noon–11 p.m. daily.

The hard-to-find **Ye Olde Mitre Tavern** (Ely Court, Hatton Garden, EC1; ☎ 0207-405-4751; tube: Chancery Lane) has been around since 1547. It's an atmospheric little hideaway with a pervasive sense of Elizabethan England. Open 11 a.m.–11 p.m.; closed weekends. A different time period is evoked in the **Old Bank of England** (194 Fleet Street, EC4; ☎ 0207-430-2255; tube: Temple), a majestic Italianate temple to Mammon, built as a branch of the Bank of England in 1888. Marble, soaring ceilings and huge chandeliers make this a pub of a very different color. Open 11 a.m.–11. p.m.; closed weekends. The **Cittie of York Tavern** (22 High Holborn, WC1; ☎ 0871-223-1801;

tube: Chancery Lane) is in a building that's been there since 1430, when it was part of a monastery. Although not impressive on entry, take a walk to the back where a vaulted ceiling covers intimate booths and suspended wine barrels. Open 11 a.m.–11 p.m.; closed Sundays.

One venue worth visiting, with three great individual bars under one roof, is the **Hilton Hotel** (Park Lane, W1; ☎ 0207-493-8000; **www.hilton.com;** tube: Hyde Park Corner or Green Park). If Britain's inclement weather causes you to yearn for sunnier climes, you might enjoy the hotel's **Trader Vic's** (☎ 0207-208-4113) for an ersatz night on a South Pacific island. Home of the Mai Tai cocktail and delicious food, Vic's is something of a mood lagoon. It's open Monday–Saturday, 5 p.m.–12:45 a.m. and Sunday, 5–10:30 p.m. Alternately, you could venture up to the 28th floor to the chichi and romantic **Windows Bar and Restaurant** (☎ 0207-208-4021), which offers a great view of London. Please note smart/casual dress code (no jeans or sneakers), and you will need to make reservations if you wish to dine. Windows' hours are Monday–Friday, 12:30–2:30 p.m. and 5:30 p.m.–2 a.m.; Saturday, 5:30 p.m.–3 a.m. Finally, the latest addition to the Hilton bar scene is the Zen-trendy **Zeta Bar** (it has a separate entrance on Hertford Street; ☎ 0207-208-4067). Cocktails are the specialty here—either nonalcoholic, delicious, health-inducing "liquid lunches," or the more lethal, alcoholic variety. Good bar food is also available. As the night wears on, a stricter door code is operated—but as long as you look affluent or trendy, you'll have no problem getting in. Zeta Bar is open Monday–Tuesday, noon–1 a.m.; Wednesday–Friday, noon–3 a.m.; Saturday, 5 p.m.–3 a.m.; and Sunday, 5–10:30 p.m.

SEX *in the* CITY

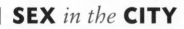

THE OLDEST PROFESSION HAS LONG FLOURISHED in London, with some of its more accomplished practitioners establishing links with the greatest names in England. Indeed, many noble lines were started by the illegitimate progeny of a royal sire and his concubine—an argument the Labour Party used in its abolishment of the right of hereditary peers to sit in the House of Lords.

Although prostitution is not as endemic as it was during its Victorian heyday (when even Tory Prime Minister Gladstone used to prowl the streets, in quest of fallen women in need of reforming), one cannot enter a telephone box in the central London of today without noticing the slew of salacious cards deposited within.

Soho is the sex center of London, and the area around Old Compton Street hosts quite a few sex shops and strip clubs. Beware of unlicensed venues, though, for they are, quite literally, tourist traps. A common practice of these establishments is to plant a siren-like hostess at the door who lures her victim inside for a drink and a show. The hapless fellow subsequently discovers that the bill for her orange juice and his beer comes to some astronomically unreasonable figure—and there are always a number of belligerent security staff on hand to ensure that customers pay up.

If you don't fancy the Soho scene, which is frankly still a bit sleazy, despite local cleanup campaigns, the next safest bet would be the erotic shows held at the following venues. These are mainly "saucy" cabaret shows or lap-dance clubs.

For Your Eyes Only (11 White Horse Street, W1; ☎ 0808-100-8899; tube: Green Park; and 28 Abbey Road, Park Royal, NW10; ☎ 0208-965-7699; **www.fyeo.co.uk;** tube: Park Royal) is the place to go if you want your dancers to go the "full monty." It's open Monday–Wednesday, 7:30 p.m.–2:30 a.m.; Thursday–Saturday, 7:30 p.m.–3 a.m.

Stringfellow's (16 Upper St. Martin's Lane, Covent Garden, WC2; ☎ 0207-240-5534; **www.stringfellows.com;** tube: Leicester Square) Peter Stringfellow's club pays host to the mass-market sort of celebrity: soap stars, footballers, and AWMs (actress/model/whatevers). The place is rife with 1980s glamour and pleasant enough in its way, particularly since Stringfellow's came into possession of a table-dancing license. It's open Monday–Saturday, 7:30 p.m.–3 a.m.

Sophisticats at Voltane (1 Marylebone Lane, W1; ☎ 0208-201-8804 or 201-8968; tube: Bond Street) is presided over by the amiable Cat-man, David Simones, and was recently the subject of a seven-part television documentary; it features ballerinas and showgirls from all over the world. Indeed, Sophisticats has a distinctly Parisian decadence about it; in addition to the twice-nightly Catgirl cabaret, the club also provides table dancing, caviar girls, and cocktail waitresses. It is recommended, since it is a private club, that you call first to see if you can get a reservation. It's open Monday–Friday, 8:30 p.m.–3 a.m.

GAMING *in the* UNITED KINGDOM

THE GAMING INDUSTRY IN GREAT BRITAIN is one of the most carefully regulated in the world. All casinos across England, Scotland, and Wales are licensed under the Gaming Act of 1968, which stipulates that unless already a member or the guest of a member, a player must register at the casino 24 hours before entering to play. The Gaming Act is designed to protect the public purse from the perils of compulsive gambling. Or, in the strictest legalese: it is a legal requirement that the membership application form is signed on the premises of the casino. A passport, driver's license, or other suitable identification is required. Authorization of all new memberships takes 24 hours. The casinos of London Clubs International begin with the magnificent **50 St. James** (50 St. James Street, SW1; ☎ 0207-491-4678; tube: Piccadilly), which opened as London's first club built for the purpose of gaming, in 1828, and is, along with the legendary **Les Ambassadeurs Club** (5 Hamilton Place, W1; ☎ 0207-495-5555; **www.clublci.com;** tube: Hyde Park), at the top end of the market. These exclusive and lavishly appointed clubs are frequented by royalty, the aristocracy, and celebrated figures from the world of entertainment. Both clubs are open daily, 2 p.m.–4 a.m. The dress code prohibits jeans, and men are expected to wear coats and ties in the evenings.

Midmarket venues include the **Rendezvous Casino** (14 Old Park Lane, W1; ☎ 0207-491-8586; **www.clublici.com;** tube: Hyde Park), with its spacious gaming floor, French-influenced bistro, and relaxed sports bar; and **The Sportsman Casino** (40 Bryanston Street, W1; ☎ 0207-414-0061; **www.clublci.com;** tube: Hyde Park), designed in the style of a Mississippi riverboat. As well as offering roulette, blackjack, and baccarat, the Sportsman boasts a dice game that has proven to be particularly popular with American visitors. Both clubs are open from about noon until 6 a.m.; gaming begins at 2 p.m. The dress code is smart/casual; no jeans are allowed. Coats and ties are required for men in the evening.

The mass-market **Golden Nugget Casino** (22 Shaftesbury Avenue, W1; ☎ 0207-439-0099; **www.clublci.com;** tube: Piccadilly) is the largest and busiest casino in the London Clubs group. It offers a fast-moving environment and fast food to go with it. The atmosphere of this casino is both friendly and informal. Games include roulette, baccarat, blackjack, and stud poker; it is open daily, 2 p.m.–6 a.m.

FREELOADER'S FORUM

VISITORS TO LONDON RAPIDLY DISCOVER the disparity in prices between goods and services purchased in England and pretty much anywhere else in the world. British merchandise is far more expensive due to, among other things, the legalized swindle called the Recommended Retail Price Index, whereby prices are fixed at scandalously high levels by agreement between manufacturers and retail outlets. But please do not complain about Britain's rip-off prices to those working on the shop floor, because although company bosses are raking it in, the poor worker at the checkout counter makes considerably less than he or she would in America. Yet the British can also be generous, as evidenced by the bonanza of free activities taking place throughout London.

FREE MUSIC

MANY CHURCHES IN CENTRAL LONDON, such as **St. John's** (Waterloo Road; tube: Waterloo), **St. Martin-in-the-Fields** (St. Martin's Place; tube: Leicester Square or Charing Cross), and **St. Pancras Church** (Euston Road; tube: Euston) offer free lunchtime classical concerts and recitals, as do music schools such as the **Royal College of Music**

(Prince Consort Road, SW7; ☎ 0207-591-4314; **www.rcm.ac.uk;** tube: Gloucester Road or High Street Kensington) and the **Royal Academy of Music** (Marylebone Road; ☎ 0207-873-7300; **www.ram.ac.uk;** tube: Marylebone or Baker Street). Performances at the Royal College of Music are held Monday–Thursday at 1:05 p.m., and during term time they are held evenings at 7 p.m. Performances at the Royal Academy of Music are held daily at 1:05 and 5:05 p.m.

You can also hear a mixture of musical delights at the aptly named **Freestage at the Barbican** (Silk Street, EC2; ☎ 0207-638-8891; **www.barbican.org.uk;** tube: Barbican) and at the **South Bank's National Theatre** (South Bank, SE1; ☎ 0207-452-3000; **www.nationaltheatre. org.uk;** tube: Waterloo or Westminster) and **Royal Festival Hall** (South Bank, SE1; ☎ 0207-960-4242; **www.sbc.org.uk;** tube; Westminster or Waterloo). Performances at the Barbican are held daily at 1 p.m.; the National Theatre features music in the foyer area daily at 6 p.m. Performances in the foyer of the Royal Festival Hall run daily from 12:30–2:30 p.m.; they also feature jazz on Friday evenings at 7 p.m.

The **100 Club** (100 Oxford Street, W1; ☎ 0207-636-0933; tube: Oxford Street) presents a well-liked series of swing and traditional gigs during Friday lunchtimes. Some bookshops also present free music. Try **Borders Books & Music** (197 Oxford Street, W1; ☎ 0207-292-1600; tube: Oxford Circus) every Friday night, upstairs, at 6:30 p.m.; **Helter Skelter Music Bookshop** (4 Denmark Street, WC2; ☎ 0207-836-1151; tube: Tottenham Court Road); and **Filthy Mac-Nasty's Whiskey Café** (68 Amwell Street, EC1; ☎ 0207-837-6067; **www.philkav@globalnet.co.uk;** tube: Angel) for a DJ on Friday nights and live music on Saturday evenings and Sunday afternoons.

Free Friday can be found at the **Cock Tavern** (Phoenix Road, NW1; ☎ 0207-387-1884; tube: Euston), where you can enjoy a variety of music and pints and alco-pops (frozen liquor on a stick) costing only £4, which is as cheap as can be found in London. Numerous bars, restaurants, and pubs also supply the customer with free music. Check *Time Out, What's On,* and *Metro Life* for listings.

FREE COMEDY

SINCE THE PRACTICE OF ADDING CANNED laughter to television soundtracks was universally condemned, the BBC now requires a constant supply of jolly spectators willing to be audience members for their comedy productions. For free tickets—just imagine the fun you'll have telling everyone back home that you appeared on British TV—contact the BBC Ticket Unit at Room 30, Design Building, BBC TV Centre, Wood Lane, W12 7RJ; ☎ 0208-576-1227, or go to **www.bbc.co.uk/whatson/tickets.**

London Nightclubs

NAME	DESCRIPTION	NEIGHBORHOOD
Bagleys	Gigantic disco and bar	Camden
Bar Rumba	International tunes and salsa	Soho
Browns Club	Glamorous disco	St. Holborn
Café de Paris	London's most renowned club	Soho
Cirque at the Hippodrome	Revamped old tourist trap is now over-the-top superclub	Leicester Square
Destino	Mexican food and top floor club	Mayfair
Dover Street Restaurant and Bar	Large jazz restaurant and bar	Mayfair
Embargo	Chelsea dance club	Chelsea
Emporium	Most discos would love to have the design and sound of this place	Soho
The Fridge Bar	Brixton's most celebrated disco	Brixton Hill
Grill Room @ Café Royal	Dress-up nights and cocktails	Piccadilly
Hanover Grand	Popular discotheque	Mayfair
Heaven	Gay dance club	Charing Cross
Jazz Café	Modern jazz club	Camden Town
Kabaret's Prophecy	Award-winning Soho celeb spot	Soho
Metro Night Club	Venerable live rock 'n' roll dive	Marylebone
Ministry of Sound	U.K.'s most famous disco	Elephant & Castle
Notting Hill Arts Club	Arty and intimate clubhouse	Notting Hill
Pizza Express	Intimate jazz club and restaurant	Soho
Ronnie Scott's	London's premier jazz club	Soho
606 Club	Jazz club and restaurant	Chelsea
333	3 floors of fun in trendy Hoxton	Hoxton
Turnmills	Late-night disco	Clerkenwell
Zoo Bar	Bar and dance club	Leicester Square

NIGHTCLUB PROFILES

Bagleys Studio

WEEKEND-ONLY GIGANTIC UNDERGROUND RAVE SITE

King's Cross Depot, York Way, Camden, N1; ☎ 0207-278-2777; tube: King's Cross

west end nightlife

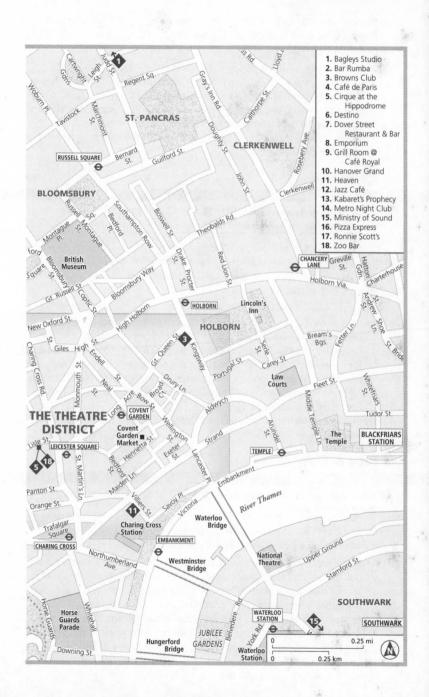

1. Bagleys Studio
2. Bar Rumba
3. Browns Club
4. Café de Paris
5. Cirque at the Hippodrome
6. Destino
7. Dover Street Restaurant & Bar
8. Emporium
9. Grill Room @ Café Royal
10. Hanover Grand
11. Heaven
12. Jazz Café
13. Kabaret's Prophecy
14. Metro Night Club
15. Ministry of Sound
16. Pizza Express
17. Ronnie Scott's
18. Zoo Bar

Cover Friday, £6–£20; Saturday, £14. **Prices** Cheap by club standards. **Dress** Smart/casual. **Food available** Snacks. **Hours** Friday, 10:30 p.m.–6:30 a.m.; Saturday, 10:30 p.m.–7:30 a.m.

WHO GOES THERE Youthful dancers and soaks.

WHAT GOES ON Sweat rises like smoke off the dance floor. Different fun on different nights. Thursday is disco roller-skating from 7 to 10:30 p.m.

SETTING AND ATMOSPHERE Bagleys is colossal, with five dance floors, six bars, and something different going on in every room.

IF YOU GO Enter a trance in a heaving, throbbing mob of young movers in one of the many rooms.

Bar Rumba

SWEATY SOHO DANCETERIA

36 Shaftsbury Avenue, Soho, W1; ☎ 0207-287-6933; www.barrumba.co.uk; tube: Piccadilly Circus

Cover £3–£12; free before 9 p.m. Tuesday, 10 p.m. Wednesday, 8 p.m. Thursday, 9 p.m. Friday. **Prices** Fair to middling. **Food available** Nibbles and snacks. **Hours** Monday, 9 p.m.–3.30 a.m.; Tuesday and Wednesday, 6 p.m.–3 a.m.; Thursday and Friday, 6 p.m.–3.30 a.m.; Saturday, 9 p.m.–5 a.m.

WHO GOES THERE Cool eclectic crowd.

WHAT GOES ON Eleven years old and still going strong, this basement club celebrated its first decade with a good-looking renovation. Although it's in the middle of tourist-land, it's where clubbing cognoscenti head for some of the most respected nights in town, even letting down their hair for free salsa lessons. From international sounds on a Monday night, drum and bass on a Thursday, to an eclectic mix of hip-hop and R & B on four turntables on Fridays.

SETTING AND ATMOSPHERE Recent face-lift makes the dark basement look ten years younger in strobe light.

Browns Club

GLAMOROUS DISCO

4 Great Queen Street, St. Holborn, WC2; ☎ 0207-831-0802; tube: Covent Garden

Cover £20. **Prices** Expensive. **Dress** Fashionable. **Food available** Dinner; catering available for large parties. **Hours** Friday and Saturday, 10:30 p.m.–4 a.m.

WHO GOES THERE Although its heyday was in the glamo 1980s, Browns can still pull in the odd celebrity or two with its Dynasty-like décor and comfort, spread over three floors. Although ostensibly a private members' club, the public is permitted entrance on Friday and Saturday nights.

WHAT GOES ON The club has a three-tiered social system: The downstairs dance floor is Midgard; the second floor is the Rainbow Bridge; and the VIP members' bar on the third floor is Asgard, home of the gods.

SETTING AND ATMOSPHERE Loud, glamorous, and urgent.

IF YOU GO Call to get on guest list.

Café de Paris

LONDON'S MOST RENOWNED CLUB

3–4 Coventry Street, Soho, W1; ☎ 0207-734-7700; www.cafedeparis.com; tube: Piccadilly Circus

Cover £10–£20. **Prices** Expensive but worth it. **Dress** Elegant. **Food available** French cuisine, of course. **Hours** Closes at 3 a.m.

WHO GOES THERE Everyone who is anyone in London.

WHAT GOES ON What doesn't go on? It's got cabaret, theme nights, and champagne-sipped-from-golden-slippers-type decadence and splendor. Live jazz music accompanies dinner, after which a DJ spins records for the more athletically inclined. The café is furnished with numerous bars, all terribly chic and deliciously sexy.

SETTING AND ATMOSPHERE Since its launch in the 1920s, Café de Paris has been synonymous with high society—even the queen has given a party there. Such luminous performers as Marlene Dietrich, Maurice Chevalier, Fred Astaire, Noël Coward, Frank Sinatra, Edith Piaf, and the divine ecdysiast Dita von Teese. Plush, opulent, and elegant, the café's art deco design was influenced by the operas *Don Giovanni* and *La Bohème*. A 50-foot bar encompasses the oval ballroom, and the restaurant is highly regarded.

IF YOU GO Dress up to the nines: you will be dining, drinking, and dancing in style. You may, however, need to know the right people to get in. Therefore we suggest that you circumvent all of the nonsense at the door by booking a table for dinner. Please do not turn up in your baseball cap and sneakers.

Cirque at the Hippodrome

REVAMPED OLD TOURIST TRAP IS NOW OVER-THE-TOP SUPERCLUB

Leicester Square, W1; ☎ 0207-437-4311; www.cirquehippodrome.com; tube: Leicester Square

Cover £15–£20, depending on night. **Prices** Slightly pricey. **Dress** Smart. **Food available** La Plume restaurant serves upscale posh food; cover fee to club is included with dinner. **Hours** Tuesday–Saturday, 9 p.m.–4 a.m.

WHO GOES THERE Hearty clubbers and entertainment junkies.

WHAT GOES ON The old warhorse of Leicester Square has got a shot in the arm that must have been megavitamins and amphetamine. The dreary bits of the old place have been ripped out, but they wisely went in for some nice restoration of Edwardian details. The food is deluxe (and expensive) and the club is fabulous, winning awards for best superclub of 2004, and dragging in a whole new generation of party people. There are theme nights with gaiety and debauchery, and Saturday must not be missed: daring young men and women on the flying trapeze float above you while celebrity DJs spin a mad mix of throbbing music. In 1900, the building was home to a circus; it's very appropriate that the venue has returned to its roots.

SETTING AND ATMOSPHERE Once a circus, now a cirque; this says it all. French Moulin-rouge type luxury and spectacle; good drinks and plenty of eye-popping entertainment and music fed through a superior sound system.

IF YOU GO Make it a Saturday night; reserve a table for dinner, and bring plenty of friends for the postprandial circus.

Destino

UPSCALE LATIN AMERICAN FIESTA ON THREE FLOORS

25 Swallow Street, Mayfair, W1; ☎ 0207-437-9895; www.destino.co.uk; tube: Piccadilly Circus

Cover None. **Prices** Not too bad, for London. **Dress** Casual. **Food available** Latin American full meals and grazing menu. **Hours** Daily, lunch to 3 a.m.

WHO GOES THERE Twentysomethings, salsa fiends, boisterous parties.

WHAT GOES ON Dinner and DJs spinning Latin electric house tunes that will make even the self-conscious get up to dance. There's no cover charge, no velvet rope, and lots of fun. Book a table for dinner and repair to the upstairs groove afterward. Salsa lessons prepare you for the late night revelries, as do the excellent margaritas.

SETTING AND ATMOSPHERE Truly gorgeous decor of handpainted tiles that are rumored to have been nicked from the King of Portugal a hundred years ago.

IF YOU GO Try the spicy food, down tequila shots, and try to salsa.

Dover Street Restaurant and Bar

8–10 Dover Street, Mayfair, W1; ☎ 0207-491-7509; www.doverst.co.uk; tube: Green Park

Cover £10–£20. **Prices** Reasonable. **Dress** Smart/casual; jeans and sneakers are not permitted. **Food available** Lunch menu offers a good deal; French and Mediterranean cuisine served until 2 a.m. **Hours** Monday–Friday, 5:30 p.m.–3 a.m.; Saturday, 7 p.m.–3 a.m.

WHO GOES THERE Numerous personalities from the worlds of stage, film, television, and sport mingle with white-collar workers.

WHAT GOES ON Fine dining, live music, dancing, and DJs.

SETTING AND ATMOSPHERE Dover Street has been established as one of London's most atmospheric restaurants and jazz, blues, and R & B venues for over 25 years and has recently been refurbished to become the largest venue of its kind in the capital. This place swings.

IF YOU GO Remember to adhere to the dress code.

Embargo

CHELSEA'S ALWAYS-IN-VOGUE DESIGNER DANCE CLUB

533B King's Road, Chelsea, SW10; ☎ 0207-351-5038; www.ponona.com; tube: Sloane Square

Cover £10 on weekends; £5 after 10 p.m. Thursday; free rest of the week. **Prices** Slightly pricey. **Dress** Stylish, smart casual. **Food available** A modern European restaurant serves dinner. **Hours** Daily, 9:30 p.m.–2 a.m.

WHO GOES THERE The young single Chelsea set.

WHAT GOES ON Despite the occasionally sadistic doorkeepers, Embargo still draws a very young and trendy crowd that dances the night away to thunderous house DJs. SETTING AND ATMOSPHERE A modern designer club with clean, hard surfaces and mirrors, Embargo is often attended by beautiful young women of posh pedigree.

IF YOU GO Don't disturb the beautiful young people.

Emporium

MOST DISCOS WOULD LOVE TO HAVE THE DESIGN AND SOUND OF THIS PLACE

62 Kingly Street, Soho, W1; ☎ 0207-734-3190; tube: Tottenham Court Road

Cover £10–£20. **Prices** Expensive. **Dress** Smart casual—no sneakers or jeans. **Food available** Chermoula serves expensive French and Mediterranean food. **Hours** Closes on Saturday at 4 a.m.

WHO GOES THERE Sports stars and soap stars.

WHAT GOES ON The pop celebrities discuss show biz and football over deafening DJs while waiters dance attendance on them.

SETTING AND ATMOSPHERE A high-tech and ultramodern club glistening with the sheen of success.

IF YOU GO Browse through a few tabloids beforehand so that you'll be able to recognize the subjects of the latest scandals.

The Fridge Bar

BRIXTON'S MOST CELEBRATED DISCO

Town Hall Parade, Brixton Hill, SW2; ☎ 0207-326-5100; www.fridge.co.uk; tube: Brixton

Cover From £5–£16 depending on night; see Web site for details. **Prices** Average. **Dress** Casual. **Food available** Fast. **Hours** Daily, 10 p.m.–6 a.m.

WHO GOES THERE The clientele varies according to what is on during any given night, but the Fridge has been playing host to the gay and lesbian market for some time now.

WHAT GOES ON Dancing and trancing out to techno, transvestite nights, disco, you name it.

SETTING AND ATMOSPHERE With a vast dance floor, a huge bar, capacious balconies, and plenty of variety in the theme nights, the Fridge is a place to really let it all hang out. Highly recommended for the open-minded. Renowned DJs spinning every night. Call for special-event information. Some nights only those over 22 or 23 are admitted.

IF YOU GO Call a respectable minicab company to get home.

Grill Room @ Café Royal

DRESS-UP THEME NIGHTS IN ELEGANT SURROUNDINGS

68 Regent Street, Piccadilly, W1; ☎ 0207-439-1865; tube: Piccadilly or Oxford Circus

Cover Depends on night. **Prices** Expensive. **Dress** Smart casual or appropriate to the theme of the night. **Food** Expensive menu. **Hours** Tuesday–Saturday, 10 p.m.–3 a.m.

WHO GOES THERE The young well-heeled set out for a party.

WHAT GOES ON Inside this grand, well-known establishment, is a host of exciting and fun nights, depending on your choice of music. Tuesday hosts the very popular Modern Times, a 1920s night—dress like guys or dolls and you'll be sure to get in; Wednesdays is for private parties; Thursdays is Rock 'n' Roll night—again dressing the part (rockabilly style) helps entry. Fridays and Saturdays mix up a dance-worthy musical cocktail of hip-hop and R *&* B.

SETTING AND ATMOSPHERE Exquisitely restored *belle-époque* splendor.

IF YOU GO Get on a guest list, or book a table for dinner.

Hanover Grand

A POPULAR DISCOTHEQUE

6 Hanover Street, Mayfair, W1; ☎ 0207-499-7977; www.hanovergrand.com; tube: Oxford Circus

Cover £8–£20. **Prices** Uppish. **Dress** Smart/casual. **Food available** No. **Hours** Daily, 10:30 p.m.–5 a.m.

WHO GOES THERE Fashionistas during the week, while the house set attends on Friday and Saturday.

WHAT GOES ON Different evenings include Fresh 'n' Funky on Wednesday, schooldisco.com on Friday, Carwash on Saturday and plenty of good dancing any day of the week.

SETTING AND ATMOSPHERE The club has a capacity for 800 people, with two dance floors and five bars on three levels.

IF YOU GO Don't dress down on the weeknights.

 ## Heaven

GAY PARADISE THAT STRAIGHTS LINE UP FOR

The Arches, Villiers Street, Charing Cross, WC2; ☎ 0207-930-2020; www.heaven-london.com; tube: Embankment or Charing Cross

Cover £6–£15. **Prices** Average. **Dress** Flamboyant. **Food available** Coffee bar–type sandwiches and munchies. **Hours** Daily, 10:30 p.m.–3 a.m.; Friday and Saturday, 10 p.m.–6 a.m.

WHO GOES THERE Party animals of both hetero- and homosexual persuasion.

WHAT GOES ON Originally a gay club, London quickly twigged that the fun quotient was sky-high here, and now everyone is dying to get into Heaven. Check Web site for special nights.

SETTING AND ATMOSPHERE The crowded rooms pulsate to techno music.

IF YOU GO Arrive before 10:30 p.m. Heaven is notorious for the length of its queues.

Jazz Café

MODERN CLUB GEARED TOWARD RAP, SOUL, FUNK, AND JAZZ

5 Parkway, Camden Town, N1; ☎ **0207-916-6060; www.jazzcafe.co.uk; tube: Camden Town**

Cover £8–£27.50 according to the popularity of the act. **Prices** Average. **Dress** Anything goes. **Food available** Dinner is offered via a modern European menu. **Hours** The Jazz Café remains open until 2 a.m. on Friday and Saturday.

WHO GOES THERE 20–55-year-olds, depending on whether jazz or rap is featured.

WHAT GOES ON This club's name is something of a misnomer, as is the radio station Jazz FM's. Both entities attempt to confer the superior artistic status of jazz on lesser forms of music. Thus the Jazz Café, on any given night, may have rap, soul, or funk bands performing rather than jazz groups. I therefore suggest that you consult the listings pages of *Time Out* or *Metro Life* magazine before going, or you may end up with Vonda Shepherd or Blackalicious when you were up for a Michael Brecker–type evening.

SETTING AND ATMOSPHERE The bar leads onto the dance floor, where there are some seats available. The restaurant is situated on the balcony overlooking the stage, and projectors transmit arty neon images onto the awnings.

IF YOU GO Tell the soul band that is performing that you thought you were coming to a jazz club and then ask them to attempt a rendition of John Coltrane's "Giant Steps."

Kabaret's Prophecy

ARTFUL DECOR AND SOPHISTICATED CROWD IN MEMBER'S AWARD-WINNING NIGHTSPOT

16–18 Beak Street, Soho, W1; ☎ **0207-439-2229; www.kabaretsprophecy.com; guest list e-mail: thegaffer@kabaret-sprophecy.com; tube: Piccadilly**

Cover No, but you *must* be on the guest list; call or e-mail. **Prices** High; minimum bills for a table is £500! **Dress** This year's designer gear or vintage. **Food available** Dinner and late-night snacks. **Hours** Monday, Wednesday–Saturday, 10:30 p.m.–3 a.m.

WHO GOES THERE A slightly older, very fashionable mix of society and celebs on the weekends; Monday at Kabaret is Paris Hilton's fave night out in London (consider yourself warned).

WHAT GOES ON This member's club with a reasonable attitude toward non-members (call or e-mail to be put on guest list) was awarded World's Best Nightclub by *Wallpaper** magazine and won best Cocktail Bar in the UK by the *Independent* newspaper. Kabaret's Prophecy is the ultimate, deluxe playpen in the heart of Soho. Its technology is awe-inspiring, with sounds and lights that are almost space-age in their cutting edge. It's got a maximum capacity of 200, which makes it both intimate and exclusive, so don't take it personally if you can't get on the guest list on a weekend night. An eclectic mix of people and great music are brought together to create perfect synergy.

SETTING AND ATMOSPHERE The interior boasts a great LED backdrop, graphics by Jamie Hewlett, the acclaimed cartoonist and creator of Tank Girl and Gorillaz, and the bar motif is studded with Swarovski crystals.

IF YOU GO No ogling the celebs, and definitely no mobile phone camera clicking (except perhaps in the case of Miss Hilton).

Metro Night Club

AUTHENTIC HEADBANGER DIVE WITH IMPRESSIVE ROCK AND ROLL HISTORY

19 Oxford Street, Marylebone, W1; ☎ 0207-437-0964; tube: Oxford Circus

Cover Depends on who's playing. **Prices** Cheap. **Dress** Very casual. **Food available** None. **Hours** Depends on who's playing; closes at 4 a.m.

WHO GOES THERE Live music lovers who aren't particular about fashion or decor.

WHAT GOES ON This is a good old Soho rock and roller, where Queen and Black Sabbath played in the early days, and where you just might catch the next big act. After 11, a DJ spins punk, metal, and rock till the wee hours.

SETTING AND ATMOSPHERE It's not going to win any design awards, which is part of its old-fashioned down-and-dirty funky-bar charm. No one's out to impress here except the performers. You can drink cheaply here, and you can hear some new artists and possibly some great music.

IF YOU GO Make sure you're up for the live act that's playing.

 ## Ministry of Sound

THE UNITED KINGDOM'S MOST FAMOUS DISCO

103 Gaunt Street, Elephant and Castle, SE1, ; ☎ 0207-378-6562; www.ministryofsound.com; tube: Elephant and Castle

Cover Friday and Saturday, £15–£20, depending on the gig. **Prices** Slightly expensive. **Dress** Glamorous. **Food available** None. **Hours** Friday, 10:30 p.m.–6 a.m.; Saturday, midnight–8 a.m.

WHO GOES THERE Regulars who've been coming for years, as well as newcomers.

WHAT GOES ON Young to youngish clubbers bopping to monotonously loud and repetitious drum 'n' bass grooves.

SETTING AND ATMOSPHERE Ministry of Sound is a vast converted warehouse located in the not exactly salubrious boondocks of Elephant and Castle, so you must be sure to take a cab both there and back. You will need plenty of energy because this place will blow your head off. Check the listings pages of the press to see what's on. You'll find yourself dancing to everything from U.K. garage to R & B hits. Get ready for a fun time!

IF YOU GO Wear your dancing shoes.

Notting Hill Arts Club

WICKED MUSIC AND ART IN CASUAL AND INTIMATE BASEMENT

21 Notting Hill Gate, Notting Hill, W11; ☎ 0207-460-4459; www.nottinghillartsclub.com; tube: Notting Hill Gate

Cover Free before 8 p.m., £5–£8 thereafter. **Prices** Cheap. **Dress** Casual to paint-spattered. **Food available** Bar snacks and toasted sandwiches. **Hours** Monday–Wednesday, 6 p.m.–1 a.m.; Thursday and Friday, 6 p.m.–2 a.m.; Saturday, 4 p.m.–2 a.m.; Sunday, 4 p.m.–1 a.m.

WHO GOES THERE Trendy Notting Hillbillies, artists, musicians, and party people.

WHAT GOES ON This small basement club situated in the heart of trendy West London's Notting Hill has far more diversity and creativity than other clubs combined. This is where artists, musos, and DJs get together, put on parties, stage exhibitions, swap ideas, and go global. You're sure to find whatever rocks your world here, from hip-hop and disco to Brazilian beats.

SETTING AND ATMOSPHERE Battered couches and peeling paint make this an authentically arty old Notting Hill haunt. The stars here are the art, the performers, the music, and the just-big-enough dance floor.

IF YOU GO Dress down.

Pizza Express

AN INTIMATE JAZZ CLUB AND RESTAURANT

10 Dean Street, Soho, W1; ☎ **0207-439-8722; www.pizzaexpress.co.uk; tube: Tottenham Court Road**

Cover £15–£27, depending on the band. **Prices** Average. **Dress** Casual. **Food available** Pizza, pasta, lasagna, salad niçoise, and so on. **Hours** Opens at 7:45 p.m., with shows beginning at 9 p.m., and closes at midnight.

WHO GOES THERE Pizza and jazz lovers of both the tourist and local variety.

WHAT GOES ON Eighty percent of the bands booked are Americans of the status of Tal Farlow, Art Farmer, Kenny Garret, and Roy Haynes. Pizza Express also books top British talent such as Martin Taylor and Guy Barker.

SETTING AND ATMOSPHERE Pizza Express is an intimate basement club equipped with modern stage lighting and sound. The environment is friendly, sophisticated, and relaxed.

IF YOU GO Order pizza—it's what they do best.

 ## Ronnie Scott's

LONDON'S PREMIER JAZZ CLUB

47 Frith Street, Soho, W1; ☎ **0207-643-4525; www.ronniescotts.co.uk; tube: Tottenham Court Road**

Cover Varies; £20–£25 is normal for a Saturday; £10 for students. **Prices** A little lower than average. **Dress** Smart. **Food available** A full menu of modern European cuisine and à la carte as well. **Hours** Daily, 8 p.m.–3 a.m.

WHO GOES THERE Yuppies, buppies, musicians, jazz junkies, arty types.

WHAT GOES ON Affluent diners and drinkers come to hear the world's best jazz musicians in the downstairs club, while the younger set tends to congregate around the upstairs dance floor. Doors open at 8 p.m., and the live shows start at 9:30 p.m. Cover price usually includes both sets.

SETTING AND ATMOSPHERE Since it opened in 1959, Ronnie's has been the number one jazz club in the U.K., inspired in atmosphere and setting by the old smoky jazz dives of Greenwich Village in its beatnik heyday, where Ronnie Scott performed in the 1950s. It's as close as London will ever get to the classic sort of jazz club you've seen in films; and although the founder died in 1996, his spirit lives on.

IF YOU GO Prepare for an enjoyable evening.

606 Club

A HIGHLY REGARDED JAZZ CLUB AND RESTAURANT OPEN FOR OVER 25 YEARS

90 Lots Road, Chelsea, SW10; ☎ 0207-352-5953; www.606club.co.uk; tube: Sloane Square

Cover No cover per se, but there is a music charge of £7 per person Monday–Thursday; £9 on Friday and Saturday; and £8 on Sunday, which is added onto the bill at the end of the night. **Prices** Modest to reasonable. **Dress** Casual. **Food available** An extensive European-based menu, featuring a wide selection of meat, fresh fish, and vegetarian meals. The cuisine at the 606 has been praised by the *Sunday Times* and TV's *The Restaurant Show,* among others. **Hours** Friday and Saturday, 8 p.m.–2 a.m.; Sunday, 8 p.m.–midnight; Monday–Wednesday, 7:30 p.m.–midnight; Thursday, 8 p.m.–1:30 a.m.

WHO GOES THERE Beboppers and bohemians, young and old.

WHAT GOES ON There are two jazz groups on each night from Monday through Wednesday playing from 7:30 p.m. until midnight. One band is featured, playing from around 8 p.m. until 11 p.m. The groups are selected from a variety of up-and-coming players and more established musicians. The music ranges from traditional to contemporary, with an emphasis on the modern.

SETTING AND ATMOSPHERE A basement club with a relaxed atmosphere, the 606 is a great place to take a date for a late supper and a bottle of wine.

IF YOU GO Don't ask any of the bands to play "Tie a Yellow Ribbon."

333

THREE FLOORS OF FUN IN HIP, HAPPENING HOXTON

333 Old Street, Hoxton, EC1; ☎ 0207-739-5949; www.333mother.com; tube: Old Street

Cover £5–£10. **Prices** Middling. **Dress** Something cool, in both senses of the word. **Food available** Snack and food. **Hours** Bar: Monday–Wednesday, 8 p.m.–3 a.m.; Friday, 8 p.m.–4 a.m.; Thursday, 8 p.m.–1 a.m. Club and bar: Friday and Saturday, 10 p.m.–5 a.m.

WHO GOES THERE Serious clubbers, dancers, and music maniacs.

WHAT GOES ON This old building in trendy Hoxton houses a no-frills three-story music-fest—something different every night. Expect queues. The basement usually plays techno, drum 'n' bass, whilst the main room bounces from house to electro to reggae. Upstairs is Mother Bar for a more chilled and plush environment, a great place to hang out.

SETTING AND ATMOSPHERE Charming yet weirdly retro club with flocked wall-paper, quilted Naugahyde doors and furniture, plus a great dance floor and a sense of humor. Go to the Web site to get a sense of the kind of joint this is.

IF YOU GO Like Goldilocks, try out all the rooms to see where you belong.

Turnmills

THE DISCO WHERE ALL NIGHTCLUBBERS END UP

63B Clerkenwell Road, Clerkenwell, EC1; ☎ 0207-250-3409; www.turnmills.co.uk; tube: Farringdon

Cover £5–£15, depending on the night. **Prices** Lowish. **Dress** Casual. **Food available** Yes, bar food. **Hours** Friday, 10:30 p.m.–7:30 a.m.; Saturday, 10 p.m.–5 a.m.

WHO GOES THERE Hard-core clubhoppers; Turnmills also hosts Trade, Britain's top gay night.

WHAT GOES ON In addition to the mandatory drinking and dancing, this club provides a few pinball machines.

SETTING AND ATMOSPHERE Candlelit tables and an Electronica bar area provide a refreshing contrast to the throbbing chaos of the dance floor.

IF YOU GO Take a taxi both there and back—if you last until 7 a.m. you will be in no condition to find your way home.

Zoo Bar

BAR AND DANCE CLUB

13–17 Bear Street, Leicester Square, WC2; ☎ 0207-839-4188; www.zoobar.co.uk; tube: Leicester Square

Cover Monday–Wednesday after 9 p.m., £3; Thursday, £4; Friday and Saturday after 9 p.m., £5, after 11 p.m., £8. **Prices** Average; about £4 a drink and less at happy hour. **Dress** Trendy. **Food available** Snacks. **Hours** Daily, 4 p.m.–3 a.m.

WHO GOES THERE Eclectic range of regulars, from laborers to lawyers, and plenty of young tourists. Over 21 only.

WHAT GOES ON A mixed bag, very laid-back. Everyone is there to have a great time. There are happy hours every night, and good dance music, too. Free entrance for women most nights, and all kinds of promos. They recently finished a much-needed face-lift and added air-conditioning, which can come in handy on the dance floor even in the middle of winter.

SETTING AND ATMOSPHERE Two floors of fun. On the first floor, there is a bar area in which to mingle and meet friends. The basement floor has a huge dance floor surrounded by a few smaller bars to ease traffic flow.

IF YOU GO Beware of the throngs of Leicester Square on the weekends—it's a zoo, so hold on to your valuables.

PART TEN

SHOPPING

LONDON'S ONE OF THE MOST COSTLY PLACES on the planet, and at a time when the pound is strong and the U.S. dollar weak, it may seem like madness to spend money on anything but hotel, food, theater tickets, and museum fees. The last few years have been particularly dreadful. The cost of one pound went as high as $1.95, and the rate hovered there throughout early 2005, the highest I've seen since I moved here in 1996. Thankfully, it has eased up a bit, and as of this writing the pound costs £1.77. The exchange rate is something we can't control, any more than we can control the weather, but in the same way we know how to make the best of a rainy day with umbrellas or raincoats, we can learn to spend our money wisely in the shops of London.

The first rule is to not buy anything here that is available at a lower cost elsewhere. Right off the bat, you've eliminated a lot of goods, especially global brand-name clothing. I know well the shock of looking at, say, a shirt from the Gap that costs £18, doing the calculation in my head, and realize that I may be spending as much as $35 American dollars for something that would cost $15 in the States. It puts a damper on shopping, let me tell you.

It's common for any penny-wise Londoner going abroad—from taxi drivers to investment bankers—to bring a roomy suitcase and load up on inexpensive clothing basics; toiletries; household goods; electronic equipment; accessories; batteries, film, printer ink; basic stationery; sewing goods; or any of well-priced household products from the bargain emporia found in Anytown, USA, Australia, New Zealand, or Canada. Even prices in Paris are better than in London, which is presently the most expensive city in the European Union. This has something to do with the fact that England is an island without much manufacturing, and goods must be delivered. There is also a shocking tradition of noncompetitive price fixing among big retailers, but that is being challenged by some newcomers. And the sky-high rents that central London shops must pay don't help prices either.

So as not to completely dash your shopping dreams, let me hasten to emphasize that London has a vibrant shopping scene, with stores, stalls, and shops as far as the eye can see and plenty of goods that are difficult to find elsewhere. Some of these things, like the hundreds of items with the Harrods name and logo plastered on them, you wouldn't necessarily want to find anywhere else, but others, like Liberty scarves, bespoke shirts from Harvie & Hudson, interesting clothing from up-and-coming British designers, books published only in England, some of the museum gift shop items, or European products that enjoy EU tariff breaks are catnip to the worldly shopper. If you come during the big sales, the best being during the month of January (there's also one in August), you just might be able to pay fair-to-good prices for stuff you can't readily get at home. These January and August sales are a retail tradition to make way for the next season of goods, but you can also expect some closing-down sales, minor spur-of-the-moment sales, or just plain desperate-to-sell sales in any given month.

WISE BUYS *in* LONDON

THE FOLLOWING ITEMS ARE WORTH BUYING in London because of their high quality or their unavailability elsewhere. See our "Where to Find" section later in this chapter for information on shops that sell these items.

Antiques

If you're an early bird and can get up before dawn to get to the early-morning Bermonsey Market, or check out the Camden Passage on Wednesdays, you'll find a huge selection in London at relatively decent prices. At one time you did not have to pay VAT on antiques, but alas, those days are over. You can bargain around the VAT by paying cash to some vendors. (We'll discuss the use of credit cards later in the chapter.) There are also Antique Centers, wonderful warrens of individual stalls selling everything from military artifacts to antique charms for bracelets.

Bath Products and Perfumes

Bath oils, salts, soaps, and scents abound in London, made by Culpepper the Herbalist, Neal's Yard Remedies, Molton Brown, Floris, Jo Malone, Lush, and Penhaligon; and there are always some less well-known products making a name for themselves in stores such as Space.NK or Harvey Nichols. Of course, some brands, like Crabtree & Evelyn, are exported everywhere and may even cost less elsewhere, but chances are that the range will be more limited, and they'll only be available in luxury department stores in big cities. There are many new and creative perfumeries in business who will whip up a unique fragrance just for you, or who sell interesting concoctions of their own. Not cheap, but you won't find them anywhere outside of Paris or Grasse.

Bone China

Look in the stalls on Portobello Road in Notting Hill on Saturday market day, or at the Reject China Shops (☎ 0207-434-2502) for patterns you can't find at home. Even Harrods has deals at sale times, and their stock is enormous. I know that you can get Spode china in T.J. Maxx for about ten dollars a plate, but you won't find the old stuff in discontinued patterns there, or any of the beautiful Staffordshire china you can pick up in antique stalls. Crystal goods, too, can be cheaper in London than elsewhere, except maybe in Waterford, Ireland.

unofficial **TIP**
Around the British Museum there are specialist book shops that have managed to keep in business despite the steady encroachment of the big chain bookshops, like Waterstone's or W. H. Smith.

Books

London is a city of readers, and there are thousands of bookstores that cater to all possible interests. You can get books here that are only published in England, antiquarian volumes in gorgeous sets, and crates full of secondhand books. The Harry Potter or Lord of the Rings books published here are more attractive to the serious fan because of the un-Americanized English spelling, punctuation, vocabulary, and idioms (the first Harry Potter book, for example, is entitled *Harry Potter and the Philosopher's Stone,* rather than the less historically precise *Sorcerer's Stone,* as it's called in America).

kids Children's Clothing

Some children's clothing may be, if not cheaper, of better quality and value than in the States. English smock dresses and French baby clothes are beautiful, and you don't have to pay VAT. There is a new trend of designers (Dior, Jigsaw, Paul Smith, to name a few) making children's clothing, which well-heeled Londoners have taken to enthusiastically. **Lillywhites**, the sporting goods emporium in Piccadilly Circus, sells the soccer shirts of British teams that they will personalize with your kid's name (sporty children will love this, but make sure you know which team they're into).

Designer Clothing

Secondhand, that is. There are tons of resale shops in which you can get "preowned" Chanel, Prada, Dolce & Gabbana, Gucci, Matthew Williamson, Westwood, Armani, Voyage, and more for a fraction of the original price. A lot of ladies seem to have worn these clothes twice and moved on to the next big thing, and it's a happy day indeed when someone of your size and taste drops off bags of discarded clothes, or a shoe collection. The hunting is part of the fun; and if nothing else, you'll find the original prices hilarious. There are outlets in which you might find semi-good deals on brand new English and French designer clothes, but it's an iffy business, dependent on exchange rates and available sizes.

Fabrics

England has long been known for its gorgeous fabrics: the Tudor crewel work is reproduced as often as the exquisite designs of William Morris & Co. Try John Lewis or Peter Jones for the best deals on locally made material and things like elaborate trim and curtain swags. Antique fabrics, ribbons, and trimming are also available at specialty shops or at auction.

Souvenirs of London

Yes, cheaper here than anywhere, naturally. The best buys are on the street in stalls; Oxford Street, Leicester Square, Soho (Tottenham Court Road), and Piccadilly Circus are the places to look. For more quirky or upscale souvenirs of London, hit the gift shops of Westminster Abbey, British Museum, Queen's Gallery, Hampton Court Palace, Victoria and Albert Museum, and the Tower of London.

Stationery

Filofax, the personal organizer so well loved by professionals in the States, is an indigenous English product and cheaper here than anywhere else, especially at sale time. Which is not to say it's all that affordable. **Smythson's** of Bond Street sells beautiful little leather-bound note books, the size of a Post-it, for £40!

▌ TIME *to* SHOP

STORES IN CENTRAL LONDON OPEN LATE and close early. The usual times are 10 a.m. to 6 p.m., with a few opening at 9 a.m. (but closing at 5 p.m.), and a very few, like Waterstone's Bookstores, staying open until 9:30 p.m. (the Piccadilly branch stays open until 11:30 p.m.). Some places, such as those in Covent Garden and some fashionable stores, don't open until 10:30 or 11 a.m.

There is a "late" night for shopping. Stores stay open until 7 or 8 p.m. on Thursdays on Oxford Street, Regent Street, and the West End. Just to keep you on your toes, Knightsbridge's and Chelsea's late night is Wednesday. Sunday has finally joined the rest of the week as a shopping day, with most stores (except for some big department stores and small businesses) opening for at least a half day, from noon to 5 or 6 p.m. Shockingly, Harrods has broken with tradition to open on Sundays after tiring of the competition from neighbor Harvey Nichols. It also extended it's hours Monday through Saturday until 7 p.m. Street markets follow their own muse as far as opening hours and days go; some markets are weekend only (Portobello Market takes place on Saturday).

PAYING UP

ALL THE MAJOR CREDIT CARDS ARE TAKEN at most shops. Some stores will take traveler's checks in British sterling, but they don't even want to hear about U.S. dollar traveler's checks. If they are kind enough to cash them, it may not be at a rate favorable to you. (Bring a passport to cash traveler's checks at an American Express office.) A good exchange rate is available at Harrods and at Marks and Spencer.

The credit card is a mixed blessing. On the plus side, you'll have a record of your purchases, and the exchange rate will be the same as the day the credit purchase clears the credit card company or bank, not the day you bought something. Go to **www.xe.com** to find out the daily exchange rate, or to do calculation. Be careful about which card you use: Many credit cards now hit you with a "foreign currency exchange" charge of 1–2.5% on each purchase made in a foreign country. This is a total rip-off and can run into a huge amount of money between hotel costs, restaurants, and shopping trips. The best solution to this highway robbery is to put lots of money in your bank account and use your bank card to get cash to pay for the bulk of your purchases. Paying by cash at some small shops, antique stalls, and the occasional hotel, could net you a bit of a discount—give it a try.

AS FOR VAT

VALUE-ADDED TAX IS THE MIND-BOGGLING 17.5% the British government adds on to the cost of all goods and services except for books, food, and children's clothing. Most goods will have the VAT already figured into the price on the tags, but other items, especially those sold at fancy knickknack stores and other high-priced shops, try to prevent total sticker shock by placing a discreet "+VAT" after all those zeros. If you have your goods shipped directly from the store, the VAT will be deducted from the price, but you'd have to be paying a lot of money to balance the costs of shipping. There's also the added cost of duty on expensive imported goods when you arrive in the United States. You are allowed $400 per person of goods duty free, and families may combine this allowance, so that a family of five is allowed $2,000 worth of goods. The next $1,000 worth of goods gets charged a flat 10%—after that it will vary according to what type of import you're bringing.

Yes, you may be able to get a refund of some of the VAT you've paid, but it requires a little footwork. Let me sketch it out briefly for you, and you'll get more detail below: First be sure that the shop where you make your purchase participates in the refund scheme—it's a completely voluntary retail service. Then the shop must fill out the official form or their own version of the VAT 407 form or a VAT Retail Export Scheme sales receipt (a regular sales receipt is not accepted). You have to show the goods to customs at the airport, so don't pack them in your check-in luggage or wrap them too well—they have to examine your purchases to make sure the form matches the goods before they'll certify the forms. Once armed with the stamped forms, you take them to a VAT Refund counter in the airport, and you'll get the refund, minus some handling fees. For more details, I'll let Her Majesty's Customs and Excise Department explain it all.

VALUE-ADDED TAX REFUNDS: THE OFFICIAL STORY

HERE ARE THE HIGHLIGHTS FROM A PAMPHLET entitled "Guide to Tax Free Shopping—the VAT Refund Scheme" (VAT/704/3/93), produced by Her Majesty's Ministry of Customs and Excise and published here by her kind permission.

WHAT IS THE RETAIL-EXPORT SCHEME? When you visit the United Kingdom, you pay value-added tax (VAT) on most things you buy. The retail-export scheme allows you to obtain a refund of the tax on certain goods you intend to export from the European Community (EC).

CAN I BUY GOODS UNDER THIS SCHEME? Yes, if you are an overseas visitor who:
- has not been in the EC for more than 365 days in the two years before the date you buy the goods; and
- you intend to leave the EC with all the goods in your personal luggage, within three months of the date you bought them.

HOW DO I KNOW WHICH SHOPS OPERATE THE SCHEME? The shops that operate the scheme usually have a sign in the window advertising the scheme as "tax-free shopping." If in doubt, ask for the "tax-free" sales assistant.

WHAT MUST I DO TO OBTAIN A VAT REFUND?
- ask the shop to complete a VAT or tax-free shopping form (this is very important, as without the form from the shop, you cannot get a refund);
- obtain an EC certification stamp when you leave the EC;
- mail back or hand in your stamped forms to obtain your VAT refund.

unofficial **TIP**
You'll find that lots of sales clerks are only too happy to inform you about this refund option, especially if it helps close the deal.)

DO I GET ALL THE TAX BACK? Most shops charge a small administrative fee which will be deducted from the tax refunded to you.

WHAT EXPORT DOCUMENTS WILL I BE GIVEN? The shop will give you one of the following VAT-refund documents:
- an official customs form VAT 407; or
- a shop's or refund company's tax-free shopping form; or
- a retail-export scheme sales invoice.

These documents are available only from shops operating the scheme, and the shop from which you purchase the goods on which you intend to claim a refund must fill out a portion of the form it provides.

WHEN MUST I EXPORT THE GOODS? You must permanently export the goods from the EC within three months of purchase.

DO I HAVE TO CARRY ALL THE GOODS BOUGHT UNDER THE SCHEME IN MY HAND BAGGAGE? You should always carry items of high value, including jewelry, furs, cameras, watches, silverware, and small antiques, in your hand baggage. However, if the goods are too large to carry on board an aircraft, you may pack them in your hold baggage. If you do this, you must contact the British Customs export officer before you check in. The airline will tell you how to do this.

unofficial **TIP**
Allow three-and-a-half hours for document certification at the airport in summer months.

DO I GET THE VAT-REFUND DOCUMENT BACK? You must give the document and show the goods to Customs at the port or airport when you finally leave the EC. The Customs export officer will certify the document and return it to you so that you can get a refund. These procedures may take some time, so please arrive at least two hours before you are due to depart.

WHAT IF I LEAVE THE EC ON A THROUGH (TRANSIT) FLIGHT VIA ANOTHER MEMBER STATE? There are special rules for goods being carried on through flights that leave the EC via another member state.

Hand baggage: Goods carried on as hand baggage and VAT-refund documents must be produced to Customs in the member state of final transfer before leaving the EC. You would process your VAT goods in the United Kingdom, but keep the goods and documents handy for inspection when leaving the EC. The same applies for check-in luggage.

Hold baggage: If you will be leaving the United Kingdom on such a flight and intend carrying large or heavy goods in hold baggage, you should ask the shopkeeper for a separate VAT-refund document for those goods. The goods and VAT-refund document must be produced to U.K. Customs before departure from the United Kingdom.

HOW DO I GET A REFUND? There are several methods to try for getting a refund. You may:
- mail the certified document back to the shopkeeper; or
- mail the certified document to a VAT-refunding company; or
- hand the certified document to a cash-refund booth at the point of departure, if the shopkeeper has authorized you to do so (a charge may be made for this service).

IMPORTANT REMINDER If you do not produce the goods and VAT-refund document to the Customs export officer when you finally leave the EC, you will not get a refund of VAT.

The Unofficial Version

Only those who are *not* British subjects or citizens of other EU countries qualify for VAT refund, and they have to leave the country with their goods within six months.

You will not get the entire 17.5% back—it's more like 10–15% (plus an additional fee that you pay for the processing of the papers) and can actually be as little as 4% with some refund companies.

Ask what is the minimum you must spend in a given shop to qualify for the papers being filled out—it can vary, although the law puts the minimum at £50. Some shops will refuse outright, and some will charge at least £5 for issuing the papers.

You must have the refund form filled out at the place of purchase! You cannot get it done anywhere else by anyone else. Bring your passport to the store.

There are refund companies that handle the VAT refund, and they have set the refund at different rates. The clerk can tell you which company the shop uses and help you decide whether it's worth your while or not.

You must show your VAT-refund purchases at the airport Customs, usually (and most easily) in carry-on luggage. Factor the size of the item against the amount of the refund, times the degree of hassle you're willing to go through to get some money back.

Go to the Customs official to get the VAT papers **before** you check in your luggage.

Allow time for all the forms to be filled out—about five minutes for each one.

After you go through passport control, line up at the VAT desk to show them what you've bought and the papers that go with them.

You then get the papers back, mail them to the shop, or take them to the Tax-Free Europe desk. Tax-Free Europe is a tax-refund company that many stores are starting to use to expedite the VAT returns. They give you a cash refund at the airport, but a lot of your money stays in their hands. There's also VatBack, which will do a credit card refund by mail; this takes about three months, but you'll get a bigger percentage back. They also give immediate cash back, at £8.60 for over £100 of goods or £18.50 for over £500 of goods.

If your VAT-refund items are too big to carry on, budget an extra hour at the airport, as you will need to have a security guard watch you go through passport control and then return the items to your airline for checking.

In the summer and after sales, there are often long lines at the VAT-refund desk at Heathrow, and this is getting worse all the time as people have started working the VAT-refund scheme in earnest.

There is also the possibility of getting a VAT refund from a hotel or holiday apartment, or from a car-rental agency; ask the concierge or the person with whom you book your travel arrangements for the forms and the information.

SALESPEOPLE'S ATTITUDES
and BEHAVIOR

SALESPEOPLE IN LONDON ARE (although one hates to make a generalization about such things) among the most laid-back in the world. It's not that they don't want to make a sale; it's just that they don't want to be perceived as pushing anyone to buy something. Except in a few upscale stores, where the staff is rigorously trained to look like they give a damn, the salespeople in London will surprise and perhaps bewilder you with their laissez-faire attitudes. Personally, I find it a relief from the kind of sales style in which you are forced to engage in banter (read: pressured to buy) with salespeople when all you want to do is have a look, but if you are in need of assistance, you will have to get used to approaching them. There's nothing malicious or lackadaisical about them; it's just that this is not a culture in which overeager selling is admired. Even the famous funny Cockney sales patter that you might still hear in some East End Markets or from street vendors is more a tradition of being quick and clever than it is of making a sale. The correct response is to be equally laid-back and not be demanding and rude—London salespeople are masters of the cold dismissal, and you won't win.

THE CHAIN REACTION

ONE OF THE GREATEST THINGS ABOUT LONDON used to be the unique character of its many little villages, with each "high street," as they call the main drag, bursting with the individual flavors of its quirky little shops. These were stores you knew about and traveled across the city to get to; some are still here: an umbrella store established in 1830 (**James Smith & Sons,** 53 New Oxford Street, WC1; ☎ 0207-836-4731) in Bloomsbury; a button shop (**The Button Queen,** 19 Marylebone Lane, WC1; ☎ 0207-935-1505) in Marylebone; a cake-baking and decorating center (**Jane Asher,** 24 Cale Street, SW3; ☎ 0207-584-6177) in Chelsea Green. Nowadays, just about every shopping street in every post code seems to be dominated by chain stores: Tesco's or Sainsbury's grocery outlet; Starbucks or Costa Coffee; McDonald's or Burger King; Pizza Express; Car Phone Warehouse; Pret a Manger; Prime Time Video; Boots the Chemist; Accessorize; Mark and Spencer; Waterstones Books; or Ryman's stationery. The statistics are chilling to small business retailers: in the six years between 1994 and 2000, London lost a fifth of its local shops. At this rate, economists estimate that by 2050 the independent mom and pop shop is likely to be as obsolete as the telegraph office or the chimney sweep. Politicians are unable to staunch the bleeding: it's all about capital and rent increases. In the time I have lived in South

Kensington, I have seen the sad demise of a little newspaper store, a wonderful curio and antique sshop, an open-till-midnight grocer, a hairdresser who'd been in business for 45 years, an Indian restaurant, a vegetarian restaurant, a quirky women's clothing shop, a friend's jewelry store, a flower shop that had been in the same place since 1901; the list of defunct businesses grows along with the rent and local taxes. But there's a slowly growing backlash: many of the proud independents have re-opened their specialty shops in less expensive areas of London, such as the East End, Hoxton, Camden, Clerkenwell, Brick Lane (Cheshire Street), Greenwich; or they've set themselves up in a stall at a covered market, which functions as an eccentric shopping mall. There are still plenty of the kind of Old Curiosity Shops that Dickens wrote about; they just may be a bit more off the beaten track than they used to be.

The following shopping areas are mostly in and around central London. I've tried to show you the flavor of the area rather than concentrating on what is on which street. With stores changing as fast and as often as they do, I hesitate to name all but the more stable-seeming shops, lest you get all excited and go there to find it boarded up. Please note that all these areas may have a wide range of possibilities: you may find an on-sale bargain on the very chic Bond Street, and run into nothing but rip-offs in the market stalls. We can't predict these things. But even if you're just window-shopping, I think you'll like the vibe and the energy of this briskly commercial city. London started out as a trading post and has kept the tradition of wheeling and dealing alive ever since. Whether you're into Jimmy Choo or Birkenstock, Paul Smith or H&M, London's got you covered.

THE BIG SHOPPING NEIGHBORHOODS

COVENT GARDEN
(tube: Covent Garden or Leicester Square)

Covent Garden has been largely taken over by branches of high street shops, mostly by clothing boutiques and shops, such as the **Gap, Monsoon, Whistles,** and **Accessorize.** Stay away from the Gap—even at sale time their prices are insane, and not in the good way. Whistles and Monsoon have good quality clothing, at high prices, so when they have a sale, it's worth a look. The area has been vastly remodeled and updated, and is one of the more fun places to wander around. There's usually a remarkable busker somewhere around the piazza entertaining with music, sidewalk art, or daredevilry. There are plenty of places to sit with a cuppa and take in the urban energy around the elegant Georgian arcade, the very site where Henry Higgins met his

Cockney flower girl, Eliza Doolittle. There's the exquisite **Benjamin Pollack's Toy Shop,** whose marvelous merchandise features re-creations of popular old toys, with an emphasis on toy theaters and puppets, a big trend in the mid 19th century when Pollock was in business. You'd be surprised how many kids, raised on the miracles of PlayStation and DVDs, are enchanted by these simple but unusual Victorian toys. **Neal Street** and **Neal's Yard** is a fun shopping area as well, with plenty of hip little shops, such as the makeup store **Pout,** which is an amusement park for young beauties; feet-friendly shoes from the **Natural Shoe Store;** and some really good vegetarian cafés and take-away. You can get your horoscope chart cast at **The Astrology Shop;** or fulfill all your crystal and New Age needs in **Mysteries** on Monmouth Street (cool retro clothes stores on that street, too). There are also plenty of clothing and shoe stores for the urban cool cat and teenager, and **Filofax** for the busy professional.

WESTBOURNE GROVE, NOTTING HILL, KENSINGTON, KENSINGTON CHURCH STREET
(tube: High Street Kensington)

This is the street of antiques, with shops stretching from Kensington High Street all the way to Notting Hill Gate. It's a great place to window-shop and cruise in and out of the stores that have displays that strike your fancy. As with all antiques stores, the inventory is always changing, but there are a few places that specialize in certain periods and styles, be it Georgian, Victorian, art nouveau, or art deco. There are also wonderful mirror stores and a great crystal chandelier place. The prices can be quite high on this street, as the rents have gone through the roof, but it's fun to look, and you never know when you'll find something you really love. There are a couple of charity and thrift shops here that are definitely worth a look in, being as they are in such an upscale neighborhood.

KENSINGTON HIGH STREET (tube: High Street Kensington)

This neighborhood is a horse of a different color, with nothing but the latest fashions at **Topshop, Miss Sixty, Diesel,** and **Urban Outfitters.** For older tastes there's **Laura Ashley, Monsoon, Ecco Shoes, Zara,** and **Next.**

PORTOBELLO ROAD (tube: Notting Hill Gate)

This area is home to the world-famous antiques and what-not market on Saturday, but every day of the week there are antiques shops, clothing and shoe shops, and the fabulous vintage clothing shop **One of a Kind Too.**

WESTBOURNE GROVE
(tube: Notting Hill Gate and Queensway)

Heading east from Portobello is a retail and residential area that's experienced a real renaissance in the past few years. While it used to be known chiefly for the well-stocked health food store, **Planet Organic,** it's now got chic and wonderful shops all up and down it, including a good restaurant called **202** that doubles as a clothing and design shop for **Nicole Farhi.** The **Notting Hill Charity Shop** on this street also has rich pickings, and there's a bounteous flower stall located by a grade-listed public loo. Designer boutiques abound, the biggest one with the most cutting-edge designers is the three-story boutique called **Question Air.** If you head up Ledbury Road to Artesian Road, you can drop in on the new perfumery **Miller Harris,** who will mix up a personal scent for you. Down the street is **Alice & Astrid,** for wild, retro lingerie. There are also great bakeries, antiques shops, and specialist food stores in this vibrant area.

KNIGHTSBRIDGE (tube: Knightsbridge)

Well, you can pretty much forget about Knightsbridge shopping if you want to get a deal, unless you go to the little neighborhood north of the Brompton Road, which has three designer consignment shops. The best, or at least biggest and most likely to have sales, is **Pandora,** and up the street is **Salou,** and **The Dress Box.** Off the north side of Brompton Road is **Beauchamp Place** (pronounced "Beecham"), a swiftly changing street these days, due to the punishing high rents and an ever-changing economy. The **Reject China Shop** dominates the entrance to Beauchamp Place at Brompton Road, with two floors of china plates and accessories. As you make your way up the street, you'll find jewelry, shoes, purses, and secondhand and clearance designer clothes at **Bertie Golightly;** deluxe underwear from **Janet Reger;** an old-fashioned stove at the **Aga Shop;** and, of course, designers (**Bruce Oldfield, Isabel Kristiansen, Caroline Charles, Paddy Campbell,** and others). This is also the street on which to see fashionable women push food around on their plates at the posh Italian restaurant **San Lorenzo.** You'll know when someone famous is inside by the scrum of paparazzi outside, and maybe a chauffeured Bentley parked illegally.

On **Walton Street** there are jewelers, a slew of interior decorators' shops full of wonderful curiosities, and a couple of decent restaurants. Try **Patrizia Wigan Designs** for Alice-in-Wonderland smocked dresses and other classic children's clothing. There's **Stephanie Hopper,** who features old portraits whose faces have been erased and replaced with dog faces—very strange, and very popular with Americans apparently. **Chelsea Textiles Ltd.** has fiercely expensive and awesomely beautiful hand-embroidered reproductions of 17th- and 18th-century linens. Reasonably priced monogrammed linens and unreasonably expensive Porthault sheets are at the **Monogrammed Linen Shops,** as are candles and soaps. Everyone on the street is happy to ship their products all around the world, so if you want to buy new or antique children's furniture at **Dragons of Walton Street,** you can get the VAT refund and have something sent home.

Sloane Street connects Knightsbridge with Sloane Square in Chelsea (on Sloane Square and Sloane Street is a new **Tiffany's,** which looks over at the department store **Peter Jones**). The Knightsbridge end of the street is teeming with every hot designer you can think of. It's like a mini Bond Street, and home to **Chanel, Dior, Dolce & Gabbana, Valentino, Prada, Lacroix, Tomasz Starzewski, Max Mara, Katharine Hamnett, Fendi, Yves Saint Laurent, Gianfranco Ferre, Armani, Alberta Ferretti, Tommy Hilfiger, Hermès,** and **Gucci.** If you're looking for less obvious designers, there's always **Harvey Nichols** on the east corner of Sloan Street, or **Harrods,** just a few blocks west on the Brompton Road. Sloane Street just smells of money, which is sweetened with the perfumes of the fabulous flagship shop of *scenteur* **Jo Malone**).

OXFORD AND REGENT STREETS AND MARYLEBONE VILLAGE
(tube: Oxford Circus and Marble Arch)

These streets have far too many chain stores for my taste and are hideously crowded. However, **Selfridges** is pretty fantastic, inside and out, and getting better all the time—you can even get a tattoo there these days. **John Lewis, Marks and Spencer, Dixons Electronics, Debenhams, The Body Shop, The Gap, Virgin Megastores**—these are not places that a visitor to London would really need to go (except maybe Marks and Spencer for their famously comfy underwear). A little past Oxford Circus is the multifloored, always busy **Topshop,** with fab clothes for young fashionables, but others will prefer to head down **Regent Street,** to stop in at **Liberty,** the Tudor-style department store that has fascinating architecture and some interesting goods. **Fenwicks** is an august department store that has been trying (successfully) to update its genteel, old-school reputation. **Hamley's,** the big toy store, is worth a look for toys and children's book only found in England. **Burberry's, Jaeger,** and **Aquascutum** offer some high-class and high-priced clothing. The famous **Carnaby Street** is worth a look-in (it's off Regent Street) but the old days of groovy independent designers and head shops are long gone; now it's got **Puma, O'Neill, Diesel, Soccerscene, Rugby Scene,** and young street wear labels in **High Jinks** and **Mambo.** Take a teen, and have a coffee on a sidewalk café while they do their thing.

Off Oxford Street is **St. Christopher's Place,** a charming pedestrian alley that leads to **Marylebone Village,** which has been given the old gentrification slap of paint and retail upgrades over the past few years. It's now got the ubiquitous **Starbucks, Gap, Ryman's, Boots,** and **Waitrose** supermarket, but it also has won a nod from *Time Out* as one of their Best Shopping Streets. It must be acknowledged that this was once a rather frumpish street, but my natural inclination against developers' ideas of what a neighborhood needs (that is, more expensive shops) makes me resent somewhat the gilding of this particular lily. However, it's true that there is a decent mix of old and new:

Daunt Books is an old independent bookshop that has an eclectic and interesting stock of titles, and **Aveda** offers natural beauty and bath products, as well as a health food café whose food is divine. **Rococo** has expanded from its King's Road chocolate shop to open a branch here, and it's an excellent place to buy nicely presented gifts or to feed your cocoa addiction. **Shoon** is a new take on the general store concept, with clothes, books, and interesting gewgaws and what-nots from all over the world. **calmia** (yes, it's a small 'c'), at the northernmost end of the street, is where rich spiritual seekers go to drop a few hundred quid on yoga props and clothing, or to schedule soothing body treatments. Check out **Moxton Street** for its specialty food shops. There are plenty of patisseries and restaurants along this high street; a hearty breakfast is served at **Providores & Tapas Room.**

CHELSEA: THE KING'S ROAD (tube: Sloane Square)

This was the place to be in the 1960s and 1970s, when Mary Quant set up shop to sell her revolutionary miniskirts, and Vivienne Westwood kept changing the name of her and Malcolm MacLaren's punk chic boutique. The Mary Quant place is now a coffee and snack shop, but the **Vivienne Westwood** store still has the fast-moving backward clock outside, and the floor inside still slants dangerously. King's Road is long and full of quickly changing boutiques and trendy stores, but there are some places that will, one can only hope, always be there. Starting at the Vivienne Westwood end (the western part near World's End) and heading to Sloane Square, you'll find thrift shops; **Oxfam, Trinity Hospice,** and **Imperial Cancer Fund** will have the occasional great buys. Some fabric stores along the way include **Anna French, Thomas Dave, Osbourne & Little,** and the **Designer's Guild. Wilde Ones** is a fun shop to browse in, very peaceful and full of crystals, incense, and New Age books. **Lello Bracio, Johnny Moke,** and the **Natural Shoe Store** offer the latest in shoes, both comfortable and stylish. **Old Church Galleries** has wonderful old and rare prints, and there are some good antiques and reproduction places along the way, including **Antiquarius,** a market housing many stalls with lots of goods. Check out **Steinberg and Tolkien** and be sure to go downstairs—they have the most amazing selection of vintage clothes in London, though it's more like a museum than a store, with prices to match. Other stores include **Marks and Spencer, Lush, Daisy & Tom's Children's Store,** lots of clothing and shoe boutiques. **The Duke of York Square** opened in 2003 and continues to fill its mall space with upscale stores. **The London Furniture Store** is at the moment the largest emporium on the complex, with reasonably priced and interesting house decor. There's also a **Patisserie Valerie** for cappuccino, **Yves Delorme** for luscious sheets and towels, and a large **Joseph** boutique. At the end of King's Road, at Sloane Square, is **Peter Jones,** the stolid department store. Good restaurants are plentiful, and there are two Starbucks at last count; I reckon there will be more by the time you read this, or even by the time I finish typing this sentence. To the south of the King's Road is **Chelsea Green,** a very smart area, with shops that include my favorite, **Jane Asher Cakes,** for all your baking needs; **Cath Kidson,** purveyor of clothing, wallets, duvets, and pillows dressed in her trademark cheerful prints; and the very hot designer **Colette Dinnegan,** whose prices will leave you gasping for air. Down **Elystan Street** there's a brilliant designer resale shop, **Sign of the Times,** where you might just find a Voyage dress for 45 quid, and lots of great high-price shoes at a fraction of their original price.

NEW AND OLD BOND STREETS (tube: Bond Street)

Wow, what a stretch of retail real estate these streets are! Starting from Oxford Street, New Bond Street begins with a battery of designer shops and clothing boutiques, such as **Warehouse, Cecil Gee, Next, Guess, Emma Somerset, Armani, Cerruti 1881, Versace, Herbie Frogg** (this one's the so-called Sale Shop—the really expensive one is down the way on Old Bond), **Calvin Klein, Hermès, Joseph, Tommy Hilfiger, Miu Miu (Prada), Lanvin, Guy LaRouche, Thierry Mugler, Donna Karan, Burberry, Yves Saint Laurent, Ermenegildo Zegna, Chanel, Ralph Lauren, Valentino, Nicole Farhi**—the list goes on and on. Suffice it to say they're all here. Not to mention designer shoes, fine art, jewelry (**Asprey, Tiffany,** and **Cartier,** natch), Hermès scarves, and so on. **Smythson of Bond Street** is a stationery store that begs your jaw to drop with its £25 pigskin mini note holder, or the blank writing book for £59. There's a bench on the great divide (a pedestrian walkway) between New and Old Bond Streets, on which you will see two very realistic statues of Winston Churchill and Franklin Roosevelt hanging out, no doubt talking about who makes the best bespoke shoes. Old Bond is more of the same: exactly the same, in fact, in the cases of **Donna Karan, Chanel, Joseph, Ralph Lauren, Armani, Versace,** and others. Old Bond is also home to **Prada, Dolce & Gabbana, Gucci** and the chauffeured Rolls Royces of such world-class shoppers as the Beckhams and Elton John. You might even get to see some shopaholic bag-laden celeb wandering around in a spending trance. Recently opened shops in this area, also known as the "Golden T," include **Stella McCartney, Gibo,** and **Alexander McQueen.** At the end of the street is the historic and charming **Burlington Arcade,** whose tenants wax and wane as regularly as the credit rating of a shopping addict.

SOUTH KENSINGTON: BROMPTON CROSS (tube: South Kensington)

The area is marked by the old Michelin Building that houses **Conrans** (housewares, toiletries, fabrics, furniture, stationery, children's stuff, and books) and the restaurants **Bibendum** and its sister, the **Oyster Bar,** and is known as the Brompton Cross. Here you will find **Chanel, Jimmy Choo Shoes,** designers **Jean Paul Gaultier, Betsy Johnson, Joseph, Ralph**

Lauren, Jigsaw, and other smaller haut monde stores: **Whistles, Paul &**
Joe, Tokio, The Library, and **Space.NK Cosmetics.** From the Brompton
Cross to Edith Grove, **Fulham Road** features a stretch of shops whose
goods cover the gamut, from the height of fashion, antiques, and
housewares, to the best used treasures, at the **Notting Hill Charity Shop.**
Ralph Lauren recently opened a beautiful three-story shop there,
crammed with goods from first-edition books (with very New York–
centric topics and costing a bundle) to an English saddle. And, of
course, clothes. Moving west on Fulham you pass **Agnes B, Jigsaw,** and
Jigsaw Junior for women's and children's fashions. **Butler & Wilson** is a
fun place to browse and shop, as many of its prices are not over the
moon. They have a small selection of antique clothes, and lots of accessories. The jewelry there is wonderful and includes all the tiaras you
could desire as well as a huge one on the top of the building. The jew-
eler **Theo Fennell;** the smart idea of the **Wedding Shop** with its worn-
once, secondhand dresses; and the upscale stationery store **Papyrus** all
precede the block devoted to expensive antiques. There's a good independent bookstore, **Pan Books,** past the **UGC Cinema,** which has an impressive assortment of books signed by the authors.

There are many other smaller and perfectly fascinating areas for
shopping; you're bound to come across your own personal preferences as you wander around. Don't neglect the more far-flung
neighborhoods, such as the East End, Greenwich, Hampstead, or
Putney Green; there are plenty of places all over London where you
can do some serious damage to your credit card.

MARKETS

MARKETS COVER A FAIR AMOUNT OF SPACE, so rather than
addresses, we've given the tube stop, from which signs will direct you
most efficiently.

APPLE MARKET (tube: Covent Garden) Open daily from 9 a.m. to 5
p.m., this is a permanent market on the south side of the piazza. The
market is set up in stalls and includes everything from crafts to
woolens, with a juice bar and other food stalls thrown in. The brick
structure that once housed the fruit, vegetable, and flower sellers is
now given over to clothing, silverware, old photos and prints, hand-
crafts, jewelry, and whatever else the wind blows in that day. A variety
of craftspeople set up stalls depending on the day, and at Christmas
even more stalls are set up around the piazza. At the **Jubilee Market,**
in the west end of the main arcade of Covent Garden, you'll find a
medium-size antiques market, with bric-a-brac, jewelry, antique
prints, and curios on Mondays only from 7 a.m. to 5 p.m.

 BERMONDSEY MARKET (Bermondsey Square; tube: London
Bridge and Borough) goes way back to 1855, and originally
took place in Islington. Open only Friday from 4 a.m. to

2 p.m., this market, also known as the **New Caledonian Market,** gives preference to the early bird, and that means arriving in pitch darkness to vie with dealers buying antiques of every description and value, including clothing and jewelry. It's a serious place, and supposedly the "really good" stuff is gone before 9 a.m., but if you're not a dealer that shouldn't bother you. No credit cards are taken here; bring plenty of cash. And you should take a taxi before sunrise as the tube doesn't start running until around 5:30 a.m., not to mention the fact that a taxi is the safest option. Ask to be let off at the corner of Bermondsey Street and Long Lane. If you do go later by tube, take the Northern Line to London Bridge, exiting on Tooley Street and walking past the London Dungeon until you get to Bermondsey Street, where you will make a right and walk down it for about ten minutes till you see the market. Many stalls are closed by 9 a.m., but some remain open till 2 p.m. There are also lots of antiques shops on the nearby **Tower Bridge Road** that have regular business hours.

BRICK LANE MARKET (Brick Lane; tube: Aldgate East, Shoreditch, or Liverpool Street) This East End market is open only on Sundays from 8 a.m. to 1 p.m. It is still kind of basic, without much of the sexy stuff, like antiques or curios, but it does have its fans. As the East End becomes more fashionable, the market shares in the gentrification with hip, young designer gear vying with chipped crockery for your attention. For lunch, walk down Brick Lane and prepare to be accosted by Pakistanis and Indians touting their restaurants with offers of discounts—there are scores of curry joints and restaurants here.

CAMDEN MARKET (Camden Town; tube: Camden Town) This has become one of London's biggest tourist attractions, which means big crowds on weekdays and weekends. An absolute must for teens and twentysomethings, this market has cheap and trendy clothing, jewelry, records, and lots of curious-looking young people to watch. Camden is sort of a latter-day Haight-Ashbury, complete with head shops, local crafts, incense, and Indian fabrics. There are plenty of good food stalls and cafés in the area and lots of outdoor seating in warm weather. The **Victorian Market Hall** is open daily and has three floors of shops and stalls of everything from London souvenirs to antiques to books—something for everyone in a charming and festive atmosphere. The street part of Camden Market is open Thursday and Friday from 9 a.m. to 5 p.m. and weekends from 10 a.m. to 6 p.m. Then there's the weightier goods of **Stables Yard,** a weekend market of antique furniture and interesting secondhand goods.

CAMDEN PASSAGE MARKET (Camden Passage, off Upper Street; tube: Angel) Not to be confused with the above Camden Market, this market offers an interesting array of antiques and collectibles in outdoor stalls. It's open Wednesday from 10 a.m. to 2 p.m. and Saturday from 10 a.m. to 5 p.m., but the Passage itself has permanent antiques stores open all week. You can visit **www.antiquescamdenpassage.co.uk.**

GREENWICH MARKETS (take Greenwich Docklands Light Rail (DCR), Jubilee line to Cutty Sark station, Cutty Sark DLR from Tower Tube, or ferry from Westminster pier) There's no better way to pass a Sunday than by taking a boat up the Thames from Westminster to Greenwich. There are a few good, well-priced markets in Greenwich that are open on Saturday and Sunday from 9 a.m. to 6 p.m. You should have no trouble finding them, because the town is small and you just can't miss them. There's the crafts market in the center of town; the **Bosun's Yard** market, which also sells crafts and such; the **Canopy Antiques Market,** which is really a flea market with plenty of interesting junk; and the **Greenwich Antiques Market,** which has many stalls of vintage clothes, as well as a variety of collectibles and antiques. And if crowds are not your thing, trot over to the wonderful **Greenwich Park,** where in summer you'll find a fresh juice kiosk and all year, at the top of the hill, is the free **Royal Observatory.**

LEATHER LANE MARKET (tube: Chancery Lane) There has been a market on this site on Leather Lane for more than 300 years. As you may guess, it does have leather goods, and they're not too expensive either. Besides the clothing, the other stuff probably won't get your attention; it's mostly electrical and household items, CDs, and so on, but the market itself has an interesting atmosphere. It's open Monday through Friday from 10:30 a.m. to 2 p.m.

PETTICOAT LANE MARKET (Middlesex Street and environs; tube: Liverpool Street) Open only on Sunday from 9 a.m. to 2 p.m., Petticoat Lane Market used to be located on a street of that name until the Victorian sensibilities became too delicate to handle the reference to ladies' unmentionables. Now there are tons of stalls selling clothing, shoes, household goods, crafts, you name it, lining a number of streets in the area.

PORTOBELLO MARKET (tube: Notting Hill Gate) Located on Portobello Road, from the Notting Hill end to the Ladbroke Grove end, this market is really several markets in one. The **antiques market** is held on Saturday from 7 a.m. to 6 p.m.; the **general market** is open Monday through Wednesday from 9 a.m. to 5 p.m.; the **organic market** takes place Thursday from 11 a.m. to 6 p.m.; and **clothing and knickknacks** are for sale on Friday from 7 a.m. to 4 p.m., Saturday from 8 a.m. to 5 p.m., and Sunday from 9 a.m. to 4 p.m. On Saturday, at the Notting Hill end, in addition to the stalls galore of antiques, the stores that are often closed on weekdays are open for business. It's a major scene, so come early. As you head toward **Ladbroke Grove,** clothing takes over, and at the end of the street, you turn left on Westbourne Grove Road and walk through densely packed stalls of secondhand clothes, head shop–type paraphernalia, vintage shoes, food, and loud music.

ST. MARTIN-IN-THE-FIELDS MARKET (St. Martin's Lane; tube: Charing Cross) Have a look around when you're in the Trafalgar Square area, as this market is in the same area. It's mostly clothing and teenage items, although one might find some nice and inexpensive second-hand velvet jackets from the 1970s. Lots of neo-hippie gear. While you're at it, go see the gift shops in the crypt of St. Martin-in-the-Fields Church and make a brass rubbing of one of the many Celtic and other designs.

SPITALFIELDS MARKET (Commercial Street between Lam and Brushfield; tube: Liverpool Street) is alas, no more. The old Sunday Market has been disbanded in favor of more regular shops and permanent stalls. There are interesting shops to be sure, but the good old days of fried food stalls and the occasional dog show on Sundays are gone. You may want to have a look there if you're going to the Petticoat Lane and/or Brick Lane Markets.

WALTHAMSTOW (Walthamstow High Street; tube: Walthamstow Central) Open Monday through Saturday from 8 a.m. to 6 p.m., Walthamstow is billed as Europe's **longest daily street market,** with 450 stalls and 300 shops. It's mostly ordinary consumer goods for a bargain, including food, clothes, electrical equipment, and the like, but it is fun to see. It also offers lots of stalls serving delicious food and, in the summer, live entertainment. It's far off the beaten track, but if you combine it with a visit to the **William Morris House** or **Hatfield House,** it could be a good day out.

DEPARTMENT STORES

THESE ARE MOST LIKE THE AMERICAN stores we know so well, although they're more expensive. **John Lewis** and **Peter Jones** (different names, same company) have everything you might need in life, and they claim to beat all other department store prices. **Harrods** pretends to have everything under the sun but really doesn't and charges at least a few quid more than John Lewis. **Marks and Spencer** has clothes and food and a limited selection of grocery items. **Selfridges, Debenhams,** and **Harvey Nichols** are somewhat similar to each other, all with lots of fashions, cosmetics, and a café or two.

DEBENHAMS (334–338 Oxford Street, West End, W1; ☎ 0207-580-3000; www.debenhams.com; tube: Bond Street) It has the usual fashion, cosmetics, and a few designers. The store has numerous locations.

FORTNUM & MASON (181 Piccadilly, Mayfair, W1; ☎ 0207-734-8040; www.fortnumandmason.co.uk; tube: Green Park) You might not think of this as anything other than a food emporium, but in fact F&M has floors that carry clothing, clocks, and gifts above its ground floor stocked with jellies and jams. The interior is beautiful, and the cream tea is classic. Make sure you cross the street a few minutes before the hour to see the enchanting movement of the mechanical clock on the building, with its velvet-coated Georgian-era mannequin popping out for a look at the pullulating traffic on Piccadilly.

HARRODS (87 Brompton Road, Knightsbridge, SW1; ☎ 0207-730-1234; **www.harrods.com;** tube: Knightsbridge) Harrods made its reputation in the mid-19th century as a goods emporium unparalleled in the empire, capable of satisfying every possible whim: it once famously delivered a camel to a customer. It still has an impressive array of stock, but in my opinion, it takes itself too seriously with its dress code: an American woman was once ejected for her poor dress sense, but she believed it was because she was overweight. She *was* strangely discriminated against, as she was dressed perfectly well, and I believe they offered her an apology and god knows what in gift certificates. Security guards will check your bags once in a while upon entering, and you must carry any backpack in your hand, so as to avoid knocking over the merchandise. Kids go mad (literally: stark raving lunacy) for the overwhelming World of Toys, with its miniature automobiles and all the toy demonstrations done by staff. There's a rustic plastic play tree for small kids to explore, and a special restaurant just for young 'uns. The food halls are filled with overpriced (but often worth it, the pesto is the best in London) produce and prepared food from all over the world, and there's a new, mysteriously popular Krispy Kreme doughnut outlet in the bakery— they seem to think these nutrient-free, calorie-packed stomach bombs are a quaint American delicacy. There are ethnic restaurants on the perimeters of the produce and prepared-foods stalls.

HARVEY NICHOLS (109–125 Knightsbridge, SW1; ☎ 0207-235-5000; **www.harveynichols.com;** tube: Knightsbridge) Beloved by fashionistas, Harvey Nichols offers floors of designer clothes, plus a good restaurant on the fifth-floor flood hall. The window displays are out of this world, and change regularly.

JOHN LEWIS/PETER JONES (John Lewis, 278–306 Oxford Street, West End, W1; ☎ 0207-629-7711; **www.johnlewis.co.uk;** tube: Oxford Circus. Peter Jones, Sloane Square, SW1; ☎ 0207-730-3434; tube: Sloane Square) There's nothing fancy or trendy here, but they actually do carry everything at good prices, from picture hooks to computers.

LIBERTY (210–220 Regent Street, West End, W1; ☎ 0207-734-1234; **www.liberty-of-london.co.uk;** tube: Oxford Circus) A wonderful store in the Tudor style that perks up the Georgian cool of Regent Street, Liberty is full of interesting items and home to the famous Liberty fabrics and to antiques.

MARKS AND SPENCER (main branch, 458 Oxford Street, Marble Arch, W1; ☎ 0207-935-7954; **www.marks-and-spencer.co.uk;** tube: Bond Street) M&S, or Marks and Sparks as it's known, carries a lot of good stuff. Under its own St. Michel name brand, it provides food and fashion. Apparently, their underwear is worn by 70% of all Londoners, and I can vouch for its comfort and design. I know of a few Americans who stock up whenever they're in town. Solid if unimaginative clothing is offered in every possible size, and **Per Una** is a recently added line of clothing that is a bit more fashionable, and does have some well-made, reasonably prices clothes, but the biggest size they make is U.K. size 16, and the occasional size 18 (American size 14 or 16). Branches are everywhere.

 SELFRIDGES (400 Oxford Street, Marble Arch, W1; ☎ 0870-837-7377; **www.selfridges.co.uk;** tube: Marble Arch) Thanks to a £100 million face-lift in 1999 and the reorganizing efforts of a new director, Selfridges has regained a grip on its identity and now thoroughly lives up to the grand promise of its extravagant facade. I love it, especially for the crazy promotions they throw each year—Las Vegas was the theme this year, and there were showgirls on the street and neon dice hanging from the ceilings. The window displays are a gas: they once had all live human "mannequins" in the windows, actors paid to hang out, chat with each other, talk on the phone, watch TV, and ignore us gawpers on the street outside. Wonderful. (Harrods did the same thing once, with the people communicating with the outside world via Internet.) Designer wear, silver, beauty products, furniture, as well as restaurants and a glorious food hall, make this a fun and satisfying shopping experience. In 2003, Selfridges gave new meaning to cutting-edge by opening its very own tattoo and body-piercing parlor.

WHERE *to* FIND . . .

ANTIQUES

THERE ARE SO MANY ANTIQUES STORES IN London, from White Chapel to Hammersmith, that an entire book could be—in fact there are many such books—devoted to listing them. What we will point you toward are the antiques arcades that are plentiful in London, and let you wander through the great variety of antiques to be had among the stalls, including jewelry, books, clothing, furniture, clocks, silver, decorative arts, knickknacks, and more. See pages 403–406 for information about the larger markets that include antiques—Bermondsey, Camden Passage, and Portobello. Other antiques markets include the following:

Alfie's Antique Market (13–5 Church Street, Marylebone, NW8; ☎ 0207-723-6066; **www.alfiesantiques.com;** tube: Edgeware Road) is open Tuesday–Saturday, 10 a.m.–6 p.m.

Antiquarius (131–141 King's Road, Chelsea, SW3; ☎ 0207-351-5353; **www.antiquarius.co.uk;** tube: Sloane Square) is open Monday–Saturday, 10 a.m.–6 p.m.

Bourbon-Hanby Antiques Centre (151 Sydney Street, Chelsea, SW3, on the corner of King's Road; ☎ 0207-352-2106; **www.antiques.co.uk/bourbon-hanby;** tube: Sloane Square) is open Monday–Saturday, 10 a.m.–6 p.m. and Sunday, 11 a.m.–5 p.m.

Gray's Antiques Market and **Gray's Mews Market** (off Oxford Street at 58 Davies Street, Mayfair, W1; ☎ 0207-629-7034; **www.graysantiques. com;** tube: Bond Street) is open Monday–Friday, 10 a.m.–6 p.m.

London hosts a lot of antiques fairs over the course of the year. Check out the following Web sites for more information.

www.antiques-london.com   www.antiquesnews.co.uk

www.antiquesweb.co.uk   www.portobelloroad.co.uk

www.lapada.co.uk   www.bada.org

AUCTION HOUSES

THESE CAN BE A LOT OF FUN, AND YOU CAN also get some amazing items, as the treasures of the empire continue to pass through acquisitive hands. Bargains are not to be had by the likes of common folk, because the dealers know what they're doing and how to do it, but you can give it a go. Call to find out what is being sold and when, and go take a look at the catalogs to familiarize yourself with the prices. The giants of the auction business in London (and in the world) are the following:

Bonhams has two London auction houses: the one in Knightsbridge (Montpelier Street, SW7; ☎ 0207-629-1602, **www.bonhams. com;** tube: Knightsbridge) and the head office in Mayfair (101 New Bond Street, W1; ☎ 0207-629-6602; tube: Bond Street); **Christie's** (85 Old Brompton Road, SW7; ☎ 0207-581-7611; **www.christies.com;** tube: South Kensington); and **Sotheby's** (34–35 New Bond Street, W1; ☎ 0207-293-5000; **www.sothebys.com;** tube: Bond Street; and Sotheby's Olympia, (Hammersmith Road, W14; ☎ 0207-293-5555; tube: Olympia Kensington).

There's also the less expensive and just-as-fun auction house off the New King's Road (the westernmost end of King's Road in Chelsea), **Lots Road** (71-71-73 Lots Road, SW10; ☎ 0207-376-6800; **www.lotsroad.com;** tube: Sloane Square, then bus 11; or Fulham Broadway and walk 10 or 15 minutes, but a cab is probably the best way). There are two sales on Sundays, one of modern furniture and the other of antique furniture or household items. Viewing starts on Thursday morning until the auction starts at 2 p.m. Sunday. This is not where you'll find museum-quality goods, but neither is it where you'll be bankrupted.

A newcomer to the scene is the **Criterion Riverside Auctions,** started in 2004 and doing very well in its outpost south of the Thames, on the border of Wandsworth and Battersea; there's also one in Islington, specializing mostly in furniture (41–47 Chatfield Road, SW11; ☎ 0207-228-5563; **www.criterionauctions.co.uk/riverside;** tube: Clapham Common and taxi). Viewings are on Friday from 10 a.m. to 7 p.m., Saturday and Sunday from 10 a.m. to 6 p.m., and Monday from 10 a.m. until the auction commences at 5 p.m. Prices are good, and merchandise is diverse.

How it's done: For each of the hundreds of auctions these houses hold, there is an exhibition of the goods to be sold. These exhibitions are open to one and all for free. They will be listed on the Web sites, and they are worth a visit even if you aren't in the market for treasure. A catalog is produced for the goods, and is available at the auction house (for a small to middling cost) or for free (sometimes without illustrations) online. This is where you can get a handle on provenance, price, and possibility of purchase. You can buy without attending the auction through the absentee bidding service or by telephone. Going in person to the auction is the most fun, however, whether you buy or not. When you arrive at the auction, you must register and receive your numbered bidding paddle (these have eliminated the old slapstick humor of a person with a chronic nervous tic unwittingly buying a million-dollar spittoon). Lots are brought out in numerical order; the auctioneer will describe the item and start the bidding at about two-thirds of the estimated price in the catalog. Raise your paddle to bid and the auctioneer will acknowledge it and continue asking for higher bids. Bids increase in approximately 10% increments. When no more bids are accepted, the hammer comes down and the auctioneer pronounces the item "sold" and names the number of the winning paddle. If you have won, go to the cashier and pay for your new toy with credit card, cash, bank transfer, or an approved personal check. The total cost is your bid, plus tax, plus a buyers' premium (a percentage of the cost paid to the auction house). The auction house will deliver your goods for a fee; some things may be brought home that very day, but it may be a few days before you can pick it up. Be sure to discuss this when you pay for it; some auction houses have the nerve to start charging you for storage after a couple of days.

BEAUTY AND BATH STORES

Culpepper the Herbalist (8 The Market, Covent Garden Piazza, WC2; ☎ 0207-379-6698—hang on, it switches from fax to telephone; **www.culpepper.co.uk;** tube: Covent Garden) sells bath salts, oils, teas, spices, essential oils—they've got it all here. Another branch is located at 21 Bruton Street, Mayfair, W1; ☎ 0207-629-4559. **Shu Uemura** (55 Neal Street, West End, WC2, ☎ 0207-240-7635; **www.shuuemura.com;** tube: Covent Garden) is held in high esteem by many professional make-up artists; this shop has everything the international beauty wants, from cosmetics to massages. **Lush** (7 and 11 The Market, Covent Garden Piazza, WC2; ☎ 0207-240-4570; **www. lush.co.uk;** tube: Covent Garden) is a wonderful place for chocolate massage bars, soaps by the hunk, fizzy bath bombs, and homemade oatmeal masks. The design is witty and ecologically sound: it looks like a delicatessen, with wheels of soap resembling cheeses, and minimal packaging; great gifts here. There are multiple branches all over London. **MAC Cosmetics** (109 King's Road, Chelsea, SW3; ☎ 0207-534-9222; **www.maccosmetics.com;** tube: Sloane Square) is a Canadian company that offers trendy makeup that doesn't cost the world. **Neal's Yard Remedies** (15 Neal's Yard, West End, WC2; ☎ 0207-379-7222; **www.nealsyardremedies.com;** tube: Covent Garden) is a great place for homeopathic remedies, fresh herbs, essential oils, soaps, and haircare products, all in beautiful blue glass bottles. Other branches are too numerous to mention, so call for information. **Space.NK Apothecary** (37 Earlham Street, West End, WC2; ☎ 0207-379-7030; **www.spacenk.co.uk;** tube: Covent Garden) is a body and beauty products boutique, with cutting-edge lotions, scents, facial products, and cosmetics from a wide variety of independent companies, mostly into natural ingredients. The apothecary also has many branches, so call for additional locations. For **Dr. Hauschka** products, stop into **The Life Centre** (15 Edge Street, Kensington, W8; ☎ 0207-221-4602; **www.thelifecentre.com;** tube: Notting Hill), a yoga studio that stocks pretty much the full range of the all-natural lotions and cosmetics at close to European prices. In the Chelsea Market there's a health food store called **Here** (Chelsea Market, 125 Sydney Street, SW3, ☎ 0207- 351-4321; tube: Sloane Square or South Kensington), which also has some of Dr. Hauska's creams and cosmetics, as well as some other holistic-type products.

For men's gifts or men's pampering treatments, don't miss the genteel, traditional Mayfair establishment, **Geo. F. Trumper** (9 Curzon Street, Mayfair, W1; ☎ 0207-499-1850; **www.trumpers.com;** tube: Green Park). It's like stepping into a time capsule, with gleaming dark oak and glass cases displaying the highest quality shaving and personal care accessories in the world. They offer a deluxe straight razor shave that's light years away from your usual daily lather and scrape.

BOOKSTORES

THERE ARE MANY CHAIN BOOKSTORES IN London, which have branches everywhere. Call to find the one nearest you: **Books Etc.** (☎ 0207-404-0261; **www.booksetc.co.uk**); **Borders Books & Music** (☎ 0207-379-6838; **www.borders.com**); **WH Smith** (☎ 0207-261-1708; **www.whsmith.co.uk**); and **Waterstone's** (☎ 0207-434-4291; **www.waterstones.co.uk**). I think Waterstone's is the best of that lot.

 Pan Bookstore (158 Fulham Road, Chelsea, SW10; ☎ 0207-373-4997; tube: South Kensington, then bus 14 toward Fulham) has lots of signed editions of recently published books. **Daunt Books** (83 Marylebone High Street, Marylebone, W1; ☎ 0207-224-2295; tube: Baker Street) is a beautiful store to browse in, with recently published titles, and good travel books. No trip to London would be complete without a look in at **Hatchards** (187 Piccadilly, Mayfair, W1; ☎ 0207-439-9921; **www.hatchards.co.uk;** tube: Piccadilly Circus). It's London's oldest bookstore, established in this beautiful, four-story building in 1797. It has an endearingly serious atmosphere and stocks some very weighty tomes. All you fans of the madcap Mitford sisters must make a beeline to **Heyward Hill** (10 Curzon Street, Mayfair, W1; ☎ 0207-629-0647; **www.heywoodhill.co.uk;** tube: Green Park), where shop girl Nancy Mitford held court with the Bright Young Things set during the Blitz. It feels historic to those of us who've already spent imaginary time there in the biographies of Nancy and the whole clan, or who've read the little autobiographical gem called *Hons and Rebels* by her sister Jessica. And we can't forget the famous **Foyles** (113–119 Charing Cross, Soho, WC2; ☎ 0207-437-5660; **www.foyles.co.uk;** tube: Tottenham Court). It used to be a mad teetering pile of all kinds of books, old and new, but it has been updated to four floors (with a lift, no less) of soberly organized books on every subject under the sun.

Then there are the more unusual specialty bookstores: **Atlantis Bookshop** (49A Museum Street, Bloomsbury, WC1; ☎ 0207-405-2120; **www.theatlantisbookshop.com;** tube: Tottenham Court Road) caters to a clientele interested in psychic research, witchcraft, and supernatural phenomena. **Book Thrift** (22 Thurloe Street, South Kensington, SW7; ☎ 0207-589-2916; tube: South Kensington) specializes in fine-arts books for a fraction of the original cost. Buy immediately: When the stock is gone, it's gone for good. **European Bookshop** (5 Warwick Street, Soho, W1; ☎ 0207-734-5259; **www.esb.co.uk;** tube: Piccadilly Circus) sells books and mags in most European languages. **Grant & Cutler** (55–57 Great Marlborough Street, Marylebone, W1; ☎ 0207-734-2012; **www.grantandcutler.com;** tube: Oxford Street) has books, videos, cassettes, and more. About 200 languages are represented, so you're certain to find something you can understand.

Henry Sotheran (on the ground floor at 2 Sackville Street, Mayfair, W1; ☎ 0207-629-6517; **www.southerans.co.uk;** tube: Green Park) is the place to look for rare antiquarian books of staggering value. Within Henry Sotheran is **The Folio Society Gallery,** where reproductions of fine antiquarian books are available. The books are magnificent, well bound, and illustrated as in the old days, with classic titles of every genre. The only catch is you have to join the society with the obligation to buy four books as the price of membership (the difficulty is limiting yourself to only four). The society, at the same address as Henry Sotheran, can be reached at ☎ 0207-439-6151 or on the Internet at **www.sotherans.co.uk.** One of the oldest rare book dealer is located in a grand, spooky old town house in Berkeley Square, and has been in business since 1853. **Maggs Brothers** (50 Berkeley Square, Mayfair, W1; ☎ 0207-493-7160; **www.maggs.com;** tube: Green Park) has a staff of 20 specialists in seven departments, and first editions of old, important books. The prices on some of their precious stock can hit six figures. (Incidentally, in the early 19th century, 50 Berkeley Square was known as "the most haunted house in London," a reputation that repelled tenants for decades, and these days it probably attracts almost as many tour guides, ghost hunters, parapsychologists, and BBC TV journalists as rare book seekers.)

Forbidden Planet (179 Shaftsbury Avenue, West End, WC2; ☎ 0207-420-3666; **www.forbiddenplanet.com;** tube: Tottenham Court Road), billed as The Science Fiction Entertainment Store, has got it all, from toys to videos to every kind of printed matter you can imagine. **French's Theatre Bookshop** (52 Fitzroy Street, West End, W1; ☎ 0207-387-9373; **www.samuelfrench-london.co.uk;** tube: Warren Street) has play scripts beyond compare and is a must for the theater student or aficionado.

Librairie La Page French Booksellers has everything for the French student, young and old (7 Harrington Road, South Kensington, SW7; ☎ 0207-589-5991; tube: South Kensington). **Politicos** (8 Artillery Row, Mayfair, SW1; ☎ 0207-828-0010; **www.politicos.co.uk;** tube: St. James's Park) has great political paraphernalia, plus a fine selection of books on biography, reference, and history. **Stanfords** (12–14 Long Acre, West End, WC2; ☎ 0207-836-1321; **www.stanfords.co.uk;** tube: Leicester Square) has the biggest collection of maps, globes, and travel books you'll ever see. **Talking Bookshop** (11 Wigmore Street, Marylebone, W1; ☎ 0207-491-4117; **www.talkingbooks.co.uk;** tube: Bond Street) is one of my favorites, with hours and hours of unabridged great fiction and nonfiction, from cassette taped classics to this year's best-sellers as well as books on CD. Theirs are not cheaper than those sold in the United States, but they do offer more unabridged books than you'll see outside of a library. **Dover Bookshop** (18 Earlham Street, West End, WC2; ☎ 0207-836-2111; **www.doverbooks.co.uk;** tube: Covent Garden) is a fabulous resource for arcane books of old and interesting copyright-free illustrations, with CD-ROMs included with many of them.

SECONDHAND BOOKSHOPS

IT WOULD BEHOOVE ANYONE INTERESTED in idle browsing through out-of-print books to take a stroll down Charing Cross Road or around Soho to look in the many secondhand bookshops spilling over with the titles of yesteryear. The prices are reasonable; sometimes there's a bargain bin selling six books for a fiver or some such deal. (Not that they'll be anything of objective value in there—these booksellers know their biz. But you never know, you may have a joyful reunion with a long-lost favorite novel) You might even get your hands on some very fine antique books for a couple of quid. Antiques neighborhoods, markets, and arcades, as listed in this book, will also have many shops and stalls featuring old and beautiful books. On the South Bank by the National Theatre, you'll find stalls of secondhand books at dirt-cheap prices; they remain open till around sundown. Many of the secondhand bookstores listed below also have rare and antiquarian books in locked glass cabinets. Check out any or all of the following shops:

Any Amount of Books (62 Charing Cross Road, West End, WC2; ☎ 0207-240-8140; **www.anyamountofbooks.com;** tube: Leicester

Square); **Gloucester Road Bookshop** (123 Gloucester Road, South Kensington, SW7; ☎ 0207-370-3503; **www.gloucesterbooks.co.uk;** tube: Gloucester Road); **Skoob Books** (15 Sicilian Avenue, Holborn, WC1; ☎ 0207-404-3063; **www.skoob.com;** tube: Holborn); and **Unsworths Booksellers** (15 Bloomsbury Street, Bloomsbury, WC1; ☎ 0207-436-9836; **www.unsworths.com;** tube: Tottenham Court Road).

DECORATIVE HOME ACCESSORIES

Architectural Components (8 Exhibition Road, South Kensington, SW7; ☎ 0207-581-2401; tube: South Kensington) has brass fittings for every possible household use with an emphasis on the bathroom. **The Conran Shop** (Michelin House, 81 Fulham Road, South Kensington, SW3; ☎ 0207-589-7401; **www.conran.com;** tube: South Kensington) has furniture, household goods, fabric, and all manner of modern bric-a-brac for bed, bath, kitchen, and nursery. **India Jane** (131 Kings Road, Chelsea, SW3; ☎ 0207-351-1060; tube: Sloane Square) has some good buys in the way of Indian silver lamps and picture frames, as well as bibelots and furniture.

   The London Silver Vaults (53–64 Chancery Lane, The City, WC2; ☎ 0207-242-3844; tube: Chancery Lane) is actually 40 shops selling silver, old and new, and for every budget.

   The Reject China Shop (183 Brompton Road, Knightsbridge, SW3; ☎ 0207-581-0739; **www.chinacraft.co.uk;** tube: Knightsbridge) is a great place to replace missing Spode or Wedgwood plates or to pick up a cow creamer. It has numerous branches. If you're into modern design, the **Design Museum Shop** (Design Museum, Shad Thames, SE1; ☎ 0207-940-8753; **www.designmuseum.org;** tube: Tower Hill) is a repository of elegantly space-age (and museum-worthy) household goods, designed by big names, such as Stefan Lindfors or Aldo Rossi. Or you could step back in time at **Thomas Goode and Co.** (19 South Audley Street, Mayfair, W1; ☎ 0207-499-2823; **www.thomasgoode.co.uk;** tube: Green Park), where you're guaranteed an authentic upper-crust English shopping experience, with exquisite fine china, silver, and crystal as well as knickknacks. Have a spot of tea there, too.

DESIGNER CLOTHES

BELOW IS A LIST OF SOME OF LONDON'S homegrown designers. They are certainly London's best-known designers, and not all sell their clothes in other countries. Some have their own boutiques, but unless you just want to see what they have to offer, you're better off buying in the department stores and boutiques that carry their clothes. If it's an internationally known designer, you're better off buying in the United States, if possible.

   Antoni & Alison, Blaak, Boudicca, Hussein Chalayan, Caroline Charles, Jasper Conran, Emma Cook, English Eccentrics, John Galliano, Ghost, Joseph, Katherine Hamnett, Justin Oh, Nicole Farhi, Bella Freud, Betty Jackson, Sophia Kokosalaki, Markus Lupfer, Stella McCartney, Julian Mac-

Donald, **Alexander McQueen, Hamish Morrow, Bruce Oldfield, Red or Dead, Pierce Fionda, Lainey Keogh, Zandra Rhodes, Paul Smith, Tomasz Starzewski, Phillip Treacy** (hats only), **Catherine Walker, Amanda Wakeley, Vivienne Westwood,** and **Matthew Williamson** have stores here or can be found in Selfridges, Harvey Nichols, Harrods, or smaller boutiques (see below). Check the phone book for locations and numbers.

DESIGNER BOUTIQUES

HARVEY NICHOLS, HARRODS, SELFRIDGES, and Liberty will likely carry some or all of the above designers' clothes (see the section "Department Stores" (pages 406–408). Here are a few smaller boutiques that carry many of England's designers:

Browns (23–27 South Molton Street, Mayfair, W1; ☎ 0207-491-7833; **www.brownsfashions.com;** tube: Bond Street) keeps up-to-the-minute creation of all the big-name designers. Other stores are: **A La Mode** (10 Symons Street, Chelsea, SW3; ☎ 0207-730-7180; tube: Sloane Square); **Feathers** (176 Westbourne Grove, Notting Hill, W11; ☎ 0207- 243-8800; tube: Notting Hill Gate); **Koh Samui** (50 Monmouth Street, West End, WC2; ☎ 0207-240-4280; **www.kohsamui.co.uk;** tube: Covent Garden); **Question Air** (38 Floral Street, West End, WC2; ☎ 0207-836-8220; tube: Covent Garden; five other branches); **Whistles** (12 St. Christopher's Place, Marylebone, W1; ☎ 0207-487-4484; tube: Bond Street).

DESIGNER RESALE SHOPS

SUCH A GOOD IDEA, THESE SHOPS. IT'S HIT or miss, but you can ease into some world-class designer threads and shoes for a fraction of what they'd cost new. Unfortunately, there tend to be more size 4s than 14s, but shoes and purses will work for anyone. Some good places to try are **Bang Bang** (21 Goodge Street, Soho, W1; ☎ 0207-631-4191; tube: Goodge Street); **Bertie Golightly** (48 Beauchamp Place, Knightsbridge, SW3; ☎ 0207-584-7270; **www.bertiego.co.uk;** tube: Knightsbridge); **Catwalk** (52 Blandford Street, Marylebone, W1; ☎ 0207-935-1052; tube: Baker Street); **The Dresser** (10 Porchester Place, Bayswater, W2; ☎ 0207-724-7212; tube: Marble Arch); **The Loft** (35 Monmouth Street, West End, WC2; ☎ 0207-240-3807; **www.the-loft.co.uk;** tube: Covent Garden); and **Sign of the Times** (17 Elystan Street, Chelsea, SW3; ☎ 0207-589-4774; tube: Sloane Square). When visiting **Pandora** (16–22 Cheval Place, Knightsbridge, SW7; ☎ 0207-589-5289; tube: Knightsbridge), see also, along this same street, **The Dress Box** (8 Cheval Place, Knightsbridge, SW3; ☎ 0207-589-2240 and **Salou** (6 Cheval Place, Knightsbridge, SW3; ☎ 0207-581-2380).

FABRICS

Anna French (343 King's Road, Chelsea, SW3; ☎ 0207-351-1126; **www.annafrench.co.uk;** tube: Sloane Square, then bus 11 or 22) sells children's room fabrics, as well as sheer, lacy, and flowery textiles. **Beaumont & Fletcher** (261 Fulham Road, Chelsea, SW3; ☎ 0207-352-5594;

www.beaumontandfletcher.com; tube: South Kensington, then bus 14) stocks mind-blowing, museum-quality antique fabric (18th- and 19th-century) and sells reproduction fabrics of perfect verisimilitude. **Colefax & Fowler** is one of the mighty giants in traditional English decoration, with elegant fabrics designed for use as upholstery, to cover walls, or for curtains (110 Fulham Road, Chelsea, SW3; ☎ 0207-244-7427; **www.colefax.com;** tube: South Kensington, then bus 14). **Osbourne & Little** (304–308 King's Road, Chelsea, SW3; ☎ 0207-352-1456; **www.osbourneandlittle.com;** tube: Sloane Square) sells traditional and modern designs, all of high quality. **VV Rouleaux** (6 Marylebone High Street, Marylebone, W1; ☎ 0207-224-5179; **www.vvrouleaux.com;** tube: Bond Street) has an incomparable stock of exotic ribbons, trimmings, and braids for use in upholstery, as curtain tie-backs, or to jazz up a boring piece of clothing.

LINENS

Irish Linen Company (35–36 Burlington Arcade, Mayfair, W1; ☎ 0207-493-8949; tube: Piccadilly Circus) stocks Irish linen and Egyptian cotton sheets and table clothes. **The Linen Merchant** (11 Montpelier Street, Knightsbridge, SW7; ☎ 0207-584-3654; tube: Knightsbridge) has a range of beautiful bathrobes and bed linens. **Monogrammed Linen Shop** (168 Walton Street, Chelsea, SW3; ☎ 0207-589-4033; tube: South Kensington) is where to go to order a personal monogram on expensive, high quality linen. **The White Company** (8 Symons Street, Chelsea, SW3; ☎ 0207-823-5322; **www.thewhitecompany.com;** tube: Sloane Square) sells lovely bedclothes, table linen, and some clothing. Ditto the French sheet designer **Yves Delorme** (54 Duke of York Square, King's Road, Chelsea, SW3; ☎ 0207-730-3435; **www.yvesdelorme.com;** tube: Sloane Square), where elegant patterns are combined with rich, practically edible, cotton.

MUSEUM SHOPS

MY FAVORITE STORES IN LONDON ARE the gift shops at museums. The **British Museum's** shop(s) is the place to find excellent facsimiles of its museum treasures such as the Lewis chess pieces and Roman coins or jewelry. **Hampton Court Palace's** shop has the best all-around selection of housewares, books, food, and decorative arts. **Museum of London's** shop has the best books on London, plus tube maps printed on boxer shorts or T-shirts. The **National Gallery** and **National Portrait Gallery** shops have gorgeous reproductions of their art treasures on clothing, mugs, notebooks, stationery, calendars, fridge magnets, and of course on the more pedestrian postcards and posters. Look for the lusciously printed catalogues from temporary exhibits past; you can't find these anywhere else, and they focus closely on the subject or theme of the exhibition. The **Natural History Museum** shop is a kid's paradise, with tons of plastic and stuffed animals. The **Queen's Gallery** shop and the **Buckingham Palace** shop (open only in August and September) have the best royal-related items and a good range of tin plates in antique designs, an excellent gift. The **Royal Academy** has art books and cool

T-shirts. If you can't find a fun, educational gift for an inquisitive child at the **Science Museum** for reasonable prices, then you don't know kids. Both **Tate Museums** have shops with good art books and postcards. I always break the bank at the **Victoria and Albert Museum,** stocking up on gift items on sale: reproduction jewelry, decorative arts, and books on design and interior decoration reflect the glory of the collection. The **Tower of London** has a number of gift shops featuring everything from kid's medieval costumes to reproductions of the royal jewels. **Westminster Abbey** has a quirky shop full of cheap tourist stuff as well as genuinely interesting souvenirs. All the gift shops in England have excellent chocolate in whimsical packaging.

PERFUMERIES

ONE OF THE GREAT THINGS ABOUT LONDON is its proximity to France, home of a thousand scents. The interest in aromas has wafted across the English Channel, and you can find some of the best perfumes in the world at the following stores. **L'Artisan Parfumeur** (17 Cale Street, Chelsea, SW3; ☎ 0207-352-4196; **www.artisanparfumeur.com;** tube: South Kensington) has scents for men, women, and children(!); candles, too. **Floris** (89 Jermyn Street, Mayfair, SW1; ☎ 0207-930-2885; **www.florislondon.co.uk;** tube: Piccadilly Circus) is the classic English fragrance and soap maker, in business since 1730. Also offered are potpourri and candles. **Jo Malone** (150 Sloane Street, Chelsea, SW1; ☎ 0207-730-2100; **www.jomalone.co.uk;** tube: Sloane Square) is a wildly popular store with remarkable, imaginative scents and creams. **Penhaligons** (41 Wellington Street, West End, WC2; ☎ 0207-836-2150; **www.penhaligons.co.uk;** tube: Covent Garden) has been a garden of lovely aromas since 1870. It's great for gifts and has numerous branches. **Les Senteurs** (71 Elizabeth Street, Victoria, SW1; ☎ 0207-730-2322; **www.lessenteurs.com;** tube: Victoria or Sloane Square) retails unusual fragrances, straight from France, as well as fine skin-care products. If you're the type of individualist woman who has strong feelings about what she likes best in a fragrance, you can have your very own bespoke, signature scent whipped up at either one of the **Miller Harris** branches in Mayfair or Notting Hill (21 Bruton Street, Notting Hill, W1; ☎ 0207-629-7750; **www.millerharris.com;** tube: Bond Street or Green Park). But trust me, you won't be disappointed by any of the exotic fragrances already mixed; go have a sniff.

SHOES

Birkenstock (37 Neal Street, West End, W2; ☎ 0207-240-2783; **www.birkenstock.co.uk;** tube: Covent Garden), the hippie shoe from the 1960s, has never been so popular or mainstream. The real thing costs a bundle in the United States, but here you can get such styles as the Vegan, which contains no animal parts, or the Classic for slightly, and in some cases much, less. **Emma Hope** (53 Sloane Square, Chelsea, SW1; ☎ 0207-259-9566; **www.emmahope.co.uk;** tube: Sloane Square) makes up-to-date, elegant shoes, as does the less expensive shop of the young English designer **L.K. Bennett** (130 Long Acre, West End, WC2; ☎ 0207-379-1710; **www.lkbennett.com;** tube: Covent Garden). **Jimmy Choo** (169 Draycott Avenue, South Kensington, SW3; ☎ 0207-584-6111; **www.jimmy choo.com;** tube: South Kensington) has become the designer of choice for the wealthy, fashionable young women; his shoes have probably trod more red carpets than pavement. The red-soled pumps of **Christian Louboutin** (23 Motcomb Street, Belgravia, SW1; ☎ 0207-823-2234; tube: Knightsbridge) are the must-have of the deep-pocketed diva set. And while we're at it, how about **Manolo Blahnik** (49–51 Old Church Street, Chelsea, SW3; ☎ 0207-352-3863; tube: Sloane Square), whose shoes were described by a devotee as "better than sex"? Apparently, he is one cobbler who can combine glamour with comfort, which goes to explain the eye-popping prices. The newest shoe master on the block is **Georgina Goodman** (12–14 Shepherd Street, Mayfair, W1; ☎ 0207-499-8599; **www.georginagoodman.com;** tube: Green Park), whose Mayfair shop is a fabulous space in which to admire the artful, individual handmade shoes, created to last a lifetime. **John Lobb** (9 St. James Street, Mayfair, SW1; ☎ 0207-930-3664; **www.johnlobbltd.co.uk;** tube: Green Park) is the oldest, grandest, and most expensive of the bespoke shoemakers; one of these classic pairs of English leather shoes will set you back about £1,500, and it will take months to get them, but they say it's well worth it. **Natural Shoe Store** (325 King's Road, Chelsea, SW3; ☎ 0207-351-3721; **www.naturesko.com;** tube: Sloane Square) has the best in comfort shoes: Ecco, Birkenstock, Arche, Krone Clogs, and American brands such as Bass, Dexter, and Rockport. Don't even think of getting the American brands, but check the prices on the Europeans.

VINTAGE CLOTHING

Steinberg and Tolkien (193 King's Road, Chelsea, SW3; ☎ 0207-376-3660; tube: Sloane Square) has an astonishing, wonderful range of vintage clothing, from the Victorian period to that worn during the 1970s, and from Worth to Balmain to Schiaparelli to Biba to Halston. It's the place where costume designers from films come to dress their actors, where actors come to play, and where designers come for inspiration. Go for the fun of seeing the largest vintage clothing collection in London, and be sure to go downstairs. **The Antique Clothing Store** (282 Portobello Road, Notting Hill, W10; ☎ 0208-964-4830; tube: Ladbroke Grove) also has a large selection; you may even find antique christening gowns. **Virginia** (98 Portland Road, Kensington, W11; ☎ 0207-727-9908; tube: Holland Park) is a visually gorgeous shop, with aristocratic fashions and accessories from the late Victorian period, which means that unless you've got a corset and a very deep pocket, you'll just want to look. For a number of retro-clothing shops, go to **Alfie's Antique Market** (13–25 Church Street, Marylebone, NW8; ☎ 0207-724-7366; **www.alfiesantiques.com;** tube: Edgeware Road), where you'll find stalls specializing in various eras, with the 1940s and 1950s particularly well represented. Plenty of accessories, too.

WOOL AND CASHMERE

WOOL AND CASHMERE IN LONDON ARE from Scotland or Ireland and are more expensive and of better quality than the Chinese kind. The best time to buy is during sales. Many of the department stores' wool departments shift a lot of pull-over sweaters, wraps, and cardigans during the summer, thanks to the influx of tourists, many of whom aren't prepared for the chilly summer and need woolens. Liberty, Harrods, Marks and Spencer, Debenhams, and other big stores have good wool departments (see "Department Stores," page 406). It's a sign of the times that so many of the old shops have gone out of business (the Scotch House is sorely missed) and manufacturers now sell straight to department stores. But cashmere is still a luxury.

Shi Cashmere (30 Lowndes Street, Knightsbridge, SW1; ☎ 0207-235-3829; ww.shicashmere.com; tube: Knightsbridge) has an elegant selection of cashmeres, wools, and silks, and if you don't see it, you can order it from the Scottish factory.

MISCELLANEOUS PERSONAL FAVORITE SHOPS
Can't Get Enough Stained Glass

When I first moved to London, my favorite haunt was the Phillips Stained Glass shop on Portobello, where Neil Phillips gave me my first fix of what was to become a real addiction, when I bought four perfect neo-Gothic trefoils. I had to wait to take them home, as they were scheduled for the opening scene of a little movie called *Notting Hill,* with Julia Roberts. I learned a lot about stained glass by popping in to see what was hanging and chatting with the amiable, learned Neil and his staff. Well, sad to say, he's given up on the rents of London, but the good news is that he's part of an empire in the East End where everything to do with stained glass is covered: restoration, installations, new design, classes, and material falls under the leaded-glass umbrella of **Goddard & Gibbs,** a company founded in 1868 (Marlborough House, Cooks Road, Stratford–East End, E15; ☎ 0208-536-0300; www.goddard.co.uk; tube: Stratford). Have a look at **www.neilphillips.co.uk** to see what portable delights you can buy and have shipped home to enliven your windows.

My most recent purveyor of small pieces of antique stained glass is Ollie Curran of **The Gothic Revival Limited** (Longdon Hall, Longdon Green, Lichfield, Staffordshire, WS15; ☎ 0797-129-5277; **www.thgothic revival.com;** British rail: Lichfield). He's done a Herculean job of sorting out the hundreds of thousands of pieces of stained glass salvaged from churches and stately homes of England, and he can read your taste like a psychic. There are, of course, the superior pieces for which millionaires only need apply, but he also finds exquisite fragments and roundels for the tight-budgeted obsessive collector like me. The company does a lot of business in the U.S. and ships anywhere. Strike up an e-mail correspondence with him before you come to London, and he'll forward photos to consider. Shipping to London takes one day, so if your piece is small enough you needn't pay overseas postage or suffer from delayed gratification. Alternatively, you could plan a day into the countryside, traveling by train to the charming, historic village of Lichfield, where you can see Dr. Samuel Johnson's birthplace, or go to the magnificent Lichfield Cathedral for a look at some *really* ancient stained glass. Ollie will pick you up from the train and let you loose in a stained-glass Aladdin's cave, with treasures of every size and from every era. We have never seen the like in North America or Down Under. Tell him I sent you.

Preferred Shops

Ganesha (6 Park Walk, Chelsea, SW10; ☎ 0207-352-8972, tube: Earl's Court or South Kensington) Filled with wonderful semiprecious jewels and artifacts of India, this is a great place to browse and to buy gifts. With silk pajamas, silver jewelry, artifacts from the days of the Raj, incense, and house decor, this is a well-filled small shop.

Summerhill and Bishop (100 Portland Road, Kensington, W11; ☎ 0207-221-4566; tube: Holland Park) has kitchen goods from France, and unusual gifts such as candles spelling "amour" and "ange," or glasses etched with "Amitie." A fun place to browse.

Cross the street from here to pop into **The Cross** (141 Portland Road, Kensington, W11; ☎ 0207-727-6760; tube: Holland Park). This place can get expensive, but it's a groove for browsing. Sourced from all over the world, there are kids' clothes and toys, embroidered silk and cotton clothing, shoes, candles, quilts, and labels from hip designers. (The vintage clothing store **Virginia** is next to Summerhill and Bishop.)

calmia (52–54 Marylebone High Street, Marylebone, W1; ☎ 0207-224-3585; **www.calmia.com;** tube: Baker Street) As its name promises, it is calming just to walk into this shrine to the hip urban yoga lifestyle— just don't look at the prices on the clothes, or you won't be feeling so calmia yourself. A wonderful place for natural cosmetics, soothing CDs, incense, and beauty/health treatments. Great neighborhood, too.

Fake Landscapes (164 Old Brompton Road, South Kensington, SW5; ☎ 0207-835-1500; **www.fake.com;** tube: South Kensington) Only a silk flower shop supremely convinced of its superiority would dare to give itself such a name; the gamble works, as the riot of flowers and plants in this shop looks anything but fake. Not cheap, but if you amortize the cost of real flowers, a pretty good deal. And you'll end up absentmindedly watering the flowering plants, I promise.

Jane Asher Party Cakes & Sugarcraft (22–4 Cale Street, Chelsea, SW3; ☎ 0207-584-6177; **www.jane-asher.co.uk;** tube: Sloane Square) This shop in charming Chelsea Green is a favorite of amateur bakers: It has the best cake mixes going, plus an amazing array of unusually shaped pans (such as number pans), adorable sugar or marzipan, as well as nonedible cake decorations, and very sophisticated baking gear. Browsing or buying, you get a sugar high just being here.

Any of the **Notting Hill Charity Shops, Oxfams, Sue Ryder Shops,** and other secondhand thrift shops, especially in the upscale neighborhoods, are a blast to breeze through. You never know what you'll find.

PART ELEVEN

EXERCISE *and* RECREATION

SPECTATOR SPORTS

THE NATIONAL JUBILATION AND PLANNED celebrations were abruptly and horribly deflated by the terrorist attacks that came the day after London won the bid to host the 2012 Olympics, and it is with a somber determination that the games will go on. The city seemed a bit divided over hosting the event, with many arguing that it's the last thing our overloaded public transport needs; and others pointing to the rejuvenation of Athens as proof of the ultimate benefit the Olympics bring to a city. Even the Queen, somewhat impolitically, was said to believe that Paris would be the perfect place for it. She, and everyone else, have accepted the challenge, and there is a good chance that London will rise admirably to the task. However, London being what it is, I foresee disgruntlement and gaffes for the next few years. But the idea of seeing world-class baseball and basketball played by the banks of the River Thames in the once underutilized Millennium Dome area is somewhat enchanting, as currently there aren't many opportunities to watch those sports played in the U.K. Yes, there are leagues, but I would strongly suggest that you use your visit to see the *real* sports of England: soccer, rugby and cricket.

FOOTBALL

SOCCER, OR FOOTBALL ("FOOTIE") AS THE English call it, is more than a national obsession—it is a religion with serious and often deranged devotees. The days when rival fans would do bloody battle in the streets are mostly gone due to CCTV, hi-tech detective work, well-organized policing at games, and reconstruction of the grounds themselves. However, the fever burns as strong as ever. (To see just how bad it was, try to rent a copy of *The Football Club*, a movie directed by Nick Love, and only available in the U.K., in U.K. format.) There is huge money in football these days, and the top teams, which belong to the Premiership league, are all locked into cable TV deals that have the exclusives on their matches. Consequently, tickets for these games are expensive (£20–£60), whereas tickets for the teams further down the league are cheaper (£10–£18). It is well worth a visit to a Premiership game, as the class (and price) of players these days is phenomenal. The spectators themselves are also worthy of close attention. Listen to their songs and chants filled with venomous derision of the visiting team.

unofficial **TIP**
Avoid the standing seats at the clubs further down the league, as this is where trouble, if it breaks out, is more likely to occur.

The soccer season runs from August to May. Games are 90 minutes long, with injury time and extra time if it is important that there be a winner (as in, for a cup final). Most of the clubs will take credit-card bookings over the phone, which is crucial for Premiership games. They take place on Saturday afternoons and in the evenings on weekdays. Wrap up warmly, and bring a rain poncho. Premiership teams include the following:

ARSENAL AT ARSENAL STADIUM (Avenall Road, N5; ☎ 0207-704-4000; **www.arsenal.co.uk**) Take the tube to Arsenal. Tickets are £33–£51; children are full price.

CHELSEA AT STAMFORD BRIDGE (Fulham Road, SW6; ☎ 0207-386-7799; **www.chelseafc.co.uk**) Take the tube to Fulham Broadway. Tickets are £28–£48 for adults and from £15 for children.

TOTTENHAM HOTSPURS (at White Hart Lane, High Road, N17; ☎ 0870-011-2222; **www.spurs.co.uk**) Take British Rail to White Hart Lane. Tickets are £25–£55 for adults and children.

WEST HAM UNITED (at Boleyn Ground, Green Street, E13; ☎ 0208-548-2700; **www.westhamunited.co.uk**) Take the tube to Upton Park. Adult tickets are £26–£50; children's tickets begin at £15.50.

CRICKET

DESPITE THE FACT THAT IT IS A TRULY international sport (at which the Brits have not excelled for years), there is something quintessentially English about the game of cricket. It is sedate, difficult to understand, and full of quaint language. For example, a "maiden over" is a series of six balls, bowled in a swinging over-arm motion, during which no runs are scored. The games sometimes last for days, interrupted frequently by rain and tea. It is considered vulgar to thrash one's opponent by too many runs; when it is clear the losing team cannot win, the winning side "declares" and gives the other team a chance to recover some of their dignity. You can see this game played by men in white clothing on many a village green during

unofficial **TIP**
Tickets for international games need to be booked well in advance, but the league games, played between local counties, are much easier to get tickets for, and are sometimes free.

the season, which runs from mid-April to early September, but there are two main venues in London, Lords and the Oval:

LORDS AT ST. JOHN'S WOOD ROAD (St. John's Wood, NW8; ☎ 0207-432-1000; **www.lords.org**) Take the tube to St. John's Wood. This is the home of the Marylebone Cricket Club (MCC) and is often considered the home of cricket. Tickets range £5–£40; children's tickets are half price.

OVAL CRICKET GROUNDS (Kennington Oval, SE11; ☎ 0207-582-6660; **www.surreycricket.com**) Take the tube to Oval. International cricket is often played here; tickets range £15–£50. Tickets for county matches are less expensive.

RUGBY

THIS IS A BRUTAL AND VIOLENT GAME SIMILAR to American football but without the padding. Again, the rules are characteristically British: the ball, shaped like an American football, is passed backward or sideways, never forward; during the scrum, the players crouch with their faces or shoulders between the thighs and against the buttocks of the player in front and push against a similarly tightly packed huddle of the opposition. The ball is thrown into this mass of steaming, muddy flesh, from which it is booted out. Whoever catches it then dashes along the field to score a "try" (touchdown), which is then converted by kicking it over the goalposts for extra points. Like cricket, it is a quintessentially British sport at which the natives no longer truly excel. The New Zealanders, French, South Africans, and Fijians are marvelous rugby players, but tickets for international games are hard to get. The season runs from September to May, and the game is enjoying something of a resurgence in popularity due to the amount of money it now attracts.

Rugby League is the professional form of rugby football. This is a fast-moving collision game with lots of open running, big hits, and tackles (the closest thing to American football). There are 13 players on a team.

Rugby Union is traditionally the amateur form of rugby football with the characteristic scrums, timeouts, and touchdowns, and 15 players per team. However, it now boasts a professional status, with the Allied Dunbar Premiership and the Jewson National League, which draw major crowds. The season runs from August to May. Watch out for the Harlequins, London Irish, Saracens, and the Wasps. Wrap up warmly if you go. The primary rugby venues are as follows:

ATHLETIC GROUND (Kew Foot Road, Richmond, Surrey, TW9; ☎ 0208-940-0397; **www.the-raa.co.uk;** tube: Richmond) These amateur games are free.

ROSSLYN PARK (Upper Richmond Road, Priory Lane, Roehampton, SW15; ☎ 0208-876-6044; **www.rosslynpark.co.uk**) Take British Rail to Barnes. Tickets are approximately £10 for adults, £5 for seniors, and £3 for children.

TWICKENHAM RUGBY HOUSE (21 Rugby Road, Twickenham, Middlesex, TW1; ☎ 0208-892-2000; **www.rfu.com**) Tickets vary in price depending on the game. Tickets for the Six Nations series held here are very difficult to get and are distributed to the faithful via the various clubs. You can see cup finals for the leagues here, too, for which tickets range between £15 and £35.

Clubs

BLACKHEATH AT RECTORY FIELD (Charlton Road, Blackheath, SE3; ☎ 0208-293-0853; **www.blackheathrugby.co.uk**)

N.E.C. HARLEQUINS AT STOOP MEMORIAL GROUND (Langhorn Drive, Twickenham, Middlesex; ☎ 0208-410-6000; **www.quins.co.uk**)

LONDON WELSH AT OLD DEER PARK (Kew Road, Richmond, Surrey; ☎ 0208-940-2368; **www.london-welsh.co.uk**)

SARACENS AT VICARAGE ROAD (Watford; ☎ 0192-347-5222; **www.saracens.com**)

LONDON WASPS (Loftus Road Stadium, South Africa Road, W12; ☎ 0208-740-2545; **www.wasps.co.uk**)

BOXING

BIG FIGHTS TAKE PLACE IN BIG VENUES, LIKE the newly renovated and re-opened Wembley Arena, Royal Albert Hall, London Arena, and Earl's Court. Publicity will be large scale, and tickets are always expensive. There are smaller venues for amateur or semiprofessional fights, and these will be advertised in local papers, *Time Out,* or on posters. You can catch a good pro or amateur fight at York Hall, Old Ford Road, E2 (☎ 0208-980-4171; **www.gll.org**). This place has a serious East End vibe and has hosted amateur matches since 1929. Tickets start at £10. Tickets for pro fights are priced by the promoters. Call Boxing News at ☎ 0207-882-1040, or see **www.sporting-life.com/boxing** for details on what's on, where, and when.

TENNIS

WIMBLEDON FORTNIGHT STARTS THE LAST WEEK in June, and demand for tickets always far exceeds the supply. Tickets must be applied for well in advance and are awarded by ballot. To get tickets for Centre Court or Number One Court you have to write, enclosing a self-addressed envelope, for an application form, between September 1 and December 31: The All England Tennis Club, P.O. Box 98, Church Road, London, SW19; ☎ 0208-946-2244; **www.wimbledon.com**. Tick-

*un*official **TIP**
You can usually get in by showing up on the day of the event and waiting to buy tickets for the outer courts; you can also buy returned tickets for the next day at a good price.

ets range between £32–£79 for Centre Court and £22–£59 for Number One Court. All tickets for the last four days are presold; all other days there are a total of 500 tickets held back for sale at the turnstile on the day, cash only. Take the tube to Wimbledon (District line). Bring a hat or umbrella and plenty of sunblock. June is a fickle month for weather.

RACING

HORSE RACING IS VERY POPULAR IN BRITAIN. You can see it almost every day on television, and every high street has at least one betting shop, or "turf accountant," as the Brits like to call them. Gambling is legal in Britain, and bookies will give odds on almost anything, from the gender of the next royal birth to whether it will snow on Christmas Day. A day at the races is as popular with the upper classes (members of which own the horses and can be seen at Ascot wearing hilarious hats that are never worn anywhere else) as it is with the hoi polloi.

The flat season runs from April to September, and the jumps or steeplechase runs from October to April. As well as branches of the major corporate bookies like William Hill and Coral, there are many trackside bookies with whom it is much more fun to bet. They usually take win-only bets, with a minimum stake of £5. Watch the extraordinary ballet of arm swinging and hand signaling as they establish the odds. More complicated bets (exactas, trifectas, accumulators, and so on) can be made at the corporate bookies, or tote, as mentioned before.

All the tracks are just outside London and are well serviced by rail. Take a coat and umbrella, just in case. Most tracks have bars and restaurants, which serve notoriously bad food, so be warned. A day at the races is exactly that; be prepared for a longish haul. Racing venues include those listed below:

ASCOT RACE COURSE (High Street, Ascot, Berks; ☎ 0134-462-2211; **www.ascot.co.uk**) Take British Rail to Ascot rail. Admission is £7–£52, depending on whether you sit in the grandstand or the silver ring. (The royal enclosure is closed to commoners.) Good competitive racing can always be seen here. One of the highlights of the year is the Royal Meeting with Ladies Day on the Thursday of that week, which is when the really mad hatters come out: one or two outrageous chapeaus inevitably make it to the front page of the paper. The 185 million pound in-progress renovation of the race course will open up many more much-desired tickets.

EPSOM (Epsom Downs, Epsom, Surrey; ☎ 0137-247-0047; **www. epsomderby.co.uk**) Take British Rail to Epsom Downs. Admission is £6–£23. This is where the Oaks and the Derby (pronounced "Darby") are held in June, and other races take place throughout the summer. Derby Day is a big betting day in England and is something of a national mood lifter. Some races will feature live music, making it a nice way to spend a summer evening, even if you know nothing about horses. The winner is always part of the headline news, and most people have a bet. Tickets in the Queen's Stand and Derby Day cost up to £100. Don't forget your top hat and tails.

KEMPTON PARK (Staines Road East, Kempton Park; ☎ 0137-247-0047; **www.kempton.co.uk**) Take British Rail to Sunbury on Thames or to Kempton Park. Admission is £15–£21. This course hosts the King George VI stakes on Boxing Day, and has events all year. The summer evenings are particularly fun, with themes such as James Bond, Irish music, or fireworks. You can bet on and watch the race from the restaurant in the sleek exhibition hall.

WINDSOR MAIDENHEAD ROAD (Windsor, Berks; ☎ 0175-349-8400; **www.windsor-racecourse.co.uk**) Take British Rail to Windsor and Eton Riverside. Admission is £6–£20. This is a pretty part of England and worth a visit in its own right. The castle (very much in use by Her Majesty) looms beautifully over the course and can be toured as part of your day out.

GREYHOUND RACING

THESE SLEEK ANIMALS TEAR ROUND THE TRACK after a wooden hare on a rail. They run amazingly fast, and the race is over in a minute or less. There's a lot of beer drinking at the dog races, and you're ensured a very entertaining evening out, featuring lots of characters and florid language. Again, all tracks are well serviced by public transport but are far from the center of London.

ROMFORD STADIUM (London Road, Romford, Essex; ☎ 0170-876-2345; **www.coraleurobet.co.uk**) Take British Rail to Romford. Admission is £1.50–£6 and free on the popular side of the stadium on Thursday afternoon and Saturday morning. All races start at 7:30 p.m. and are held Mondays, Wednesdays, Fridays, and Saturdays.

WIMBLEDON STADIUM (Plough Lane, SW17; ☎ 0208-946-8000; **www.wimbledonstadium.co.uk**) Take the tube to Wimbledon. Admission is £3–£5.50, and races start at 7:30 p.m. on Tuesdays and Thursdays through Saturdays.

▐ PARTICIPATION SPORTS

GYMS AND LEISURE CENTERS

THE GYM CULTURE OF WORKING OUT AND staying in shape has grown proportionally as the Britons make their way up the scale of overweight nations. Though the Germans have them beaten in the pudgy stakes, England is experiencing the same alarming statistics of obesity as the United States. Nevertheless, London is full of exercise options, some of them quite entertaining, such as Friday night inline skating events, organized sunrise runs in Hyde Park, and the increasingly popular London Marathon. The visitor to London who needs to pump up their endorphins or maintain a training program will have no problem finding parks to run in or gyms to work out at, for a day-pass charge that can run from £20–£50. There are far too many to list here, so look in the Yellow Pages under Leisure Centres to find one nearest you, or speak to your concierge. Many hotels, even the budget ones, have access to a gym or sports facility, or else their own exercise room, which will vary in quality. What follows is a small list of sport and leisure in central London (please note that most of the leisure centers will expect you to do an "induction" to the gym (at a small cost); and some of the busier centers have had to limit the gym facilities to members only):

CHELSEA SPORTS CENTER (Chelsea Manor Street, Chelsea, SW3, ☎ 0207-352-6985; **www.rbkc.gov.uk/sport;** tube: Sloane Square) Offers a 25-meter pool and aerobics classes, but you have to be a member to use the gym. They charge £2.85 to swim, £4.10–£5.10 for studio classes, and £3.70 for a half hour on the badminton court.

JUBILEE HALL LEISURE CENTER (30 The Piazza, Covent Garden, WC2; ☎ 0207-836-4835; **www.jubileehallclubs.co.uk;** tube: Covent Garden) This fully equipped gym (called the Gym at Covent Garden) has been refurbished with a new cardio theater, free weights, and resistance machines, and is in an excellent location. There are also yoga, Pilates, and various exercise classes at reasonable prices. The cost is £8 for a day visit.

LONDON CENTRAL YMCA (112 Great Russell Street, Bloomsbury, WC1; ☎ 0207-343-1700; **www.ymcaclub.co.uk;** tube: Tottenham Court Road). This is also very central, and totally comprehensive, with lots of classes. The cost is £15 for a "taster" day visit.

QUEEN MOTHER SPORTS CENTER (223 Vauxhall Bridge Road, Victoria, SW1; ☎ 0207-630-5522; **www.westminster.gov.uk/leisureandculture;** tube: Victoria) Very central, this center has been modernized to the tune of over £1 million and has a complete range of facilities, equipment, and classes; £8 gym, £4.75 class, and £2.65 pool.

PORCHESTER CENTER IN QUEENSWAY (Queensway, Bayswater, W2; ☎ 0207-792-2919; **www.westminster.gov.uk/leisureandculture;** tube: Queensway or Bayswater) Facilities include a 30-meter pool, gym, classes, and a wonderful health spa (Russian steam room, Turkish hot room, sauna, Jacuzzi, and plunge pool). The gym, pool, and spa are open daily; £8 gym, £2.65 pool, £4.75 class.

SEYMOUR LEISURE CENTER (Seymour Place, Marylebone, W1; ☎ 0207-723-8019; **www.westminster.gov.uk/leisureandculture;** tube: Marble Arch) This center has an Olympic-size pool, steam rooms, cardiovascular machines, and exercise classes. Fees are £2.65 pool, £9.10 sauna/steam rooms, £8 gym, and £4.75 class.

BICYCLING

YOU TAKE YOUR LIFE INTO YOUR HANDS bicycling around the streets of London, even with the marked bicycle lanes, but there are plenty of parks to bike in that are wonderfully stress free and interest rich. The London Bicycle Tour Company is the best, with a huge inventory of bikes to rent as well as fun guided tours. They are open from 10 a.m. to 6 p.m. and are located on the Thames at 1a Gabriels Wharf, 56 Upper Gorund, SE1. Call ☎ 0207-928-6838 or visit **www. londonbicycle.com**.

INLINE SKATING

ROLLERBLADES ARE POPULAR IN LONDON, with plenty of good paths throughout Hyde Park and Battersea Park. There are hotdoggers with ramps and cones, as well as serious hockey players alongside the Albert Memorial, and on the north side of the Serpentine in Hyde Park, which makes for good spectator sport. On Wednesday and Friday nights in the warmer months, there is a huge group skating with hundreds of skaters starting at Hyde Park Corner and gliding down London streets in a pack, pumped up by music and whistles; a sight not to be missed. Check out **www.thefns.com** for meeting times and locations (for intermediate and above skaters only—they move fast). You can rent roller skates/blades at a number of sports stores; **www.easy peaseyskate.co.uk** has links to a number of skate-rental shops around London. You can visit **London Skate Centre** (21 Leinster Terrace, W2; ☎ 0207-7706- 8769; **www.lonskate.com;** tube: Queensway or Bayswater) or **Slick Willies** (12 Gloucester Road, South Kensington, SW7; ☎ 0207-225-0004; **www.slickwillies.co.uk;** tube: Gloucester Road). Both stores are conveniently located near Hyde Park. Prices are around £10 per day, £15 for a weekend, and £30 per week, with a credit card deposit of £100. They stock the newest models.

HORSEBACK RIDING

THOUGH NOT EXACTLY THE SPORT OF CHOICE for the masses, there are beautiful places to ride in London. Hyde Park is an old favorite, with well-trodden riding paths like Rotten Row. The beasts are mostly of the warhorse variety, but you can occasionally get a bolter, and there's one straightaway on which they are inclined to canter, unless you have them firmly in hand. You may want to see the British Horse Society Web site at **www.bhs.org.uk** for a comprehensive list of stables around London. The most central are the following stables, which share the same mews location:

ROSS NYE STABLES (8 Bathurst Mews, Bayswater, W2; ☎ 0207-262-3791; tube: Lancaster Gate or Paddington). The price is £40 per hour for a ride around Hyde Park (closed Monday) and £50 for individual lessons (Tuesday through Friday only). They won't take anyone under age 6 or anyone who weighs over 200 pounds. The stables are closed for a couple of months in the summer. Beginners and experienced riders are allowed, and children are encouraged. The horses here are gorgeous and well cared for, and they have plenty of ponies.

unofficial TIP

Do not assume that riding in Hyde Park is without danger. You have to traverse a few streets and cross a busy main road to get into the park.

HYDE PARK STABLES (63 Bathurst Mews, Bayswater, W2; ☎ 0207-723-2813; **www.hydeparkstables. com;** tube: Lancaster Gate or Paddington). The cost is £42 for groups and £50 for a solo ride.

WIMBLEDON VILLAGE STABLES (24 High Street, Wimbledon, SW19, ☎ 0208-946-8579; **www.wvstables.com;** tube: Wimbledon. The price is £35 per hour during the week, £40 on weekends. Expect to pay £20 extra for an individual lesson. This is outside London but worth a trip if you want to avoid automobile traffic. They have small classes for beginners, and you will be taken on a rugged ride through Wimbledon Common, Putney Heath, and Richmond Park, all of which are semi-wild expanses. Look out for deer. This is a much more beautiful experience than Hyde Park, though less convenient.

ICE-SKATING

ALTHOUGH IT'S NEVER COLD ENOUGH IN LONDON for any natural bodies of water to ice over, the city looks after its budding Olympians with a fair number of year-round and winter-only rinks. Admission and skate rental are cheap, and skating can be a fun night out. During December and January there is a wonderful skating venue in the courtyard of the grand old Somerset House on the Strand (☎ 0207-845-4600; **www.somerset-house.org.uk**), and a smaller outdoor rink next to Marble Arch.

BROADGATE ICE RINK (Broadgate Circus, Eldon Street, EC2; ☎ 0207-505-4068; tube: Liverpool Street) Admission plus skate rental is £7 adult, £4 child. This tiny outdoor rink in the middle of London, among the glass castles of the financial district, is open late October through April. There's plenty of room to watch if you don't skate.

QUEENS ICE AND BOWL (17 Queensway, W2; ☎ 0207-229-0172; **www. queensiceandbowl.co.uk;** tube: Bayswater or Queensway) Admission is £7, which includes skate hire. Friday and Saturday nights are disco nights. Good Middle Eastern, Chinese, and Indian restaurants are in the immediate neighborhood for après skate. For those who aren't so keen on skating, there are bowling lanes and arcade games at the same venue.

SWIMMING

MOST OF THE LEISURE CENTERS LISTED EARLIER include swimming pools, but it is worth noting that almost every borough of London has at least one municipally run pool, some of which are more salubrious than others. To find your nearest municipal pool, outdoor pool, or lido, have a look at the interesting Web sites www.lidos.org.uk or www.londonpoolscampaign.com, both of which will give you an idea of how passionately some Londoners feel about swimming and their glorious history of public pools. Bearing in mind that no one comes to London for the great swimming, here's a list of some of the better dipping holes, and they're worth checking out when it's hot, although they can get crowded:

unofficial **TIP**
There are no facilities except a basic changing area, so bring refreshments and a picnic.

HAMPSTEAD MIXED PONDS AND THE HIGHGATE MEN'S AND LADIES' PONDS (Millfield Lane, NW3; ☎ 0207-485-3873; tube: Hampstead or Hampstead Heath or British Rail: Gospel Oak) Admission is free to these ponds that have been in use for a hundred years, though by the time you read this, there may be a small fee (in fact, by the time you read this, the ponds may be closed to swimmers, but we expect a huge popular resistance). These are three ponds in picturesque surroundings: one for men, one for women, and one for both. The segregated ponds are open all year. Try not to look shocked by the skinny-dipping, which is not compulsory. The mixed pond opens April through September only. The ponds are popular hangouts for gays.

THE PARLIAMENT HILL LIDO Known as the Hampstead Heath Lido Hampstead Heath at Gordon House Road, NW3; ☎ 0207-485-3873; British Rail to Gospel Oak) This 200 X 90 foot pool on the edge of Hampstead Heath was first opened to the public in 1938, and was upgraded in 2005 and 2006. Admission is £3.50, £1.50 for concessions. This is London's biggest outdoor pool and is recommended for hot days (it's unheated). Open daily, April through September.

THE OASIS (32 Endell Street, West End, WC2; ☎ 0207-831-1804; tube: Covent Garden or Holborn) Opened originally in 1852 as the Bloomsbury Baths & Washhouses, the completion in 1960 of the indoor facility made it the first all-weather swimming complex in the country. Admission is £2.90 for adults, £1.10 for children over age 5, and free for children under age 5. There is an indoor pool, an outdoor pool, and a bathing deck for basking on those rare sunny days.

RICHMOND POOLS IN THE PARK (Old Deer Park, Twickenham Road, Richmond, Surrey; ☎ 0208-940-0561; www.springhealthleisure.com; tube: Richmond) Admission is £3 for adults, £2.40 for children, and free for kids under age 5. There is an indoor pool, an outdoor pool, and a lush grassy area for flopping upon.

SERPENTINE LIDO (Hyde Park; ☎ 0207-706-3422; www.serpentine lido.com; tube: Hyde Park Corner, Lancaster Gate, or Marble Arch) The Lido is open July through September only, from 10 a.m. to 6 p.m. daily, although the famous polar bears do take their Christmas Day dip there faithfully. This is the most centrally located lido, and includes fun for the kids in the form of a playground, occasional entertainment, and plenty of people-watching possibilities. It's near the Princess Diana Memorial. Admission is £3.50 for adults and 80p for children.

WATER SPORTS

FOR THOSE WHO ENJOY THE WATER, THERE is plenty to do on the Thames and in the surrounding reservoirs and docklands. Thanks to insurance problems, many of the old watersports clubs no longer offer drop-in fun. But there is still one place that is full-service:

DOCKLANDS SAILING AND WATERSPORTS CENTRE (235A Westferry Road, E14; ☎ 0207-537-2626; **www.dswc.org;** Docklands Light Rail to Crossharbour/London Arena) offers sailing, Dragon-boat racing, power boating, rowing, canoeing and more. Day passes cost £20. Open daily 9 a.m. to 9 p.m.

GOLF

THE ENGLISH GOLF UNION IS AN EXCELLENT resource for all golf information and can be reached at ☎ 0152-635-4500, or by surfing to **www.englishgolfunion.org.** Weekends get very, very crowded, so you need to hit the green quite early in the morning. Courses outside the city include the following:

RICHMOND PARK PUBLIC GOLF CLUB (Roehampton Gate, Richmond Park, SW15; ☎ 0208-876-3205; **www.richmondparkgolf.co.uk;** British Rail to Barnes) There are two 18-hole courses that cost £15 on weekdays and £18 on weekends. The price drops for games played late in the day.

ROYAL MID-SURREY GOLF CLUB (Old Deer Park, Twickenham Road, Richmond, Surrey; ☎ 0208-940-1894; **www.rmsgc.co.uk;** British Rail or the tube to Richmond) There are two 18-hole courses here, and although it is a private club, visitors are welcome. Admission is £72 in summer, £48 in winter for a full day; £30 after 4:30 p.m.

DUKES MEADOWS GOLF CLUB AND CHISWICK BRIDGE GOLF RANGE (Dukes Meadows, Dan Mason Drive (formerly Great Chartsey Road), Chiswick, W4; ☎ 0208-994-3314; **www.golflessons.co.uk;** tube: Hammersmith, then bus 190 to Hartington Road) The club is open daily 9 a.m. to 10 p.m. There is something for everyone here: a nine-hole course, a 50-bay driving range, a six-hole academy course (child-friendly), and a full teaching center. You can rent golf clubs here, too. Wind down afterward in the restaurant and bar. The cost to play the nine-hole course is £9.50 on weekdays, £11 on weekends. On the driving range, you'll pay £4.50 for a bucket of balls.

TENNIS

ALMOST ALL LONDON PARKS HAVE TENNIS COURTS, which cost very little to play on, but you must bring your own racket and balls. There is usually a grass court or two and a few asphalt ones. It's very informal; just turn up on any weekday, and you will almost certainly be able to play. The serious player should look into the **Queens Club** (Palliser Road, West Kensington, W14; ☎ 0207-385-3421; **www.queens club.co.uk**) or contact the Lawn Tennis Association at ☎ 0207-381-7000 or **www.lta.org.uk** for a listing of all London venues.

HOTEL INDEX

Abbey Court, 83, 85, 94–95
Academy Bloomsbury Town House, 83, 84, 95–96

Baglioni Hotel, 76–77
Barkston Gardens, 83, 84, 97–98
Basil Street Hotel, 83, 84, 96–97
The Berkeley, 77
Blakes, 77
The Brompton Hotel, 84, 98–99
Brown's Hotel, 77, 82, 84, 99–100

Cadogan Hotel, 83, 84, 100–101
Charlotte Street Hotel, 83, 84, 101–2
Claridges, 77–78
The Claverley, 83, 84, 102–3
Collingham Apartments, 83, 84, 103–4
The Colonnade Hotel, 82, 85, 105–6
The Columbia Hotel, 83, 85, 106–7
Comfort Inn Notting Hill, 84, 85, 107–8
The Connaught, 78
Covent Garden Hotel, 82, 84, 108–9, 186

The Dorchester, 78
The Draycott Hotel, 82, 84, 109–10
Dukes Hotel, 82, 84, 110–11
Durrants, 83, 85, 111–12

Edward Lear Hotel, 84, 85, 112–13
11 Cadogan Gardens, 82, 84, 113-14

Fielding Hotel, 84, 114–15
Five Sumner Place Hotel, 83, 84, 115
The Four Seasons, 78
Franklin Hotel, 83, 84, 116

The Gainesborough, 83, 84, 117
The Gallery Hotel, 83, 84, 117–18
The Gore, 82, 84, 118–19, 186
Goring Hotel, 82, 84, 120
Grange White Hall Hotel, 83, 84, 121
Great Eastern Hotel, 83, 84, 121–23

Hazlitt's Hotel, 83, 84, 123-24

Holiday Inn Mayfair, 83, 84, 124
Hotel Russell, 82, 84, 125

The Landmark, 78
The Lanesborough, 78–79
L'Hotel, 82, 84, 125–26
Lincoln House Hotel, 83, 85, 126–27
London Marriott Hotel County Hall, 83, 84,
    127–28

Mandarin Oriental Hotel, 79
The Metropolitan, 79
Miller's Residence, 83, 85, 128–29
The Montague on the Gardens, 83, 84, 129–30
Morgan Hotel, 83, 84, 130–31

Number Sixteen, 83, 85, 131–32

One Aldwych, 79

Parkes Hotel, 83, 85, 132
The Pelham, 83, 85, 133
Pembridge Court Hotel, 83, 85, 134
The Portobello Hotel, 83, 85, 134–35, 186

Quality Hotel, 84, 135–36

Radisson Edwardian Hampshire, 83, 84, 136–37
The Rembrandt Hotel, 83, 85, 137–38
The Ritz, 79, 186
The Rookery, 83, 84, 138–39
Royal Adelphi Hotel, 84, 139–40
Ruskin Hotel, 84, 140–41

Sanderson, 79–80
The Savoy, 80
St. Margaret's Hotel, 83, 84, 141–42
Strand Palace Hotel, 83, 84, 142–44

Thistle Hotel Victoria, 82, 84, 144–45
Threadneedles Hotel, 82, 84, 145–46

The Zetter Restaurant & Rooms, 82, 84, 146–47

RESTAURANT INDEX

Al Hamra, 304
Angela Hartnett at the Connaught, 298, 300, 305–7
Arkansas Café, 298, 300, 307
Aubaine, 298, 301, 307–14

Back to Basics, 302
Baltic, 300, 314–15
Bank Aldwych, 299, 300, 315–16
Belgo Centraal, 298, 300, 316
Benares, 301
Bibendum, 299, 301, 316–17
Big Easy, 288
Blueprint Café, 299, 300, 317–18
Boisdale of Belgravia, 298, 301, 318
Brasserie St. Quentin, 298, 301, 318–19

Café Carluccio's, 299, 301, 320–21
Café Corfu, 303
Café Primo, 300, 301, 319–20
Café Spice Namaste, 299, 300, 320
Cambio de Tercio, 300, 301, 321–22
Cantina Vinopolis, 299, 300, 322
Chez Gérard at the Opera Terrace, 298, 300, 323
Chinese Experience, 298, 300, 324
Clarke's, 299, 301, 324–25
Condotti, 303–4
Cork & Bottle Wine Bar, 303
Corney and Barrow, 299, 300, 325
The Cow, 303
Crêperie d'Hampstead, 298, 326
Cuba, 298, 326–27

Dan's, 299, 301, 327–28

The Eagle, 303
E & O, 298, 328–29

Fakhredine, 304
Fifteen, 298, 329–30
fish!, 300, 330–31
Food for Thought, 300, 331–32
Fung Shing, 301

Geales, 302
Good Earth, 301
Gordon Ramsay, 302–3

Halepi Restaurant, 303
Harbour City, 301
Hard Rock Café, 288
The Havelock Tavern, 303
Hunan, 301

Itsu, 304
The Ivy, 299, 300, 333

Joe Allen, 298, 300, 333–34

Kulu Kulu, 304

La Porte des Indes, 299, 334–35
Le Caprice, 299, 300, 301, 322–23
Le Gavroche, 298, 300, 332–33
Locanda Locatelli, 304

Masala Zone, 299, 300, 335–36
Mash, 299, 301, 336
Matsuri, 299, 301, 336–37
Maxwells, 288
Mildreds, 288
Misato, 304
Momo, 186
Mon Plaisir, 302
Moro, 300, 301, 337
Mr. Kong, 298, 300, 337–38

Nahm, 305
Nathalie's, 298, 301, 340
Navajo Joe's, 300, 338–39
Nobu, 299, 300, 339
North Sea Fish Restaurant, 300, 340–41
1 Lombard Street, 302
Orrery, 299, 301, 341–42
Orsini's Café, 299, 301, 342–43

Patara, 305

Patogh, 304
Pied à Terre, 301
Pizza Express, 299, 301, 343, 367, 375, 385
Poissonerie de l'avenue, 302
Pont de la Tour, 186
Pret à Manger, 300, 301, 343–44
Providores and Tapa Room, 299, 301, 344–45
Racine, 302
Rainforest Café, 289
Ranoush Juice Bar, 305
Rasa, 299, 300, 345
Richard Corrigan at Lindsay House, 298, 300, 345–46
Riva, 304
The River Café, 299, 346–47
Royal China, 298, 301, 347–48
Rules, 298, 300, 348–49

Shezan, 302
Smollensky's, 289

The Square, 303
Sri Siam, 305
Star of India, 302
Sticky Fingers, 289
Strada, 299, 300, 349

Tamarind, 299, 300, 349–50
The Tea Palace, 298, 350–51
Texas Embassy Cantina, 289, 300, 351
TGI Friday's, 289
Tootsie's, 289

Veeraswamy, 299, 300, 351–52

Wagamama, 298, 300, 352–53
The Wolseley, 299, 353–54
World Food Café, 300, 354

Yautcha, 298, 355

SUBJECT INDEX

Access in London, 56
Access to the Underground, 56
Accommodations
  air-conditioning, 50
  amenities, 68
  apartments, 74–75
  bed-and-breakfasts, 73–74
  deals and discounts, 67, 68, 72–73
  for the disabled, 56
  hotel comparisons, 81–84
  hotel profiles, 85–147
  hotel ratings, 80–81
  luxury hotels, 75–80
  by neighborhoods, 69–72, 84–85
  out of Central London, 72
  overview, 7
  room sizes, 68
  selecting, 66–67
  service, 68
  tipping, 158
  value-added tax (VAT), 55, 68
Air-conditioning, 50
Air travel and airlines
  airlines, 44
  consolidators, 44–45
  deals, 44–46
  luggage, 46
  medications/prescriptions, 46, 54, 149
  personal electronics, 47
  valuables, 46
Albert Memorial, 198, 199–208
Alcoholics Anonymous, 59
Almeida theatre, 360
Ambulances, 58
American Airlines, 44
American Embassy, 55
Amused Moose Soho, 363
Apartments. See Accommodations
Apsley House (The Wellington Museum), 198, 208–9
Arrival cards, 148
Artslines, 56

ATMs (cashpoints), 47, 150
Attractions. See Sightseeing and attractions

Bagley's Studio, 375–78
Bank of England Museum, 197, 209
Barbican Centre, 364, 366
Bar Rumba, 375, 378
Bath, 184
Bayswater neighborhood, 72
Beating Retreat Household Division, 62
Bed-and-breakfasts. See Accommodations
Big Ben Clock Tower, 197, 209–10
Big Issue magazine, 164
Bloomsbury neighborhood, 71–72
Bonfire Night and Guy Fawkes Day Fireworks
    Displays, 64
Boxing, 424
Brighton, 184
British Airways, 44
British Airways London Eye, 185, 197, 210–11, 282
British Library at St. Pancras, 198, 211–12, 283
British Museum, 185, 196, 212–13, 282
BritRail Pass, 47
Brixton Academy, 368
Browns Club, 375, 378
Buckingham Palace, 63, 197, 198, 213–14, 245–46, 248
The Bulldog Club, 73–74
Burgh House and Hampstead Museum, 199, 214–15
Buses
  air-conditioning, 50
  from airports, 152, 153
  fares, 170
  routes, 170
  touring, 180–82
  types, 169
Bush Theatre, 360

The Cabinet War Rooms and Churchill Museum, 197, 215–16, 282
Café de Paris, 369, 375, 379

Cambridge, 184
Can Be Done, 56
Canterbury, 184
Carlyle's House, 198, 216, 283
Car rentals, 47, 150, 154, 175–76
Casinos, 372–73
Cell phones, 47
Celsius *vs.* Fahrenheit, 47–48
Central London Apartments, 75
Changing of the Guard, 198, 216–17
Charles I Commemoration, 59
Chelsea Flower Show, 61
Chelsea neighborhood, 13–14
Chelsea Theatre, 361
Children, traveling with
    activities, 284–87
    attractions, 210–11, 215–16, 218–19, 223, 231–
        32, 233–35, 237–39, 243, 247–48, 251–52,
        258–61
    festivals and events, 60, 61, 64–65
    hotels, 79–80, 97–98, 103–7, 135–36, 137–38,
        141–42
    least popular sights, 283
    most popular sights, 282
    parks, 269–71, 272, 273–74
    planning and touring tips, 277–81
    playgrounds, 286–87
    rental equipment and childcare, 284–85
    restaurants, 288–89, 307, 316, 319–21, 323,
        326–27, 330–31, 337–39, 340–41, 342–44,
        349, 350–51, 352–53, 354
    sample itinerary, 283–84
    shopping for, 289–92, 390, 397–98, 407
    side trips, 184
    theaters, 287, 359
    transportation, 170, 288
    before you go, 276–277
Chinese New Year Celebrations, 60
Chiswick House, 199, 217–18
Christmas Lights and Tree, 65
Cirque at the Hippodrome, 375, 379–80
Cittie of York Tavern, 370–71
City neighborhood
    attractions, 197
    hotels, 84
    maps, 89, 157, 203, 306
    overview, 11–12
    restaurants, 300–301
    walking, 189–91
Clinics, 58
Clink Exhibition, 197, 218
Clore Studios, 366–67
Clothing and dress codes, 49–51, 362
Comedy Café, 363
Comedy Store, 363
Costermongers Pearly Harvest Festival, 64
Courtauld Institute, 283
Credit cards, 47, 150, 166, 392
Cricket, 422–23
Crime, 163–64
Culture, 36–40
Customs, 54, 149–50
Cutty Sark, 199, 218–19

Daily Mail Ideal Home Exhibition, 60
Dali Universe, 197, 219
Dance Umbrella, 365
Delta Airlines, 44
Dental Emergency Care Service, 58
Design Museum, 197, 220, 283
Destino, 375, 380
Dickens House, 196, 220–21, 283
Dining. *See* Restaurants and dining
Disabled travelers, 56
Docklands Light Rail, 175
Docklands neighborhood, 199
Doctors Direct, 58
Donmar Warehouse theatre, 360
Dover Streer Restaurant and Bar, 375, 380
Dr. Johnson's House, 197, 227–28
Drill Hall, 360
Driving
    driver's license, 176
    National Car Parks (NCP), 176
    overview, 154, 175–76
    parking, 176
    roundabouts, 176
Duty-free items, 54, 149

Earl's Court Exhibition Centre, 367
Earl's Court neighborhood, 70, 72
East End neighborhood, 197
Electricity, adapters, converters and transformers,
    47, 49, 54
Embargo, 369, 375, 380–81
Emergency rooms, 58
Emporium, 375, 381
English National Opera (ENO), 366
Entertainment and nightlife
    adult entertainment, 371–72
    bars and pubs, 369–71
    casinos and gaming, 372–73
    classical music, 363–65
    comedy clubs, 362–63
    dance and ballet, 365–66
    dance clubs, 368–69
    freebies, 373–75
    list of nightclubs and profiles, 375–87
    live jazz, pop and rock, 367–68
    opera, 366–67
    overview, 10, 356–57
    theater, 357–62
Eurostar, 153–54
Evening Standard, 157
Excercise and recreation
    bicycling, 428
    golf, 431
    gyms and leisure centers, 426–27
    horseback riding, 428–29
    ice-skating, 429
    inline skating, 428
    spectator sports, 421–26
    swimming, 429–30
    tennis, 431
    water sports, 431

Fast Track Pass, 148
Festivals and Events, calendar, 59–65
50 St. James, 372–73
The Finborough theatre, 361
Florence Nightingale Museum, 283
Football, 421–22
Freud Museum, 199, 221
The Fridge Bar, 375, 381

The Gate theatre, 360
Gatwick Express, 150–51
Gay and lesbian issues and organizations, 165–66
Gay & Lesbian London (Parker), 166
Geography of the City, 155–57
The Globe Theatre, 185, 197, 221–22, 359–60
Golden Nugget Casino, 373
Great River Race, 63
Great Spitalfields Pancake Race, 60
Green Park, 266, 267
Greenwich, 199, 274–75
Greyhound racing, 426
Grill Room @ Café Royal, 375, 381–82
Guards Museum, 282
Guildhall, 197, 222–23
Gun Salute to Mark the Queen's Birthday, 61

Hampstead Heath, 266, 267–68
Hampton Court Palace, 185, 199, 223–25
Hampton Court Palace Festival, 365
Hanover Grand, 369, 375, 382
Hatfield House, 184
Head of the River Boat Race, 60
Health Insurance Finders, 58
Heathrow Express Train, 152
Heaven, 375, 382
Henry Wood Promenade Concerts (the Proms), 63, 364
High Commissions, 55–56
Highgate Cemetery, 266, 268–69
Highway to Health Insurance, 58
History, 16–36
HMS Belfast, 197, 223, 282
Hogarth's House, 199, 225
Holiday Care Service, 56
Holland Park, 267, 269
Holland Park Theatre, The, 365
Home From Home, 74–75
Homeless and beggars, 164
Horse Guard's Parade, 62
Horse racing, 425–26
Hotelink, 151
Hotels. *See* Accommodations
Houses of Parliament, 198, 225–27
Hyde Park, 156, 185, 267, 269–70

Immigration, 148–49
Imperial War Museum, 197, 227, 282
Information
    Britain and London Visitor Center, 180
    British Tourist Authority, 52–53
    Department of State Bureau of Consular Afffairs, 53
    Excise and Inland Customs Advice Centre, 149

London Tourist Board, 59, 64, 65
    London Transport, 168, 177
    National Passport Information Center, 53
    Travel Information Center, 170
Information for Wheelchair Users Visiting London (pamphlet), 56
Insurance
    medical, 58
    travel, 46

Jazz Café, 375, 383
Jermyn Street Theatre, 361–62
Jet lag, 57–58
Jongleurs, 363
Jongleurs Camden Lock, 363

Kabaret's Prophecy, 375, 383–84
Kensington Gardens, 267, 271
Kensington neighborhood, 70, 198, 398
Kensington Palace State Rooms, 198, 228–29
Kenwood House (The Iveagh Bequest), 62, 199, 229–30
Kenwood Lakeside Concerts, 62, 365
Kew Gardens (The Royal Botanic Gardens), 267, 271–72
King's Head theatre, The, 360–61
Knightsbridge neighborhood
    attractions, 198
    hotels, 84–85
    maps, 90–91, 204–5, 310–11
    overview, 13–14
    restaurants, 301
    shopping, 399–400

Language, British/English glossary, 40–43
Laptop computers, 54, 161
Laycock, 184
Leighton House Museum and Art Gallery, 198, 230–31, 283
Les Ambassadeurs Club, 375
Linbury Studio Theater, 366
Linley Sambourne House, 198, 231
London Aquarium, 197, 231–32, 282
London Arena, 367–68
London A to Z, 48, 156–57, 167
London Bridge Experience, 282
London Coliseum, 366, 367
London Comedy Festival, 363
London Dungeon, 197, 232–33, 282
London First Choice Apartments, 74
London Harness Horse Parade, 61
London Homestead Services, 74
London International Boat Show, 60
London Marathon, 61
London Philharmonic Orchestra, 364
London Symphony Orchestra, 364
London to Brighton Veteran Car Run, 64
London Transport Museum, 196, 233–34, 282
London Transport Unit for Disabled Visitors, 56
London Zoo, 199, 234, 282
Lord Mayor's Show, 64
Lost and found, 177

Madame Tussaud's Waxworks and the London Planetarium, 198, 235–36
Magazines, 159–60
Mail, 162
Marylebone to Notting Hill Gate neighborhood
attractions, 198
hotels, 85
maps, 92–93, 206–7, 312–13
overview, 14–15
restaurants, 301
May Fair and Puppet Festival, 61
Mayfair neighborhood, 70–71
Medic Alert tag, 46
Medical Express, 58
Metro Life, 157
Metro Night Club, 375, 384
Millennium Bridge, 197, 236–37
Minicabs, 151, 174–75
Ministry of Sound, 369, 375, 384
Money
exchange rates, 54, 55, 388, 392
pounds and pence, 54–55
The Monument, 197, 237–38
Motorcycle taxis, 174
Museum of Childhood at Bethnal Green, 197, 238, 282
Museum of London, 185, 197, 238–39, 282

Narcotics Anonymous, 59
National Army Museum, 282
National Express, 152, 153
National Film Theatre, 287
National Gallery, 196, 239–41
National Health Service, 58–59
National Maritime Museum and Queen's House, 199, 241–42
The National Portrait Gallery, 185, 242
National Theatre, 357–59
Natural History Museum, 198, 243, 282
New End Theatre, 362
Newspapers, 158–59
New Year's Day London Parade, 59
Nicholsons London Street Atlas, 48
Nightlife. *See* Entertainment and nightlife
North London neighborhood, 198–99, 301
Notes from a Small Island (Bryson), 173
Notting Hill Arts Club, 375, 384–85
Notting Hill Carnival, 63, 367

Old Bailey (Central Criminal Courts), 197, 244
Old Bank of England, 370
Old Hampstead Village, 191–93
Old Operating Theatre, Museum, and Herb Garret, 197, 245
Old Red Lion theatre, 362
Olympia International Show Jumping Champions, 65
Open House London, 64
Oris London Jazz Festival, 367
Overeaters Anonymous, 59
Oxford, 184
Oxford *vs.* Cambridge Boat Race, 60–61

Passports, 53–54, 55, 148
Peacock Theatre, 366
Pharmacies, 58
Piccadilly neighborhood, 70–71
The Place Theatre, 366
Polka Theatre for Children, 287
Pollock's Toy Museum, 282
Post codes, 155
Prescriptions, 46, 54, 149
Prospect of Whitby, 370
Puppet Theatre Barge, 287

Queen's Gallery, Buckingham Palace, 198, 245–46, 283
Queues, 37

Radio, 160–61
Regent's Park, 267, 272
Regent's Park Open Air Theatre, 361
Religion, 164–65
Remembrance Day, 64–65
Rendezvous Casino, 373
Restaurants and dining
air-conditioning, 50
gastro-pubs, 295
listed by cuisine, 298–305
listed by neighborhood, 300–301
overview, 10, 293–96
profiles, 305–55
ratings, 296–97
service, 38, 295
tipping, 158
Richmond Park, 267, 272–73
Riverside Studios, 361
River Thames, 155–56
Ronnie Scott's, 367, 375, 385–86
Royal Academy of Arts, 62, 196, 246–47, 283
Royal Academy Summer Exhibition, 62
Royal Albert Hall, 364
Royal Ascot, 62
Royal Ballet, 366
Royal Court Theatre, 359
Royal Greenwich Observatory, 199, 247–48
Royal Mews, Buckingham Palace, 198, 248, 282
The Royal Observatory, 282
Royal Opera House, 364, 366–67
Royal Windsor Horse Show, 61–62
Rugby, 423–24

Saatchi Gallery, 197, 249
Sadler's Wells, 366
Safety tips, 163–64
Salisbury, 184, 185
The Science Museum, 185, 198, 251–52, 282
Shepherd's Bush Empire, 368
Sherlock Holmes Museum, 198, 252
Shopping
air-conditioning, 50
antiques, 389, 408–9
auction houses, 409–10
baby goods, 292
bath products and perfumes, 389–90, 410–11, 417

bone china, 390
books and bookstores, 159–60, 286, 290, 390, 411–14
chain stores, 396–97
children's clothing and shoes, 290–92, 390
decorative home accessories, 414
department stores, 406–8
designer clothing and boutiques, 390–91, 414–15
designer resale shops, 415
fabrics, 391, 415–16
hours of operation, 163, 391–92
linens, 416
maps, 157
markets, 403–4
museum shops, 416–17
by neighborhoods, 397–403
overview, 388–89
preferred shops, 420
romantic items, 186
salespeople, 396
shoes, 417–18
souvenirs, 391
stained glass, 419–20
stationery, 391
toys, 289–90
vintage clothing, 418
wool and cashmere, 419
Sightseeing and attractions
attractions by neighborhood, 196–99
museum and attraction profiles, 199–206
for museum lovers, 195–96
not to be missed in London, 185
outside London, 184
overview, 178–79
parks, 266–74
romantic London, 185–86
sample itinerary, 186–88
side trips, 184–85
touring, 180–83
tourist information centers, 179–80
Sir John Soane's Museum, 196, 252–53, 283
606 Club, 367, 375, 386
Smoking, 172, 173
Soho Jazz Festival, 367
Soho neighborhood, 71, 371–72
Soho Theatre, 361
Somerset House, 196, 253–55
South Bank Centre, 282, 364–65, 366
South Eastern Trains, 151
South Kensington neighborhood
hotels, 69–70, 84–85
maps, 90–91, 204–5, 310–11
overview, 13–14
restaurants, 301
South London neighborhood, 197
South Thames neighborhood, 300–301
Southwark Cathedral, 197, 255
The Sportsman Casino, 373
St. Albans, 184
St. James Park, 185, 267, 273–74
St. John's Smith Square, 364
St. Patrick's Day Celebations, 60

St. Paul's Cathedral, 185, 197, 249–51
Stansted Express, 152–53
Stonehenge, 184
Stratford-Upon-Avon, 184, 185

Tate Britain, 198, 256
The Tate Modern, 185, 197, 256–57
Taxis
from airports, 151, 153
companies, 174
drivers, 173–74
etiquette, 173–74
overview, 172–73
smoking, 173
tipping, 158
Telephones and phone cards, 161–62
Television, 160
Tennis, 424–25
Thameslink train, 151, 153
Theatre Museum, 282, 333, 375, 386–87
Ticketmaster, 358
Time Out London, 157
Time Out magazine, 52, 59, 157
Toilets, public, 162
Tourist seasons, 50–52
Tower Bridge Experience, 197, 257–58
The Tower of London, 185, 197, 258–60, 282
Trader Vic's, 371
Trafalgar Day Parade, 64
Traffic, 167–68
Trains
air-conditioning, 50
from Gatwick Airport, 150–51
from Heathrow Airport, 152
from Luton Airport, 153
from Stansted Airport, 152
Transportation
from airports, 150–53
discount cards, 175
overview, 167–68
Oyster Cards, 168
rail service, 175
by ship from America, 154
Travel Cards, 47, 49, 168–69, 175
travel zones, 168
Travel advisories, 46
Traveler's checks, 47, 392
Trooping the Colour, 62
The Tube (The Underground), 56, 152, 170–72
Turnmills, 375, 387

UNICEF Change Collection, 55
United Airlines, 44
Uptown Reservations, 74

Value-added tax (VAT), 55, 68, 392–95
Victoria and Albert Museum, 185, 198, 260–61, 282
Victoria neighborhood
attractions, 197–98
hotels, 72, 84
maps, 88, 202

Victoria neighborhood *(continued)*
   overview, 12–13
   restaurants, 301
Virgin Atlantic Airways, 44, 46
Visas, 54, 148–49

Walking, 177
   City of London, 189–91
   Old Hamstead Village, 191–93
   Royal London from Palace to Parliament, 193–95
   tour companies, 189
Wallace Collection, 198, 261–62
Warwick Castle, 184
Weather, 37–38, 47–48
The Wellington Arch, 198, 262–63
Wellington Museum, 198, 208–9
Wembley Arena, 367
West End neighborhood
   attractions, 196
   hotels, 71, 84
   maps, 86–87, 200–201, 308–9, 376–77
   overview, 10–11
   restaurants, 300
   theater, 357–61

West London neighborhood, 199
Westminster Abbey, 185, 198, 263–65
Westminster neighborhood
   attractions, 197–98
   hotels, 84
   maps, 88, 202
   overview, 12–13
   restaurants, 301
What's On magazine, 52, 157
Wigmore Hall, 364
Wimbledon Lawn Tennis Championships, 62–63
Windsor, 185
Windsor Castle, 197, 265–66

Ye Old Cheshire Cheese, 370
Ye Old Mitre Tavern, 370
YoungVic, 361

Zeta Bar, 371
Zoo Bar, 375, 387